Neuropsychology of Women

Erin Sullivan-Baca • Rachael L. Ellison
Editors

Neuropsychology of Women

Considerations for Clinical Care & Research

Springer

Editors
Erin Sullivan-Baca
Neurocognitive Specialty Group
Dallas, TX, USA

Rachael L. Ellison
Department of Psychology
Rosalind Franklin University of Medicine and Science
North Chicago, IL, USA

ISBN 978-3-031-87227-3 ISBN 978-3-031-87228-0 (eBook)
https://doi.org/10.1007/978-3-031-87228-0

This Springer imprint is published by the registered company Springer Nature Switzerland AG
The registered company address is: Gewerbestrasse 11, 6330 Cham, Switzerland

Acknowledgements

Dr. Sullivan-Baca: To all the women in neuropsychology who have been my teachers, my mentors, my colleagues, and my friends. Special thanks to Y.M. for her partnership on fellowship, on epilepsy research, and on navigating our early careers as women and mothers. To A.C. who paved the way through graduate school and is often my biggest cheerleader. To my internship mentor (A.Z.) and fellowship mentors (N.P. & B.M.) who are fantastic allies and always let my feminist light shine. To my co-editor R.E. who will dive head and heart first into any project that lifts up women. And to my husband, A.B., my endless source of support, and my daughter, K.B., who is only 2 but is poised to take over the world.

Dr. Ellison: To the members of APA Division 40 (Society of Clinical Neuropsychology; SCN)'s Women in Neuropsychology (WIN) committee and former chair K.L. for taking a chance on me and allowing me the incredible opportunity to serve as WIN Chair. To the women who mentored throughout fellowship (A.U., A.W., M.S.), internship (A.J. & J.J.), and graduate school (K.G.), who truly shaped my professional career as a neuropsychologist. To my co-editor E.S.B., there is no one else I would rather choose to jump head first into new and uncharted professional journeys with. To my husband J.E., who has championed my career and passions every step of the way, and to my 'little meatballs' M.E. and N.E., who have opened my eyes to the wonderful complexities of motherhood.

Together, we would like to thank everyone who helped make this book a reality. Thank you to our colleagues at APA Division 40 (SCN) and on the WIN committee who offer unlimited support, encouragement, and helping hands to carry the load. Thank you to Catherine Thoms and everyone at Springer Nature for trusting us to develop this work. And thank you to all of the chapter authors for being diligent, thoughtful, and passionate in their writing. We truly could not have done this without you.

Contents

Contributors

Demy Alfonso Children's Healthcare of Atlanta, Atlanta, GA, USA

Ece Bayram University of Colorado Anschutz, Aurora, CO, USA

Anna Brugulat-Serrat BarcelonaBeta Brain Research Center, Barcelona, Spain

Lauren Bush The Center for Pediatric Neuropsychology, Palm Beach Gardens, FL, USA

Rush University Medical Center, Chicago, IL, USA

Cheryl Bushnell Wake Forest University School of Medicine, Winston-Salem, NC, USA

Hannah Combs Baylor College of Medicine, Houston, TX, USA

Rachael L. Ellison Rosalind Franklin University of Medicine and Science, North Chicago, IL, USA

Sheina Emrani Perelman School of Medicine, University of Pennsylvania, Philadelphia, PA, USA

Asish Gulati The George Washington University School of Medicine, Washington, DC, USA

Robin C. Hilsabeck UT Health San Antonio, San Antonio, TX, USA

Amy Jak Center of Excellence for Stress and Mental Health, VA San Diego Healthcare System, University of California San Diego, San Diego, CA, USA

Erin Logue The University of Texas at Austin Dell Medical School, Austin, TX, USA

Francesca Lopez Center of Excellence for Stress and Mental Health, VA San Diego Healthcare System, University of California San Diego, San Diego, CA, USA

Yosefa Modiano University of Texas Health Neurosciences, Houston, TX, USA

Maddy Myers University of Utah School of Medicine, Salt Lake City, UT, USA

Kritika Nayar Hassenfeld Children's Hospital at NYU Langone, New York, NY, USA

Elisabeth Netherton Rock Springs Behavioral Health, Georgetown, TX, USA

Mary Jo Pugh VA Salt Lake City, University of Utah School of Medicine, Salt Lake City, UT, USA

Jessica Rohr Houston Methodist, Houston, TX, USA

Lauren Rynar Rush University Medical Center, Chicago, IL, USA

Megan N. Scott Ann & Robert H. Lurie Children's Hospital of Chicago, Northwestern University Feinberg School of Medicine, Chicago, IL, USA

C. Elizabeth Shaaban University of Pittsburgh School of Public Health, Pittsburgh, PA, USA

Erin Sullivan-Baca Neurocognitive Specialty Group, Dallas, TX, USA

Erin Sundermann University of California San Diego, San Diego, CA, USA

Joyce W. Tam Rush University Medical Center, Chicago, IL, USA

Hannah B. VanLandingham Rosalind Franklin University of Medicine and Science, North Chicago, IL, USA

Chapter 1
Introduction

Erin Sullivan-Baca and Rachael L. Ellison

Introduction

If you are taking the time to read this book for your own professional development, or to integrate in formal didactics, supervision, or other coursework, we as a field are already one step closer to addressing a long history of reduced attention to women's and gender issues in medical research. These gaps, from training, to study design and methodological approach, to a history of biases in the peer review process, compound one another and reduce both the quality of our research and generalizable knowledge, and ultimately impact patient care and do a disservice to our students and trainees. We, the editors of the present book, have personally experienced such gaps, from lack of inclusion of these topics across our doctoral training, clinical internships, and/or post-doctoral fellowships, to, experiences in our professional lives; for example, receiving a culturally insensitive response from peer reviewers stating, "*I do not find the statistical comparison between men and women particularly informative or interesting*." Such a statement came from but one of many voices across various facets of the scientific community which continue to influence how research is disseminated, how education and training is structured, and how clinical care is performed. Overall, we aim to bring to this book our personal and professional passions for instigating change in our field, and dismantling the current historical precedents of marginalization and minimization of women in research, particularly related to cognition.

E. Sullivan-Baca (✉)
Neurocognitive Specialty Group, Dallas, TX, USA
e-mail: sullivan-baca@nsgdallas.com

R. L. Ellison
Rosalind Franklin University of Medicine and Science, North Chicago, IL, USA

E. Sullivan-Baca, R. Ellison (eds.), *Neuropsychology of Women*,
https://doi.org/10.1007/978-3-031-87228-0_1

Specifically, in *Neuropsychology of Women,* we aim to fill crucial gaps in the literature on women's issues in our field and provide a resource to anyone seeking to learn more about how women are uniquely influenced by neuropsychological conditions. In this introductory chapter, we will place the book in the larger context of the medical field by providing an overview of historical biases in research, which have led to current discrepancies in our knowledge based on how various conditions affect women and their cognitive functioning. We will incorporate discussions of policy changes and current initiatives aimed at comprehensive gender inclusion across research, which provide an optimistic outlook for the downstream future of women's health. We will next specifically zoom into the current state of the field of neuropsychology, including broad lessons of what we know about women and what we are yet to elucidate about their neurocognitive health. Finally, we will discuss our overall aims of this book, including recommendations for how it can be used in various contexts, spanning research, clinical care, and education/training.

Underrepresentation of Women in Medical Research

Women have long been underrepresented in medical research. Women of color and transgender populations have historically experienced even greater rates of underrepresentation (e.g., Bierer et al., 2022; Boehmer, 2002). The reasons for this lack of representation are multifactorial and stem from policy, access, and research focus, among other complex variables.

Relevant policy factors over the past 50 years are described in Fig. 1.1.

Policy is not, however, the only influence on inclusion of women in research. In a 2018 article, authors laid out pitfalls in clinical drug trials that led to

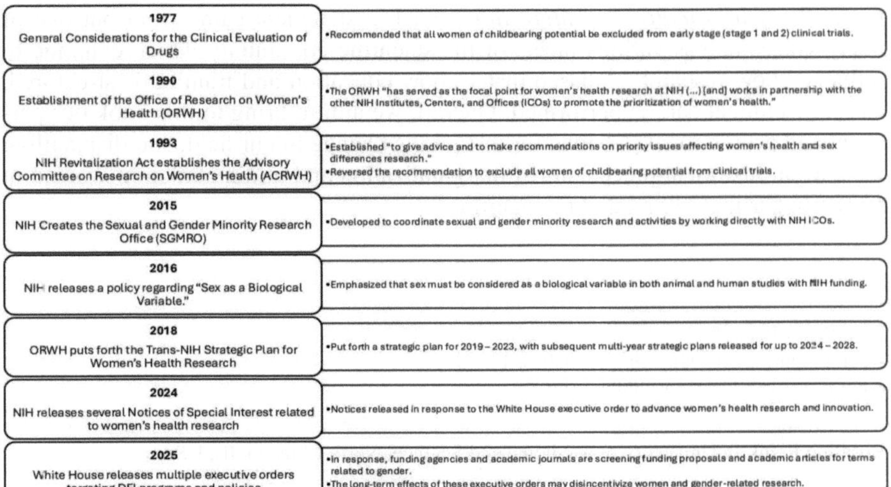

Fig. 1.1 Policy factors influencing women's involvement in medical research, 1977—Present. *Note:* Information gathered from the National Institutes of Health (NIH; www.nih.gov)

underrepresentation of women (Pilote & Raparelli, 2018). While these pitfalls were related to women's inclusion in cardiovascular clinical trials, the lessons they describe are relevant for other healthcare issues. Such barriers included a lack of knowledge and awareness of sex and gender by the researchers, including a knowledge gap in terminology (e.g., sex vs. gender), and gender-related barriers to engage in research, including access to care and parenting/caregiver responsibilities. Barriers were also acknowledged at the editorial level, including lack of specific editorial requirements for sex-specific reporting. Additional researcher-level factors have also been discerned to interfere with inclusion of women, including misperceptions that women will respond to the same treatment as men and the view that women's hormonal cycles bring increased complexity that could influence results (Mazure & Jones, 2015).

The effects of underrepresentation of women in medical research are vast and include impacts on time to diagnosis, accuracy of diagnosis, efficacy of treatment, and acknowledgement of potential side effects of medication for conditions that affect both men and women, but for which men have been overrepresented in research (Antequera et al., 2022; Bierer et al., 2022). Additionally, research on conditions that primarily affect women, including migraine, eating disorders, endometriosis, and gynecological cancers, is underfunded compared to conditions that primarily affect men, leading to disparities in healthcare knowledge when treating these conditions (Mirin, 2021). A striking and relevant example of the downstream effects of this research disparity is a low level of knowledge among healthcare professionals about the increased risk of cardiovascular disease after hypertensive disorders of pregnancy (Roth et al., 2019), a phenomenon discussed further in Chaps. 3 and 11 of this book.

Current Initiatives to Advance Women's Health Research

While policies have been implemented over the past several decades to address existing research gaps, with varying levels of success, we are currently in an especially exciting time for both policy changes and public attention to disparities in women's medical research and healthcare. In March 2024, President Biden issued an executive order and announced new actions to advance women's health research and innovation. Goals within this order include (1) integrate women's health across the federal research portfolio; (2) prioritize investments in women's health research; (3) galvanize new research on women's midlife health; and (4) access unmet needs to support women's health research.

In September 2024, the U.S. Department of Defense committed to spend $500 million per year on women's health research, primarily through the Congressionally Directed Medical Research Programs. Additionally, they pledged to adopt a new research policy to ensure that women's health is considered during each step of the research process for all projects funded through their programs. The U.S. Department of Health and Human Services Healthy People 2030 initiative also highlights several objectives related to women's health, including objectives related to women's experiences of cancer, family planning, osteoporosis, pregnancy, and childbirth. While there is still ample ground to cover to promote gender equity in healthcare, these large-scale initiatives, at the time, provided a cautiously hopeful outlook for the future of women's medical research and healthcare. More recently, in 2025, women's related research has encountered difficulties related to reductions in prioritization of funding, administrative barriers with NIH funding, and broad disincentives for conducting gender-focused research.

Women as a Focus of Neuropsychology Research, Training, and Clinical Care

Gender disparities in neuropsychology research and healthcare have been less well documented; although there are indicators that our field is not immune to the same history and trends inherent to the larger healthcare system. Biases in sex and gender inclusion in research are particularly prevalent in neuroscience and related fields, perhaps due to the perception that hormonal fluctuations in women may introduce unnecessary noise into the study of already complex topics, such as cognition (Shansky & Woolley, 2016). In a recent article, Prieto and colleagues examined the representation of women as participants in research across publications in eight major neuropsychology journals in 2019 (Prieto et al., 2024). Findings suggest that while the number of women included in neuropsychology studies is similar to that of men (48.24% women vs. 51.76% men), gender-focused neuropsychology research is extremely limited (3% of studies) and research is more likely to include only men or majority men compared to only women or majority women.

While research is only one facet of neuropsychology, it is an important driver of what information is disseminated into neuropsychology education, training, and clinical practice. While studies have not specifically been performed to estimate the rate of inclusion of women's topics into neuropsychology training, speaking anecdotally, we would assert that coverage of these topics is likely minimal. Sparse education and training on women's issues in neuropsychology has far-reaching effects, including (1) reduced understanding of how women and men with the same neuropsychological condition may present differently, leading to diagnostic inaccuracies; (2) reduced understanding of how women-specific issues (e.g., pregnancy and menopause) may influence neuropsychological functioning; and (3) limited to no training on gender-specific questions to ask during the clinical interview or to consider in interpretation and recommendations, which could lead to insufficient care for women patients.

Structure and Aim of *Neuropsychology of Women*

In this book, we aim to provide a resource to neuropsychologists at all levels of training and career, spanning work settings, to better understand how neuropsychological conditions affect women. In structuring the chapters, we drew inspiration from other fundamental neuropsychology texts and identified nine key categories of conditions often encountered by neuropsychologists: neurodevelopmental disorders, stroke and vascular dementia, traumatic brain injury, Alzheimer's disease and other dementias, movement disorders, epilepsy, cancer, autoimmune disorders, and chronic health conditions. We also included a final chapter focused on issues specific to women, including pregnancy, menopause, and other hormonal factors. Within each chapter, authors aimed to provide an overview of the condition followed by a critical examination of how gender influences base rates and prevalence rates, risk factors, symptom presentation, diagnosis, and prognosis. Each chapter concludes with research and clinical takeaways, which we hope will provide succinct messages that can easily be incorporated into educational or didactic settings.

This book is unique within our field and comes at a time of burgeoning focus, interest, and funding into women's healthcare issues. We sincerely hope that it will lay the groundwork for inclusion of gender into discussions of neuropsychological concepts and promote gender-informed healthcare for all of our women patients.

References

Antequera, A., Cuadrado-Conde, M. A., Roy-Vallejo, E., Montoya-Martínez, M., León-García, M., Madrid-Pascual, O., Calderón-Larrañaga, S., & Collaboration, on Behalf of Research for Gender Equity. (2022). Lack of sex-related analysis and reporting in Cochrane Reviews: A cross-sectional study. *Systematic Reviews, 11*, 281. https://doi.org/10.1186/s13643-021-01867-3

Bierer, B. E., Meloney, L. G., Ahmed, H. R., & White, S. A. (2022). Advancing the inclusion of underrepresented women in clinical research. *Cell Reports Medicine, 3*(4), 4. https://doi.org/10.1016/j.xcrm.2022.100553

Boehmer, U. (2002). Twenty years of public health research: Inclusion of lesbian, gay, bisexual, and transgender populations. *American Journal of Public Health, 92*(7), 1125–1130.

Mazure, C. M., & Jones, D. P. (2015). Twenty years and still counting: Including women as participants and studying sex and gender in biomedical research. *BMC Women's Health, 15*(1), 1. https://doi.org/10.1186/s12905-015-0251-9

Mirin, A. A. (2021). Gender disparity in the funding of diseases by the U.S. National Institutes of Health. *Journal of Women's Health, 30*(7), 956–963. https://doi.org/10.1089/jwh.2020.8682

Pilote, L., & Raparelli, V. (2018). Participation of women in clinical trials: not yet time to rest on our laurels. *Journal of the American College of Cardiology, 71*(18), 1970–1972. https://doi.org/10.1016/j.jacc.2018.02.069

Prieto, S., Bangen, K. J., Riegler, K., Kim, S. H., Mahmood, Z., Kaseda, E. T., Ellison, R. L., & Sullivan-Baca, E. (2024). Representation of women in neuropsychology research prior to the COVID-19 pandemic. *Journal of Clinical and Experimental Neuropsychology, 46*(3), 173–186. https://doi.org/10.1080/13803395.2024.2335109

Roth, H., LeMarquand, G., Henry, A., & Homer, C. (2019). Assessing knowledge gaps of women and healthcare providers concerning cardiovascular risk after hypertensive disorders of pregnancy—A scoping review. *Frontiers in Cardiovascular Medicine, 6*, 178. https://doi.org/10.3389/fcvm.2019.00178

Shansky, R. M., & Woolley, C. S. (2016). Considering sex as a biological variable will be valuable for neuroscience research. *The Journal of Neuroscience, 36*(47), 47. https://doi.org/10.1523/JNEUROSCI.1390-16.2016

Chapter 2
Neurodevelopmental Disorders

Kritika Nayar, Lauren Bush, and Megan N. Scott

Introduction

Neurodevelopmental disorders encompass a wide range of lifelong disorders that are characterized by developmental delays in motor, language, physical, social, learning, or behavior. These disorders present early in development and impact an individual's course of development, causing impairments in multiple areas of functioning (e.g., academic, personal, social, occupational). Research indicates that sex and gender are important considerations when considering the diversity and range of presentations in neurodevelopmental disorders.

There are significant differences in prevalence rates of neurodevelopmental diagnoses based on gender (Table 2.1). In a recent U.S. population-based survey, the overall prevalence rate of any neurodevelopmental disorder in children between the ages of 3 and 17 years was 17.8% based on parent report (Zablotsky et al., 2019). However, female children are much less likely to be diagnosed with neurodevelopmental conditions than male children, with gender ratios ranging from 1.2:1 to 4:1 males to females being reported across developmental conditions (Zablotsky et al., 2019; Bolte et al., 2023). Zablotsky et al. (2019) reported a prevalence rate of any neurodevelopmental disorder in 12.6% in females, while it was 22.7% in males.

K. Nayar
Hassenfeld Children's Hospital at NYU Langone, New York, NY, USA

L. Bush
The Center for Pediatric Neuropsychology, Palm Beach Gardens, FL, USA

Rush University Medical Center, Chicago, IL, USA

M. N. Scott (✉)
Ann & Robert H. Lurie Children's Hospital of Chicago, Northwestern University Feinberg School of Medicine, Chicago, IL, USA
e-mail: mnscott@luriechildrens.org

E. Sullivan-Baca, R. Ellison (eds.), *Neuropsychology of Women*,
https://doi.org/10.1007/978-3-031-87228-0_2

Table 2.1 Ratio of females to males with neurodevelopmental disorders

Neurodevelopmental disorder	Ratio (female:male)
Intellectual disability/intellectual developmental disorder	1:1.2 to 1:1.6
Specific learning disorders	1:1.67
Attention-deficit/hyperactivity disorder	1:2.1 to 1:4
Autism spectrum disorder	1:3 to 1:4

This discrepancy is also well documented in the literature. Historically, gender ratios are largely attributed to the sex-linked genetic factors as well as to increased vulnerability to brain insult in males (American Psychiatric Association, 2013). There is, however, concern that there are sex-based differences in phenotypic presentations, delayed diagnosis, and underdiagnosis in certain neurodevelopmental conditions that may be contributing to these gender ratios.

In this chapter we will focus on intellectual disability (ID), learning disorders (LDs), attention deficit hyperactivity disorder (ADHD), and autism spectrum disorder (ASD). The focus on these specific presentations is based on available research in these areas which indicates that there are notable differences in phenotypical presentation, outcomes, or prognosis in females, or that there are concerns with regard to delayed diagnosis or under-identification of these presentations in females. We will highlight the two most common genetic causes of intellectual disability (Down syndrome and fragile X) and two genetic disorders that have a higher incidence rate in females (Rett syndrome and Turner syndrome). Other genetic syndromes will not be individually discussed beyond the broader intellectual disabilities section due to limitations in research in sex-differences within these specific conditions. Given that neurodevelopmental disorders initially present early in development and are typically identified in childhood, the bulk of this chapter will focus on the pediatric literature with some focus on adult presentations and outcomes.

Intellectual Disability (Intellectual Developmental Disorder) (ID/IDD)

Intellectual disability (ID) is a neurodevelopmental disorder with onset in the early developmental period. Individuals with intellectual disability demonstrate deficits in intellectual functioning (reasoning, academic functioning, problem solving, planning, etc.) as well as deficits in adaptive functioning (conceptual, social, and practical domains) that limit one's ability to attain culturally appropriate levels of independence and social functioning (American Psychiatric Association, 2013). On assessments of intellectual functioning, IQ scores of 70 and below characterize intellectual disability; though, there is acknowledgement of statistical variation. Individuals with IQ of 75 can be diagnosed with intellectual disability when deficits of adaptive functioning are clearly demonstrated. Conversely, individuals with IQ scores around 70 who do not demonstrate adaptive impairment would not meet criteria for this diagnosis. While severity of intellectual disability had previously been determined by IQ, in the DSM-5-TR severity level of intellectual disability (mild, moderate, severe, profound) is determined by the level of adaptive functioning impairment in the conceptual, social, and practical domains (American Psychiatric Association, 2022). The majority of cases of intellectual disability fall in the mild ID range, with less than 0.5% of cases of ID falling in the severe range (Rrauch et al., 2012).

This section provides an overview of gender differences in ID/IDD. The following information focuses primarily on children with some focus on gender differences in outcomes in adulthood in ID. Given the vastness of this topic and the range of etiologic factors and syndromic presentations of ID, the majority of the information provided below examines ID/IDD as a whole without differentiating between idiopathic and syndromic ID. Two of the most common IDDs with a genetic basis are Down syndrome and fragile X. Due to their higher prevalence rate, there is more research on gender differences, and thus these specific populations will be discussed as follows (see Boxes 2.1 and 2.2, respectively). Turner syndrome and Rett syndrome are reviewed separately as these genetic syndromes occur almost exclusively in women (se Boxes 2.3 and 2.4).

Box 2.1 Fragile X Syndrome (FXS)

Fragile X syndrome (FXS) is the most commonly known inherited cause of ID (Huddleston et al., 2014). Prevalence estimates vary depending on mutation status, but the overall prevalence of FXS is approximately 1/4000 males and 1/5000 to 8000 females (Jin & Chen, 2015). Because FXS is an X-linked disorder, the presence of a second unaffected X chromosome in girls results in a healthy copy of *FMR1*. This oftentimes contributes to a milder clinical phenotype in girls as compared to boys (Hagerman & Hagerman, 2002; Loesch et al., 2002). Indeed, differences in cognitive functioning have been reported between boys and girls, such that while boys with FXS typically meet diagnostic criteria for IDD (Bartholomay et al., 2019; Cornish et al., 2008), girls with FXS show more borderline to low average IQs (Gallagher & Hallahan, 2012; Huddleston et al., 2014). Girls with FXS are at risk for math-specific deficits (Hodapp et al., 1992; Mazzocco, 2001; Murphy, 2009), a finding which is similar to the learning profile of boys with FXS and may be related to weaknesses in short-term memory, non-verbal sequencing, and aspects of attention and executive functioning (Freund & Reiss, 1991; Huddleston et al., 2014; Murphy, 2009; Rivera et al., 2002).

Autism is diagnosed in approximately 20% of girls with FXS and occurs at even higher rates in boys (Clifford et al., 2007; Hall et al., 2008; Kaufmann et al., 2017; Philofsky et al., 2004; Rogers et al., 2001). This likely exacerbates a number of difficulties with social communication and functioning (Bush et al., 2021; Lesniak-Karpiak et al., 2003). Beyond this, high levels of social anxiety and extreme shyness are well documented (Cordeiro et al., 2011; Freund et al., 1993), further contributing to difficulties in social, academic, and adaptive functioning among this population.

Box 2.2 Down Syndrome

Down syndrome (trisomy 21) is one of the most common genetic causes of intellectual disability. Down syndrome (DS) is caused by the presence by part or all of a third chromosome 21. Patients with DS present with characteristic facial dysmorphology, developmental delays, typically mild-to-moderate intellectual disability, and increased risk of congenital heart defect, gastrointestinal abnormalities, hematological disorders, hypotonia, seizures, and early onset Alzheimer's disease (AD) (Akhtar & Bokhari, 2024). Prevalence rates of DS vary across populations with the current prevalence rate in the United States reported to be 1 in 691 live births (Parker et al., 2010).

While prevalence rates of DS do not differ significantly by sex, differences in health outcomes have been identified. Although males are at higher risk of congenital heart disease (CHD), a recent meta-analysis revealed females with DS are at higher risk of hypertension, ischemic heart disease, and cerebrovascular disease (Bates et al., 2023). This is particularly notable given that CHD and cardiovascular disease are common causes of death for those with DS. In contrast to the general population, life expectancy is longer in males than females which may relate to these cardiovascular differences (Bates et al., 2023). Adults with ID report high rates of psychiatric comorbidity (23%) though this is a lower finding than in the general ID literature (Tassé et al., 2016). The most commonly reported diagnoses in a cohort of adults were depression, anxiety, and dementia with no gender differences reported (Tassé et al., 2016).

With respect to cognition, research has identified some differences in developmental trajectories and outcomes. In a Japanese study, children with DS were found to progress at a slower rate in terms of development across language, motor, and cognitive domains, but girls with DS were found to have higher cognitive and language abilities in early childhood than boys (Aoki et al., 2018). Research has identified relative strengths in nonverbal cognitive abilities in ID while relative weaknesses have been identified in language, phonological processing, aspects of executive functioning, short-term verbal memory and verbal working memory though findings related to memory are mixed (Godfrey & Lee, 2018; Loveall et al., 2017). DS is associated with higher risk of autism with co-morbidity rates ranging from 16 to 42% (Soriano et al., 2024). No gender differences were identified in prevalence of autism in DS, but girls with DS (without autism) have higher scores on verbal IQ measures than those with DS and comorbid autism (Soriano et al., 2024). This finding was not seen in males. Some research has found that men with DS perform significantly poorer than women with DS on assessments of episodic memory, executive processing, and functional academics but reported higher quality of life (de Sola et al., 2015). Risk of Alzheimer's disease (AD) is well documented in the Down syndrome literature and is thought to be related to overexpression of the amyloid beta gene which leads to earlier and increased development of amyloid beta in the brain. While gender differences have not been identified with regard to risk of AD or rate of cognitive decline, women with DS have been found to live with AD for a significantly longer time than men (Lai et al., 2020).

Box 2.3 Rett Syndrome

Rett syndrome is an X-linked neurodevelopmental disorder that occurs in 1 in every 10,000 to 15,000 live female births (Chahil & Bollu, 2024). While Rett can occur in males, it is generally not compatible with viability, and most will not survive beyond birth or infancy. The majority of Rett syndrome cases are caused by *MECP2* mutations linked to the gene methyl-CpG-binding protein (Chahil & Bollu, 2024). While there is heterogeneity in the presentation, the typical course of Rett syndrome is characterized by a four phase as described by Hagberg et al. (1986). The first is a period of typical development in infancy and early childhood (6–18 months of age) followed by a period of developmental plateau. Early signs include lack of eye contact, deceleration in head growth, and hypotonia. There is then a period of rapid regression of cognitive and motor skills, the onset of stereotypic motor movements or hand wringing, and the onset of autistic features occurs between the ages of 1 and 4 years. The third phase (ages 2–10 years) is characterized by stability with some minor improvement in behavior and communication though children remain very impaired. In addition, onset of epilepsy may occur during this stage. Finally, the fourth stage (after the age of 10) is characterized by motor decline, dystonia, and scoliosis. The neurocognitive presentation is characterized by severe cognitive impairment, loss of speech and purposeful. In addition to the cognitive impact, Rett syndrome is associated with high risk of sleep disturbances, poor growth, seizures, feeding difficulties, and behavioral challenges (Bricker & Vaughn, 2024).

Box 2.4 Turner Syndrome

Turner syndrome is a genetic disorder caused by the partial or complete absence of one of the X chromosomes. Turner syndrome occurs in 1 in 2000 to 1 in 2500 live female births though this is likely an underestimate as individuals with mild phenotypes may not be identified at all or until adulthood (Cui et al., 2018; Gunther et al., 2004). Recent research has indicated that prevalence of Turner syndrome is not impacted by maternal age. There are differences in prevalence rate based on race or ethnicity with higher rates for those who identify as white though there are concerns that ascertainment biases may contribute to differences in rates by race and ethnicity (Martin-Giacalone et al., 2023). Turner syndrome has characteristic features of short stature and webbed neck and is associated with higher risk of cardiac abnormalities, renal abnormalities, hearing loss, ovarian failure, and poor bone health among others (Shankar Kikkeri & Nagalli, 2024). From a neurocognitive perspective, Turner syndrome is commonly characterized by generally

(continued)

age-appropriate cognitive functioning with a pattern of common neurocognitive strengths and weaknesses. Specifically, strengths are found in verbal abilities while weaknesses are commonly found in visual–spatial reasoning and memory, attention, executive functioning, motor skills, and math skills (Hutaff-Lee et al., 2019). Those with Turner syndrome are at much higher risk of comorbid diagnoses of attention deficit hyperactivity disorder and specific learning disorder with impairment in mathematics (Russell et al., 2006; Hutaff-Lee et al., 2019). From a social–emotional perspective, females with Turner syndrome experience higher level of anxiety, depression, and social difficulties (Hutaff-Lee et al., 2019). Given these findings, practice guidelines include the integration of cognitive and neurocognitive evaluations and screening of social–emotional and behavioral health into regular care for individuals with Turner syndrome (Gravholt et al., 2024). The need for adaptation and examination of the evidence-based intervention to address cognitive and psychosocial needs of females with Turner syndrome was also identified (Gravholt et al., 2024).

Prevalence Rates

There are methodological differences across studies assessing the prevalence and incidence rate of intellectual disability (ID) leading to some variability. The global prevalence of ID is often reported as approximately 1% though recent review raises concern that the global rate may actually be less than 1% (McKenzie et al., 2016). The rate of ID is reported as lower in adults (0.5) as compared to children (1.8) (Bolte et al., 2023). Data from the most recent National Health Interview Survey (NHIS) from 2019 to 2021 indicated a prevalence rate of 1.85 for children ages 3–17 years (Zablotsky et al., 2023). Findings indicated that ID was diagnosed at a lower rate in girls (1.37%) than in boys (2.31%). Rates were also higher in older children (2.35% in 13–17 year olds) as compared to younger children (1.39% in 3–7 year olds).

Additionally, ID was reported at higher rates in Black/African American children as compared to other racial/ethnic groups (Zablotsky et al., 2023). Li et al. (2023) reported that rates of ID were higher non-Hispanic/Latinx White or non-Hispanic/Latinx Black/African American individuals and those with lower family income level. Overall prevalence from the NHIS study was reported by Li and colleagues as 1.72% overall; 1.26 for females and 2.16% for males (Li et al., 2023). Of note, limitations of the survey studies, such as the National Health Interview Survey, are that they rely on parent report. When reviewing data collected in the United States as part of the Autism and Developmental Disabilities Monitoring Network including IQ assessment data, a prevalence rate of 1.2% was found in 8-year-old children across nine geographic regions of the United States (Patrick et al., 2021). The prevalence rate for males was twice as large as the rate for females. Consistent with other data, rates of ID were highest among non-Hispanic/Latinx Black/African American males (23.5 per 1000), then Hispanic/Latinx males (15.9 per 1000), then non-Hispanic/Latinx Black/African American females (11.8 per 1000), Asian males (11.6 per 1000), white males (10.8), Hispanic/Latinx females (7.7 per 1000), Asian females (5.4 per 1000), and finally white females (5.2 per 1000) (Patrick et al., 2021). It was hypothesized that disparities across racial and ethnic groups were attributed in part to sociodemographic differences that impact outcomes (Patrick et al., 2021). It is important to note that the studies described above do not differentiate syndromic and idiopathic ID.

When examining non-syndromic ID, gender differences are attenuated (Bolte et al., 2023). Female-to-male ratios in mild ID have been reported as 1 to 1.6 and even closer in severe presentations 1 to 1.2. This pattern mirrors shifts to closer gender ratios in other neurodevelopmental disorders (e.g., autism spectrum disorder) in more severe presentations. Interestingly, gender ratios are reported as closer 1 to 1.1–1.4 in adulthood as compared to childhood (Bolte et al., 2023).

Risk Factors

ID is multi-causal and a single known etiological cause of ID is unknown in many of cases. Findings are variable with research suggesting 25–50% of cases are related to genetic syndromes (Kaufman et al., 2010; Ruach et al., 2012; Srour & Shevell, 2014). Srour and Shevell (2014) reported 400 genes that contributed to syndromic ID/IDD and 50 known contribute to non-syndromic ID. There are etiological factors to consider outside of genetics. In addition, the American Association on Intellectual and Developmental Disabilities (AAIDD) describes four classes of causes or contributions in intellectual disability including biomedical (genetic, infection, traumatic brain injury (TBI), other health factors), social (parental neglect, healthcare disparities, family stress, etc.), behavioral (in utero exposure, child abuse, exposure to intimate partner violence), and educational (parental education, access to education, etc.) (Schalock, Luckasson, & Tasse, 2021). These risk factors can impact individuals during the prenatal, perinatal, and/or postnatal periods (AAIDD, 2010). This outline of etiological factors and timing highlight the complexity of IDD and the challenges with identifying causal and contributing factors in these cases.

As previously discussed, females are generally less impacted by ID than males. Increased rate of ID among males is thought to be due in part to biological and genetic risk factors such as X-linked genetic disorders and to increased vulnerability to prenatal, perinatal, and postnatal complications in males. Within certain genetic syndromes such as fragile X, females tend to have less severe phenotypic presentations (see Box 2.1). In addition, there are several genetic disorders that occur almost exclusively in women (Rett syndrome and Turner syndrome). While severe presentations of ID are more often related to biological causes including genetic syndromes, mild presentations of ID are more often associated with socioeconomic, educational, and family variables (Cicek et al., 2020; Reichenberg et al.,

2016). Outside of genetic disorders that occur almost in women, there is limited data that has identified risk factors that are specific to or more significant for women.

Research examining intellectual disabilities is complicated by the high rate of comorbidity in ID/IDDs. Research finds higher rates of comorbidity in girls with ID/IDDs (Polyak et al., 2015). Specifically, girls have higher rates of comorbidity overall as well as higher rates of epilepsy (Polyak et al., 2015). Girls with IDD or autism also show increased rates of large copy number variants in ID/IDD compared to males (Polyak et al., 2015). When examining family histories, girls have more developmental disorders in their family history (e.g., growth delays). In contrast, boys tend to have more behavioral/psychiatric history in the family such as autism or learning disorders (Polyak et al., 2015).

Symptom Presentation

Intellectual disability is a highly heterogenous presentation with varying etiological contributions and symptom severity. There is limited research related to gender differences in symptom presentation of ID. When looking along the severity continuum of ID, the prevalence rates across sexes become more even with higher levels of symptom severity. From a neurocognitive perspective, individuals with ID have difficulty with executive functioning based on ratings on the Behavior Rating of Executive Function (BRIEF; as self-report of executive functioning), with no significant gender differences identified (Memisevic & Sinanovic, 2014); though, the level of ID had a significant effect on executive function deficit. Furthermore, a meta-analysis showed that ID was associated with inhibition deficits with a medium-to-large effect size identified (Bexkens et al., 2014). Specifically, this analysis highlighted deficits in behavioral inhibition and interference control, while deficits in cognitive inhibition and motivational inhibition were not found to be significant in ID (Bexkens et al., 2014). There was no analysis of gender as a variable.

Diagnosis and Prognosis

There are high rates of comorbidity with other neurodevelopmental and psychiatric disorders in intellectual disability. Children with ID are at much higher risk for a co-occurring psychiatric disorder; though, there is high variability reported (i.e., 10–50%; Dekker et al., 2002; Einfeld et al., 2011). Common co-morbid diagnoses are also reported, including disruptive behavior disorders, ADHD, depression, anxiety, as well as enuresis/encopresis (Munir, 2016). Internalizing disorders are more common in children and teens with mild ID and among girls with intellectual disability while externalizing symptoms were associated with moderate-to-severe ID and are more common among boys with ID (Cicek et al., 2020). Inconsistent findings regarding risk of depression in women are reported. Several studies have indicated higher reports of depression, loneliness, and stress in women with ID and in teens with ID (Lunsky, 2003). Women are at higher risk for adjustment reaction, dementia, while men had higher risk of personality disorders and psychosis (Tsakanikos et al., 2006).

There is limited research indicating differences in diagnosis by sex. There are, however, important findings about outcomes in ID that are important when treating women. From a medical perspective, ID, as a whole, is associated with poorer access to medical care (David et al., 2015). In addition to poor access, women with ID are less physically active (Westrop et al., 2018), have higher rates of cardiovascular risk factors (De Winter et al., 2012a), and have higher rates of obesity (De Winter et al., 2012b) compared to men with ID and the general population. Research on life expectancy in women with ID is mixed. Some data has suggested that females with ID have lower life expectancy (Heslop et al., 2014), while other research has suggested that women with ID have a longer life expectancy than men with intellectual disability, meaning that they are more impacted by aging and potentially dementia (Dew et al., 2006).

Poor access to medical care impacts women with ID differently. Specifically, women with ID have fewer mammograms and pap smears as well as higher risk of not having pelvic examinations by 21–25 years of age when compared to typically developing peers (Parish et al., 2015). Research also finds that mothers of teens with ID introduced discussions about sexual topics at a later age, discussed fewer topics, and were more concerned about vulnerability than mothers of typically developing peers. This lack of gender education may place women at higher risk for abuse. However, research on this topic has been challenged by problems with tracking, reporting, and operationalizing abuse and assault. Overall, data suggests that rates of lifetime abuse, including sexual abuse, is between 25% and 53%, and 11.5–28% in children and teens with ID (Horner-Johnson & Drum, 2006). When examining depressive symptoms in individuals with ID, women with ID and higher depression scores were more likely to report a number of contributing factors including a history of abuse, poor social support, poorer coping skills, and unemployment when compared to women with ID and low IQ scores (Lunsky, 2003). This pattern was not the same for men.

Transition outcomes for youth with ID are poorer than those of many peers with other disabilities. The National Longitudinal Transition Study-2 found that approximately a quarter of youth with ID were enrolled in post-secondary education within 4 years of completing high school and had half the rate of post-secondary educational enrollment and employment than peers with disabilities (Newman et al., 2009). However, participation in inclusion-based education is a significant predictor of post-secondary education for youth with ID (Baer et al., 2011). In addition, females and Black/African American students with disabilities enrolled in post-secondary education at higher rates compared to peers. One hypothesized explanation was that Black/African American students are overrepresented in the mild ID category (Baer et al., 2011).

Learning Disorders (LD)

Specific learning disorders (SLDs) are defined in the DSM-5/DSM-5-TR as difficulties "learning and using academic skills … that have persisted for at least 6 months, despite the provision of interventions that target these difficulties" (p. 66 American Psychiatric Association, 2013; American Psychiatric Association, 2022). Academic or LDs must be identified in at least one of the following areas: word reading accuracy or fluency; reading comprehension; spelling; written expression; number sense, math facts, calculation; or math reasoning. For individuals with LDs, academic achievement must be substantially below what is expected for an individuals' age based on standardized assessment and impair academic functioning, occupational functioning, and/or daily living abilities. In addition, academic difficulties must begin in childhood and must not be better accounted for by another diagnosis (American Psychiatric Association, 2022). Although there is no specific definition of impairment on assessments, academic achievement scores that are at least 1.5 standard deviations below the mean provide higher certainty of substantial impairment in this area (American Psychiatric Association, 2022). There is, however, allowance for flexibility when reviewing assessment data and standardized assessment findings; it should be interpreted within the context of a broader clinical assessment that reviews the individual's educational history, grades, school-based test scores, etc. (American Psychiatric Association, 2022).

Response to intervention (RTI) is another model for identification of children with learning disorders and is used in schools many for identification of LDs to determine eligibility of special education services or individualized education programs (IEPs). In the RTI approach, all students should be provided with evidence-based education and their progress should be monitored. Children who are not progressing as expected then receive a higher level of intervention or instruction for a specified period of time. If children make sufficient gains in response to this intervention, they do not require additional support. Children who do not respond to the intervention then receive intensive intervention as well as additional evaluation to clarify areas of challenge and the appropriateness of an educational label of specific learning disability. While RTI has many strengths, this model can result in delays in intensive intervention, limited assessment, and under-identification of comorbid presentations (Pennington et al., 2019).

This section will focus on learning disorders as a group and on specific learning disorders with impairment in reading and mathematics (referred to as reading LD and math LD for the remainder of this section). These specific diagnoses/presentations have the most research to support them as individual constructs. Nonverbal learning disorder will not be reviewed as it is not included in the DSM-5/DSM-5-TR. In addition, there are inconsistencies in how nonverbal learning disorder is defined, which has led to inconsistencies in research literature. Similarly, there is limited research on specific learning disorder with impairment in written expression and inconsistencies in methodology and definitions as well as poor correlation between assessments of written expression which complicates research and outcomes in this area (Pennington et al., 2019). Thus, this diagnosis will also not be reviewed.

Prevalence Rates

The lifetime prevalence of LDs across gender and age is 9.7% (Altarac & Saroha, 2007). In the National Health Interview Survey, US parents reported higher rates of LDs among boys, non-Hispanic white or non-Hispanic Black children, and those with lower family income level (Li et al., 2023; Zablotsky et al., 2019). Recent prevalence rate of LDs as a whole is 7.45%. Prevalence rate is lower among females (5.57%) as compared to males (9.31%; Li et al., 2023). Research on prevalence rate is complicated by methodological differences (e.g., survey vs. standardized assessment) as well as differences in operational definitions. Despite these challenges, there are consistent findings indicating higher rates of learning disorders in males than females.

Specific LD with impairment in reading or dyslexia is the most commonly diagnosed LD. A recent systematic review and meta-analysis (Yang et al., 2022) indicated world-wide pooled prevalence of dyslexia of 7.10% with rates being significantly lower in girls (4.66%) than in boys (9.22%). Population prevalence of developmental dyslexia/reading LD ranges from 3 to 12%, with consistently higher prevalence rates in boys. The female:male ratio ranges from 1:1.93 to 1:3.29 (Gu et al., 2018; Moll et al., 2014; Rutter et al., 2004).

There is much less data on specific LD with impairment in mathematics or dyscalculia specifically. Devine et al. (2013) reported a wide range of prevalence rates (1.3–13.8%) in their review based on variable definitions of math LD. Despite this wide range, Devine et al. (2013) did not identify significant gender differences. Other studies have found slightly higher rates in boys or slightly higher rates in girls depending on how math LD was defined. One international study found that identification of math LD with diagnostic tests led to lower prevalence rate in girls, while identification of math LD based on teacher report led to higher prevalence rates in girls (Ramma & Gowramma, 2002). When using cut-off criteria on standardized assessments to define math LDs, Devine et al. (2013) found no gender differences in prevalence rates. In contrast, when discrepancy models were applied to define math LD (math being discrepant from reading), girls were identified at a higher rate (Devine et al., 2013). An Irish sample revealed no significant gender differences in rates of math LD, but when controlling for IQ, English scores, or special education status, girls demonstrated lower math achievement scores (Morsanyi et al., 2018). Despite inconsistent findings regarding gender differences in prevalence rates as a whole, women with fragile X syndrome (Box 2.1) and Turner syndrome (Box 2.3) experience much higher rates of math LD than the general population.

Reading and math LDs are highly comorbid with reports of comorbidity in either presentation ranging from 30 to 70% (Kovas et al., 2007; Landerl & Moll, 2010). This level of comorbidity impacts research and clinical application of findings.

Risk Factors

There are a number of environmental factors that increase the risk for specific LDs, including prenatal exposure and prematurity. In addition, certain genetic disorders have higher rates of LDs. There is also a high heritability of LDs as a whole (American Psychiatric Association, 2022). Risk factors for specific LDs with impairment in reading and math will be discussed independently.

In reading disorders, twin studies have estimated heritability rates at 40 to 70% (Paracchini et al., 2007). A number of susceptibility genes have been identified for reading disorders (Granocchio et al., 2023). Two candidate genes for reading LD are found to have differential impacts in females either increasing risk (DYX1C1) or reducing risk (CNTNAP2), though more research is warranted in this area (Dandouh et al., 2009; Granocchio et al., 2023; Gu et al., 2018). It is important to note that while candidate genes have been identified, reading LD is thought to be complex and likely polygenetic (Miciak & Fletcher, 2023). Regarding neuroanatomical findings, imaging studies have shown that reading primarily involves the left hemisphere with recruitment of the frontal, temporoparietal, and occipitotemporal regions (Granocchio et al., 2023). However, these findings come from imaging studies that overrepresent males with reading disorders (Richlan et al., 2011), with males accounting for the majority of the sample in both pediatric and adult samples. Neuroimaging research in reading LD finds that for males the perisylvian reading network is involved (Evans et al., 2014). In contrast, research suggests that reading LD in girls may be characterized by involvement of early sensory and motor cortices and the right hemisphere (Evans et al., 2014). Some researchers have also hypothesized that a relationship between gray matter volume and fetal testosterone may play a role in gender differences in dyslexia (Krafnick & Evans, 2019; Lombardo et al., 2012). This pattern of findings suggests differing neurobiological contributions to reading disorder by sex; though, this warrants continued evaluation and replication in research.

There is less research on risk factors and neurobiological bases of specific LDs in mathematics (math LD). Importantly, many children with a math LD have a comorbid diagnosis of a reading LD which complicates research in this presentation. Heritability estimates for math LD have been found to be 0.47, although genetic factors relevant in math LD overlap with reading LD (Cirino, 2022; Kovas et al., 2007). In terms of neuropathology, research shows math LD is associated with decreased white and gray matter in numerous brain regions (parietal cortex, frontal cortex, and occipital cortex); though, there are relatively few studies (Cirino, 2022). A longitudinal study found persistent bilateral reduction in gray matter in the inferior parietal lobe (McCaskey et al., 2020). White matter reduction was found to be persistent in the inferior and superior longitudinal fasciculus, inferior fronto-occipital fasciculus, corticospinal tracts, and right anterior thalamic radiation (McCaskey et al., 2020). Many of these findings were consistent with other structural studies, but highlighted persistence over a 4-year period for children. Importantly, gender differences have not been examined in many of these studies with relatively small sample sizes. Functional studies in math LD have found differences in frontal and parietal areas (Kaufmann et al., 2011). While children typically show front-parietal activation on number processing and calculation tasks, those with math LDs showed differences in activation in parietal, frontal, and occipital regions (Kaufmann et al., 2011). Again, functional studies have not reported or examined gender differences.

In females, certain genetic disorders have a significantly increased risk of math LD. Specifically, females with Turners syndrome and fragile X experience much higher rates of math LDs than the general population (Murphy et al., 2006; see Boxes 2.1 and 2.3).

Symptoms

LDs are defined by academic achievement that falls well-below age-based expectations. When examining symptoms of specific LDs, there are a number of disorder specific and broader neurocognitive symptoms that are common to these disorders. IQ has been strongly associated with academic *g* or an overall general factor that encompasses foundational literacy skills as well as reading comprehension, math, and written expressions skills (Peterson et al., 2021). Children with specific LDs have higher scores on the Verbal Comprehension Index (VCI) and Perceptual Reasoning Index (PRI) of the Wechsler Intelligence Scale for Children - 4th Edition (WISC-IV), and lower scores on the Working Memory Index (WMI) and Processing Speed Index (PSI) (Giofrè et al., 2017). When examining differences in performance on the WISC-IV across LD categories, Toffalini et al. (2017) found that reading LDs were associated with more difficulty on aspects of the verbal comprehension index, while children with mathematics LDs had more difficulty with visual spatial or nonverbal reasoning on the perceptual reasoning and better performance on verbal tasks. Children with co-occurring reading and math LDs had lower intellectual functioning across all indices and subtests (Toffalini et al., 2017). When looking across children with reading LD, math LD, and comorbid reading and math LDs, Giofrè and colleagues (2022) found that females outperformed mains on the WMI and PSI with differences being more notable on the PSI. That said, these gender differences were small despite being clinically significant and more notable when comparing children with math LD to those with reading LD or comorbid reading and math LDs (Giofrè et al., 2022).

Numerous cognitive processes are implicated in reading LDs. Specifically, early delays in speech or language development, phonological processing, working memory, and rapid naming are associated with increased risk of reading LDs (American Psychiatric Association, 2013). Deficits in phonological processing are also identified in reading LDs, and are historically thought of as a primary deficit in this disorder (Miciak & Fletcher, 2023). That said, this is not a unitary and common deficit among all who have reading LDs, and thus a single deficit explanation for reading LDs is not appropriate (Peterson & Pennington, 2015). Weaknesses in phonological memory, verbal short-term memory, processing speed, and visual attention have been linked with reading LDs (Peterson & Pennington, 2015). Research suggests that females have stronger literacy skills as well as better verbal processing speed, working memory, conceptualization, visuospatial decoding, and orthographic decoding (Bolte et al., 2023). Arnett et al. (2015) concluded that sex-related differences in reading were due to differences in processing speed and inhibitory control and not due to deficits in working memory and phonological abilities.

There are inconsistent findings as it relates to gender differences in mathematics. This is complicated by variability in research examining differing aspects of math as well as math at achievement at different points in development/education. A recent large scales study found no significant gender differences in math achievement when using individually administered measures (Scheiber et al., 2015). Some studies have indicated minimal or no sex-differences in mathematics in early childhood and school age years (Lachance & Mazzocco, 2006; Robinson & Lubienski, 2011), but there has been some research that differences are reported more frequently as children advances into later school years (Lindberg et al., 2010). Consistent with this trajectory, gender differences are found on complex mathematical problem solving with females performing slightly better (Lindberg et al., 2010). Importantly, recent research has largely disputed the idea that women are worse at math than males. In countries where there is more gender equality, there is little data to support differences in mathematics achievement in general (Else-Quest et al., 2010).

A number of neurocognitive processes are implicated in math LDs. In addition to weaknesses in numerosity or number sense, studies find poorer performance in phonological processing (Cirino et al., 2018; Geary et al., 2007), rapid naming (Koponen et al., 2017), processing speed (Andersson & Lyxell, 2007; Geary et al., 2007), working memory (Friso-van den Bos et al., 2013), set-shifting (Van der Sluis et al., 2004; Yeniad et al., 2013), and fine motor skills (Carlson et al., 2013; Flores et al., 2023), though findings have been inconsistent in some of these areas. Visual spatial skills have commonly been thought of as related to mathematics, but research findings are mixed and results are variable depending on assessment tasks and age (Cirino, 2022; Cirino et al., 2002, 2007). Those with comorbid math LDs and reading LDs have more difficulty with processing speed, language, and mathematics measures than those with math LD alone, reading LD alone, and no LD (Cirino et al., 2015).

There is relatively little research on gender differences in the neurocognitive processes involved in math LD though some research has examined gender differences in processes involved in math achievement/performance. Research has found that phonological processing has an effect on children's number recognition and larger math performance (not specific to math LD). Kuzmina et al. (2019) found that in the first year of schooling girls had lower number recognition and math performance than boys at the start and end of the school year. Phonological processing had a larger effect on number recognition for girls than boys. Several studies have examined gender differences in approach to mathematics tasks showing that boys used more verbal retrieval strategies to solve math problems, while girls relied on more visual spatial strategies (Carr & Alexeev, 2011; Carr & Davis, 2001). That said, as math tasks became more complex, both sexes tended to shift toward a higher reliance on visual spatial strategies (Carr & Alexeev, 2011). One study found that boys relied more on verbal working memory when solving complex math problems than girls (van de Weijer-Bergsma et al., 2022).

Diagnosis and Prognosis

Though the research is old, data examining school identification versus research identification of students with dyslexia revealed that schools were much more biased to identify dyslexia in boys vs. girls (Shaywitz, 1990). This has been thought to be related to higher report of co-occurring externalizing behaviors in boys (Shaywitz, 1990). Quinn and Wagner examined differences in school identification compared to identification of reading impairment on standardized testing (2015). They found that far fewer girls who had reading impairment were identified by the school (1 in 7) as compared to boys (1 in 4). There is limited research on gender differences in diagnosis in math LD.

In the review on gender differences, Bolte et al. (2023) reported that across LDs females had higher rates of inattention and internalizing symptoms while males had higher rates of hyperactivity and externalizing behaviors at large. ADHD is highly comorbid with LDs as a whole. Population-based research has reported high rates of comorbidity with LD with higher rates reported in clinic referred studies (Kerner auch Koerner et al., 2021). When gender differences in rates of ADHD comorbidity with specific LDs were examined in a population-based study, females with ADHD had higher rates of comorbid math LDs than males with ADHD. No differences were identified in reading LD (Kerner auch Koerner et al., 2021). Research has historically found that LDs are more strongly associated with inattention as compared to hyperactivity and impulsivity. Consistent with this, Kerner auch Koerner and colleagues (Kerner auch Koerner et al., 2021) found that mathematics performance was predicted by both gender and inattentive symptoms with girls and those with inattention demonstrating poorer performance. In a clinic sample, Aro et al. (2022) found higher rates of ADHD, affective, and anxiety symptoms across LDs. When looking at gender and specific LD types (reading LD alone, math LD alone, and reading and math LD), they found reading LD alone was associated with increased risk of affective symptoms in girls (Aro et al., 2022). Math LD as a whole was associated with the highest endorsement of behavioral–emotional symptoms. For boys with math LD, specific concerns regarding anxiety and ADHD were reported (Aro et al., 2022).

Research has identified that girls with ADHD had higher risk of math LD than boys with ADHD, but this gender difference was not seen when examining reading LD (math LDs are diagnosed earlier when there is comorbid attentional or reading difficulties (American Psychiatric Association, 2013)). Math anxiety is thought to impact outcomes in math achievement and can exacerbate underlying challenges.

Research has found that females experience more math anxiety than males (Else-Quest et al., 2010) and research has found a modest relationship between math anxiety and math performance (Ma, 1999). Findings related to the causal relationship between math anxiety and math performance are inconsistent, and thus Carey et al. (2016) have described the relationship between math performance and math anxiety to be bidirectional. When examining comorbid diagnoses and symptoms, math LD has been associated with increased risk of language or communication difficulties, and autism spectrum disorder (Morsanyi et al., 2018).

Overall, the findings are inconsistent regarding gender differences in comorbidity for those with LDs. These findings are complicated by recruitment differences (clinic vs. population-based studies), definitions of LDs, and time at which comorbidity is examined. That said, it is clear that children with LDs are at risk for a number of comorbid diagnoses and neurocognitive challenges. These comorbidities impact prognosis. From a learning perspective, significant inattention in the preschool years is predictive of later difficulties in reading and mathematics achievement and poorer response to academic interventions (American Psychiatric Association, 2013). ADHD comorbidity with LDs is associated with poorer mental health outcomes than LDs without comorbid ADHD (American Psychiatric Association, 2013).

Research has supported the use of intervention services that support phonological processing skills for foundational word reading weaknesses in reading LDs (Miciak & Fletcher, 2023; Peterson & Pennington, 2015). Though there is limited data on gender differences in response to intervention in developmental dyslexia, a recent study found that when controlling for reading ability, girls were less likely to have an adequate response to intervention as compared to boys (Middleton et al., 2021). Research on gender differences in response to intervention for math LD was limited. Effective treatment of LDs is important as those with LDs are at risk for poorer outcomes as they transition into adulthood. SLDs in adolescence are associated with an increased risk of depressive symptoms in adulthood, with risk being higher women (Rim et al., 2024). The National Longitudinal Transition Study-2 (NLTS2) has reported poor postsecondary outcomes for students with LDs. Wagner et al. (2005) found that 32.7% of students with LDs as compared to 61.8% of peers without disabilities attended any form of postsecondary education, though more recent publications have indicated that this gap has narrowed (Sanford et al., 2011). The type of postsecondary setting does vary with fewer students with LDs attending 4-year university settings as compared to students with LDs while those with LDs were more likely to attend community college, vocational, technical, business, or 2-year programs (Sanford et al., 2011). While there is older research on gender differences, there is little current research on this relationship which is crucial given the well-documented close in the gender gap in students seeking post-secondary education.

Attention-Deficit/Hyperactivity Disorder (ADHD)

Attention-deficit/hyperactivity disorder (ADHD) is a neurodevelopmental disorder marked by persistent patterns of inattention and/or hyperactivity/impulsivity (American Psychiatric Association, 2013). As is the case with any clinical diagnosis, primary symptoms of ADHD must cause a degree of functional impairment, such that individuals with ADHD experience a direct impact on their social, adaptive, and/or academic/occupational functioning. The DSM-5-TR describes symptoms of inattention (e.g., often fails to give close attention to details or makes careless mistakes; difficulty sustaining attention in tasks or play; does not seem to listen when spoken to directly; difficulty organizing tasks and activities) and hyperactivity/impulsivity (e.g., often fidgets with or taps hands or feet or squirms in seat; runs about or climbs in situations where it is inappropriate; "on the go"; difficulty waiting his or her turn). A minimum of six symptoms need to present for at least 6 months prior to the age of 12 years, and to a "degree that is inconsistent with developmental level," in order to appropriately make a diagnosis of ADHD (American Psychiatric Association, 2013). Symptoms must present in at least two settings (e.g., home and school). Within ADHD, individuals can present with a predominately inattentive subtype, a predominately hyperactive/impulsive subtype, or a combined subtype (i.e., criterion for both inattention and hyperactivity/impulsivity are met). Diagnoses are additionally classified by severity, with clinicians rating whether the ADHD presentation is mild, moderate, or severe.

In what follows is a broad-based overview of gender differences in ADHD, based largely off meta-analytic reviews or population-based studies. The information below focuses primarily on children, but in some cases includes studies with adult samples. Given the vastness of this topic, readers are directed to more comprehensive texts for additional detail (e.g., Oxford Textbook of Attention Deficit Hyperactivity Disorder; Carucci et al., 2023).

Prevalence Rates

Among children aged 5–17 years, 11.3% have ever been diagnosed with ADHD between 2020 and 2022 (Reuben & Elgaddal, 2024). Notably, there is a higher prevalence of ADHD among boys (14.5%) relative to girls (8.0%), a pattern that presents early in childhood and persists throughout adolescence (Reuben & Elgaddal, 2024). Higher rates of diagnosis are also documented among white non-Hispanic children (13.4%) relative to Black/African American non-Hispanic (10.8%) and Hispanic/Latinx (8.9%) children (Reuben & Elgaddal, 2024).

The ratio of female to male diagnosis in children is approximately 1:4 in clinical studies (Martin, 2024). In contrast, community or population studies suggest this ratio is closer to 2:1, highlighting the fact that diagnoses among women may be missed in many clinical settings (Martin, 2024). Indeed, girls with ADHD are not as readily identified by parents and teachers, in part due to differences in symptomatology (Staller & Faraone, 2006).

Relative to childhood, the prevalence of ADHD in adulthood decreases with age (Song et al., 2021). This is the case of those with symptomatic adult ADHD, as well as those with a childhood onset. Recent systematic review and meta-analysis reported a prevalence of 6.76% in symptomatic adult ADHD and 2.58% of persistent adult ADHD (Song et al., 2021).

Risk Factors

While ADHD is less common among females than males, there are no differences in familial risk patterns between boys and girls (Nussbaum, 2012; Staller & Faraone, 2006). There are also no known gender differences in the genetic factors thought to be implicated in ADHD (Martin, 2024), although some research has suggested the possible explanation of an overexpression of Y-linked genes (see Greven et al., 2018). Relatedly, females with a single X chromosome (i.e., Turner syndrome) are at a higher risk for ADHD, suggesting that the additional X chromosome in females could be a protective factor against ADHD (Carucci et al., 2023). To this end, Klinefelter syndrome, in which males carry an extra X chromosome (XXY), is associated with higher rates of ADHD, specifically the ADHD inattentive subtype (Carucci et al., 2023). This finding is similar to what is observed among women and may suggest that the number of X chromosomes could also be related to the gender differences seen in ADHD (Carucci et al., 2023).

Regarding neuroanatomical differences, there is yet to be a clear consensus in terms of gender differences. Despite this, atypical development of many brain structures, including the prefrontal cortex, amygdala, caudate, putamen, globus pallidus, and cerebellum are well documented (e.g., Carucci et al., 2023). Both structural and functional studies suggest cortical and subcortical differences between girls and boys (see Carucci et al., 2023); however, majority of studies have relied on male participants and thus limit the conclusions that can be drawn.

Children with ADHD show difficulties with social, academic, adaptive, and behavioral functioning, with a number of meaningful gender differences (Carucci et al., 2023). Specifically, boys with ADHD are more likely to experience comorbid externalizing disorders, tic disorder, and difficulties with language, learning, and/or motor development, while girls are at a higher risk for internalizing symptoms and eating disorders (Greven et al., 2018). Studies are mixed regarding whether comorbid autism spectrum disorder and/or ID are less common in males vs. males, with some studies suggesting this to occur at lower rates in girls (Greven et al., 2018), and others suggesting it occurs at higher rates in girls (Ottosen et al., 2019). There is also variability in risk factors across the lifespan. For example, substance use disorders impact females and males at equal rates during childhood, but this may be of greater risk for males with ADHD during adulthood (Greven et al., 2018). Notably, these findings should be interpreted with a degree of caution, as it is not clear the extent to which ADHD poses additional risk for psychiatric comorbidity beyond gender alone, as many studies do not include sex-specific comparisons between clinical and control groups (Greven et al., 2018). In addition, oppositional defiant disorder and conduct disorder are more common in children with ADHD, while mood and anxiety disorders, and antisocial personality disorders are more common in adolescence and adulthood (Carucci et al., 2023). Adults with ADHD also show a higher risk of suicidal behavior, particularly those with comorbid psychiatric conditions (Carucci et al., 2023).

Symptom Presentation

Girls with ADHD show higher rates of the inattentive subtype compared to boys and are usually less hyperactive (Martin, 2024; Nussbaum, 2012). Indeed, boys are more prone to experiencing symptoms of hyperactivity and impulsivity, and more often meet criteria for all ADHD subtypes (Greven et al., 2018). In part because of the behavioral differences that accompany the latter, girls often receive a diagnosis of ADHD later than boys and are less likely to be prescribed medication for ADHD symptomatology (Martin, 2024).

Both boys and girls with ADHD experience neurocognitive difficulties relative to controls. Indeed, compared to controls, boys and girls with ADHD show differences in intellectual abilities, achievement, reaction time, vigilance, working memory, and many aspects of executive function (Pievsky & McGrath, 2018). There is significant heterogeneity in the neuropsychological profile of ADHD, and the presence of comorbid neurodevelopmental or psychiatric conditions must always be considered. Temporal processing deficits (including motor timing, perceptual timing, and temporal predication) tend to be a consistent area of concern among individuals with ADHD (Carucci et al., 2023), and may subsequently have downstream effects on other neurocognitive domains.

Some studies have suggested sex-specific differences across neurocognitive domains, but these findings overall are inconclusive, with even some contradictory findings reported in the literature (Greven et al., 2018). However, studies find that females with ADHD may show poorer working memory, vocabulary, and visual spatial skills relative to boys with ADHD, while boys show more impulsive errors, slower processing speed, and more motor functioning deficits (Carucci et al., 2023). Performance on the continuous performance test (CPT) shows greater commission errors among boys and no differences in rates of omission errors (Carucci et al., 2023).

Boys and girls with ADHD can experience difficulties with social functioning and peer relationships. The presentation of these difficulties differs between boys and girls; boys can become more aggressive with peers, while girls are usually more verbally aggressive and have a tendency toward relational aggression (Carucci et al., 2023). Girls with ADHD are also at an increased risk of being bullied, whereas boys are more likely to bully others (Carucci et al., 2023).

Diagnosis and Prognosis

As a result of many of the symptom differences between males and females, diagnosis of ADHD among girls tends to be more difficult than for boys. Indeed, ADHD is diagnosed 3–16 times more frequently in males compared to females during the childhood years; however, these findings level off and become more similar by adulthood (Babinski, 2024; Martin, 2024). Given this striking difference, concerns about the appropriateness of the ADHD diagnostic criteria for girls as a group have been raised. Girls tend to present with lower symptom counts on rating scales and lab measures compared to boys (e.g., Carucci et al., 2023; Nussbaum, 2012). As a result, for girls to be identified as meeting threshold for ADHD, they need to present with significantly more attention symptoms when compared with female peers than do males when compared with male peers (Nussbaum, 2012). This puts girls at risk for being missed and not receiving a diagnosis and subsequent treatment, which has led to suggestions for a "corrected" criterion that would include gender-specific thresholds (McGee & Feehan, 1991).

The symptom presentation of girls also tends to be better tolerated by parents and teachers since girls are less likely to show problematic or disruptive behaviors (Carucci et al., 2023). Thus, it is often the case that girls are only diagnosed when their ADHD presentation is quite severe, and/or when they experience a clinically concerning comorbid condition (e.g., anxiety and depression; Carucci et al., 2023), which may be secondary to untreated ADHD.

Perhaps because of a later and more difficult diagnostic process, girls with ADHD are therefore less likely to be prescribed ADHD medication (Martin et al., 2023), despite the known effectiveness of pharmacotherapy as a first-line treatment in ADHD (Kok et al., 2020). This finding shifts in adulthood, such that there are no gender differences in the frequency of pharmacotherapy among adults with ADHD (Kok et al., 2020). Possible gender differences related to pharmacological intervention have been suggested, with at least one review finding that atomoxetine may be more promising for girls and women with ADHD than a single daily use of methylphenidate (Kok et al., 2020). Further research in this area is needed, however.

Possibly secondary to a later diagnosis and/or treatment, there are a number of areas in adulthood in which women tend to be more adversely affected than men (Faheem et al., 2022). For example, a number of studies have found that women are more impaired in social functioning, adaptive functioning, and stress management in adulthood compared to men (Faheem et al., 2022). These results are not necessarily consistent across studies and many studies have also found that both men and women with ADHD show equal rates of impairment in these areas, as well as in educational outcomes (Faheem et al., 2022). However, in one recent longitudinal study, relative to a control group of girls without ADHD, girls with ADHD were found to be at a higher risk of poorer outcomes over a 16-year period (Owens et al., 2017). By their mid-20s, girls with a history of childhood ADHD were more likely to experience internalizing/externalizing problems, self-injury, poorer educational achievement and occupational attainment, health problems, and social problems

(Owens et al., 2017). Interestingly, a small subset of these girls experienced childhood-limited ADHD and were not at risk for the extent of problems in adulthood that was found among the girls with more persistent ADHD symptoms, although, some differences were still found among this group relative to controls (Owens et al., 2017).

Autism Spectrum Disorder (ASD)

Autism spectrum disorder (ASD) is a neurodevelopmental disorder characterized by social communication difficulties (i.e., reduced social-emotional reciprocity, impaired nonverbal communicative behaviors, and difficulty with developing or understanding relationships) and the presence of restricted interests and repetitive behaviors (RRBs; e.g., repetitive motor movements, having an inflexible adherence to routines, having intense and fixated interests, or experiencing sensory sensitivities/interests) (American Psychiatric Association, 2013). The DSM-5 (American Psychiatric Association, 2013) indicates that the "symptoms must be present in the early developmental period (but may not become fully manifest until social demands exceed limited capacities, or may be masked by learned strategies in later life)" (p. 50). It is also necessary that the "symptoms cause clinically significant impairment in social, occupational, or other important areas of current functioning" (p. 50) and cannot be explained by intellectual disability or global developmental delay.

Below we offer details on gender differences in ASD, which has been an area of growing clinical and research focus given the vast discrepancy in age of diagnosis, presenting symptoms, and genetic architecture between autistic individuals assigned male versus female at birth. Of note, throughout this chapter both identity-first and person-first language are used to incorporate the varied preferences of autism terminology among the autism stakeholder community.

Prevalence Rates

At present, approximately 1 in 36 individuals under the age of 8 years meets diagnostic criteria for ASD (Maenner, 2023), according to the Center for Disease Control (CDC). The prevalence of ASD has increased dramatically over the past few decades. In the 1990s, the rate was about 1 in 1000 children, which rose to approximately 1 in 100 by 2010. By 2018, ASD had become the second most common psychiatric condition among children, affecting around 2.7% of boys and 1.7% of all 8-year-olds. Recent data from the Autism and Developmental Disabilities Monitoring (ADDM) Network in 2020 suggests an even higher prevalence, with 1 in 36 children aged 8 years being diagnosed (Maenner, 2023). The diagnostic gap between boys and girls has also narrowed, with about 4% of boys and 1% of girls being identified, indicating an increased recognition of ASD in girls (Maenner, 2023).

ASD diagnostic estimates show a male-to-female ratio ranging from 3:1 to 4:1 (Loomes et al., 2017; Maenner, 2023; Posserud et al., 2021). While the CDC reports a 4:1 ratio, a rigorous meta-analysis from 54 studies highlights that the male-to-female ratio in ASD is closer to 3:1 (Loomes et al., 2017). Moreover, in Norway, the ratio varies by age and comorbidities (e.g., intellectual disability and ADHD), with 2.57:1 in adults and 3.67:1 in adolescents (Posserud et al., 2021). The gap widens in verbally fluent individuals or those with higher cognitive abilities, reaching up to 7:1 (Fombonne, 2003). These differences highlight potential sex-related genetic effects on ASD symptoms. Notably, a meta-analysis revealed that ID affects ASD symptomatology. Specifically, all females with ASD with or without ID generally display fewer restricted interests and repetitive behaviors than their male counterparts. Conversely, relative to their male counterparts, females with ASD who do not have an ID exhibit better social communication skills (Saure et al., 2023) while females with ASD also with ID experience more social communication difficulties.

Risk Factors

Numerous theories have been proposed to explain the gender disparity in ASD. The *female protective effect* posits that females need a greater genetic or neurological impact to show ASD symptoms compared to males (Hull et al., 2020; Lai et al., 2015). Studies indicate that females with ASD often have higher rates of intellectual and comorbid difficulties and more copy number variants than males (Sebat et al., 2007; Wigdor et al., 2022). Additionally, females in the top percentile for ASD traits exhibit greater symptom severity, suggesting a higher genetic load in families with a female with ASD (Robinson et al., 2013). This implies that females may be more resistant to developing ASD.

Proposed by Baron-Cohen (2002), the *extreme male brain theory* suggests that ASD represents an exaggerated form of the male brain, characterized by strengths in pattern recognition and weaknesses in social intelligence. It links fetal testosterone to brain development and ASD traits. However, the theory is criticized for reinforcing harmful stereotypes, oversimplifying gender differences, and failing to capture the complexity of the ASD phenotype (Botha et al., 2022; Ridley, 2019; Joel, 2021; Sanderson, 2021; Santos et al., 2022; van Eijk & Zietsch, 2021; Whitehouse, 2016).

The *gender incoherence theory* suggests that males with ASD display female traits, while females with ASD exhibit male traits (Bejerot et al., 2012). Some brain imaging studies support this by showing neural patterns in ASD individuals that resemble those of the opposite gender (Deng & Wang, 2021; Floris et al., 2018; Lee et al., 2020; Smith et al., 2019). However, other studies challenge this theory, indicating it may not fully explain the observed gender differences in ASD (Olson et al., 2020).

Table 2.2 Key findings for neuropsychological performance in autism spectrum disorder

Domain	Key takeaways
Development, cognitive, and adaptive functioning	Females with ASD often show more impairment in daily living skills. Mixed findings on gender differences in cognitive abilities
Executive functioning	Parent reports suggest greater impairments in girls, while self-reports show no gender differences. Females outperform males in some standardized tasks
Language	Females often show better narrative competence and pragmatic language skills. Language gaps between sexes tend to close over time
Visual perception and visual attention	Some studies show higher visual reception scores in girls. Females may exhibit social attention patterns similar to non-autistic peers
Theory of mind and social cognition	No significant gender differences in theory of mind. Males show lower empathy levels. Females may have slightly stronger social cognitive skills
Memory	Females recall more details about autobiographical and emotional memories. Neural correlates during memory tasks vary by gender
Sensori-motor	Males with ASD often show worse motor skills compared to controls. Females may outperform males in fine motor skills but not gross motor skills

Note. *ASD* autism spectrum disorder

Finally, and a highly prevalent theory, *camouflaging theory* proposes that females with ASD can imitate non-autistic behaviors, resulting in a more concealed expression of their ASD traits (Hull et al., 2017). Research shows that females with ASD often report higher levels of symptoms than what clinical assessments reveal, likely due to behaviors such as linguistic masking, reduced stimming, and increased eye contact (Lai et al., 2017; Parish-Morris et al., 2017). This may lead to underdiagnosis in females. However, camouflaging is also associated with increased anxiety and depression (Cook et al., 2021; Tubío-Fungueiriño et al., 2021). A meta-analysis supports the notion that ASD traits are both less expressed and less perceived in females (Chen et al., 2020). Camouflaging is very common in adults with ASD and is an area of enormous clinical relevance for neuropsychologists and clinicians to consider in their diagnostic process.

Symptom Presentation

As noted earlier, ASD is highly heterogeneous, and its symptoms and severity vary widely among individuals. This variability complicates clinical diagnosis and treatment, as well as research efforts to delineate a consistent symptom profile. As a result, clinicians should tailor their approaches to each person's unique needs for best practice, while researchers face challenges in identifying common mechanisms and effective interventions due to the diverse presentation. Additionally, symptoms can differ significantly between males and females, further adding to the complexity. As such, research is ongoing, and the following review highlights past and current efforts to characterize ASD traits and the corresponding neuropsychological profiles across sexes.

Core Symptoms

There is a recent growing body of literature that aims to disentangle the sex/gender differences of the core features of autism and the neuropsychological profile; however, there is substantial variability. Overall, higher functioning females with ASD tend to have camouflaged/masked symptoms, with compensatory peer behaviors such as physical proximity, and fewer or more socially appropriate RRBs (Bitsika et al., 2018; Dean et al., 2017; Frazier et al., 2014; Hartley & Sikora, 2009; Lai et al., 2019; Osório et al., 2021; Postorino et al., 2015; Ros-Demarize et al., 2020; Schuck et al., 2019). Specifically, relative to males with ASD, females with ASD demonstrate either better or greater difficulty in social communication when using gold-standard clinical assessments (ADOS, ADI-R), with findings differing by age (Beggiato et al., 2017; Frazier et al., 2014; Lawson et al., 2018; Postorino et al., 2015; Tillmann et al., 2018). Females with ASD similarly show comparable or greater impairments in social communication on parent-rating scales and clinical observation screeners, with different developmental trajectories (Backer van Ommeren et al., 2017; Fulton et al., 2017; Grove et al., 2017; Head et al., 2014; Kaat et al., 2021; Nishimura et al., 2023; Rodgers et al., 2019; Ros-Demarize et al., 2020), as well as better play-based and friendship skills particularly in older children due to camouflaging (Dean et al., 2017; Lai et al., 2019; Schuck et al., 2019). In terms of RRBs, females with autism tend to have more socially appropriate circumscribed interests relative to males with ASD, which tend to also vary across development (Antezana et al., 2019; McFayden et al., 2019; Nowell et al., 2019; Tillmann et al., 2018). As such, understanding and clarifying gender differences in ASD symptoms is crucial for improving early diagnosis and customizing both assessment tools and treatment strategies.

Internalizing Symptoms

Research on gender differences in mood and anxiety comorbidities in ASD shows mixed results. Many studies find no significant differences between males and females (Frazier et al., 2014; Park et al., 2012; Postorino et al., 2015; Simonoff et al., 2008; Solomon et al., 2012). However, some studies suggest subtle differences, particularly during school-age and adolescence. For instance, autistic girls may exhibit greater anxious/depressed affect as toddlers (Hartley & Sikora, 2009), but lower anxiety as preschoolers (Prosperi et al., 2021). Subsequently, school-age girls exhibit higher rates of specific phobia (Gadow et al., 2005), and adolescent females with ASD frequently experience more severe depression, anxiety, and self-harm concerns than their male counterparts. Large cohort studies also suggest that autistic females are more prone to mood or anxiety disorders and psychiatric hospitalizations compared to males in general.

Externalizing Symptoms

ADHD (Arnett et al., 2015; Biederman et al., 2002; Loyer Carbonneau et al., 2021; Rucklidge, 2010) and oppositional-defiant disorder (ODD) (Rynkiewicz & Lucka, 2018) occur at higher rates among males with ASD versus females. Interestingly, parents report no differences in externalizing symptoms during toddlerhood via standardized questionnaires (Hartley & Sikora, 2009), but greater externalizing symptoms in school-age among girls versus boys with ASD (Frazier et al., 2014; Holtmann et al., 2007; Mandy et al., 2012).

Neuropsychological Domains (Table 2.2)

Development, Cognitive, and Adaptive Functioning ASD is highly heterogeneous, with varying intellectual and neuropsychological abilities, and many individuals have comorbid intellectual disability (Lai et al., 2015). Females with ASD may be more readily identified when they have intellectual disability, as significant difficulties with daily living prompt clinical treatment (Lai et al., 2015). Among those without intellectual disability, gender differences in cognitive domains have been reported, such as faster processing speed in girls with ASD compared to boys (Koyama et al., 2009), and a greater verbal–nonverbal cognitive split in boys (Ankenman et al., 2014). However, some studies found no gender differences in cognition (Duvall et al., 2020; Hartley & Sikora, 2009; Reinhardt et al., 2015). Developmentally, females initially show lower cognitive abilities but greater gains over time (Postorino et al., 2015). Adaptive skills are generally more impaired in females with ASD, particularly in daily living skills (Frazier et al., 2014; Ratto et al., 2018; White et al., 2017), although some studies found no gender differences (Reinhardt et al., 2015). The gap between IQ and adaptive abilities is similar between autistic males and females but larger compared to non-autistic individuals (McQuaid et al., 2022).

Executive Functioning Studies examining executive functioning in males and females with ASD show mixed results, varying by assessment method. Parent reports indicate greater executive function impairments in school-aged girls with ASD than boys (White et al., 2017), while self-reports show no gender differences in adolescents and adults (Demetriou et al., 2021). Parent-reported executive functions were linked to social reciprocity in females with ASD but not males with ASD (Torske et al., 2023). Neuropsychological assessment reveals no gender differences in mental rotation tasks in adults with ASD, although underlying neural circuitry differs between sexes (Beacher et al., 2012; Rohde et al., 2018). In working memory tasks, females with ASD produced longer digit sequences, while males excelled in letter-number sequencing (Kiep & Spek, 2017). School-aged autistic girls without IDs performed worse than boys on response inhibition and planning tasks (Lemon et al., 2011; Nyden et al., 2000), though other studies found no gender differences in planning (Bolte et al., 2011; Kiep & Spek, 2017). Finally, adolescent females with ASD outperformed males in set-shifting tasks (Bolte et al., 2011; Kiep & Spek, 2017).

Language Empirical studies on language in ASD also reveal mixed findings—some report lower language skills in females compared to males (Carter et al., 2007; Holtmann et al., 2007), while others find that high-IQ females have fewer social-communicative impairments (Lai et al., 2011). In storytelling, girls demonstrate better narrative competence, using more cognitive devices (Boorse et al., 2019). Conversational studies show females use more words and social language, while males use more fillers (Cho et al., 2023; Cola et al., 2022; Kauschke et al., 2016). Overall, females with ASD tend to exhibit stronger pragmatic language skills than males (den Hartog et al., 2023). Additionally, autobiographical memory studies suggest higher verbal fluency in females (Goddard et al., 2014). Some review studies similarly indicate that males with ASD have a higher prevalence of speech and language conditions (Adani & Cepanec, 2019). In ASD, despite initial differences, language gaps between sexes tend to close over time (Carter et al., 2007; Postorino et al., 2015).

Visual Perception and Visual Attention Visual processing and attention in ASD similarly present complex patterns, with limited understanding in females. While studies using the Mullen Scale of Early Learning find no visual reception differences (Duvall et al., 2020; Reinhardt et al., 2015), Carter et al. (2007) report higher scores in preschool girls with ASD. High-risk infant girls display increased attention to social stimuli, potentially mitigating ASD symptoms and perhaps contributing to camouflaging behaviors (Chawarska et al., 2016). Likewise, females with SD exhibit social attention visual patterns similarly to their non-autistic peers, which is in contrast to the reduced social attention observed in males with ASD (Harrop et al., 2018a, 2018b, 2020).

Theory of Mind and Social Cognition Theory of mind deficits are prevalent in ASD (Baron-Cohen et al., 2001). While no significant gender differences are noted in theory of mind abilities in ASD (Lai et al., 2012), males with ASD exhibit lower empathy levels compared to females (Auyeung et al., 2009; Baron-Cohen & Wheelwright, 2004). Females with ASD may possess slightly stronger social cognitive skills than males with ASD (Corbett et al., 2021).

Memory Very few studies have investigated memory differences between males and females with ASD. Goddard et al. (2014) found that males with ASD had more difficulty retrieving specific autobiographical memories compared to male controls, while females with and without ASD recalled more details about autobiographical and emotional memories.

Sensori-Motor Autistic individuals often display motor deficits (Fournier et al., 2010; Green et al., 2009; Jansiewicz et al., 2006; Mari et al., 2003; Pan et al., 2009), yet research on gender differences in motor function is limited. A large SPARK study found that males with ASD plateau in development by around the age of 7 years, while females plateau earlier but show increased growth by the age of 13 years (Bhat, 2020). Lai et al. (2012) noted that males with ASD performed worse on motor tasks than controls, while females with ASD showed no significant differences from female controls. Motor development scores in male preschoolers with ASD were reported to be better than in females (Carter et al., 2007), although other studies found that females outperformed males in fine motor skills (Craig et al., 2020; Zwaigenbaum et al., 2012). Finally, gross motor skills were found to be stronger among males with ASD than females (Craig et al., 2020).

Diagnosis and Prognosis

Detecting and intervening early is crucial for improving outcomes in individuals with ASD (Corsello, 2005; Rogers, 1996). Although a diagnosis can be made as young as 2 years (Lord, 1995), and instances of early identification have risen in recent years (Hertz-Picciotto & Delwiche, 2009), there are significant disparities in diagnosis age across different demographic groups and sexes. To ensure accurate diagnosis, comprehensive clinical evaluations that encompass various assessment domains are recommended as best practices for identifying ASD (Huerta & Lord, 2012). Such evaluations typically consist of detailed clinical, developmental, and medical interviews, along with questionnaires from multiple informants. Critically, gold-standard clinical-behavioral assessments targeting ASD symptoms, including the Autism Diagnostic Observation Schedule (ADOS; Lord et al., 2000; Lord et al., 2012) and the Autism Diagnostic Interview-Revised (ADI-R; Lord et al., 1994), are utilized.

However, the ADOS and/or ADI-R may exhibit reduced sensitivity in identifying ASD symptoms in females compared to males (Bitsika et al., 2018; Rynkiewicz & Lucka, 2018). The reported gender disparity in ASD prevalence has led to an underrepresentation of females in research studies, potentially generating a male bias in understanding and assessing the disorder. Studies indicate diagnostic tools like the ADOS-2 and ADI-R may exhibit differences in scoring males and females, especially those with high cognitive abilities (Kaat et al., 2021; Kalb et al., 2022; Ratto et al., 2018). Population-based studies suggest lower gender ratio differences compared to clinic-based studies, possibly due to biases in assessment and diagnosis or greater likelihood of females with co-occurring conditions seeking treatment. As a result, females with ASD are more likely to be misdiagnosed, and more likely to have a delay in diagnosis compared to males with ASD (McDonnell et al., 2021; McQuaid et al., 2022; Rutherford et al., 2016).

Conclusions

In general, females tend to fair better in terms of prevalence and severity of presentations in neurodevelopmental disorders. Examination for gender differences in diagnosis, symptom presentation, and prognosis has been limited in many neurodevelopmental populations with recent research most notably in autism spectrum disorders and attention deficit hyperactivity disorder have highlighted important differences in phenotypic presentations and neuropsychological profiles. Historical ascertainment biases in research examining neurodevelopmental disorders have hindered our understanding and ability to appropriately define and diagnose these presentations in females. Continued examination of gender differences in neurodevelopmental disorders in imperative to better characterize, diagnoses, and support females with neurodevelopmental disorders and improve outcomes for women across the lifespan.

Research Takeaways

ID/IDD

- There is very limited research looking at gender differences in terms of presentation and long-term outcomes in the IDD population beyond syndromic profiles (e.g., Rett syndrome). Future research should examine gender-based differences.
- There is also limited reporting on gender differences in rates or outcomes across racial and ethnic groups which is an important consideration when thinking about intersectionality.
- Research is complicated by the heterogeneity of this population and methodological challenges with regard to how ID/IDD is defined.
- Gender differences have been identified in terms of comorbid psychiatric presentations, but this research has not yet expanded to explore gender differences in treatment response for these psychiatric presentations. Expanding research in this area would greatly inform clinical care.
- While there is some data on postsecondary education and vocational outcomes in ID, this has not thoroughly examined by gender and there is limited understanding of protective factors for young adults with ID.

Learning Disorders

- Due to ascertainment biases as well as higher prevalence rates of reading disorders in males as compared to females, much of the research in reading LD has focused more on males.
- Research examining dyslexia or reading disorders in females does not yet have sufficient replication with regard to recruitment of differing neuroanatomy.
- Research needs to be expanded to determine whether there are female/male phenotypes and understand what implication this has in terms of response to intervention.
- Research is very limited in specific learning disorders with impairment in mathematics and written expression. Research to understand population base and prevalence rates in these disorders when using consistent definitions with regard to these diagnoses is warranted.
  - Addressing this dearth of research across genders would then allow for a more thorough examination of gender-based prevalence rates and gender differences in presentation as well as etiology in these SLDs.
- Research in sex-based differences in response to intervention is essential. Given the report of poorer response to intervention for women in one study, it is imperative that this be further evaluated to clarify this differential response. If this finding is replicated, it is important to understand whether this difference is related to greater preponderance of males in dyslexia and intervention research biasing this intervention. Differential intervention approaches should be explored to assess and identify evidence-based interventions to address LDs across presentations.

ADHD

- More research examining sex-specific differences related to ADHD is necessary, with more direct comparisons of male ADHD cases with male controls and female ADHD cases with female controls.
- Research focused on females with ADHD remains warranted across domains (e.g., diagnosis, treatment, etiology, related correlates).

ASD

- Existing research on gender differences in ASD highlights areas of divergence and overlap across various neuropsychological domains.

- Findings remain largely inconclusive due to the disorder's inherent heterogeneity and variations in research methodologies, such as inconsistent comparison groups and sample sizes.
- Methodological differences contribute to observed disparities in ASD symptomatology between sexes (Van Wijngaarden-Cremers et al., 2014).
- There is no research on sex-based differences across different ethnic and cultural groups, where socioeconomic and cultural factors have been shown to influence ASD detection and diagnosis.
- Research has demonstrated disparities among racial and ethnic minorities (Elsabbagh et al., 2012; Maenner, 2023), which may stem from differences in symptom reporting, clinician biases, and healthcare access.
- Findings highlight the urgent need for more equitable diagnostic practices (Fiscella et al., 2000; Hertz-Picciotto & Delwiche, 2009; Mandell et al., 2007).
- Future research on gender differences in ASD should address several key limitations:

  – Given the behavioral definition of ASD, diagnostic criteria should be adjusted to account for sex-specific differences, necessitating a clearer characterization of autistic females. Employ less biased instrumentation and incorporate various assessment methods.
  – Population-based studies can elucidate diagnostic challenges and compensatory mechanisms in females.
  – Understanding protective factors unique to autistic females may refine screening tools and treatment strategies.
  – Cross-cultural investigations are needed to untangle biological and cultural influences on ASD and sex.
  – Redefining ASD to accommodate sex-specific variations and exploring unique symptom clusters in females are crucial for a comprehensive understanding of the disorder's heterogeneity in addition to informing targets of intervention for autistic females.

Clinical Takeaways

ID/IDD

- Females with intellectual disability have high rates of comorbid medical, psychiatric, and neurodevelopmental disorders that increase risk of poor outcomes as they transition to adulthood.
- It is imperative for psychologists to provide comprehensive evaluations given increased risk of co-morbid diagnoses in women.
- To appropriately support the needs of this population, the assessment and recommendations should go beyond cognitive functioning and include interview and

associated related to access to the medical system, co-morbid psychiatric conditions, and current health behaviors to understand multiple levels of need.

- Recommendations provided to families should address the cognitive presentation as well as provide psychoeducation and recommendations related to physical activity, health, access to medical care, and access to social services and vocational services.
- Clinicians working with children and adults with ID should be integrating developmentally appropriate, trauma informed care given the rates of abuse in this population.
  - Safety interviewing as well as interviewing about past trauma should be a part of all diagnostic interviews and intakes given the impact that trauma can have on psychosocial and cognitive presentations.
  - Providers should be prepared to provide parents with appropriate resources for gender education and encourage families to start introducing these topics at the same age as typically developing peers at a level that is accessible for the child, teen, or young adult.

Learning Disorders

- Research has identified gender differences in prevalence rates in reading LD.
- Providers should be aware of documented differences in rates of identification of girls with LDs based on teacher report or school emphasizing the importance of gathering information from multiple informants.
- Girls tend to be identified at higher rates across LDs when standardized assessments are utilized.
- Thorough interviewing around the development of early language, phonological processing, and motor skills is an important piece of identify risk factors associated with higher rates of both reading and math LDs.
- Given rates of comorbid diagnosis for children and adults with LDs, it is important to integrate diagnostic evaluations and screenings that include assessment of externalizing and internalizing symptoms as well as ADHD screens. Early ADHD and inattentive symptoms have led to earlier identification of girls with LDs, but the comorbidity also raises concerns about poorer outcomes thus necessitating efficient access to appropriate intervention services following identification.
- Women with LDs have higher rates of internalizing symptoms as well as higher rates of math anxiety. Thorough evaluation of potential psychiatric symptoms or comorbidity when completing LD evaluations should be standard practice with efficient referral for appropriate interventions to target comorbid symptomatology is important to minimize the bidirectional impact of these symptoms on academic performance.

ADHD

- Sex differences play an important role in ADHD.
- ADHD is diagnosed at higher rates among boys, although this is likely a result of diagnostic bias (Carucci et al., 2023), a fact that should be considered in clinical evaluations of girls.
- The diagnostic criteria is largely informed by the presentation of boys with ADHD (and not girls).
- Girls with ADHD are more likely to show inattentive symptoms. Perhaps secondary to misdiagnosis, girls are at a higher risk for experiencing comorbid internalizing disorders, while boys are more likely to show externalizing symptomatology.
- Significant individual variability exists related to the neuropsychological phenotype associated with ADHD, with many factors contributing to these individual differences.
- Sex differences shift over the course of development, such that important differences in childhood may equalize by adulthood. Despite this, there may be emerging evidence to suggest that women have more difficulties in social and adaptive functioning in adulthood relative to men, which could be secondary to missed opportunities for intervention in childhood.
- Pharmacological and behavioral interventions are known to be effective among individuals with ADHD, but further review is needed to determine whether specific treatments may be better suited for females relative to males (Kok et al., 2020).

ASD

- Autistic females are more likely to be misdiagnosed and experience delays in diagnosis compared to autistic males.
- A comprehensive evaluation that applies a multi-method approach, such as using a combination of questionnaires, behavioral assessments, and diagnostic interviews, can help to capture the full spectrum of behaviors and traits (especially those that may be masked or camouflaged in females).
- Given the substantial variability in neuropsychological findings between autistic males and females, it is crucial to understand areas of strengths and weaknesses at an individual level.
- Tailoring assessments to the unique profile of each patient can lead to more accurate diagnoses (and subsequently more effective targets for intervention).
- Applying existing theories such as the female protective effect and camouflaging can provide valuable insights into the female autistic phenotype. Understanding these theories can inform both diagnosis and intervention strategies, helping clinicians to recognize subtler manifestations of ASD in females.

- Females with ASD may exhibit more socially appropriate restricted interests and may engage in camouflaging behaviors which can be easily overlooked in structured clinical settings. As such, behavioral observations in naturalistic settings can provide rich clinical information to inform diagnoses.
- Incorporating reports from multiple informants, including parents and teachers, is essential to gain a comprehensive understanding of the child's behavior across different contexts. These reports can provide valuable insights into social communication difficulties and repetitive behaviors that may not be evident during clinical assessments, particularly among females.
- Clinicians may also consider the developmental trajectories of ASD symptoms, which differ between males and females (e.g., females may initially show lower cognitive abilities but exhibit greater gains over time). An understanding of these trajectories can aid in early identification.
- Comorbid conditions such as anxiety, depression, and ADHD, which present differently in females with ASD, are also important considerations as they can obscure the core ASD symptomatology.
- Recognizing the influence of cultural and socioeconomic factors on ASD detection and diagnosis is also crucial. Clinicians should be aware of potential biases and disparities in healthcare access that may affect the diagnostic process for females from diverse backgrounds.
- Ongoing training and increased awareness among clinicians about the latest research and best practices for diagnosing and treating autistic females can lead to more accurate diagnoses and better-targeted interventions.

References

Adani, S., & Cepanec, M. (2019). Gender differences in early communication development: Behavioral and neurobiological indicators of more vulnerable communication system development in boys. *Croatian Medical Journal, 60*(2), 141–149. Retrieved from https://www.ncbi.nlm.nih.gov/pubmed/31044585

Altarac, M., & Saroha, E. (2007). Lifetime prevalence of learning disability among US children. Pediatrics, 119 Suppl 1, S77–S83. https://doi.org/10.1542/peds.2006-2089L

Akhtar, F., & Bokhari, S. R. A. (2024, January–). Down Syndrome. [Updated 2023 Aug 8]. In *StatPearls [Internet]*. StatPearls Publishing. Retrieved from https://www.ncbi.nlm.nih.gov/books/NBK526016/

American Psychiatric Association. (2013). *Diagnostic and statistical manual of mental disorders* (5th ed.). American Psychiatric Association.

American Psychiatric Association. (2022). *Diagnostic and statistical manual of mental disorders* (5th ed., text rev.). https://doi.org/10.1176/appi.books.9780890425787

Andersson, U., & Lyxell, B. (2007). Working memory deficit in children with mathematical difficulties: A general or specific deficit? *Journal of Experimental Child Psychology, 96*(3), 197–228.

Ankenman, K., Elgin, J., Sullivan, K., Vincent, L., & Bernier, R. (2014). Nonverbal and verbal cognitive discrepancy profiles in autism spectrum disorders: Influence of age and gender. *American Journal on Intellectual and Developmental Disabilities, 119*(1), 8.

Antezana, L., Factor, R. S., Condy, E. E., Strege, M. V., Scarpa, A., & Richey, J. A. (2019). Gender differences in restricted and repetitive behaviors and interests in youth with autism. *Autism Research, 12*(2), 274–283.

Aoki, S., Yamauchi, Y., & Hashimoto, K. (2018). Developmental trend of children with Down's syndrome—How do gender and neonatal conditions influence their developmental patterns? *Brain and Development, 40*(3), 181–187.

Arnett, A. B., Pennington, B. F., Willcutt, E. G., DeFries, J. C., & Olson, R. K. (2015). Gender differences in ADHD symptom severity. *Journal of Child Psychology and Psychiatry and Allied Disciplines, 56*(6), 632–639. https://doi.org/10.1111/jcpp.12337

Aro, T., Eklund, K., Eloranta, A. K., Ahonen, T., & Rescorla, L. (2022). Learning disabilities elevate children's risk for behavioral-emotional problems: Differences between LD types, genders, and contexts. *Journal of Learning Disabilities, 55*(6), 465–481. https://doi.org/10.1177/00222194211056297

Auyeung, B., Wheelwright, S., Allison, C., Atkinson, M., Samarawickrema, N., & Baron-Cohen, S. (2009). The children's Empathy Quotient and Systemizing Quotient: Gender differences in typical development and in autism spectrum conditions. *Journal of Autism and Developmental Disorders, 39*(11), 1509–1521. https://doi.org/10.1007/s10803-009-0772-x

Babinski D. E. (2024). Sex Differences in ADHD: Review and Priorities for Future Research. *Current psychiatry reports, 26*(4), 151–156. https://doi.org/10.1007/s11920-024-01492-6

Backer van Ommeren, T., Koot, H. M., Scheeren, A. M., & Begeer, S. (2017). Gender differences in the reciprocal behaviour of children with autism. *Autism, 21*(6), 795–803.

Badian, N. A. (1999). Persistent arithmetic, reading, or arithmetic and reading disability. *Annals of Dyslexia, 49*, 43–70.

Baer, R. M., Daviso, A. W., Flexer, R. W., Queen, R. M., & Meindi, R. S. (2011). Students with intellectual disabilities: Predictors of transition outcomes. *Career Development for Exceptional Individuals, 34*(3), 132–141.

Baron-Cohen, S. (2002). The extreme male brain theory of autism. *Trends in Cognitive Sciences, 6*(6), 248–254. https://doi.org/10.1016/s1364-6613(02)01904-6

Baron-Cohen, S., & Wheelwright, S. (2004). The empathy quotient: An investigation of adults with Asperger syndrome or high functioning autism, and normal gender differences. *Journal of Autism and Developmental Disorders, 34*(2), 163–175.

Baron-Cohen, S., Wheelwright, S., Hill, J., Raste, Y., & Plumb, I. (2001). The "Reading the Mind in the Eyes" Test revised version: A study with normal adults, and adults with Asperger syndrome or high-functioning autism. *Journal of Child Psychology and Psychiatry and Allied Disciplines, 42*(2), 241–251.

Bartholomay, K. L., Lee, C. H., Bruno, J. L., Lightbody, A. A., & Reiss, A. L. (2019). Closing the gender gap in Fragile X syndrome: Review on females with FXS and preliminary research findings. *Brain Science, 9*(1), 11. https://doi.org/10.3390/brainsci9010011

Bates, M. L., Vasileva, A., Flores, L. D. M., Pryakhina, Y., Buckman, M., Tomasson, M. H., & DeRuisseau, L. R. (2023). Sex differences in cardiovascular disease and dysregulation in Down Syndrome. *American Journal of Physiology-Heart and Circulatory Physiology, 324*(4), H542–H552.

Beacher, F. D., Radulescu, E., Minati, L., Baron-Cohen, S., Lombardo, M. V., Lai, M. C., et al. (2012). Sex differences and autism: Brain function during verbal fluency and mental rotation. *PLoS One, 7*(6), e38355. https://doi.org/10.1371/journal.pone.0038355

Beggiato, A., Peyre, H., Maruani, A., Scheid, I., Rastam, M., Amsellem, F., et al. (2017). Gender differences in autism spectrum disorders: Divergence among specific core symptoms. *Autism Research, 10*(4), 680–689.

Bejerot, S., Eriksson, J. M., Bonde, S., Carlstrom, K., Humble, M. B., & Eriksson, E. (2012). The extreme male brain revisited: Gender coherence in adults with autism spectrum disorder. *British Journal of Psychiatry, 201*, 116–123.

Bexkens, A., Ruzzano, L., Collot D' Escury-Koenigs, A. M., Van der Molen, M. W., & Huizenga, H. M. (2014). Inhibition deficits in individuals with intellectual disability: a meta-regression analysis. *Journal of intellectual disability research: JIDR, 58*(1), 3–16. https://doi.org/10.1111/jir.12068

Bhat, A. N. (2020). Is motor impairment in autism spectrum disorder distinct from developmental coordination disorder? A report from the SPARK study. *Physical Therapy, 100*(4), 633–644.

Biederman, J., Mick, E., Faraone, S. V., Braaten, E., Doyle, A., Spencer, T., et al. (2002). Influence of gender on attention deficit hyperactivity disorder in children referred to a psychiatric clinic. *American Journal of Psychiatry, 159*(1), 36–42. https://doi.org/10.1176/appi.ajp.159.1.36

Bitsika, V., Sharpley, C. F., & Mills, R. (2018). Sex differences in sensory features between boys and girls with Autism Spectrum Disorder. *Research in Autism Spectrum Disorders, 51*, 49–55.

Bolte, S., Duketis, E., Poustka, F., & Holtmann, M. (2011). Sex differences in cognitive domains and their clinical correlates in higher-functioning autism spectrum disorders. *Autism, 15*(4), 497–511. https://doi.org/10.1177/1362361310391116

Bolte, S., Neufeld, J., Marschick, P. B., Williams, Z. J., Gallagher, L., & Lai, M. (2023). Sex and gender in neurodevelopmental conditions. *Nature Reviews Neurology, 19*, 136–159.

Boorse, J., Cola, M., Plate, S., Yankowitz, L., Pandey, J., Schultz, R. T., & Parish-Morris, J. (2019). Linguistic markers of autism in girls: Evidence of a "blended phenotype" during storytelling. *Molecular Autism, 10*, 14. https://doi.org/10.1186/s13229-019-0268-2

Botha, M., Dibb, B., & Frost, D. M. (2022). "Autism is me": An investigation of how autistic individuals make sense of autism and stigma. *Disability & Society, 37*(3), 427–453.

Bricker, K., & Vaughn, B. V. (2024). Rett syndrrome: A review of clinical manifestations and therapeutic approaches. *Frontiers in Sleep, 3*, 1373489.

Bush, L., Martin, G. E., Landau, E., & Losh, M. (2021). A longitudinal study of parent-child interactions and language outcomes in Fragile X syndrome and other neurodevelopmental disorders. *Fronters in Psychiatry, 12*, 718572. https://doi.org/10.3389/fpsyt.2021.718572

Carr, M., & Davis, H. (2001). Gender differences in arithmetic strategy use: A function of skill and preference. *Contemporary educational psychology, 26*(3), 330–347.

Carr, M., & Alexeev, N. (2011). Fluency, accuracy, and gender predict developmental trajectories of arithmetic strategies. *Journal of Educational Psychology, 103*(3), 617–631. https://doi.org/10.1037/a0023864

Carey, E., Hill, F., Devine, A., & Szücs, D. (2016). The chicken or the egg? The direction of the relationship between mathematics anxiety and mathematics performance. *Frontiers in Psychology, 6*, 1987.

Carlson, A. G., Rowe, E. W., & Curby, T. W. (2013). Disentangling fine motor skills' relation to academic achievement: The differential impact of visual-spatial integration and visual motor coordination. *Journal of Genetic Psychology, 174*, 514–533. https://doi.org/10.1080/00221325.2012.717122

Carter, A. S., Black, D. O., Tewani, S., Connolly, C. E., Kadlec, M. B., & Tager-Flusberg, H. (2007). Sex differences in toddlers with autism spectrum disorders. *Journal of Autism and Developmental Disorders, 37*(1), 86–97. https://doi.org/10.1007/s10803-006-0331-7

Carucci, S., Narducci, C., Bazzoni, M., Balia, C., Donno, F., Gagliano, A., & Zuddas, A. (2023). Clinical characteristics, neuroimaging findings, and neuropsychological functioning in attention-deficit hyperactivity disorder: Sex differences. *Journal of Neuroscience Research, 101*(5), 704–717.

Chahil, G., & Bollu, P. C. (2024, January–). Rett Syndrome. [Updated 2023 Aug 8]. In *StatPearls [Internet]*. StatPearls Publishing. Retrieved from https://www.ncbi.nlm.nih.gov/books/NBK482252/

Chawarska, K., Macari, S., Powell, K., DiNicola, L., & Shic, F. (2016). Enhanced social attention in female infant siblings at risk for autism. *Journal of the American Academy of Child and Adolescent Psychiatry, 55*(3), 188–195. https://doi.org/10.1016/j.jaac.2015.11.016

Chen, M., Marraccini, M. E., Simeonsson, R. J., Lu, X., & Chang, Y. (2020). Modeling and explaining sex differences in the prevalence of autism spectrum disorder. https://doi.org/10.31219/osf.io/kbev3

Cho, S., Cola, M., Knox, A., Pelella, M. R., Russell, A., Hauptmann, A., et al. (2023). Sex differences in the temporal dynamics of autistic children's natural conversations. *Molecular Autism, 14*(1), 13.

Cicek, A. U., Sari, S. A., & Isik, C. M. (2020). Sociodemographic characteristics, risk factors, and prevalence of comorbidity among children and adolescents with intellectual disability: A cross-sectional study. *Journal of Mental Health Research in Intellectual Disabilities, 13*(2), 66–85.

Cirino, P. T. (2022). Math disability. In R. L. Beauchamp, M. D. Ris, H. G. Taylor, & K. O. Yeates (Eds.), *Pediatric neuropsychology: Research theory, and practice* (3rd ed., pp. 279–299).

Cirino, P. T., Morris, M. K., & Morris, R. D. (2002). Neuropsychological concomitants of calculation skills in college students referred for learning difficulties. *Developmental Neuropsychology, 21*(2), 201–218.

Cirino, P. T., Morris, M. K., & Morris, R. D. (2007). Semantic, executive, and visuospatial abilities in mathematical reasoning of referred college students. *Assessment, 14*(1), 94–104.

Cirino, P. T., Fuchs, L. S., Elias, J. T., Powell, S. R., & Schumacher, R. F. (2015). Cognitive and mathematical profiles for different forms of learning difficulties. *Journal of Learning Disabilities, 48*(2), 156–175. https://doi.org/10.1177/0022219413494239

Cirino, P. T., Child, A. E., & Macdonald, K. T. (2018). Longitudinal predictors of the overlap between reading and math skills. *Contemporary Educational Psychology, 54*, 99–111.

Clifford, S., Dissanayake, C., Bui, Q. M., Huggins, R., Taylor, A. K., & Loesch, D. Z. (2007). Autism spectrum phenotype in males and females with fragile X full mutation and premutation. *Journal of Autism and Developmental Disorders, 37*(4), 738–747. https://doi.org/10.1007/s10803-006-0205-z

Cola, M., Yankowitz, L. D., Tena, K., Russell, A., Bateman, L., Knox, A., et al. (2022). Friend matters: Sex differences in social language during autism diagnostic interviews. *Molecular Autism, 13*, 1–16.

Cook, J., Hull, L., Crane, L., & Mandy, W. (2021). Camouflaging in autism: A systematic review. *Clinical Psychology Review, 89*, 102080. https://doi.org/10.1016/j.cpr.2021.102080

Corbett, B. A., Schwartzman, J. M., Libsack, E. J., Muscatello, R. A., Lerner, M. D., Simmons, G. L., & White, S. W. (2021). Camouflaging in autism: Examining sex-based and compensatory models in social cognition and communication. *Autism Research, 14*(1), 127–142.

Cordeiro, L., Ballinger, E., Hagerman, R., & Hessl, D. (2011). Clinical assessment of DSM-IV anxiety disorders in fragile X syndrome: Prevalence and characterization. *Journal of Neurodevelopmental Disorders, 3*(1), 57–67. https://doi.org/10.1007/s11689-010-9067-y

Cornish, K., Turk, J., & Hagerman, R. (2008). The fragile X continuum: New advances and perspectives. *Journal of Intellectual Disability Research, 52*(Pt 6), 469–482. https://doi.org/10.1111/j.1365-2788.2008.01056.x

Corsello, C. M. (2005). Early intervention in autism. *Infants & Young Children, 18*(2), 74–85. https://doi.org/10.1097/00001163-200504000-00002

Craig, F., Crippa, A., De Giacomo, A., Ruggiero, M., Rizzato, V., Lorenzo, A., et al. (2020). Differences in developmental functioning profiles between male and female preschoolers children with autism spectrum disorder. *Autism Research, 13*(9), 1537–1547.

Cui, X., Cui, Y., Shi, L., Luan, J., Zhou, X., & Han, J. (2018). A basic understanding of Turner syndrome: Incidence, complications, diagnosis, and treatment. *Intractable & Rare Diseases Research, 7*(4), 223–228.

Dandouh, F., Anthoni, H., Tapia-Paez, I., Peyrard-Janvid, M., Schulte-Korne, G., Warnke, A., Remschmidt, H., Ziegler, A., Kere, J., Mullerr-Myhsok, B., Nothen, M. M., Schumacherr, J., & Zucchlli, M. (2009). Furtheer vidnc for DYX1C1 as a suscptibility facto for dyslexia. *Psychiatric Genetics, 19*(2), 59–63.

David, N., Rahlff, P., König, H., Dückert, S., Gewohn, P., Erik, F., Vogeley, K., Schöttle, D., Konnopka, A., Schulz, H., & Peth, J. (2025). Barriers to healthcare predict reduced health-related quality of life in autistic adults without intellectual disability. Autism: the international *journal of research and practice, 29*(2), 476–489. https://doi.org/10.1177/13623613241275406

Dekker, M. C., Koot, H. M., van der Ende, J., & Verhulst, F. C. (2002). Emotional and behavioral problems in children and adolescents with and without intellectual disability. *Journal of child psychology and psychiatry, and allied disciplines, 43*(8), 1087–1098. https://doi.org/10.1111/1469-7610.00235

de Sola, S., de la Torre, R., Sánchez-Benavides, G., Benejam, B., Cuenca-Royo, A., del Hoyo, L., Rodríguez, J., Catuara-Solarz, S., Sanchez-Gutierrez, J., Dueñas-Espin, I., Hernandez, G., Peña-Casanova, J., Langohr, K., Videla, S., Blehaut, H., Farre, M., Dierssen, M., & The TESDAD Study Group. (2015). A new cognitive evaluation battery for Down syndrome and its relevance for clinical trials. *Frontiers in Psychology, 6*, 708. https://doi.org/10.3389/fpsyg.2015.00708

Dew, A., Llewellyn, G., & Gorman, J. (2006). Having the time of my life: an exploratory study of women with intellectual disability growing older. *Health care for women international, 27*(10), 908–929. https://doi.org/10.1080/07399330600880541

De Winter, C., Bastiaanse, L., Hinlgenkamp, T., Evenhuis, H., & Echteld, M. (2012a). Cardiovascular risk factors (diabetes, hypertension, hypercholesterolemia and metabolic syndrome) in older people with intellectual disability: Results of the HAID study. *Research in Developmental Disabilities, 33*, 1722–1731.

De Winter, C., Bastiaanse, L., Hinlgenkamp, T., Evenhuis, H., & Echteld, M. (2012b). Overweight and obesity in older people with intellectual disability. *Research in Developmental Disabilities, 38*(2), 398–405.

Dean, M., Harwood, R., & Kasari, C. (2017). The art of camouflage: Gender differences in the social behaviors of girls and boys with autism spectrum disorder. *Autism, 21*(6), 678–689.

Demetriou, E. A., Pepper, K. L., Park, S. H., Pellicano, L., Song, Y. J. C., Naismith, S. L., et al. (2021). Autism spectrum disorder: An examination of sex differences in neuropsychological and self-report measures of executive and non-executive cognitive function. *Autism, 25*(8), 2223.

den Hartog, A., de la Roche, L., Derby, B., Psaradellis, E., & Kelley, E. (2023). A scoping review of sex/gender differences in pragmatic language and friendship characteristics in autistic children and adolescents. *Research in Autism Spectrum Disorders, 108*, 102229.

del Hoyo Soriano, L., Sterling, A., Edgin, J., Hamilton, D. R., Berry-Kravis, E., Dimachkie Nunnally, A., ... & Abbeduto, L. (2024). Associations among sex, cognitive ability, and autism symptoms in Individuals with Down syndrome. *Journal of autism and developmental disorders, 54*(1), 301–311.

Deng, Z., & Wang, S. (2021). Sex differentiation of brain structures in autism: Findings from a gray matter asymmetry study. *Autism Research, 14*(6), 1115–1126.

Devine, A., Soltész, F., Nobes, A., Goswami, U., & Szűcs, D. (2013). Gender differences in developmental dyscalculia depend on diagnostic criteria. *Learning and Instruction, 27*, 31–39.

Duvall, S. W., Huang-Storms, L., Presmanes Hill, A., Myers, J., & Fombonne, E. (2020). No sex differences in cognitive ability in young children with autism spectrum disorder. *Journal of Autism and Developmental Disorders, 50*, 1770–1785.

Einfeld, S. L., Ellis, L. A., & Emerson, E. (2011). Comorbidity of intellectual disability and mental disorder in children and adolescents: a systematic review. *Journal of intellectual & developmental disability, 36*(2), 137–143. https://doi.org/10.1080/13668250.2011.572548

Elsabbagh, M., Divan, G., Koh, Y. J., Kim, Y. S., Kauchali, S., Marcín, C., Montiel-Nava, C., Patel, V., Paula, C. S., Wang, C., Yasamy, M. T., & Fombonne, E. (2012). Global prevalence of autism and other pervasive developmental disorders. *Autism Research: Official Journal of the International Society for Autism Research, 5*(3), 160–179. https://doi.org/10.1002/aur.239

Else-Quest, N. M., Hyde, J. S., & Linn, M. C. (2010). Cross-national patterns of gender differences in mathematics: A meta-analysis. *Psychological Bulletin, 136*, 103–127.

Evans, T. M., Flowers, D. L., Napoliello, E. M., & Eden, G. F. (2014). Sex-specific gray matter volume differences in females with developmental dyslexia. *Brain Structure and Function, 219*(3), 1041–1054.

Faheem, M., Akram, W., Akram, H., Khan, M. A., Siddiqui, F. A., & Majeed, I. (2022). Gender-based differences in prevalence and effects of ADHD in adults: A systematic review. *Asian Journal of Psychiatry, 75*, 103205.

Fiscella, K., Franks, P., Gold, M. R., & Clancy, C. M. (2000). Inequality in quality: Addressing socioeconomic, racial, and ethnic disparities in health care. *JAMA, 283*(19), 2579–2584.

Flores, P., Coelho, E., Mourão-Carvalhal, M. I., & Forte, P. (2023). Association between motor and math skills in preschool children with typical development: Systematic review. *Frontiers in Psychology, 14*, 1105391. https://doi.org/10.3389/fpsyg.2023.1105391

Floris, D. L., Lai, M. C., Nath, T., Milham, M. P., & Di Martino, A. (2018). Network-specific sex differentiation of intrinsic brain function in males with autism. *Molecular Autism, 9*, 17. https://doi.org/10.1186/s13229-018-0192-x

Fombonne, E. (2003). Epidemiological surveys of autism and other pervasive developmental disorders: An update. *Journal of Autism and Developmental Disorders, 33*(4), 365–382. https://doi.org/10.1023/a:1025054610557

Fournier, K. A., Hass, C. J., Naik, S. K., Lodha, N., & Cauraugh, J. H. (2010). Motor coordination in autism spectrum disorders: A synthesis and meta-analysis. *Journal of Autism and Developmental Disorders, 40*(10), 1227–1240. https://doi.org/10.1007/s10803-010-0981-3

Frazier, T. W., Georgiades, S., Bishop, S. L., & Hardan, A. Y. (2014). Behavioral and cognitive characteristics of females and males with autism in the Simons Simplex Collection. *Journal of the American Academy of Child and Adolescent Psychiatry, 53*(3), 329–340.e321–323.

Freund, L. S., & Reiss, A. L. (1991). Cognitive profiles associated with the fra(X) syndrome in males and females. *American Journal of Medical Genetics, 38*(4), 542–547. https://doi.org/10.1002/ajmg.1320380409

Freund, L. S., Reiss, A. L., & Abrams, M. T. (1993). Psychiatric disorders associated with fragile X in the young female. *Pediatrics, 91*(2), 321–329. Retrieved from http://www.ncbi.nlm.nih.gov/pubmed/8380924

Friso-Van den Bos, I., Van der Ven, S. H., Kroesbergen, E. H., & Van Luit, J. E. (2013). Working memory and mathematics in primary school children: A meta-analysis. *Educational Research Review, 10*, 29–44.

Fulton, A. M., Paynter, J. M., & Trembath, D. (2017). Gender comparisons in children with ASD entering early intervention. *Research in Developmental Disabilities, 68*, 27–34.

Gadow, K. D., Devincent, C. J., Pomeroy, J., & Azizian, A. (2005). Comparison of DSM-IV symptoms in elementary school-age children with PDD versus clinic and community samples. *Autism, 9*(4), 392–415. https://doi.org/10.1177/1362361305056079

Gallagher, A., & Hallahan, B. (2012). Fragile X-associated disorders: A clinical overview. *Journal of Neurology, 259*(3), 401–413. https://doi.org/10.1007/s00415-011-6161-3

Geary, D. C., Hoard, M. K., Byrd-Craven, J., Nugent, L., & Numtee, C. (2007). Cognitive mechanisms underlying achievement deficits in children with mathematical learning disability. *Child Development, 78*(4), 1343–1359.

Giofrè, D., Toffalini, E., Altoè, G., & Cornoldi, C. (2017). Intelligence measures as diagnostic tools for children with specific learning disabilities. *Intelligence, 61*, 140–145. https://doi.org/10.1016/j.intell.2017.01.014

Giofrè, D., Allen, K., Toffalini, E., Mammarella, I. C., & Caviola, S. (2022). Decoding gender differences: Intellectual profiles of children with specific learning disabilities. *Intelligence, 90*, 101615.

Goddard, L., Dritschel, B., & Howlin, P. (2014). A preliminary study of gender differences in autobiographical memory in children with an autism spectrum disorder. *Journal of Autism and Developmental Disorders, 44*(9), 2087–2095. https://doi.org/10.1007/s10803-014-2109-7

Godfrey, M., & Lee, N. R. (2018). Memory profiles in Down syndrome across development: A review of memory abilities through the lifespan. *Journal of Neurodevelopmental Disorders, 10*, 1–31.

Granocchio, E., DeSalvatore, M., Bonanomi, E., & Sarti, D. (2023). Sex-related differences in reading achievement. *Journal of Neuroscience Research, 101*, 668–678.

Gravholt, C. H., Andersen, N. H., Christin-Maitre, S., Davis, S. M., Duijnhouwer, A., Gawlik, A., Maciel-Guerra, A. T., Gutmark-Little, I., Fleischer, K., Hong, D., Klein, K. O., Prakash, S. K., Shankar, R. K., Sandberg, D. E., Sas, T. C. J., Skakkebæk, A., Stochholm, K., van der Velden,

J. A., International Turner Syndrome Consensus Group, & Backeljauw, P. F. (2024). Clinical practice guidelines for the care of girls and women with Turner syndrome. *European Journal of Endocrinology, 190*(6), G53–G151. https://doi.org/10.1093/ejendo/lvae050

Green, D., Charman, T., Pickles, A., Chandler, S., Loucas, T., Simonoff, E., & Baird, G. (2009). Impairment in movement skills of children with autistic spectrum disorders. *Developmental Medicine and Child Neurology, 51*(4), 311–316. https://doi.org/10.1111/j.1469-8749.2008.03242.x

Greven, C. U., Richards, J. S., & Buitelaar, J. K. (2018). Sex differences in ADHD. In T. Banaschewski, D. Coghill, & A. Zuddas (Eds.), *Oxford textbook of attention deficit hyperactivity disorder* (p. 0). Oxford University Press.

Grove, R., Hoekstra, R. A., Wierda, M., & Begeer, S. (2017). Exploring sex differences in autistic traits: A factor analytic study of adults with autism. *Autism, 21*(6), 760–768.

Gunther, D. F., Eugster, E., Zagar, A. J., Bryant, C. G., Davenport, M. L., & Quigley, C. A. (2004). Ascertainment bias in Turner syndrome: New insights from girls who were diagnosed incidentally in prenatal life. *Pediatrics, 114*(3), 640–644. https://doi.org/10.1542/peds.2003-1122-L

Gu, H., Hou, F., Liu, L., Luo, X., Nkomola, P. D., Xie, X., ... & Song, R. (2018). Genetic variants in the CNTNAP2 gene are associated with gender differences among dyslexic children in China. EBioMedicine, 34, 165–170.

Hagberg, B., Witt-Engerström, I., Opitz, J. M., & Reynolds, J. F. (1986). Rett syndrome: A suggested staging system for describing impairment profile with increasing age towards adolescence. *American Journal of Medical Genetics, 25*(S1), 47–59.

Hagerman, R. J., & Hagerman, P. J. (2002). *Fragile X syndrome: Diagnosis, treatment, and research* (3rd ed.). Johns Hopkins University Press.

Hall, S. S., Lightbody, A. A., & Reiss, A. L. (2008). Compulsive, self-injurious, and autistic behavior in children and adolescents with fragile X syndrome. *American Journal of Mental Retardation, 113*(1), 44–53. https://doi.org/10.1352/0895-8017(2008)113[44:CSAABI]2.0.CO;2

Harrop, C., Jones, D., Zheng, S. T., Nowell, S., Boyd, B. A., & Sasson, N. (2018a). Circumscribed interests and attention in autism: The role of biological sex. *Journal of Autism and Developmental Disorders, 48*(10), 3449–3459. https://doi.org/10.1007/s10803-018-3612-z

Harrop, C., Jones, D., Zheng, S. T., Nowell, S. W., Boyd, B. A., & Sasson, N. (2018b). Sex differences in social attention in autism spectrum disorder. *Autism Research, 11*(9), 1264–1275. https://doi.org/10.1002/aur.1997

Harrop, C., Jones, D. R., Sasson, N. J., Zheng, S. T., Nowell, S. W., & Parish-Morris, J. (2020). Social and object attention is influenced by biological sex and toy gender-congruence in children with and without autism. *Autism Research, 13*(5), 763–776. https://doi.org/10.1002/aur.2245

Hartley, S. L., & Sikora, D. M. (2009). Sex differences in autism spectrum disorder: An examination of developmental functioning, autistic symptoms, and coexisting behavior problems in toddlers. *Journal of Autism and Developmental Disorders, 39*(12), 1715–1722.

Head, A. M., McGillivray, J. A., & Stokes, M. A. (2014). Gender differences in emotionality and sociability in children with autism spectrum disorders. *Molecular Autism, 5*(1), 19. https://doi.org/10.1186/2040-2392-5-19

Hertz-Picciotto, I., & Delwiche, L. (2009). The rise in autism and the role of age at diagnosis. *Epidemiology, 20*(1), 84–90.

Heslop, P., Blair, P., Fleming, P., Hoghton, M., Marriot, A., & Russ, L. (2014). The confidential inquiry into premature deaths of people with intellectual disabilities in the UK: A population-based study. *The Lancet, 383*(9920), 889–895.

Hodapp, R. M., Leckman, J. F., Dykens, E. M., Sparrow, S. S., Zelinsky, D. G., & Ort, S. I. (1992). K-ABC profiles in children with fragile X syndrome, Down syndrome, and nonspecific mental retardation. *American Journal of Mental Retardation, 97*(1), 39–46. Retrieved from https://www.ncbi.nlm.nih.gov/pubmed/1386742

Holtmann, M., Bolte, S., & Poustka, F. (2007). Autism spectrum disorders: Sex differences in autistic behaviour domains and coexisting psychopathology. *Developmental Medicine and Child Neurology, 49*(5), 361–366. https://doi.org/10.1111/j.1469-8749.2007.00361.x

Horner-Johnson, W., & Drum, C. E. (2006). Prevalence of maltreatment of people with intellectual disabilities: A review of recently published research. *Mental Retardation and Developmental Disabilities Research Reviews, 12*(1), 57–69. https://doi.org/10.1002/mrdd.20097

Huddleston, L. B., Visootsak, J., & Sherman, S. L. (2014). Cognitive aspects of fragile X syndrome. *Wiley Interdisciplinary Reviews: Cognitive Science, 5*(4), 501–508. https://doi.org/10.1002/wcs.1296

Huerta, M., & Lord, C. (2012). Diagnostic evaluation of autism spectrum disorders. *Pediatric Clinics of North America, 59*(1), 103–111. https://doi.org/10.1016/j.pcl.2011.10.018

Hull, L., Mandy, W., & Petrides, K. V. (2017). Behavioural and cognitive sex/gender differences in autism spectrum condition and typically developing males and females. *Autism, 21*(6), 706–727.

Hull, L., Petrides, K. V., & Mandy, W. (2020). The female autism phenotype and camouflaging: A narrative review. *Review Journal of Autism and Developmental Disorders, 7*(4), 306–317. https://doi.org/10.1007/s40489-020-00197-9

Hutaff-Lee, C., Bennett, E., Howell, S., & Tartaglia, N. (2019). Clinical developmental, neuropsychological, and social-emotional features of Turner syndrome. American journal of medical genetics. *Part C, Seminars in medical genetics, 181*(1), 126–134. https://doi.org/10.1002/ajmg.c.31687

Jansiewicz, E. M., Goldberg, M. C., Newschaffer, C. J., Denckla, M. B., Landa, R., & Mostofsky, S. H. (2006). Motor signs distinguish children with high functioning autism and Asperger's syndrome from controls. *Journal of Autism and Developmental Disorders, 36*(5), 613–621. https://doi.org/10.1007/s10803-006-0109-y

Jin, X., & Chen, L. (2015). Fragile X syndrome as a rare disease in China—Therapeutic challenges and opportunities. *Intractable & Rare Diseases Research, 4*(1), 39–48. https://doi.org/10.5582/irdr.2014.01037

Joel, D. (2021). Beyond the binary: Rethinking sex and the brain. *Neuroscience and Biobehavioral Reviews, 122*, 165–175. https://doi.org/10.1016/j.neubiorev.2020.11.018

Kaat, A. J., Shui, A. M., Ghods, S. S., Farmer, C. A., Esler, A. N., Thurm, A., et al. (2021). Sex differences in scores on standardized measures of autism symptoms: A multisite integrative data analysis. *Journal of Child Psychology and Psychiatry, 62*(1), 97–106.

Kalb, L. G., Singh, V., Hong, J. S., Holingue, C., Ludwig, N. N., Pfeiffer, D., et al. (2022). Analysis of race and sex bias in the Autism Diagnostic Observation Schedule (ADOS-2). *JAMA Network Open, 5*(4), e229498–e229498.

Kaufman, L., Ayub, M., & Vincent, J. B. (2010). The genetic basis of non-syndromic intellectual disability: A review. *Journal of Neurodevelopmental Disorders, 2*(4), 182–209.

Kaufmann, L., Wood, G., Rubinsten, O., & Henik, A. (2011). Meta-analyses of developmental fMRI studies investigating typical and atypical trajectories of number processing and calculation. *Developmental neuropsychology, 36*(6), 763–787.

Kaufmann, W. E., Kidd, S. A., Andrews, H. F., Budimirovic, D. B., Esler, A., Haas-Givler, B., Stackhouse, T., Riley, C., Peacock, G., Sherman, S. L., Brown, W. T., & Berry-Kravis, E. (2017). Autism Spectrum Disorder in Fragile X Syndrome: Cooccurring Conditions and Current Treatment. *Pediatrics, 139*(Suppl 3), S194–S206. https://doi.org/10.1542/peds.2016-1159F

Kauschke, C., van der Beek, B., & Kamp-Becker, I. (2016). Narratives of girls and boys with autism spectrum disorders: Gender differences in narrative competence and internal state language. *Journal of Autism and Developmental Disorders, 46*, 840–852.

Kerner auch Koerner, J., Visser, L., Rothe, J., Schulte-Koerne, G., & Hasselhorn, M. (2021). Gender differences in the comorbidity of ADHD symptoms and specific learning disorders in a population-based sample. *Sustainability, 13*(15), 8440.

Kiep, M., & Spek, A. A. (2017). Executive functioning in men and women with an autism spectrum disorder. *Autism Research, 10*(5), 940–948. https://doi.org/10.1002/aur.1721

Kok, F. M., Groen, Y., Fuermaier, A. B. M., & Tucha, O. (2020). The female side of pharmacotherapy for ADHD: A systematic literature review. *PLoS One, 15*(9), e0239257. https://doi.org/10.1371/journal.pone.0239257

Koponen, T., Georgiou, G., Salmi, P., Leskinen, M., & Aro, M. (2017). A meta-analysis of the relation between RAN and mathematics. *Journal of Educational Psychology, 109*(7), 977.

Kovas, Y., Haworth, C. M., Dale, P. S., & Plomin, R. (2007). The genetic and environmental origins of learning abilities and disabilities in the early school years. *Monographs of the Society for Research in Child Development, 72*(3), vii–144. https://doi.org/10.1111/j.1540-5834.2007.00439.x.

Kovas, Y., Haworth, C. M. A., Harlaar, N., Petrill, S. A., Dale, P. S., & Plomin, R. (2007). Overlap and specificity of genetic and environmental influences on mathematics and reading disability in 10-year-old twins. *Journal of Child Psychology and Psychiatry, 48*(9), 914–922.

Koyama, T., Kamio, Y., Inada, N., & Kurita, H. (2009). Sex differences in WISC-III profiles of children with high-functioning pervasive developmental disorders. *Journal of Autism and Developmental Disorders, 39*(1), 135–141. https://doi.org/10.1007/s10803-008-0610-6

Krafnick, A. J., & Evans, T. M. (2019). Neurobiological Sex Differences in Developmental Dyslexia. *Frontiers in psychology, 9*, 2669. https://doi.org/10.3389/fpsyg.2018.02669.

Kuzmina, Y., Ivanova, A., & Kaiky, D. (2019). The effect of phonological processing on mathematics performance in elementary school varies for boys and girls: Fixed-effects longitudinal analysis. *British Educational Research Journal, 45*(3), 640–661.

Lachance, J. A., & Mazzocco, M. M. (2006). A longitudinal analysis of sex differences in math and spatial skills in primary school age children. *Learning and Individual Differences, 16*(3), 195–216.

Lai, M. C., Lombardo, M. V., Pasco, G., Ruigrok, A. N., Wheelwright, S. J., Sadek, S. A., et al. (2011). A behavioral comparison of male and female adults with high functioning autism spectrum conditions. *PLoS One, 6*(6), e20835. https://doi.org/10.1371/journal.pone.0020835

Lai, M. C., Lombardo, M. V., Ruigrok, A. N., Chakrabarti, B., Wheelwright, S. J., Auyeung, B., et al. (2012). Cognition in males and females with autism: Similarities and differences. *PLoS One, 7*(10), e47198. https://doi.org/10.1371/journal.pone.0047198

Lai, M. C., Lombardo, M. V., Auyeung, B., Chakrabarti, B., & Baron-Cohen, S. (2015). Sex/gender differences and autism: Setting the scene for future research. *Journal of the American Academy of Child and Adolescent Psychiatry, 54*(1), 11–24. https://doi.org/10.1016/j.jaac.2014.10.003

Lai, M. C., Lombardo, M. V., Ruigrok, A. N., Chakrabarti, B., Auyeung, B., Szatmari, P., Happé, F., Baron-Cohen, S., & MRC AIMS Consortium. (2017). Quantifying and exploring camouflaging in men and women with autism. *Autism: The International Journal of Research and Practice, 21*(6), 690–702. https://doi.org/10.1177/1362361316671012

Lai, M. C., Lombardo, M. V., Chakrabarti, B., Ruigrok, A. N. V., Bullmore, E. T., Suckling, J., et al. (2019). Neural self-representation in autistic women and association with 'compensatory camouflaging'. *Autism, 23*(5), 1210–1223.

Lai, F., Mhatre, P. G., Yang, Y., Wang, M. C., Schupf, N., & Rosas, H. D. (2020). Sex differences in risk of Alzheimer's disease in adults with Down syndrome. *Alzheimer's & Dementia: Diagnosis, Assessment & Disease Monitoring, 12*(1), e12084.

Landerl, K., & Moll, K. (2010). Comorbidity of learning disorders: prevalence and familial transmission. *Journal of child psychology and psychiatry, and allied disciplines, 51*(3), 287–294. https://doi.org/10.1111/j.1469-7610.2009.02164.x

Lawson, L., Joshi, R., Barbaro, J., & Dissanayake, C. (2018). Gender differences during toddlerhood in autism spectrum disorder: A prospective community-based longitudinal follow-up study. *Journal of Autism and Developmental Disorders, 48*(8), 2619–2628.

Lee, J. K., Amaral, D. G., Solomon, M., Rogers, S. J., Ozonoff, S., & Nordahl, C. W. (2020). Sex differences in the amygdala resting-state connectome of children with autism spectrum disorder. *Biological Psychiatry: Cognitive Neuroscience and Neuroimaging, 5*(3), 320–329.

Lemon, J. M., Gargaro, B., Enticott, P. G., & Rinehart, N. J. (2011). Executive functioning in autism spectrum disorders: A gender comparison of response inhibition. *Journal of Autism and Developmental Disorders, 41*(3), 352–356. https://doi.org/10.1007/s10803-010-1039-2

Lesniak-Karpiak, K., Mazzocco, M. M., & Ross, J. L. (2003). Behavioral assessment of social anxiety in females with Turner or fragile X syndrome. *Journal of Autism and Developmental Disorders, 33*(1), 55–67. Retrieved from http://www.ncbi.nlm.nih.gov/pubmed/12708580

Li, Q., Yanmei, L., Zheng, J., Yan, X., Huang, J., Xu, Y., Zeng, X., Shen, T., Xin, X., Chen, Q., & Yang, W. (2023). Prevalence and trends of developmental disabilities among US children and adolescents aged 3 to 17 years, 2018–2021. *Scientific Reports, 13*, 17254.

Lindberg, S. M., Hyde, J. S., Petersen, J., & Linn, M. C. (2010). New trends in gender and mathematics performance: A meta-analysis. *Psychological Bulletin, 136*(6), 1123–1135. https://doi.org/10.1037/a0021276

Loesch, D. Z., Huggins, R. M., Bui, Q. M., Epstein, J. L., Taylor, A. K., & Hagerman, R. J. (2002). Effect of the deficits of fragile X mental retardation protein on cognitive status of fragile x males and females assessed by robust pedigree analysis. *Journal of Developmental and Behavioral Pediatrics, 23*(6), 416–423. Retrieved from https://www.ncbi.nlm.nih.gov/pubmed/12476071

Loomes, R., Hull, L., & Mandy, W. P. L. (2017). What is the male-to-female ratio in autism spectrum disorder? A systematic review and meta-analysis. *Journal of the American Academy of Child & Adolescent Psychiatry, 56*(6), 466–474.

Lombardo, M. V., Ashwin, E., Auyeung, B., Chakrabarti, B., Taylor, K., Hackett, G., Bullmore, E. T., & Baron-Cohen, S. (2012). Fetal testosterone influences sexually dimorphic gray matter in the human brain. *The Journal of neuroscience: the official journal of the Society for Neuroscience, 32*(2), 674–680.

Lord, C. (1995). Follow-up of two-year-olds referred for possible autism. *Journal of Child Psychology and Psychiatry, 36*(8), 1365–1382.

Lord, C., Rutter, M., & Le Couteur, A. (1994). Autism Diagnostic Interview-Revised: A revised version of a diagnostic interview for caregivers of individuals with possible pervasive developmental disorders. *Journal of Autism and Developmental Disorders, 24*(5), 659–685.

Lord, C., Risi, S., Lambrecht, L., Cook, E. H., Jr., Leventhal, B. L., DiLavore, P. C., Pickles, A., & Rutter, M. (2000). The autism diagnostic observation schedule-generic: A standard measure of social and communication deficits associated with the spectrum of autism. *Journal of Autism and Developmental Disorders, 30*(3), 205–223.

Lord, C., Luyster, R. J., Gotham, K., & Guthrie, W. (2012). *ADOS-2. Autism diagnostic observation schedule* (2nd ed.). Western Psychological Services.

Loveall, S. J., Conners, F. A., Tungate, A. S., Hahn, L. J., & Osso, T. (2017). A cross-sectional analysis of executive function in Down syndrome from 2 to 35 years. *Journal of Intellectual Disability Research, 61*(9), 877–887.

Loyer Carbonneau, M., Demers, M., Bigras, M., & Guay, M. C. (2021). Meta-analysis of sex differences in ADHD symptoms and associated cognitive deficits. *Journal of Attention Disorders, 25*(12), 1640–1656.

Lunsky Y. (2003). Depressive symptoms in intellectual disability: does gender play a role?. *Journal of intellectual disability research: JIDR, 47*(Pt 6), 417–427. https://doi.org/10.1046/j.1365-2788.2003.00516.x

Ma X. (1999). A meta-analysis of the relationship between anxiety toward mathematics and achievement in mathematics. *Journal for Research in Mathematics Education, 30*, 520–540.

Maenner, M. J. (2023). Prevalence and characteristics of autism spectrum disorder among children aged 8 years—Autism and Developmental Disabilities Monitoring Network, 11 sites, United States, 2020. *MMWR Surveillance Summaries, 72*, 1–14.

Mandell, D. S., Ittenbach, R. F., Levy, S. E., & Pinto-Martin, J. A. (2007). Disparities in diagnoses received prior to a diagnosis of autism spectrum disorder. *Journal of Autism and Developmental Disorders, 37*, 1795–1802.

Mandy, W., Chilvers, R., Chowdhury, U., Salter, G., Seigal, A., & Skuse, D. (2012). Sex differences in autism spectrum disorder: Evidence from a large sample of children and adolescents. *Journal of Autism and Developmental Disorders, 42*(7), 1304–1313. https://doi.org/10.1007/s10803-011-1356-0

Mari, M., Castiello, U., Marks, D., Marraffa, C., & Prior, M. (2003). The reach-to-grasp movement in children with autism spectrum disorder. *Philosophical Transactions of the Royal Society of London. Series B: Biological Sciences, 358*(1430), 393–403. https://doi.org/10.1098/rstb.2002.1205

Martin, J. (2024). Why are females less likely to be diagnosed with ADHD in childhood than males? *Lancet Psychiatry, 11*(4), 303–310. https://doi.org/10.1016/s2215-0366(24)00010-5

Martin, J., Langley, K., Cooper, M., Rouquette, O. Y., John, A., Sayal, K., et al. (2023). Sex differences in ADHD diagnosis and clinical care: A national study of population healthcare records in Wales. *medRxiv*, 2023–10.

Martin-Giacalone, B. A., Lin, A. E., Rasmussen, S. A., Kirby, R. S., Nestoridi, E., Liberman, R. F., Agopian, A. J., Carey, J. C., Cragan, J. D., Forestieri, N., Leedom, V., Boyce, A., Nembhard, W. N., Piccardi, M., Sandidge, T., Shan, X., Shumate, C. J., Stallings, E. B., Stevenson, R., & Lupo, P. J. (2023). Prevalence and descriptive epidemiology of Turner syndrome in the United States, 2000–2017: A report from the National Birth Defects Prevention Network. *American Journal of Medical Genetics. Part A, 191*(5), 1339–1349. https://doi.org/10.1002/ajmg.a.63181

Mazzocco, M. M. (2001). Math learning disability and math LD subtypes: Evidence from studies of Turner syndrome, fragile X syndrome, and neurofibromatosis type 1. *Journal of Learning Disabilities, 34*(6), 520–533. https://doi.org/10.1177/002221940103400605

McCaskey, U., Von Aster, M., O'Gorman, R., & Kucian, K. (2020). Persistent differences in brain structure in developmental dyscalculia: A longitudinal morphometry study. *Frontiers in Human Neuroscience, 14*, 272.

McDonnell, C. G., DeLucia, E. A., Hayden, E. P., Penner, M., Curcin, K., Anagnostou, E., et al. (2021). Sex differences in age of diagnosis and first concern among children with autism spectrum disorder. *Journal of Clinical Child & Adolescent Psychology, 50*(5), 645–655.

McFayden, T. C., Albright, J., Muskett, A. E., & Scarpa, A. (2019). Brief report: Sex differences in ASD diagnosis—A brief report on restricted interests and repetitive behaviors. *Journal of Autism and Developmental Disorders, 49*, 1693–1699.

McGee, R., & Feehan, M. (1991). Are girls with problems of attention underrecognized? *Journal of Psychopathology and Behavioral Assessment, 13*(3), 187–198. https://doi.org/10.1007/BF00960783

McKenzie, K., Milton, M., Smith, G., & Ouellette-Kuntz, H. (2016). Systematic review of the prevalence and incidence of intellectual disabilities: Current trends and issues. *Current Developmental Disorders Reports, 3*, 104–115.

McQuaid, G. A., Lee, N. R., & Wallace, G. L. (2022). Camouflaging in autism spectrum disorder: Examining the roles of sex, gender identity, and diagnostic timing. *Autism, 26*(2), 552–559.

Memisevic, H., & Sinanovic, O. (2014). Executive function in children with intellectual disability—The effects of sex, level and aetiology of intellectual disability. *Journal of Intellectual Disability Research, 58*(9), 830–837.

Miciak, J., & Fletcher, J. M. (2023). Specific reading disabilities. In G. G. Brown, T. Z. King, K. Y. Haaland, & B. Crosson (Eds.), *APA handbook of neuropsychology: Neurobehavioral disorders and conditions: Accepted science and open questions* (pp. 79–102). American Psychological Association.

Middleton, A. E., Farris, E. A., Ring, J. J., & Odegard, T. N. (2021). Predicting and Evaluating Treatment Response: Evidence Toward Protracted Response Patterns for Severely Impacted Students With Dyslexia. *Journal of Learning Disabilities, 55*(4), 272–291. https://doi.org/10.1177/00222194211047633 (Original work published 2022)

Moll, K., Kunze, S., Neuhoff, N., Bruder, J., Schulte-Körne, G. (2014). Specific learning disorder: Prevalence and gender differences. *PLoS ONE, 9*(7), e103537. https://doi.org/10.1371/journal.pone.0103537

Morsanyi, K., van Bers, B., McCormack, T., & McGGourty, J. (2018). The prevalence of specific learning disorder in mathematics and comorbidity with other developmental disorders in primary school-age children. *British Journal of Psychology, 109*, 917–940.

Munir K. M. (2016). The co-occurrence of mental disorders in children and adolescents with intellectual disability/intellectual developmental disorder. *Current opinion in psychiatry, 29*(2), 95–102. https://doi.org/10.1097/YCO.0000000000000236

Murphy, M. M. (2009). A review of mathematical learning disabilities in children with fragile X syndrome. *Developmental Disabilities Research Reviews, 15*(1), 21–27.

Murphy, M. M., Mazzocco, M. M., Gerner, G., & Henry, A. E. (2006). Mathematics learning disability in girls with Turner syndrome or fragile X syndrome. *Brain and cognition, 61*(2), 195–210.

Newman, L., Wagner, M., Cameto, R., & Knokey, A. M. (2009). *The post-high school outcomes of youth with disabilities up to 4 years after high school: A report from the national longitudinal transition study-2 (NLTS2)*. NCSER 2009-3017. National Center for Special Education Research.

Nishimura, T., Takahashi, N., Okumura, A., Harada, T., Iwabuchi, T., Nakayasu, C., et al. (2023). Sex differences in neurodevelopmental trajectories in children with different levels of autistic traits. *Psychiatry and Clinical Neurosciences, 77*(5), 282–289.

Nowell, S. W., Jones, D. R., & Harrop, C. (2019). Circumscribed interests in autism: Are there sex differences? *Advances in Autism, 5*(3), 187–198.

Nussbaum, N. L. (2012). ADHD and female specific concerns: A review of the literature and clinical implications. *Journal of Attention Disorders, 16*(2), 87–100. https://doi.org/10.1177/1087054711416909

Nyden, A., Hjelmquist, E., & Gillberg, C. (2000). Autism spectrum and attention-deficit disorders in girls. Some neuropsychological aspects. *European Child and Adolescent Psychiatry, 9*(3), 180–185. Retrieved from https://www.ncbi.nlm.nih.gov/pubmed/11095040

Olson, L. A., Mash, L. E., Linke, A., Fong, C. H., Müller, R. A., & Fishman, I. (2020). Sex-related patterns of intrinsic functional connectivity in children and adolescents with autism spectrum disorders. *Autism, 24*(8), 2190–2201.

Osório, J. M. A., Rodríguez-Herreros, B., Richetin, S., Junod, V., Romascano, D., Pittet, V., et al. (2021). Sex differences in sensory processing in children with autism spectrum disorder. *Autism Research, 14*(11), 2412–2423.

Ottosen, C., Larsen, J. T., Faraone, S. V., Chen, Q., Hartman, C., Larsson, H., et al. (2019). Sex differences in comorbidity patterns of attention-deficit/hyperactivity disorder. *Journal of the American Academy of Child and Adolescent Psychiatry, 58*(4), 412–422.e413.

Owens, E. B., Zalecki, C., Gillette, P., & Hinshaw, S. P. (2017). Girls with childhood ADHD as adults: Cross-domain outcomes by diagnostic persistence. *Journal of Consulting and Clinical Psychology, 85*(7), 723–736. https://doi.org/10.1037/ccp0000217

Pan, C. Y., Tsai, C. L., & Chu, C. H. (2009). Fundamental movement skills in children diagnosed with autism spectrum disorders and attention deficit hyperactivity disorder. *Journal of Autism and Developmental Disorders, 39*(12), 1694–1705. https://doi.org/10.1007/s10803-009-0813-5

Paracchini, S., Scerri, T., & Monaco, A. P. (2007). The genetic lexicon of dyslexia. *Annual Review of Genomics and Human Genetics, 8*(1), 57–79.

Parish, S. L., Mitra, M., Son, E., Bonardi, A., Swoboda, P. T., & Igdalsky, L. (2015). Pregnancy Outcomes Among U.S. Women With Intellectual and Developmental Disabilities. *American journal on intellectual and developmental disabilities, 120*(5), 433–443. https://doi.org/10.1352/1944-7558-120.5.433

Parish-Morris, J., Liberman, M. Y., Cieri, C., Herrington, J. D., Yerys, B. E., Bateman, L., et al. (2017). Linguistic camouflage in girls with autism spectrum disorder. *Molecular Autism, 8*, 1–12.

Parker, S. E., Mai, C. T., Canfield, M. A., Rickard, R., Wang, Y., Meyer, R. E., Anderson, P., Mason, C. A., Collins, J. S., Kirby, R. S., Correa, A., & National Birth Defects Prevention Network (2010). Updated National Birth Prevalence estimates for selected birth defects in the United States, 2004-2006. Birth defects research. Part A, Clinical and molecular teratology, 88(12), 1008–1016. https://doi.org/10.1002/bdra.20735

Park, S., Cho, S. C., Cho, I. H., Kim, B. N., Kim, J. W., Shin, M. S., et al. (2012). Sex differences in children with autism spectrum disorders compared with their unaffected siblings and typically developing children. *Research in Autism Spectrum Disorders, 6*(2), 861–870. https://doi.org/10.1016/j.rasd.2011.11.006

Patrick, M. E., Shaw, K. A., Dietz, P. M., Baio, J., Yeargin-Allsopp, M., Bilder, D. A., Kirby, R. S., Hall-Lande, J. A., Harrington, R. A., Lee, L.-C., Lopez, M. L. C., Daniels, J., & Maenner, M. J. (2021). Prevalence of intellectual disability among eight-year-old children from selected communities in the United States, 2014. *Disability and Health Journal, 14*(2), 101023.

Peterson, R. L., & Pennington, B. F. (2015). Developmental dyslexia. *Annual review of clinical psychology, 11*, 283–307. https://doi.org/10.1146/annurev-clinpsy-032814-112842.

Pennington, B. F., McGrath, L. M., & Peterson, R. L. (2019). *Diagnosing learning disorders: From Science to Practice* (3rd ed.). Guilford Press.

Peterson, R. L., McGrath, L. M., Willcutt, E. G., Keenan, J. M., Olson, R. K., & Pennington, B. F. (2021). How Specific Are Learning Disabilities?. *Journal of learning disabilities, 54*(6), 466–483. https://doi.org/10.1177/0022219420982981

Philofsky, A., Hepburn, S. L., Hayes, A., Hagerman, R., & Rogers, S. J. (2004). Linguistic and cognitive functioning and autism symptoms in young children with fragile X syndrome. *American Journal of Mental Retardation, 109*(3), 208–218. https://doi.org/10.1352/0895-8017(2004)109<208:LACFAA>2.0.CO;2

Pievsky, M. A., & McGrath, R. E. (2018). The neurocognitive profile of attention-deficit/hyperactivity disorder: A review of meta-analyses. *Archives of Clinical Neuropsychology, 33*(2), 143–157.

Polyak, A., Rosenfeld, J. A., & Girirajan, S. (2015). An assessment of sex bias in neurodevelopmental disorders. *Genome Medicine, 7*, 1–11.

Posserud, M. B., Skretting Solberg, B., Engeland, A., Haavik, J., & Klungsøyr, K. (2021). Male to female ratios in autism spectrum disorders by age, intellectual disability and attention-deficit/hyperactivity disorder. *Acta Psychiatrica Scandinavica, 144*(6), 635–646.

Postorino, V., Fatta, L. M., De Peppo, L., Giovagnoli, G., Armando, M., Vicari, S., & Mazzone, L. (2015). Longitudinal comparison between male and female preschool children with autism spectrum disorder. *Journal of Autism and Developmental Disorders, 45*(7), 2046–2055.

Prosperi, M., Turi, M., Guerrera, S., Napoli, E., Tancredi, R., Igliozzi, R., et al. (2021). Sex differences in autism spectrum disorder: An investigation on core symptoms and psychiatric comorbidity in preschoolers. *Frontiers in Integrative Neuroscience, 14*, 594082.

Quinn, J. M., & Wagner, R. K. (2015). Gender differences in reading impairment and in the identification of impaired readers: Results from a large-scale study of at-risk readers. *Journal of Learning Disabilities, 48*(4), 433–445.

Ramma, S., & Gowramma, I. P. (2002). A systematic procedure for identifying and classifying children with dyscalculia among primary school children in India. *Dyslexia, 8*(1), 67–85.

Ratto, A. B., Kenworthy, L., Yerys, B. E., Bascom, J., Wieckowski, A. T., White, S. W., et al. (2018). What about the girls? Sex-based differences in autistic traits and adaptive skills. *Journal of Autism and Developmental Disorders, 48*, 1698–1711.

Reichenberg, A., Cederlöf, M., McMillan, A., Trzaskowski, M., Kapra, O., Fruchter, E., et al. (2016). Discontinuity in the genetic and environmental causes of the intellectual disability spectrum. *Proceedings of the National Academy of Sciences, 113*(4), 1098–1103.

Reinhardt, V. P., Wetherby, A. M., Schatschneider, C., & Lord, C. (2015). Examination of sex differences in a large sample of young children with autism spectrum disorder and typical development. *Journal of Autism and Developmental Disorders, 45*(3), 697–706. https://doi.org/10.1007/s10803-014-2223-6

Reuben, C., & Elgaddal, N. (2024). *Attention-deficit/hyperactivity disorder in children ages 5–17 years: United States, 2020–2022*. NCHS Data Brief. No. 499. National Center for Health Statistics.

Richlan, F., Kronbichler, M., & Wimmer, H. (2011). Meta-analyzing brain dysfunctions in dyslexic children and adults. *Neuroimage, 56*(3), 1735–1742.

Ridley, R. (2019). Some difficulties behind the concept of the 'Extreme male brain' in autism research. A theoretical review. *Research in Autism Spectrum Disorders, 57*, 19–27.

Rim, H., Son, H., & Kim, J. (2024). From classroom to life: Gender differences in the persistent effect of learning disabilities on adult depressive symptoms. *Social Science & Medicine, 349*, 116886.

Rivera, S. M., Menon, V., White, C. D., Glaser, B., & Reiss, A. L. (2002). Functional brain activation during arithmetic processing in females with fragile X Syndrome is related to FMR1 protein expression. *Human Brain Mapping, 16*(4), 206–218.

Robinson, J. P., & Lubienski, S. T. (2011). The development of gender achievement gaps in mathematics and reading during elementary and middle school: Examining direct cognitive assessments and teacher ratings. *American Educational Research Journal, 48*(2), 268–302.

Robinson, E. B., Lichtenstein, P., Anckarsater, H., Happe, F., & Ronald, A. (2013). Examining and interpreting the female protective effect against autistic behavior. *Proceedings of the National Academy of Sciences of the United States of America, 110*(13), 5258–5262.

Rodgers, J. D., Lodi-Smith, J., Donnelly, J. P., Lopata, C., McDonald, C. A., Thomeer, M. L., et al. (2019). Brief report: Examination of sex-based differences in ASD symptom severity among high-functioning children with ASD using the SRS-2. *Journal of Autism and Developmental Disorders, 49*, 781–787.

Rogers, S. J. (1996). Brief report: Early intervention in autism. *Journal of Autism and Developmental Disorders, 26*(2), 243–246. https://doi.org/10.1007/Bf02172020

Rogers, S. J., Wehner, D. E., & Hagerman, R. (2001). The behavioral phenotype in fragile X: Symptoms of autism in very young children with fragile X syndrome, idiopathic autism, and other developmental disorders. *Journal of Developmental and Behavioral Pediatrics, 22*(6), 409–417. Retrieved from http://www.ncbi.nlm.nih.gov/pubmed/11773805

Rohde, M. S., Georgescu, A. L., Vogeley, K., Fimmers, R., & Falter-Wagner, C. M. (2018). Absence of sex differences in mental rotation performance in autism spectrum disorder. *Autism, 22*(7), 855–865.

Ros-Demarize, R., Bradley, C., Kanne, S. M., Warren, Z., Boan, A., Lajonchere, C., et al. (2020). ASD symptoms in toddlers and preschoolers: An examination of sex differences. *Autism Research, 13*(1), 157–166.

Rrauch, A., Wieczorek, D., Ggraf, E., Wieland, T., Endele, S., Schwarzmayr, T., et al. (2012). Range of genetic mutations associated with severe non-syndromic sporadic intellectual disability: An Exome sequencing study. *Lancet, 380*(9854), 1674–1682.

Rucklidge, J. J. (2010). Gender differences in attention-deficit/hyperactivity disorder. *Psychiatric Clinics of North America, 33*(2), 357–373. https://doi.org/10.1016/j.psc.2010.01.006

Rutter, M., Caspi, A., Fergusson, D., Horwood, L. J., Goodman, R., Maughan, B., ... & Carroll, J. (2004). Sex differences in developmental reading disability: New findings from 4 epidemiological studies. *JAMA, 291*(16), 2007–2012.

Rutherford, M., McKenzie, K., Johnson, T., Catchpole, C., O'Hare, A., McClure, I., et al. (2016). Gender ratio in a clinical population sample, age of diagnosis and duration of assessment in children and adults with autism spectrum disorder. *Autism, 20*(5), 628–634.

Russell, H. F., Wallis, D., Mazzocco, M. M., Moshang, T., Zackai, E., Zinn, A. R., Ross, J. L., & Muenke, M. (2006). Increased prevalence of ADHD in Turner syndrome with no evidence of imprinting effects. *Journal of pediatric psychology, 31*(9), 945–955. https://doi.org/10.1093/jpepsy/jsj106

Rynkiewicz, A., & Lucka, I. (2018). Autism spectrum disorder (ASD) in girls. Co-occurring psychopathology. Sex differences in clinical manifestation. *Psychiatria Polska, 52*(4), 629–639. https://doi.org/10.12740/PP/OnlineFirst/58837

Sanderson, K. (2021). High-profile autism genetics project paused amid backlash. *Nature, 598*(7879), 17–18.

Sanford, C., Newman, L., Wagner, M., Cameto, R., Knokey, A. M., & Shaver, D. (2011). *The post-high school outcomes of young adults with disabilities up to 6 years after high school: Key findings from the National Longitudinal Transition Study-2 (NLTS2)*. NCSER 2011-3004. National Center for Special Education Research.

Santos, S., Ferreira, H., Martins, J., Goncalves, J., & Castelo-Branco, M. (2022). Male sex bias in early and late onset neurodevelopmental disorders: Shared aspects and differences in Autism Spectrum Disorder, Attention Deficit/hyperactivity Disorder, and Schizophrenia. *Neuroscience & Biobehavioral Reviews, 135*, 104577.

Saure, E., Castrén, M., Mikkola, K., & Salmi, J. (2023). Intellectual disabilities moderate sex/gender differences in autism spectrum disorder: A systematic review and meta-analysis. *Journal of Intellectual Disability Research: JIDR, 67*(1), 1–34. https://doi.org/10.1111/jir.12989

Schalock, R. L., Luckasson, R., & Tassé, M. J. (2021). An overview of intellectual disability: Definition, diagnosis, classification, and systems of supports. *American journal on intellectual and developmental disabilities, 126*(6), 439–442.

Scheiber, C., Reynolds, M. R., Hajovsky, D. B., & Kaufman, A. S. (2015). Gender differences in achievement in a large, nationally representative sample of children and adolescents. *Psychology in the Schools, 52*(4), 335–348. https://doi.org/10.1002/pits.21827

Schuck, R. K., Flores, R. E., & Fung, L. K. (2019). Brief report: Sex/gender differences in symptomology and camouflaging in adults with autism spectrum disorder. *Journal of Autism and Developmental Disorders, 49*(6), 2597–2604.

Sebat, J., Lakshmi, B., Malhotra, D., Troge, J., Lese-Martin, C., Walsh, T., Yamrom, B., Yoon, S., Krasnitz, A., Kendall, J., Leotta, A., Pai, D., Zhang, R., Lee, Y. H., Hicks, J., Spence, S. J., Lee, A. T., Puura, K., Lehtimaki, T., et al. (2007). Strong association of de novo copy number mutations with autism. *Science, 316*(5823), 445–449.

Shaywitz, S. E., & Shaywitz, B. A. (1990). Prevalence of reading disability in boys and girls: Results of the Connecticut Longitudinal Study. *JAMA, 264*(8), 998–1002.

Shankar Kikkeri, N., & Nagalli, S. (2024, January–). Turner Syndrome. [Updated 2023 Aug 8]. In *StatPearls [Internet]*. StatPearls Publishing. Retrieved from https://www.ncbi.nlm.nih.gov/books/NBK554621/

Simonoff, E., Pickles, A., Charman, T., Chandler, S., Loucas, T., & Baird, G. (2008). Psychiatric disorders in children with autism spectrum disorders: Prevalence, comorbidity, and associated factors in a population-derived sample. *Journal of the American Academy of Child and Adolescent Psychiatry, 47*(8), 921–929. https://doi.org/10.1097/CHI.0b013e318179964f

Smith, R. E., Avery, J. A., Wallace, G. L., Kenworthy, L., Gotts, S. J., & Martin, A. (2019). Sex differences in resting-state functional connectivity of the cerebellum in autism spectrum disorder. *Frontiers in Human Neuroscience, 13*, 104.

Solomon, M., Miller, M., Taylor, S. L., Hinshaw, S. P., & Carter, C. S. (2012). Autism symptoms and internalizing psychopathology in girls and boys with autism spectrum disorders. *Journal of Autism and Developmental Disorders, 42*(1), 48–59. https://doi.org/10.1007/s10803-011-1215-z

Song, P., Zha, M., Yang, Q., Zhang, Y., Li, X., & Rudan, I. (2021). The prevalence of adult attention-deficit hyperactivity disorder: A global systematic review and meta-analysis. *Journal of Globalization and Health, 11*, 04009.

Srour, M., & Shevell, M. (2014). Genetics and the investigation of developmental delay/intellectual disability. *Archives of Disease in Childhood, 99*(4), 386–389.

Staller, J., & Faraone, S. V. (2006). Attention-deficit hyperactivity disorder in girls: Epidemiology and management. *CNS Drugs, 20*(2), 107–123. https://doi.org/10.2165/00023210-200620020-00003

Tassé, M. J., Navas Macho, P., Havercamp, S. M., Benson, B. A., Allain, D. C., Manickam, K., & Davis, S. (2016). Psychiatric conditions prevalent among adults with Down syndrome. *Journal of Policy and Practice in Intellectual Disabilities, 13*(2), 173–180.

Tillmann, J., Ashwood, K., Absoud, M., Bölte, S., Bonnet-Brilhault, F., Buitelaar, J. K., et al. (2018). Evaluating sex and age differences in ADI-R and ADOS scores in a large European multi-site sample of individuals with autism spectrum disorder. *Journal of Autism and Developmental Disorders, 48*, 2490–2505.

Toffalini, E., Giofrè, D., & Cornoldi, C. (2017). Strengths and weaknesses in the intellectual profile of different subtypes of specific learning disorder: A study on 1,049 diagnosed children. *Clinical Psychological Science, 5*(2), 402–409.

Torske, T., Nærland, T., Quintana, D. S., Hypher, R. E., Kaale, A., Høyland, A. L., et al. (2023). Sex as a moderator between parent ratings of executive dysfunction and social difficulties in children and adolescents with autism spectrum disorder. *Journal of Autism and Developmental Disorders, 53*(10), 3847–3859.

Tsakanikos, E., Bouras, N., Sturmey, P., & Holt, G. (2006). Psychiatric co-morbidity and gender differences in intellectual disability. *Journal of Intellectual Disabilities Research, 50*, 582–587.

Tubío-Fungueiriño, M., Cruz, S., Sampaio, A., Carracedo, A., & Fernández-Prieto, M. (2021). Social camouflaging in females with autism spectrum disorder: A systematic review. *Journal of Autism and Developmental Disorders, 51*, 2190–2199.

van de Weijer-Bergsma, E., Van Luit, J. E., & Moeller, K. (2022). Sex differences in the association of math achievement with visual-spatial and verbal working memory: Does the type of math test matter? *British Journal of Psychology, 113*(3), 798–819.

Van der Sluis, S., De Jong, P. F., & Van der Leij, A. (2004). Inhibition and shifting in children with learning deficits in arithmetic and reading. *Journal of Experimental Child Psychology, 87*(3), 239–266.

van Eijk, L., & Zietsch, B. P. (2021). Testing the extreme male brain hypothesis: Is autism spectrum disorder associated with a more male-typical brain? *Autism Research, 14*(8), 1597–1608.

Van Wijngaarden-Cremers, P. J., van Eeten, E., Groen, W. B., Van Deurzen, P. A., Oosterling, I. J., & Van der Gaag, R. J. (2014). Gender and age differences in the core triad of impairments in autism spectrum disorders: A systematic review and meta-analysis. *Journal of Autism and Developmental Disorders, 44*, 627–635.

Wagner, M., Newman, L., Cameto, R., Garza, N., & Levine, P. (2005). After high school: A first look at the postschool experiences of youth with disabilities. A report from the National Longitudinal Transition Study-2 (NLTS2). Online submission.

Westrop, S. C., Melville, C. A., Muirhead, F., & McGary, A. M. (2018). Gender differences in physical activity and sedentary behavior in adults with intellectual disabilities: A systematic review and meta-analysis. *Journal of Applied Research in Intellectual Disabilities, 32*, 1359–1374.

White, E. I., Wallace, G. L., Bascom, J., Armour, A. C., Register-Brown, K., Popal, H. S., et al. (2017). Sex differences in parent-reported executive functioning and adaptive behavior in children and young adults with autism spectrum disorder. *Autism Research, 10*(10), 1653–1662. https://doi.org/10.1002/aur.1811

Whitehouse, A. J. (2016). Commentary: Are we expecting too much from the extreme male brain theory of autism? A reflection on Kung et al. *Journal of Child Psychology and Psychiatry, 57*(12), 1463–1464.

Wigdor, E. M., Weiner, D. J., Grove, J., Fu, J. M., Thompson, W. K., Carey, C. E., Baya, N., van der Merwe, C., Walters, R. K., Satterstrom, F. K., Palmer, D. S., Rosengren, A., Bybjerg-Grauholm, J., iPSYCH Consortium, Hougaard, D. M., Mortensen, P. B., Daly, M. J., Talkowski, M. E., Sanders, S. J., Bishop, S. L., et al. (2022). The female protective effect against autism spectrum disorder. *Cell Genomics, 2*(6), 100134. https://doi.org/10.1016/j.xgen.2022.100134

Yang, L., Li, C., Li, X., Zhai, M., An, Q., Zhang, Y., et al. (2022). Prevalence of developmental dyslexia in primary school children: A systematic review and meta-analysis. *Brain Sciences, 12*(2), 240.

Yeniad, N., Malda, M., Mesman, J., Van IJzendoorn, M. H., & Pieper, S. (2013). Shifting ability predicts math and reading performance in children: A meta-analytical study. *Learning and Individual Differences, 23*, 1–9.

Zablotsky, B., et al. (2019). Prevalence and trends of developmental disabilities among children in the United States: 2009–2017. *Pediatrics, 144*, e20190811.

Zablotsky, B., Ng, A. E., Black, L. I., & Blumberg, S. J. (2023). Diagnosed developmental disabilities in children aged 3–17 years: United States, 2019–2012. *NCHS Data Brief, 473*, 1–7.

Zwaigenbaum, L., Bryson, S. E., Szatmari, P., Brian, J., Smith, I. M., Roberts, W., et al. (2012). Sex differences in children with autism spectrum disorder identified within a high-risk infant cohort. *Journal of Autism and Developmental Disorders, 42*, 2585–2596.

Chapter 3
Stroke and Vascular Dementia

Asish Gulati and Cheryl Bushnell

Introduction

Stroke is a leading cause of death and disability within the United States and worldwide. Annually, approximately 15 million people suffer a stroke worldwide, of which more than 795,000 occur within the United States (CDC, 2024c; World Health Organization, 2024). Approximately half of the individuals affected by stroke are women (Yoon & Bushnell, 2023). Stroke is often the first presentation of cardiovascular disease in women, while men most often present with coronary artery disease (Rexrode et al., 2022). Although prevalence is similar between sexes, women are disproportionately affected by stroke with a higher total lifetime risk of stroke and poorer stroke outcomes than men (Yoon & Bushnell, 2023). Understanding and identifying cardiovascular disease in women is particularly important because it often presents differently than in men, leading to misdiagnosis and delayed treatment; by recognizing these unique patterns, we can improve prevention strategies, enhance care, and ultimately save lives. In this chapter, we review the types of stroke (i.e., ischemic and hemorrhagic), and the impact that strokes have on women worldwide, including sequelae of cognitive impairment, epilepsy, post-stroke depression (PSD), and vascular dementia.

A. Gulati (✉)
The George Washington University School of Medicine, Washington, DC, USA
e-mail: agulati@mfa.gwu.edu

C. Bushnell
Wake Forest University School of Medicine, Winston-Salem, NC, USA

E. Sullivan-Baca, R. Ellison (eds.), *Neuropsychology of Women*,
https://doi.org/10.1007/978-3-031-87228-0_3

Epidemiology

Stroke is the fifth leading cause of death in women with approximately 1 in 5 women suffering a stroke annually (American Heart Association, 2024c). Globally, the lifetime risk of stroke is 25.1% in women and 24.7% in men, with a higher lifetime risk noted in women in Eastern Europe and East Asia (Rexrode et al., 2022; Yoon & Bushnell, 2023).

Ischemic Stroke

Within the United States, approximately 87% of strokes are due to ischemia, or loss of blood flow to a blood vessel within the brain (John Hopkins Medicine, 2024). The cause of ischemic stroke can be further characterized by the Trial of Org 10,172 in Acute Stroke Treatment (TOAST) criteria, which recognizes five subtypes of ischemic stroke: (1) large-artery atherosclerosis, (2) cardioembolism, (3) small-vessel occlusion, (4) stroke of other determined etiology, and (5) stroke of undetermined etiology (Adams et al., 1993).

Though increased age has historically been associated with a higher risk of stroke, recent studies find that young women aged 25–44 years are at a higher risk of developing ischemic strokes than men (Leppert et al., 2020). After the age of 45 years, however, men have a higher risk of ischemic stroke than women with this difference narrowing and becoming equivocal after the age of 75 years and even higher in women (Leppert et al., 2020) (Table 3.1).

Hemorrhagic Stroke

Hemorrhagic strokes are caused by rupture of a blood vessel within the brain resulting in bleeding. When compared to ischemic strokes, hemorrhagic strokes within the United States are rarer. While they account for only 13% of all strokes, they are

Table 3.1 Comparison of ischemic stroke risk among women and men by age

Age group (years)	Risk of ischemic stroke (women)	Risk of ischemic stroke (men)	Notes
25–34	Higher	Lower	Young women at higher risk
35–44	Higher	Lower	Young women at higher risk
45–54	Similar	Higher	Men begin to have a higher risk
55–64	Lower	Higher	Men maintain higher risk
65–74	Lower	Higher	Men have a more significant risk
75 and older	Higher	Similar	Risk increases in women; difference narrows

associated with a higher morbidity and mortality (Fernando et al., 2021). Intracerebral hemorrhage (ICH) or bleeding within the brain tissue accounts for approximately 10% of hemorrhagic stroke while aneurysmal subarachnoid hemorrhage (SAH) accounts for approximately 3% (Salvadori et al., 2020).

As the rates of ischemic and hemorrhagic stroke are often combined, limited data is available regarding the exact rate of hemorrhagic stroke within women. However, data from the Women's Health Initiative (WHI) found that of women who presented with a stroke, 18.7% were hemorrhagic (Wassertheil-Smoller, 2010). When combined data is evaluated, there remains a trend toward lower risk of hemorrhagic stroke among women when compared with men. A study assessing the nationwide incidence of primary intracranial hemorrhage among 803,230 adults from 2004 to 2018 found the average incidence to be lower in women at 66.72 per 100,000 compared to men at 72.6 per 100,000 over a 3-year period (Bako et al., 2022). When assessing the overall trend over time, the incidence increased in both genders but remained lower in women with women having an incidence of 61.31 per 100,000 in 2004–2006 increasing to 74.22 per 100,000 from 2016 to 2018, while men had an incidence of 64.39 per 100,000 from 2004 to 2006 increasing to 83.77 per 100,000 from 2016 to 2018 (Bako et al., 2022).

When separated by race and ethnicity, the average incidence rate per 100,000 was higher in non-Hispanic/Latinx Black/African Americans at 103.41 followed by non-Hispanic/Latinx Whites at 68.71, Asian Americans at 66.47, and Hispanic/Latinx at 47.35 (Bako et al., 2022). Similarly, several other studies have found a higher risk of intracerebral hemorrhage among Black/African American and Hispanic/Latinx patients when compared to White patients (Broderick et al., 1992; Brott et al., 1986; Bruno et al., 1996; Flaherty et al., 2006; Morgenstern et al., 2004).

While the overall prevalence of hemorrhagic stroke is lower in women than in men, women have a higher prevalence and incidence of intracranial aneurysms leading to a higher incidence of subarachnoid hemorrhage when compared to men (Rexrode et al., 2022). Notably, the increased rates of aneurysm formation and rupture is thought to be directly correlated with a decrease in estrogen level after menopause (Fuentes et al., 2022; Yoon & Bushnell, 2023).

Risk Factors

The most common modifiable risk factors for ischemic stroke include hypertension, diabetes, dyslipidemia, tobacco use, diet, physical inactivity, obesity, excessive alcohol consumption, cardiac disease, and the ratio of apolipoprotein B to A1. Similarly, the most common modifiable risk factors for hemorrhagic stroke include hypertension, tobacco use, excessive alcohol consumption, obesity, and diet. Several of these risk factors can be summed up into Life's Essential 8, eight key elements defined by the American Heart Association that can be adapted to improve and maintain cardiovascular health. These elements include the following: eat better, be more active, quit tobacco, get healthy sleep, manage weight, control cholesterol,

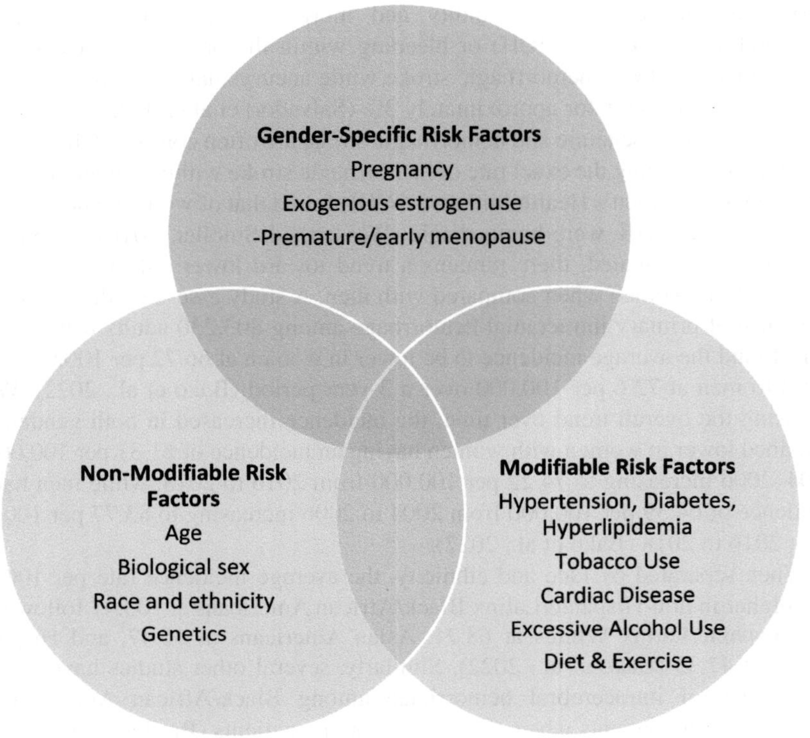

Fig. 3.1 Risk factors for stroke in women, including non-modifiable, modifiable, and gender-specific risk factors

manage blood sugar, and manage blood pressure (American Heart Association, 2024b). Non-modifiable risk factors include age, biological sex, race and ethnicity, and genetics (O'Donnell et al., 2010). These risk factors will be discussed in more thorough detail in the following sections, as well as the interaction between modifiable and non-modifiable risk factors (Fig. 3.1).

Non-Modifiable Risk Factors

Age is one of the primary non-modifiable risk factors for stroke. Stroke is commonly considered a disease of aging with the incidence doubling for each decade after the age of 55 years (Roger et al., 2012). Similarly, in hemorrhagic stroke, the incidence was found to increase after the age of 45 years (van Asch et al., 2010).

Biological sex can interact with age and also play a role in the risk of stroke. At younger ages, women have a higher risk of stroke compared to men. The higher stroke risk at younger age is likely due to women-specific risk factors, which we will discuss in more detail later. At an older age, the difference between the risk of stroke among both genders narrows. However, overall a higher number of strokes occur in women due to their longer lifespan when compared to men (Reeves et al., 2009a, 2009b).

Race and ethnicity also affect stroke risk. Within the United States, the overall prevalence of stroke in non-Hispanic/Latinx White individuals is approximately 2.3%, while the prevalence in non-Hispanic/Latinx Black/African American individuals is approximately 4.0% (Cruz-Flores et al., 2011). Non-Hispanic/Latinx Black/African American children are also at a higher risk of ischemic stroke, most commonly due to sickle cell disease. Black/African American stroke survivors are more likely to have recurrent strokes and greater disability post-stroke (CDC, 2005; Kennedy, 2005).

The overall prevalence of stroke in Hispanic/Latinx individuals is approximately 2.6% with a higher incidence among Mexican American individuals (CDC, 2007). The incidence of transient ischemic attacks (TIA), ICH, and SAH is also higher in Mexican Americans when compared to non-Hispanic/Latinx Whites, with this population also found to have a higher rate of recurrent stroke (Lisabeth et al., 2006; Morgenstern et al., 2004). Native Americans have the highest prevalence of stroke at approximately 6.0% (CDC, 2007). Among those aged 65 years and older, there is a higher rate of new and recurrent stroke in Native American women compared to men with the annual rate per 1000 being 6.1 for men and 6.6 for women (NIH, 2001). Racial-ethnic minorities also have higher rates of stroke mortality within the United States, with the highest mortality rates in non-Hispanic/Latinx Black/African Americans (CDC, 2005; Cruz-Flores et al., 2011). The cause of racial-ethnic disparities is often multifactorial, including decreased access to care, lower socioeconomic status, cultural variations in perception of the healthcare system, disadvantages in early childhood, genetic factors, and educational level (Cruz-Flores et al., 2011).

The ability to recognize warning signs of a stroke is low among the general population with 30–60% of the population unable to recognize a single warning sign (Nicol & Thrift, 2005). However, discrepancies in the ability to recognize the warning signs of a stroke exist and vary based on gender, age, and race and ethnicity. Specifically, among women aged 45–54 years, Hispanic/Latinx women were more than 4 times as likely and non-Hispanic/Latinx Black/African Americans were 2.5 times as likely than non-Hispanic/Latinx Whites to have low scores on assessments of stroke knowledge (Lutfiyya et al., 2009). The rate of compliance with medication is also lower in minorities; this is often influenced by factors including denial of disease, concern for side effects, difficulty filling prescriptions or attending appointments, and lower health literacy (Cruz-Flores et al., 2011).

Compounding and contributing to racial-ethnic disparities, access to healthcare varies widely among minorities. Non-Hispanic/Latinx Black and African Americans and Hispanic/Latinx were found to use emergency transport services less, resulting in delayed arrival to the Emergency Department and delayed care (Lacy et al., 2001). Non-Hispanic/Latinx Black and African Americans are also found to have significantly longer wait times resulting in delayed access to acute stroke treatment.

Strategies to mitigate racial-ethnic disparities should continue to remain at the forefront of stroke care and research.

Modifiable Risk Factors

Hypertension is one of the most common risk factors for a stroke. According to the American Heart Association, Stage 1 hypertension is defined as a systolic blood pressure greater than 130 and/or diastolic blood pressure greater than 80 (American Heart Association, 2024a). A systemic analysis of hypertension published in 2016 analyzed the rate of hypertension globally with hypertension defined as a systolic blood pressure greater than 140 and diastolic blood pressure greater than 90. The study found that the prevalence of hypertension in adults greater than 20 years of age was 31.1% with a rate of 30.1% in women and 31.9% in men. In high income countries, the rate was found to be 28.5% with a rate of 25.3% in women and 31.6% in men. In middle and low income countries, the rate was approximately 31.5% with a rate of 31.2% in women and 31.7% in men (Mills et al., 2016). In high income countries, the greatest burden was seen in older age groups greater than 60 years of age, whereas in low and middle income countries, the greatest burden was seen in middle age groups aged 40–59 years old (Mills et al., 2016).

A similar study published in 2021 evaluated the rates of hypertension worldwide from 1990 to 2019. The study found that the prevalence of hypertension in 2019 was overall similar to the prevalence in 1990 with 32% of women and 34% of men aged 30–79 years with hypertension in 2019 compared to 32% of both women and men in 1990 (Zhou et al., 2021). Though the overall prevalence of hypertension was generally found to be lower in women than men, women within the postmenopausal phase were found to have an increased prevalence of hypertension (Zhou et al., 2021).

Low and middle income countries have the highest prevalence of hypertension with almost 82% of individuals with hypertension residing within these countries (Zhou et al., 2021). Hypertension was found to be a new diagnosis in 47% of women and 38% of men. Among those treated for hypertension, less than half achieved control with control rates of 23% in women and 18% in men globally (Zhou et al., 2021). Control rates were found to improve in most countries since 1990 with the largest improvement seen in high-income countries and central Europe. Among the countries with the lowest difference in improvement were countries in sub-Saharan Africa and Oceania. In most countries, the rate of hypertension treatment was found to be higher in women than men (Zhou et al., 2021).

Within the United States, a lower percentage of women than men have hypertension (44% vs 50%, respectively). These rates were found to differ among race with non-Hispanic/Latinx Black/African American adults having a higher rate at 56% followed by 48% in non-Hispanic/Latinx White adults, 46% in non-Hispanic/Latinx Asian adults, and 39% in Hispanic/Latinx adults. Blood pressure control was highest among non-Hispanic/Latinx White adults at 32% followed by non-Hispanic/Latinx Black/African American adults and Hispanic/Latinx adults at 25%, and non-Hispanic/Latinx Asian adults at 19%. The highest rates of hypertension were seen in the southeast region of the United States (CDC, 2024a).

In addition to being one of the most common risk factors for a stroke, hypertension is also one of the greatest modifiable risk factors. Prior studies have shown a similar risk of cardiovascular disease worldwide in both women and men with hypertension (Peters et al., 2013). Specifically, for every 10 mmHg increase in systolic blood pressure, the risk of stroke has been found to increase by 23% in women and 24% in men (Peters et al., 2013). However, more recent studies, such as the REGARDS study, found higher rates of stroke in women with hypertension in the United States than in men, with the incidence of stroke almost twice as high in women (Madsen et al., 2019). As such, future research on the biological mechanisms for variations in stroke incidence and sex-specific guidelines for management and treatment are warranted.

Diabetes mellitus is another important modifiable risk factor implicated in cardiovascular disease. In 2021, the prevalence of diabetes within the United States was 11.6%. The percentage of adults with diabetes increased with age with a prevalence of 29.2% among individuals aged 65 years or higher. The prevalence among women was slightly lower than in men (14.1% vs 15.4%, respectively) (CDC, 2024b). The rates of treatment and control were similar in women and men within the United States (Peters et al., 2014). However, women with diabetes were found to have a 27% greater relative risk of stroke when compared to men in a pooled analysis of 64 population-based cohort studies published in between 1966 and 2013 with a total of 775,385 patients, of whom 12,539 were patients with stroke (Peters et al., 2014). In a meta-analysis published in 2018 evaluating 68 prospective observational studies included in the Prospective Studies Collaboration and Asia Pacific Cohort Studies Collaboration from 1949 to 2002 involving 980,793 patients, women with diabetes were found to have a higher relative risk of death following an ischemic stroke compared to men (Gnatiuc et al., 2018).

Atrial fibrillation is a major risk factor for stroke with the incidence of stroke related to atrial fibrillation nearly tripling in the past three decades (Yiin et al., 2014). Though women have a lower prevalence and incidence of atrial fibrillation than men, the lifetime risk is similar to men due to the longer life expectancy of women (Ko et al., 2016). In a meta-analysis of 30 cohort studies published in between 1966 and 2015 with a total of 4,371,714 participants, atrial fibrillation was found to be associated with a significantly higher risk of stroke, cardiovascular mortality, cardiac events, and heart failure, as well as all-cause mortality in women compared to men (Emdin et al., 2016). In another cohort study performed within the United Kingdom, atrial fibrillation was also associated with a higher hazard ratio of hemorrhagic stroke in women than in men at 2.80, with hazard ratio defined as a measure used in survival analysis to compare the rate at which an event occurs in two groups over time (Peters et al., 2020).

Though associated with a higher risk of stroke in women, women with atrial fibrillation were found to have lower anticoagulation use than men. An analysis of the PINNACLE study in 2017 found that women were significantly less likely to receive oral anticoagulation than men (56.7% vs 61.3%) (Thompson et al., 2017).

Women were also less likely than men to undergo catheter ablation for atrial fibrillation (Avgil Tsadok et al., 2015). These discrepancies in management may explain why the stroke risk is higher in women with atrial fibrillation and should be evaluated further in future studies.

Hyperlipidemia is defined as elevated lipid levels in the form of total cholesterol or low-density lipoprotein cholesterol (LDL-C). It is one of the major risk factors for cardiovascular disease and stroke. In a survey performed within the United States, a lower percentage of women than men with cardiovascular disease had dyslipidemia, while the rates were similar in those without cardiovascular disease (Peters et al., 2019). Nonetheless, in a prospective study of women greater than 45 years of age within the United States, the multivariable-adjusted hazard ratio of ischemic stroke was 2.27 for total cholesterol and 1.74 for LDL-C (Kurth et al., 2007). Statin therapy is the mainstay of treatment of hyperlipidemia. However, similar to oral anticoagulation in atrial fibrillation, women were less likely than men to be treated with any statin or at the guideline-recommended dose (Nanna et al., 2019).

Tobacco use is associated with higher rates of stroke. Though the prevalence of smoking is lower in women than men, there was a greater risk of stroke in women who smoked tobacco with an odds ratio (OR) of 1.88 in women compared to 1.54 in men in a meta-analysis of 14 studies published in between 1980 and 2018 with a total of 303,134 participants (Pan et al., 2019). Similarly, in a cohort study performed in the United Kingdom, smoking was associated with a higher hazard ratio (HR) of any stroke in women than in men (HR 1.18) (Peters et al., 2020).

Migraine and its particular subtype—migraine with aura—is associated with a higher risk of stroke. In a narrative review published in 2022, the global prevalence of migraine was found to be 20.7% in women and 9.7% in men. Several mechanisms have been proposed linking migraine and stroke; these include genetic predisposition, endothelial dysfunction, coagulation abnormalities, arterial dissection, and paradoxical embolism through a patent foramen ovale (PFO) (Lee et al., 2016). Women are shown to have a higher association of migraine with ischemic stroke when compared to men (RR 2.08 vs. 1.37, respectively) (Schurks et al., 2009). This risk was most prevalent in women under the age of 45 years (RR 3.65), women on oral contraceptives (RR 7.02), and individuals with current tobacco use (RR 9.03 in smokers vs. 1.56 in non-smokers) (Schurks et al., 2009).

Obesity, diet, and physical activity are all factors that contribute to the risk of stroke. Obesity, in itself, is a risk factor for stroke in both women and men. However, the prevalence of obesity is higher in women (Garawi et al., 2014). An elevated body mass index, clinical obesity defined as greater than or equal to 30 kg/m^2, and a high waist-to-hip ratio are all associated with higher risk of ischemic stroke in both women and men, though a stronger association was noted in women (Kroll et al., 2016; Peters et al., 2020). There is conflicting data on the relationship between obesity and hemorrhagic stroke with some data suggesting a decreased risk (Kroll et al., 2016).

Lifestyle modifications, including diet and physical activity, are associated with reduction in the risk of stroke. In a cross-sectional study published in 2022, any amount of activity, whether light to moderate or vigorous, was associated with a decreased risk of stroke. In contrast, a sedentary lifestyle was associated with a higher risk of stroke (Ghozy et al., 2022). Adherence to diets, such as the Mediterranean diet and DASH diet, can lower the risk of stroke (Foroughi et al., 2013). Further studies need to determine the gender-differences in adopting such lifestyle modifications and the potential barriers or challenges that are faced.

Women-Specific Risk Factors

Pregnancy can induce a hypercoagulable state that can result in a four to ten times increased thrombotic risk (Bremme, 2003). This, in addition to other physiological changes that occur during pregnancy, can result in an increased risk of stroke. The risk of maternal stroke is higher in the peripartum and postpartum periods than during the antepartum period (Sullivan-Baca et al., 2024). A population-based cohort study performed in the United Kingdom in 2017 found that the rate of any stroke, ischemic or hemorrhagic, was ninefold higher in the peripartum period (defined as 2 days before and 1 day after delivery) and threefold higher in the early postpartum period (defined as the first 6 weeks following delivery) when compared to age-matched non-pregnant women (Ban et al., 2017). Common stroke etiologies during pregnancy include hemorrhagic stroke, reversible cerebral vasoconstrictive syndrome (RCVS), cervical arterial dissection, cardioembolism, and cerebral sinus thrombosis. Of these stroke etiologies, hemorrhagic stroke accounts for approximately 60% of maternal strokes.

According to a retrospective population-based cohort study performed in Canada in 2019, risk factors for stroke in pregnancy included older maternal age defined as greater than or equal to 40, pre-eclampsia, eclampsia, maternal congenital heart disease, connective tissue disorders, sepsis, severe postpartum hemorrhage, and thrombophilia (Liu et al., 2019). Black/African American race is also found to increase the risk of pregnancy-related stroke (Miller & Leffert, 2020). Among pregnant women with hypertensive disorders of pregnancy, Black/African American patients were found to have twice the risk of stroke compared to White patients. Without hypertension, this trend remained with Black/African American patients having a 17% higher risk of stroke (Miller & Leffert, 2020; Sullivan-Baca et al., 2024).

Hypertensive disorders of pregnancy, including chronic hypertension (diagnosed prior to 20 weeks of pregnancy), gestational hypertension (diagnosed after 20 weeks of pregnancy), and pre-eclampsia, are associated with both maternal stroke and an increased long-term risk of stroke (Hung et al., 2022; Sullivan-Baca et al., 2024). A cross-sectional study performed within the United States in 2015 evaluated 81,983,216 pregnancy hospitalizations from 1994 to 2011. During this time period, the study found that the rate of stroke with hypertensive disorders in pregnancy increased from 0.8 per 10,000 from 1994 to 1995 to 1.6 per 10,000 from 2010 to 2011 with women with hypertensive disorders of pregnancy at an approximately 5.2 times higher risk of maternal stroke than those without (Leffert et al., 2015). When further broken down by race, the study found that White women had the highest rate of hypertensive disorders of pregnancy and stroke at 29.1% followed by Black/ African American at 26.7%, Hispanic/Latinx at 15%, and other at 6.6%. The rates were also higher within certain geographical locations with the South being the highest at 50% followed by the West at 22.4%, the Midwest at 20.3%, and the Northeast at 15.3% (Leffert et al., 2015).

Furthermore, a meta-analysis published in 2017 evaluated the association of pre-eclampsia and cardiovascular disease across 22 studies, of which greater than 6.4 million women including greater than 258,000 women with pre-eclampsia were identified. It found that pre-eclampsia was associated with a fourfold increase in future incident of heart failure and twofold increase in future incidence of coronary heart disease, stroke, and death due cardiovascular disease. The increase in risk was particularly highest during the first 10 years after a pregnancy complicated by pre-eclampsia compared with those beyond 10 years (Wu et al., 2017). Similarly, in a nationwide study performed in Taiwan in 2022, the risk of hemorrhagic stroke continued to increase over time with a hazard ratio of 4.64 approximately 10–15 years after childbirth, while the risk of ischemic stroke peaked around 1–3 years postpartum with a hazard ratio of 2.14 (Hung et al., 2022). In addition to hypertensive disorders of pregnancy, other factors associated with increased long-term risk of stroke include gestational diabetes, smoking, migraine headaches, and preterm delivery (Sullivan-Baca et al., 2024; Yoon & Bushnell, 2023).

Exogenous estrogen use, in particular estrogen-containing oral contraceptive pills, are associated with an increased risk of stroke. In a meta-analysis of 18 studies published in 2015, women on oral contraceptive pills had a 2.5-fold increased risk of an ischemic stroke with the risk decreasing with lower estrogen concentrations. The risk of an ischemic stroke was further increased when combined with tobacco use, hypertension, history of migraine, and age greater than 35 (Xu et al., 2015). Another meta-analysis, published in 2018, evaluated 15 studies with a total of 4271 hemorrhagic stroke cases. It found that the risk of hemorrhagic stroke was approximately 1.4-fold higher in women on oral contraceptive pills (Xu et al., 2018). This risk was further increased by other associated risk factors including hypertension, migraine, and tobacco use (Xu et al., 2015, 2018).

Similar to estrogen-containing oral contraceptives, oral menopausal hormone replacement therapy (HRT) is associated with an increased risk of ischemic stroke (Manson et al., 2013). The risk of stroke is higher in the first year of use, but remains elevated in the years after (Johansson et al., 2022). Unlike oral HRT, transdermal therapy containing low doses of estrogen have been found to have a lower risk of stroke (Pinkerton, 2020).

Endogenous estrogen exposure occurs from menarche to menopause. Age at menarche is associated with variable rates of stroke. Women with early menarche, defined as age less than or equal to 10 years, and late menarche, defined as age greater than or equal to 16 years, have a 27% and 25% increased risk of stroke, respectively (Mishra et al., 2020). Early menarche combined with a shorter reproductive lifespan defined as less than 33 years had the highest risk of cardiovascular disease (HR 2.06) (Mishra et al., 2020).

Similarly, age at menopause has variable associations with stroke. Women with premature menopause, defined as age less than 40 years, and early menopause, defined as age 40–44 years, have a 98% and 49% higher risk of stroke, respectively (Mishra et al., 2020). This risk can be mitigated in those with late menopause occurring at age 56 years or older with a 28% lower risk of cardiovascular disease (HR 0.72). Surgical menopause, completed by performing a bilateral oophorectomy with or without a hysterectomy, is also associated with a higher risk of stroke with the risk most significant in women under the age of 48 years (Bushnell & Kapral, 2023; Poorthuis et al., 2017, 2022).

Presentation

Early and rapid recognition of the signs and symptoms of a stroke is essential in providing prompt management and treatment. Traditional signs and symptoms of a stroke include sudden onset dizziness or difficulty with balance, change in vision, difficulty producing or comprehending speech, and unilateral numbness or weakness. Prior studies evaluating the gender difference in acute stroke presentation conflict with some population studies suggesting that women were more likely to present with non-traditional signs of stroke such as altered mental status and pain. A population based study in Rochester, MN, corroborated these findings, indicating higher rates of disorientation, confusion, generalized weakness, fatigue, and changes in mental status in women upon presentation (Gardener et al., 2020). Similarly, in a Michigan-based study evaluating 1922 acute stroke cases, of whom 54.2% were women, women were found to be significantly less likely than men to present with any stroke warning sign or suspected stroke (87.5% vs 91.4%) and less likely to report trouble with walking, balance, or dizziness (9.5% vs 13.7%) (Gargano et al., 2009).

Comorbid conditions can often influence and delay the diagnosis of stroke. The Diagnosis of Uncertain Origin Benign Transient Events (DOUBT) study published in 2019 was a prospective cohort study involving nine sites within Canada, Australia, and the Czech Republic that evaluated a total of 1028 patients with transient or minor stroke symptoms of whom 51% were women (Coutts et al., 2019). It found that women were more likely to report a history of migraine and recent stressors on presentation (33% women vs. 17% men and 19% women vs. 12% men, respectively) (Coutts et al., 2019; Rexrode et al., 2022). These conditions can often overlap with and mimic stroke and, thus, result in delayed diagnosis. As such, it is essential to account for variations in presentation to prevent delays in both the diagnosis and treatment of stroke in women.

Diagnosis and Treatment

Diagnosis

The diagnostic evaluation of stroke is multifaceted involving a thorough neurological examination and grading of symptoms using the National Institutes of Health Stroke Scale (NIHSS). Brain imaging is then performed using either computed tomography (CT) or magnetic resonance (MR) imaging. The cranial vasculature is then evaluated, typically using CT or MR angiography (Wityk & Beauchamp, 2000). Several studies show variations in the diagnostic assessment of stroke in women when compared to men. A retrospective cohort study published in 2020 evaluated Medicare claims submitted from 2008 to 2016 and included patients age greater than or equal to 65 years who were hospitalized with an acute ischemic stroke. Of the 78,822 patients admitted with an acute ischemic stroke, 58.3% were women. Within the study, women were less likely to be evaluated by a stroke specialist and less likely to undergo standard diagnostic testing when compared to men (Bruce et al., 2020). In addition, female sex was also associated with decreased odds of intracranial vessel imaging, extracranial vessel imaging, heart-rhythm monitoring, echocardiography, evaluation by a neurologist, and evaluation by a vascular neurologist (Bruce et al., 2020). Similar findings have been reported in prior studies (Bruce et al., 2020; Di Carlo et al., 2003; Roquer et al., 2003). In addition to variations in diagnostic assessment, delays in care are also reported (Centers for Disease & Prevention, 2007; Jungehulsing et al., 2006; Rose et al., 2008; Yu et al., 2002). A study in 2009 involving a statewide stroke registry in Michigan covering 15 hospitals evaluated a total of 1922 acute stroke cases, of whom 54.2% were women. It found that women had an 11% longer door-to-doctor interval and 15% longer door-to-image time interval (Gargano et al., 2009).

This delay can be even more pronounced in pregnant individuals due to variations in recommendations and the desire to avoid potential harm to the mother and fetus. Though ultrasonography and MR imaging are the modalities of choice in pregnancy, the American College of Obstetricians and Gynecologists recommend that CT scans can be considered if rapid diagnosis is required or depending on availability of imaging as the radiation exposure is at a dose much lower than that associated with fetal harm (Elgendy et al., 2021; Gynecologists, 2017). If using MR imaging, the use of gadolinium contrast should be limited as its use remains controversial due to the ability of the molecules to cross the placenta and cause possible fetal harm (American College of Obstetricians and Gynecologists & Committee on Obstetric Practice, 2017). Further studies should be performed to evaluate disparities in stroke evaluation and mitigate the delays upon presentation.

Treatment

Thrombolytics in Acute Stroke

The 2019 American Heart Association guidelines recommend rapid treatment of patients presenting with symptoms of an acute stroke with thrombolytics within 4.5 hours from last known normal (LKN). The thrombolytics typically used in acute stroke include IV alteplase and IV tenecteplase (Powers et al., 2019). Similar to the differences seen in stroke diagnosis, women are also less likely to receive thrombolysis than men (Deng et al., 2006; Reed et al., 2001; Reeves et al., 2009a; Reid et al., 2008; Turtzo & McCullough, 2008). A meta-analysis published in 2020 evaluating 24 studies published in between 2008 and 2018 found that women were 13% less likely to receive IV thrombolytics than men (Strong et al., 2020). These differences may be due to women being older at onset with higher baseline modified Rankin score (mRS), presenting with atypical syndromes, delays in time from symptom onset to hospital or from door to needle, greater likelihood of living independently and thus presenting outside of the time window or with an unknown last known normal, or being more unwilling to accept thrombolysis (Gargano et al., 2009).

Uncertainty regarding the administration of thrombolytics in pregnant individuals can also lead to delays in care within this population. Though pregnancy was historically considered a contraindication to IV thrombolytics, these medications are not known to be teratogenic and are too large to travel across the placenta. However, there remains a high concern for complications including uterine bleeding, placental abruption, premature labor, and fetal demise (Demchuk, 2013; Elgendy et al., 2021). Current guidelines recommend consideration of IV thrombolytics in pregnancy when the benefits of treating moderate-to-severe stroke outweigh the potential risks (Demaerschalk et al., 2016; Elgendy et al., 2021; Powers et al., 2019). The use of IV thrombolytics in the early postpartum period, defined as less than 14 days following delivery, remains uncertain (Powers et al., 2019). Early involvement of a multidisciplinary team involving obstetricians, neurologists, and potentially a perinatologist to assist with management is essential (Demaerschalk et al., 2016; Powers et al., 2019).

Endovascular Therapy in Acute Stroke

Endovascular treatment (EVT) is guideline-recommended therapy for individuals with an acute ischemic stroke due to large-vessel occlusion (LVO). Variations in utility and outcomes following EVT based on gender have been previously studied. A recent meta-analysis published in 2022 evaluated 51 studies and did not find any differences in utilization of EVT among women and men (Ouyang et al., 2023). In addition, the study did not show any gender differences in outcomes following EVT (Ouyang et al., 2023). These findings are similar to a previous meta-analysis performed using data from the Highly Effective Reperfusion Using Multiple Endovascular Devices (HERMES) trial that did not show any changes in treatment effect or outcome based on gender, noting that women and men benefited equally (Chalos et al., 2019; Goyal et al., 2016). However, a post hoc analysis of the Multicenter Randomized Clinical Trial of Endovascular Treatment for Acute Ischemic Stroke in the Netherlands (MR CLEAN) trial indicated that women had a higher 90-day mortality and adverse events when compared to men (De Ridder et al., 2016). Further studies are needed to determine whether any disparity exists in the utilization of EVT and in post-thrombectomy outcomes based on gender.

Outcomes

Gender differences have been found to exist in stroke outcomes. Women often have worse outcomes post-stroke with increased disability and decreased quality of life (Bushnell et al., 2018). The Framingham Heart Study was a longitudinal community-based cohort study that began in Framingham, Massachusetts, in 1948 and initially involved 5209 men and women aged 30–62 years old who were free of cardiovascular disease. Of the participants who were living in 1999, 220 participants between the age of 65 and 94 years experienced their first stroke. The study evaluated the variation in deficits post-stroke based on gender and found that 34% of women were disabled at 6 months post-stroke compared to only 16% of men (Kelly-Hayes et al., 2003). In addition, women were found to be more dependent in activities of daily living (ADLs) (33.9% vs 15.6%), less likely to walk unassisted (40.3% vs 17.8%), and more likely to reside in nursing homes (34.9% vs 13.3%). When adjusted for age and stroke subtype, older age was the main factor that accounted for the severity in disability. As strokes tend to occur later in life in women, age at presentation is often the main contributor of post-stroke disability (Kelly-Hayes et al., 2003).

Lower quality of life in women post-stroke is often impacted by stroke-related anxiety, depression, pain and discomfort, and decreased mobility compared to men (Bushnell et al., 2014b). Post-stroke mortality has also been reported to be higher in women when compared to men (Phan et al., 2017; Yoon & Bushnell, 2023). The International Stroke Outcomes Study (INSTRUCT), a meta-analysis published in 2017 evaluating 13 population-based incidence studies in Europe, Australia, South America, and the Caribbean between 1987 and 2013, found that women have greater long-term mortality than men after stroke. Factors associated with an increase in mortality include advanced age, stroke severity, lower pre-stroke function, higher baseline mRS, and the presence of atrial fibrillation (Phan et al., 2017) (Table 3.2).

Table 3.2 Comparison of gender differences in post-stroke outcomes

Outcome category	Men	Women
Stroke incidence	Slightly higher incidence than women, especially at younger ages	Lower overall incidence, but higher in very old age groups (85+ years)
Age at stroke	Typically younger age at first stroke	Typically older age at first stroke
Stroke severity	Often lower stroke severity at presentation	Often higher stroke severity at presentation
Functional recovery	Generally faster recovery and better functional outcomes	Slower recovery and more significant functional impairments
Disability and dependence	Lower rates of long-term disability	Higher rates of long-term disability, often due to worse initial deficits
Mortality rate	Slightly lower mortality rates, especially in younger age groups	Higher mortality rates, particularly in older age groups
Recurrence risk	Generally lower recurrence risk than women	Slightly higher recurrence risk, especially post-menopause
Post-stroke depression	Lower rates of post-stroke depression	Higher rates of post-stroke depression
Response to rehabilitation	Better tolerance to physical rehabilitation	Often slower improvement and higher support needs in rehabilitation
Quality of life post-stroke	Quality of life outcomes often better	Quality of life outcomes typically lower
Comorbidities impact	Comorbid conditions like smoking, heart disease impact outcomes more heavily	Comorbid conditions like hypertension, atrial fibrillation, and post-menopausal factors contribute more significantly to outcomes

Post-Stroke Depression

Post-stroke depression (PSD) is one of the most common complications following a stroke, affecting approximately one-third of stroke survivors (Hackett & Pickles, 2014). Pregnant individuals may be more prone to developing PSD due to the co-occurrence of postpartum depression (PPD) and postpartum anxiety (PPA) (Rai et al., 2015; Sullivan-Baca et al., 2024). Those affected have a higher risk of decreased functional outcome, poorer quality of life, recurrent vascular events, and mortality (Towfighi et al., 2017). The frequency of PSD is highest in the first year following stroke and then gradually declines (Towfighi et al., 2017). A multitude of studies have shown five main predictors of PSD. These include (1) a history of mental disorder prior to stroke onset, (2) stroke severity, (3) physical disability, (4) cognitive impairment, and (5) lack of social support (Ladwig et al., 2023). A validation study published in 2023 evaluated two prospective longitudinal studies of stroke survivors: the Berlin PSD sample and the post-stroke depression early assessment for improved management (PoStDAM) sample. The study found that a history of psychiatric disorder prior to stroke onset, physical disability, and lack of social support were independent risk factors for the development of PSD (Ladwig et al., 2023).

Women are at higher risk of physical disability following stroke, which can increase the risk of developing PSD. In addition, women are more likely to have a history of depression pre-stroke which can further contribute to their risk. A population study published in 2020 evaluating 786 patients with first-time strokes from the Brain Attack Surveillance in Corpus Christi project from 2011 to 2016 found that approximately one-fourth of women were on medication for depression at the time of stroke onset, while one-fifth were not on medication but reported a history of depression, which was significantly higher than the rates in men (Dong et al., 2020). The gender difference in rates of pre-stroke depression may be accounted for by the higher likelihood of women to seek treatment than men. Within the study, the prevalence of depression at the first 90 days following stroke onset was 32.7% in women and 28.2% in men; though not significant, the prevalence was numerically higher in women than in men (Dong et al., 2020). Of the patients without a history of depression at stroke onset, approximately two-fifths were women. Compared to men, these women were typically older, more likely to be widowed, have a higher stroke severity and a higher burden of medical comorbidities (Dong et al., 2020). Fatigue and sleep disturbance were the most common symptoms experienced among both women and men with PSD. The prevalence of fatigue and changes in appetite was higher in women, whereas the prevalence of psychomotor changes was higher in men. Factors associated with first-onset depression following stroke included lack of insurance coverage, number of medical conditions, and tobacco use at the time of stroke onset (Dong et al., 2020).

A cross-sectional study published in 2023 evaluated the gender-specific association between stroke status and depression in South Korea with a total of 5746 men and 7608 women. The study found that the prevalence of PSD in women was 22.2% compared to 8.8% in men. Compared with the non-stroke participants, women with stroke had a 2.49-fold higher risk of depression (Kim & Lee, 2023). In addition, the study found that women with a younger age at stroke onset (<60 years; OR 4.05) and stroke duration of greater than 10 years had a stronger association with PSD (OR 3.12) (Kim & Lee, 2023). Actively screening for depression and providing treatment in stroke survivors is of vital importance and may greatly impact their quality of life. Further research is needed to better understand the gender differences of PSD and the interventions that may be best suited for each individual.

Post-Stroke Epilepsy

Stroke is one of the leading causes of acquired epilepsy in adults, particularly in older adults (Luhdorf et al., 1986). The incidence of post-stroke epilepsy (PSE) can range from 6% to 15% with the risk being highest in the first few years after stroke onset (Galovic et al., 2021). A meta-analysis performed in 2015 analyzed post-stroke seizures in 34 cohort studies involving 102,008 patients from 1990 to 2013.

The study found that the pooled incidence of post-stroke seizures was approximately 7% and post-stroke epilepsy was approximately 5% with no significant difference between women and men (Zou et al., 2015). Acute symptomatic seizures occurring within 7 days from stroke onset have been seen in up to 4% of patients with ischemic stroke and 16% of those with intracerebral hemorrhage (Beghi et al., 2011; Galovic et al., 2021). In addition to hemorrhagic strokes, cortical lesions can be predictors of acute symptomatic seizures (Beghi et al., 2011). Recurrent seizures following stroke can also affect stroke rehabilitation and recovery by leading to a decreased quality of life, potential injuries and physical impairments, cognitive changes, and decreased independence (Baranowski, 2018; Verducci et al., 2019).

While we have some insights into general trends, there is a gap in comprehensive data specifically addressing how gender might affect the prognosis, treatment response, and quality of life in patients with PSE. Further research is crucial for understanding these nuances and could help tailor interventions that account for gender-specific factors, potentially improving outcomes for both women and men.

Post-Stroke Cognitive Impairment

Post-stroke cognitive impairment (PSCI) can range in severity from mild to severe and affects approximately 60% of stroke survivors in the first year following stroke onset (El Husseini et al., 2023). Approximately 10% of stroke survivors can progress to developing dementia within 1 year following stroke onset (Moulin et al., 2016). Pre-stroke cognitive impairment, PSCI, and dementia are also frequently seen in patients with intracranial hemorrhage (Banerjee et al., 2018; Moulin et al., 2016). These rates are particularly higher in those with lobar hemorrhages, which are often seen in a condition associated with dementia called cerebral amyloid angiopathy. In patients with subarachnoid hemorrhage, impairment in at least one cognitive domain is commonly seen with the rates of impairment on global cognitive tests ranging between 26% and 43% at 3 months and 21% at 12 months (Mayer et al., 2002; Springer et al., 2009).

Risk factors for PSCI include older age, stroke severity, history of prior strokes, multiple comorbidities, lower educational status, and social isolation (Pendlebury & Rothwell, 2009). Black/African American patients have been found to have a greater cognitive decline and higher rates of dementia within the first 5 years following an ischemic stroke when compared to White patients (Clark et al., 2018). A multicenter study evaluated patients with acute ischemic strokes from nine cohorts including France, Hong Kong, Republic of Korea, the Netherlands, and Singapore with a total of 2343 patients. The study did not find any difference in the rate of women and men affected by PSCI; however, it did note a difference in the cognitive domains impacted (Exalto et al., 2023). Women were more likely to have impairments in the domains of attention, executive function, and language, whereas men were more likely to have impairments in verbal memory (Exalto et al., 2023). Pregnant individuals may be more prone to developing cognitive changes due to the co-occurrence of postpartum depression, anxiety, or psychosis in addition to lifestyle and environmental changes including sleep deprivation, new responsibilities, as well as changes in identity (Sullivan-Baca et al., 2024).

Management of PSCI is usually multifaceted and involves interdisciplinary collaboration between neurologists, gerontologists, primary care physicians, speech language pathologists, occupational therapists, neuropsychologists, and other healthcare providers. Approaches for management include physical activity, cognitive rehabilitation, and pharmaceutical management (El Husseini et al., 2023). Additional targeted studies are needed to determine how peripartum and postpartum periods, as well as other life stages specific to women, might impact cognitive recovery and management strategies.

Vascular Dementia

Vascular dementia is the second most common form of dementia following Alzheimer's disease, accounting for approximately 20% of dementia cases, with the risk doubling every 5 years after the age of 65 years (Korczyn et al., 2012; Roman, 2003). Vascular dementia following stroke is typically defined as a stepwise cognitive decline that occurs within 3 months of stroke onset. However, many stroke survivors can develop a delayed dementia outside of the 3-month period or following recurrent strokes (Kalaria et al., 2016). Pooled estimates show that 1-in-10 patients have pre-stroke dementia, 1-in-10 patients develop post-stroke dementia following their initial stroke, and over 1-in-3 patients develop post-stroke dementia after recurrent strokes (Pendlebury, 2009). Female sex, family history, and medial temporal lobe atrophy are strongly associated with pre-stroke dementia (Pendlebury, 2009; Pendlebury & Rothwell, 2009). The development of post-stroke dementia, in contrast, depends on several factors including the degree of stroke burden and neuronal damage, complications from the stroke, and the presence of pre-existing cognitive impairment or other cerebral pathology (Kalaria et al., 2016; Pendlebury & Rothwell, 2009). In addition, lower education, older age, diabetes mellitus, myocardial infarction, atrial fibrillation, epileptic seizures, sepsis, cardiac arrhythmias, congestive heart failure, global cerebral atrophy, medial temporal lobe atrophy, white matter changes, and post-stroke depression, which is more commonly seen in women than in men, are all linked to an increased risk of dementia following a stroke (Pendlebury & Rothwell, 2009; Pinkston et al., 2009).

Environmental factors can also contribute to the development of dementia. These factors can include poor air quality, toxic metals, trace elements, and work hazards that can involve the use of pesticides, fertilizers, and solvents (Killin et al., 2016). Though unlikely to directly cause dementia, these factors can exacerbate other risk factors that can contribute to the development (Kamel & Hoppin, 2004).

Types of Vascular Dementia

Gender differences are variable based on the type of vascular dementia, which include (1) subcortical, (2) stroke-related, (3) multi-infarct, and (4) mixed, and are outlined as follows.

Subcortical Vascular Dementia The most common type of vascular dementia, subcortical vascular dementia, is caused by damage to the small vessels within the subcortex of the brain over time. The cerebrovascular white matter lesions that are ordinarily seen with this disease correlate with advanced age, female gender, and vascular risk factors such as hypertension, diabetes mellitus, tobacco use, and lower income (Tomimoto, 2011). However, other studies have not shown a significant gender difference (Akhter et al., 2021).

Stroke-Related Vascular Dementia Stroke-related vascular dementia can occur after an initial stroke event. Though many individuals can develop transient cognitive impairment in the weeks or months following the initial stroke event, approximately 20% will go on to develop vascular dementia by 6 months (Alzheimer's Society, 2024a). While current data show no significant gender differences in stroke-related vascular dementia prevalence, theoretically, women might have a higher risk due to their longer life expectancy and often higher age at stroke onset. This age factor could mean more accumulated cerebrovascular burden by the time of stroke, potentially predisposing women to a higher risk of post-stroke cognitive impairment. More targeted studies could clarify whether there are subtle differences in pathophysiology or outcomes between genders in this dementia subtype.

Multi-Infarct Vascular Dementia Multi-infarct dementia occurs when a series of multiple minor strokes occur leading to cognitive dysfunction. It is most common in individuals aged 55–75 years and less likely to occur in women than men (Lechner & Bertha, 1991; McKay & Scott, 2017). Factors that increase the risk of multi-infarct dementia include atrial fibrillation, rapid heartbeat, previous strokes, heart failure, pre-stroke cognitive decline, hypertension, diabetes mellitus, atherosclerosis, tobacco use, alcohol use, low level of education, poor diet, and limited physical activity (Lechner & Bertha, 1991).

Mixed Vascular Dementia Mixed dementia refers to vascular dementia caused by more than one underlying cerebral pathology, such as a combination of vascular dementia and Alzheimer's disease. Approximately 1-in-10 patients with dementia have mixed dementia (Alzheimer's Society, 2024b). Generally, vascular dementia and mixed dementias occur less frequently in women than in men with approximate rates of 25% vs. 31%, respectively (Podcasy & Epperson, 2016). However, this difference is most noticeable at a younger age, whereas women over the age of 85–90 years have a higher risk of occurrence of vascular dementia, likely accounted for by the higher longevity of women (Lucca et al., 2020).

Risk Factors for Vascular Dementia

Female-specific factors for developing vascular dementia are hypothesized to include pregnancy-related disorders such as pre-eclampsia, menopause, and delayed hormone replacement therapy (HRT) (Gannon et al., 2019). Several studies have found postmenopausal estrogen deficiency to be a risk factor for vascular dementia (Robusto-Leitao & Ferreira, 2006). Though some studies have suggested that the use of HRT can decrease the risk of dementia, risks associated with the use of HRT such as increased risk of gynecologic malignancies and breast cancer as well as stroke may negate these benefits (D'Alonzo et al., 2019; Hogervorst et al., 2000; Yaffe et al., 1998). As such, no clear consensus or guidelines exist on the use and proper timing of HRT in postmenopausal women. In addition, women with concurrent diabetes mellitus, obesity, and hypertension are at higher risk for developing vascular dementia than males (Gannon et al., 2019). These risk factors provide areas that can be specifically targeted to decrease the potential risk of developing vascular dementia in women (Fig. 3.2).

Underlying genetic variants can also predispose patients to developing vascular dementia. Specifically, mutations in the Notch Receptor 3 (NOTCH3) gene can predispose individuals to developing cerebral autosomal dominant arteriopathy with subcortical infarcts and leukoencephalopathy (CADASIL), a rare form of vascular dementia (Akhter et al., 2021; Papakonstantinou et al., 2019). Both genders have an equal risk of developing CADASIL; however, their clinical presentations can differ (Ruitenberg et al., 2001; Singhal, 2004). In a study of 313 CADASIL patients from a large prospective cohort study in Paris and Munich published in 2011, women were found to be more likely to present with migraine with aura while

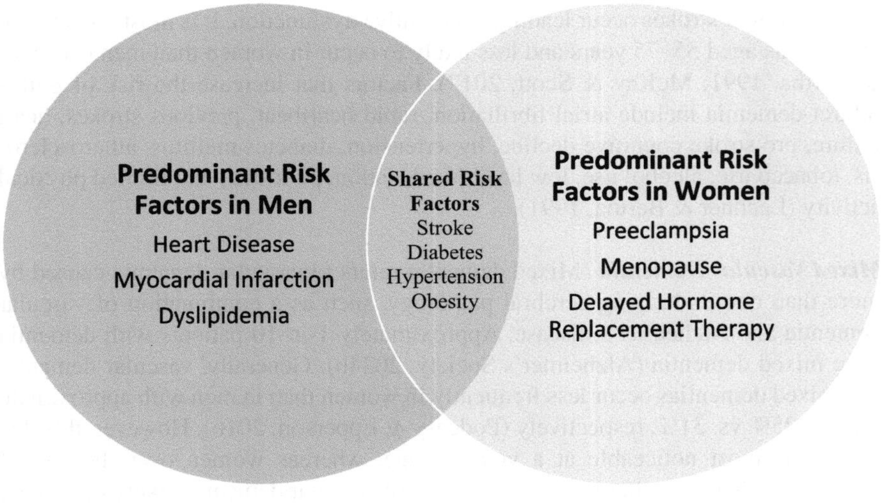

Fig. 3.2 Overview of gender-specific risk factors for vascular contributions to cognitive impairment and dementia (VCID)

men were more likely to present with strokes before the age of 51 years; however, this difference disappeared as individuals aged (Bushnell et al., 2014a; Gunda et al., 2012). Variants in apolipoprotein E (APOE) are also linked to vascular dementia, though their impact on the development of vascular dementia is less when compared to their impact on Alzheimer's disease. In addition, studies show that the risk of vascular dementia increases by at least tenfold with the presence of homozygous APOE4 (Akhter et al., 2021). Women with homozygous APOE4 have the highest risk of developing dementia when compared to men with the same homozygous pattern (Davidson et al., 2006; Molero et al., 2001; Rasmussen et al., 2018). Unlike APOE4, APOE2 shows some unique protective effects against dementia and cognitive decline in women, an effect that was not seen in men (Volgman et al., 2019).

Treatment

Currently, there is no cure for vascular dementia. Therapies and treatments are similar to those available for Alzheimer's dementia and aim to slow the progression of the disease. Pharmaceutical treatments can include cholinesterase inhibitors such as donepezil and rivastigmine, NMDA antagonists such as memantine, and aggressive medical management of stroke risk factors.

Focus on eliminating and decreasing risk factors is of utmost importance. Adequate and consistent blood pressure control decreases the risk of vascular dementia by 55% (Sierra, 2020). In addition to blood pressure management, primary prevention should include diet and lifestyle modifications with a special focus on high-risk groups such as the elderly, patients with hypertension and/or diabetes, smokers, individuals with TIA or prior strokes, as well as patients with hypercholesterolemia and atrial fibrillation (Eggink et al., 2019; Vijayan & Reddy, 2016). Management of vascular dementia and dementia-related complications often requires a multidisciplinary team involving the primary care physician, gerontologist, vascular neurologist, and rehabilitation specialists.

Research Takeaways

- Racial and ethnic minorities, particularly Black/African American and Hispanic/Latinx women, have higher stroke risks and poorer outcomes due to factors such as lower access to healthcare, socioeconomic disadvantages, and lower health literacy. Further research into methods to minimize disparities is of significant importance to combat the unequal distribution of stroke in minority populations.
- Common modifiable risk factors for stroke include hypertension, diabetes, hyperlipidemia, tobacco use, and lifestyle factors such as diet and physical inactivity. Further research should focus on the implementation of gender-

specific programs to address lifestyle modifications and mitigate the risk of stroke.
- Women-specific risk factors, such as pregnancy-related complications and hormonal factors, significantly impact stroke risk, highlighting the need for targeted prevention strategies.
- Women often present with non-traditional signs of stroke, such as altered mental status and generalized weakness, leading to potential delays in diagnosis and treatment. This highlights the importance of education on the variations in stroke presentation to decrease delays in identification.
- Women have higher rates of post-stroke disability and lower quality of life compared to men, influenced by factors such as older age at stroke onset and higher prevalence of comorbid conditions. Further research should be aimed toward a multifactorial approach to individuals in addressing not only stroke management and prevention, but also focusing on the psychosocial impact of stroke.

Clinical Takeaways

- Early and rapid recognition of stroke symptoms is crucial for effective treatment. Differences in symptom presentation between genders necessitate tailored approaches to improve diagnostic accuracy and reduce treatment delays.
- Thrombolytics and endovascular treatments are effective for acute ischemic stroke, but women are less likely to receive these treatments due to various barriers, including age and atypical symptom presentation.
- Strategies to mitigate racial and ethnic disparities in stroke care should focus on improving access to healthcare, increasing awareness of stroke symptoms, and addressing socioeconomic barriers.
- Post-stroke depression, cognitive impairment, and epilepsy are common complications that require comprehensive management strategies. Women are at higher risk for these complications, necessitating gender-specific care plans.
- Vascular dementia, a common outcome of stroke, requires ongoing management to slow disease progression and improve quality of life. Multifaceted approaches involving lifestyle modifications, pharmaceutical treatments, and multidisciplinary care are essential.

References

Adams, H. P., Bendixen, B. H., Kappelle, L. J., Biller, J., Love, B. B., Gordon, D. L., & Marsh, E. E. (1993). Classification of subtype of acute ischemic stroke. Definitions for use in a multicenter clinical trial. TOAST. Trial of Org 10172 in Acute Stroke Treatment. *Stroke, 24*(1), 35–41. https://doi.org/10.1161/01.str.24.1.35

Akhter, F., Persaud, A., Zaokari, Y., Zhao, Z., & Zhu, D. (2021). Vascular dementia and underlying sex differences. *Frontiers in Aging Neuroscience, 13*, 720715. https://doi.org/10.3389/fnagi.2021.720715

Alzheimer's Society. (2024a). *Types of vascular dementia.* Retrieved from https://www.alzheimers.org.uk/about-dementia/types-dementia/types-of-vascular-dementia#2
Alzheimer's Society. (2024b). *What is mixed dementia?* Retrieved from https://www.alzheimers.org.uk/blog/what-is-mixed-dementia
American Heart Association. (2024a). *High blood pressure.* Retrieved from https://www.heart.org/en/health-topics/high-blood-pressure
American Heart Association. (2024b). *Life's essential 8.* Retrieved from https://www.heart.org/en/healthy-living/healthy-lifestyle/lifes-essential-8
American Heart Association. (2024c). *Risk of stroke in women infographic.* Retrieved from https://www.goredforwomen.org/en/know-your-risk/risk-factors/risk-of-stroke-in-women-infographic
American College of Obstetricians and Gynecologists & Committee on Obstetric Practice. (2017). Committee opinion no. 656 summary: guidelines for diagnostic imaging during pregnancy and lactation. *Obstetrics and gynecology, 127*(2), 418.
Avgil Tsadok, M., Gagnon, J., Joza, J., Behlouli, H., Verma, A., Essebag, V., & Pilote, L. (2015). Temporal trends and sex differences in pulmonary vein isolation for patients with atrial fibrillation. *Heart Rhythm, 12*(9), 1979–1986. https://doi.org/10.1016/j.hrthm.2015.06.029
Bako, A. T., Pan, A., Potter, T., Tannous, J., Johnson, C., Baig, E., Meeks, J., Woo, D., & Vahidy, F. S. (2022). Contemporary trends in the nationwide incidence of primary intracerebral hemorrhage. *Stroke, 53*(3), e70–e74. https://doi.org/10.1161/strokeaha.121.037332
Ban, L., Sprigg, N., Abdul Sultan, A., Nelson-Piercy, C., Bath, P. M., Ludvigsson, J. F., Stephansson, O., & Tata, L. J. (2017). Incidence of first stroke in pregnant and nonpregnant women of childbearing age: A population-based cohort study from England. *Journal of the American Heart Association, 6*(4), e004601. https://doi.org/10.1161/jaha.116.004601
Banerjee, G., Wilson, D., Ambler, G., Osei-Bonsu Appiah, K., Shakeshaft, C., Lunawat, S., Cohen, H., Yousry, T., Lip, G. Y. H., Muir, K. W., Brown, M. M., Al-Shahi Salman, R., Jäger, H. R., Werring, D. J., Shaw, L., Sword, J., Mohd Nor, A., Sharma, P., Veltkamp, R., et al. (2018). Cognitive impairment before intracerebral hemorrhage is associated with cerebral amyloid angiopathy. *Stroke, 49*(1), 40–45. https://doi.org/10.1161/strokeaha.117.019409
Baranowski, C. J. (2018). The quality of life of older adults with epilepsy: A systematic review. *Seizure, 60*, 190–197. https://doi.org/10.1016/j.seizure.2018.06.002
Beghi, E., D'Alessandro, R., Beretta, S., Consoli, D., Crespi, V., Delaj, L., Gandolfo, C., Greco, G., La Neve, A., Manfredi, M., Mattana, F., Musolino, R., Provinciali, L., Santangelo, M., Specchio, L. M., Zaccara, G., & Epistroke, G. (2011). Incidence and predictors of acute symptomatic seizures after stroke. *Neurology, 77*(20), 1785–1793. https://doi.org/10.1212/WNL.0b013e3182364878
Bremme, K. A. (2003). Haemostatic changes in pregnancy. *Best Practice & Research Clinical Haematology, 16*(2), 153–168. https://doi.org/10.1016/s1521-6926(03)00021-5
Broderick, J. P., Brott, T., Tomsick, T., Huster, G., & Miller, R. (1992). The risk of subarachnoid and intracerebral hemorrhages in Blacks as compared with Whites. *New England Journal of Medicine, 326*(11), 733–736. https://doi.org/10.1056/nejm199203123261103
Brott, T., Thalinger, K., & Hertzberg, V. (1986). Hypertension as a risk factor for spontaneous intracerebral hemorrhage. *Stroke, 17*(6), 1078–1083. https://doi.org/10.1161/01.str.17.6.1078
Bruce, S. S., Merkler, A. E., Bassi, M., Chen, M. L., Salehi Omran, S., Navi, B. B., & Kamel, H. (2020). Differences in diagnostic evaluation in women and men after acute ischemic stroke. *Journal of the American Heart Association, 9*(5), e015625. https://doi.org/10.1161/jaha.119.015625
Bruno, A., Carter, S., Qualls, C., & Nolte, K. B. (1996). Incidence of spontaneous intracerebral hemorrhage among Hispanics and non-Hispanic whites in New Mexico. *Neurology, 47*(2), 405–408. https://doi.org/10.1212/wnl.47.2.405
Bushnell, C. D., & Kapral, M. K. (2023). Stroke in women and unique risk factors. *Stroke, 54*(2), 587–590. https://doi.org/10.1161/strokeaha.122.041734
Bushnell, C., McCullough, L. D., Awad, I. A., Chireau, M. V., Fedder, W. N., Furie, K. L., Howard, V. J., Lichtman, J. H., Lisabeth, L. D., Piña, I. L., Reeves, M. J., Rexrode, K. M., Saposnik, G., Singh, V., Towfighi, A., Vaccarino, V., & Walters, M. R. (2014a). Guidelines

for the prevention of stroke in women. *Stroke, 45*(5), 1545–1588. https://doi.org/10.1161/01.str.0000442009.06663.48

Bushnell, C. D., Reeves, M. J., Zhao, X., Pan, W., Prvu-Bettger, J., Zimmer, L., Olson, D., & Peterson, E. (2014b). Sex differences in quality of life after ischemic stroke. *Neurology, 82*(11), 922–931. https://doi.org/10.1212/wnl.0000000000000208

Bushnell, C. D., Chaturvedi, S., Gage, K. R., Herson, P. S., Hurn, P. D., Jiménez, M. C., Kittner, S. J., Madsen, T. E., McCullough, L. D., McDermott, M., Reeves, M. J., & Rundek, T. (2018). Sex differences in stroke: Challenges and opportunities. *Journal of Cerebral Blood Flow & Metabolism, 38*(12), 2179–2191. https://doi.org/10.1177/0271678x18793324

CDC. (2005). Differences in disability among black and white stroke survivors—United States, 2000–2001. *MMWR Morbidity and Mortality Weekly Report, 54*, 3–6.

CDC. (2007). Prevalence of stroke—United States, 2005. *MMWR Morbidity and Mortality Weekly Report, 56*, 469–474.

CDC. (2024a). *High blood pressure facts*. Retrieved from https://www.cdc.gov/high-blood-pressure/data-research/facts-stats/?CDC_AAref_Val=https://www.cdc.gov/bloodpressure/facts.htm

CDC. (2024b). *National diabetes statistics report*. Retrieved from https://www.cdc.gov/diabetes/php/data-research/?CDC_AAref_Val=https://www.cdc.gov/diabetes/data/statistics-report/index.html

CDC. (2024c). *Stroke*. Retrieved from https://www.cdc.gov/stroke/data-research/facts-stats/?CDC_AAref_Val=https://www.cdc.gov/stroke/facts.htm

Chalos, V., De Ridder, I. R., Lingsma, H. F., Brown, S., Van Oostenbrugge, R. J., Goyal, M., Campbell, B. C. V., Muir, K. W., Guillemin, F., Bracard, S., White, P., Dávalos, A., Jovin, T. G., Hill, M. D., Mitchell, P. J., Demchuk, A. M., Saver, J. L., Van Zwam, W. H., & Dippel, D. W. J. (2019). Does sex modify the effect of endovascular treatment for ischemic stroke? *Stroke, 50*(9), 2413–2419. https://doi.org/10.1161/strokeaha.118.023743

Clark, D. G., Boan, A. D., Sims-Robinson, C., Adams, R. J., Amella, E. J., Benitez, A., Lackland, D. T., & Ovbiagele, B. (2018). Differential impact of index stroke on dementia risk in African-Americans compared to Whites. *Journal of Stroke and Cerebrovascular Diseases, 27*(10), 2725–2730. https://doi.org/10.1016/j.jstrokecerebrovasdis.2018.05.048

Coutts, S. B., Moreau, F., Asdaghi, N., Boulanger, J. M., Camden, M. C., Campbell, B. C., et al. (2019). Rate and prognosis of brain ischemia in patients with lower-risk transient or persistent minor neurologic events. *JAMA Neurology, 76*(12), 1439–1445.

Cruz-Flores, S., Rabinstein, A., Biller, J., Elkind, M. S. V., Griffith, P., Gorelick, P. B., Howard, G., Leira, E. C., Morgenstern, L. B., Ovbiagele, B., Peterson, E., Rosamond, W., Trimble, B., & Valderrama, A. L. (2011). Racial-ethnic disparities in stroke care: The American experience. *Stroke, 42*(7), 2091–2116. https://doi.org/10.1161/str.0b013e3182213e24

D'Alonzo, M., Bounous, V. E., Villa, M., & Biglia, N. (2019). Current evidence of the oncological benefit-risk profile of hormone replacement therapy. *Medicina, 55*(9), 573. https://doi.org/10.3390/medicina55090573

Davidson, Y., Gibbons, L., Purandare, N., Byrne, J., Hardicre, J., Wren, J., Payton, A., Pendleton, N., Horan, M., Burns, A., & Mann, D. M. (2006). Apolipoprotein E epsilon4 allele frequency in vascular dementia. *Dementia and Geriatric Cognitive Disorders, 22*(1), 15–19. https://doi.org/10.1159/000092960

De Ridder, I. R., Fransen, P. S. S., Beumer, D., Berkhemer, O. A., Van Den Berg, L. A., Wermer, M. J., Lingsma, H., Van Zwam, W. H., Roos, Y. B., Van Oostenbrugge, R. J., Majoie, C. B., Van Der Lugt, A., & Dippel, D. W. J. (2016). Is intra-arterial treatment for acute ischemic stroke less effective in women than in men. *Interventional Neurology, 5*(3–4), 174–178. https://doi.org/10.1159/000447331

Demaerschalk, B. M., Kleindorfer, D. O., Adeoye, O. M., Demchuk, A. M., Fugate, J. E., Grotta, J. C., Khalessi, A. A., Levy, E. I., Palesch, Y. Y., Prabhakaran, S., Saposnik, G., Saver, J. L., & Smith, E. E. (2016). Scientific rationale for the inclusion and exclusion criteria for intravenous alteplase in acute ischemic stroke. *Stroke, 47*(2), 581–641. https://doi.org/10.1161/str.0000000000000086

Demchuk, A. M. (2013). Yes, intravenous thrombolysis should be administered in pregnancy when other clinical and imaging factors are favorable. *Stroke, 44*(3), 864–865. https://doi.org/10.1161/strokeaha.111.000134

Deng, Y. Z., Reeves, M. J., Jacobs, B. S., Birbeck, G. L., Kothari, R. U., Hickenbottom, S. L., Mullard, A. J., Wehner, S., Maddox, K., Majid, A., & Paul Coverdell National Acute Stroke Registry Michigan Prototype Investigators. (2006). IV tissue plasminogen activator use in acute stroke: Experience from a statewide registry. *Neurology, 66*(3), 306–312. https://doi.org/10.1212/01.wnl.0000196478.77152.fc

Di Carlo, A., Lamassa, M., Baldereschi, M., Pracucci, G., Basile, A. M., Wolfe, C. D. A., Giroud, M., Rudd, A., Ghetti, A., & Inzitari, D. (2003). Sex differences in the clinical presentation, resource use, and 3-month outcome of acute stroke in Europe. *Stroke, 34*(5), 1114–1119. https://doi.org/10.1161/01.str.0000068410.07397.d7

Dong, L., Sánchez, B. N., Skolarus, L. E., Stulberg, E., Morgenstern, L. B., & Lisabeth, L. D. (2020). Sex difference in prevalence of depression after stroke. *Neurology, 94*(19), e1973–e1983. https://doi.org/10.1212/wnl.0000000000009394

Eggink, E., Moll Van Charante, E. P., Van Gool, W. A., & Richard, E. (2019). A population perspective on prevention of dementia. *Journal of Clinical Medicine, 8*(6), 834. https://doi.org/10.3390/jcm8060834

El Husseini, N., Katzan, I. L., Rost, N. S., Blake, M. L., Byun, E., Pendlebury, S. T., Aparicio, H. J., Marquine, M. J., Gottesman, R. F., & Smith, E. E. (2023). Cognitive impairment after ischemic and hemorrhagic stroke: A scientific statement from the American Heart Association/American Stroke Association. *Stroke, 54*(6), e272–e291. https://doi.org/10.1161/str.0000000000000430

Elgendy, I. Y., Bukhari, S., Barakat, A. F., Pepine, C. J., Lindley, K. J., & Miller, E. C. (2021). Maternal stroke. *Circulation, 143*(7), 727–738. https://doi.org/10.1161/circulationaha.120.051460

Emdin, C. A., Wong, C. X., Hsiao, A. J., Altman, D. G., Peters, S. A., Woodward, M., & Odutayo, A. A. (2016). Atrial fibrillation as risk factor for cardiovascular disease and death in women compared with men: Systematic review and meta-analysis of cohort studies. *BMJ, 532*, h7013. https://doi.org/10.1136/bmj.h7013

Exalto, L. G., Weaver, N. A., Kuijf, H. J., Aben, H. P., Bae, H.-J., Best, J. G., Bordet, R., Chen, C. P. L. H., Van Der Giessen, R. S., Godefroy, O., Gyanwali, B., Hamilton, O. K. L., Hilal, S., Huenges Wajer, I. M. C., Kim, J., Kappelle, L. J., Kim, B. J., Köhler, S., De Kort, P. L. M., et al. (2023). Sex differences in poststroke cognitive Impairment: A multicenter study in 2343 patients with acute ischemic stroke. *Stroke, 54*(9), 2296–2303. https://doi.org/10.1161/strokeaha.123.042507

Fernando, S. M., Qureshi, D., Talarico, R., Tanuseputro, P., Dowlatshahi, D., Sood, M. M., Smith, E. E., Hill, M. D., McCredie, V. A., Scales, D. C., English, S. W., Rochwerg, B., & Kyeremanteng, K. (2021). Intracerebral hmorrhage Inicidence, mortality, and association with oral anticoagulation use. *Stroke, 52*(5), 1673–1681. https://doi.org/10.1161/strokeaha.120.032550

Flaherty, M. L., Woo, D., & Broderick, J. (2006). The incidence of deep and lobar intracerebral hemorrhage in whites, blacks, and Hispanics. *Neurology, 66*(6), 956–957; author reply 956–957. https://doi.org/10.1212/01.wnl.0000218670.19577.4c

Foroughi, M., Akhavanzanjani, M., Maghsoudi, Z., Ghiasvand, R., Khorvash, F., & Askari, G. (2013). Stroke and nutrition: A review of studies. *International Journal of Preventative Medicine, 4*(Suppl 2), S165–S179. Retrieved from https://www.ncbi.nlm.nih.gov/pubmed/23776719

Fuentes, A. M., Stone Mcguire, L., & Amin-Hanjani, S. (2022). Sex differences in cerebral aneurysms and subarachnoid hemorrhage. *Stroke, 53*(2), 624–633. https://doi.org/10.1161/strokeaha.121.037147

Galovic, M., Ferreira-Atuesta, C., Abraira, L., Döhler, N., Sinka, L., Brigo, F., Bentes, C., Zelano, J., & Koepp, M. J. (2021). Seizures and epilepsy after stroke: Epidemiology, biomarkers and management. *Drugs & Aging, 38*(4), 285–299. https://doi.org/10.1007/s40266-021-00837-7

Gannon, O. J., Robison, L. S., Custozzo, A. J., & Zuloaga, K. L. (2019). Sex differences in risk factors for vascular contributions to cognitive impairment & dementia. *Neurochemistry International, 127*, 38–55. https://doi.org/10.1016/j.neuint.2018.11.014

Garawi, F., Devries, K., Thorogood, N., & Uauy, R. (2014). Global differences between women and men in the prevalence of obesity: Is there an association with gender inequality? *European Journal of Clinical Nutrition, 68*(10), 1101–1106. https://doi.org/10.1038/ejcn.2014.86

Gardener, H., Sacco, R. L., Rundek, T., Battistella, V., Cheung, Y. K., & Elkind, M. S. V. (2020). Race and ethnic disparities in stroke incidence in the Northern Manhattan Study. *Stroke, 51*(4), 1064–1069. https://doi.org/10.1161/strokeaha.119.028806

Gargano, J. W., Wehner, S., & Reeves, M. J. (2009). Do presenting symptoms explain sex differences in emergency department delays among patients with acute stroke? *Stroke, 40*(4), 1114–1120. https://doi.org/10.1161/strokeaha.108.543116

Ghozy, S., Zayan, A. H., El-Qushayri, A. E., Parker, K. E., Varney, J., Kallmes, K. M., Morsy, S., Abbas, A. S., Diestro, J. D. B., Dmytriw, A. A., Shah, J., Hassan, A. E., & Islam, S. M. S. (2022). Physical activity level and stroke risk in US population: A matched case–control study of 102,578 individuals. *Annals of Clinical and Translational Neurology, 9*(3), 264–275. https://doi.org/10.1002/acn3.51511

Gnatiuc, L., Herrington, W., Halsey, J., Tuomilehto, J., Fang, X., Kim, H., De Bacquer, D., Dobson, A., Criqui, M., Jacobs, D., Leon, D., Peters, S., Ueshima, H., Sherliker, P., Peto, R., Collins, R., Huxley, R., Emberson, J., Woodward, M., et al. (2018). Sex-specific relevance of diabetes to occlusive vascular and other mortality: A collaborative meta-analysis of individual data from 980 793 adults from 68 prospective studies. *The Lancet Diabetes & Endocrinology, 6*(7), 538–546. https://doi.org/10.1016/s2213-8587(18)30079-2

Goyal, M., Menon, B. K., van Zwam, W. H., Dippel, D. W., Mitchell, P. J., Demchuk, A. M., Davalos, A., Majoie, C. B., van der Lugt, A., de Miquel, M. A., Donnan, G. A., Roos, Y. B., Bonafe, A., Jahan, R., Diener, H. C., van den Berg, L. A., Levy, E. I., Berkhemer, O. A., Pereira, V. M., et al. (2016). Endovascular thrombectomy after large-vessel ischaemic stroke: A meta-analysis of individual patient data from five randomised trials. *Lancet, 387*(10029), 1723–1731. https://doi.org/10.1016/S0140-6736(16)00163-X

Gunda, B., Hervé, D., Godin, O., Bruno, M., Reyes, S., Alili, N., Opherk, C., Jouvent, E., Düring, M., Bousser, M.-G., Dichgans, M., & Chabriat, H. (2012). Effects of gender on the phenotype of CADASIL. *Stroke, 43*(1), 137–141. https://doi.org/10.1161/strokeaha.111.631028

Hackett, M. L., & Pickles, K. (2014). Part I: Frequency of depression after stroke: An updated systematic review and meta-analysis of observational studies. *International Journal of Stroke, 9*(8), 1017–1025. https://doi.org/10.1111/ijs.12357

Hogervorst, E., Williams, J., Budge, M., Riedel, W., & Jolles, J. (2000). The nature of the effect of female gonadal hormone replacement therapy on cognitive function in post-menopausal women: A meta-analysis. *Neuroscience, 101*(3), 485–512. https://doi.org/10.1016/s0306-4522(00)00410-3

Hung, S.-K., Lee, M.-S., Lin, H.-Y., Chen, L.-C., Chuang, C.-J., Chew, C.-H., Yu, B.-H., Yang, H.-J., Hsu, F.-C., & Chiou, W.-Y. (2022). Impact of hypertensive disorders of pregnancy on the risk of stroke stratified by subtypes and follow-up time. *Stroke, 53*(2), 338–344. https://doi.org/10.1161/strokeaha.121.034109

Johansson, T., Fowler, P., Ek, W. E., Skalkidou, A., Karlsson, T., & Johansson, Å. (2022). Oral contraceptives, hormone replacement therapy, and stroke risk. *Stroke, 53*(10), 3107–3115. https://doi.org/10.1161/strokeaha.121.038659

John Hopkins Medicine. (2024). *Types of stroke*. Retrieved from https://www.hopkinsmedicine.org/health/conditions-and-diseases/stroke/types-of-stroke

Jungehulsing, G. J., Rossnagel, K., Nolte, C. H., Muller-Nordhorn, J., Roll, S., Klein, M., Wegscheider, K., Einhaupl, K. M., Willich, S. N., & Villringer, A. (2006). Emergency department delays in acute stroke: Analysis of time between ED arrival and imaging. *European Journal of Neurology, 13*(3), 225–232. https://doi.org/10.1111/j.1468-1331.2006.01170.x

Kalaria, R. N., Akinyemi, R., & Ihara, M. (2016). Stroke injury, cognitive impairment and vascular dementia. *Biochimica et Biophysica Acta (BBA)-Molecular Basis of Disease, 1862*(5), 915–925. https://doi.org/10.1016/j.bbadis.2016.01.015

Kamel, F., & Hoppin, J. A. (2004). Association of pesticide exposure with neurologic dysfunction and disease. *Environmental Health Perspectives, 112*(9), 950–958. https://doi.org/10.1289/ehp.7135

Kelly-Hayes, M., Beiser, A., Kase, C. S., Scaramucci, A., D'Agostino, R. B., & Wolf, P. A. (2003). The influence of gender and age on disability following ischemic stroke: The Framingham study. *Journal of Stroke and Cerebrovascular Disease, 12*(3), 119–126.

Kennedy, B. S. (2005). Does race predict stroke readmission? An analysis using the truncated negative binomial model. *Journal of the National Medicine Association, 97*, 699–713. https://doi.org/10.1016/S1052-3057(03)00042-9

Killin, L. O. J., Starr, J. M., Shiue, I. J., & Russ, T. C. (2016). Environmental risk factors for dementia: A systematic review. *BMC Geriatrics, 16*(1), 175. https://doi.org/10.1186/s12877-016-0342-y

Kim, M., & Lee, Y.-H. (2023). Gender differences in the risk of depression in community-dwelling stroke survivors compared to the general population without stroke. *Chonnam Medical Journal, 59*(2), 134. https://doi.org/10.4068/cmj.2023.59.2.134

Ko, D., Rahman, F., Schnabel, R. B., Yin, X., Benjamin, E. J., & Christophersen, I. E. (2016). Atrial fibrillation in women: Epidemiology, pathophysiology, presentation, and prognosis. *Nature Reviews Cardiology, 13*(6), 321–332. https://doi.org/10.1038/nrcardio.2016.45

Korczyn, A. D., Vakhapova, V., & Grinberg, L. T. (2012). Vascular dementia. *Journal of the Neurological Sciences, 322*(1–2), 2–10. https://doi.org/10.1016/j.jns.2012.03.027

Kroll, M. E., Green, J., Beral, V., Sudlow, C. L. M., Brown, A., Kirichek, O., Price, A., Yang, T. O., & Reeves, G. K. (2016). Adiposity and ischemic and hemorrhagic stroke. *Neurology, 87*(14), 1473–1481. https://doi.org/10.1212/wnl.0000000000003171

Kurth, T., Everett, B. M., Buring, J. E., Kase, C. S., Ridker, P. M., & Gaziano, J. M. (2007). Lipid levels and the risk of ischemic stroke in women. *Neurology, 68*(8), 556–562. https://doi.org/10.1212/01.wnl.0000254472.41810.0d

Lacy, C. R., Suh, D.-C., Bueno, M., & Kostis, J. B. (2001). Delay in presentation and evaluation for acute stroke. *Stroke, 32*(1), 63–69. https://doi.org/10.1161/01.str.32.1.63

Ladwig, S., Werheid, K., Südmeyer, M., & Volz, M. (2023). Predictors of post-stroke depression: Validation of established risk factors and introduction of a dynamic perspective in two longitudinal studies. *Frontiers in Psychiatry, 14*, 1093918. https://doi.org/10.3389/fpsyt.2023.1093918

Lechner, H., & Bertha, G. (1991). Multiinfarct dementia. In V. Springer (Ed.), *Age-associated neurological diseases*. Springer.

Lee, M. J., Lee, C., & Chung, C.-S. (2016). The migraine–stroke connection. *Journal of Stroke, 18*(2), 146–156. https://doi.org/10.5853/jos.2015.01683

Leffert, L. R., Clancy, C. R., Bateman, B. T., Bryant, A. S., & Kuklina, E. V. (2015). Hypertensive disorders and pregnancy-related stroke. *Obstetrics & Gynecology, 125*(1), 124–131. https://doi.org/10.1097/aog.0000000000000590

Leppert, M. H., Ho, P. M., Burke, J., Madsen, T. E., Kleindorfer, D., Sillau, S., Daugherty, S., Bradley, C. J., & Poisson, S. N. (2020). Young women had more strokes than young men in a large, United States claims sample. *Stroke, 51*(11), 3352–3355. https://doi.org/10.1161/strokeaha.120.030803

Lisabeth, L. D., Smith, M. A., Brown, D. L., Moyé, L. A., Risser, J. M. H., & Morgenstern, L. B. (2006). Ethnic differences in stroke recurrence. *Annals of Neurology, 60*(4), 469–475. https://doi.org/10.1002/ana.20943

Liu, S., Chan, W.-S., Ray, J. G., Kramer, M. S., & Joseph, K. S. (2019). Stroke and cerebrovascular disease in pregnancy. *Stroke, 50*(1), 13–20. https://doi.org/10.1161/strokeaha.118.023118

Lucca, U., Tettamanti, M., Tiraboschi, P., Logroscino, G., Landi, C., Sacco, L., Garrì, M., Ammesso, S., Biotti, A., Gargantini, E., Piedicorcia, A., Mandelli, S., Riva, E., Galbussera, A. A., & Recchia, A. (2020). Incidence of dementia in the oldest-old and its relationship with

age: The Monzino 80-plus population-based study. *Alzheimer's & Dementia, 16*(3), 472–481. https://doi.org/10.1016/j.jalz.2019.09.083
Luhdorf, K., Jensen, L. K., & Plesner, A. M. (1986). Etiology of seizures in the elderly. *Epilepsia, 27*(4), 458–463. https://doi.org/10.1111/j.1528-1157.1986.tb03567.x
Lutfiyya, M. N., Ng, L., Asner, N., & Lipsky, M. S. (2009). Disparities in stroke symptomology knowledge among US midlife women: An analysis of population survey data. *Journal of Stroke and Cerebrovascular Diseases, 18*(2), 150–157. https://doi.org/10.1016/j.jstrokecerebrovasdis.2008.09.009
Madsen, T. E., Howard, G., Kleindorfer, D. O., Furie, K. L., Oparil, S., Manson, J. E., Liu, S., & Howard, V. J. (2019). Sex differences in hypertension and stroke risk in the REGARDS Study. *Hypertension, 74*(4), 749–755. https://doi.org/10.1161/hypertensionaha.119.12729
Manson, J. E., Chlebowski, R. T., Stefanick, M. L., Aragaki, A. K., Rossouw, J. E., Prentice, R. L., Anderson, G., Howard, B. V., Thomson, C. A., Lacroix, A. Z., Wactawski-Wende, J., Jackson, R. D., Limacher, M., Margolis, K. L., Wassertheil-Smoller, S., Beresford, S. A., Cauley, J. A., Eaton, C. B., Gass, M., et al. (2013). Menopausal hormone therapy and health outcomes during the intervention and extended poststopping phases of the Women's Health Initiative Randomized Trials. *JAMA, 310*(13), 1353. https://doi.org/10.1001/jama.2013.278040
Mayer, S. A., Kreiter, K. T., Copeland, D., Bernardini, G. L., Bates, J. E., Peery, S., Claassen, J., Du, Y. E., & Connolly, E. S., Jr. (2002). Global and domain-specific cognitive impairment and outcome after subarachnoid hemorrhage. *Neurology, 59*(11), 1750–1758. https://doi.org/10.1212/01.wnl.0000035748.91128.c2
McKay, E., & Scott, S. E. (2017). Multi-infarct dementia: A historical perspective. *Dementia and Geriatric Cognitive Disorders Extra, 7*(1), 160–171. https://doi.org/10.1159/000470836
Miller, E. C., & Leffert, L. (2020). Stroke in pregnancy: A focused update. *Anesthesia & Analgesia, 130*(4), 1085–1096. https://doi.org/10.1213/ANE.0000000000004203
Mills, K. T., Bundy, J. D., Kelly, T. N., Reed, J. E., Kearney, P. M., Reynolds, K., Chen, J., & He, J. (2016). Global disparities of hypertension prevalence and control. *Circulation, 134*(6), 441–450. https://doi.org/10.1161/circulationaha.115.018912
Mishra, S. R., Chung, H.-F., Waller, M., Dobson, A. J., Greenwood, D. C., Cade, J. E., Giles, G. G., Bruinsma, F., Simonsen, M. K., Hardy, R., Kuh, D., Gold, E. B., Crawford, S. L., Derby, C. A., Matthews, K. A., Demakakos, P., Lee, J. S., Mizunuma, H., Hayashi, K., et al. (2020). Association between reproductive life span and incident nonfatal cardiovascular disease. *JAMA Cardiology, 5*(12), 1410. https://doi.org/10.1001/jamacardio.2020.4105
Molero, A. E., Pino-Ramirez, G., & Maestre, G. E. (2001). Modulation by age and gender of risk for Alzheimer's disease and vascular dementia associated with the apolipoprotein E-epsilon4 allele in Latin Americans: Findings from the Maracaibo Aging Study. *Neuroscience Letters, 307*(1), 5–8. https://doi.org/10.1016/s0304-3940(01)01911-5
Morgenstern, L. B., Smith, M. A., Lisabeth, L. D., Risser, J. M., Uchino, K., Garcia, N., Longwell, P. J., McFarling, D. A., Akuwumi, O., Al-Wabil, A., Al-Senani, F., Brown, D. L., & Moye, L. A. (2004). Excess stroke in Mexican Americans compared with non-Hispanic Whites: The brain attack surveillance in Corpus Christi project. *American Journal of Epidemiology, 160*(4), 376–383. https://doi.org/10.1093/aje/kwh225
Moulin, S., Labreuche, J., Bombois, S., Rossi, C., Boulouis, G., Henon, H., Duhamel, A., Leys, D., & Cordonnier, C. (2016). Dementia risk after spontaneous intracerebral haemorrhage: A prospective cohort study. *Lancet Neurology, 15*(8), 820–829. https://doi.org/10.1016/S1474-4422(16)00130-7
Nanna, M. G., Wang, T. Y., Xiang, Q., Goldberg, A. C., Robinson, J. G., Roger, V. L., Virani, S. S., Wilson, P. W. F., Louie, M. J., Koren, A., Li, Z., Peterson, E. D., & Navar, A. M. (2019). Sex differences in the use of statins in community practice. *Circulation: Cardiovascular Quality and Outcomes, 12*(8), e005562. https://doi.org/10.1161/circoutcomes.118.005562
Nicol, M. B., & Thrift, A. G. (2005). Knowledge of risk factors and warning signs of stroke. *Vascular Health and Risk Management, 1*(2), 137–147. https://doi.org/10.2147/vhrm.1.2.137.64085
NIH. (2001). Strong Heart Study Data Book: A report to American Indian Communities.

O'Donnell, M. J., Xavier, D., Liu, L., Zhang, H., Chin, S. L., Rao-Melacini, P., et al. (2010). Risk factors for ischaemic and intracerebral haemorrhagic stroke in 22 countries (the INTERSTROKE study): A case-control study. *The Lancet, 376*(9735), 112–123.

Ouyang, M., Shajahan, S., Liu, X., Sun, L., Carcel, C., Harris, K., Anderson, C. S., Woodward, M., & Wang, X. (2023). Sex differences in the utilization and outcomes of endovascular treatment after acute ischemic stroke: A systematic review and meta-analysis. *Frontiers in Global Women's Health, 3*, 1032592. https://doi.org/10.3389/fgwh.2022.1032592

Pan, B., Jin, X., Jun, L., Qiu, S., Zheng, Q., & Pan, M. (2019). The relationship between smoking and stroke: A meta-analysis. *Medicine (Baltimore), 98*(12), e14872. https://doi.org/10.1097/MD.0000000000014872

Papakonstantinou, E., Bacopoulou, F., Brouzas, D., Megalooikonomou, V., D'Elia, D., Bongcam-Rudloff, E., & Vlachakis, D. (2019). NOTCH3 and CADASIL syndrome: A genetic and structural overview. *EMBnet.Journal, 24*, e921. https://doi.org/10.14806/ej.24.0.921

Pendlebury, S. T. (2009). Stroke-related dementia: Rates, risk factors and implications for future research. *Maturitas, 64*(3), 165–171. https://doi.org/10.1016/j.maturitas.2009.09.010

Pendlebury, S. T., & Rothwell, P. M. (2009). Prevalence, incidence, and factors associated with pre-stroke and post-stroke dementia: A systematic review and meta-analysis. *Lancet Neurology, 8*(11), 1006–1018. https://doi.org/10.1016/S1474-4422(09)70236-4

Peters, S. A. E., Huxley, R. R., & Woodward, M. (2013). Comparison of the sex-specific associations between systolic blood pressure and the risk of cardiovascular disease. *Stroke, 44*(9), 2394–2401. https://doi.org/10.1161/strokeaha.113.001624

Peters, S. A., Huxley, R. R., & Woodward, M. (2014). Diabetes as a risk factor for stroke in women compared with men: A systematic review and meta-analysis of 64 cohorts, including 775,385 individuals and 12,539 strokes. *Lancet, 383*(9933), 1973–1980. https://doi.org/10.1016/S0140-6736(14)60040-4

Peters, S. A. E., Muntner, P., & Woodward, M. (2019). Sex differences in the prevalence of, and trends in, cardiovascular risk factors, treatment, and control in the United States, 2001 to 2016. *Circulation, 139*(8), 1025–1035. https://doi.org/10.1161/circulationaha.118.035550

Peters, S. A. E., Carcel, C., Millett, E. R. C., & Woodward, M. (2020). Sex differences in the association between major risk factors and the risk of stroke in the UK Biobank cohort study. *Neurology, 95*(20), e2715–e2726. https://doi.org/10.1212/WNL.0000000000010982

Phan, H. T., Blizzard, C. L., Reeves, M. J., Thrift, A. G., Cadilhac, D., Sturm, J., Heeley, E., Otahal, P., Konstantinos, V., Anderson, C., Parmar, P., Krishnamurthi, R., Barker-Collo, S., Feigin, V., Bejot, Y., Cabral, N. L., Carolei, A., Sacco, S., Chausson, N., et al. (2017). Sex differences in long-term mortality after stroke in the INSTRUCT (INternational STRoke oUtComes sTudy). *Circulation: Cardiovascular Quality and Outcomes, 10*(2), e003436. https://doi.org/10.1161/circoutcomes.116.003436

Pinkerton, J. V. (2020). Hormone therapy for postmenopausal women. *New England Journal of Medicine, 382*(5), 446–455. https://doi.org/10.1056/nejmcp1714787

Pinkston, J. B., Alekseeva, N., & Gonzalez Toledo, E. (2009). Stroke and dementia. *Neurology Research, 31*(8), 824–831. https://doi.org/10.1179/016164109X12445505689643

Podcasy, J. L., & Epperson, C. N. (2016). Considering sex and gender in Alzheimer disease and other dementias. *Dialogues in Clinical Neuroscience, 18*(4), 437–446. https://doi.org/10.31887/dcns.2016.18.4/cepperson

Poorthuis, M. H., Algra, A. M., Algra, A., Kappelle, L. J., & Klijn, C. J. (2017). Female- and male-specific risk factors for stroke: A systematic review and meta-analysis. *JAMA Neurology, 74*(1), 75–81. https://doi.org/10.1001/jamaneurol.2016.3482

Poorthuis, M. H. F., Yao, P., Chen, Y., Guo, Y., Shi, L., Li, L., Chen, Z., Clarke, R., Yang, L., Chen, J., Collins, R., Lv, J., Peto, R., Walters, R., Avery, D., Bennett, D., Boxall, R., Bragg, F., Chang, Y., et al. (2022). Risks of stroke and heart disease following hysterectomy and oophorectomy in Chinese premenopausal women. *Stroke, 53*(10), 3064–3071. https://doi.org/10.1161/strokeaha.121.037305

Powers, W. J., Rabinstein, A. A., Ackerson, T., Adeoye, O. M., Bambakidis, N. C., Becker, K., Biller, J., Brown, M., Demaerschalk, B. M., Hoh, B., Jauch, E. C., Kidwell, C. S., Leslie-Mazwi, T. M., Ovbiagele, B., Scott, P. A., Sheth, K. N., Southerland, A. M., Summers, D. V., & Tirschwell, D. L. (2019). Guidelines for the early management of patients with acute ischemic stroke: 2019 Update to the 2018 Guidelines for the Early Management of Acute Ischemic Stroke: A Guideline for Healthcare Professionals from the American Heart Association/American Stroke. *Stroke, 50*(12), e344–e418. https://doi.org/10.1161/str.0000000000000211

Rai, S., Pathak, A., & Sharma, I. (2015). Postpartum psychiatric disorders: Early diagnosis and management. *Indian Journal of Psychiatry, 57*(Suppl 2), S216–S221. https://doi.org/10.4103/0019-5545.161481

Rasmussen, K. L., Tybjærg-Hansen, A., Nordestgaard, B. G., & Frikke-Schmidt, R. (2018). Absolute 10-year risk of dementia by age, sex and APOE genotype: A population-based cohort study. *Canadian Medical Association Journal, 190*(35), E1033–E1041. https://doi.org/10.1503/cmaj.180066

Reed, S. D., Cramer, S. C., Blough, D. K., Meyer, K., & Jarvik, J. G. (2001). Treatment with tissue plasminogen activator and inpatient mortality rates for patients with ischemic stroke treated in community hospitals. *Stroke, 32*(8), 1832–1840. https://doi.org/10.1161/01.str.32.8.1832

Reeves, M., Bhatt, A., Jajou, P., Brown, M., & Lisabeth, L. (2009a). Sex differences in the use of intravenous rt-PA thrombolysis treatment for acute ischemic stroke. *Stroke, 40*(5), 1743–1749. https://doi.org/10.1161/strokeaha.108.543181

Reeves, M. J., Fonarow, G. C., Zhao, X., Smith, E. E., & Schwamm, L. H. (2009b). Quality of care in women with ischemic stroke in the GWTG Program. *Stroke, 40*(4), 1127–1133. https://doi.org/10.1161/strokeaha.108.543157

Reid, J. M., Dai, D., Gubitz, G. J., Kapral, M. K., Christian, C., & Phillips, S. J. (2008). Gender differences in stroke examined in a 10-Year cohort of patients admitted to a Canadian teaching hospital. *Stroke, 39*(4), 1090–1095. https://doi.org/10.1161/strokeaha.107.495143

Rexrode, K. M., Madsen, T. E., Yu, A. Y. X., Carcel, C., Lichtman, J. H., & Miller, E. C. (2022). The impact of sex and gender on stroke. *Circulation Research, 130*(4), 512–528. https://doi.org/10.1161/CIRCRESAHA.121.319915

Robusto-Leitao, O., & Ferreira, H. (2006). Hormones and dementia: A comparative study of hormonal impairment in post-menopausal women, with and without dementia. *Neuropsychiatric Disease and Treatment, 2*(2), 199–206. https://doi.org/10.2147/nedt.2006.2.2.199

Roger, V. L., Go, A. S., Lloyd-Jones, D. M., Benjamin, E. J., Berry, J. D., Borden, W. B., Bravata, D. M., Dai, S., Ford, E. S., Fox, C. S., Fullerton, H. J., Gillespie, C., Hailpern, S. M., Heit, J. A., Howard, V. J., Kissela, B. M., Kittner, S. J., Lackland, D. T., Lichtman, J. H., et al. (2012). Heart disease and stroke statistics—2012 update. *Circulation, 125*(1), e2–e220. https://doi.org/10.1161/cir.0b013e31823ac046

Roman, G. (2003). Vascular dementia: A historical background. *International Psychogeriatrics, 15*(S1), 11–13. https://doi.org/10.1017/S1041610203008901

Roquer, J., Campello, A. R., & Gomis, M. (2003). Sex differences in first-ever acute stroke. *Stroke, 34*(7), 1581–1585.

Rose, K. M., Rosamond, W. D., Huston, S. L., Murphy, C. V., & Tegeler, C. H. (2008). Predictors of time from hospital arrival to initial brain-imaging among suspected stroke patients. *Stroke, 39*(12), 3262–3267. https://doi.org/10.1161/strokeaha.108.524686

Ruitenberg, A., Ott, A., van Swieten, J. C., Hofman, A., & Breteler, M. M. (2001). Incidence of dementia: Does gender make a difference? *Neurobiological Aging, 22*(4), 575–580. https://doi.org/10.1016/s0197-4580(01)00231-7

Salvadori, E., Papi, G., Insalata, G., Rinnoci, V., Donnini, I., Martini, M., Falsini, C., Hakiki, B., Romoli, A., Barbato, C., Polcaro, P., Casamorata, F., Macchi, C., Cecchi, F., & Poggesi, A. (2020). Comparison between ischemic and hemorrhagic strokes in functional outcome at discharge from an intensive rehabilitation hospital. *Diagnostics, 11*(1), 38. https://doi.org/10.3390/diagnostics11010038

Schurks, M., Rist, P. M., Bigal, M. E., Buring, J. E., Lipton, R. B., & Kurth, T. (2009). Migraine and cardiovascular disease: Systematic review and meta-analysis. *BMJ, 339*, b3914–b3914. https://doi.org/10.1136/bmj.b3914

Sierra, C. (2020). Hypertension and the risk of dementia. *Frontiers in Cardiovascular Medicine, 7*, 5. https://doi.org/10.3389/fcvm.2020.00005

Singhal, S. (2004). The influence of genetic and cardiovascular risk factors on the CADASIL phenotype. *Brain, 127*(9), 2031–2038. https://doi.org/10.1093/brain/awh223

Springer, M. V., Schmidt, J. M., Wartenberg, K. E., Frontera, J. A., Badjatia, N., & Mayer, S. A. (2009). Predictors of global cognitive impairment 1 year after subarachnoid hemorrhage. *Neurosurgery, 65*(6), 1043–1050; discussion 1050–1041. https://doi.org/10.1227/01.NEU.0000359317.15269.20

Strong, B., Lisabeth, L. D., & Reeves, M. (2020). Sex differences in IV thrombolysis treatment for acute ischemic stroke: A systematic review and meta-analysis. *Neurology, 95*(1), e11–e22. https://doi.org/10.1212/WNL.0000000000009733

Sullivan-Baca, E., Modiano, Y. A., McKenney, K. M., & Carlew, A. R. (2024). Pregnancy-related stroke through a neuropsychology lens. *Clinical Neuropsychology, 38*(6), 1293–1312. https://doi.org/10.1080/13854046.2022.2131631

Thompson, L. E., Maddox, T. M., Lei, L., Grunwald, G. K., Bradley, S. M., Peterson, P. N., Masoudi, F. A., Turchin, A., Song, Y., Doros, G., Davis, M. B., & Daugherty, S. L. (2017). Sex differences in the use of oral anticoagulants for atrial fibrillation: A report from the National Cardiovascular Data Registry (NCDR®) PINNACLE Registry. *Journal of the American Heart Association, 6*(7), e005801. https://doi.org/10.1161/jaha.117.005801

Tomimoto, H. (2011). Subcortical vascular dementia. *Neuroscience Research, 71*(3), 193–199. https://doi.org/10.1016/j.neures.2011.07.1820

Towfighi, A., Ovbiagele, B., El Husseini, N., Hackett, M. L., Jorge, R. E., Kissela, B. M., Mitchell, P. H., Skolarus, L. E., Whooley, M. A., & Williams, L. S. (2017). Poststroke depression: A scientific statement for healthcare professionals from the American Heart Association/American Stroke Association. *Stroke, 48*(2), STR.000000000000. https://doi.org/10.1161/str.0000000000000113

Turtzo, L. C., & McCullough, L. D. (2008). Sex differences in stroke. *Cerebrovascular Diseases, 26*(5), 462–474. https://doi.org/10.1159/000155983

van Asch, C. J., Luitse, M. J., Rinkel, G. J., van der Tweel, I., Algra, A., & Klijn, C. J. (2010). Incidence, case fatality, and functional outcome of intracerebral haemorrhage over time, according to age, sex, and ethnic origin: A systematic review and meta-analysis. *Lancet Neurology, 9*, 167–176. https://doi.org/10.1016/S1474-4422(09)70340-0

Verducci, C., Hussain, F., Donner, E., Moseley, B. D., Buchhalter, J., Hesdorffer, D., Friedman, D., & Devinsky, O. (2019). SUDEP in the North American SUDEP Registry: The full spectrum of epilepsies. *Neurology, 93*(3), e227–e236. https://doi.org/10.1212/WNL.0000000000007778

Vijayan, M., & Reddy, P. H. (2016). Stroke, vascular dementia, and Alzheimer's disease: Molecular links. *Journal of Alzheimer's Disease, 54*(2), 427–443. https://doi.org/10.3233/jad-160527

Volgman, A. S., Bairey Merz, C. N., Aggarwal, N. T., Bittner, V., Bunch, T. J., Gorelick, P. B., Maki, P., Patel, H. N., Poppas, A., Ruskin, J., Russo, A. M., Waldstein, S. R., Wenger, N. K., Yaffe, K., & Pepine, C. J. (2019). Sex differences in cardiovascular disease and cognitive impairment: Another health disparity for women? *Journal of the American Heart Association, 8*(19), e013154. https://doi.org/10.1161/jaha.119.013154

Wassertheil-Smoller, S. (2010). Stroke in women. *Nutrition, Metabolism and Cardiovascular Diseases, 20*(6), 419–425. https://doi.org/10.1016/j.numecd.2010.02.017

Wityk, R. J., & Beauchamp, N. J. (2000). Diagnostic evaluation of stroke. *Neurologic Clinics, 18*(2), 357–378. https://doi.org/10.1016/s0733-8619(05)70197-3

World Health Organization. (2024). *Stroke, cerebrovascular accident*. Retrieved from https://www.emro.who.int/health-topics/stroke-cerebrovascular-accident/index.html

Wu, P., Haththotuwa, R., Kwok, C. S., Babu, A., Kotronias, R. A., Rushton, C., Zaman, A., Fryer, A. A., Kadam, U., Chew-Graham, C. A., & Mamas, M. A. (2017). Preeclampsia and future cardiovascular health. *Circulation: Cardiovascular Quality and Outcomes, 10*(2), e003497. https://doi.org/10.1161/circoutcomes.116.003497

Xu, Z., Li, Y., Tang, S., Huang, X., & Chen, T. (2015). Current use of oral contraceptives and the risk of first-ever ischemic stroke: A meta-analysis of observational studies. *Thrombosis Research, 136*(1), 52–60. https://doi.org/10.1016/j.thromres.2015.04.021

Xu, Z., Yue, Y., Bai, J., Shen, C., Yang, J., Huang, X., Zhao, Y., & Li, Y. (2018). Association between oral contraceptives and risk of hemorrhagic stroke: A meta-analysis of observational studies. *Archives of Gynecology and Obstetrics, 297*(5), 1181–1191. https://doi.org/10.1007/s00404-018-4723-7

Yaffe, K., Sawaya, G., Lieberburg, I., & Grady, D. (1998). Estrogen therapy in postmenopausal women: Effects on cognitive function and dementia. *JAMA, 279*(9), 688–695. https://doi.org/10.1001/jama.279.9.688

Yiin, G. S. C., Howard, D. P. J., Paul, N. L. M., Li, L., Luengo-Fernandez, R., Bull, L. M., Welch, S. J. V., Gutnikov, S. A., Mehta, Z., & Rothwell, P. M. (2014). Age-specific incidence, outcome, cost, and projected future burden of atrial fibrillation–related embolic vascular events. *Circulation, 130*(15), 1236–1244. https://doi.org/10.1161/circulationaha.114.010942

Yoon, C. W., & Bushnell, C. D. (2023). Stroke in women: A review focused on epidemiology, risk factors, and outcomes. *Journal of Stroke, 25*(1), 2–15. https://doi.org/10.5853/jos.2022.03468

Yu, R. F., San Jose, M. C., Manzanilla, B. M., Oris, M. Y., & Gan, R. (2002). Sources and reasons for delays in the care of acute stroke patients. *Journal of the Neurological Sciences, 199*(1–2), 49–54. https://doi.org/10.1016/s0022-510x(02)00103-x

Zhou, B., Carrillo-Larco, R. M., Danaei, G., Riley, L. M., Paciorek, C. J., Stevens, G. A., Gregg, E. W., Bennett, J. E., Solomon, B., Singleton, R. K., Sophiea, M. K., Iurilli, M. L., Lhoste, V. P., Cowan, M. J., Savin, S., Woodward, M., Balanova, Y., Cifkova, R., Damasceno, A., et al. (2021). Worldwide trends in hypertension prevalence and progress in treatment and control from 1990 to 2019: A pooled analysis of 1201 population-representative studies with 104 million participants. *The Lancet, 398*(10304), 957–980. https://doi.org/10.1016/s0140-6736(21)01330-1

Zou, S., Wu, X., Zhu, B., Yu, J., Yang, B., & Shi, J. (2015). The pooled incidence of post-stroke seizure in 102,008 patients. *Topics in Stroke Rehabilitation, 22*(6), 460–467. https://doi.org/10.1179/1074935715Z.00000000062

Chapter 4
Traumatic Brain Injury

Amy Jak and Francesca Lopez

Introduction

Traumatic brain injury (TBI) affects individuals of all genders, but women may experience TBI differently from men, in terms of both physiological responses and long-term outcomes. This chapter, therefore, will place a spotlight on TBI in women, a historically under-researched and under-recognized area. It is important to center the discussion in the broader context of TBI and so the chapter will begin with a brief introduction to the basics of TBI, including defining clinical characteristics and pathophysiology, prevalence and incidence rates, mortality and morbidity, and demographic-related risk factors. This general discussion will give way to the unique factors that play a role in the risk of TBI for women, and how these factors may influence differences in symptom presentation, recovery trajectories, and long-term outcomes post-injury. We will address special populations and settings where head injuries commonly occur but are particularly understudied among women including sports-related concussion, military service, and intimate partner violence. Finally, we will detail clinical and research takeaways. By understanding these nuanced gender differences, healthcare providers can better address the unique needs of women who have sustained a TBI and improve their overall quality of care and life.

A. Jak (✉) · F. Lopez
Center of Excellence for Stress and Mental Health, VA San Diego Healthcare System, University of California San Diego, San Diego, CA, USA
e-mail: ajak@health.ucsd.edu

E. Sullivan-Baca, R. Ellison (eds.), *Neuropsychology of Women*,
https://doi.org/10.1007/978-3-031-87228-0_4

Epidemiology and Presentation

TBI is a serious public health concern that results in death and disability for thousands of people each year (Maas et al., 2022). Worldwide there are approximately 27 million new TBI cases annually with an additional 49 million prevalent cases, resulting in over 7 million years lived with TBI-related disability (Guan et al., 2023). Specifically in the U.S., estimates of TBI range anywhere from 1.5 to 2.5 million brain injuries per year. More than 2.5 million hospital emergency department visits, 288,000 hospitalizations, and 60,000 deaths result from TBI annually (Centers for Disease Control and Prevention, 2022) with 5.3 million individuals living with significant disabilities resulting from TBI (Popescu et al., 2015).

TBI is defined as a traumatically induced structural injury and/or physiological disruption of brain function as a result of an external force, resulting in new onset or worsening of at least one of the following clinical signs immediately after the event: (1) loss or alteration of consciousness (LOC/AOC); (2) memory gap consistent with post-traumatic amnesia (PTA); or (3) any neurological deficits (VA/DoD, 2021). The determination of TBI severity (mild, moderate, or severe) is based on available acute injury characteristics including presence and duration of LOC/AOC and PTA, Glasgow Coma Scale (GCS; Teasdale & Jennett, 1974), and any acutely acquired neuroimaging. TBI severity tends to be a robust predictor of morbidity and mortality in moderate and severe TBI cases, but less so in mild TBI (mTBI) cases. The terms "concussion" and "mTBI" are largely used interchangeably; there are no distinct symptom profiles, diagnostic criteria, or objective biomarkers that distinguish concussion from mTBI. Mild TBI by far is the most common severity sustained in both civilian and military populations with approximately 80% of all TBI sustained classified as mild (Taylor et al., 2017; Williamson & Rajajee, 2021).

Leading causes of TBI include falls, blunt force trauma, and motor vehicle accidents/pedestrian collisions. Depending on the severity and location of the TBI, individuals may experience motor, cognitive, mood, personality, or other changes and, particularly in the case of moderate-to-severe TBI, are unlikely to return to preinjury baseline (Azouvi et al., 2017). Similarly, cognitive symptoms and neuropsychological profiles can vary depending on injury location and severity, but processing speed deficits and mental fatigue are hallmark symptoms. Deficits in memory, attention/working memory, and executive function are also common following TBI, and will be discussed later in further detail with attention to gender differences (Azouvi et al., 2017).

Risk Factors

Common demographic factors associated with increased risk of TBI include age, gender, and occupation. Regarding age, risk is highest for children, young adults, and adults over the age of 65 years (Cassidy et al., 2004; Styrke et al., 2007). Men are over twice as likely as women to sustain a TBI, with approximately 17% of men having sustained a TBI in their lifetime (Biegon, 2021). The nature of the work in occupations such as construction, transportation, law enforcement/first responders, athletes, and the military all increase risk for TBI (Centers for Disease Control and Prevention, 2024). Women are more likely to incur TBI from falls and in instances of intimate partner violence (IPV), while men are more likely to experience trauma resultant from contact collision, motor vehicle accidents, or in military combat (Biegon, 2021). However, with a larger proportion of women entering the armed forces and engaged in sports, including contact sports, the occurrence of TBI in women is increasing.

Racial and ethnic minoritized groups also have a disproportionately higher risk and rate of sustaining TBIs (Maldonado et al., 2022; Miller et al., 2021; Ritchie et al., 2001). Both women and men of American Indian and Alaskan native descent have the highest average annual age-adjusted rate of TBI-related deaths (24.5 per 100,000 population in 2018 and 23.1 in 2019) when compared to Black/African American, Hispanic/Latinx, or White persons (Centers for Disease Control and Prevention, 2022).

Emerging evidence further underscores the need for a more nuanced look at the intersection of these demographic risk factors and gender differences in TBI. For example, young adult men have 2–3 times higher odds of sustaining a mTBI as compared to same-aged women. However, women who are 65 years or older have higher rates of TBI than same-aged men (Centers for Disease Control and Prevention, 2022) even though women are at greatest risk of TBI during young and middle adulthood (21–50 years old), as compared to women 65 years and older or girls 10 years and younger (Munivenkatappa et al., 2016). Understanding these unique aspects for women is critical for enhancing identification and treatment of TBI.

Unique Considerations for Women

Physical/Biological

There are elements of sexual dimorphism that are hypothesized to play a role in differential experience of and outcomes from TBI between women and men. Physically, muscle neck strength and neck dimensions differ between women and men. As compared to men, women tend to have smaller and weaker neck muscles that in turn leads to vulnerability of greater acceleration by the neck and head upon impact (McGroarty et al., 2020; Merritt et al., 2019; Tierney et al., 2008, 2005). Moreover, neuroimaging studies suggest that skull thickness and intracranial volumes varies as a function of sex, which may increase vulnerability of damage to the brain in women as compared to men (Escorial et al., 2015; Martínez et al., 2017; Ruigrok et al., 2014). Women and men also exhibit brain differences in neuronal structure (Dollé et al., 2018; McGroarty et al., 2020; Merritt et al., 2019). Specifically, axons are smaller with a fewer number of microtubules in women relative to men. Together, the combination of sexual dimorphism among anatomical and neuronal structure may place women at greater risk of physical and axonal injury following TBI.

Sex Hormones

Given that women who are aged 21–50 years tend to have a higher risk of sustaining TBI as compared to young girls and post-menopausal women, a question has been raised as to whether vulnerability of TBI may vary with biological age due to patterns of circulating hormones. This has led to one of the most widely debated hypotheses as to whether/to what degree hormonal fluctuations at the time of the TBI impact recovery and outcomes. Briefly, there are low hormonal levels after birth across sex, and both girls and boys experience an increase in female and male sex hormones during puberty, respectively. Men experience incremental declines in testosterone production over time. In contrast, women continue to experience menstrual cycles (fluctuations in progesterone and estrogen) until menopause. It is hypothesized that both normal fluctuations across the lifespan (e.g., adolescence, pregnancy, oral contraceptive use) as well as declines in production during mid-life influence vulnerability and post-injury outcomes. Support for this hypothesis primarily comes from animal studies; human studies have not fully supported this hypothesis.

There is some evidence to suggest women are more susceptible to physical injury during the luteal phase (rapid decrease in progesterone and estrogen) of their menstrual cycle rather than during the follicular phase (increases in progesterone and estrogen; Belanger et al., 2013; Möller-Nielsen & Hammar, 1989). Estrogen plays a key role in skeletal formation and reabsorption (Almeida et al., 2017; Mirza & Canalis, 2015; Schiavi et al., 2021) as well as structure and function of smooth muscles (Sinder et al., 2024). Transition to menopause disrupts these vital functions, leads to decreases in bone strength and quality and redistribution of adipose tissue, and increased susceptibility to fall-related TBIs in older adulthood for women but not men (Blaya et al., 2022).

Sex hormones are also thought to play a large role in post-injury response, which is primarily supported by evidence derived from animal models (*see* Ma et al., 2019). Female sex hormones down-regulate proinflammatory responses and up-regulate nerve growth factor production. Males tend to express a greater number of neuroglia including microglia and astrocytes. In turn, this leads to decreased neuroinflammation, improved cerebral perfusion, reduced intracranial pressure, and enhanced neurological and cognitive function in females as compared to males following TBI (Caplan et al., 2017; Lenz & McCarthy, 2014).

There are differential alterations in dopaminergic symptoms, ischemia, and mitochondrial function observed between the sexes. Males tend to have lower levels of dopamine whereas females tend to have a greater degree of dopaminergic-related deficits (Wagner et al., 2005; Xu et al., 2016). In addition, females tend to have higher vessel density, increased cerebral blood volume, and increased gene transcription production as compared to males (Valera et al., 2021; Wagner et al., 2004). Together, this suggests the degree of vulnerability post-injury is greater for males as compared to females.

Overall, most animal studies using mTBI models reported females fare better than males (44%), but some have found females fared worse (14%); still, a large proportion of studies reported no differences (28%) or mixed findings (14%). This pattern persisted in moderate and severe TBI models (Gupte et al., 2019). In contrast, most human studies reported worse outcomes for women as compared to men (47%); roughly a quarter of studies (26%) reported worse outcomes for men, and a sizeable portion reported no differences (18%) or mixed findings (9%). The following trends in long-term outcomes emerged when categorized by injury severity: (1) women fared worse than men in mTBI cases and (2) women had comparable if not slightly better outcomes in moderate-to-severe TBI cases (Gupte et al., 2019). Possible reasons for discrepant findings between animal and human models include limited translation of TBI models and differences in outcome measures (e.g., mostly molecular and cellular in animals versus mostly social and behavioral in humans).

Given decreased levels of progesterone are associated with worse outcomes acutely post-TBI, this hormone has been a particular target of research. Trials examining progesterone as a potential therapy to improve outcomes post-TBI have been mixed with some showing promising outcomes, while others have shown no therapeutic effects (Blaya et al., 2022). Investigators found improved outcomes in moderate TBI, and mixed outcomes in severe TBI (Wright et al., 2007; Xiao et al., 2008), though one of the largest Phase III clinical trials showed no therapeutic effects (Skolnick et al., 2014). Ultimately, the role of sex hormones as a neuroprotective factor in humans remains equivocal (see Fig. 4.1).

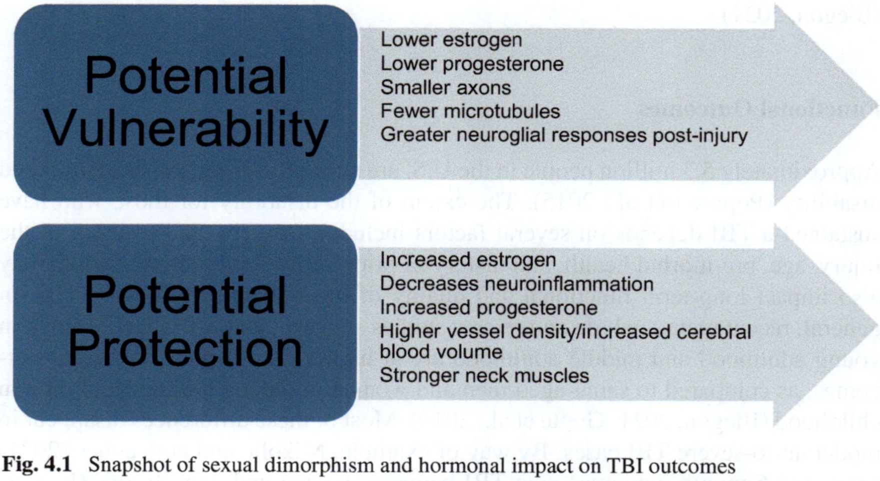

Fig. 4.1 Snapshot of sexual dimorphism and hormonal impact on TBI outcomes

Diagnosis and Prognosis

Acute Symptom Presentation, and Initial Treatment Pathways

Following a TBI event, persons may present to the emergency department with a host of physical (e.g., headache, nausea/vomiting, onset of neurologic deficit), neurobehavioral (e.g., confusion, memory problems, poor sleep, irritability), and/or sensory (e.g., sensitivity to light or sound, blurred vision, dizziness) symptoms in addition to loss of consciousness and/or post-traumatic amnesia. Of these, headache, fatigue, confusion, and dizziness are most commonly reported acutely (Cole & Bailie, 2016). A recent study by Mikolić and colleagues (2021) examined the relationship between gender and initial care and treatment pathways in a community sample of individuals 16 years and older (median age_{Women} = 58; median age_{Men} = 50) for all severity of TBI across 63 centers in Europe and Israel. In mTBI cases (based on baseline GCS of 13–15), women were less likely to be admitted and more likely to be discharged home after presenting to the emergency department, and less likely to receive a secondary referral as compared to men. However, there were no significant differences between men and women across initial care and treatment pathways in moderate and severe TBI cases (Mikolic et al., 2021).

In general, epidemiological studies demonstrate men have higher mortality rates than women following TBI due to more lethal mechanisms of injury. However, findings from a recent review by Biegon (2021) suggest that mortality rate gender differences may depend on injury severity to some extent. Despite similar presenting symptoms, GCS scores within the mild range, and abnormal (i.e., contusion, edema, herniation) computed tomography scans, mortality rate tends to be twice as high in women as compared to men (though mortality resultant from mTBI is exceptionally rare). In moderate-to-severe TBI, there are no gender differences in mortality rate (Biegon, 2021).

Functional Outcomes

Approximately 5.3 million people in the U.S. are currently living with a TBI-related disability (Popescu et al., 2015). The extent of the disability for those who have sustained a TBI depends on several factors including severity and location of the injury, age, pre-morbid health, and history of prior TBIs. Sociocultural factors may also impact long-term functional and quality of life outcomes following TBI. In general, recent meta-analytic and review studies suggest that post-mTBI, women in young adulthood and middle adulthood are at higher risk of poor functional outcomes, as compared to same-aged men and women in older adulthood and girls in childhood (Biegon, 2021; Gupte et al., 2019). Most of these differences disappear in moderate-to-severe TBI cases. By way of example, Mikolić and colleagues (2021) examined 6-month outcomes post-TBI between women and men. In mTBI cases, women had worse functional outcomes as compared to men including being less likely to return to work and lower self-reported quality of life. When stratied by age, the most pronounced gender differences were observed in those in middle and older adulthood. In moderate-to-severe TBI cases, women in older adulthood had the worst functional outcomes (Mikolic et al., 2021).

Post-Concussive Symptoms

Acute symptoms following mTBI, also referred to as post-concussive symptoms, are expected to resolve and return to baseline within at most 12 weeks following mTBI. Despite this, a sizeable minority of people continue to experience symptoms well beyond the time of expected recovery. These include a combination of persistent physical (e.g., headache, fatigue, dizziness), cognitive (e.g., memory and attention problems, executive dysfunction), and/or mood (e.g., depression, anxiety, irritability) symptoms. Post-mTBI, women tend to report a greater number and severity of persistent post-concussive symptoms relative to men. Most common are depressive symptoms, pain, sleep problems, and/or subjective cognitive changes; differences that persist when accounting for pre-morbid health (i.e., emotional, physical), age, and recovery rate (Gupte et al., 2019; Haynes & Goodwin, 2023; Jak et al., 2024). In terms of objective cognitive or neuropsychological changes following TBI, findings are mixed. Some studies reported women perform worse on global measures of cognition as well as objective cognitive measures of memory (visual, verbal) and executive function, while others reported men performed worse on these measures (Gupte et al., 2019; Haynes & Goodwin, 2023).

As with much of the literature on sex differences in TBI, there are also studies reporting mixed findings or lack of differences in post-concussive symptoms between men and women (Haynes & Goodwin, 2023). Differences in gender and sociocultural norms likely influence symptom reporting to some extent. Following an index event, women in the U.S. are more likely to report post-concussive symptoms when directly asked (Merritt et al., 2019). One possible explanation for this observation relates to traditional gender norms in the U.S. In childhood, help-seeking behaviors are emphasized for young girls, particularly when experiencing discomfort; toughness and composure are emphasized for young boys (e.g., "stiff upper lip"; Casper, 2021). Given that men are more likely to sustain moderate-to-severe TBIs, the time-to-reporting is more likely than not also influenced by severity and mechanism of injury.

Special Topics

While not an exhaustive list, women have been historically under-studied in several settings where head injuries commonly occur including sports-related concussion, military service, and intimate partner violence. These special topics are explored in more detail in the following sections (see also Table 4.1).

Table 4.1 Settings in which head injuries commonly occur where women have been historically understudied

Special topic	Key point(s)
Sports-related concussion (SRC)	• **Higher SRC Risk for Women Athletes:** Women face higher concussion risk than men in comparable sports; under-researched in women-dominated sports like cheerleading and gymnastics • **Symptom Reporting:** Women report more symptoms and worse long-term outcomes; tend to express somatic/neurobehavioral symptoms, while men report cognitive symptoms • **Cognitive Outcomes:** Mixed results highlighting the need for more comprehensive assessments to detect subtle differences post-concussion
Military service	• **Injury Mechanisms:** Men in the military are more likely to sustain combat-related traumatic brain injuries (TBIs; e.g., from blasts and bullets), while women experience more non-combat injuries, including falls and TBIs from in imate partner violence (IPV) • **Symptom Reporting:** Women report more neurobehavioral symptoms (e.g., depression, cognitive issues), whereas men are more likely to report chronic pain following military-related TBI • **Cognitive and Mental Health Outcomes:** Women generally perform better on cognitive tasks post-TBI compared to men. However, men have a higher risk for post-traumatic stress disorder (PTSD) and other mental health conditions linked to TBI
Intimate Partner Violence (IPV)	• **Injury Mechanisms:** IPV frequently causes head injuries, with up to 92% of survivors suffering head trauma and 19–100% sustaining a TBI. Non-fatal strangulation (NFS) is also common, leading to significant brain injury • **Symptom Reporting:** Women experiencing IPV often report cognitive issues like memory loss and confusion, but these are frequently complicated by co-occurring conditions such as PTSD and depression • **Cognitive and Mental Health Outcomes:** There are high rates of PTSD and depression among women with histories of IPV-related TBI. Although more work is needed, IPV-related TBIs may be linked to cognitive impairments (i.e., memory, executive function)
Intersecting identities	• **Research Gaps:** Marginalized and minoritized groups (e.g., racial-ethnic, sexual and gender) are underrepresented in TBI research, leading to gaps in understanding their specific risks and health outcomes • **Intersectionality and Health Disparities:** The intersection of various identities can compound health disparities and increase vulnerability to TBI among women across diverse racial-ethnic, gender, and socioeconomic status backgrounds
Chronic Traumatic Encephalopathy (CTE)	• **Research Gaps:** Most CTE research is based on male samples, limiting applicability to women • **Inclusive Research Needed:** Future studies must include women to inform clinical criteria and avoid generalizing male-focused findings

Sports-Related Concussion (SRC)

Sports-related concussion (SRC) is common, and risk of SRC among athletes is 20% (Clay et al., 2013). While much of the initial research on SRC was androcentric reflecting focus on men-dominated contact sports, the number of women athletes participating in sports is steadily rising. As of 2023, approximately 43% of high school athletes in the U.S. are girls (NFHS, 2023), and 42% of National Collegiate Athletic Association (NCAA) athletes are young women (NCAA, 2023). As research has evolved to include women, it has come to light that women athletes are more likely to sustain a concussion following an injury to the head or neck than men athletes (Covassin et al., 2012; McGroarty et al., 2020; Merritt et al., 2019; Tierney et al., 2008). This increased risk persists even when considering gender-equivalent sports, particularly in soccer, basketball, and softball/baseball (Covassin et al., 2016). Women and men athletes who play hockey also have similar concussion incidence rates despite differences in contact rules. Many women-dominated sports, including cheerleading and gymnastics, have the highest rates of SRC (11% of all concussions in girls' sports occur in competitive cheer), though still fail to receive the attention that men-dominated contact sports have (Bretzin et al., 2024).

There are a limited (but growing) number of high quality and powered studies examining gender differences among susceptibility to and outcomes following SRC. In these studies, women athletes have a greater number of post-concussive symptoms as compared to men athletes (Biegon, 2021; Bunt et al., 2022; Covassin et al., 2012; Van Pelt et al., 2021). The nature of symptoms reported may also differ. Women athletes are more likely to report somatic and neurobehavioral symptoms, whereas men athletes are more likely to report cognitive symptoms (Koerte et al., 2020). Moreover, women athletes tend to have poorer long-term outcomes as compared to men athletes (Biegon, 2021; Bunt et al., 2022; Covassin et al., 2012; Van Pelt et al., 2021). However, at least one meta-analysis of 26 studies from 2004–2017 argues concussion-like symptoms are under-reported by both women and men athletes (Ferdinand Pennock et al., 2023). This finding was observed across childhood, adolescence, and young adulthood. Delayed onset of symptoms and/or lack of recognition of symptoms (McGroarty et al., 2020), as well as return-to-play motivations (Kerr et al., 2016) are possible explanations for under- or lack of reporting. At present, it remains unclear whether women and men athletes experience similar vulnerability to sub-concussive or repetitive hits by returning to play too soon.

Regarding cognitive outcomes, Immediate Post-Concussion Assessment and Cognitive Testing (ImPACT; (Lovell, 2022) is one of the most commonly used measures in SRC research. ImPACT is a brief computer-based test used to assess cognitive function (i.e., memory, processing speed, reaction time, attention) before (i.e., prior to or the start of the season as a "baseline") and immediately following an SRC to manage symptoms and inform return to play decisions (Manderino & Gunstad, 2018). Nevertheless, ImPACT testing has its own unique set of advantages (i.e., early detection, guides return to play) and caveats (i.e., validity of baseline testing, specificity and sensitivity). In general, gender difference findings have been twofold but discrepant: either (1) women athletes tend to have worse ImPACT cognitive scores (i.e., visual memory, reaction time) as compared to men athletes acutely following concussion (i.e., within 3 days), or (2) ImPACT cognitive scores are comparable among women and men athletes with a history of concussion (Koerte et al., 2020). It is more likely than not that sensitive, comprehensive neuropsychological assessment is needed to characterize and detect subtle gender differences following concussion (if such differences exist), highlighting a major limitation of most studies.

Military Service

TBI is a common injury among military personnel, particularly among Veterans involved in more recent conflicts in Iraq and Afghanistan (Helmick et al., 2015). Explosive blasts are a common cause of TBI for service members in addition to penetrating wounds, severe blows to the head with shrapnel or debris, and falls or bodily collisions with objects following a blast. Given improvements in vehicle armor, protective gear, including head protection, and other technological safety and medical advances, service members across genders are surviving events that would have previously been fatal, which has contributed to an increase in the rate of TBIs. Like civilian TBI, of the almost 500,000 medically diagnosed military TBIs recorded between 2000 and 2023, more than 80% were classified as mild in severity (DoD, 2023).

Similar to early work in SRC, military TBI research has historically been predominantly focused on male service members and Veterans. However, there are an increasing number of women serving in the military. Currently in the U.S. military, up to 17% of personnel identify as women, with female representation in the military growing by 20% over the last 20 years (Department of Defense, 2022). Moreover, the number of women enrolled in the U.S. Veterans Health Administration (VHA) has increased by almost 50% over the last decade (Department of Veterans Affairs, 2023). Generally, women service members and Veterans are somewhat less likely to sustain a head injury compared to men. Although limited, prevalence estimates range from 11 to 65% among men and 8 to 58% among women (Merritt et al., 2023; Schneiderman et al., 2008).

While overall rate of military TBI may be similar between men and women, mechanism of injuries shows more divergence. In a recent study, men Veterans were more likely to sustain bullet- and blast-related injuries (with alteration of consciousness), whereas women Veterans were more likely to sustain falls (Merritt et al., 2023). Although men Veterans sustained higher rates of deployment-related TBI (Jackson et al., 2016), women were more likely to sustain non-deployment related TBI (Merritt et al., 2023). Regarding post-concussive symptoms, women are more likely to report neurobehavioral symptoms (e.g., depression, headache, poor sleep, cognitive problems), whereas men are more likely to report chronic pain (Valera et al., 2021). In terms of severity of symptoms, some studies report severity is greater among women Veterans, while others suggest gender differences disappear after controlling for blast exposure, symptom validity, and post-traumatic stress disorder (PTSD) symptoms (Valera et al., 2021).

Additionally, there is a tendency for men service members and Veterans to both screen positive for TBI (Hendricks et al., 2013), as well as have their history of TBI confirmed by a clinician (Merritt et al., 2023). Thus, it is more likely than not rates of head injuries among women Veterans and service members are higher than currently estimated due to a combination of more accessible combat roles and under-recognition of non-combat-related mechanisms of injury (e.g., military sexual assault and interpersonal violence) that may place women at greater risk in military settings. Despite this, there are a limited number of high quality and powered studies examining gender differences.

There are a host of acute and long-term health outcomes associated with military-related TBI. Of these, PTSD is one of the most widely studied psychiatric comorbidities followed by neurological, metabolic, and endocrine conditions (Greer et al., 2020; Stein & McAllister, 2009). PTSD and mTBI commonly co-occur in military/veteran samples; military-related mTBI is both physically and emotionally traumatic, increasing risk for developing PTSD following mTBI (Hendrickson et al., 2018). In general, Veterans and service-members have a fourfold increased risk of developing PTSD following TBI as compared to civilians who have twofold increased risk (Loignon et al., 2020). Women Veterans with a history of TBI are at lower risk for developing mental health conditions (e.g., PTSD, depression) as compared to men Veterans (Merritt et al., 2024).

Regarding neuropsychological outcomes, there are two main findings. First, remote history of mTBI alone does not contribute to persistent or progressive cognitive impairment (Nelson et al., 2012; Shandera-Ochsner et al., 2013). By way of example, Walker et al. (2023) found that there was not a relationship between remote history of mTBI and cognitive performance among a large sample of Veterans and service members with combat exposure (Walker et al., 2023). Women Veterans and service members with mTBI histories tend to perform better than men on several cognitive domains including memory, processing speed, and fine motor dexterity. Second, it is more likely than not mental health conditions (e.g., PTSD, depression) are the primary influence on persistent post-TBI cognitive complaints and performance regardless of severity and mechanism of injury (Jak, 2017; Lange et al., 2013).

Intimate Partner Violence (IPV)

Intimate partner violence (IPV) refers to physical, sexual, or psychological harm levied by current or former partners within an intimate relationship (WHO definition). IPV disproportionately impacts women including both cisgender and transgender women (Jain et al., 2024; Toccalino et al., 2022). The US Centers for Disease Control (CDC) report approximately 41% of women (compared to approximately 26% of men) have experienced IPV in the U.S. (Leemis et al., 2022), rates that increased during the COVID-19 pandemic quarantine and stay at home orders (Smith-Clapham et al., 2023). Worldwide, one third of women will experience IPV in their lifetime and almost 40% of deaths among women are committed by intimate partners (WHO, 2021). Despite this alarming rate, it is a largely unrecognized public health crisis.

The head is one of the most commonly targeted/injured sites in IPV with up to 92% of individuals experiencing IPV endorsing a history of being hit in the head/face by a partner; the vast majority of which further indicated the targeting of the head/face was ongoing and repetitive (Campbell et al., 2022) with fractures being most common to the face (Loder & Momper, 2020). Following from this common targeting of the head and face, anywhere from 19 to 100% of women experiencing IPV sustain a TBI (Haag et al., 2022) and up to half have reported TBI with LOC (Campbell et al., 2022).

TBI among those experiencing IPV is often overlooked and therefore under-counted and under-researched. Challenges for identifying TBI in the context of IPV are varied but include differing definitions for both IPV and TBI, variable measures to identify TBI, recall bias (as with all TBI/TBI injury details), and use of often small and/or convenience samples (Campbell et al., 2022). Despite exceptionally high rates of IPV-related TBI in sexual and gender minorities, this is a particularly overlooked demographic in research and clinical care for TBI (Stranges et al., 2024). Transgender individuals may be at particularly high risk for IPV; in a recent study, they were shown to be 1.66 times more likely to experience IPV than cisgender individuals (Peitzmeier et al., 2020). To date, however, there is no known data detailing specific rates of TBI in transgender individuals experiencing IPV.

Questions that have traditionally been used to elicit non-IPV TBI histories may be less effective in eliciting IPV-related TBI. Specific prompts asking about TBI in the context of IPV need to be a part of screening. IPV survivors tend to prefer self-report questionnaires that do not require face-to-face responses (Goldin et al., 2016). Common TBI questionnaires/interviews (e.g., the Brain Injury Screening Questionnaire [BISQ]; Research and Training Center on Community Integration of Individuals with Traumatic Brain Injury, 1997); the Ohio State University TBI Identification Method (Corrigan & Bogner, 2007)) can be amended to better align with the needs of the IPV population; most existing instruments are worded to assume injury from accident rather than assault and often lack questions about facial injuries, violent shaking, or strangulation injuries that are common in IPV (Goldin et al., 2016). The BISQ has been amended in this way (BISQ-IPV) and is shown to enhance detection of IPV-related TBI history (Dams-O'Connor et al., 2023). Women's shelter staff or others with high IPV knowledge are typically well aware of the risk for TBI in their residents but feel they lack training in how to appropriately screen for TBI (Campbell et al., 2022) so questionnaires or other information gathering tools should offer ease of administration by IPV knowledgeable staff who may not have specialty training in TBI (Haag et al., 2022). Broadly, collaborative efforts with neuropsychology, social work, healthcare workers, dental professionals, etc. are needed for early identification and system-level support for integrated and coordinated IPV-related TBI care (Toccalino et al., 2022).

While the focus of this chapter is on *traumatic* brain injury, other *acquired* brain injuries via hypoxia/anoxia also commonly present in IPV populations due to non-fatal strangulation (NFS; Bichard et al., 2022; Costello & Greenwald, 2022; Monahan et al., 2022). Anywhere from 68 to 89% of those experiencing IPV reported strangulation (Nemeth et al., 2019; Raskin et al., 2024), with 17–82% of those resulting in LOC (Campbell et al., 2022; Karr et al., 2024). Similar to TBI, NFS events in IPV are frequently repetitive with 38–88% of respondents endorsing repetitive strangulation incidents (Campbell et al., 2022).

Neuropsychological consequences of TBI in the context of IPV are also woefully understudied. Cognitive concerns such as mental fatigue, confusion, memory changes, executive dysfunction, and difficulty concentrating have been reported (Monahan et al., 2022; Raskin et al., 2024; Zieman et al., 2017). Disentangling the precise etiology of these cognitive symptoms is challenging as they are also frequently reported in the context of depression, anxiety, irritability, and/or PTSD that are highly comorbid in those who are experiencing IPV. Hypoxia has potential cognitive consequences including memory, attention, and/or executive functioning deficits (Anderson & Arciniegas, 2010) and NFS in the context of IPV also commonly results in cognitive changes (Raskin et al., 2024). Specifically, in one study of mostly White women (34% Black/African American; 3% Latina; 3% Native American, 1% Other), those with alteration of consciousness following NFS evidenced significantly lower recall (as measured by the CVLT) and working memory (via WAIS-IV Digit Span Total Score) than those without (Valera et al., 2022).

Certainly, it is challenging to identify with certainty the etiology of cognitive deficits as being directly related to TBI/hypoxia versus mental health comorbidities, though the research literature to date suggests that both contribute (Lifshitz et al., 2019; Monahan et al., 2022; Raskin et al., 2024). For example, Raskin et al. (2024) examined neuropsychological performance among women who identified as Black or Latina with and without IPV histories. Findings suggested that women who had experienced IPV performed more poorly than those without IPV histories on measures of working memory, executive functioning, and visuoconstruction. Those with IPV histories and comorbid PTSD also showed poorer set-shifting performance on Trails B, an aspect of executive functioning. While those with a history of NFS also evidence lower scores across a neuropsychological battery as compared to those without NFS, the number of impaired scores (2 SD criteria) did not differ between groups (Raskin et al., 2024). However, significant differences were still found in memory and executive functioning even after controlling for mental health symptoms (Raskin et al., 2024). Certainly, additional research is needed to more fully understand how histories of IPV might affect cognitive and emotional health, but to date, the literature suggests that similar to concussions sustained via other means, there may be subtle group differences between those with and without IPV, but widespread severe cognitive impairments do not appear to be common.

Intersecting Identities

The special populations above, as well as other identity characteristics, are often overlapping. Looking at multiple identity characteristics in concert as opposed to in isolation in TBI is also important. For example, women Veterans are up to twice as likely to experience IPV than non-Veterans in the U.S. (Iverson et al., 2020). While women Veterans experiencing or with a history of experiencing IPV have more mental and physical health concerns than Veterans with no IPV history (Iverson et al., 2020), they are not more likely to have sustained a TBI than Veterans without IPV history. However, those with IPV and TBI do report more neurobehavioral symptoms. Certainly, more work needs to be done; a national survey of 6000 Iraq/Afghanistan-era Veterans who had undergone a VA Comprehensive TBI Evaluation resulted in only a 16% response rate, only 127 of whom were women and answered questions about IPV (Iverson et al., 2020).

Persons from groups that have been historically and systematically marginalized are underrepresented and underserved in TBI clinical practice and research. More recent research has begun to examine racial and ethnic TBI-related health disparities. Racial and ethnic minoritized groups have a disproportionately higher risk and rate of sustaining TBIs (Maldonado et al., 2022; Miller et al., 2021; Ritchie et al., 2001). As previously noted, both women and men of American Indian and Alaskan Native descent have the highest average annual age-adjusted rate of TBI-related deaths (24.5 per 100,000 population in 2018 and 23.1 in 2019) when compared to Black/African American, Hispanic/Latinx, or White persons (Centers for Disease Control and Prevention, 2022). Additionally, the ongoing crisis of missing and endangered Indigenous women exacerbates health disparities, including the risk of TBI, within these communities (Amnesty International, 2014; Kubik et al., 2009).

Regarding other vulnerable populations, women working in street-based sex work (Baumann et al., 2019; Church et al., 2001; Deering et al., 2014), with histories of involvement in criminal activities (Church et al., 2001; Deering et al., 2014), and/or incarceration (Colantonio et al., 2014) are at increased risk of TBI (Muldoon et al., 2015). There is a possible relationship between childhood TBI and subsequent involvement in violent relationships, highlighting yet another area of intersection that impact TBI risk for women (Farley et al., 2018; Haag et al., 2022; St Ivany & Schminkey, 2016).

To date, there is not sufficient data on rates of TBIs among sexual and gender minoritized persons (Giordano et al., 2020), such as the Two Spirit, Lesbian, Gay, Bisexual, Transgender, Queer or Questioning (2S/LGBTQ) community. Given that persons who experience housing instability have higher rates of injuries related to physical assaults (approximately 42% of women and 58% of men; Mollayeva et al., 2018), and persons from sexual and gender minoritized groups are more likely to experience physical assaults (Truman et al., 2024) and housing instability (LoSchiavo et al., 2020), it is more likely than not that TBI is an underrecognized cause of morbidity and mortality among this underserved population (Giordano et al., 2020). Indeed, as demonstrated by Stranges et al. (2024), an overwhelming majority of 2S/LGBTQ persons reported symptoms consistent with IPV-related TBI, highlighting how the intersection of various identities can compound health disparities and increase vulnerability to TBI.

Chronic Traumatic Encephalopathy (CTE)

Chronic traumatic encephalopathy (CTE) is a neurodegenerative condition characterized by abnormal accumulation of hyperphosphorylated tau in the brains of individuals with a history of repetitive brain trauma; post-mortem examination of brain tissue is required for definitive diagnosis (McKee et al., 2016) and there are no validated criteria for clinical diagnosis of CTE (Iverson et al., 2019). Notably, at this time, CTE research and prevalence data is almost entirely from male samples and the translation from research to clinical practice is not yet firmly established. With this context, it is beyond the scope of this chapter generally and may be premature to address CTE, particularly in women. However, it will be imperative in this emerging area of research and in development of future clinical criteria for adequate data from women to be considered before generalizing results from predominantly male samples to women.

Clinical Takeaways

- Because TBI research has been androcentric, resultant clinical care for concussed women has been, by extension, far less evidenced-based and adjustments may need to be made in clinical care for women with a history of TBI; women may experience, recover, and report TBI events and symptoms differently than men.
- Women may be at higher risk for sport-related concussions including those in women-dominated high-risk sports.
- Multiple traumatic events can have an additive effect (e.g., combat deployments, IPV, TBI) and women Veterans may need differently tailored interventions to address this unique context and aggregate impact.
- In IPV-specific TBI, cognitive deficits cannot be explained entirely by comorbid PTSD or other mood/anxiety disorder.
- Screen all adult (both cis- and transgender) women for IPV and TBI; the BISQ-IPV and the Ohio State University TBI Identification Method amended to better align with the needs of the IPV population may be particularly effective choices.
- Concussion risk/prevention and associated safety protocols and medical support is well highlighted in sports; there are no analogous protocols or ready access to concussion care for IPV. This area of needed growth will require "cross-pollination" of knowledge between neuropsychologists, social work, healthcare workers, dental professionals, etc.

Research Takeaways

- To answer many lingering questions about gender differences in TBI outcomes, it will be essential to prospectively include cis- and transgender women in TBI research, attending to age, endogenous sex hormone levels, as well as racial, ethnic, cultural, and geographic diversity; intersectional work is also paramount.
- Women generally endorse higher rates of post-concussive symptoms and determining the underlying reason(s) *why* (e.g., gender differences in endorsement styles or genuine differences in symptom presentation) will further advance capability to mitigate development of symptoms and/or intervene more appropriately with women post-TBI.
- TBI in the context of IPV remains understudied, despite its high prevalence rates and more research is warranted and desperately needed, particularly focusing on long-term outcomes in this population.
- IPV-related TBI and women with sport-related concussions need to be included in research on repetitive head trauma or chronicity research.
- Incarcerated populations remain a woefully understudied population at high risk for TBI events. Better understanding the relationship between childhood TBI and subsequent involvement in violent relationships may provide insight into prevention as well as treatment.

References

Almeida, M., Laurent, M. R., Dubois, V., Claessens, F., O'Brien, C. A., Bouillon, R., Vanderschueren, D., & Manolagas, S. C. (2017). Estrogens and androgens in skeletal physiology and pathophysiology. *Physiological Reviews, 97*(1), 135–187. https://doi.org/10.1152/physrev.00033.2015

Amnesty International. (2014). Violence against indigenous women and girls in Canadea: A summary of Amnesty International's concerns and call to action.

Anderson, C. A., & Arciniegas, D. B. (2010). Cognitive sequelae of hypoxic-ischemic brain injury: A review. *NeuroRehabilitation, 26*(1), 47–63.

Azouvi, P., Arnould, A., Dromer, E., & Vallat-Azouvi, C. (2017). Neuropsychology of traumatic brain injury: An expert overview. *Revue Neurologique, 173*(7–8), 461–472. https://doi.org/10.1016/j.neurol.2017.07.006

Baumann, R. M., Hamilton-Wright, S., Riley, D. L., Brown, K., Hunt, C., Michalak, A., & Matheson, F. I. (2019). Experiences of violence and head injury among women and transgender women sex workers. *Sexuality Research and Social Policy, 16*(3), 278–288. https://doi.org/10.1007/s13178-018-0334-0

Belanger, L., Burt, D., Callaghan, J., Clifton, S., & Gleberzon, B. J. (2013). Anterior cruciate ligament laxity related to the menstrual cycle: An updated systematic review of the literature. *The Journal of the Canadian Chiropractic Association, 57*(1), 76.

Bichard, H., Byrne, C., Saville, C. W. N., & Coetzer, R. (2022). The neuropsychological outcomes of non-fatal strangulation in domestic and sexual violence: A systematic review. *Neuropsychological Rehabilitation, 32*(6), 1164–1192. https://doi.org/10.1080/09602011.2020.1868537

Biegon, A. (2021). Considering biological sex in traumatic brain injury. *Frontiers in Neurology, 12*, 576366. https://doi.org/10.3389/fneur.2021.576366
Blaya, M. O., Raval, A. P., & Bramlett, H. M. (2022). Traumatic brain injury in women across lifespan. *Neurobiology of Disease, 164*, 105613. https://doi.org/10.1016/j.nbd.2022.105613
Bretzin, A. C., Pollard-McGrandy, A. M., Davis, E. R., Wiebe, D. J., & Covassin, T. (2024). Avenues for prevention using the epidemiology of sport-related concussion from a large high school surveillance study. *Neurosurgical Focus, 57*(1), E3. https://doi.org/10.3171/2024.4.FOCUS24153
Bunt, S. C., Didehbani, N., LoBue, C., Stokes, M., Heinzelmann, M., Rossetti, H., Miller, S. M., Nakonezny, P. A., Bell, K., Batjer, H., & Cullum, C. M. (2022). Sex differences in reporting of concussion symptoms in adults. *The Clinical Neuropsychologist, 36*, 1290–1303. https://doi.org/10.1080/13854046.2020.1842500
Campbell, J. K., Joseph, A. C., Rothman, E. F., & Valera, E. M. (2022). The prevalence of brain injury among survivors and perpetrators of intimate partner violence and the prevalence of violence victimization and perpetration among people with brain injury: A scoping review. *Current Epidemiology Reports, 9*(4), 290–315. https://doi.org/10.1007/s40471-022-00302-y
Caplan, H. W., Cox, C. S., & Bedi, S. S. (2017). Do microglia play a role in sex differences in TBI? *Journal of Neuroscience Research, 95*(1–2), 509–517. https://doi.org/10.1002/jnr.23854
Casper, S. T. (2021). The intertwined history of malingering and brain injury: An argument for structural competency in traumatic brain injury. *Journal of Law, Medicine & Ethics, 49*(3), 365–371. https://doi.org/10.1017/jme.2021.55
Cassidy, J. D., Carroll, L. J., Peloso, P. M., Borg, J., von Holst, H., Holm, L., Kraus, J., & Coronado, V. G. (2004). Incidence, risk factors and prevention of mild traumatic brain injury: Results of the WHO Collaborating Centre Task Force on Mild Traumatic Brain Injury. *Journal of Rehabilitation Medicine*, (43 Suppl), 28–60. PMID: 15083870. https://doi.org/10.1080/16501960410023732
Centers for Disease Control and Prevention. (2022). Surveillance report of traumatic brain injury-related deaths by age group, sex, and mechanism of injury—United States, 2018 and 2019.
Centers for Disease Control and Prevention. (2024). *TBI in the workplace facts*. Centers for Disease Control and Prevention, CDC. Retrieved from https://www.cdc.gov/traumatic-brain-injury/data-research/facts-stats/tbi-in-the-workplace.html
Church, S., Henderson, M., Barnard, M., & Hart, G. (2001). Violence by clients towards female prostitutes in different work settings: Questionnaire survey. *British Medical Journal, 322*(7285), 524–525. https://doi.org/10.1136/bmj.322.7285.524
Clay, M. B., Glover, K. L., & Lowe, D. T. (2013). Epidemiology of concussion in sport: A literature review. *Journal of Chiropractic Medicine, 12*(4), 230–251. https://doi.org/10.1016/j.jcm.2012.11.005
Colantonio, A., Kim, H., Allen, S., Asbridge, M., Petgrave, J., & Brochu, S. (2014). Traumatic brain injury and early life experiences among men and women in a prison population. *Journal of Correctional Health Care, 20*(4), 271–279. https://doi.org/10.1177/1078345814541529
Cole, W. R., & Bailie, J. M. (2016). Frontiers in neuroscience neurocognitive and psychiatric symptoms following mild traumatic brain injury. In D. Laskowitz & G. Grant (Eds.), *Translational research in traumatic brain injury*. Taylor & Francis.
Corrigan, J. D., & Bogner, J. (2007). Initial reliability and validity of the Ohio State University TBI Identification Method. *The Journal of Head Trauma Rehabilitation, 22*(6), 318–329. https://doi.org/10.1097/01.HTR.0000300227.67748.77
Costello, K., & Greenwald, B. D. (2022). Update on domestic violence and traumatic brain injury: A narrative review. *Brain Science, 12*(1), 122. https://doi.org/10.3390/brainsci12010122
Covassin, T., Elbin, R. J., Harris, W., Parker, T., & Kontos, A. (2012). The role of age and sex in symptoms, neurocognitive performance, and postural stability in athletes after concussion. *American Journal of Sports Medicine, 40*(6), 1303–1312. https://doi.org/10.1177/0363546512444554
Covassin, T., Moran, R., & Elbin, R. J. (2016). Sex differences in reported concussion injury rates and time loss from participation: An update of the national collegiate athletic association injury

surveillance program from 2004–2005 through 2008–2009. *Journal of Athletic Training, 51*(3), 189–194. https://doi.org/10.4085/1062-6050-51.3.05

Dams-O'Connor, K., Bulas, A., Haag, H. L., Spielman, L. A., Fernandez, A., Frederick-Hawley, L., Hoffman, J. M., & Goldin Frazier, Y. (2023). Screening for brain injury sustained in the context of intimate partner violence (IPV): Measure development and preliminary utility of the brain injury screening questionnaire IPV module. *Journal of Neurotrauma, 40*(19–20), 2087–2099. https://doi.org/10.1089/neu.2022.0357

Deering, K. N., Amin, A., Shoveller, J., Nesbitt, A., Garcia-Moreno, C., Duff, P., Argento, E., & Shannon, K. (2014). A systematic review of the correlates of violence against sex workers. *American Journal of Public Health, 104*(5), e42–e54. https://doi.org/10.2105/ajph.2014.301909

Department of Defense. (2022). Demographics profile of the military community.

Department of Veterans Affairs. (2023). *VetPop2020 state estimates 2000 to 2020*. Retrieved from https://www.data.va.gov/stories/s/Veterans-Day-2023/4gqv-ddx7/#:~:text=Overall%2C%20the%20population%20of%20female,from%2010%25%20to%2017%25

DoD. (2023). *DOD numbers for traumatic brain injury worldwide*. Retrieved August 1, from https://health.mil/Military-Health-Topics/Centers-of-Excellence/Traumatic-Brain-Injury-Center-of-Excellence/DOD-TBI-Worldwide-Numbers

Dollé, J. P., Jaye, A., Anderson, S. A., Ahmadzadeh, H., Shenoy, V. B., & Smith, D. H. (2018). Newfound sex differences in axonal structure underlie differential outcomes from in vitro traumatic axonal injury. *Experimental Neurology, 300*, 121–134. https://doi.org/10.1016/j.expneurol.2017.11.001

Escorial, S., Román, F. J., Martínez, K., Burgaleta, M., Karama, S., & Colom, R. (2015). Sex differences in neocortical structure and cognitive performance: A surface-based morphometry study. *NeuroImage, 104*, 355–365. https://doi.org/10.1016/j.neuroimage.2014.09.035

Farley, M., Banks, M. E., Ackerman, R. J., & Golding, J. M. (2018). Screening for traumatic brain injury in prostituted women. *Dignity: A Journal of Analysis of Exploitation and Violence, 3*(2), 5. https://doi.org/10.23860/dignity.2018.03.02.05

Ferdinand Pennock, K., McKenzie, B., McClemont Steacy, L., & Mainwaring, L. (2023). Under-reporting of sport-related concussions by adolescent athletes: A systematic review. *International Review of Sport and Exercise Psychology, 16*(1), 66–92. https://doi.org/10.1080/1750984X.2020.1824243

Giordano, K. R., Rojas-Valencia, L. M., Bhargava, V., & Lifshitz, J. (2020). Beyond binary: Influence of sex and gender on outcome after traumatic brain injury. *Journal of Neurotrauma, 37*(23), 2454–2459. https://doi.org/10.1089/neu.2020.7230

Goldin, Y., Haag, H. L., & Trott, C. T. (2016). Screening for history of traumatic brain injury among women exposed to intimate partner violence. *Physical Medicine and Rehabilitation, 8*, 1104–1110.

Greer, N., Sayer, N. A., Spoont, M., Taylor, B. C., Ackland, P. E., MacDonald, R., McKenzie, L., Rosebush, C., & Wilt, T. J. (2020). Prevalence and severity of psychiatric disorders and suicidal behavior in service members and veterans with and without traumatic brain injury: Systematic review. *The Journal of Head Trauma Rehabilitation, 35*(1), 1–13. Retrieved from https://journals.lww.com/headtraumarehab/fulltext/2020/01000/prevalence_and_severity_of_psychiatric_disorders.1.aspx

Guan, B., Anderson, D. B., Chen, L., Feng, S., & Zhou, H. (2023). Global, regional and national burden of traumatic brain injury and spinal cord injury, 1990–2019: A systematic analysis for the Global Burden of Disease Study 2019. *BMJ Open, 13*(10), e075049. https://doi.org/10.1136/bmjopen-2023-075049

Gupte, R., Brooks, W., Vukas, R., Pierce, J., & Harris, J. (2019). Sex differences in traumatic brain injury: What we know and what we should know. *Journal of Neurotrauma, 36*(22), 3063–3091. https://doi.org/10.1089/neu.2018.6171

Haag, H. L., Jones, D., Joseph, T., & Colantonio, A. (2022). Battered and brain injured: Traumatic brain injury among women survivors of intimate partner violence—A scoping review. *Trauma, Violence, & Abuse, 23*(4), 1270–1287.

Haynes, N., & Goodwin, T. (2023). Literature review of sex differences in mTBI. *Military Medicine, 188*(5–6), e978–e984. https://doi.org/10.1093/milmed/usab472

Helmick, K. M., Spells, C. A., Malik, S. Z., Davies, C. A., Marion, D. W., & Hinds, S. R. (2015). Traumatic brain injury in the US military: Epidemiology and key clinical and research programs. *Brain Imaging and Behavior, 9*(3), 358–366. https://doi.org/10.1007/s11682-015-9399-z

Hendricks, A. M., Amara, J., Baker, E., Charns, M. P., Gardner, J. A., Iverson, K. M., Kimerling, R., Krengel, M., Meterko, M., Pogoda, T. K., Stolzmann, K. L., & Lew, H. L. (2013). Screening for mild traumatic brain injury in OEF-OIF deployed US military: An empirical assessment of VHA's experience. *Brain Injury, 27*(2), 125–134. https://doi.org/10.3109/02699052.2012.729284

Hendrickson, R. C., Schindler, A. G., & Pagulayan, K. F. (2018). Untangling PTSD and TBI: Challenges and strategies in clinical care and research. *Current Neurology and Neuroscience Reports, 18*(12), 106. https://doi.org/10.1007/s11910-018-0908-5

Iverson, G. L., Gardner, A. J., Shultz, S. R., Solomon, G. S., McCrory, P., Zafonte, R., Perry, G., Hazrati, L. N., Keene, C. D., & Castellani, R. J. (2019). Chronic traumatic encephalopathy neuropathology might not be inexorably progressive or unique to repetitive neurotrauma. *Brain, 142*(12), 3672–3693. https://doi.org/10.1093/brain/awz286

Iverson, K. M., Sayer, N. A., Meterko, M., Stolzmann, K., Suri, P., Gormley, K., Nealon Seibert, M., Yan, K., & Pogoda, T. K. (2020). Intimate partner violence among female OEF/OIF/OND veterans who were evaluated for traumatic brain injury in the veterans health administration: A preliminary investigation. *Journal of Interpersonal Violence, 35*(13–14), 2422–2445. https://doi.org/10.1177/0886260517702491

Jackson, C. E., Green, J. D., Bovin, M. J., Vasterling, J. J., Holowka, D. W., Ranganathan, G., Rosen, R. C., Keane, T. M., & Marx, B. P. (2016). Mild taumatic brain injury, PTSD, and psychosocial functioning among male and female U.S. OEF/OIF veterans. *Journal of Traumatic Stress, 29*(4), 309–316. https://doi.org/10.1002/jts.22110

Jain, D., Safer, J. D., Ovalles, A., Dorman, K., Gurrapu, S., Dams-O'Connor, K., & Esopenko, C. (2024). Preliminary evidence of intimate partner violence-related head trauma among transgender and gender-diverse adults. *Violence and Gender, 11*(3), 149–158. https://doi.org/10.1089/vio.2023.0071

Jak, A. J. (2017). The primary role of mental health treatment in resolution of persistent postconcussive symptoms. *Current Treatment Options in Psychiatry, 4*(3), 231–240. https://doi.org/10.1007/s40501-017-0119-8

Jak, A. J., Merritt, V. C., Thomas, M. L., Witten, C., Talbert, L., Agyemang, A., & Pugh, M. J. (2024). Sex differences in postconcussive symptom reporting in those with history of concussion: Findings from the federal interagency traumatic brain injury research (FITBIR) database. *The Clinical Neuropsychologist, 38*(6), 1468–1480. https://doi.org/10.1080/13854046.2024.2371007

Karr, J. E., White, A. E., Leong, S. E., & Logan, T. K. (2024). The neurobehavioral symptom inventory: Psychometric properties and symptom comparisons in women with and without brain injuries due to intimate partner violence. *Assessment, 32*(1), 102–118. https://doi.org/10.1177/10731911241236687

Kerr, Z. Y., Register-Mihalik, J. K., Kroshus, E., Baugh, C. M., & Marshall, S. W. (2016). Motivations associated with nondisclosure of self-reported concussions in former collegiate athletes. *American Journal of Sports Medicine, 44*(1), 220–225. https://doi.org/10.1177/0363546515612082

Koerte, I. K., Schultz, V., Sydnor, V. J., Howell, D. R., Guenette, J. P., Dennis, E., Kochsiek, J., Kaufmann, D., Sollmann, N., Mondello, S., Shenton, M. E., & Lin, A. P. (2020). Sex-related differences in the effects of sports-related concussion: A review. *Journal of Neuroimaging, 30*(4), 387–409. https://doi.org/10.1111/jon.12726

Kubik, W., Bourassa, C., & Hampton, M. (2009). Stolen sisters, second class citizens, poor health: The legacy of colonization in Canada. *Humanity and Society, 33*(1–2), 18–34. https://doi.org/10.1177/016059760903300103

Lange, R. T., Brickell, T., French, L. M., Ivins, B., Bhagwat, A., Pancholi, S., & Iverson, G. L. (2013). Risk factors for postconcussion symptom reporting after traumatic brain injury in U.S. military service members. *Journal of Neurotrauma, 30*(4), 237–246. https://doi.org/10.1089/neu.2012.2685

Leemis, R. W., Friar, N., Khatiwada, S., Chen, M. S., Kresnow, M., Smith, S. G., Caslin, S., & Basile, K. C. (2022). The national intimate partner and sexual violence survey: 2016/2017 report on intimate partner violence.

Lenz, K. M., & McCarthy, M. M. (2014). A starring role for microglia in brain sex differences. *The Neuroscientist, 21*(3), 306–321. https://doi.org/10.1177/1073858414536468

Lifshitz, J., Crabtree-Nelson, S., & Kozlowski, D. A. (2019). Traumatic brain injury in victims of domestic violence. *Journal of Aggression, Maltreatment & Trauma, 28*(6), 655–659. https://doi.org/10.1080/10926771.2019.1644693

Loder, R. T., & Momper, L. (2020). Demographics and fracture patterns of patients presenting to US emergency departments for intimate partner violence. *JAAOS Global Research & Reviews, 4*(2), e20.00009. https://doi.org/10.5435/JAAOSGlobal-D-20-00009

Loignon, A., Ouellet, M., & Belleville, G. (2020). A systematic review and meta-analysis on PTSD following TBI among military/veteran and civilian populations. *The Journal of Head Trauma Rehabilitation, 35*(1), E21–E35. Retrieved from https://journals.lww.com/headtraumarehab/fulltext/2020/01000/a_systematic_review_and_meta_analysis_on_ptsd.12.aspx

LoSchiavo, C., Krause, K. D., Singer, S. N., & Halkitis, P. N. (2020). The confluence of housing instability and psychosocial, mental, and physical health in sexual minority young adults: The P18 cohort study. *Journal of Health Care for the Poor and Underserved, 31*(4), 1693–1711. https://doi.org/10.1353/hpu.2020.0127

Lovell, M. R. (2022). *ImPACT administration and interpretation manual (version 4)*. ImPACT Applications.

Ma, C., Wu, X., Shen, X., Yang, Y., Chen, Z., Sun, X., & Wang, Z. (2019). Sex differences in traumatic brain injury: A multi-dimensional exploration in genes, hormones, cells, individuals, and society. *Chinese Neurosurgical Journal, 5*(1), 24. https://doi.org/10.1186/s41016-019-0173-8

Maas, A. I. R., Menon, D. K., Manley, G. T., Abrams, M., Åkerlund, C., Andelic, N., Aries, M., Bashford, T., Bell, M. J., Bodien, Y. G., Brett, B. L., Büki, A., Chesnut, R. M., Citerio, G., Clark, D., Clasby, B., Cooper, D. J., Czeiter, E., Czosnyka, M., et al. (2022). Traumatic brain injury: Progress and challenges in prevention, clinical care, and research. *The Lancet Neurology, 21*(11), 1004–1060. https://doi.org/10.1016/s1474-4422(22)00309-x

Maldonado, J., Huang, J. H., Childs, E. W., & Tharakan, B. (2022). Racial/ethnic differences in traumatic brain injury: Pathophysiology, outcomes, and future directions. *Journal of Neurotrauma, 40*(5–6), 502–513. https://doi.org/10.1089/neu.2021.0455

Manderino, L. M., & Gunstad, J. (2018). Performance of the immediate post-concussion assessment and cognitive testing protocol validity indices. *Archives of Clinical Neuropsychology, 33*(5), 596–605. https://doi.org/10.1093/arclin/acx102

Martínez, K., Janssen, J., Pineda-Pardo, J. Á., Carmona, S., Román, F. J., Alemán-Gómez, Y., Garcia-Garcia, D., Escorial, S., Quiroga, M. Á., Santarnecchi, E., Navas-Sánchez, F. J., Desco, M., Arango, C., & Colom, R. (2017). Individual differences in the dominance of interhemispheric connections predict cognitive ability beyond sex and brain size. *Neuroimage, 155*, 234–244. https://doi.org/10.1016/j.neuroimage.2017.04.029

McGroarty, N. K., Brown, S. M., & Mulcahey, M. K. (2020). Sport-related concussion in female athletes: A systematic review. *Orthopaedic Journal of Sports Medicine, 8*(7), 2325967120932306. https://doi.org/10.1177/2325967120932306

McKee, A. C., Cairns, N. J., Dickson, D. W., Folkerth, R. D., Keene, C. D., Litvan, I., Perl, D. P., Stein, T. D., Vonsattel, J. P., Stewart, W., Tripodis, Y., Crary, J. F., Bieniek, K. F., Dams-O'Connor, K., Alvarez, V. E., & Gordon, W. A. (2016). The first NINDS/NIBIB consensus meeting to define neuropathological criteria for the diagnosis of chronic traumatic encephalopathy. *Acta Neuropathologica, 131*(1), 75–86. https://doi.org/10.1007/s00401-015-1515-z

Merritt, V. C., Padgett, C. R., & Jak, A. J. (2019). A systematic review of sex differences in concussion outcome: What do we know? *The Clinical Neuropsychologist, 33*(6), 1016–1043. https://doi.org/10.1080/13854046.2018.1508616

Merritt, V. C., Chanfreau-Coffinier, C., Sakamoto, M. S., Jak, A. J., & Delano-Wood, L. (2023). Characterizing sex differences in clinical and functional outcomes among military veterans with a comprehensive traumatic brain injury evaluation (CTBIE): A million veteran program (MVP) study. *Clinical Psychological Science, 11*(2), 253–270. https://doi.org/10.1177/21677026221100230

Merritt, V. C., Gasperi, M., Yim, J., Ly, M. T., & Chanfreau-Coffinier, C. (2024). Exploring interactions between traumatic brain injury history and gender on medical comorbidities in military veterans: An epidemiological analysis in the VA Million Veteran Program. *Journal of Neurotrauma, 41*(5–6), 623–634. https://doi.org/10.1089/neu.2023.0174

Mikolic, A., Groeniger, J. O., Zeldovich, M., Wilson, L., van Lennep, J. R., van Klaveren, D., & Polinder, S. (2021). Explaining outcome differences between men and women following mild traumatic brain injury. *Journal of Neurotrauma, 38*(23), 3315–3331. https://doi.org/10.1089/neu.2021.0116

Miller, G. F., Daugherty, J., Waltzman, D., & Sarmiento, K. (2021). Predictors of traumatic brain injury morbidity and mortality: Examination of data from the national trauma data bank: Predictors of TBI morbidity & mortality. *Injury, 52*(5), 1138–1144. https://doi.org/10.1016/j.injury.2021.01.042

Mirza, F., & Canalis, E. (2015). Management of endocrine disease: Secondary osteoporosis: Pathophysiology and management. *European Journal of Endocrinology, 173*(3), R131–R151. https://doi.org/10.1530/eje-15-0118

Mollayeva, T., Mollayeva, S., & Colantonio, A. (2018). Traumatic brain injury: Sex, gender and intersecting vulnerabilities. *Nature Reviews Neurology, 14*(12), 711–722. https://doi.org/10.1038/s41582-018-0091-y

Möller-Nielsen, J., & Hammar, M. (1989). Women's soccer injuries in relation to the menstrual cycle and oral contraceptive use. *Medicine and Science in Sports and Exercise, 21*(2), 126–129.

Monahan, K., Bannon, S., & Dams-O'Connor, K. (2022). Nonfatal strangulation (NFS) and intimate partner violence: A brief overview. *Journal of Family Violence, 37*(1), 75–86. https://doi.org/10.1007/s10896-020-00208-7

Muldoon, K. A., Deering, K. N., Feng, C. X., Shoveller, J. A., & Shannon, K. (2015). Sexual relationship power and intimate partner violence among sex workers with non-commercial intimate partners in a Canadian setting. *AIDS Care, 27*(4), 512–519. https://doi.org/10.1080/09540121.2014.978732

Munivenkatappa, A., Agrawal, A., Shukla, D. P., Kumaraswamy, D., & Devi, B. I. (2016). Traumatic brain injury: Does gender influence outcomes? *International Journal of Critical Illness and Injury Science, 6*(2), 70–73. https://doi.org/10.4103/2229-5151.183024

NCAA. (2023). National Collegiate Athletic Association Demographics Database. Retrieved from https://www.ncaa.org/sports/2018/12/13/ncaa-demographics-database.aspx

Nelson, N. W., Hoelzle, J. B., Doane, B. M., McGuire, K. A., Ferrier-Auerbach, A. G., Charlesworth, M. J., Lamberty, G. J., Polusny, M. A., Arbisi, P. A., & Sponheim, S. R. (2012). Neuropsychological outcomes of U.S. veterans with report of remote blast-related concussion and current psychopathology. *Journal of the International Neuropsychological Society, 18*(5), 845–855. https://doi.org/10.1017/S1355617712000616

Nemeth, J. M., Mengo, C., Kulow, E., Brown, A., & Ramirez, R. (2019). Provider perceptions and domestic violence (DV) survivor experiences of traumatic and anoxic-hypoxic brain injury: Implications for DV advocacy service provision. *Journal of Aggression, Maltreatment & Trauma, 28*(6), 744–763. https://doi.org/10.1080/10926771.2019.1591562

NFHS. (2023). National Federation of High Schools High School Athletics Participation Survey. Retrieved from https://www.nfhs.org/media/7212351/2022-23_participation_survey.pdf

Peitzmeier, S. M., Malik, M., Kattari, S. K., Marrow, E., Stephenson, R., Agénor, M., & Reisner, S. L. (2020). Intimate partner violence in transgender populations: Systematic review and meta-analysis of prevalence and correlates. *American Journal of Public Health, 110*(9), e1–e14. https://doi.org/10.2105/ajph.2020.305774

Popescu, C., Anghelescu, A., Daia, C., & Onose, G. (2015). Actual data on epidemiological evolution and prevention endeavours regarding traumatic brain injury. *Journal of Medicine and Life, 8*(3), 272–277.

Raskin, S. A., DeJoie, O., Edwards, C., Ouchida, C., Moran, J., White, O., Mordasiewicz, M., Anika, D., & Njoku, B. (2024). Traumatic brain injury screening and neuropsychological functioning in women who experience intimate partner violence. *The Clinical Neuropsychologist, 38*(2), 354–376. https://doi.org/10.1080/13854046.2023.2215489

Research and Training Center on Community Integration of Individuals with Traumatic Brain Injury. (1997). *Brain injury screening questionnaire*. Research and Training Center.

Ritchie, K., Artero, S., & Touchon, J. (2001). Classification criteria for mild cognitive impairment: A population-based validation study. *Neurology, 56*(1), 37–42. Retrieved from http://www.neurology.org/cgi/content/abstract/56/1/37

Ruigrok, A. N., Salimi-Khorshidi, G., Lai, M. C., Baron-Cohen, S., Lombardo, M. V., Tait, R. J., & Suckling, J. (2014). A meta-analysis of sex differences in human brain structure. *Neuroscience and Biobehavioral Review, 39*, 34–50. https://doi.org/10.1016/j.neubiorev.2013.12.004

Schiavi, J., Fodera, D. M., Brennan, M. A., & McNamara, L. M. (2021). Estrogen depletion alters osteogenic differentiation and matrix production by osteoblasts in vitro. *Experimental Cell Research, 408*(1), 112814. https://doi.org/10.1016/j.yexcr.2021.112814

Schneiderman, A. I., Braver, E. R., & Kang, H. K. (2008). Understanding sequelae of injury mechanisms and mild traumatic brain injury incurred during the conflicts in Iraq and Afghanistan: Persistent postconcussive symptoms and posttraumatic stress disorder. *American Journal of Epidemiology, 167*(12), 1446–1452. https://doi.org/10.1093/aje/kwn068

Shandera-Ochsner, A. L., Berry, D. T. R., Harp, J. P., Edmundson, M., Graue, L. O., Roach, A., & High, W. M. (2013). Neuropsychological effects of self-reported deployment-related mild TBI and current PTSD in OIF/OEF veterans. *The Clinical Neuropsychologist, 27*(6), 881–907. https://doi.org/10.1080/13854046.2013.802017

Sinder, S. B., Sharma, S. V., Shirvaikar, I. S., Pradhyumnan, H., Patel, S. H., Cabeda Diaz, I., Perez, G. G., Bramlett, H. M., & Raval, A. P. (2024). Impact of menopause-associated frailty on traumatic brain injury. *Neurochemistry International, 176*, 105741. https://doi.org/10.1016/j.neuint.2024.105741

Skolnick, B. E., Maas, A. I., Narayan, R. K., Van Der Hoop, R. G., MacAllister, T., Ward, J. D., Nelson, N. R., & Stocchetti, N. (2014). A clinical trial of progesterone for severe traumatic brain injury. *New England Journal of Medicine, 371*(26), 2467–2476.

Smith-Clapham, A. M., Childs, J. E., Cooley-Strickland, M., Hampton-Anderson, J., Novacek, D. M., Pemberton, J. V., & Wyatt, G. E. (2023). Implications of the COVID-19 pandemic on interpersonal violence within marginalized communities: Toward a new prevention paradigm. *American Journal of Public Health, 113*(S2), S149–s156. https://doi.org/10.2105/ajph.2023.307289

St Ivany, A., & Schminkey, D. (2016). Intimate partner violence and traumatic brain injury: State of the science and next steps. *Family and Community Health, 39*(2), 129–137. https://doi.org/10.1097/fch.0000000000000094

Stein, M. B., & McAllister, T. W. (2009). Exploring the convergence of posttraumatic stress disorder and mild traumatic brain injury. *American Journal of Psychiatry, 166*(7), 768–776. https://doi.org/10.1176/appi.ajp.2009.08101604

Stranges, T. N., Marshall, R. A., Godard, R., Simonetto, D., & van Donkelaar, P. (2024). Characterizing intimate partner violence-caused brain injury in a sample of survivors in the two spirit, lesbian, gay, bisexual, transgender, queer or questioning community. *Journal of Interpersonal Violence, 40*(3–4), 906–927. https://doi.org/10.1177/08862605241256390

Styrke, J., Stålnacke, B. M., Sojka, P., & Björnstig, U. (2007). Traumatic brain injuries in a well-defined population: Epidemiological aspects and severity. *Journal of Neurotrauma, 24*(9), 1425–1436. PMID: 17892405. https://doi.org/10.1089/neu.2007.0266

Taylor, C. A., Bell, J. M., Breiding, M. J., & Xu, L. (2017). Traumatic brain injury-related emergency department visits, hospitalizations, and deaths—United States, 2007 and 2013. *Morbidity and Mortality Weekly Report. Surveillance Summaries, 66*(9), 1–16. https://doi.org/10.15585/mmwr.ss6609a1

Teasdale, G., & Jennett, B. (1974). Assessment of coma and impaired consciousness: A practical scale. *The Lancet, 304*(7872), 81–84. https://doi.org/10.1016/S0140-6736(74)91639-0

Tierney, R. T., Sitler, M. R., Swanik, C. B., Swanik, K. A., Higgins, M., & Torg, J. (2005). Gender differences in head-neck segment dynamic stabilization during head acceleration. *Medicine and Science in Sports and Exercise, 37*(2), 272–279. https://doi.org/10.1249/01.mss.0000152734.47516.aa

Tierney, R. T., Higgins, M., Caswell, S. V., Brady, J., McHardy, K., Driban, J. B., & Darvish, K. (2008). Sex differences in head acceleration during heading while wearing soccer headgear. *Journal of Athletic Training, 43*(6), 578–584. https://doi.org/10.4085/1062-6050-43.6.578

Toccalino, D., Haag, H. L., Estrella, M. J., Cowle, S., Fuselli, P., Ellis, M. J., Gargaro, J., & Colantonio, A. (2022). The intersection of intimate partner violence and traumatic brain injury: Findings from an emergency summit addressing system-level changes to better support women survivors. *Journal of Head Trauma Rehabilitation, 37*(1), E20–e29. https://doi.org/10.1097/htr.0000000000000743

Truman, J. L., Morgan, R. E., & Coen, E. J. (2024). Characteristics and consequences of violent victimization in sexual and gender minority communities: An analysis of the 2017–2021 national crime victimization survey. *LGBT Health, 11*(7), 552–562. https://doi.org/10.1089/lgbt.2023.0110

VA/DoD. (2021). VA/DoD clinical practice guideline for the management and rehabilitation of post-acute mild traumatic brain injury.

Valera, E. M., Joseph, A. C., Snedaker, K., Breiding, M. J., Robertson, C. L., Colantonio, A., Levin, H., Pugh, M. J., Yurgelun-Todd, D., Mannix, R., Bazarian, J. J., Turtzo, L. C., Turkstra, L. S., Begg, L., Cummings, D. M., & Bellgowan, P. S. F. (2021). Understanding traumatic brain injury in females: A state-of-the-art summary and future directions. *Journal of Head Trauma Rehabilitation, 36*(1), E1–e17. https://doi.org/10.1097/htr.0000000000000652

Valera, E. M., Daugherty, J., Scott, O. C., & Berenbaum, H. (2022). Strangulation as an acquired brain injury in intimate–partner violence and its relationship to cognitive and psychological functioning: A preliminary study. *The Journal of Head Trauma Rehabilitation, 37*(1), 15–23. https://doi.org/10.1097/htr.0000000000000755

Van Pelt, K. L., Puetz, T., Swallow, J., Lapointe, A. P., & Broglio, S. P. (2021). Data-driven risk classification of concussion rates: A systematic review and meta-analysis. *Sports Medicine, 51*(6), 1227–1244. https://doi.org/10.1007/s40279-021-01428-7

Wagner, A. K., Bayir, H., Ren, D., Puccio, A., Zafonte, R. D., & Kochanek, P. M. (2004). Relationships between cerebrospinal fluid markers of excitotoxicity, ischemia, and oxidative damage after severe TBI: The impact of gender, age, and hypothermia. *Journal of Neurotrauma, 21*(2), 125–136. https://doi.org/10.1089/089771504322778596

Wagner, A. K., Chen, X., Kline, A. E., Li, Y., Zafonte, R. D., & Dixon, C. E. (2005). Gender and environmental enrichment impact dopamine transporter expression after experimental traumatic brain injury. *Experimental Neurology, 195*(2), 475–483. https://doi.org/10.1016/j.expneurol.2005.06.009

Walker, W. C., O'Neil, M. E., Ou, Z., Pogoda, T. K., Belanger, H. G., Scheibel, R. S., Presson, A. P., Miles, S. R., Wilde, E. A., Tate, D. F., Troyanskaya, M., Pugh, M. J., Jak, A. J., & Cifu, D. X. (2023). Can mild traumatic brain injury alter cognition chronically? A LIMBIC-CENC multicenter study. *Neuropsychology, 37*(1), 1–19. https://doi.org/10.1037/neu0000855

WHO. (2021). Violence against women Prevalence Estimates, 2018. Global, regional and national prevalence estimates for intimate partner violence against women and global and regional prevalence estimates for non-partner sexual violence against women.

Williamson, C., & Rajajee, V. (2021). Traumatic brain injury: Epidemiology, classification, and pathophysiology. In M. J. M. Aminoff, & M. E. (Ed.), *UpToDate* (2023/05/16 ed.).

Wright, D. W., Kellermann, A. L., Hertzberg, V. S., Clark, P. L., Frankel, M., Goldstein, F. C., Salomone, J. P., Dent, L. L., Harris, O. A., Ander, D. S., Lowery, D. W., Patel, M. M., Denson, D. D., Gordon, A. B., Wald, M. M., Gupta, S., Hoffman, S. W., & Stein, D. G. (2007). ProTECT: A randomized clinical trial of progesterone for acute traumatic brain injury. *Annals of Emergency Medicine, 49*(4), 391–402. https://doi.org/10.1016/j.annemergmed.2006.07.932

Xiao, G., Wei, J., Yan, W., Wang, W., & Lu, Z. (2008). Improved outcomes from the administration of progesterone for patients with acute severe traumatic brain injury: A randomized controlled trial. *Critical Care, 12*(2), R61. https://doi.org/10.1186/cc6887

Xu, X., Cao, S., Chao, H., Liu, Y., & Ji, J. (2016). Sex-related differences in striatal dopaminergic system after traumatic brain injury. *Brain Research Bulletin, 124*, 214–221. https://doi.org/10.1016/j.brainresbull.2016.05.010

Zieman, G., Bridwell, A., & Cárdenas, J. F. (2017). Traumatic brain injury in domestic violence victims: A retrospective study at the Barrow Neurological Institute. *Journal of Neurotrauma, 34*(4), 876–880. https://doi.org/10.1089/neu.2016.4579

Chapter 5
Alzheimer's Disease and Other Dementias

Anna Brugulat-Serrat, C. Elizabeth Shaaban, Sheina Emrani, and Erin Sundermann

Introduction

Dementia

Dementia is a general term for a group of neurological conditions caused by irreversible degeneration of the structure and function of the central and peripheral nervous system (Wilson et al., 2023) and characterized by the loss of memory, reasoning, language, attention, and concentration as well as behavioral changes, resulting in an impairment in daily functioning. The Diagnostic and Statistical Manual of Mental Disorders, 5th Edition, Text Revision (DSM-5-TR) introduced the classification of major neurocognitive disorder (NCD) to describe conditions that significantly impair cognitive function, aligning closely with the traditional definition of dementia (American Psychiatric Association, 2022). The diagnosis of NCD in DSM-5-TR requires evidence of significant cognitive decline from a previous level of functioning in one (or more) domains, impacting daily independence and necessitating assistance with complex tasks. However, unlike the traditional definitions of dementia, the DSM-5-TR Major NCD criteria allows for a broader scope that

A. Brugulat-Serrat
BarcelonaBeta Brain Research Center, Barcelona, Spain

C. E. Shaaban
University of Pittsburgh School of Public Health, Pittsburgh, PA, USA

S. Emrani
Perelman School of Medicine, University of Pennsylvania, Philadelphia, PA, USA

E. Sundermann (✉)
University of California San Diego, San Diego, CA, USA
e-mail: esundermann@health.ucsd.edu

E. Sullivan-Baca, R. Ellison (eds.), *Neuropsychology of Women*,
https://doi.org/10.1007/978-3-031-87228-0_5

extends beyond age-associated neurodegenerative disorders, including conditions impacting younger individuals.

Worldwide, there are over 55 million people living with age-related dementia (Gauthier et al., 2021). Globally, dementia prevalence is greater for women (8.1%) vs. men (5.4%), and this pattern is true across all age bands 65 years and older and across all World Health Organization geographic regions (WHO, 2021). The most common types of dementia among adults aged 65 years and older are Alzheimer's disease (AD) and vascular dementia, followed by frontotemporal dementia and Lewy body dementia, which includes dementia with Lewy bodies and Parkinson's disease dementia.

AD will be a central focus of this chapter because of the prominent gender differences in not only AD rates but also in risk factors, clinical trajectory, diagnostic accuracy and pathology as well as the extensive literature devoted to the gender influence in AD. We also discuss protective, lifestyle factors that not only reduce AD risk but also promote healthy aging. The limited findings thus far of the women-specific experience for frontotemporal dementia (FTD) will also be discussed herein while a comprehensive review of the unique experience of vascular dementia and movement disorder-related dementias (e.g., Parkinson's dementia, Lewy body dementia) in women is provided in Chaps. 3 and 6, respectively.

Alzheimer's Disease (AD)

AD is characterized by a progressive cognitive decline with memory impairment typically being the earliest and most pronounced clinical feature, followed by declines in executive functions and language, and eventually extending to all cognitive domains (2024 Alzheimer's Disease Facts and Figures, 2024). AD ultimately leads to a loss of autonomy (2024 Alzheimer's Disease Facts and Figures, 2024); however, in some cases, depending on etiology, symptoms can be treated, and progression slowed to extend the quality of life for affected individuals. AD is the most common cause of dementia, accounting for 50–70% of cases (*Dementia - Key Facts*, 2023). In consequence, AD is considered one of the greatest healthcare challenges of the twenty-first century (Alzheimer's Disease International et al., 2015). Women are at the epicenter of the AD epidemic, as they comprise two thirds of AD dementia cases (2017 Alzheimer's Disease Facts and Figures, 2017). Therefore, the study of women-specific health factors across the lifespan is needed to further understand the risk/protective factors and mechanisms that contribute to the disease in this highest risk group.

Over the years, researchers have identified many changes in the brain that may contribute to AD. The two hallmark pathologies of AD are the abnormal protein aggregations of amyloid-β (Aβ) plaques and hyperphosphorylated tau that comprise the neurofibrillary tangles (NFTs). It is the tau pathology that is more closely linked to cognitive function with the earliest NFT deposition occurring in brain regions responsible for memory function including the medial temporal lobe structures of the hippocampus and entorhinal cortex (Weintraub et al., 2012). Other defining features of AD include neuronal and synaptic loss and glial proliferation (Ball et al., 1997; Dubois et al., 2016; Montine et al., 2012; Sperling et al., 2011). Importantly, AD pathology typically occurs in conjunction with other dementia pathology types, particularly vascular dementia pathologies, and often labeled as "mixed dementia". Pure AD and vascular dementia pathology are present in as few as 10% of patients (Iadecola, 2013; Rizzi et al., 2014). Women have more mixed AD and cerebrovascular pathology than men (Barnes et al., 2019).

Aβ plaques may damage neurons by interfering with neural synapses and activating immune cells triggering neuroinflammation. Inside neurons, tau tangles block the transportation of nutrients and other molecules essential for the normal function and survival of neurons. Longitudinal models of the temporal order of these markers have hypothesized that Aβ plaque accumulation is an early initiating event in the AD cascade (Hardy & Selkoe, 2002), followed by the spread of tau within the medial temporal lobe into neocortex that synergistically leads to neuronal and synaptic loss followed by cognitive decline and dementia (Jack et al., 2013; Price & Morris, 1999). However, the mechanisms by which these pathological aggregations influence neuronal integrity and clinical symptoms remain unclear.

AD has been classically conceptualized and diagnosed as a clinical pathological syndrome. Accordingly, initial diagnostic criteria only considered a "definite" AD diagnosis when post-mortem confirmation was available (Snyder et al., 2016). Otherwise, a "probable" AD diagnosis was provided that only required the presence of a clinical picture of dementia after ruling out other potential etiologies. However, in the last decades, the identification of AD biomarkers either in cerebrospinal fluid or blood or via neuroimaging has enabled a shift in AD diagnosis from a clinical–pathological entity toward a clinical biological one (Pais et al., 2023)

AD is defined as a continuum that can be divided into three stages: preclinical, mild cognitive impairment (MCI), and AD dementia. Prospective clinical and biomarker studies have shown that AD pathology is present 10–20 years before symptoms of the disease emerge (Sutphen et al., 2015; Villemagne et al., 2011). This silent stage of AD, when AD biomarkers indicate the presence of AD pathology but there is no or only subtle cognitive impairment, has been termed "preclinical AD" (Sperling et al., 2011). MCI is characterized by mild cognitive deficits that are not severe enough to interfere with everyday function. Amnestic MCI (aMCI) is a subtype of MCI that is characterized by episodic memory deficits and is specifically linked to a higher risk of progression to AD dementia. In the DSM-5-TR, the diagnosis of mild neurocognitive disorder was introduced (American Psychiatric Association, 2022). Similar to MCI, mild neurocognitive disorder also represents mild cognitive deficits; however, it is defined based on decline from a prior measure of cognitive function. Measurement of AD biomarkers can be used with cognitive testing and MCI classification to help distinguish MCI due to AD from other causes of cognitive decline; thereby, improving diagnostic accuracy and guiding more targeted treatment and intervention strategies. While AD refers to the trajectory of the disease or pathological process that takes years to develop and progress, AD dementia refers to a late-stage, detrimental outcome of this disease (Ward et al., 2013).

Epidemiology of Alzheimer's Disease

Currently, there are 6.9 million AD dementia cases in the U.S. (2024 Alzheimer's Disease Facts and Figures, 2024). Barring any breakthroughs in research leading to a cure, estimated global dementia cases are expected to almost double every 20 years, increasing from 55 million in 2021 to 78 million cases in 2030 and 139 million in 2050 (*ADI - Reports & Resources*, n.d.). The rising prevalence of dementia is due to increased life expectancy leading to greater numbers of older adults. U.S. AD dementia prevalence increases with age, more than doubling with each 10-year age band age 65–85+: 5% of people ages 65–74 years; 13% of those 75–84 years; and 33% of those 85 years or older (2024 Alzheimer's Disease Facts and Figures, 2024). Global patterns in overall dementia prevalence mirror this age-related pattern (World Health Organization, 2021). While dementia is growing globally, the greatest increases will occur in low- and middle-income countries (Gauthier et al., 2021). Table 5.3 provides an overview of the gender differences in prevalence rates for AD.

It is well known that women bear the greatest burden of this disease as they represent 55% of the U.S. population 65 years or older and yet represent 67% of U.S. AD dementia cases aged 65 years or older (2024 Alzheimer's Disease Facts and Figures, 2024). Among U.S. adults aged 65+ years, AD dementia prevalence is 11% of women and 9% of men. Globally, dementia prevalence is greater in women vs. men across all age bands from age 65 years up (World Health Organization, 2021) (Table 5.1). Conversely, studies commonly report a higher prevalence of MCI, the precursor AD stage, in men vs. women (Brodaty et al., 2013; Roberts et al., 2012). Potential reasons for this paradox are discussed in the section titled, *Gender Differences in Diagnosis and Prognosis of Alzheimer's Disease*. Studies examining rates of AD in transgender adults are sparse; however, the limited evidence indicates higher prevalence and risk of AD and subjective cognitive decline in transgender versus cisgender older adults (Flatt et al., 2021; Guo et al., 2022). In a study examining electronic health records and claims data from the OneFlorida Clinical Research Consortium among 1784 older (age $\geq$ 50 years) transgender adults and a matched cisgender control group, Kingdom found that the prevalence of AD and related dementias was 3.5% in the transgender adults versus 2.2% in cisgender controls and this difference was a statistical trend ($p = 0.067$; Guo et al., 2022). Using data from the 2019 Behavioral Risk Factor Surveillance System, cisgender and transgender groups were age-matched by gender and dementia risk scores a matched-cohort approach was used to develop sex and gender identity cohorts (cisgender men, cisgender women, transgender men, transgender women, and non-binary adults) for comparison. Dementia risk scores were calculated using established mid-life and late-life risk score algorithms and the late-life dementia risk scores were significantly higher in transgender men and women, and non-binary compared to both cisgender men and women (Brady et al., 2023). This disparity highlights the pressing need for more research on AD risk in the transgender community along with the unique AD risk factors among the aging transgender and other sexual/gender minority populations.

Table 5.1 Gender differences in the risk and protective factors for Alzheimer's disease

Factor	Influence on dementia	Gender differences	
Low education	Low early-life education is strongly associated with a higher risk of dementia due to lower cognitive reserve	W > M	Gender norms historically limited women's education access, especially in low- and middle-income countries
Physical activity and exercise	Physical activity protects brain health by promoting blood flow and reducing the risk of obesity, diabetes, and cardiovascular disease	W > M	Women tend to experience greater cognitive benefits from exercise than men, particularly for executive function and hippocampal volume, but not consistently
Stress	High lifetime stress is linked with poorer cognitive performance and/or faster longitudinal cognitive decline	W > M	Women report higher stress levels than men, possibly explaining part of the gender disparity in dementia rates
Depression	Depression increases risk for AD and vascular dementia	W > M	Depression rates are twice as high in women
APOE genotype	The *APOE*-ε4 allele increases the risk of AD and lowers age at onset	W > M	Women who carry the APOE-ε4 allele have higher risk than men who carry this allele
Marital status	Being married tends to be associated with a lower risk for developing dementia	W < M	Married status is less protective of AD risk in women versus men
Dementia caregiving	Long-term caregiving is associated with stress, poorer health outcomes, and potentially cognitive decline	W > M	Women represent 60% of primary caregivers for people with dementia and report higher caregiving burden than men caregivers, with potential cognitive effects

Overall, evidence regarding gender differences in AD dementia risk suggests that incidence is greater in women than men, especially among older adults aged 80+ years. Results from a meta-analysis of 11 European cohorts from Denmark, France, Greece, Italy, Spain, Sweden, and the United Kingdom found that incidence in women was 13.25 cases per 1000 person-years (95% confidence interval (CI), 12.05–14.51) vs. 7.02 cases per 1000 person-years (95% CI, 6.06–8.05) in men (Niu et al., 2017). A meta-analysis of 16 cohorts in Asia, Australia, Europe, and North and South America similarly found that incidence of AD was non-significantly greater in women. Though differences were not significant, the effect sizes were notable suggesting that many existing studies were not statistically powered to test for gender differences (Fiest et al., 2016).

Women's lifetime risk of AD dementia is also greater than men's. Assuming survival to age 65 years, women have a 21.1% risk of developing AD dementia vs. men's 11.6% risk (Chêne et al., 2015). This difference in risk may be due in part to women's greater longevity (Bureau, 2021) or selective survival by gender (e.g., men die younger due to cardiovascular disease, a factor which is also related to dementia; Shaw et al., 2021), but these factors are unlikely to fully explain gender-based differences. Women also represent the majority of AD dementia care partners, both in the U.S. and globally (Alzheimer's Association, 2024).

Alzheimer's Disease Rates Across Race/Ethnicity by Gender Groups

In addition to gender, there are a variety of factors associated with disparities in dementia risk, including race/ethnicity, socioeconomic status, environment, culture, geographic location, and sexual orientation. Individuals who are non-White, less educated, rural-dwelling and with fewer economic resources and limited access to quality healthcare bear a disproportionate burden of dementia. In terms of race/ethnicity, there are stark differences in dementia prevalence. Compared to non-Hispanic/Latinx Whites, the risk of AD is two times higher in Black/African Americans and 1.5 times higher in Hispanic/Latinx Americans (Alzheimer's Association, 2024; Rajan et al., 2021). In an epidemiological study of dementia incidence in the U.S. from 2000 to 2013, incidence was highest for Black/African Americans (26.6/1000 person-years) and American Indian/Alaska Native (22.2/1000 person-years); intermediate for Hispanic/Latinx (19.6/1000 person-years), Pacific Islanders (19.6/1000 person-years), and Whites (19.3/1000 person-years) and lowest among Asian-Americans (15.2/1000 person-years; Mayeda et al., 2020). How gender differences may differ by ethnoracial group requires an understanding of how systems of oppression overlap to multiply disadvantage to some groups, and this is critical for understanding risk stratification and development of appropriate interventions. We consider such intersectional perspectives further in a later section titled, *Current State of Gender-Based Dementia Research and Remaining Questions.*

The precise reasons for the increased burden of dementia in the Black/African American, American Indian/Alaska Native, and Hispanic/Latinx communities are unknown but believed to be driven by structural/ social determinants of health (S/SDOH) unique to marginalized communities including discrimination, environmental risks, individual and structural racism and barriers to quality education and healthcare (Stradford et al., 2024; Zsembik & Peek, 2001). The higher risk of AD in women has the potential of intersecting with these various levels of disparities leading to multiple layers of disadvantage and compounding dementia risk. For example, Black/African American women are an exceptionally high-risk group for AD as demonstrated by Matthews et al. (2019) who examined AD prevalence rates by gender and race/ethnicity (African American, Hispanic/Latinx, non-Hispanic white, American Indian and Alaska Native and Asian and Pacific Islander) among Medicare Fee-for-Service beneficiaries aged 65 years or more. Among these groups, they found that AD prevalence is highest in Black/African American women and second highest in Hispanic/Latinx women.

Interestingly, studies within Australian and Canadian Indigenous populations show that the gender disparity in dementia is actually reversed with men showing higher rates of cognitive decline and dementia than women (R. Henderson et al., 2024; Jacklin et al., 2012; Lavrencic et al., 2022; Smith et al., 2008). Underscoring the importance of gender-related sociocultural factors in dementia disparities, the authors speculate that this may be due to the higher rates of the dementia risk factors of head injury, heavy alcohol use, history of police custody or incarceration, and low education in men versus women in this community (Lavrencic et al., 2022).

Gender Differences in Alzheimer's Disease Clinical Presentation

The clinical trajectory and symptom presentation of AD is yet another aspect of the disease that shows gender differences, and these differences seem to depend on disease stage. In the preclinical to early MCI phase, studies suggest that women actually have a cognitive advantage over men (Caldwell et al., 2017, 2019; Sundermann, Biegon, et al., 2016; Sundermann et al., 2017, 2020; Sundermann, Maki, et al., 2016), particularly in the domain of verbal memory. However, among individuals with MCI, women tend to show more rapid decline than men (Holland et al., 2013; Lin et al., 2015). This pattern of findings is depicted in Fig. 5.1 and suggestive of a waterfall effect in women whereby they are better able to sustain normal cognitive function than men in early AD stages; however, once a tipping point of pathology burden is reached, women are no longer able to compensate and accelerated cognitive decline begins.

To help us understand these gender differences in the clinical presentation of AD, it is important to understand how women and men differ on average in terms of healthy cognitive function. It is well established that gender differences in cognitive abilities occur across the lifespan. Men typically have an advantage in visuospatial abilities, mathematical reasoning, and gross motor skills, whereas women tend to excel at tasks involving verbal and fine motor skills and processing speed (Elst et al., 2005; Halari et al., 2005; J. H. Kramer et al., 1988; Mann et al., 1990; Mous et al., 2017; Snow & Weinstock, 1990). In terms of verbal skills, the female advantage in verbal memory, memory for verbally presented material (e.g., stories, word lists), has been reliably demonstrated across the adult lifespan (Elst et al., 2005) as well as in children (J. H. Kramer et al., 1997; Mous et al., 2017).

Because these gender differences are observed across the lifespan, a prevailing theory is that these differences are rooted in the organizational effects of sex hormones on brain development in utero (Gurvich et al., 2018; Halari et al., 2005). Another possibility is that sociocultural factors of disparities in educational and recreational exposures, as well as differences in social cues encountered during childhood may contribute to gender differences in cognition (McCarthy & Konkle, 2005). Although the female advantage in verbal memory is beneficial to women, ironically, it may put women at a disadvantage in terms of detecting AD and intervening at the earliest stages. This is because memory is a cognitive domain that shows the earliest and most pronounced deficits in AD and, therefore, clinical tests of verbal memory are commonly used in MCI and AD diagnostic criteria. Despite the gender difference in verbal memory, the normative data and cut-points for impairment on our clinical tests of verbal memory typically account for the influence of age and education, but not sex, which likely has implications for the clinical detection of MCI and AD.

It is hypothesized that the female advantage in verbal memory enables women to sustain "normal" memory performance, as defined by our clinical cut-points, despite advancing AD neuropathology and delaying an MCI diagnosis until a more advanced disease state compared to men. However, once AD pathology reaches a level of severity at which women are no longer able to compensate and sustain their memory function, they tend to decline faster than men as the disease is more advanced.

In support of this theory, a series of studies across AD biomarkers (hippocampal atrophy, brain glucose hypometabolism, Aβ plaque burden, pathological tau burden) report that women sustain their verbal memory advantage over men despite evidence of moderate AD pathology, but women show a greater decrease in verbal memory when comparing those with severe versus mild/moderate AD pathology suggestive of a more rapid decline in women (Caldwell et al., 2019; Digma et al., 2020; Sundermann, Biegon, et al., 2016; Sundermann et al., 2017; Sundermann, Maki, et al., 2016). This more aggressive profile of late-stage AD in women is supported by an autopsy study that found that AD pathology is more likely to be clinically expressed as dementia in women than in men among 141 postmortem cases with antemortem cognitive data (Barnes et al., 2005). The clinical implications of a delayed onset of clinically evident memory impairment in women are weighty as it limits the opportunity for early diagnosis and intervention when our currently available pharmaceutical and non-pharmaceutical interventions have the greatest potential of altering the disease course and life planning is better implemented.

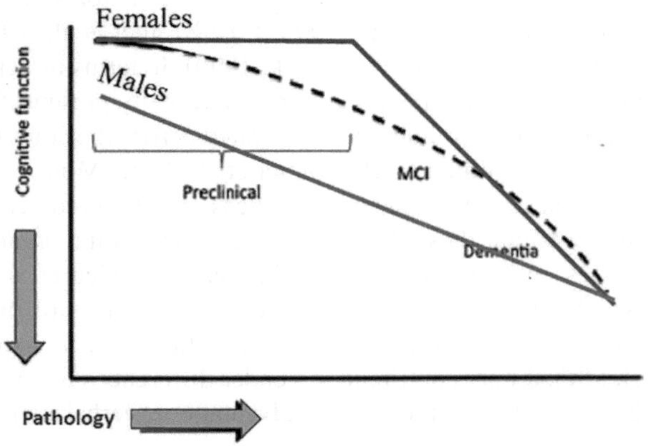

Fig. 5.1 Gender differences in the clinical presentation of Alzheimer's disease by disease stage

Gender Differences in Risk and Protective Factors for Dementia

Education

Education may be associated with late-life cognition both via education duration and quality and is thought to impart its benefits to cognition by increasing cognitive reserve (Clouston et al., 2020; Stern, 2002). Low early-life education is strongly associated with greater risk of later-life dementia (Caamaño-Isorna et al., 2006). A meta-analysis of 14 studies found a relative risk (RR) of 1.80 (95% CI: 1.43, 2.27) of AD dementia and 1.59 (1.26, 2.01) of all-cause dementia for those with low vs. high education. Lower education quality is also associated with poor late-life cognitive performance and incident dementia (Seblova et al., 2023; Soh et al., 2023). In the Project Talent Aging Study, in which participants originally recruited from 42 states in the U.S. during high school were also followed up on later life ($N = 2289$; mean age, years: 74.8±1.2; 52.6% women; 80.3% non-Hispanic White, 10.6% non-Hispanic Black, 3.3% Hispanic, and 4.5% Asian), some associations of high school education quality indicators with late-life cognition were driven by women vs. men, though this was inconsistent (Seblova et al., 2023).

It is likely that gender-based differences in dementia related to education are due to gender norms in which women have historically been given less access to education, and this is still the case for many women and girls in low- and middle-income countries and conflict settings. Low education is more common in low- and middle-income countries overall, and thus intervening to reduce or remove this risk factor would have a larger population level benefit on dementia in such countries (Livingston et al., 2024; Shaaban & Rosso, 2024).

Physical Activity and Exercise

Physical activity is defined as any bodily movement that results in energy expenditure (e.g., occupational, sports, household activities), whereas exercise is a subset of physical activity that is planned, structured, and repetitive with the goal of improving or maintaining physical fitness (Caspersen et al., 1985). Sedentary behavior and the related cardiovascular risk factors of obesity (Kim et al., 2017), diabetes (Colberg et al., 2010), and cardiovascular diseases (Carnethon, 2009) are some of the strongest and well-evidenced risk factors for dementia (Meng et al., 2020). A key reason for this is that our brains are massively vascularized organs and healthy blood flow to the brain is crucial for the delivery of oxygen and nutrients essential for neuron function and overall brain health, while also removing waste products. Physical activity/exercise also helps to improve sleep and mood and reduce inflammation (Pujari, 2024) and, thus, serves as a multi-benefit lifestyle factor for brain health.

A growing body of literature indicates that physical activity and related cardiovascular risk factors do not impact women's and men's brains equally, although the direction of effects varies depending on the specific risk factor and brain health outcome examined (Barha et al., 2017; Dufouil et al., 2014; A. F. Kramer & Colcombe, 2018; Meng et al., 2020). Some evidence suggests that women benefit more cognitively from exercise compared to men (Barha et al., 2017; Dufouil et al., 2014; A. F. Kramer & Colcombe, 2018). Furthermore, multimodal exercise, including aerobic and resistance training, has been shown to benefit women more, especially in executive function performance (Barha et al., 2017, 2020). Research also indicates that daily walking may have structural benefits to the hippocampus, particularly in women (Varma et al., 2016). On the other hand, some studies have reported that men experience more exercise-related benefits in hippocampal volume (Carlson et al., 2015), global cognitive function, and executive functioning (Lindwall et al., 2008; Tolppanen et al., 2015). Discrepancies in the benefits of exercise may be partly explained by gender roles, as women generally exercise less than men over their lifespans (Mielke et al., 2022) and may have a greater influence by factors such as parenthood and caregiving (Nomaguchi & Bianchi, 2004; Verhoef et al., 1992). The understanding of potential moderators such as biological sex and gender will help in developing more targeted and effective exercise-based interventions for AD prevention in the future.

Stress

Results from community-based studies of older adults suggest that greater stress is associated with poorer cognitive performance at baseline and/or faster longitudinal decline in global cognition, episodic memory, executive function, and visuospatial ability (Aggarwal et al., 2014; Troxel et al., 2024; Turner et al., 2017). While associations of stress with cognition did not vary by gender or race in a study of Black/African American and White older adults, women reported greater levels of stress than men and Black/African American participants reported greater levels of stress than White participants indicating that stress may be an explanatory pathway for gender and racial disparities in dementia (Aggarwal et al., 2014). Although associations of stress with poorer cognitive performance were found, the Think PHRESH study found that stress was not associated with clinically adjudicated cognitive impairment (MCI or dementia) among Black/African American older adults (N = 204 Black/African American adults; mean age, years: 63.7±9.3; 78.6% women; Troxel et al., 2024).

Studies including childhood and midlife data suggest the need for a life course approach to understand associations of stress with late-life cognition and dementia and that cumulative lifetime stress exposures are important to consider. For example, analyses carried out in a midlife U.S. cohort found that greater cumulative stress as well as stress in childhood alone and stress in adulthood alone, were associated with poorer baseline global cognition, episodic memory, and executive function and slower global and executive decline (R. Chen et al., 2022; D'Amico et al., 2023), Furthermore, exploratory analyses suggested these relationships were present in women, but not in men (D'Amico et al., 2023). Emerging evidence from a Spanish study of cognitively unimpaired adults aged 48–77 years (99% White, 61% women) suggests possible mechanistic pathways of these associations. The study found that early and midlife stressful events are associated with Alzheimer's Disease and Related Dementias (ADRD) pathologies such as CNS inflammation, plasma p-tau_{181}, and neurodegeneration (Palpatzis et al., 2024). Gender differences were found in this study such that stressful events were associated with brain amyloid accumulation in men and more neurodegeneration in women (Palpatzis et al., 2024).

Depression

Meta-analyses including both men and women document an increased risk of dementia including AD dementia (hazard ratio [HR] ranging from 1.65 to 1.90), vascular dementia (HR: 2.52–2.71), and all cause dementia (HRs ranging from 1.85 to 1.97) associated with depression (Alzheimer's Disease International [ADI], 2014; Diniz et al., 2013; Stafford et al., 2022), with differences not noted by gender when evaluated (Stafford et al., 2022). These studies cannot completely rule out the possibility that part of this relationship is explained by depression being an early symptom of dementia rather than a cause of it, and associations appear stronger for studies linking late-life depression with dementia or for studies with shorter follow-up (Stafford et al., 2022).

However, a recent study using a Danish patient registry suggests associations of depression with later dementia remain strong and significant whether the depression was diagnosed in early, mid, or late-life, and suggests, consistent with the prior studies, that those with a history of depression diagnosis have nearly double the risk of dementia (Elser et al., 2023). This relationship of depression with dementia may be slightly weaker in women than men (Elser et al., 2023). Yet, women have approximately double the odds of a depression diagnosis as men, making depression an important possible source of dementia gender disparities (Salk et al., 2017). Potential mechanisms of the relationship of late-life depression, including both new onset depression in late-life and depression with onset earlier in life, which is recurrent in later life, include factors such as cerebrovascular disease, hypothalamic–pituitary–adrenal (HPA axis) and glucocorticoid changes, and reduced brain and cognitive reserve (Butters et al., 2008). Gender differences in the relation of depression and AD, as well as mechanisms have been recently reviewed (Y.-H. Chen et al., 2024).

APOE *Genotype*

The ε4 allele of the apolipoprotein E (*APOE-ε4*) gene is the strongest genetic risk factor for late-onset AD, which often confers its risk in individuals aged 65 years and older (Blacker et al., 1997). The human APOE gene exists as three polymorphic alleles (ε2, ε3, and ε4) which have a worldwide frequency in healthy Caucasians of 8.4%, 77.9% and 13.7%, respectively, across ages between 40 and 90 years. However, the frequency of the ε4 allele dramatically increases to ~40%, in patients with AD (Farrer et al., 1997). The *APOE* protein is involved in the transport of cholesterol and other lipids in the periphery of the brain (Caspersen et al., 1985). The human *APOE* gene exists as three polymorphic alleles, ε2, ε3, and ε4 with frequencies in the global population of 8.4%, 77.9% and 13.7%, respectively (Farrer et al., 1997). Each individual has a combination of two *APOE* alleles (one from the paternal side and one from the maternal side) leading to a variety of combinations among the ε2, ε3, and ε4 alleles.

While the infrequent ε2 allele has a protective effect against AD, the ε4 allele increases risk and the ε3 allele is risk neutral. A large body of evidence indicates that women are more vulnerable to the adverse effects of *APOE*- ε4 on AD risk. A meta-analytic study across nearly 58,000 older adults from 12 research institutions in the Global Alzheimer's Association Interactive Network (from North America, Europe, Asia, and Australia) found that women with *ε3/ε4* have a higher age-specific odds ratio of AD than men with the same *APOE* genotype between 65 and 75 years (4.4 times increased odds of AD in women vs. 3.8 increased odds in men; Neu et al., 2017). The authors suggest that the mechanisms that underlie these gender differences may be linked to physiologic changes associated with menopause and estrogen loss that begins at a mean age of 51 years (McKinlay et al., 1992) just prior to when pathogenesis is believed to commence in the AD trajectory. Furthermore, the presence of an *APOE*-ε4 allele significantly increases the risk of AD and lowers the age of onset in a dose-dependent manner based on gender (Caspersen et al., 1985; C.-C. Liu et al., 2013). The more deleterious effect of APOE-ε4 in women versus men has been shown to be driven more so by ε3/ε4 heterozygotes than ε4/ε4 homozygotes (Payami et al., 1994; Poirier et al., 1993). Specifically, a meta-analysis by Farrer et al. (1997) that collected *APOE* genotype across 40 research teams using clinical, community, and brain bank sources and including White, Black/African American, Hispanic/Latinx, and Japanese individuals showed that compared to the ε3/ε3 genotype, the ε3/ε4 genotype was associated with a 4-fold increased risk of AD in women and a 1.5 increased risk in men.

Furthermore, women ε4 carriers are significantly more likely to convert from MCI to AD than men. An analysis of over 5400 clinically normal participants from the National Alzheimer's Coordinating Center (NACC) and the Alzheimer's Disease Neuroimaging Initiative (ADNI) (mean aged 73.0, 64% women) found that the risk of clinical conversion conferred by the ε4 allele was significantly greater in women than men (Altmann et al., 2014).

While the reasons for the more adverse effect of the *APOE*-ε4 allele in women are not fully understood, various research groups suggest that *APOE*-ε4 females may exhibit higher levels of AD pathology, compromising brain network integrity, and/or accelerating long-term decline relative to their level of AD pathology (Altmann et al., 2014; Caspersen et al., 1985; Heise et al., 2014; Sampedro et al., 2015). Some evidence suggests that this gender disparity in the level of AD pathology may be due to an interaction between the *APOE*-ε4 genotype and the sex hormone estrogen (Kang & Grodstein, 2012; Yaffe et al., 2000). Evidence of this possibility is discussed below in the *Menopause Hormone Therapy* section.

Marital Status

The association between marital status and risk for dementia differs by gender, whereby women who have never married or are widowed have a lower risk of developing AD compared to men (Najar et al., 2021; Pankratz et al., 2015; Van Gelder et al., 2006). This observation may be due to the historical responsibility of women for the healthcare of their family, ensuring that their family members receive regular checkups and maintain a healthy diet sometimes at the expense of their own health (Rosende-Roca et al., 2021). Moreover, compared to single men, single women are more likely than men to seek healthcare and participate in social activities, which are beneficial for cognition (H. Liu et al., 2020; Nebel et al., 2018; K. Williams & Umberson, 2004). An important question yet to be addressed is how marital status influences risk of dementia among the LGBTQ population. While some data suggest that the risk of MCI and dementia is similar among older adults in same-sex relationship versus adults in opposite sex relationships in the U.S. (Perales-Puchalt et al., 2019), it remains unknown how risk of dementia may differ for LGBTQ individuals based on martial or partnership status.

Caregiving Patterns

A diagnosis of dementia has a profound impact not only on the individuals with the condition but also on their family and friends. The emergence and progression of dementia, along with the challenges and new responsibilities it brings, often lead to changes in family dynamics (Teel & Carson, 2003). Women are often the primary caregivers for people with dementia, providing the majority of informal care globally, estimated at 55–91% (Wimo et al., 2018). In the U.S., around 65% of the more than 15 million unpaid caregivers for individuals with AD are women (Alzheimer & Association, 2009). Additionally, women caregivers experience a higher level of burden compared to men caregivers (Gallicchio et al., 2002).

Because dementia typically lasts for 5–15 years and the nature of symptoms is variable, a caregiver must learn to adapt continually to the patient's needs (Carter et al., 2012), which has consequences for health, relationships, and financial status. Several studies have explored the impact of caregiving on physical and emotional health and well-being. Informal caregivers for patients with dementia suffer more significant stress with elevated levels of cortisol than other types of caregivers (Allen et al., 2017; Dauphinot et al., 2015; Godfrey & Warshaw, 2009; World Health Organization, 2011), and impaired attention and executive function (Allen et al., 2017). There is a hypothesis that spousal caregivers may have a higher risk of cognitive impairment or dementia compared to non-caregiver spouses due to various factors such as psychosocial issues (e.g., depression, social isolation, and sleep problems), life-style factors (such as exercise and diet), and physiological variables (like metabolic syndrome and inflammation; Vitaliano et al., 2011).

The differences between women and men in caregiver health outcomes are underexplored. Women caregivers tend to experience higher levels of depression and anxiety (H. D. Davies et al., 2012; Gallicchio et al., 2002; Ma et al., 2018) as well as higher levels of burden as a result of an imbalance of care demands relatives to caregiver's role (social time, physical and emotional states or financial resources) (Papastavrou et al., 2009) compared to men caregivers. Additionally, nearly three-quarters of women caregivers express concerns about the ability to maintain their own physical and mental health since taking on the caregiving role (Alzheimer's Association, 2022; Peacock et al., 2020).

Women caregivers are also likely to face adverse consequences in the workplace due to their caregiving duties. Using data from the 1984 and 1987 National Longitudinal Surveys of Mature Women, including more than 5000 women aged between 30 and 44 years, Pavalko and Artis (1997) investigated the causal relationship between women's caregiving responsibilities and paid employment. Their findings indicated that employment status did not influence whether women decided to take on caregiving roles. However, once women became caregivers, they were more likely to reduce their paid working hours or exit the workforce. Furthermore, ending caregiving duties did not lead to an increase in their work hours, implying challenges in regaining the employment opportunities lost during midlife (Pavalko & Artis, 1997). Overall, more research, including longitudinal studies, is needed to understand the long-term impact of the dementia journey on the brain health of women caregivers (Rosie et al., 2015).

Regarding sexual and gender minority (SGM) caregivers, previous literature found that SGM caregivers experience higher levels of stress, health disparities, and discrimination compared to non-SGM caregivers. SGM caregivers reported greater psychological distress and feelings of isolation, partly due to a lack of targeted support and inclusivity in caregiving resources (Anderson et al., 2021). (Table 5.1)

Women-Specific Risk Factors for Dementia

Pregnancy

The impact of pregnancy on the risk of dementia and cognitive decline later in life is not yet fully understood, with inconsistencies in the literature. Some studies suggest that a higher number of pregnancies are associated with poorer late-life cognition (Jung et al., 2020; Ptok et al., 2002), higher risk of cognitive decline (Lee et al.,

2024; L. Zhou et al., 2024) and MCI (Xi et al., 2022), greater AD pathology (Beeri et al., 2009), and an earlier onset of AD (Colucci et al., 2006; Sobow & Kloszewska, 2004). Among 9756 nondemented and community-dwelling older women from six population-based, prospective cohort studies from four European and two Asian countries, grand multiparity (five or more parities) increased the risk of dementia by 30% compared to 1–4 parities; however, parity was not associated specifically with AD (Bae et al., 2020). In contrast, among 7100 older (age $\geq$ 65 years) women from the Women's Health Initiative Memory Study, higher parity was associated with reduced risk for MCI/dementia and less cognitive decline (R. Zhou et al., 2022). In a cross-sectional study with 95 British women, a higher number of months spent pregnant in the lifetime was associated with a 20% reduced risk of AD (Fox et al., 2018). Interestingly, among 273,240 women and 228,957 men from the U.K. Biobank cohort, having 2 children was associated with a slightly lower dementia risk compared to having no or 4 or more children, suggesting that the relationship between parity and dementia risk may not be linear (Gong et al., 2022). The fact that the relationship between number of children and dementia risk was similar between men and women suggests that psychosocial factors associated with parenting are likely contributors to this relationship that are important to account for.

Pregnancy complications are also linked to a higher risk of AD. Hypertensive disorders of pregnancy, including gestational hypertension and preeclampsia, are associated with brain atrophy and cognitive decline detected as early as 5–15 years after the pregnancy (Mielke et al., 2016; Shaaban et al., 2021; Siepmann et al., 2017; Wiegman et al., 2014) and with higher risk for dementia (Andolf et al., 2017; Basit et al., 2018; Garovic et al., 2020; Schliep et al., 2023). See Chap. 3 (Stroke and Vascular Dementia) for more details about the relationship between hypertensive disorders of pregnancy and overall vascular risk.

The biological mechanisms connecting pregnancy and dementia risk are unclear. One overarching hypothesis suggests that women who spend more time pregnant in their lives will experience a reduction in AD risk via improvement in immunoregulation caused by a dramatic increase in T-regulatory cells during the first trimester followed by more gradual increases for at least a year post-partum (Fox et al., 2018; Heikkinen et al., 2004; Lima et al., 2017; Somerset et al., 2004). Relatedly, evidence suggests that pregnancy induces protection and relief from autoimmune diseases (Buyon, 1998). Pregnancy-related immune adaptations, together with endocrinological changes, may impact maternal brain plasticity during pregnancy and the postpartum period, potentially influencing the trajectory of neurobiological aging (Barth & de Lange, 2020) later in life. However, other mechanisms involving social factors and modifiable risk factors of AD related to parenting should be considered (Callaghan et al., 2024; Giudicessi et al., 2022). In this regard, a recent cross-sectional study with 1016 cognitively unimpaired women from the National Health and Nutrition Examination study found an association between greater number of term pregnancies and worse cognitive performance and that this association was partially mediated by socioeconomical status (Giudicessi et al., 2022).

These studies highlight the importance of acknowledging and understanding the long-term implications of both the biological and psychosocial aspects of parity on brain health and dementia risk in women. By understanding these links, we can better understand dementia etiology, assess dementia risk and develop targeted risk reduction and treatment strategies in women (Galea et al., 2018).

Menopause

The timing of menopause shows an impact on the risk of dementia. An earlier age at menopause occurring spontaneously, before 45 years old, is associated with cognitive decline (Kuh et al., 2018; Lindseth et al., 2022). Early or premature menopause is often caused by the surgical removal of the ovaries, i.e., bilateral oophorectomy, prior to the natural cessation of ovarian function for medical reasons such as ovarian cancer, endometriosis or uterine fibroids (Sochocka et al., 2023). Multiple studies show associations between surgical menopause and cognitive decline and increased risk of dementia (Georgakis et al., 2019; Gervais et al., 2020; Phung et al., 2010; Rocca et al., 2011). Specifically, in a study by Gervais et al. (2020), bilateral oophorectomy was associated with an increased AD risk by up to 70%. Further, an earlier age at menopause due to surgical menopause is associated with lower gray matter volume in the medial temporal lobe (Zeydan et al., 2019), higher white matter hyperintensities load (Lohner et al., 2022), and greater neuropathological burden (Bove et al., 2014; Coughlan et al., 2023; Rahman et al., 2020) than spontaneous menopause.

The effects of menopause transition on AD risk are also highlighted by neuroimaging studies. These studies have shown that women in midlife, during perimenopause and postmenopause, who have family history of AD, exhibit increased AD biomarkers, including higher Aβ deposition (Mosconi et al., 2017, 2018, 2021), brain glucose hypometabolism (Mosconi et al., 2017, 2018), and gray matter loss in AD-vulnerable regions (Mosconi et al., 2017, 2018, 2021; Schelbaum et al., 2021) compared to premenopausal women and age-matched men. Additionally, Aβ deposition is found to be exacerbated in postmenopausal, women *APOE-ε4* carriers compared to premenopausal and perimenopausal, women *APOE-ε4* carriers (Mosconi et al., 2017). With the hypothesized model of the AD trajectory in mind, it is notable that the timing of menopause aligns with the beginning stages of AD pathogenesis (Sperling et al., 2011). It is theorized that menopause and its effects on the brain may exacerbate or accelerate these early pathological processes, potentially increasing the risk of developing AD later in life in women. In this context, growing evidence supports the idea that menopausal transition is an optimal window of opportunity for AD preventive interventions in women (Mosconi & Brinton, 2018).

Menopause Hormone Therapy (MHT)

MHT, often referred to as hormone replacement therapy, relieves the symptoms of menopause by supplementing the body with estrogen, and sometimes progesterone, to replace the diminished levels of ovarian hormones (Sindi et al., 2021). Although there is significant evidence from animal models demonstrating the neuroprotective effects of estrogen (Brinton, 2008; Brinton et al., 2015), the use of MHT for dementia risk reduction has been a topic of controversy due to inconsistent evidence in the literature suggesting both beneficial and harmful (and neutral) effects of MHT on dementia risk. Over the past two decades, several studies have suggested the existence of a critical window or period during which MHT exerts neuroprotective effects, known as the "window of opportunity" hypothesis (V. W. Henderson & Rocca, 2012; Maki, 2008; Maki & Sundermann, 2009; Whitmer et al., 2011; Zandi et al., 2002). This hypothesis implies that the effect of MHT depends on when treatment is initiated, with more beneficial effects likely when treatment starts closer in time to menopause.

A recent meta-analysis covering over 20,000 MHT-treated women found an association between MHT use and risk of AD or dementia, with the association varying based on the timing of initiation and the therapy formulation. In midlife, estrogen-only therapy use was associated with a 32% reduction in dementia risk, while estrogen-plus-progestogen therapy use showed a non-significant 23% risk reduction as compared to non-use. Conversely, late-life use of both formulations was associated with an increased dementia risk, although neither reached statistical significance (Nerattini et al., 2023). These results are in line with previous observational studies, which indicated that introducing MHT in midlife reduced the risk of AD by 22% and the risk of all-cause dementia by 19% (Nerattini et al., 2023).

This evidence was promising and led to the first randomized clinical trial of the effects of MHT on dementia risk in older (aged ≥ 65 years), postmenopausal women conducted by the Women's Health Initiative Memory Study (WHIMS). Specifically, the WHIMS investigated the impact of conjugated equine estrogen (CEE) in women with prior hysterectomy over age 65 years and the impact of CEE combined with progesterone therapy (medroxyprogesterone acetate [MPA]) in naturally postmenopausal women over age 65 years (Shumaker et al., 2003, 2004). The trials were surprisingly stopped prematurely due to a lack of evidence that CEE lowered the risk of all-cause dementia in postmenopausal women with prior hysterectomy (Shumaker et al., 2004) and combination CEE/MPA actually doubled the risk for all-cause dementia among naturally postmenopausal women (Shumaker et al., 2003). This finding came as a shock to many researchers and led to the "window of opportunity" hypothesis as this trial was in women aged 65 years and older whereas most of the earlier observational studies were in women who were closer to the menopause transition. The window of opportunity hypothesis suggests that starting MHT close to the onset of menopause (within about 5 years) may help protect cognitive function, while delaying therapy until later in life could increase the risk of adverse effects on brain health (Maki, 2013; Nerattini et al., 2023; see Fig. 5.2).

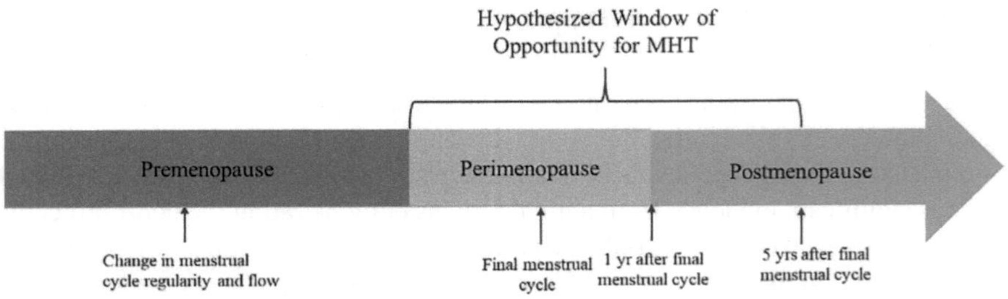

Fig. 5.2 Window of opportunity hypothesis

Consistent with the "window of opportunity" hypothesis, the evidence of a beneficial effect of MHT on dementia risk is most robust and consistent for women who recently underwent surgical menopause and only require estrogen-only therapy as the there is no need for a progesterone to protect the uterus against endometrial hyperplasia (The North American Menopause Society, 2022). However, the "window of opportunity" hypothesis was not supported by some prospective studies that found that MHT use did not benefit cognition in recently postmenopausal women (spontaneous only or combined spontaneous and surgical), although MHT use also did not have an adverse effect on cognition (Ryan et al., 2009; Weber et al., 2014). More long-term follow-up data is needed in these cohorts to examine the "window of opportunity" hypothesis on late-life dementia risk.

Further evidence supports the link between MHT and its impact on cognition and AD biomarkers in postmenopausal women. Research findings indicate that MHT initiated during early postmenopause may help maintain certain cognitive domains, such as verbal memory (LeBlanc et al., 2001; Maki, 2005) as well as learning and processing speed (Maki & Sundermann, 2009). Notably, a recent prospective interventional study involving 224 cognitively unimpaired postmenopausal women who had not previously used MHT, assessed plasma biomarkers of Aβ pathology, tauopathy, and neurodegeneration. The study found that MHT use was linked with lower rates of AD biomarker change as reflected in a smaller reduction in Aβ2/ptau231 ratios, with more pronounced effect in *APOE-e4* allele carrier (Depypere et al., 2023). Therefore, it is essential for future research to focus on gaining a better understanding of MHT efficacy, timing, type, and modality of MHT for timely and precision medicine interventions (Depypere et al., 2023; Sindi et al., 2021).

Other studies have also indicated that the effects of MHT on women's cognition are influenced by *APOE* genotype, although the direction has been inconsistent (Burkhardt et al., 2004; Valen-Sendstad et al., 2010; Yaffe et al., 2000). Some studies report that MHT has a more beneficial effect for ε4 non-carriers. For instance, among 3393 Medicare-eligible women from the Cardiovascular Health Study, past or current estrogen use was associated with reduced risk of developing cognitive impairment and reduced thickening of the common and internal carotid artery walls (named carotid atherosclerosis) only among APOE-ε4 non-carriers (Yaffe et al., 2000). Other studies suggest that MHT reduces AD risk in ε4 carriers (Tang et al., 1996), or have found a beneficial effect of MHT regardless of *APOE* genotype (Zandi et al., 2002). Therefore, more research is essential to uncover the mechanisms behind the stronger effects of the *APOE*-ε4 allele in women and the interaction between *APOE* and endocrine-related health events in women to understand their implications for targeted risk reduction and treatment interventions.

The impact of hormone therapy on dementia risk is especially relevant to the transgender and gender diverse (TGD) population due to the integral role of sex hormones in gender-affirming care (Brady et al., 2023). However, there is limited research exploring the impact of aging on gender-affirming intervention. Increasing evidence suggests that gender-affirming hormone therapies may increase cardiometabolic risk (Aranda et al., 2021; Dutra et al., 2019; Swe et al., 2022), which in turn could contribute to a higher risk of dementia. In contrast, a meta-analysis of 10 studies involving 234 birth-assigned males and 150 birth-assigned females found no evidence to support an adverse impact of gender-affirming hormone therapy on cognitive function. Notably, the analysis revealed a statistically significant improvement in visuospatial ability among birth-assigned females (Karalexi et al., 2020) on gender-affirming hormone therapy. Another cross-sectional study including 73 transgender women and 39 transgender men (age between 56 and 84 years) suggests the importance of accounting for psychological factors when examining the relationships of TGD status and gender-affirming hormone therapy to cognitive function including the high rates of anxiety, depression or loneliness found among TGD individuals (van Heesewijk et al., 2025). Future studies should focus on long-term, longitudinal research to clarify these relationships and inform evidence-based guidelines that support cognitive health and overall well-being in the TGD population (Table 5.2).

Table 5.2 Women-specific risk factors for dementia: key take-home messages

Pregnancy	• The relationship between pregnancy and dementia risk is mixed: some studies link a higher number of pregnancies to poorer cognition, while others report protective effects. • Pregnancy complications like preeclampsia may increase dementia risk.
Menopause	• Early or surgical menopause increases dementia risk, potentially due to loss of neuroprotective hormones. • The menopause is a neurological transition state characterized by changes in brain structure, connectivity, and metabolism that may exacerbate or accelerate early AD pathologic processes.
MHT	• MHT shows neuroprotective effects when started soon after menopause, but it may increase dementia risk if initiated later. • The timing and type of MHT are critical to its potential benefits on cognition and AD risk.

Note. AD = Alzheimer's disease; MHT = menopause hormone therapy

Gender Differences in Diagnosis and Prognosis of Alzheimer's Disease

A Gender Paradox in MCI versus AD Prevalence

There are a couple of contributing factors that may underlie the paradox of higher rates of MCI in men despite the higher rates of AD dementia in women. First, the previously described gender differences in AD clinical trajectory may contribute, whereby the female cognitive advantage in early-stage AD followed by a steeper decline may lead to a delayed diagnosis of MCI and a shorter timespan in the MCI stage. This has motivated development of gender-specific verbal memory norms. In ADNI and the Rush University Memory and Aging Project, Sundermann et al. (2019) showed that when these gender-specific norms are incorporated into the MCI diagnostic criteria, about 10% of women previously classified as cognitively unimpaired, were reclassified as MCI (false negatives), and 10% of men, previously classified as MCI were reclassified as cognitively normal (false positives). The comparison of AD biomarkers and rates of progression to dementia across diagnostic groups suggested that the new diagnostic classification derived from sex-adjusted norms are more accurate (Sundermann et al., 2019, 2021). Moreover, consistent with other studies, the prevalence of MCI was lower in women vs. men when using the conventional MCI diagnostic criteria, but this difference was either eliminated or reversed when using sex-specific diagnostic criteria (Sundermann et al., 2019, 2021).

These results suggest that prior reports of lower MCI rates in women vs. men may be an artifact of the use of non-sex-adjusted in MCI criteria. The incorporation of sex-specific norms into MCI diagnostic criteria may improve diagnostic accuracy and avoid diagnostic errors in approximately 20%. Importantly, applying sex-based norms may help to identify women at an earlier disease stage when they can more likely benefit from the interventional studies that typically recruit MCI individuals. Similarly, Banks et al. (2019) found that women-specific cognitive composites increase the statistical power to detect cognitive changes over time among AD biomarker positive cognitively normal and MCI women and, thus, reduce the sample size needed in clinical trials.

Gender Differences in AD Mortality Rates

Together with incidence and prevalence of a disease, mortality rates and time to death are important epidemiologic measures of disease. Mortality is defined as deaths attributable to disease (Dubal, 2020). Several studies show that women progress to death at a later age than men in both early (Liang et al., 2016; Ueki et al., 2001) and late-onset AD (Lapane et al., 2001). In addition, the rapid progression to death in men is observed to closely correlate with higher rate of cognitive decline

(Hui et al., 2003; Stern et al., 1997). However, Buckley et al. (Buckley, Waller, et al., 2019) examined over 180,000 dementia mortality cases in Australia based on death certificates and found that deaths with AD were higher for women, whereas rates of death with vascular dementia were higher for men. These controversial results highlight the presence of methodological challenges for research examining gender differences in risk of AD, including challenges in measurement, survival bias and competing risks (Buckley, Waller, et al., 2019). A large and in-depth study of over 9000 individuals with probable AD diagnosis in the U.S. found that significant predictors of death in women were those related to disability, an impairment in activities of daily living, malnutrition, and other medical comorbidities. In contrast, significant predictors of AD mortality in men were those related to AD itself, such as dementia severity and presence of delirium episodes (Lapane et al., 2001).

Frontotemporal Dementia (FTD)

Introduction

FTD is one the most common clinical forms of early-onset neurodegenerative disease. FTD clinical syndromes span multiple phenotypes including (a) social and behavioral changes, known as behavioral variant FTD (bvFTD); (b) impairments of speech and language, known as primary progressive aphasia (PPA); (c) extrapyramidal motor disorders including progressive supranuclear palsy-Richard's syndrome (PSP-RS) and corticobasal syndrome (CBS); and (d) pyramidal motor disorders like amyotrophic lateral sclerosis (ALS). Similar to AD, studies show phenotypic and prevalence gender differences in FTD, although much fewer studies have directly interrogated these differences.

Frontotemporal lobar degeneration (FTLD) is the main pathology type responsible for these conditions, accounting for roughly 95% of the clinical FTD syndromes described above. FTLD is divided into two major pathology classes: misfolded tau (FTLD-tau) and TAR DNA-binding protein of ~43 kDa (FTLD-TDP) (Wilson et al., 2023). The main risk factors associated with FTLD include age and family history (Wilson et al., 2023), with mixed results and limited studies on other potential risk factors including sex, race, and geographic variation. Throughout this part of the chapter, we will review the literature on the unique experience of sporadic bvFTD, PPA, and PSP-RS/CBS in women and briefly summarize these FTD types in the following sections.

bvFTD is typically associated with social and personality changes and the underlying pathology can be either FTLD-tau or FTLD-TDP. The two major types of PPA associated with FTLD include non-fluent/agrammatic PPA (nvPPA) and semantic-variant PPA (svPPA). nvPPA is typically associated with deficits in speech (effortful), grammar, and word output, with FTLD-tau as the underlying pathology (Wilson et al., 2023). svPPA includes a progressive disorder of semantic knowledge and naming and is characteristically associated with left anterior temporal lobe atrophy with FTLD-TDP type C as the underlying pathology (Wilson et al., 2023). Finally, PSP is a sporadic neurodegenerative Parkinsonism disorder characterized by predominant axial rigidity, bradykinesia, and supranuclear gaze palsy (Price & Morris, 1999), with histopathologic patterns of widespread glial tau inclusions and neurofibrillary tangles in subcortical gray matter (Villemagne et al., 2011).

Epidemiology

As described above, FTD is less common compared to AD. Consequently, there is a dearth of epidemiological studies examining gender differences in the prevalence and incidence of bvFTD (Onyike & Diehl-Schmid, 2013) (Table 5.1). In a study examining sporadic FTD, defined by those who met clinical diagnostic criteria for probable or definite bvFTD or PPA (Gorno-Tempini et al., 2011; Rascovsky et al., 2011) without a genetic mutation, age of symptom onset was later in women compared to men with FTD, primarily driven by bvFTD and non-fluent/agrammatic PPA syndromes (de Boer et al., 2021). Additionally, sporadic bvFTD was less predominant in women (38.4% women, total bvFTD $N = 654$) compared to genetic bvFTD (47.1%; de Boer et al., 2021). Many other studies have similarly found sporadic bvFTD to have a lower incidence in women compared to men (Diehl & Kurz, 2002; Heuer et al., 2020; Johnson et al., 2005; Pengo et al., 2022; Ratnavalli et al., 2002), although mixed (Onyike & Diehl-Schmid, 2013) and conflicting (Gustafson et al., 2001) results have been reported as well.

nvPPA is typically seen in women, while men have a higher prevalence of svPPA, as described in both clinical (de Boer et al., 2021; Johnson et al., 2005; Pengo et al., 2022; Rogalski et al., 2007) and pathologically confirmed PPA cohorts (Johnson et al., 2005; Spinelli et al., 2017). Similar to the syndromes described above, most studies find a lower incidence of PSP in women (Bower et al., 1997; Chiu et al., 2010; Driver-Dunckley et al., 2023; Litvan, Mangone, et al., 1996; Nasri et al., 2024; Santacruz et al., 1998; Stang et al., 2020), although not all have been pathologically confirmed (D. R. Williams et al., 2005). See Table 5.3 for a summary of gender differences in AD and FTD rates.

Gender Differences in Clinical Presentation

Few studies have interrogated gender differences in clinical symptoms of bvFTD. In a cohort of 216 individuals with definitive bvFTD, a subset of whom had autopsy confirmed FTLD, women with bvFTD had worse atrophy in frontotemporal regions compared to men in the presence of similar clinical characteristics (Illán-Gala et al.,

Table 5.3 Gender-based differences in prevalence rates for Alzheimer's disease and frontotemporal dementia

Type of dementia	Gender with higher prevalence	Notes
Alzheimer's disease	Women	Women represent ~67% of U.S. AD cases in adults 65+; lifetime AD risk is ~21.1% for women versus 11.6% for men.
Behavioral variant frontotemporal dementia	Men (bvFTD)	Sporadic bvFTD has higher incidence and prevalence in men (61.6%) versus women (38.4%) (de Boer et al., 2021).
Primary progressive aphasia	nvPPA: Women; svPPA: Men	nvPPA is more common in women, while svPPA is more common in men (Johnson et al., 2005; Rogalski et al., 2007).
Progressive supranuclear palsy	Men	PSP prevalence is generally higher in men, though findings vary, and not all studies are pathologically confirmed (Driver-Dunckley et al., 2023; Litvan, Mangone et al., 1996; Nasri et al., 2024).

Note. AD = Alzheimer's disease; bvFTD = behavioral variant of frontotemporal dementia; nvPPA = non-fluent/agrammatic variant of primary progressive aphasia; PSP = progressive supraenuclear palsy; svPPA= semantic variant of primary progressive aphasia

2021). Women and men with bvFTD were diagnosed at similar disease stage and had a similar disease trajectory after diagnosis. Overall, for a given amount of atrophy, women performed better than expected on executive function tasks and had fewer changes in apathy, sleep, and appetite, suggesting greater resilience in women (Illán-Gala et al., 2021).

A study from the Northwestern Alzheimer's Disease Center comparing severity of language impairment in men vs. women with PPA found that verbal fluency performance at baseline and rates of decline over time were worse for women, although the difference was not statistically significant (Rogalski et al., 2007). A similar comparison in AD, who on average were older and less educated than the PPA group, did not reveal differences in language test scores by gender at any time point suggesting the uniqueness of this gender disparity to PPA (Rogalski et al., 2007). In another study of a combined cohort of bvFTD and PPA (svPPA and nfPPA) examining neuropsychiatric symptoms, there were no gender differences in overall neuropsychiatric symptoms (Silvestri et al., 2024); however, delusions, hallucinations, and depression were more frequently reported in women, while agitation/aggression, apathy/indifference, and irritability/lability were more frequently reported in men (Silvestri et al., 2024).

A large study of 334 hospital patients in South India with PSP were evaluated on clinical symptoms using the National Institute of Neurological Disorders and Stroke and the Society for PSP criteria (1996) (Litvan, Agid, et al., 1996) and, retrospectively, the Movement Disorders Society criteria for PSP (2017) (Höglinger et al., 2017) to diagnose subtypes. Of note, the clinical syndromes included both PSP-RS, as well as other syndromes including PSP-Parkinsonism, PSP-frontal, PSP-corticobasal syndrome, PSP-speech/language syndrome, and others (Mahale et al., 2022). Falls within one year, apathy, executive dysfunction, and pyramidal signs (hyperreflexia) were more frequent in women, while there was no difference on other motor symptoms like rigidity, bradykinesia, dystonia, apraxia, or vertical saccade slowing and gaze palsy. Finally, women were more likely to reach aphasia, and severe dysphagia and cognitive impairment earlier than men (Mahale et al., 2022). Comparatively, other studies among PSP patients found women to have a less dominant motor symptom phenotype than men (Santacruz et al., 1998), and that women had longer disease duration than men (O'Sullivan et al., 2008), while others found no gender differences in baseline cognitive performance or longitudinal change in PSP-RS (Digma et al., 2023) or in disease onset, duration or motor symptoms (Baba et al., 2006). Finally, an examination of the distribution of co-pathologies (e.g., small vessel disease, cerebral amyloid angiopathy, beta-amyloid, neurofibrillary tangles, TDP-43) found no differences between women and men (Jecmenica Lukic et al., 2020).

Gender-Based Risk and Protective Factors for FTD/FTLD

Overall, FTD and FTLD diagnostic incidence was found to be lower in women than in men (Logroscino et al., 2023). While not discussed in this chapter, women seem to have a decreased risk of developing ALS, as well (Manjaly et al., 2010; Mata et al., 2023). In pursuing a better understanding of why women are less likely to develop ALS, a few studies found head trauma as a risk factor, incurred more frequently by men (Ingre et al., 2015; Pearce et al., 2015) and, therefore, may be one reason for the gender differences observed in the broad spectrum of FTLD. Other possible explanations include (1) sex-specific vulnerability in left frontal regions for women and right frontal and bilateral temporal regions for men (Flaherty et al., 2018) in diseases like PPA; (2) higher cognitive social reserve in women as demonstrated by their greater atrophy in FTD-sensitive brain regions despite similar clinical characteristics to men suggesting delayed symptom onset in women (de Boer et al., 2021; Heuer et al., 2020); (3) underrepresentation of women in non-epidemiologic studies (e.g., females are referred at later stages due to factors like social roles; de Boer et al., 2021); (4) higher psychiatric misdiagnosis in women (J. D. Woolley et al., 2011); and (5) a predilection for women to recognize social cognitive deficits in spouses earlier than vice versa (Devenney et al., 2018; Gossink et al., 2016).

Current State of Gender-Based Dementia Research and Remaining Questions

Intersection of Gender with Race/Ethnicity and SDOH

There is a need for more research examining the intersectionality of race/ethnicity, sex/gender, and sociocultural factors in dementia risk factors and clinical presentations in diverse populations worldwide. A better understanding of these intersecting disparities is essential for advancing our understanding of the disease and improving health outcomes across diverse populations, and yet this research is scarce. Complicating investigations into the gender and race/ethnicity intersection is the limited diversity of large, aging cohort studies and the underrepresentation of communities of color, particularly Black/African Americans, in clinical research on dementia. Only 5% of participants in observational studies and 8% in drug trials are Black or African American (Alegria et al., 2021). The reasons for this are multifactorial and include resource and access limitations, study design issues and medical and scientific mistrust resulting from historical unjust treatment of minoritized communities in medical care (Stradford et al., 2024). It is essential for the scientific community to use both study design-based approaches to enhance diversity of samples—principles of good recruitment and representation science approaches such as developing inclusive and accessible research designs and appointment times and conducting culturally appropriate community outreach strategies to establish trust with minoritized communities—and analytic approaches that can improve external validity such as inverse probability of selection weighting (Shaaban & Rosso, 2024). Only by doing so will our research be relevant and useful in real-world applications and serve the general population.

Few studies have examined the gender by race/ethnicity and other intersections, and the results demonstrate the importance of the question. A qualitative review of the literature on race by gender differences in AD and related dementias pathology reports that the higher prevalence of AD and related dementias in women versus men of the same race may be due to both higher pathological tau burden and greater vulnerability to cognitive decline when amyloid pathology and cerebral small vessel disease is present. Greater neurodegeneration and cerebral small vessel disease were also observed in Black/African American women relative to non-Hispanic/Latinx White older individuals (Royse et al., 2021). Avila et al. (2019) examined whether cognitive trajectories differ between women and men across and within racial/ethnic groups within the diverse aging cohort of the Washington/Hamilton Heights-Inwood Columbia Aging Project. They found that older Black/African American women showed steeper memory and visuo-spatial decline over time compared to Hispanic/Latinx men and non-Hispanic/Latinx White women, respectively (Avila et al., 2019). More recent work has examined intersectionality of gender, race/ethnicity, and lifecourse financial mobility. This work found that consistently low and downward lifecourse mobility were associated with poorer late-life memory function and that this did not vary across intersectional gender-race/ethnicity identities among the ethnoracially diverse pooled KHANDLE and STAR cohorts from an integrated health system in northern California ($N = 2340$; mean age, years: 73.6 ± 8.1; 62.4% women; 16.6% Asian, 48.5% Black, 14.3% Latinx, and 20.6% White; Kobayashi et al., 2024). Altogether these results indicate that examining the intersections of gender with other structural and identity-based factors can add critical insights into our understanding of AD health disparities and contribute to the development of personalized medicine approaches to prevent or delay dementia.

A Need for More Inclusive Definitions of Sex/Gender and the Inclusion of Sex and Gender Minority Populations in Clinical Research

A limitation of sex and gender research more broadly is the over reliance on the binary classification of sex and gender that fails to capture the fluidity and diversity that can occur for sex and gender both within and among individuals. Historically, sex has been a binary classification defined by sex chromosomes, reproductive organs and sex hormones; however, sex chromosomes, hormones, and secondary sexual characteristics do not always align in a straightforward way. Intersex refers to a range of conditions (e.g., Turner syndrome [XO], Klinefelter syndrome [XXY]) where individuals may have chromosomes, gonads, or genitalia that do not fit typical definitions of male or female. Binary sex classification excludes the intersex community, which represents about 1.7 to 4% of the population (Fausto-Sterling, 1993; Sears, 2005) with estimates varying depending upon the criteria for what constitutes an intersex condition and the population studied. Gender involves complex social and psychological dimensions, including roles, expectations, and self-perception. These factors contribute to a range of gender experiences that are not limited to a binary framework. The historical exclusion of those with sex or gender identities outside of the binary classification has several consequences including incomplete understanding of how dementia manifests across diverse populations, missed insights into how the full spectrum of genetic, hormonal or sociocultural aspects contribute to dementia risk and the perpetuation of health inequities and the marginalization of these individuals (Mielke et al., 2022).

Sexual orientation also occurs on a spectrum and has shown influences on brain health and dementia outcomes. Growing evidence suggests that sexual orientation and its intersection with sex and gender identity influences brain health and dementia outcomes via the consequences of social marginalization (Flatt, 2020). Numerous studies have reported that sexual and gender minority (SGM; e.g., lesbian, gay, bisexual, transgender, non-binary, gender fluid) individuals are more likely to have a modifiable risk factor (e.g., heavy alcohol use, smoking, cardiovascular risk factors, depression) for dementia compared to their non-SGM counterparts (Caceres et al., 2017; Corliss et al., 2018; Fredriksen-Goldsen et al., 2013; Jackson et al., 2016; Lee et al., 2009; Pharr, 2021). In a scoping review of the literature on cognitive impairment in SGM groups, Romanelli et al. (2024) reported that among eight studies examining self-reported cognitive impairment, seven found a higher prevalence among some SGM groups versus non SGM groups (Romanelli et al., 2024). Among three studies with clinician-provided dementia diagnoses based on objective cognitive assessments, two reported a higher likelihood of dementia diagnosis in transgender versus cisgender individuals (Romanelli et al., 2024). However, the review also notes the considerable variability in the literature on dementia-related outcomes in SGM groups including a longitudinal study from the National Alzheimer's Coordinating Center that found no difference in risk of dementia between SGM and non-SGM groups in the overall sample or stratified by sex (Perales-Puchalt et al., 2019). The authors comment that comparison across these studies is challenging due to variability in how SGM groups and cognitive impairment were defined and the factors adjusted for in statistical models with some studies observing null findings due to adjustment for the psychological and sociocultural factors that may be driving a higher risk of cognitive impairment in SGM groups (Romanelli et al., 2024).

Perhaps the largest limitation of dementia research in SGM populations is the underrepresentation of SGM groups in clinical research as well as the lack of inclusion of sexual and gender minority status questions in research studies (Romanelli et al., 2024). Efforts are needed to recruit SGM populations into research as their inclusion is crucial to identify factors that may put these groups at higher risk so that we can better address unique health disparities, ensure culturally competent care, and develop tailored interventions.

Influence of the X Chromosome

An interesting new area of research regarding sex differences in dementia relates to the influence of the X chromosome. There are several potential mechanisms for these differences (see Lopez-Lee and colleagues, for a recent review; Lopez-Lee et al., 2024), but one important source of dementia-relevant X-linked differences is greater gene expression of some genes in women versus men. This is because one of the two X chromosomes in women is randomly inactivated to equalize gene expression between women and men who only have one X chromosome; however, sometimes the X chromosome on certain genes can escape inactivation. In these instances, women will have greater expression of those X-linked genes, which can have implications for immunity and neurodegeneration pathways in which X-linked genes play a role. An autopsy study found a general pattern suggesting that greater expression of X chromosome-related genes was associated with better cognitive trajectories (less decline) over time in women. In men, expression of several X chromosome-related genes was associated with tau pathology, but not cognition (E. J. Davis et al., 2021). Human application of this work is in early stages but growing rapidly.

Biological Mechanism Underlying Female Cognitive Advantage in the Preclinical Stage

There is considerable evidence supporting the female cognitive advantage in the preclinical AD stage and the steeper decline in women after MCI diagnosis; however, the biological mechanisms that may support better resilience to early AD pathology burden in women followed by a steeper decline remain unclear. One study that examined gender differences in positron emission tomography (PET)-measured brain glucose metabolism, a measure of brain energy utilization or function, in older adults across the spectrum of healthy aging, MCI and AD dementia might offer a clue as to a contributing factor. They found that gender differences in cognition paralleled gender differences in brain glucose metabolism across AD pathology levels (i.e., Aβ plaques and hippocampal volume). More specifically, among those with a mild-to-moderate burden of AD pathology markers, women showed higher levels of cognitive function and brain glucose metabolism but not at more severe levels of AD biomarkers suggesting a steeper decline in cognition and brain glucose metabolism in women versus men (Sundermann et al., 2020). Moreover, the female cognitive advantage at mild-to-moderate AD pathology levels was eliminated/attenuated after adjusting for brain metabolism, suggesting a mediating role of brain metabolism in the female cognitive advantage (Sundermann et al., 2020), although longitudinal studies are needed to more definitively test this hypothesis.

There are also well-known gender differences in the immune response to brain insults with women having a more robust response (Cannon & St Pierre, 1997). It is notable that women comprise 80% of those with autoimmune disorders in which an immune response is overactive and dysregulated (Moulton, 2018; Oertelt-Prigione, 2012; Ortona et al., 2016). Neuroinflammation, mediated by the innate immune cells of the brain, microglia, is a critical pathologic mechanism in AD and related dementias with bidirectional effects with hallmark AD pathologies (Amelimojarad et al., 2024; Deng et al., 2024; Eikelenboom et al., 2010). Whereas an initial inflammatory response is typically beneficial as it reflects the body removing harmful pathogens and promoting tissue repair, this response can become harmful if it becomes chronic, leading to excessive inflammation and tissue damage. How the role of neuroinflammation in AD and related dementias may differ for women versus men is a key knowledge gap in the field.

The Influence of Gender in Other Dementia Types

In addition to AD, this chapter focused on the FTD dementia type in which the literature on the influence of gender is minimal and inconsistent, likely due, in part, to variability in the diagnostic criteria and whether diagnosis was autopsy-confirmed. Far more work is needed using universal clinical criteria with biomarker or autopsy confirmation to gain a clearer picture of gender disparities in FTD and to understand the biological and sociocultural factors that contribute to these differences. In general, research examining the influence of gender on dementia types other than AD is far less prolific than with AD representing a major knowledge gap. The research available indicates that gender differences in the prevalence, clinical presentation and prognosis of dementia vary by dementia type suggesting that gender-related factors differentially impact and interact with specific disease mechanisms that underlie different dementia types (Podcasy & Epperson, 2016). On the other hand, there are certain lifestyle factors such as diet, exercise, and sleep that promote brain health and reduce dementia risk more generally; however, their degree of influence and the specific recommendations for these lifestyle factors can differ for women versus men. It is critical that we further our understanding of how gender influences risk and resilience across all dementia types.

Research Challenges in Women's Brain Health

Throughout the chapter, it is clear that dementia, particularly AD, shows significant gender differences in pathophysiology and progression. However, the field has yet to fully acknowledge dementia as a women's health issue. This delay has hindered the development of targeted preventative strategies and treatments for the gender that bears the greatest burden of disease. Additionally, while researchers in the cognitive aging field often consider various factors throughout a person's lifespan when studying their sample population (e.g., education, physical activity, or smoking history), the endocrine lifespan is usually overlooked despite the well-established neuroprotective effects of sex hormones (Taylor et al., 2019). As has been mentioned, reproductive life events involving hormonal changes are of particular interest in relation to age-related cognitive changes and dementia risk in women. The existing literature suggests that pregnancy, menopause, and MHT use represent women-specific risk or protective factors for AD (Nerattini et al., 2023), underscoring the crucial role that sex hormones play in understanding women' brain health. However, the inconsistency in the literature regarding how reproductive life events impact dementia risk suggests that these relationships are not straightforward but nuanced and dependent on multiple individual and environmental factors. Further research in large, diverse samples that integrate biomarker, genetic, epigenetic, and multidisciplinary approaches are needed to unravel these complex relationships.

Over the last decade, medical research has been shifting toward precision medicine due to lackluster therapeutic options despite tens of billions of dollars invested in dementia treatment trials. Precision medicine is an emerging integrative approach for disease prevention, early detection, and treatment, which consider individual variability in genetics, epigenetics, sex, environment, and lifestyle (Miramontes et al., 2024). Advancements in precision medicine have improved our understanding of the physiological changes involved in the development and progression of dementia (Nebel et al., 2018). However, gender has not yet been fully integrated into precision medicine approaches, which has slowed down progress in detecting and treating dementia.

Enhancements in this area are crucial for optimizing healthcare resources and reducing the high costs associated with dementia care. To this end, it is critical for dementia studies to conduct gender-stratified analyses. By combining analyses across genders, researchers do a disservice to those we are trying to help as it dilutes findings of therapeutic targets and risk reduction strategies that may be specific to or optimal for each gender. In addition to advancing personalized medicine, gender differences provide information about the disease overall. These differences give us a clue that gender-disparate factors are likely at play in the disease including sex hormones, genetic factors, or gender-based sociocultural factors. By researching these factors and the mechanisms they influence, we use gender differences as a window into disease etiology overall.

Additional important areas of research include establishing infrastructure for precision medicine in low-resource settings and assessing its social and economic impacts on diverse populations (Miramontes et al., 2024). There are ethnic disparities in pregnancy and menopause. For example, non-Hispanic/Latinx Black/African American women generally undergo menopause transition at younger age (Walker et al., 2019), experience more frequent hot flashes (Gilsanz et al., 2017), and have a higher likelihood of developing hypertensive disorders of pregnancy and undergoing premenopausal bilateral oophorectomy, compared to White women (Mielke et al., 2022). However, the impact of these differences on the risk of dementia is not well understood. The same holds true for the variation in dosage, duration, and access to MHT among different race/ethnic groups, and the role of these factors in the risk of dementia remains unknown. Therefore, future studies need to employ mixed methodologies in diverse samples among various world regions to explore how the constructs of sex and gender differ in behavioral roles and norms across cultural contexts, and their complex intersection with aging throughout the life course (Mielke et al., 2022).

Considering AD as a women's health challenge can lead to a significant transformation in AD research and care. This shift would involve improved diagnostic accuracy, targeted interventions, and ultimately, better clinical outcomes (Miramontes et al., 2024). Therefore, it is important to consider gender differences in AD research across all levels, including basic science studies, clinical research, and clinical trials. Despite the challenges, acknowledging these differences rather than ignoring them will bring us closer to developing and providing better care for both women and men (Mielke et al., 2018).

The State of Gender-Based Clinical Practice and Remaining Questions

Gender differences in dementia have critical implications for clinical practice and for the development of refined diagnostic approaches, disease tracking strategies and treatment, and risk reduction interventions that are optimal for each gender. The medical field in general is understanding more and more the value and need for personalized medicine to apply the right treatments to the right patients at the right time. Our understanding of how the experience of ADRD differs between men and women is a critical piece in this shift toward personalized and targeted treatment. While there have been major strides in the research addressing gender differences in dementia, particularly AD, and their biological and sociocultural underpinnings, a number of questions remain unknown. We discuss a few of these questions as follows.

Questions Regarding Clinical Guidelines for MHT Use

The value of MHT use in dementia risk reduction remains a highly controversial topic in clinical medicine. Whether to initiate MHT during or after the menopause transition is a challenging and nuanced decision for women that should be made after in-depth risk/benefit assessments with health care providers. Evidence suggests that a number of factors influence the effect of MHT on the brain including the MHT formulation, the age at initiation of the MHT, the mode of delivery, and one's prior medical history. The interplay of these factors refutes the "one-size-fits-all" approach to MHT and argues for individualized MHT choices that carefully weighs a women's menopause experience, medical history, family medical history, needs, and concerns. For instance, the benefits of MHT may weigh more heavily for women undergoing surgical menopause as the evidence of a beneficial effect of estrogen-only therapy on ADRD risk is most consistent for this group (The North American Menopause Society, 2022). In contrast, the risks of MHT use may weigh more heavily for women with a personal or family history of breast, ovarian, or uterine or who are more than five years from their menopause transition.

A major limitation in the development of clinical guidelines for MHT use is the paucity of data from randomized controlled trials (RCTs), the gold standard in determining clinical effectiveness of an intervention. To date, the only RCT examining the effect of MHT use on ADRD risk is the previously mentioned WHIMS trial, which found that the use of estrogen plus progesterone therapy in naturally menopausal women doubled the risk for all-cause dementia (Shumaker et al., 2003). However, the WHIMS trial was conducted in women aged 65 years and older without menopause symptoms and, thus, not representative of women needing MHT in real-world clinical settings (Nerattini et al., 2023). Observational studies and retrospective analyses studies suggest that MHT may have a role in reducing dementia risk for women who are perimenopausal or recently postmenopausal, particularly those who have had surgical menopause. However, RCTs are weighted more heavily in clinical care guidelines. RCTs are needed to determine the effect of MHT use during the perimenopause and/or early postmenopause period on later-life dementia risk; however, the time, cost, and resource burden of an RCT with at least a 15-year follow-up is impractical. RCTs that utilize biomarkers known to occur early in pathogenesis as outcomes represent attractive opportunities for adding to the literature that informs clinical guidelines of mid-life MHT use (Nerattini et al., 2023).

Optimal Diagnostic Approaches for Women

Our research suggests that our conventional methods of detecting early cognitive change may not be serving women as well as they are serving men, which has clinical implications for our ability to intervene in women in the early disease stages. Research is warranted into potential strategies that may improve our ability to detect early cognitive change in women. One potential strategy is to identify cognitive tests that may be most sensitive to early cognitive change in women.

One question under investigation is whether memory tests that use visual rather than verbal stimuli which do not show a female bias in performance, may be more sensitive to early brain changes than the more conventional verbal memory tests, particularly in women. Intriguingly, Bonner-Jackson and colleagues found that among individuals with MCI from a memory clinic (57% female), hippocampal volume more strongly related to visual (Brief Visuospatial Memory Test-Revised) versus verbal memory (Hopkins Verbal Learning Test-Revised), although sex-stratified analyses were not conducted (Bonner-Jackson et al., 2015).

Above, we described how we can improve our use of the conventional verbal memory tests in detecting early MCI by applying gender-specific normative data and cut-scores for impairment to these tests. Evidence suggests that by doing so, we improve our ability to intervene earlier in more women with MCI and avoid undue stress and treatments in a proportion of men falsely diagnosed with MCI (Sundermann et al., 2019, 2021). Findings such as this have begun to motivate the development of sex-adjusted normative data for clinical use. For example, the Mayo's Older Americans Normative Studies (MOANS) recently revised and published their norms for the commonly used Rey Auditory Verbal Learning Test by including a sex adjustment (Stricker et al., 2021). However, far more work is needed in the development of sex-adjusted norms and in the adoption of these norms into research and clinical practice.

There are many other cognitive screening tasks that are commonly used in diagnosing dementia that do not consider gender differences in performance when applying cut-scores for cognitive impairment (e.g., Mini Mental State Exam, The Montreal Cognitive Assessment). There are critical implications to diagnostic accuracy if our standard clinical tests of cognitive function differentially reflect underlying brain pathology in women compared to men. Work is needed to generate and embrace the use of sex-specific cut-scores on clinical tests of cognitive function that would optimize detection of underlying disease pathology in women and men. It remains to be seen how a shift to sex-adjusted MCI diagnostic criteria may minimize sex-based disparities for dementia.

Rapid Advances in Plasma-Based Dementia Biomarkers: A Need for Gender Considerations

As mentioned earlier, evidence suggests that women present a greater burden of AD pathology in the early disease stages (Altmann et al., 2014; Buckley, Mormino, et al., 2019; Hohman et al., 2018; Jack et al., 2015; Oveisgharan et al., 2018) and this is reflected in biomarkers including tau positron emission tomography and cerebrospinal fluid p-Tau levels. Furthermore, there may also be sex differences in the ability of AD biomarkers to reflect brain neuropathology burden and overall AD risk. There is an urgent need to address these questions of sex differences among blood-based AD biomarkers, which are rapidly emerging in the field due to technical advances in assay sensitivity. Understanding sex differences in blood-based AD biomarkers will aid in the development of sex-specific guidelines for its use as a screening tool in both research and clinical trials, as well as optimizing its use in primary care settings. These questions began to be addressed by Tsiknia and colleagues in ADNI. They found that although plasma p-Tau181 concentrations were similar between women and men, higher plasma p-tau181 levels related to worse phenotypic biomarker profiles, faster cognitive decline and greater risk of developing dementia in women who met criteria for either preclinical AD or MCI compared to matched men (Tsiknia et al., 2022). The results suggest that plasma p-Tau181 may be a better proxy of overall AD risk in women versus men although far more work is needed to replicate, extend to other blood-based AD biomarkers and test generalizability in more diverse cohorts. Investigations such as this will challenge the often erroneous assumption that AD biomarkers have the same prognostic utility and temporal pattern in women as men. It is probable that sex-specific cutoffs for biomarker positivity can enhance the sensitivity of biomarkers as a prognostic tool. A better understanding of sex differences in AD biomarkers, blood-based and beyond, will improve diagnostic precision, strengthen findings from research studies utilizing biomarker outcomes, and inform the design and analysis of clinical trial studies.

Clinical Takeaways

- Evidence of the effect of MHT on dementia risk is complicated and nuanced such that decisions regarding MHT should be an informed decision with healthcare providers that factors in one's menopause experience, medical history, family medical history, needs, and concerns.

- Our current approaches to diagnosing early-stage dementia seem not to serve women as well as men. Research is needed into diagnostic approaches that are more sensitive to detecting early cognitive decline in women so as to allow more opportunities to intervene early in the disease trajectory.
- The shift in the medical field toward precision medicine approaches is paramount to optimize diagnostic, risk reduction and interventions based on gender as well as one's combination of medical diagnostic, environment, and genetic background.

Research Takeaways

- There is a need for more research examining the generalizability of gender disparities in dementia in underrepresented and underserved populations and the intersectionality of gender by race/ethnicity and SDoH.
- Research that accounts for lifespan exposures to protective/risk factors including female reproductive history is critical to understanding the higher AD risk in women.
- Improving our understanding of gender differences in dementia and their biological and sociocultural bases can serve as a window into disease etiology overall and improve dementia prevention and care in all.

References

2017 Alzheimer's disease facts and figures. (2017). *Alzheimer's & Dementia, 13*(4), 325–373. https://doi.org/10.1016/j.jalz.2017.02.001

2024 Alzheimer's disease facts and figures. (2024). https://alz-journals.onlinelibrary.wiley.com/doi/10.1002/alz.13809

ADI - Reports & resources. (n.d.). Retrieved August 22, 2024, from https://www.alzint.org/reports-resources/

Aggarwal, N. T., Wilson, R. S., Beck, T. L., Rajan, K. B., Mendes de Leon, C. F., Evans, D. A., & Everson-Rose, S. A. (2014). Perceived stress and change in cognitive function among adults 65 years and older. *Psychosomatic Medicine, 76*(1), 80–85. https://doi.org/10.1097/PSY.0000000000000016

Allen, A. P., Curran, E. A., Duggan, Á., Cryan, J. F., Chorcoráin, A. N., Dinan, T. G., Molloy, D. W., Kearney, P. M., & Clarke, G. (2017). A systematic review of the psychobiological burden of informal caregiving for patients with dementia: Focus on cognitive and biological markers of chronic stress. *Neuroscience & Biobehavioral Reviews, 73*, 123–164. https://doi.org/10.1016/J.NEUBIOREV.2016.12.006

Alegria, M., Sud, S., Steinberg, B. E., Gai, N., & Siddiqui, A. (2021). Reporting of participant race, sex, and socioeconomic status in randomized clinical trials in general medical journals, 2015 vs 2019. *JAMA Network Open, 4*(5), e2111516-e2111516.

Altmann, A., Tian, L., Henderson, V. W., & Greicius, M. D. (2014). Sex modifies the APOE-related risk of developing Alzheimer disease. *Annals of Neurology, 75*(4), 563–573. https://doi.org/10.1002/ana.24135

Alzheimer, & Association. (2009). *Caregiving across the United States caregivers of persons with Alzheimer's disease or dementia in 8 states and the district of Columbia behavioral risk factor surveillance system.*

Alzheimer's Association. (2022). *Fact sheet, women and Alzheimer's disease.*

Alzheimer's Association. (2024). 2024 Alzheimer's disease facts and figures. *Alzheimer's & Dementia, 20*(5), 3708–3821. https://doi.org/10.1002/alz.13809

Alzheimer's Disease International (ADI). (2014). *World Alzheimer Report 2014: Dementia and risk reduction. An analysis of protective and modifiable factors.* https://www.alzint.org/resource/world-alzheimer-report-2014/

Alzheimer's Disease International, Wimo, A., Ali, G.-C., Guerchet, M., Prince, M., Prina, M., & Wu, Y.-T. (2015). *World Alzheimer Report 2015: The global impact of dementia: An analysis of prevalence, incidence, cost and trends.* https://www.alzint.org/resource/world-alzheimer-report-2015/

Amelimojarad, M., Amelimojarad, M., & Cui, X. (2024). The emerging role of brain neuroinflammatory responses in Alzheimer's disease. *Frontiers in Aging Neuroscience, 16*, 1391517. https://doi.org/10.3389/fnagi.2024.1391517

American Psychiatric Association. (2022). *Diagnostic and statistical manual of mental disorders* (5th ed., text rev.). (5th ed.). American Psychiatric Association.

Anderson, J. G., Flatt, J. D., Tree, J. M. J., Gross, A. L., & Rose, K. M. (2021). Characteristics of sexual and gender minority caregivers of people with dementia. *Journal of Aging and Health, 33*(10), 838. https://doi.org/10.1177/08982643211014767

Andolf, E. G., Sydsjö, G. C. M., Bladh, M. K., Berg, G., & Sharma, S. (2017). Hypertensive disorders in pregnancy and later dementia: A Swedish National Register Study. *Acta Obstetricia Et Gynecologica Scandinavica, 96*(4), 464–471. https://doi.org/10.1111/aogs.13096

Aranda, G., Halperin, I., Gomez-Gil, E., Hanzu, F. A., Seguí, N., Guillamon, A., & Mora, M. (2021). Cardiovascular risk associated with gender ffirming Hormone thherapy in transgender population. *Frontiers in Endocrinology, 12*, 718200. https://doi.org/10.3389/fendo.2021.718200

Avila, J. F., Vonk, J. M. J., Verney, S. P., Witkiewitz, K., Arce Rentería, M., Schupf, N., Mayeux, R., & Manly, J. J. (2019). Sex/gender differences in cognitive trajectories vary as a function of race/ethnicity. *Alzheimer's and Dementia.* https://doi.org/10.1016/j.jalz.2019.04.006

Baba, Y., Putzke, J. D., Whaley, N. R., Wszolek, Z. K., & Uitti, R. J. (2006). Progressive supranuclear palsy: Phenotypic sex differences in a clinical cohort. *Movement Disorders: Official Journal of the Movement Disorder Society, 21*(5), 689–692. https://doi.org/10.1002/mds.20769

Bae, J. B., Lipnicki, D. M., Han, J. W., Sachdev, P. S., Kim, T. H., Kwak, K. P., Kim, B. J., Kim, S. G., Kim, J. L., Moon, S. W., Park, J. H., Ryu, S.-H., Youn, J. C., Lee, D. Y., Lee, D. W., Lee, S. B., Lee, J. J., Jhoo, J. H., Skoog, I., et al. (2020). Parity and the risk of incident dementia: A COSMIC study. *Epidemiology and Psychiatric Sciences, 29*, e176. https://doi.org/10.1017/S2045796020000876

Ball, M., Braak, H., Coleman, P., Dickson, D., Duyckaerts, C., Gambetti, P., Hansen, L., Hyman, B., Jellinger, K., Markesbery, W., Perl, D., Powers, J., Price, J., Trojanowski, J. Q., Wisniewski, H., Phelps, C., & Khachaturian, Z. (1997). Consensus recommendations for the postmortem diagnosis of Alzheimer's disease. *Neurobiology of Aging.* https://doi.org/10.1016/S0197-4580(97)00057-2

Banks, S. J., Shifflett, B., Berg, J., Sundermann, E., Peavy, G., Bondi, M. W., Edland, S. D., & Alzheimer's Disease Neuroimaging Initiative. (2019). Sex-specific composite scales for longitudinal studies of incipient Alzheimer's disease. *Alzheimer's & Dementia: Translational Research & Clinical Interventions, 5*(1), 508–514. https://doi.org/10.1016/j.trci.2019.07.003

Barha, C. K., Best, J. R., Rosano, C., Yaffe, K., Catov, J. M., & Liu-Ambrose, T. (2020). Sex-specific relationship between long-term maintenance of physical activity and cognition in the Health ABC Study: Potential role of hippocampal and dorsolateral prefrontal cortex volume. *The Journals of Gerontology Series A: Biological Sciences and Medical Sciences, 75*(4), 764. https://doi.org/10.1093/GERONA/GLZ093

Barha, C. K., Davis, J. C., Falck, R. S., Nagamatsu, L. S., & Liu-Ambrose, T. (2017). Sex differences in exercise efficacy to improve cognition: A systematic review and meta-analysis of randomized controlled trials in older humans. *Frontiers in Neuroendocrinology, 46*(December 2016), 71–85. https://doi.org/10.1016/j.yfrne.2017.04.002

Barnes, L. L., Lamar, M., & Schneider, J. A. (2019). Sex differences in mixed neuropathologies in community-dwelling older adults. *Brain Research, 1719*, 11–16. https://doi.org/10.1016/j.brainres.2019.05.028

Barnes, L. L., Wilson, R. S., Bienias, J. L., Schneider, J. A., Evans, D. A., & Bennett, D. A. (2005). Sex differences in the clinical manifestations of Alzheimer disease pathology. *Archives of General Psychiatry*. https://doi.org/10.1001/archpsyc.62.6.685

Barth, C., & de Lange, A.-M. G. (2020). Towards an understanding of women's brain aging: The immunology of pregnancy and menopause. *Frontiers in Neuroendocrinology, 58*, 100850. https://doi.org/10.1016/j.yfrne.2020.100850

Basit, S., Wohlfahrt, J., & Boyd, H. A. (2018). Pre-eclampsia and risk of dementia later in life: Nationwide cohort study. *BMJ, 363*, k4109. https://doi.org/10.1136/bmj.k4109

Beeri, M. S., Rapp, M., Schmeidler, J., Reichenberg, A., Purohit, D. P., Perl, D. P., Grossman, H. T., Prohovnik, I., Haroutunian, V., & Silverman, J. M. (2009). Number of children is associated with neuropathology of Alzheimer's disease in women. *Neurobiology of Aging*. https://doi.org/10.1016/j.neurobiolaging.2007.11.011

Blacker, D., Haines, J. L., Rodes, L., Terwedow, H., Go, R. C. P., Harrell, L. E., Perry, R. T., Bassett, S. S., Chase, G., Meyers, D., Albert, M. S., & Tanzi, R. (1997). ApoE-4 and age at onset of Alzheimer's disease. *Neurology, 48*(1), 139–147. https://doi.org/10.1212/WNL.48.1.139

Bonner-Jackson, A., Mahmoud, S., Miller, J., & Banks, S. J. (2015). Verbal and non-verbal memory and hippocampal volumes in a memory clinic population. *Alzheimer's Research & Therapy, 7*(1), 61. https://doi.org/10.1186/s13195-015-0147-9

Bove, R., Secor, E., Chibnik, L. B., Barnes, L. L., Schneider, J. A., Bennett, D. A., & De Jager, P. L. (2014). Age at surgical menopause influences cognitive decline and Alzheimer pathology in older women. *Neurology, 82*(3), 222–229. https://doi.org/10.1212/WNL.0000000000000033

Bower, J. H., Maraganore, D. M., McDonnell, S. K., & Rocca, W. A. (1997). Incidence of progressive supranuclear palsy and multiple system atrophy in Olmsted County, Minnesota, 1976 to 1990. *Neurology, 49*(5), 1284–1288. https://doi.org/10.1212/wnl.49.5.1284

Brady, B., Zheng, L., Kootar, S., & Anstey, K. J. (2023). Sex and gender differences in risk scores for dementia and Alzheimer's disease among cisgender, transgender, and non-binary adults. *Alzheimer's & Dementia, 20*(1), 5. https://doi.org/10.1002/alz.13317

Brinton, R. D. (2008). The healthy cell bias of estrogen action: Mitochondrial bioenergetics and neurological implications. *Trends in Neurosciences, 31*(10), 529–537. https://doi.org/10.1016/j.tins.2008.07.003

Brinton, R. D., Yao, J., Yin, F., Mack, W. J., & Cadenas, E. (2015). Perimenopause as a neurological transition state. *Nature Reviews Endocrinology, 11*(7), 393–405. https://doi.org/10.1038/nrendo.2015.82

Brodaty, H., Heffernan, M., Kochan, N. A., Draper, B., Trollor, J. N., Reppermund, S., Slavin, M. J., & Sachdev, P. S. (2013). Mild cognitive impairment in a community sample: The Sydney Memory and Ageing Study. *Alzheimer's & Dementia: The Journal of the Alzheimer's Association, 9*(3), 310–317.e1. https://doi.org/10.1016/j.jalz.2011.11.010

Buckley, R. F., Mormino, E. C., Rabin, J. S., Hohman, T. J., Landau, S., Hanseeuw, B. J., Jacobs, H. I. L., Papp, K. V., Amariglio, R. E., Properzi, M. J., Schultz, A. P., Kirn, D., Scott, M. R., Hedden, T., Farrell, M., Price, J., Chhatwal, J., Rentz, D. M., Villemagne, V. L., et al. (2019). Sex differences in the association of global amyloid and regional tau deposition measured by positron emission tomography in clinically normal older adults. *JAMA Neurology, 76*(5), 542–551. https://doi.org/10.1001/jamaneurol.2018.4693

Buckley, R. F., Waller, M., Masters, C. L., & Dobson, A. (2019). To what extent does age at death account for sex differences in rates of mortality from Alzheimer disease? *American Journal of Epidemiology, 188*(7), 1213–1223. https://doi.org/10.1093/aje/kwz048

Bureau, U. C. (2021). *Around the world, living longer and healthier depends largely on gender and countries' income*. Census.Gov. https://www.census.gov/library/stories/2021/05/long-life-does-not-always-mean-a-healthy-life-in-old-age.html

Burkhardt, M. S., Foster, J. K., Laws, S. M., Baker, L. D., Craft, S., Gandy, S. E., Stuckey, B. G. A., Clarnette, R., Nolan, D., Hewson-Bower, B., & Martins, R. N. (2004). Oestrogen replacement therapy may improve memory functioning in the absence of APOE ε4. *Journal of Alzheimer's Disease, 6*(3), 221–228.

Butters, M. A., Young, J. B., Lopez, O., Aizenstein, H. J., Mulsant, B. H., Reynolds, C. F., DeKosky, S. T., & Becker, J. T. (2008). Pathways linking late-life depression to persistent cognitive impairment and dementia. *Dialogues in Clinical Neuroscience, 10*(3), 345–357. https://doi.org/10.31887/DCNS.2008.10.3/mabutters

Buyon, J. P. (1998). The effects of pregnancy on autoimmune diseases. *Journal of Leukocyte Biology, 63*(3), 281–287. https://doi.org/10.1002/jlb.63.3.281

Caamaño-Isorna, F., Corral, M., Montes-Martínez, A., & Takkouche, B. (2006). Education and dementia: A meta-analytic study. *Neuroepidemiology, 26*(4), 226–232. https://doi.org/10.1159/000093378

Caceres, B. A., Brody, A., Luscombe, R. E., Primiano, J. E., Marusca, P., Sitts, E. M., & Chyun, D. (2017). A systematic review of cardiovascular disease in sexual minorities. *American Journal of Public Health, 107*(4), e13–e21. https://doi.org/10.2105/AJPH.2016.303630

Caldwell, J. Z. K., Berg, J.-L., Cummings, J. L., & Banks, S. J. (2017). Moderating effects of sex on the impact of diagnosis and amyloid positivity on verbal memory and hippocampal volume. *Alzheimer's Research & Therapy, 9*(1), 72. https://doi.org/10.1186/s13195-017-0300-8

Caldwell, J. Z. K., Cummings, J. L., Banks, S. J., Palmqvist, S., & Hansson, O. (2019). Cognitively normal women with Alzheimer's disease proteinopathy show relative preservation of memory but not of hippocampal volume. *Alzheimer's Research and Therapy, 11*(1). https://doi.org/10.1186/s13195-019-0565-1

Callaghan, B. L., McCormack, C., Kim, P., & Pawluski, J. L. (2024). Understanding the maternal brain in the context of the mental load of motherhood. *Nature Mental Health, 2*(7), 764–772. https://doi.org/10.1038/s44220-024-00268-4

Cannon, J. G., & St Pierre, B. A. (1997). Gender differences in host defense mechanisms. *Journal of Psychiatric Research, 31*(1), 99–113. https://doi.org/10.1016/s0022-3956(96)00055-6

Carlson, M. C., Kuo, J. H., Chuang, Y. F., Varma, V. R., Harris, G., Albert, M. S., Erickson, K. I., Kramer, A. F., Parisi, J. M., Xue, Q. L., Tan, E. J., Tanner, E. K., Gross, A. L., Seeman, T. E., Gruenewald, T. L., McGill, S., Rebok, G. W., & Fried, L. P. (2015). Impact of the Baltimore Experience Corps Trial on cortical and hippocampal volumes. *Alzheimer's & Dementia : The Journal of the Alzheimer's Association, 11*(11), 1340–1348. https://doi.org/10.1016/J.JALZ.2014.12.005

Carnethon, M. R. (2009). Physical activity and cardiovascular disease: How much is enough? *American Journal of Lifestyle Medicine, 3*(1 Suppl), 44S–49S. https://doi.org/10.1177/1559827609332737

Carter, C. L., Resnick, E. M., Mallampalli, M., & Kalbarczyk, A. (2012). Sex and gender differences in Alzheimer's disease: Recommendations for future research. *Journal of Women's Health, 21*(10), 1018–1023. https://doi.org/10.1089/jwh.2012.3789

Caspersen, C. J., Powell, K. E., & Christenson, G. M. (1985). Physical activity, exercise, and physical fitness: Definitions and distinctions for health-related research. *Public Health Reports (Washington, D.C.: 1974), 100*(2), 126–131.

Chen, R., Williams, D. R., Nishimi, K., Slopen, N., Kubzansky, L. D., & Weuve, J. (2022). A life course approach to understanding stress exposures and cognitive function among middle-aged and older adults. *Social Science & Medicine (1982), 314*, 115448. https://doi.org/10.1016/j.socscimed.2022.115448

Chen, Y.-H., Wang, Z.-B., Liu, X.-P., Xu, J.-P., & Mao, Z.-Q. (2024). Sex differences in the relationship between depression and Alzheimer's disease—Mechanisms, genetics, and therapeutic opportunities. *Frontiers in Aging Neuroscience, 16*. https://doi.org/10.3389/fnagi.2024.1301854

Chêne, G., Beiser, A., Au, R., Preis, S. R., Wolf, P. A., Dufouil, C., & Seshadri, S. (2015). Gender and incidence of dementia in the Framingham Heart Study from mid-adult life. *Alzheimer's & Dementia: The Journal of the Alzheimer's Association, 11*(3), 310–320. https://doi.org/10.1016/j.jalz.2013.10.005

Chiu, W. Z., Kaat, L. D., Seelaar, H., Rosso, S. M., Boon, A. J., Kamphorst, W., & van Swieten, J. C. (2010). Survival in progressive supranuclear palsy and frontotemporal dementia. *Journal of Neurology, Neurosurgery, and Psychiatry, 81*(4), 441–445. https://doi.org/10.1136/jnnp.2009.195719

Clouston, S. A. P., Smith, D. M., Mukherjee, S., Zhang, Y., Hou, W., Link, B. G., & Richards, M. (2020). Education and cognitive decline: An integrative analysis of global longitudinal studies of cognitive aging. *The Journals of Gerontology. Series B, Psychological Sciences and Social Sciences, 75*(7), e151–e160. https://doi.org/10.1093/geronb/gbz053

Colberg, S. R., Sigal, R. J., Fernhall, B., Regensteiner, J. G., Blissmer, B. J., Rubin, R. R., Chasan-Taber, L., Albright, A. L., & Braun, B. (2010). Exercise and type 2 diabetes: The American College of Sports Medicine and the American Diabetes Association: Joint position statement. *Diabetes Care, 33*(12). https://doi.org/10.2337/DC10-9990

Colucci, M., Cammarata, S., Assini, A., Croce, R., Clerici, F., Novello, C., Mazzella, L., Dagnino, N., Mariani, C., & Tanganelli, P. (2006). The number of pregnancies is a risk factor for Alzheimer's disease. *European Journal of Neurology, 13*(12), 1374–1377. https://doi.org/10.1111/j.1468-1331.2006.01520.x

Corliss, H. L., VanKim, N. A., Jun, H.-J., Austin, S. B., Hong, B., Wang, M., & Hu, F. B. (2018). Risk of type 2 diabetes among lesbian, bisexual, and heterosexual women: Findings from the Nurses' Health Study II. *Diabetes Care, 41*(7), 1448–1454. https://doi.org/10.2337/dc17-2656

Coughlan, G. T., Betthauser, T. J., Boyle, R., Koscik, R. L., Klinger, H. M., Chibnik, L. B., Jonaitis, E. M., Yau, W.-Y. W., Wenzel, A., Christian, B. T., Gleason, C. E., Saelzler, U. G., Properzi, M. J., Schultz, A. P., Hanseeuw, B. J., Manson, J. E., Rentz, D. M., Johnson, K. A., Sperling, R., et al. (2023). Association of age at menopause and hormone therapy use with Tau and β-amyloid positron emission tomography. *JAMA Neurology, 80*(5), 462–473. https://doi.org/10.1001/jamaneurol.2023.0455

D'Amico, D., Alter, U., & Fiocco, A. J. (2023). Cumulative stress exposure and cognitive function among older adults: The moderating ole of a healthy lifestyle. *The Journals of Gerontology. Series B, Psychological Sciences and Social Sciences, 78*(12), 1983–1991. https://doi.org/10.1093/geronb/gbad116

Dauphinot, V., Delphin-Combe, F., Mouchoux, C., Dorey, A., Bathsavanis, A., Makaroff, Z., Rouch, I., & Krolak-Salmon, P. (2015). Risk factors of caregiver burden among patients with Alzheimer's disease or related disorders: A cross-sectional study. *Journal of Alzheimer's Disease, 44*(3), 907–916. https://doi.org/10.3233/JAD-142337

Davies, H. D., Sridhar, S. B., Newkirk, L. A., Beaudreau, S. A., & Ohara, R. (2012). Gender differences in sexual behaviors of AD patients and their relationship to spousal caregiver well-being. *Aging & Mental Health, 16*(1), 89. https://doi.org/10.1080/13607863.2011.609532

Davis, E. J., Solsberg, C. W., White, C. C., Miñones-Moyano, E., Sirota, M., Chibnik, L., Bennett, D. A., De Jager, P. L., Yokoyama, J. S., & Dubal, D. B. (2021). Sex-specific association of the X chromosome with cognitive change and tau pathology in aging and Alzheimer disease. *JAMA Neurology, 78*(10), 1249–1254. https://doi.org/10.1001/jamaneurol.2021.2806

de Boer, S. C. M., Riedl, L., van der Lee, S. J., Otto, M., Anderl-Straub, S., Landin-Romero, R., Sorrentino, F., Fieldhouse, J. L. P., Reus, L. M., Vacaflor, B., Halliday, G., Galimberti, D., Diehl-Schmid, J., Ducharme, S., Piguet, O., & Pijnenburg, Y. A. L. (2021). Differences in sex distribution between genetic and sporadic frontotemporal dementia. *Journal of Alzheimer's Disease: JAD, 84*(3), 1153–1161. https://doi.org/10.3233/JAD-210688

Dementia—Key Facts. (2023). World Health Organization. https://www.who.int/news-room/fact-sheets/detail/dementia

Deng, Q., Wu, C., Parker, E., Liu, T. C.-Y., Duan, R., & Yang, L. (2024). Microglia and astrocytes in Alzheimer's disease: Significance and summary of recent Advances. *Aging and Disease, 15*(4), 1537–1564. https://doi.org/10.14336/AD.2023.0907

Depypere, H., Vergallo, A., Lemercier, P., Lista, S., Benedet, A., Ashton, N., Cavedo, E., Zetterberg, H., Blennow, K., Vanmechelen, E., Hampel, H., & Initiative (NPMI), the N. P. M. (2023). Menopause hormone therapy significantly alters pathophysiological biomarkers of Alzheimer's disease. *Alzheimer's & Dementia, 19*(4), 1320–1330. https://doi.org/10.1002/alz.12759

Devenney, E., Swinn, T., Mioshi, E., Hornberger, M., Dawson, K. E., Mead, S., Rowe, J. B., & Hodges, J. R. (2018). The behavioural variant frontotemporal dementia phenocopy syndrome is a distinct entity—Evidence from a longitudinal study. *BMC Neurology, 18*(1), 56. https://doi.org/10.1186/s12883-018-1060-1

Diehl, J., & Kurz, A. (2002). Frontotemporal dementia: Patient characteristics, cognition, and behaviour. *International Journal of Geriatric Psychiatry, 17*(10), 914–918. https://doi.org/10.1002/gps.709

Digma, L. A., Litvan, I., Del Ser, T., & Bayram, E. (2023). Sex differences for cognitive decline in progressive supranuclear palsy. *Parkinsonism & Related Disorders, 112*, 105454. https://doi.org/10.1016/j.parkreldis.2023.105454

Digma, L. A., Madsen, J. R., Rissman, R. A., Jacobs, D. M., Brewer, J. B., Banks, S. J., Weiner, M., Aisen, P., Petersen, R., Jack, C. R., Jagust, W., Trojanowki, J. Q., Toga, A. W., Beckett, L., Green, R. C., Saykin, A. J., Morris, J., Shaw, L. M., Liu, E., et al. (2020). Women can bear a bigger burden: Ante- and post-mortem evidence for reserve in the face of tau. *Brain Communications*. https://doi.org/10.1093/braincomms/fcaa025

Diniz, B. S., Butters, M. A., Albert, S. M., Dew, M. A., & Reynolds, C. F. (2013). Late-life depression and risk of vascular dementia and Alzheimer's disease: Systematic review and meta-analysis of community-based cohort studies. *The British Journal of Psychiatry: The Journal of Mental Science, 202*(5), 329–335. https://doi.org/10.1192/bjp.bp.112.118307

Driver-Dunckley, E. D., Zhang, N., Serrano, G. E., Dunckley, N. A., Sue, L. I., Shill, H. A., Mehta, S. H., Belden, C., Tremblay, C., Atri, A., Adler, C. H., & Beach, T. G. (2023). Low clinical sensitivity and unexpectedly high incidence for neuropathologically diagnosed progressive supranuclear palsy. *Journal of Neuropathology and Experimental Neurology, 82*(5), 438–451. https://doi.org/10.1093/jnen/nlad025

Dubal, D. B. (2020). Sex difference in Alzheimer's disease: An updated, balanced and emerging perspective on differing vulnerabilities. *Handbook of Clinical Neurology, 175*, 261–273. https://doi.org/10.1016/B978-0-444-64123-6.00018-7

Dubois, B., Hampel, H., Feldman, H. H., Scheltens, P., Aisen, P., Andrieu, S., Bakardjian, H., Benali, H., Bertram, L., Blennow, K., Broich, K., Cavedo, E., Crutch, S., Dartigues, J. F., Duyckaerts, C., Epelbaum, S., Frisoni, G. B., Gauthier, S., Genthon, R., et al. (2016). Preclinical Alzheimer's disease: Definition, natural history, and diagnostic criteria. *Alzheimer's and Dementia*. https://doi.org/10.1016/j.jalz.2016.02.002

Dufouil, C., Seshadri, S., & Chêne, G. (2014). Cardiovascular risk profile in women and dementia. *Journal of Alzheimer's Disease: JAD, 42*(Suppl 4), S353–S363. https://doi.org/10.3233/JAD-141629

Dutra, E., Lee, J., Torbati, T., Garcia, M., Merz, C. N. B., & Shufelt, C. (2019). Cardiovascular implications of gender-affirming hormone treatment in the transgender population. *Maturitas, 129*, 45–49. https://doi.org/10.1016/j.maturitas.2019.08.010

Eikelenboom, P., Van Exel, E., Hoozemans, J. J. M., Veerhuis, R., Rozemuller, A. J. M., & Van Gool, W. A. (2010). Neuroinflammation—An early event in both the history and pathogenesis of Alzheimer's disease. *Neurodegenerative Diseases*. https://doi.org/10.1159/000283480

Elser, H., Horváth-Puhó, E., Gradus, J. L., Smith, M. L., Lash, T. L., Glymour, M. M., Sørensen, H. T., & Henderson, V. W. (2023). Association of early-, middle-, and late-life depression with incident dementia in a Danish cohort. *JAMA Neurology, 80*(9), 949–958. https://doi.org/10.1001/jamaneurol.2023.2309

Elst, W. V. D., Boxtel, M. P. J. V., Breukelen, G. J. P. V., & Jolles, J. (2005). Rey's verbal learning test: Normative data for 1855 healthy participants aged 24–81 years and the influence of age, sex, education, and mode of presentation. *Journal of the International Neuropsychological Society, 11*(3), 290–302. https://doi.org/10.1017/S1355617705050344

Farrer, L. A., Cupples, L. A., Haines, J. L., Hyman, B., Kukull, W. A., Mayeux, R., Myers, R. H., Pericak-Vance, M. A., Risch, N., & Van Duijn, C. M. (1997). Effects of age, sex, and ethnicity on the association between apolipoprotein E genotype and Alzheimer disease: A meta-analysis. *JAMA, 278*(16), 1349–1356. https://doi.org/10.1001/jama.278.16.1349

Fausto-Sterling, A. (1993). *THE five sexes the sciences—Wiley Online Library*. https://nyaspubs.onlinelibrary.wiley.com/doi/10.1002/j.2326-1951.1993.tb03081.x

Fiest, K. M., Jetté, N., Roberts, J. I., Maxwell, C. J., Smith, E. E., Black, S. E., Blaikie, L., Cohen, A., Day, L., Holroyd-Leduc, J., Kirk, A., Pearson, D., Pringsheim, T., Venegas-Torres, A., & Hogan, D. B. (2016). The prevalence and incidence of dementia: A systematic review and meta-analysis. *Canadian Journal of Neurological Sciences*. https://doi.org/10.1017/cjn.2016.18

Flaherty, C. V., Zangeneh, A. S., & Marikunte, M. A. H. (2018). Gender differences in frontotemporal lobar degeneration (FTLD) support an estrogenic model of delayed onset. In *Sex hormones in neurodegenerative processes and diseases*. IntechOpen. https://doi.org/10.5772/intechopen.74158

Flatt, J. (2020). The epidemiology of dementia in LGBTQ older adults. *Innovation in Aging, 4*(Suppl 1), 748–749. https://doi.org/10.1093/geroni/igaa057.2695

Flatt, J. D., Cicero, E. C., Lambrou, N. H., Wharton, W., Anderson, J. G., Bouldin, E. D., McGuire, L. C., & Taylor, C. A. (2021). Subjective cognitive decline higher among sexual and gender minorities in the United States, 2015-2018. *Alzheimer's & Dementia (New York, N. Y.), 7*(1), e12197. https://doi.org/10.1002/trc2.12197

Fox, M., Berzuini, C., Knapp, L. A., & Glynn, L. M. (2018). Women's pregnancy life history and Alzheimer's risk: Can immunoregulation explain the link? *American Journal of Alzheimer's Disease & Other Dementias®, 33*(8), 516–526. https://doi.org/10.1177/1533317518786447

Fredriksen-Goldsen, K. I., Kim, H.-J., Barkan, S. E., Muraco, A., & Hoy-Ellis, C. P. (2013). Health disparities among lesbian, gay, and bisexual older adults: Results from a population-based study. *American Journal of Public Health, 103*(10), 1802–1809. https://doi.org/10.2105/AJPH.2012.301110

Galea, L. A., Qiu, W., & Duarte-Guterman, P. (2018). Beyond sex differences: Short and long-term implications of motherhood on women's health. *Current Opinion in Physiology, 6*, 82–88. https://doi.org/10.1016/j.cophys.2018.06.003

Gallicchio, L., Siddiqi, N., Langenberg, P., & Baumgarten, M. (2002). Gender differences in burden and depression among informal caregivers of demented elders in the community. *International Journal of Geriatric Psychiatry, 17*(2), 154–163. https://doi.org/10.1002/GPS.538

Garovic, V. D., White, W. M., Vaughan, L., Saiki, M., Parashuram, S., Garcia-Valencia, O., Weissgerber, T. L., Milic, N., Weaver, A., & Mielke, M. M. (2020). Incidence and long-term outcomes of hypertensive disorders of pregnancy. *Journal of the American College of Cardiology, 75*(18), 2323–2334. https://doi.org/10.1016/j.jacc.2020.03.028

Gauthier, S., Rosa-Neto, P., Morais, J. A., & Webster, C. (2021). *World Alzheimer Report 2021 Abridged version journey through the diagnosis of dementia*. Alzheimer's Disease International.

Georgakis, M. K., Beskou-Kontou, T., Theodoridis, I., Skalkidou, A., & Petridou, E. T. (2019). Surgical menopause in association with cognitive function and risk of dementia: A systematic review and meta-analysis. *Psychoneuroendocrinology, 106*, 9–19. https://doi.org/10.1016/j.psyneuen.2019.03.013

Gervais, N. J., Au, A., Almey, A., Duchesne, A., Gravelsins, L., Brown, A., Reuben, R., Baker-Sullivan, E., Schwartz, D. H., Evans, K., Bernardini, M. Q., Eisen, A., Meschino, W. S., Foulkes, W. D., Hampson, E., & Einstein, G. (2020). Cognitive markers of dementia risk in middle-aged women with bilateral salpingo-oophorectomy prior to menopause. *Neurobiology of Aging, 94*, 1–6. https://doi.org/10.1016/j.neurobiolaging.2020.04.019

Gilsanz, P., Mayeda, E. R., Glymour, M. M., Quesenberry, C. P., Mungas, D. M., DeCarli, C., Dean, A., & Whitmer, R. A. (2017). Female sex, early-onset hypertension, and risk of dementia. *Neurology, 89*(18), 1886–1893. https://doi.org/10.1212/WNL.0000000000004602

Giudicessi, A. J., Saelzler, U. G., Shadyab, A. H., Posis, A. I. B., Sundermann, E. E., Banks, S. J., & Panizzon, M. S. (2022). The mediating role of socioeconomic status on the relationship between pregnancy history and later-life cognition. *Climacteric: The Journal of the International Menopause Society, 25*(6), 627–633. https://doi.org/10.1080/13697137.2022.2129004

Godfrey, J. R., & Warshaw, G. A. (2009). Toward optimal health: Considering the enhanced healthcare needs of women caregivers. *Journal of Women's Health (2002), 18*(11), 1739–1742. https://doi.org/10.1089/jwh.2009.1720

Gong, J., Harris, K., Peters, S. A. E., & Woodward, M. (2022). Reproductive factors and the risk of incident dementia: A cohort study of UK Biobank participants. *PLOS Medicine, 19*(4), e1003955. https://doi.org/10.1371/journal.pmed.1003955

Gorno-Tempini, M. L., Hillis, A. E., Weintraub, S., Kertesz, A., Mendez, M., Cappa, S. F., Ogar, J. M., Rohrer, J. D., Black, S., Boeve, B. F., Manes, F., Dronkers, N. F., Vandenberghe, R., Rascovsky, K., Patterson, K., Miller, B. L., Knopman, D. S., Hodges, J. R., Mesulam, M. M., & Grossman, M. (2011). Classification of primary progressive aphasia and its variants. *Neurology, 76*(11), 1006–1014. https://doi.org/10.1212/WNL.0b013e31821103e6

Gossink, F. T., Dols, A., Kerssens, C. J., Krudop, W. A., Kerklaan, B. J., Scheltens, P., Stek, M. L., & Pijnenburg, Y. A. L. (2016). Psychiatric diagnoses underlying the phenocopy syndrome of behavioural variant frontotemporal dementia. *Journal of Neurology, Neurosurgery, and Psychiatry, 87*(1), 64–68. https://doi.org/10.1136/jnnp-2014-308284

Guo, Y., Li, Q., Yang, X., Jaffee, M. S., Wu, Y., Wang, F., & Bian, J. (2022). Prevalence of Alzheimer's and related dementia diseases and risk factors among transgender adults, Florida, 2012–2020. *American Journal of Public Health, 112*(5), 754–757. https://doi.org/10.2105/AJPH.2022.306720

Gurvich, C., Hoy, K., Thomas, N., & Kulkarni, J. (2018). Sex differences and the influence of sex hormones on cognition through adulthood and the aging process. *Brain Sciences*. https://doi.org/10.3390/brainsci8090163

Gustafson, L., Passant, U., Gräsbeck, A., & Brun, A. (2001). Clinical variability of frontotemporal dementia. In K. Miyoshi, C. M. Shapiro, M. Gaviria, & Y. Morita (Eds.), *Contemporary Neuropsychiatry* (pp. 152–157). Springer Japan. https://doi.org/10.1007/978-4-431-67897-7_23

Halari, R., Mines, M., Kumari, V., Mehrotra, R., Wheeler, M., Ng, V., & Sharma, T. (2005). Sex differences and individual differences in cognitive performance and their relationship to endogenous gonadal hormones and gonadotropins. *Behavioral Neuroscience*. https://doi.org/10.1037/0735-7044.119.1.104

Hardy, J., & Selkoe, D. J. (2002). The amyloid hypothesis of Alzheimer's disease: Progress and problems on the road to therapeutics. *Science, 297*(5580), 353–356. https://doi.org/10.1126/science.1072994

Heikkinen, J., Möttönen, M., Alanen, A., & Lassila, O. (2004). Phenotypic characterization of regulatory T cells in the human decidua. *Clinical and Experimental Immunology, 136*(2), 373–378. https://doi.org/10.1111/j.1365-2249.2004.02441.x

Heise, V., Filippini, N., Trachtenberg, A. J., Suri, S., Ebmeier, K. P., & Mackay, C. E. (2014). Apolipoprotein E genotype, gender and age modulate connectivity of the hippocampus in healthy adults. *NeuroImage, 98*, 23–30. https://doi.org/10.1016/j.neuroimage.2014.04.081

Henderson, R., Furlano, J. A., Claringbold, S. S., Cornect-Benoit, A., Ly, A., Walker, J., Zaretsky, L., & Roach, P. (2024). Colonial drivers and cultural protectors of brain health among Indigenous peoples internationally. *Frontiers in Public Health, 12*, 1346753. https://doi.org/10.3389/fpubh.2024.1346753

Henderson, V. W., & Rocca, W. A. (2012). Estrogens and Alzheimer disease risk: Is there a window of opportunity. *Neurology, 79*(18), 1840–1841. https://doi.org/10.1212/wnl.0b013e318271f88f

Heuer, H. W., Wang, P., Rascovsky, K., Wolf, A., Appleby, B., Bove, J., Bordelon, Y., Brannelly, P., Brushaber, D. E., Caso, C., Coppola, G., Dickerson, B., Dickinson, S., Domoto-Reilly, K.,

Faber, K., Ferrall, J., Fields, J., Fishman, A., Fong, J., et al. (2020). Comparison of sporadic and familial behavioral variant frontotemporal dementia (FTD) in a North American cohort. *Alzheimer's & Dementia: The Journal of the Alzheimer's Association, 16*(1), 60–70. https://doi.org/10.1002/alz.12046

Höglinger, G. U., Respondek, G., Stamelou, M., Kurz, C., Josephs, K. A., Lang, A. E., Mollenhauer, B., Müller, U., Nilsson, C., Whitwell, J. L., Arzberger, T., Englund, E., Gelpi, E., Giese, A., Irwin, D. J., Meissner, W. G., Pantelyat, A., Rajput, A., van Swieten, J. C., et al. (2017). Clinical diagnosis of progressive supranuclear palsy: The movement disorder society criteria. *Movement Disorders: Official Journal of the Movement Disorder Society, 32*(6), 853–864. https://doi.org/10.1002/mds.26987

Hohman, T. J., Dumitrescu, L., Barnes, L. L., Thambisetty, M., Beecham, G., Kunkle, B., Gifford, K. A., Bush, W. S., Chibnik, L. B., Mukherjee, S., De Jager, P. L., Kukull, W., Crane, P. K., Resnick, S. M., Keene, C. D., Montine, T. J., Schellenberg, G. D., Haines, J. L., Zetterberg, H., et al. (2018). Sex-specific association of apolipoprotein E with cerebrospinal fluid levels of tau. *JAMA Neurology, 75*(8), 989–998. https://doi.org/10.1001/jamaneurol.2018.0821

Holland, D., Desikan, R. S., Dale, A. M., & McEvoy, L. K. (2013). Higher rates of decline for women and apolipoprotein e ε4 carriers. *American Journal of Neuroradiology*. https://doi.org/10.3174/ajnr.A3601

Hui, J. S., Wilson, R. S., Bennett, D. A., Bienias, J. L., Gilley, D. W., & Evans, D. A. (2003). Rate of cognitive decline and mortality in Alzheimer's disease. *Neurology, 61*(10), 1356–1361. https://doi.org/10.1212/01.wnl.0000094327.68399.59

Iadecola, C. (2013). The pathobiology of vascular dementia. *Neuron, 80*(4), 844–866. https://doi.org/10.1016/j.neuron.2013.10.008

Illán-Gala, I., Casaletto, K. B., Borrego-Écija, S., Arenaza-Urquijo, E. M., Wolf, A., Cobigo, Y., Goh, S. Y. M., Staffaroni, A. M., Alcolea, D., Fortea, J., Blesa, R., Clarimon, J., Iulita, M. F., Brugulat-Serrat, A., Lladó, A., Grinberg, L. T., Possin, K., Rankin, K. P., Kramer, J. H., et al. (2021). Sex differences in the behavioral variant of frontotemporal dementia: A new window to executive and behavioral reserve. *Alzheimer's & Dementia: The Journal of the Alzheimer's Association, 17*(8), 1329–1341. https://doi.org/10.1002/alz.12299

Ingre, C., Roos, P. M., Piehl, F., Kamel, F., & Fang, F. (2015). Risk factors for amyotrophic lateral sclerosis. *Clinical Epidemiology, 7*, 181–193. https://doi.org/10.2147/CLEP.S37505

Jack, C. R., Knopman, D. S., Jagust, W. J., Petersen, R. C., Weiner, M. W., Aisen, P. S., Shaw, L. M., Vemuri, P., Wiste, H. J., Weigand, S. D., Lesnick, T. G., Pankratz, V. S., Donohue, M. C., & Trojanowski, J. Q. (2013). Tracking pathophysiological processes in Alzheimer's disease: An updated hypothetical model of dynamic biomarkers. *The Lancet. Neurology, 12*(2), 207–216. https://doi.org/10.1016/S1474-4422(12)70291-0

Jack, C. R., Wiste, H. J., Weigand, S. D., Knopman, D. S., Vemuri, P., Mielke, M. M., Lowe, V., Senjem, M. L., Gunter, J. L., Machulda, M. M., Gregg, B. E., Pankratz, V. S., Rocca, W. A., & Petersen, R. C. (2015). Age, sex, and APOE ϵ4 effects on memory, brain structure, and β-Amyloid across the adult life Span. *JAMA Neurology*. https://doi.org/10.1001/jamaneurol.2014.4821

Jacklin, K. M., Walker, J. D., & Shawande, M. (2012). The emergence of dementia as a health concern among First Nations populations in Alberta, Canada. *Canadian Journal of Public Health = Revue Canadienne DeSante Publique, 104*(1), e39–e44. https://doi.org/10.1007/BF03405652

Jackson, C. L., Agénor, M., Johnson, D. A., Austin, S. B., & Kawachi, I. (2016). Sexual orientation identity disparities in health behaviors, outcomes, and services use among men and women in the United States: A cross-sectional study. *BMC Public Health, 16*(1), 807. https://doi.org/10.1186/s12889-016-3467-1

Jecmenica Lukic, M., Kurz, C., Respondek, G., Grau-Rivera, O., Compta, Y., Gelpi, E., Troakes, C., & Barcelona Brain Bank collaborative group, the MDS-endorsed PSP study group, van Swieten, J. C., Giese, A., Roeber, S., Arzberger, T., & Höglinger, G. (2020). Copathology in progressive supranuclear palsy: Does it matter? *Movement Disorders: Official Journal of the Movement Disorder Society, 35*(6), 984–993. https://doi.org/10.1002/mds.28011

Johnson, J. K., Diehl, J., Mendez, M. F., Neuhaus, J., Shapira, J. S., Forman, M., Chute, D. J., Roberson, E. D., Pace-Savitsky, C., Neumann, M., Chow, T. W., Rosen, H. J., Forstl, H., Kurz, A., & Miller, B. L. (2005). Frontotemporal lobar degeneration: Demographic characteristics of 353 patients. *Archives of Neurology, 62*(6), 925–930. https://doi.org/10.1001/archneur.62.6.925

Jung, J. H., Lee, G. W., Lee, J. H., Byun, M. S., Yi, D., Jeon, S. Y., Jung, G. J., Joung, H., Shin, S. A., Kim, Y. K., Kang, K. M., Sohn, C.-H., & Lee, D. Y. (2020). Multiparity, brain atrophy, and cognitive decline. *Frontiers in Aging Neuroscience, 12*. https://doi.org/10.3389/fnagi.2020.00159

Kang, J. H., & Grodstein, F. (2012). Postmenopausal hormone therapy, timing of initiation, APOE and cognitive decline. *Neurobiology of Aging*. https://doi.org/10.1016/j.neurobiolaging.2010.10.007

Karalexi, M. A., Georgakis, M. K., Dimitriou, N. G., Vichos, T., Katsimpris, A., Petridou, E. T., & Papadopoulos, F. C. (2020). Gender-affirming hormone treatment and cognitive function in transgender young adults: A systematic review and meta-analysis. *Psychoneuroendocrinology, 119*, 104721. https://doi.org/10.1016/j.psyneuen.2020.104721

Kim, B. Y., Choi, D. H., Jung, C. H., Kang, S. K., Mok, J. O., & Kim, C. H. (2017). Obesity and physical activity. *Journal of Obesity & Metabolic Syndrome, 26*(1), 15–22. https://doi.org/10.7570/JOMES.2017.26.1.15

Kobayashi, L. C., Peterson, R. L., Yu, X., Avila-Rieger, J., Amofa-Ho, P. A., Vila-Castelar, C., Meza, E., Shaaban, C. E., Whitmer, R. A., Gilsanz, P., & Mayeda, E. R. (2024). Life course financial mobility and later-life memory function and decline by gender, and race and ethnicity: An intersectional analysis of the US KHANDLE and STAR cohort studies. *The Lancet. Healthy Longevity, 5*(9), 100613. https://doi.org/10.1016/S2666-7568(24)00129-6

Kramer, A. F., & Colcombe, S. (2018). Fitness effects on the cognitive function of older adults: A meta-analytic study-revisited. *Perspectives on Psychological Science: A Journal of the Association for Psychological Science, 13*(2), 213–217. https://doi.org/10.1177/1745691617707316

Kramer, J. H., Delis, D. C., & Daniel, M. (1988). Sex differences in verbal learning. *Journal of Clinical Psychology*. https://doi.org/10.1002/1097-4679(198811)44:6<907::AID-JCLP2270440610>3.0.CO;2-8

Kramer, J. H., Kaplan, E., Delis, D. C., O'Donnell, L., & Prifitera, A. (1997). Developmental sex differences in verbal learning. *Neuropsychology*. https://doi.org/10.1037/0894-4105.11.4.577

Kuh, D., Cooper, R., Moore, A., Richards, M., & Hardy, R. (2018). Age at menopause and lifetime cognition: Findings from a British birth cohort study. *Neurology, 90*(19), e1673–e1681. https://doi.org/10.1212/WNL.0000000000005486

Lapane, K. L., Gambassi, G., Landi, F., Sgadari, A., Mor, V., & Bernabei, R. (2001). Gender differences in predictors of mortality in nursing home residents with AD. *Neurology, 56*(5), 650–654. https://doi.org/10.1212/wnl.56.5.650

Lavrencic, L. M., Delbaere, K., Broe, G. A., Daylight, G., Draper, B., Cumming, R. G., Garvey, G., Allan, W., Hill, T. Y., Lasschuit, D., Schofield, P. R., & Radford, K. (2022). Dementia incidence, *APOE* genotype, and risk factors for cognitive decline in aboriginal Australians: A longitudinal cohort study. *Neurology, 98*(11), e1124–e1136. https://doi.org/10.1212/wnl.0000000000013295

LeBlanc, E. S., Janowsky, J., Chan, B. K. S., & Nelson, H. D. (2001). Hormone replacement therapy and cognition: Systematic review and Meta-analysis. *JAMA, 285*(11), 1489–1499. https://doi.org/10.1001/jama.285.11.1489

Lee, J. G. L., Griffin, G. K., & Melvin, C. L. (2009). Tobacco use among sexual minorities in the USA, 1987 to May 2007: A systematic review. *Tobacco Control, 18*(4), 275–282.

Lee, J. K., Frank, R. D., Christenson, L. R., Fields, J. A., Rocca, W. A., & Mielke, M. M. (2024). Associations of reproductive factors and exogenous estrogens with global and domain-specific cognition in later life. *Alzheimer's & Dementia: The Journal of the Alzheimer's Association, 20*(1), 63–73. https://doi.org/10.1002/alz.13394

Liang, F.-W., Chan, W., Chen, P.-J., Zimmerman, C., Waring, S., & Doody, R. (2016). Cognitively-related basic activities of daily living impairment greatly increases the risk of death in Alzheimers disease. *PLOS ONE, 11*(8), e0160671. https://doi.org/10.1371/journal.pone.0160671

Lima, J., Martins, C., Nunes, G., Sousa, M. J., Branco, J. C., & Borrego, L. M. (2017). Regulatory T cells show dynamic behavior during late pregnancy, delivery, and the postpartum period. *Reproductive Sciences*. https://doi.org/10.1177/1933719116676395

Lin, K. A., Choudhury, K. R., Rathakrishnan, B. G., Marks, D. M., Petrella, J. R., & Doraiswamy, P. M. (2015). Marked gender differences in progression of mild cognitive impairment over 8 years. *Alzheimer's and Dementia: Translational Research and Clinical Interventions*. https://doi.org/10.1016/j.trci.2015.07.001

Lindseth, L. R. S., Lange, A.-M. G. de, Meer, D. van der, Agartz, I., Westlye, L. T., Tamnes, C. K., & Barth, C. (2022). *Female-specific factors are associated with cognition in the UK Biobank cohort* (p. 2022.06.27.22276879). medRxiv. https://doi.org/10.1101/2022.06.27.22276879

Lindwall, M., Rennemark, M., & Berggren, T. (2008). Movement in mind: The relationship of exercise with cognitive status for older adults in the Swedish National Study on Aging and Care (SNAC). *Aging & Mental Health, 12*(2), 212–220. https://doi.org/10.1080/13607860701797232

Litvan, I., Agid, Y., Calne, D., Campbell, G., Dubois, B., Duvoisin, R. C., Goetz, C. G., Golbe, L. I., Grafman, J., Growdon, J. H., Hallett, M., Jankovic, J., Quinn, N. P., Tolosa, E., & Zee, D. S. (1996). Clinical research criteria for the diagnosis of progressive supranuclear palsy (Steele-Richardson-Olszewski syndrome): Report of the NINDS-SPSP international workshop. *Neurology, 47*(1), 1–9. https://doi.org/10.1212/wnl.47.1.1

Litvan, I., Mangone, C. A., McKee, A., Verny, M., Parsa, A., Jellinger, K., D'Olhaberriague, L., Chaudhuri, K. R., & Pearce, R. K. (1996). Natural history of progressive supranuclear palsy (Steele-Richardson-Olszewski syndrome) and clinical predictors of survival: A clinicopathological study. *Journal of Neurology, Neurosurgery, and Psychiatry, 60*(6), 615–620. https://doi.org/10.1136/jnnp.60.6.615

Liu, C.-C., Liu, C.-C., Kanekiyo, T., Xu, H., & Bu, G. (2013). Apolipoprotein E and Alzheimer disease: Risk, mechanisms and therapy. *Nature Reviews. Neurology, 9*(2), 106–118. https://doi.org/10.1038/nrneurol.2012.263

Liu, H., Zhang, Z., Choi, S.-W., & Langa, K. M. (2020). Marital status and dementia: Evidence from the health and retirement study. *The Journals of Gerontology. Series B, Psychological Sciences and Social Sciences, 75*(8), 1783–1795. https://doi.org/10.1093/geronb/gbz087

Livingston, G., Huntley, J., Liu, K. Y., Costafreda, S. G., Selbæk, G., Alladi, S., Ames, D., Banerjee, S., Burns, A., Brayne, C., Fox, N. C., Ferri, C. P., Gitlin, L. N., Howard, R., Kales, H. C., Kivimäki, M., Larson, E. B., Nakasujja, N., Rockwood, K., et al. (2024). Dementia prevention, intervention, and care: 2024 report of the Lancet standing Commission. *Lancet (London, England), 404*(10452), 572–628. https://doi.org/10.1016/S0140-6736(24)01296-0

Logroscino, G., Piccininni, M., Graff, C., Hardiman, O., Ludolph, A. C., Moreno, F., Otto, M., Remes, A. M., Rowe, J. B., Seelaar, H., Solje, E., Stefanova, E., Traykov, L., Jelic, V., Rydell, M. T., Pender, N., Anderl-Straub, S., Barandiaran, M., Gabilondo, A., et al. (2023). Incidence of syndromes associated with frontotemporal lobar degeneration in 9 European countries. *JAMA Neurology, 80*(3), 279–286. https://doi.org/10.1001/jamaneurol.2022.5128

Lohner, V., Pehlivan, G., Sanroma, G., Miloschewski, A., Schirmer, M. D., Stöcker, T., Reuter, M., & Breteler, M. M. B. (2022). Relation between sex, menopause, and white matter hyperintensities: The Rhineland Study. *Neurology, 99*(9), e935–e943. https://doi.org/10.1212/WNL.0000000000200782

Ma, M., Dorstyn, D., Ward, L., & Prentice, S. (2018). Alzheimers' disease and caregiving: A meta-analytic review comparing the mental health of primary carers to controls. *Aging and Mental Health, 22*(11), 1395–1405. https://doi.org/10.1080/13607863.2017.1370689

Mahale, R. R., Krishnan, S., Divya, K. P., Jisha, V. T., & Kishore, A. (2022). Gender differences in progressive supranuclear palsy. *Acta Neurologica Belgica, 122*(2), 357–362. https://doi.org/10.1007/s13760-021-01599-0

Maki, P. M. (2005). A systematic review of clinical trials of hormone therapy on cognitive function: Effects of age at initiation and progestin use. *Annals of the New York Academy of Sciences, 1052*(1), 182–197. https://doi.org/10.1196/annals.1347.012

Maki, P. M. (2008). The timing of estrogen therapy after ovariectomy—Implications for neurocognitive function. *Nature Clinical Practice Endocrinology & Metabolism, 4*(9), 494–495. https://doi.org/10.1038/ncpendmet0901

Maki, P. M. (2013). Critical window hypothesis of hormone therapy and cognition: A scientific update on clinical studies. *Menopause (New York, N.Y.), 20*(6), 695–709. https://doi.org/10.1097/GME.0b013e3182960cf8

Maki, P. M., & Sundermann, E. (2009). Hormone therapy and cognitive function. *Human Reproduction Update, 15*(6), 667–681. https://doi.org/10.1093/humupd/dmp022

Manjaly, Z. R., Scott, K. M., Abhinav, K., Wijesekera, L., Ganesalingam, J., Goldstein, L. H., Janssen, A., Dougherty, A., Willey, E., Stanton, B. R., Turner, M. R., Ampong, M.-A., Sakel, M., Orrell, R. W., Howard, R., Shaw, C. E., Leigh, P. N., & Al-Chalabi, A. (2010). The sex ratio in amyotrophic lateral sclerosis: A population based study. *Amyotrophic Lateral Sclerosis: Official Publication of the World Federation of Neurology Research Group on Motor Neuron Diseases, 11*(5), 439–442. https://doi.org/10.3109/17482961003610853

Mann, V. A., Sasanuma, S., Sakuma, N., & Masaki, S. (1990). Sex differences in cognitive abilities: A cross-cultural perspective. *Neuropsychologia*. https://doi.org/10.1016/0028-3932(90)90141-A

Mata, S., Bussotti, M., Del Mastio, M., Barilaro, A., Piersanti, P., Lombardi, M., Cincotta, M., Torricelli, S., Leccese, D., Sperti, M., Rodolico, G. R., Nacmias, B., & Sorbi, S. (2023). Epidemiology of amyotrophic lateral sclerosis in the north east Tuscany in the 2018-2021 period. *eNeurologicalSci, 31*, 100457. https://doi.org/10.1016/j.ensci.2023.100457

Matthews, K. A., Xu, W., Gaglioti, A. H., Holt, J. B., Croft, J. B., Mack, D., & McGuire, L. C. (2019). Racial and ethnic estimates of Alzheimer's disease and related dementias in the United States (2015–2060) in adults aged ≥65 years. *Alzheimer's & Dementia, 15*(1), 17–24. https://doi.org/10.1016/j.jalz.2018.06.3063

Mayeda, E. R., Mobley, T. M., Weiss, R. E., Murchland, A. R., Berkman, L. F., & Sabbath, E. L. (2020). Association of work-family experience with mid- and late-life memory decline in US women. *Neurology, 95*(23), e3072–e3080. https://doi.org/10.1212/WNL.0000000000010989

McCarthy, M. M., & Konkle, A. T. M. (2005). When is a sex difference not a sex difference? *Frontiers in Neuroendocrinology, 26*(2), 85–102. https://doi.org/10.1016/j.yfrne.2005.06.001

McKinlay, S. M., Brambilla, D. J., & Posner, J. G. (1992). The normal menopause transition. *Maturitas, 14*(2), 103–115. https://doi.org/10.1016/0378-5122(92)90003-m

Meng, Q., Lin, M.-S., & Tzeng, I.-S. (2020). Relationship between exercise and Alzheimer's disease: A narrative literature review. *Frontiers in Neuroscience, 14*, 131. https://doi.org/10.3389/fnins.2020.00131

Mielke, M. M., Aggarwal, N. T., Vila-Castelar, C., Agarwal, P., Arenaza-Urquijo, E. M., Brett, B., Brugulat-Serrat, A., DuBose, L. E., Eikelboom, W. S., Flatt, J., Foldi, N. S., Franzen, S., Gilsanz, P., Li, W., McManus, A. J., van Lent, D. M., Milani, S. A., Shaaban, C. E., Stites, S. D., et al. (2022). Consideration of sex and gender in Alzheimer's disease and related disorders from a global perspective. *Alzheimer's & Dementia, 18*(12), 2707–2724. https://doi.org/10.1002/alz.12662

Mielke, M. M., Ferretti, M. T., Iulita, M. F., Hayden, K., & Khachaturian, A. S. (2018). Sex and gender in Alzheimer's disease—Does it matter? *Alzheimer's & Dementia: The Journal of the Alzheimer's Association, 14*(9), 1101–1103. https://doi.org/10.1016/j.jalz.2018.08.003

Mielke, M. M., Milic, N. M., Weissgerber, T. L., White, W. M., Kantarci, K., Mosley, T. H., Windham, B. G., Simpson, B. N., Turner, S. T., & Garovic, V. D. (2016). Impaired cognition and brain atrophy decades after hypertensive pregnancy disorders. *Circulation. Cardiovascular Quality and Outcomes, 9*(2 Suppl 1), S70–S76. https://doi.org/10.1161/CIRCOUTCOMES.115.002461

Miramontes, S., Pereda Serras, C., Woldemariam, S. R., Khan, U., Li, Y., Tang, A. S., Tsoy, E., Oskotsky, T. T., & Sirota, M. (2024). Alzheimer's disease as a women's health challenge: A call for action on integrative precision medicine approaches. *Npj Women's Health, 2*(1), 17. https://doi.org/10.1038/s44294-024-00021-3

Montine, T. J., Phelps, C. H., Beach, T. G., Bigio, E. H., Cairns, N. J., Dickson, D. W., Duyckaerts, C., Frosch, M. P., Masliah, E., Mirra, S. S., Nelson, P. T., Schneider, J. A., Thal, D. R., Trojanowski, J. Q., Vinters, H. V., Hyman, B. T., & National Institute on Aging, & Alzheimer's Association. (2012). National Institute on Aging-Alzheimer's Association guidelines for the neuropathologic assessment of Alzheimer's disease: A practical approach. *Acta Neuropathologica, 123*(1), 1–11. https://doi.org/10.1007/s00401-011-0910-3

Mosconi, L., Berti, V., Dyke, J., Schelbaum, E., Jett, S., Loughlin, L., Jang, G., Rahman, A., Hristov, H., Pahlajani, S., Andrews, R., Matthews, D., Etingin, O., Ganzer, C., de Leon, M., Isaacson, R., & Brinton, R. D. (2021). Menopause impacts human brain structure, connectivity, energy metabolism, and amyloid-beta deposition. *Scientific Reports, 11*, 10867. https://doi.org/10.1038/s41598-021-90084-y

Mosconi, L., Berti, V., Quinn, C., McHugh, P., Petrongolo, G., Varsavsky, I., Osorio, R. S., Pupi, A., Vallabhajosula, S., Isaacson, R. S., de Leon, M. J., & Brinton, R. D. (2017). Sex differences in Alzheimer risk: Brain imaging of endocrine vs chronologic aging. *Neurology, 89*(13), 1382–1390. https://doi.org/10.1212/WNL.0000000000004425

Mosconi, L., & Brinton, R. D. (2018). How would we combat menopause as an Alzheimer's risk factor? *Expert Review of Neurotherapeutics, 18*(9), 689–691. https://doi.org/10.1080/14737175.2018.1510320

Mosconi, L., Rahman, A., Diaz, I., Wu, X., Scheyer, O., Hristov, H. W., Vallabhajosula, S., Isaacson, R. S., de Leon, M. J., & Brinton, R. D. (2018). Increased Alzheimer's risk during the menopause transition: A 3-year longitudinal brain imaging study. *PloS One, 13*(12), e0207885. https://doi.org/10.1371/journal.pone.0207885

Moulton, V. R. (2018). Sex hormones in acquired immunity and autoimmune disease. *Frontiers in Immunology, 9*, 2279. https://doi.org/10.3389/fimmu.2018.02279

Mous, S. E., Schoemaker, N. K., Blanken, L. M. E., Thijssen, S., van der Ende, J., Polderman, T. J. C., Jaddoe, V. W. V., Hofman, A., Verhulst, F. C., Tiemeier, H., & White, T. (2017). The association of gender, age, and intelligence with neuropsychological functioning in young typically developing children: The Generation R study. *Applied Neuropsychology: Child*. https://doi.org/10.1080/21622965.2015.1067214

Najar, J., Aakre, J. A., Vassilaki, M., Wetterberg, H., Rydén, L., Zettergren, A., Skoog, I., Jack, C. R., Knopman, D. S., Petersen, R. C., Kern, S., & Mielke, M. M. (2021). Sex difference in the relation between marital status and dementia risk in two population-based cohorts. *Journal of Alzheimer's Disease: JAD, 83*(3), 1269–1279. https://doi.org/10.3233/JAD-210246

Nasri, A., Sghaier, I., Neji, A., Gharbi, A., Abida, Y., Mrabet, S., Gargouri, A., Djebara, M. B., Kacem, I., & Gouider, R. (2024). Phenotypic spectrum of progressive supranuclear palsy: Clinical study and apolipoprotein E effect. *Journal of Movement Disorders, 17*(2), 158. https://doi.org/10.14802/jmd.23178

Nebel, R. A., Aggarwal, N. T., Barnes, L. L., Gallagher, A., Goldstein, J. M., Kantarci, K., Mallampalli, M. P., Mormino, E. C., Scott, L., Yu, W. H., Maki, P. M., & Mielke, M. M. (2018). Understanding the impact of sex and gender in Alzheimer's disease: A call to action. *Alzheimer's & Dementia: The Journal of the Alzheimer's Association, 14*(9), 1171–1183. https://doi.org/10.1016/j.jalz.2018.04.008

Nerattini, M., Jett, S., Andy, C., Carlton, C., Zarate, C., Boneu, C., Battista, M., Pahlajani, S., Loeb-Zeitlin, S., Havryulik, Y., Williams, S., Christos, P., Fink, M., Brinton, R. D., & Mosconi, L. (2023). Systematic review and meta-analysis of the effects of menopause hormone therapy on risk of Alzheimer's disease and dementia. *Frontiers in Aging Neuroscience, 15*, 1260427. https://doi.org/10.3389/fnagi.2023.1260427

Neu, S. C., Pa, J., Kukull, W., Beekly, D., Kuzma, A., Gangadharan, P., Wang, L. S., Romero, K., Arneric, S. P., Redolfi, A., Orlandi, D., Frisoni, G. B., Au, R., Devine, S., Auerbach, S.,

Espinosa, A., Boada, M., Ruiz, A., Johnson, S. C., et al. (2017). Apolipoprotein E genotype and sex risk factors for Alzheimer disease: A meta-analysis. *JAMA Neurology, 74*(10), 1178–1189. https://doi.org/10.1001/jamaneurol.2017.2188

Niu, H., Álvarez-Álvarez, I., Guillén-Grima, F., & Aguinaga-Ontoso, I. (2017). Prevalence and incidence of Alzheimer's disease in Europe: A meta-analysis. *Neurologia (Barcelona, Spain), 32*(8), 523–532. https://doi.org/10.1016/j.nrl.2016.02.016

Nomaguchi, K. M., & Bianchi, S. M. (2004). Exercise time: Gender differences in the effects of marriage, parenthood, and employment. *Journal of Marriage and Family, 66*(2), 413–430. https://doi.org/10.1111/J.1741-3737.2004.00029.X

O'Sullivan, S. S., Massey, L. A., Williams, D. R., Silveira-Moriyama, L., Kempster, P. A., Holton, J. L., Revesz, T., & Lees, A. J. (2008). Clinical outcomes of progressive supranuclear palsy and multiple system atrophy. *Brain: A Journal of Neurology, 131*(Pt 5), 1362–1372. https://doi.org/10.1093/brain/awn065

Oertelt-Prigione, S. (2012). The influence of sex and gender on the immune response. *Autoimmunity Reviews, 11*(6–7), A479–A485. https://doi.org/10.1016/j.autrev.2011.11.022

Onyike, C. U., & Diehl-Schmid, J. (2013). The epidemiology of frontotemporal dementia. *International Review of Psychiatry (Abingdon, England), 25*(2), 130–137. https://doi.org/10.3109/09540261.2013.776523

Ortona, E., Pierdominici, M., Maseli, A., Veroni, C., Aloisi, F., & Shoenfeld, Y. (2016). Sex-based differences in autoimmune diseases. *Annali Dell'Istituto Superiore Di Sanita, 52*(2), 205–212. https://doi.org/10.4415/ANN_16_02_12

Oveisgharan, S., Arvanitakis, Z., Yu, L., Farfel, J., Schneider, J. A., & Bennett, D. A. (2018). Sex differences in Alzheimer's disease and common neuropathologies of aging. *Acta Neuropathologica, 136*(6), 887–900. https://doi.org/10.1007/s00401-018-1920-1

Pais, M. V., Forlenza, O. V., & Diniz, B. S. (2023). Plasma biomarkers of Alzheimer's disease: A review of available assays, recent developments, and implications for clinical practice. *Journal of Alzheimer's Disease Reports, 7*(1), 355. https://doi.org/10.3233/ADR-230029

Palpatzis, E., Akinci, M., Aguilar-Dominguez, P., Garcia-Prat, M., Blennow, K., Zetterberg, H., Carboni, M., Kollmorgen, G., Wild, N., Fauria, K., Falcon, C., Gispert, J. D., Suárez-Calvet, M., Grau-Rivera, O., Sánchez-Benavides, G., Arenaza-Urquijo, E. M., & ALFA study. (2024). Lifetime stressful events associated with Alzheimer's pathologies, neuroinflammation and brain structure in a risk enriched cohort. *Annals of Neurology, 95*(6), 1058–1068. https://doi.org/10.1002/ana.26881

Pankratz, V. S., Roberts, R. O., Mielke, M. M., Knopman, D. S., Jack, C. R., Geda, Y. E., Rocca, W. A., & Petersen, R. C. (2015). Predicting the risk of mild cognitive impairment in the Mayo Clinic Study of Aging. *Neurology, 84*(14), 1433–1442. https://doi.org/10.1212/WNL.0000000000001437

Papastavrou, E., Tsangari, H., Kalokerinou, A., Papacostas, S. S., & Sourtzi, P. (2009). Gender issues in caring for demented relatives. *Health Science Journal, 3*(1), 41–53.

Pavalko, E. K., & Artis, J. E. (1997). Women's caregiving and paid work: Causal relationships in late midlife. *The Journals of Gerontology: Series B, 52B*(4), S170–S179. https://doi.org/10.1093/geronb/52B.4.S170

Payami, H., Montee, K. R., Kaye, J. A., Bird, T. D., Yu, C. E., Wijsman, E. M., & Schellenberg, G. D. (1994). Alzheimer's disease, apolipoprotein E4, and gender. *JAMA: The Journal of the American Medical Association*. https://doi.org/10.1001/jama.1994.03510410028015

Peacock, S., Bayly, M., Duggleby, W., Ploeg, J., Pollard, L., Swindle, J., Lee, H. J., Williams, A., Markle-Reid, M., & McAiney, C. (2020). Women's caregiving experience of older persons living with Alzheimer disease and related dementias and multiple chronic conditions: Using Wuest's Theory. *SAGE Open Nursing*. https://doi.org/10.1177/2377960820974816

Pearce, N., Gallo, V., & McElvenny, D. (2015). Head trauma in sport and neurodegenerative disease: An issue whose time has come? *Neurobiology of Aging, 36*(3), 1383–1389. https://doi.org/10.1016/j.neurobiolaging.2014.12.024

Pengo, M., Alberici, A., Libri, I., Benussi, A., Gadola, Y., Ashton, N. J., Zetterberg, H., Blennow, K., & Borroni, B. (2022). Sex influences clinical phenotype in frontotemporal dementia. *Neurological Sciences: Official Journal of the Italian Neurological Society and of the Italian Society of Clinical Neurophysiology, 43*(9), 5281–5287. https://doi.org/10.1007/s10072-022-06185-7

Perales-Puchalt, J., Gauthreaux, K., Flatt, J., Teylan, M. A., Resendez, J., Kukull, W. A., Chan, K. C. G., Burns, J., & Vidoni, E. D. (2019). Risk of dementia and mild cognitive impairment among older adults in same-sex relationships. *International Journal of Geriatric Psychiatry, 34*(6), 828–835. https://doi.org/10.1002/gps.5092

Pharr, J. R. (2021). Health disparities among lesbian, gay, bisexual, transgender, and nonbinary adults 50 years old and older in the United States. *LGBT Health, 8*(7), 473–485. https://doi.org/10.1089/lgbt.2021.0009

Phung, T. K. T., Waltoft, B. L., Laursen, T. M., Settnes, A., Kessing, L. V., Mortensen, P. B., & Waldemar, G. (2010). Hysterectomy, ophorectomy and risk of dementia: A nationwide historical cohort study. *Dementia and Geriatric Cognitive Disorders, 30*(1), 43–50. https://doi.org/10.1159/000314681

Podcasy, J. L., & Epperson, C. N. (2016). Considering sex and gender in Alzheimer disease and other dementias. *Dialogues in clinical neuroscience, 18*(4), 437-446.

Poirier, J., Bertrand, P., Poirier, J., Kogan, S., Gauthier, S., Poirier, J., Gauthier, S., Davignon, J., Bouthillier, D., & Davignon, J. (1993). Apolipoprotein E polymorphism and Alzheimer's disease. *The Lancet*. https://doi.org/10.1016/0140-6736(93)91705-Q

Price, J. L., & Morris, J. C. (1999). Tangles and plaques in nondemented aging and "preclinical" Alzheimer's disease. *Annals of Neurology, 45*(3), 358–368. https://doi.org/10.1002/1531-8249(199903)45:3<358::AID-ANA12>3.0.CO;2-X

Ptok, U., Barkow, K., & Heun, R. (2002). Fertility and number of children in patients with Alzheimer's disease. *Archives of Women's Mental Health, 5*(2), 83–86. https://doi.org/10.1007/s00737-002-0142-6

Pujari, V. (2024). Moving to improve mental health - The role of exercise in cognitive function: A narrative review. *Journal of Pharmacy & Bioallied Sciences, 16*(Suppl 1), S26–S30. https://doi.org/10.4103/jpbs.jpbs_614_23

Rahman, A., Schelbaum, E., Hoffman, K., Diaz, I., Hristov, H., Andrews, R., Jett, S., Jackson, H., Lee, A., Sarva, H., Pahlajani, S., Matthews, D., Dyke, J., de Leon, M. J., Isaacson, R. S., Brinton, R. D., & Mosconi, L. (2020). Sex-driven modifiers of Alzheimer risk. *Neurology, 95*(2), e166–e178. https://doi.org/10.1212/WNL.0000000000009781

Rajan, K. B., Weuve, J., Barnes, L. L., McAninch, E. A., Wilson, R. S., & Evans, D. A. (2021). Population estimate of people with clinical Alzheimer's disease and mild cognitive impairment in the United States (2020-2060). *Alzheimer's & Dementia: The Journal of the Alzheimer's Association, 17*(12), 1966–1975. https://doi.org/10.1002/alz.12362

Rascovsky, K., Hodges, J. R., Knopman, D., Mendez, M. F., Kramer, J. H., Neuhaus, J., van Swieten, J. C., Seelaar, H., Dopper, E. G. P., Onyike, C. U., Hillis, A. E., Josephs, K. A., Boeve, B. F., Kertesz, A., Seeley, W. W., Rankin, K. P., Johnson, J. K., Gorno-Tempini, M.-L., Rosen, H., et al. (2011). Sensitivity of revised diagnostic criteria for the behavioural variant of frontotemporal dementia. *Brain: A Journal of Neurology, 134*(Pt 9), 2456–2477. https://doi.org/10.1093/brain/awr179

Ratnavalli, E., Brayne, C., Dawson, K., & Hodges, J. R. (2002). The prevalence of frontotemporal dementia. *Neurology, 58*(11), 1615–1621. https://doi.org/10.1212/wnl.58.11.1615

Rizzi, L., Rosset, I., & Roriz-Cruz, M. (2014). Global epidemiology of dementia: Alzheimer's and vascular types. *BioMed Research International, 2014*, 908915. https://doi.org/10.1155/2014/908915

Roberts, R. O., Geda, Y. E., Knopman, D. S., Cha, R. H., Pankratz, V. S., Boeve, B. F., Tangalos, E. G., Ivnik, R. J., Rocca, W. A., & Petersen, R. C. (2012). The incidence of MCI differs by subtype and is higher in men: The Mayo Clinic Study of Aging. *Neurology, 78*(5), 342–351. https://doi.org/10.1212/WNL.0b013e3182452862

Rocca, W. A., Grossardt, B. R., & Shuster, L. T. (2011). Oophorectomy, menopause, estrogen treatment, and cognitive aging: Clinical evidence for a window of opportunity. *Brain Research, 1379*, 188–198. https://doi.org/10.1016/j.brainres.2010.10.031

Rogalski, E., Rademaker, A., & Weintraub, S. (2007). Primary progressive aphasia: Relationship between gender and severity of language impairment. *Cognitive and Behavioral Neurology: Official Journal of the Society for Behavioral and Cognitive Neurology, 20*(1), 38–43. https://doi.org/10.1097/WNN.0b013e31802e3bae

Romanelli, R. J., Rosenblatt, A. S., Marcum, Z. A., & Flatt, J. D. (2024). Cognitive impairment in sexual and gender minority groups: A scoping review of the literature. *LGBT Health, 11*(3), 178–192. https://doi.org/10.1089/lgbt.2023.0095

Rosende-Roca, M., Abdelnour, C., Esteban, E., Tartari, J. P., Alarcon, E., Martínez-Atienza, J., González-Pérez, A., Sáez, M. E., Lafuente, A., Buendía, M., Pancho, A., Aguilera, N., Ibarria, M., Diego, S., Jofresa, S., Hernández, I., López, R., Gurruchaga, M. J., Tárraga, L., et al. (2021). The role of sex and gender in the selection of Alzheimer patients for clinical trial pre-screening. *Alzheimer's Research & Therapy, 13*(1), 95. https://doi.org/10.1186/s13195-021-00833-4

Rosie, E., Brooker, D., & Elizabet, P. (2015). *Women and dementia. A global research review*. Alzheimer's Disease International.

Royse, S. K., Cohen, A. D., Snitz, B. E., & Rosano, C. (2021). Differences in Alzheimer's disease and related dementias pathology among African American and Hispanic women: A qualitative literature review of biomarker studies. *Frontiers in Systems Neuroscience, 15*, 685957. https://doi.org/10.3389/fnsys.2021.685957

Ryan, J., Carrière, I., Scali, J., Dartigues, J. F., Tzourio, C., Poncet, M., Ritchie, K., & Ancelin, M. L. (2009). Characteristics of hormone therapy, cognitive function, and dementia: The prospective 3C Study. *Neurology, 73*(21), 1729–1737. https://doi.org/10.1212/WNL.0b013e3181c34b0c

Salk, R. H., Hyde, J. S., & Abramson, L. Y. (2017). Gender differences in depression in representative national samples: Meta-analyses of diagnoses and symptoms. *Psychological Bulletin, 143*(8), 783–822. https://doi.org/10.1037/bul0000102

Sampedro, F., Vilaplana, E., de Leon, M. J., Alcolea, D., Pegueroles, J., Montal, V., Carmona-Iragui, M., Sala, I., Sánchez-Saudinos, M.-B., Antón-Aguirre, S., Morenas-Rodríguez, E., Camacho, V., Falcón, C., Pavía, J., Ros, D., Clarimón, J., Blesa, R., Lleó, A., Fortea, J., & Alzheimer's Disease Neuroimaging Initiative. (2015). APOE-by-sex interactions on brain structure and metabolism in healthy elderly controls. *Oncotarget, 6*(29), 26663–26674. https://doi.org/10.18632/oncotarget.5185

Santacruz, P., Uttl, B., Litvan, I., & Grafman, J. (1998). Progressive supranuclear palsy: A survey of the disease course. *Neurology, 50*(6), 1637–1647. https://doi.org/10.1212/wnl.50.6.1637

Schelbaum, E., Loughlin, L., Jett, S., Zhang, C., Jang, G., Malviya, N., Hristov, H., Pahlajani, S., Isaacson, R., Dyke, J. P., Kamel, H., Brinton, R. D., & Mosconi, L. (2021). Association of reproductive history with brain MRI biomarkers of dementia risk in midlife. *Neurology, 97*(23), e2328–e2339. https://doi.org/10.1212/WNL.0000000000012941

Schliep, K. C., Shaaban, C. E., Meeks, H., Fraser, A., Smith, K. R., Majersik, J. J., Foster, N. L., Wactawski-Wende, J., Østbye, T., Tschanz, J., Padbury, J. F., Sharma, S., Zhang, Y., Facelli, J. C., Abdelrahman, C. S., Theilen, L., & Varner, M. W. (2023). Hypertensive disorders of pregnancy and subsequent risk of Alzheimer's disease and other dementias. *Alzheimer's & Dementia (Amsterdam, Netherlands), 15*(2), e12443. https://doi.org/10.1002/dad2.12443

Sears, J. T. (James T. (with Internet Archive). (2005). *Youth, education, and sexualities: An international encyclopedia*. Greenwood Press. http://archive.org/details/youtheducationse00jame

Seblova, D., Eng, C., Avila-Rieger, J. F., Dworkin, J. D., Peters, K., Lapham, S., Zahodne, L. B., Chapman, B., Prescott, C. A., Gruenewald, T. L., Arpawong, T. E., Gatz, M., Jones, R. J., Glymour, M. M., & Manly, J. J. (2023). High school quality is associated with cognition 58 years later. *Alzheimer's & Dementia (Amsterdam, Netherlands), 15*(2), e12424. https://doi.org/10.1002/dad2.12424

Shaaban, C. E., Rosano, C., Cohen, A. D., Huppert, T., Butters, M. A., Hengenius, J., Parks, W. T., & Catov, J. M. (2021). Cognition and cerebrovascular reactivity in midlife women with history of preeclampsia and placental evidence of maternal vascular malperfusion. *Frontiers in Aging Neuroscience, 13*, 637574. https://doi.org/10.3389/fnagi.2021.637574

Shaaban, C. E., & Rosso, A. L. (2024). Racial, ethnic, and geographic diversity in population neuroscience. *Current Topics in Behavioral Neurosciences*. https://doi.org/10.1007/7854_2024_475

Shaw, C., Hayes-Larson, E., Glymour, M. M., Dufouil, C., Hohman, T. J., Whitmer, R. A., Kobayashi, L. C., Brookmeyer, R., & Mayeda, E. R. (2021). Evaluation of selective survival and sex/gender differences in dementia incidence using a simulation model. *JAMA Network Open, 4*(3), e211001. https://doi.org/10.1001/jamanetworkopen.2021.1001

Shumaker, S. A., Legault, C., Kuller, L., Rapp, S. R., Thal, L., Lane, D. S., Fillit, H., Stefanick, M. L., Hendrix, S. L., Lewis, C. E., Masaki, K., Coker, L. H., & Women's Health Initiative Memory Study. (2004). Conjugated equine estrogens and incidence of probable dementia and mild cognitive impairment in postmenopausal women: Women's Health Initiative Memory Study. *JAMA, 291*(24), 2947–2958. https://doi.org/10.1001/jama.291.24.2947

Shumaker, S. A., Legault, C., Rapp, S. R., Thal, L., Wallace, R. B., Ockene, J. K., Hendrix, S. L., Jones, B. N., Assaf, A. R., Jackson, R. D., Kotchen, J. M., Wassertheil-Smoller, S., & Wactawski-Wende, J. (2003). Estrogen plus progestin and the incidence of dementia and mild cognitive impairment in postmenopausal women—The Women's Health Initiative Memory Study: A randomized controlled rrial. *Journal of the American Medical Association*. https://doi.org/10.1001/jama.289.20.2651

Siepmann, T., Boardman, H., Bilderbeck, A., Griffanti, L., Kenworthy, Y., Zwager, C., McKean, D., Francis, J., Neubauer, S., Yu, G. Z., Lewandowski, A. J., Sverrisdottir, Y. B., & Leeson, P. (2017). Long-term cerebral white and gray matter changes after preeclampsia. *Neurology, 88*(13), 1256–1264. https://doi.org/10.1212/WNL.0000000000003765

Silvestri, C., Almici, V., Libri, I., Mattioli, I., Cosseddu, M., Turrone, R., Rivolta, J., Grassini, C., Caratozzolo, S., Alberici, A., Marengoni, A., Pilotto, A., Borroni, B., Padovani, A., & Benussi, A. (2024). Sex differences in the severity and progression of neuropsychiatric symptoms across different dementia types. *Neurology. Clinical Practice, 14*(3), e200299. https://doi.org/10.1212/CPJ.0000000000200299

Sindi, S., Toopchiani, S., Barbera, M., Håkansson, K., Lehtisalo, J., Rosenberg, A., Stephen, R., Udeh-Momoh, C., & Kivipelto, M. (2021). Chapter 10—Sex and gender differences in genetic and lifestyle risk and protective factors for dementia. In M. T. Ferretti, A. S. Dimech, & A. S. Chadha (Eds.), *Sex and gender differences in Alzheimer's disease* (pp. 269–308). Academic Press. https://doi.org/10.1016/B978-0-12-819344-0.00013-2

Smith, K., Flicker, L., Lautenschlager, N. T., Almeida, O. P., Atkinson, D., Dwyer, A., & LoGiudice, D. (2008). High prevalence of dementia and cognitive impairment in Indigenous Australians. *Neurology, 71*(19), 1470–1473. https://doi.org/10.1212/01.wnl.0000320508.11013.4f

Snow, W. G., & Weinstock, J. (1990). Sex differences among non-brain-damaged adults on the Wechsler Adult Intelligence Scales: A review of the literature. *Journal of Clinical and Experimental Neuropsychology*. https://doi.org/10.1080/01688639008401028

Snyder, H. M., Asthana, S., Bain, L., Brinton, R., Craft, S., Dubal, D. B., Espeland, M. A., Gatz, M., Mielke, M. M., Raber, J., Rapp, P. R., Yaffe, K., & Carrillo, M. C. (2016). Sex biology contributions to vulnerability to Alzheimer's disease: A think tank convened by the Women's Alzheimer's Research Initiative. *Alzheimer's & Dementia, 12*(11), 1186–1196. https://doi.org/10.1016/j.jalz.2016.08.004

Sobow, T., & Kloszewska, I. (2004). Parity, number of pregnancies, and the age of onset of Alzheimer's disease. *The Journal of Neuropsychiatry and Clinical Neurosciences, 16*(1), 120-a. https://doi.org/10.1176/jnp.16.1.120-a

Sochocka, M., Karska, J., Pszczołowska, M., Ochnik, M., Fułek, M., Fułek, K., Kurpas, D., Chojdak-Łukasiewicz, J., Rosner-Tenerowicz, A., & Leszek, J. (2023). Cognitive decline in early and premature menopause. *International Journal of Molecular Sciences, 24*(7), 6566. https://doi.org/10.3390/ijms24076566

Soh, Y., Whitmer, R. A., Mayeda, E. R., Glymour, M. M., Peterson, R. L., Eng, C. W., Quesenberry, C. P., Manly, J. J., & Gilsanz, P. (2023). State-level indicators of childhood educational quality and incident dementia in older Black and White adults. *JAMA Neurology, 80*(4), 352–359. https://doi.org/10.1001/jamaneurol.2022.5337

Somerset, D. A., Zheng, Y., Kilby, M. D., Sansom, D. M., & Drayson, M. T. (2004). Normal human pregnancy is associated with an elevation in the immune suppressive CD25+ CD4+ regulatory T-cell subset. *Immunology, 112*(1), 38–43. https://doi.org/10.1111/j.1365-2567.2004.01869.x

Sperling, R. A., Aisen, P. S., Beckett, L. A., Bennett, D. A., Craft, S., Fagan, A. M., Iwatsubo, T., Jack, C. R., Kaye, J., Montine, T. J., Park, D. C., Reiman, E. M., Rowe, C. C., Siemers, E., Stern, Y., Yaffe, K., Carrillo, M. C., Thies, B., Morrison-Bogorad, M., et al. (2011). Toward defining the preclinical stages of Alzheimer's disease: Recommendations from the National Institute on Aging-Alzheimer's Association workgroups on diagnostic guidelines for Alzheimer's disease. *Alzheimer's and Dementia, 7*(3). https://doi.org/10.1016/j.jalz.2011.03.003

Spinelli, E. G., Mandelli, M. L., Miller, Z. A., Santos-Santos, M. A., Wilson, S. M., Agosta, F., Grinberg, L. T., Huang, E. J., Trojanowski, J. Q., Meyer, M., Henry, M. L., Comi, G., Rabinovici, G., Rosen, H. J., Filippi, M., Miller, B. L., Seeley, W. W., & Gorno-Tempini, M. L. (2017). Typical and atypical pathology in primary progressive aphasia variants. *Annals of Neurology, 81*(3), 430–443. https://doi.org/10.1002/ana.24885

Stafford, J., Chung, W. T., Sommerlad, A., Kirkbride, J. B., & Howard, R. (2022). Psychiatric disorders and risk of subsequent dementia: Systematic review and meta-analysis of longitudinal studies. *International Journal of Geriatric Psychiatry, 37*(5). https://doi.org/10.1002/gps.5711

Stang, C. D., Turcano, P., Mielke, M. M., Josephs, K. A., Bower, J. H., Ahlskog, J. E., Boeve, B. F., Martin, P. R., Upadhyaya, S. G., & Savica, R. (2020). Incidence and trends of progressive supranuclear palsy and corticobasal syndrome: A population-based study. *Journal of Parkinson's Disease, 10*(1), 179–184. https://doi.org/10.3233/JPD-191744

Stern, Y. (2002). What is cognitive reserve? Theory and research application of the reserve concept. *Journal of the International Neuropsychological Society*. https://doi.org/10.1017/S1355617702813248

Stern, Y., Tang, M.-X., Albert, M. S., Brandt, J., Jacobs, D. M., Bell, K., Marder, K., Sano, M., Devanand, D., Albert, S. M., Bylsma, F., & Tsai, W.-Y. (1997). Predicting time to nursing home care and death in individuals with Alzheimer disease. *JAMA, 277*(10), 806–812. https://doi.org/10.1001/jama.1997.03540340040030

Stradford, J., Heyworth, N. C., Jackson, M., Norman, M., Banks, S. J., Sundermann, E. E., & Thames, A. D. (2024). Increasing research study engagement in minoritized populations: An example from the Black Women Inflammation and Tau Study. *Alzheimer's & Dementia: The Journal of the Alzheimer's Association*. https://doi.org/10.1002/alz.14177

Stricker, N. H., Christianson, T. J., Lundt, E. S., Alden, E. C., Machulda, M. M., Fields, J. A., Kremers, W. K., Jack, C. R., Knopman, D. S., Mielke, M. M., & Petersen, R. C. (2021). Mayo normative studies: Regression-based normative data for the auditory verbal learning test for ages 30-91 years and the importance of adjusting for sex. *Journal of the International Neuropsychological Society: JINS, 27*(3), 211–226. https://doi.org/10.1017/S1355617720000752

Sundermann, E. E., Barnes, L. L., Bondi, M. W., Bennett, D. A., Salmon, D. P., & Maki, P. M. (2021). Improving detection of amnestic mild cognitive impairment with sex-specific cognitive norms. *Journal of Alzheimer's Disease: JAD, 84*(4), 1763–1770. https://doi.org/10.3233/JAD-215260

Sundermann, E. E., Biegon, A., Rubin, L. H., Lipton, R. B., Landau, S., & Maki, P. M. (2017). Does the female advantage in verbal memory contribute to underestimating Alzheimer's disease pathology in women versus men? *Journal of Alzheimer's Disease*. https://doi.org/10.3233/JAD-160716

Sundermann, E. E., Biegon, A., Rubin, L. H., Lipton, R. B., Mowrey, W., Landau, S., & Maki, P. M. (2016). Better verbal memory in women than men in MCI despite similar levels of hippocampal atrophy. *Neurology*. https://doi.org/10.1212/WNL.0000000000002570

Sundermann, E. E., Maki, P., Biegon, A., Lipton, R. B., Mielke, M. M., Machulda, M., & Bondi, M. W. (2019). Sex-specific norms for verbal memory tests may improve diagnostic accuracy of amnestic MCI. *Neurology, 93*(20), E1881–E1889. https://doi.org/10.1212/WNL.0000000000008467

Sundermann, E. E., Maki, P. M., Reddy, S., Bondi, M. W., & Biegon, A. (2020). Women's higher brain metabolic rates compensates for early Alzheimer's pathology. *Alzheimer's & Dementia: Diagnosis, Assessment and Disese Monitoring*, 12(1), e12121.

Sundermann, E. E., Maki, P. M., Rubin, L. H., Lipton, R. B., Landau, S., & Biegon, A. (2016). Female advantage in verbal memory. *Neurology, 87*(18), 1916–1924. https://doi.org/10.1212/WNL.0000000000003288

Sutphen, C. L., Jasielec, M. S., Shah, A. R., Macy, E. M., Xiong, C., Vlassenko, A. G., Benzinger, T. L. S., Stoops, E. E. J., Vanderstichele, H. M. J., Brix, B., Darby, H. D., Vandijck, M. L. J., Ladenson, J. H., Morris, J. C., Holtzman, D. M., & Fagan, A. M. (2015). Longitudinal cerebrospinal fluid biomarker changes in preclinical Alzheimer disease during middle age. *JAMA Neurology, 72*(9), 1029–1042. https://doi.org/10.1001/jamaneurol.2015.1285

Swe, N. C., Ahmed, S., Eid, M., Poretsky, L., Gianos, E., & Cusano, N. E. (2022). The effects of gender-affirming hormone therapy on cardiovascular and skeletal health: A literature review. *Metabolism Open, 13*, 100173. https://doi.org/10.1016/j.metop.2022.100173

Tang, M. X., Maestre, G., Tsai, W. Y., Liu, X. H., Feng, L., Chung, W. Y., Chun, M., Schofield, P., Stern, Y., Tycko, B., & Mayeux, R. (1996). Relative risk of Alzheimer disease and age-at-onset distributions, based on APOE genotypes among elderly African Americans, Caucasians, and Hispanics in New York City. *American Journal of Human Genetics, 58*(3), 574–584.

Taylor, C. M., Pritschet, L., Yu, S., & Jacobs, E. G. (2019). Applying a women's health lens to the study of the aging brain. *Frontiers in Human Neuroscience, 13*, 224. https://doi.org/10.3389/fnhum.2019.00224

Teel, C. S., & Carson, P. (2003). Family experiences in the journey through dementia diagnosis and care. *Journal of Family Nursing, 9*(1), 38–58. https://doi.org/10.1177/1074840702239490

The North American Menopause Society. (2022). The 2022 hormone therapy position statement of The North American Menopause Society. *Menopause, 29*(7), 767–794. https://doi.org/10.1097/GME.0000000000002028

Tolppanen, A.-M., Solomon, A., Kulmala, J., Kåreholt, I., Ngandu, T., Rusanen, M., Laatikainen, T., Soininen, H., & Kivipelto, M. (2015). Leisure-time physical activity from mid- to late life, body mass index, and risk of dementia. *Alzheimer's & Dementia, 11*(4), 434–443.e6. https://doi.org/10.1016/j.jalz.2014.01.008

Troxel, W. M., Dubowitz, T., Haas, A., Ghosh-Dastidar, B., Butters, M. A., Gary-Webb, T. L., Weinstein, A. M., Ibeanu, A., Wagner, L., Gildengers, A., & Rosso, A. L. (2024). A preliminary analysis of stress burden and cognitive function and clinically adjudicated cognitive outcomes in Black American adults. *The Journals of Gerontology. Series A, Biological Sciences and Medical Sciences, 79*(9), glae177. https://doi.org/10.1093/gerona/glae177

Tsiknia, A. A., Edland, S. D., Sundermann, E. E., Reas, E. T., Brewer, J. B., Galasko, D., & Banks, S. J. (2022). Sex differences in plasma p-tau181 associations with Alzheimer's disease biomarkers, cognitive decline, and clinical progression. *Molecular Psychiatry, 27*(10), 4314–4322. https://doi.org/10.1038/s41380-022-01675-8

Turner, A. D., James, B. D., Capuano, A. W., Aggarwal, N. T., & Barnes, L. L. (2017). Perceived stress and cognitive decline in different cognitive domains in a cohort of older African Americans. *The American Journal of Geriatric Psychiatry: Official Journal of the American Association for Geriatric Psychiatry, 25*(1), 25–34. https://doi.org/10.1016/j.jagp.2016.10.003

Ueki, A., Shinjo, H., Shimode, H., Nakajima, T., & Morita, Y. (2001). Factors associated with mortality in patients with early-onset Alzheimer's disease: A five-year longitudinal study. *International Journal of Geriatric Psychiatry, 16*(8), 810–815. https://doi.org/10.1002/gps.419

Valen-Sendstad, A., Engedal, K., Stray-Pedersen, B., Strobel, C., Barnett, L., Nurminemi, M., Meyer, N., & ADACT Study Group. (2010). Effects of hormone therapy on depressive symptoms and cognitive functions in women with Alzheimer disease: A 12 month randomized, double-blind, placebo-controlled study of low-dose estradiol and norethisterone. *The American Journal of Geriatric Psychiatry, 18*(1), 11–20.

Van Gelder, B. M., Tijhuis, M., Kalmijn, S., Giampaoli, S., Nissinen, A., & Kromhout, D. (2006). Marital status and living situation during a 5-year period are associated with a subsequent 10-year cognitive decline in older men: The FINE study. *Journals of Gerontology - Series B Psychological Sciences and Social Sciences*. https://doi.org/10.1093/geronb/61.4.P213

van Heesewijk, J. O., Dreijerink, K. M. A., Wiepjes, C. M., Kok, A. A. L., Geurtsen, G. J., van Schoor, N. M., Huisman, M., den Heijer, M., & Kreukels, B. P. C. (2025). Cognitive functioning in older transgender individuals receiving long-term genderaffirming hormone therapy. *International Journal of Transgender Health, 26*(1), 88–104. https://doi.org/10.1080/26895269.2023.2289069

Varma, V. R., Tang, X., & Carlson, M. C. (2016). Hippocampal sub-regional shape and physical activity in older adults. *Hippocampus, 26*(8), 1051–1060. https://doi.org/10.1002/HIPO.22586

Verhoef, M., Love, E. J., & Rose, S. A. (1992). Women's social roles and their exercise participation. *Women & Health, 19*(4), 15–29. https://doi.org/10.1300/J013V19N04_02

Villemagne, V. L., Pike, K. E., Chételat, G., Ellis, K. A., Mulligan, R. S., Bourgeat, P., Ackermann, U., Jones, G., Szoeke, C., Salvado, O., Martins, R., O'Keefe, G., Mathis, C. A., Klunk, W. E., Ames, D., Masters, C. L., & Rowe, C. C. (2011). Longitudinal assessment of Aβ and cognition in aging and Alzheimer disease. *Annals of Neurology, 69*(1), 181–192. https://doi.org/10.1002/ana.22248

Vitaliano, P. P., Murphy, M., Young, H. M., Echeverria, D., & Borson, S. (2011). Does caring for a spouse with dementia promote cognitive decline? A hypothesis and proposed mechanisms. *Journal of the American Geriatrics Society, 59*(5), 900–908. https://doi.org/10.1111/J.1532-5415.2011.03368.X

Walker, K. A., Sharrett, A. R., Wu, A., Schneider, A. L. C., Albert, M., Lutsey, P. L., Bandeen-Roche, K., Coresh, J., Gross, A. L., Windham, B. G., Knopman, D. S., Power, M. C., Rawlings, A. M., Mosley, T. H., & Gottesman, R. F. (2019). Association of midlife to late-life blood pressure patterns with incident dementia. *JAMA, 322*(6), 535–545. https://doi.org/10.1001/jama.2019.10575

Ward, A., Tardiff, S., Dye, C., & Arrighi, H. M. (2013). Rate of conversion from prodromal Alzheimer's disease to Alzheimer's dementia: A systematic review of the literature. *Dementia and Geriatric Cognitive Disorders Extra, 3*(1), 320–332. https://doi.org/10.1159/000354370

Weber, M. T., Maki, P. M., & McDermott, M. P. (2014). Cognition and mood in perimenopause: A systematic review and meta-analysis. *The Journal of Steroid Biochemistry and Molecular Biology, 142*, 90–98. https://doi.org/10.1016/j.jsbmb.2013.06.001

Weintraub, S., Wicklund, A. H., & Salmon, D. P. (2012). The neuropsychological profile of Alzheimer disease. *Cold Spring Harbor Perspectives in Medicine, 2*(4), a006171. https://doi.org/10.1101/cshperspect.a006171

Whitmer, R. A., Quesenberry, C. P., Zhou, J., & Yaffe, K. (2011). Timing of hormone therapy and dementia: The critical window theory revisited. *Annals of Neurology, 69*(1), 163–169. https://doi.org/10.1002/ana.22239

WHO. (2021). Global status report on the public health response to dementia. https://www.who.int/publications/i/item/9789240033245

Wiegman, M. J., Zeeman, G. G., Aukes, A. M., Bolte, A. C., Faas, M. M., Aarnoudse, J. G., & de Groot, J. C. (2014). Regional distribution of cerebral white matter lesions years after preeclampsia and eclampsia. *Obstetrics & Gynecology, 123*(4), 790. https://doi.org/10.1097/AOG.0000000000000162

Williams, D. R., de Silva, R., Paviour, D. C., Pittman, A., Watt, H. C., Kilford, L., Holton, J. L., Revesz, T., & Lees, A. J. (2005). Characteristics of two distinct clinical phenotypes in pathologically proven progressive supranuclear palsy: Richardson's syndrome and PSP-parkinsonism. *Brain: A. Journal of Neurology, 128*(Pt 6), 1247–1258. https://doi.org/10.1093/brain/awh488

Williams, K., & Umberson, D. (2004). Marital status, marital transitions, and health: A gendered life course perspective. *Journal of Health and Social Behavior, 45*(1), 81–98. https://doi.org/10.1177/002214650404500106

Wilson, D. M., Cookson, M. R., Bosch, L. V. D., Zetterberg, H., Holtzman, D. M., & Dewachter, I. (2023). Hallmarks of neurodegenerative diseases. *Cell, 186*(4), 693–714. https://doi.org/10.1016/j.cell.2022.12.032

Wimo, A., Gauthier, S., & Prince, M. (2018). Global estimates of informal care. *Alzheimer's disease international*, 22.

Woolley, J. D., Khan, B. K., Murthy, N. K., Miller, B. L., & Rankin, K. P. (2011). The diagnostic challenge of psychiatric symptoms in neurodegenerative disease: Rates of and risk factors for prior psychiatric diagnosis in patients with early neurodegenerative disease. *The Journal of Clinical Psychiatry, 72*(2), 126–133. https://doi.org/10.4088/JCP.10m06382oli

World Health Organization. (2011). World health statistics 2011. *Estadísticas Sanitarias Mundiales, 2011*, 170.

World Health Organization. (2021). *Global status report on the public health response to dementia*. World Health Organization. https://www.who.int/publications/i/item/9789240033245

Xi, H., Gan, J., Liu, S., Wang, F., Chen, Z., Wang, X.-D., Shi, Z., & Ji, Y. (2022). Reproductive factors and cognitive impairment in natural menopausal women: A cross-sectional study. *Frontiers in Endocrinology, 13*, 893901. https://doi.org/10.3389/fendo.2022.893901

Yaffe, K., Haan, M., Byers, A., Tangen, C., & Kuller, L. (2000). Estrogen use, APOE, and cognitive decline: Evidence of gene-environment interaction. *Neurology, 54*(10), 1949–1954. https://doi.org/10.1212/wnl.54.10.1949

Zandi, P. P., Carlson, M. C., Plassman, B. L., Welsh-Bohmer, K. A., Mayer, L. S., Steffens, D. C., Breitner, J. C. S., & Cache County Memory Study Investigators. (2002). Hormone replacement therapy and incidence of Alzheimer disease in older women: The Cache County Study. *JAMA, 288*(17), 2123–2129. https://doi.org/10.1001/jama.288.17.2123

Zeydan, B., Tosakulwong, N., Schwarz, C. G., Senjem, M. L., Gunter, J. L., Reid, R. I., Gazzuola Rocca, L., Lesnick, T. G., Smith, C. Y., Bailey, K. R., Lowe, V. J., Roberts, R. O., Jack, C. R., Petersen, R. C., Miller, V. M., Mielke, M. M., Rocca, W. A., & Kantarci, K. (2019). Association of bilateral salpingo-oophorectomy before menopause onset with medial temporal lobe neurodegeneration. *JAMA Neurology, 76*(1), 95–100. https://doi.org/10.1001/jamaneurol.2018.3057

Zhou, L., Chen, X., Zhang, G., Sui, Y., Hou, L., Hu, F., Xia, X., Luo, S., Peng, X., Yue, J., Dong, B., Dong, B., & Liu, X. (2024). Associations of parity and cognitive decline, depression, and chronic comorbidity in West China: Results from WCHAT study. *International Journal of Gynaecology and Obstetrics: The Official Organ of the International Federation of Gynaecology and Obstetrics, 167*(3), 1010–1016. https://doi.org/10.1002/ijgo.15754

Zhou, R., Liu, H.-M., Zou, L.-W., Wei, H.-X., Huang, Y.-N., Zhong, Q., Gu, S.-Y., Chen, M.-F., Wang, S.-L., Sun, H.-X., & Wu, X.-B. (2022). Associations of parity with change in global cognition and incident cognitive impairment in older women. *Frontiers in Aging Neuroscience, 14*, 864128. https://doi.org/10.3389/fnagi.2022.864128

Zsembik, B. A., & Peek, M. K. (2001). Race differences in cognitive functioning among older adults. *The Journals of Gerontology. Series B, Psychological Sciences and Social Sciences, 56*(5), S266–S274. https://doi.org/10.1093/geronb/56.5.s266

Chapter 6
Movement Disorders

Ece Bayram

Introduction

Movement disorders are a group of neurological disorders impacting the production and control of movements. People experience excess movements (hyperkinetic) or paucity of voluntary and automatic movements (hypokinetic), unrelated to weakness or spasticity (Fig. 6.1). Movement disorders include some of the most common neurological diseases and diseases that can affect people of any age and gender. The basal ganglia and cerebellum, which were historically considered to primarily have motor function, are the main structures implicated in movement disorders. However, studies have continuously shown that the basal ganglia and cerebellum play a substantial role in different non-motor functions including cognition and behavior, and accordingly, movement disorders include a variety of non-motor symptoms in addition to the traditional motor features (Wichmann, 2018). In fact, several movement disorders include non-motor features in the diagnostic criteria (i.e., progressive supranuclear palsy and corticobasal degeneration).

Biological sex differences are shown in both structure and function of the basal ganglia and cerebellum. The basal ganglia are among the main brain regions with a high density of sex steroid receptors. Sex steroid hormones affect brain morphology during development and young adulthood and lead to differences in brain function and behavior (Rijpkema et al., 2012). Cerebellar subcomponents are sensitive to sex and sex chromosomes (Kaczkurkin et al., 2019). In addition to biological sex and sex hormones, interplay between biological factors, genetics, and environment differ for women and men, and impact the structure and function of basal ganglia and cerebellum. Thus, one can expect gender differences for movement disorders associated with these structures. In this section, we will provide an overview of

E. Bayram (✉)
University of Colorado Anschutz, Aurora, CO, USA
e-mail: ece.bayram@cuanschutz.edu

E. Sullivan-Baca, R. Ellison (eds.), *Neuropsychology of Women*,
https://doi.org/10.1007/978-3-031-87228-0_6

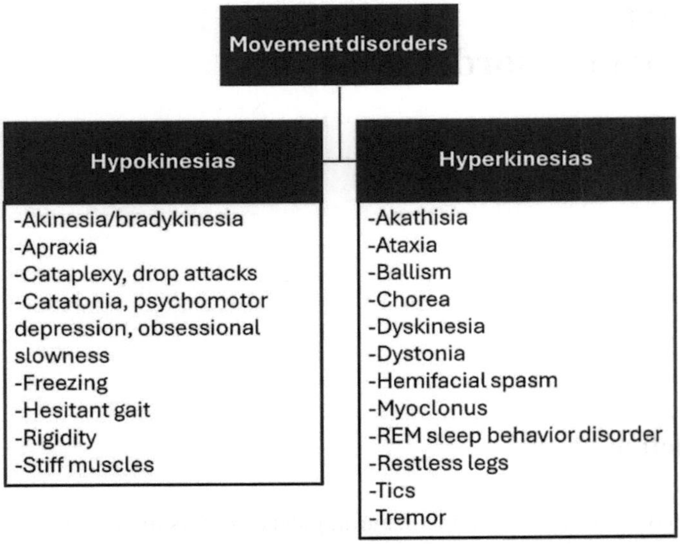

Fig. 6.1 Movement disorders classification

movement disorders, discuss the existing knowledge on gender differences, and highlight women's experiences with these disorders.

Parkinsonian Disorders (Hypokinetic Movement Disorders)

Hypokinetic movement disorders or Parkinsonian disorders are a group of disorders characterized by akinesia (absence of movement), bradykinesia (slowness of movement), or hypokinesia (decreased amplitude of movement) generally affecting voluntary movement. Parkinson's disease is the most common hypokinetic movement disorder with consistently reported gender differences. Various gender differences are also described in other hypokinetic movement disorders.

Parkinson's Disease

Epidemiology

Parkinson's disease (PD) is the second most common neurodegenerative disorder and the fastest growing neurological disease worldwide (GBD 2016 Parkinson's Disease Collaborators, 2018). Pathologically, it is characterized by Lewy bodies, neuronal inclusions of misfolded alpha-synuclein, and progressive nigral loss.

Clinically, it is characterized by parkinsonism, which is defined as bradykinesia accompanied by rest tremor and/or rigidity (Postuma et al., 2015). Clear response to dopaminergic therapy, levodopa-induced dyskinesia, rest tremor of a limb during the examination, and presence of olfactory loss or cardiac sympathetic denervation on metaiodobenzylguanidine (MIBG) scintigraphy are supportive features. Detailed history, clinical examination, and further tests are required to exclude other potential causes of parkinsonism before diagnosing the person with PD (Table 6.1). Although pathology is the gold standard for diagnosis, clinical diagnostic criteria have an accuracy rate of 92.6%, with rates increasing during follow-up (Postuma et al., 2018). Global pooled prevalence is reported as 1.51 per 1000, with lower rates for women compared to men (1.49 vs. 1.54 per 1000) (Zhu et al., 2024). In a 2024 meta-analysis including 83 studies from 37 countries from database inception (databases were PubMed, Cochrane, Web of Science, Embase, Scopus, and Global Health) to November 1, 2023, PD was more prevalent for women in the Western Pacific region, as well as in countries with very high human development index and high sociodemographic index (Zhu et al., 2024). However, globally, women consistently had a lower prevalence than men after the age of 50.

Risk Factors

Female sex is considered a protective factor for PD, with male sex being a risk factor. Other risk factors include older age, regular pesticide exposure, occupational solvent exposure, not using caffeine, not smoking, diabetes, physical inactivity, and genetic mutations including but not limited to *GBA*, *LRRK2*, and *SNCA* (Heinzel et al., 2019). Low plasma urate levels and erectile dysfunction are also associated with PD risk only for men. Genome-wide association studies have not identified gender differences in allele frequency on autosomal or X chromosomes (Blauwendraat et al., 2021; Le Guen et al., 2021). However, gender differences have been shown for expression in the brain for genetic variants (Nordengen et al., 2024).

Table 6.1 Features suggesting atypical parkinsonism over Parkinson's disease

Abnormal eye movements (progressive supranuclear palsy)
Absence/paucity of tremor
Apraxia, alien limb, myoclonus (corticobasal syndrome)
Early severe dysautonomia (multiple system atrophy)
Early gait instability, falls
Early, prominent dementia
Irregular jerky tremor, myoclonus
Poor/lack of response to levodopa
Pyramidal tract, cerebellar signs (multiple system atrophy)
Rapid disease progression
Severe dysarthria, dysphonia, stridor (multiple system atrophy)

In women, hysterectomy and bilateral oophorectomy before the age of menopause have been suggested as risk factors, whereas postmenopausal estrogen therapy may be a protective factor, without significant effects of early menopause on the risk for PD (Abdelzaher Ibrahim et al., 2022; Currie et al., 2004). Other reproductive factors such as use of oral contraceptives, age at menarche, age at menopause, parity, and type of menopause (surgical vs. natural) have not been consistently associated with PD risk (Lv et al., 2017).

Rapid eye movement (REM) sleep behavior disorder, abnormal dopaminergic functional imaging, subthreshold parkinsonism, hyposmia, constipation, orthostatic hypotension, urinary dysfunction, depression with or without anxiety, and global cognitive deficit are prodromal markers of PD (Heinzel et al., 2019), with subthreshold parkinsonism and depression being stronger predictors for women than men for future PD (Heinzel et al., 2018). Notably, women often report fewer symptoms in the prodromal phase (Gonzalez-Latapi et al., 2021). These findings support gender differences in PD risk factors and predictors with a different experience for women with prodromal PD compared to men.

Presentation

Women with PD are more likely than men to develop the more benign tremor dominant phenotype of PD, facial masking, levodopa-induced dyskinesias, restless legs syndrome, mood and sleep disturbances, depression, anxiety, apathy, fatigue, pain, as well as urogenital symptoms. In addition, they are less likely to experience cognitive decline, hallucinations, gastrointestinal symptoms, and sexual dysfunction compared to men (Subramanian et al., 2022; Table 6.2). In contrast, men are more likely to present with a postural instability and gait dysfunction phenotype associated with more widespread disease, freezing of gait, falls, impulse control disorder, and dopamine dysregulation syndrome when compared to women (Gonzalez-Latapi et al., 2021). For women with PD, more severe disease is associated with depression, *LRRK2* variant, B12 deficiency, perinatal depression, natural childbirth, and total hysterectomy (Rao et al., 2023). However, compared to men, disease progression is generally slower, and the survival rate is higher for women (Willis et al., 2012).

Disease impact on daily lives also differs by gender (Subramanian et al., 2022). Compared to men, women with PD have less social support, experience more psychological distress, and report more disability, a worse quality of life, a negative and destructive self-image, and impaired sexual intimacy. Women tend to downplay their symptoms more, have a higher risk for delayed diagnosis, feel they are not heard more often, have a higher risk of discrimination while receiving healthcare, and can experience a perceived loss of femininity (Bayram et al., 2023b; Subramanian et al., 2022).

There are special considerations regarding presentation and treatment of PD for women in accordance with reproductive stages. Specifically, symptoms can worsen during pre-menstruation, pregnancy, postpartum, and premenopause for women.

Table 6.2 Gender differences in PD

Disease features	Women	Men
Risk	Subthreshold parkinsonism, depression stronger predictors for PD Hysterectomy, oopherectomy before menopause increase risk	Male sex is a risk factor for PD Low urate levels, erectile dysfunction increase risk
Diagnosis	Higher risk for delayed diagnosis, more likely to downplay symptoms, feel unheard, perceive discrimination	Higher disease prevalence
Clinical profile	More likely tremor dominant phenotype More common facial masking, restless legs, depression, anxiety, apathy, fatigue, sleep disturbances, pain, urogenital symptoms	More likely postural instability gait dysfunction More common freezing of gait, falls, cognitive decline, hallucinations, gastrointestinal symptoms, sexual dysfunction
Daily life	More psychological stress, more disability, worse quality of life	More social support
Treatment	Levodopa-induced dyskinesia, wearing off Less likely to receive advanced therapies such as deep brain stimulation	Impulse control disorder, dopamine dysregulation syndrome
Progression	Slower disease progression	Higher death rate

Note. PD = Parkinson's disease

During pregnancy, levodopa monotherapy is the safe and the most common treatment (Seier & Hiller, 2017), while amantadine has teratogenic effects and should not be used during pregnancy.

Treatment

Multidisciplinary and personalized treatment is key in PD management (Bloem et al., 2021). Treatment can range from single medication use to advanced therapies such as deep brain stimulation. For dopaminergic treatments, different pharmacokinetics and outcomes are shown in women and men. Compared to men, women present a greater bioavailability of levodopa and pramipexole, have lower levodopa clearance levels, develop wearing-off and levodopa-induced dyskinesias more, and have a higher risk of developing dyskinesia even when treated with small amounts of levodopa (de Souza Ferreira et al., 2022; Russillo et al., 2022). Women are more likely to experience gastrointestinal and orthostatic adverse effects when using tolcapone, a COMT inhibitor used alongside levodopa. Women are also less likely to receive advanced therapies like deep brain stimulation, although they experience better quality of life improvement after surgery compared to men. Care partners also play an important role in the treatment process for PD. The majority of care partners for people with PD are women, and women care partners are more involved with daily tasks, provide more hours of care, and offer more hands-on care than men (Subramanian et al., 2022). On the other hand, women with PD are more likely to have a paid caregiver or reside in a nursing home compared to men.

Parkinson's Disease Dementia (PDD)

The cognitive profile of people with PD can range from normal cognition to subjective cognitive complaints, mild cognitive impairment, and dementia. People with PD have a higher risk for cognitive decline and cognitive decline, including mild cognitive impairment, which can also occur before the onset of motor symptoms. Thus, mild cognitive impairment is included in the prodromal PD criteria (Heinzel et al., 2019). People with PD typically have a non-amnestic cognitive decline with impairments in attention, executive function, and visuospatial functioning. Memory and language can also be affected, and people can experience impairment in single or multiple domains. Prevalence is estimated to be between 0.3 and 0.5% for people over the age of 65, and 3–4% in people with dementia (Aarsland & Kurz, 2010). Up to 80% of people with PD can develop dementia after 20 years of disease, with highly heterogeneous cognitive profiles and progression rates (Aarsland & Kurz, 2010).

Overall, women with PD have a lower risk for cognitive impairment than men. However, women are more likely to experience visuospatial deficits and less likely to experience verbal fluency decline compared to men (Gonzalez-Latapi et al., 2021). REM sleep behavior disorder and orthostatic hypotension, more prevalent in men, are associated with worse cognitive performance. Currently, available treatments for PDD have limited efficacy, and women remain underrepresented in clinical trials focused on cognition in PD (Bayram et al., 2023a).

Dementia with Lewy Bodies (DLB)

Epidemiology

Dementia with Lewy bodies (DLB) is the second most common neurodegenerative dementia following Alzheimer's disease. Compared to Alzheimer's disease, DLB is associated with faster progression and a higher level of burden (Desai et al., 2022). The gold standard for the diagnosis of DLB is the pathological confirmation of Lewy bodies in the brain, although co-pathologies including Alzheimer's are common and contribute to clinical heterogeneity (Coughlin et al., 2019; McKeith et al., 2017). The typical phenotype includes non-amnestic dementia, cognitive fluctuations, visual hallucinations early in the dementia process, REM sleep behavior disorder, and parkinsonism. Clinical misdiagnosis with Alzheimer's disease is common, particularly for women (Bayram et al., 2021, 2022, 2024a).

Lewy body dementia refers to a dementia profile with underlying Lewy body pathology, which includes both PDD and DLB (Fig. 6.2). DLB can be differentiated from PDD based on the interval between dementia and parkinsonism onset. In DLB, dementia occurs before, at, or within one year following parkinsonism onset. Parkinsonism is also not required for DLB, as some people do not experience parkinsonism despite a DLB diagnosis. Mean prevalence is estimated as 0.36% for the population over the age of 65, with a wide range from 0 to 4.99%; and 4.2% within all dementia cases, with a range from 0 to 21.9% (Vann Jones & O'Brien, 2014).

Risk Factors

DLB is considered to be less prevalent for women than men, although several studies noted a higher prevalence for women, when controlling for the gender of the sample population. Age seems to contribute to differences in prevalence; DLB is less prevalent for women than men until the age of 75, and women have similar or higher prevalence rates compared to men after the age of 75 (Chiu et al., 2023).

Presentation

Cognitive impairments in DLB typically include impairments in attention and visuospatial function with relatively preserved memory and naming compared to Alzheimer's disease (Wyman-Chick et al., 2024). Women can present with worse

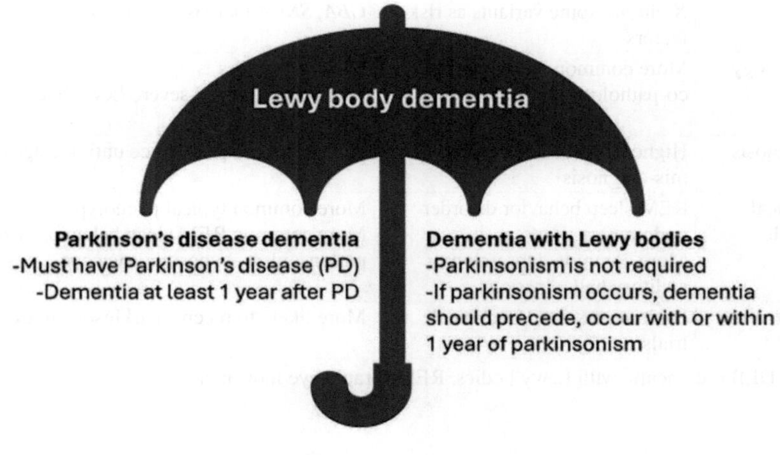

Fig. 6.2 Lewy body dementia as an umbrella term

overall cognition compared to men with similar disease duration (Chiu et al., 2023; Table 6.3). Language and memory deficits can occur in people with Alzheimer's co-pathology, which is more common in women with DLB (Barnes et al., 2019). Studies so far suggest similar rates of cognitive fluctuations for women and men.

Visual hallucinations are more common and occur earlier for women in clinically diagnosed DLB; although, pathologically defined cohorts have shown a lower prevalence of visual hallucinations for women compared to men (Chiu et al., 2023). Women develop visual hallucinations earlier in the disease process than men.

Several clinical studies suggest a lower prevalence of REM sleep behavior disorder for women; although community samples suggest a similar prevalence (Chiu et al., 2023). REM sleep behavior disorder may be under-detected in women due to bed partner reports; women have less muscle phasic activity during REM sleep and smaller movements that do not cause injury as often.

Parkinsonism is less common for women and accordingly, women are less likely to receive treatment for parkinsonism. For other features, including Capgras syndrome, severe neuroleptic sensitivity, constipation, and orthostatic hypotension, similar rates have been noted for women and men. Compared to men, depression and auditory hallucinations may be more common in women, while hyposmia and syncope in early DLB may be less common for women. Genetic risk factors including *GBA* and *SNCA* may increase the risk for DLB less for women than men (Gibbons et al., 2022). Women may have Alzheimer-related genetic risk factors on the X chromosome, putting them at a risk for DLB (Bayram et al., 2024b). As nigral loss can be less severe and Alzheimer's co-pathology more severe for women than men, biomarkers assessing dopamine imaging, amyloid, and tau levels can differ for women and men with DLB.

Table 6.3 Gender differences in DLB

Disease features	Women	Men
Risk	X chromosome variants as risk factors	*GBA*, *SNCA* increase risk more
Pathology	More common Alzheimer's co-pathology	More nigral loss More common and severe Lewy body pathology
Diagnosis	Higher risk for delayed and mis-diagnosis	Higher disease prevalence until the age of 75
Clinical profile	REM sleep behavior disorder underreported More common depression, auditory hallucinations	More common typical phenotype More common REM sleep behavior disorder, parkinsonism, hyposmia, syncope
Treatment	Underrepresented in clinical trials	More likely to receive parkinsonism treatment

Note. DLB = dementia with Lewy bodies. REM = rapid eye movement

Treatment and Prognosis

Findings on gender differences for progression and survival rates are inconsistent. The majority of the caregivers of people with DLB are women, although the gender effect on caregiving in DLB is not well investigated (Chiu et al., 2023). Women with DLB are substantially underrepresented in clinical trials with women making only 15–37% of the cohorts, limiting the interpretation of findings (Chiu et al., 2023). Currently, only symptomatic treatments are available and women with DLB are likely undertreated due to higher rates of delayed and misdiagnosis compared to men (Chiu et al., 2023).

Multiple System Atrophy (MSA)

Epidemiology

Multiple system atrophy (MSA) is a rare, adult-onset, progressive, neurodegenerative disorder characterized by motor symptoms and autonomic dysfunction. It is an oligodendroglioneural alpha-synucleinopathy, but not a Lewy body disease. Similar to PD and DLB, the gold standard for diagnosis is pathological confirmation (Wenning et al., 2022). Clinically, MSA is characterized by autonomic dysfunction accompanying parkinsonism and/or cerebellar symptoms. Based on the predominant motor profile, MSA can be classified as MSA-Parkinsonian (MSA-P) or MSA-Cerebellar (MSA-C). Autonomic dysfunction can include orthostatic hypotension (≥20/10 mmHg blood pressure drop within 3 min of standing), urinary urge continence, voiding difficulties with post-void urinary residual volume ≥100 mL, and erectile dysfunction. Parkinsonism typically has a poor levodopa response. Cerebellar symptoms can include ataxic gait, limb ataxia, dysarthria, and oculomotor dysfunction with sustained nystagmus or saccadic hypermetria. Non-motor features including sleep disturbances with high rates of REM sleep behavior disorder, pain, fatigue, depression, and cognitive changes are also common (Makawita et al., 2024). At disease onset, MSA can mimic PD and misdiagnosis is likely. Prevalence ranges from 0.5 to 17 per 100,000 (Kaplan, 2024). Although gender differences are not typically reported for the MSA prevalence, a recent meta-analysis including 24 studies from 14 European countries published between 1995 and 2022, noted a slightly lower prevalence for women than men (1.19 vs. 2.75 per 100,000; Kaplan, 2024).

Presentation

Compared to men, women are more likely to have motor features as initial symptoms and a better response to levodopa (Leys et al., 2024). Women are less likely to have autonomic symptoms at disease onset or experience widespread and severe autonomic failure, except for urinary urge incontinence and constipation, which are more common for women than men. Women are also more likely to experience pain, anxiety, depression, sarcopenia, frailty, early falls, fractures, cognitive decline, and worse quality of life.

Treatment and Prognosis

MSA typically leads to death within 6 to 10 years after symptom onset, and available treatment options are only symptomatic with limited benefit. Gender differences in clinical presentation are also depicted in differences in symptom management. Women may be more likely than men to be prescribed central nervous system targeting medications, and less likely to be prescribed antihypertensives. Progression may be faster for women with a shorter time to dependency on walking aids or wheelchair (Leys et al., 2024). While some studies noted a shorter survival for women when autonomic features are considered for disease onset, some noted a longer survival for women, and some noted no gender differences in survival.

Progressive Supranuclear Palsy (PSP)

Epidemiology

Progressive supranuclear palsy (PSP) is a 4-repeat tauopathy and a type of frontotemporal lobar degeneration. It is associated with various phenotypes that can also present with other pathologies. The most recent diagnostic criteria noted four core functional domains including oculomotor dysfunction, postural instability, akinesia, and cognitive dysfunction as characteristic clinical manifestations of PSP (Höglinger et al., 2017). Oculomotor dysfunction includes frequent macro square wave jerks or eyelid opening apraxia, slower vertical saccades, or vertical supranuclear gaze palsy. Postural instability includes more than two steps with the pull-test, tendency to fall on the pull-test, or repeated unprovoked falls within three years. Akinesia includes levodopa-responsive asymmetric parkinsonism with tremors, predominantly axial akinetic-rigid levodopa-resistant parkinsonism, or progressive freezing of gait within three years.

Cognitive dysfunction in PSP includes corticobasal syndrome, frontal cognitive/behavioral syndrome, and nonfluent/agrammatic variant of primary progressive aphasia or progressive speech apraxia. While Richardson's syndrome is the most common phenotype of PSP, other phenotypes can include predominant oculomotor dysfunction, parkinsonism, progressive gait freezing, frontal presentation including behavioral variant frontotemporal dementia, speech/language disorder, corticobasal syndrome, primary lateral sclerosis, and cerebellar ataxia (Höglinger et al., 2017). It is sporadic with an onset at or after the age of 40, a gradual progression, and a mean survival of 6 to 8 years. The prevalence of PSP ranges from 1 to 18 with a pooled estimate of 6.92 per 100,000 (Lyons et al., 2023). It is unclear whether prevalence is higher for women or men, as studies so far have conflicting findings (Park et al., 2021).

Presentation, Treatment, and Prognosis

Only a small number of studies have investigated gender differences in symptoms and prognosis for PSP. One such study from India reported that compared to men, women had more frequent falls, pyramidal signs, apathy, and executive dysfunction; less frequent tremors and PSP-parkinsonism phenotype; a shorter time to attain unintelligible speech, severe dysphagia, and cognitive impairment; and a longer time to attain wheelchair dependency (Mahale et al., 2022). Another study from the United States including 121 people with probable PSP examined at the Mayo Clinic in Florida also noted tremors were less frequent for women than men, although other gender differences in symptoms and progression were not reported (Baba et al., 2006). In a cohort including people with PSP from Europe and North America, the cognitive decline did not differ for women and men during the 1-year follow-up (Digma et al., 2023).

There are currently no disease-modifying treatment options for PSP; although, various approaches are being investigated (Boxer et al., 2017). Interestingly, one of the drugs under investigation called davunetide, which enhances tau-microtubule interaction, was reported to not have any efficacy in the pooled cohort, although there were gender-specific effects (Gozes et al., 2023). After 52 weeks of twice daily treatment, davunetide was associated with age-correlated protection against brain ventricular volume increases, significant effectiveness on daily living activities, fine motor function, functional bulbar activities, and no significant deterioration of mental activities only for women. These findings underscore the gender differences in disease mechanisms and efficacy of treatments, which need to be considered in treatment trials.

Corticobasal Degeneration (CBD)

Epidemiology and Presentation

Corticobasal degeneration (CBD) is a rare neurodegenerative disorder under the frontotemporal lobar degeneration umbrella, characterized by widespread neuronal and glial hyperphosphorylated 4-repeat tau deposition primarily affecting cortex and basal ganglia. Similar to PSP, CBD is associated with different phenotypes that also present with other pathologies. Thus, the term "CBD" is reserved for autopsy-confirmed cases. The most frequent phenotype is corticobasal syndrome (CBS), characterized by limb rigidity, bradykinesia, dystonia, and myoclonus that are more likely to present asymmetric than symmetric; orobuccal or limb apraxia, cortical sensory deficit, and alien limb phenomena (Armstrong et al., 2013). Other phenotypes include (1) frontal behavioral-spatial syndrome with executive dysfunction, behavioral or personality changes, and visuospatial deficits; (2) nonfluent/agrammatic variant of primary progressive aphasia with effortful and agrammatic speech, impaired grammar/sentence comprehension despite relatively preserved single word comprehension, and speech apraxia; and (3) PSP syndrome with axial or symmetric limb rigidity or bradykinesia, postural instability or falls, urinary incontinence, behavioral changes, and supranuclear vertical gaze palsy or slow vertical saccades. In addition to these more typical clinical phenotypes, CBD can also present with amnestic dementia (similar to Alzheimer's disease), progressive orofacial apraxia, conduction-type aphasia with repetition difficulties, posterior cortical atrophy with optic ataxia, oculomotor apraxia and simultagnosia, frontal-type gait disorder, and pseudobulbar syndrome with dysarthria and emotional lability (Constantinides et al., 2019).

Overall, the disease is predominantly sporadic, with an insidious symptom onset at or after the age of 50, a gradual progression, and a life expectancy of up to 10 years after symptom onset. Prevalence rates for CBS range from 0.83 to 25 with a pooled estimate of 3.91 per 100,000 (Lyons et al., 2023). Although a slight women predominance for prevalence has been previously suggested, a significant gender difference has not been noted in prevalence studies so far (Lyons et al., 2023; Swallow et al., 2022).

Treatment and Prognosis

Survival in CBD and CBS is estimated as about 7 years from symptom onset (Aiba et al., 2023; Pantelyat, 2022). Currently, only symptomatic treatments are available with limited benefit. Unfortunately, gender differences have not been investigated further in CBD or CBS.

Secondary Parkinsonism

Epidemiology and Presentation

Parkinsonism can also have secondary causes beyond the neurodegenerative disorders described above. The most common secondary parkinsonism is drug-induced parkinsonism. Neuroleptic drugs that impact dopaminergic transmission, as well as calcium channel blockers and other drugs, can lead to or worsen parkinsonism. Most studies suggest drug-induced parkinsonism is the second most common cause of parkinsonism following PD, with 7.9–20% of people with parkinsonism noted to have drug-induced parkinsonism (Höllerhage, 2019). In contrast to PD, women seem to have a higher risk than men for drug-induced parkinsonism (Shiraiwa et al., 2018).

Compared to PD, symmetrical symptoms, more rapid progression, relative absence of rest tremor, and oromandibular dyskinesias may be more common in drug-induced parkinsonism. However, drug-induced parkinsonism has a heterogeneous clinical presentation and people may also present with a typical PD profile. Diagnosis is based on the appearance of parkinsonism during the use of the drug and no prior parkinsonism before the drug.

Following drug-induced parkinsonism, vascular parkinsonism is another common type of secondary parkinsonism. Vascular parkinsonism, due to vascular lesions, is clinically characterized by lower body parkinsonism with pronounced gait disorder, postural instability, and minimal symptoms in the upper extremities. Vascular parkinsonism may be less common in women than men (Caslake et al., 2014). Other rare causes for secondary parkinsonism include brain tumors, trauma, chronic traumatic encephalopathy, infection, and toxin or drug exposure.

Treatment

Treatment of drug-induced parkinsonism includes withdrawal of the drug, if possible, and while symptoms can improve and resolve after six months following the withdrawal of the drug, they can also persist in up to one out of four people (Munhoz et al., 2017). The persistence of symptoms may suggest an underlying neurodegenerative parkinsonism or potential damage by the drug to the dopaminergic system. For the treatment of vascular parkinsonism, addressing vascular risk factors can help prevent further problems, and levodopa can be helpful, although response rates are lower than in PD (Miguel-Puga et al., 2017).

Stiff Person Syndrome Spectrum Disorders

Epidemiology and Presentation

Stiff person syndrome spectrum disorders (SPSD) are a group of rare neuroimmunological disorders characterized by rigidity, unpredictable and painful spasms, and hypersensitivity to external stimuli (Newsome & Johnson, 2022). SPSD includes Stiff person syndrome (SPS) and other disorders that share a wide range of clinical features and a spectrum of antibodies against neuronal proteins (e.g., antibodies to the glutamic acid decarboxylase 65-kilodalton isoform, GAD65) associated with inhibition of central hyperexcitability. The classic phenotype of SPSD is characterized by spasms or increased rigidity in response to stimuli such as abrupt loud noises, cold weather, stress, tactile stimuli, and open spaces, with the torso and lower extremities affected more commonly than upper extremities (Wang et al., 2024). Typical examination findings include hyperlordosis, rigidity, paravertebral/abdominal muscle spasm or tightness, spasticity in extremities, and/or gait hyperreflexia affecting lower extremities more commonly than upper extremities. The presence of serum GAD65 autoantibody, glycine receptor, or amphiphysin and the exclusion of other potential diagnoses are also included in the diagnostic approach for a classic phenotype. Classic SPS is the most common phenotype, found in 70–80% of the cases.

Other phenotypes include (1) partial SPS, in which symptoms are isolated to one extremity or torso; (2) SPS-plus, in which brainstem and/or cerebellar findings accompany the classic phenotype; (3) pure cerebellar ataxia, in which cerebellar findings are present without musculoskeletal symptoms or signs; and (4) progressive encephalomyelitis with rigidity and myoclonus (PERM), in which a mixture of symptoms and signs from other phenotypes can be present with encephalopathy, severe torso rigidity, and/or multifocal or generalized myoclonus, as well as generalized slowing and/or epileptic discharges on EEG (Newsome & Johnson, 2022). Some do not consider PERM as a separate phenotype and instead include it under SPS-plus, and some consider pure cerebellar ataxia as a separate condition from SPSD. Not all people with SPSD fit perfectly into the individual phenotypes and may also have overlapping syndromes such as classic SPS with limbic encephalitis or epilepsy (Saiz et al., 2008).

Although the exact cause is not known, a variety of malignancies (e.g., breast cancer, colon cancer, small-cell lung cancer, thymoma, and Hodgkin's lymphoma) have been associated with SPSD for 5–10% of the cases (Baizabal-Carvallo & Jankovic, 2015). The estimated prevalence of classic SPS is one to two per million in the general population, with women being affected twice as often as men (Hadavi et al., 2011). A majority of people with SPS develop symptoms in their 30s and 40s; although, diagnosis is often delayed.

Treatment and Prognosis

Prognosis can differ across the phenotypes and a combination of non-pharmacological and pharmacological options can be used for symptom management. Despite the prevalence being higher in women, the unique experiences of women in comparison to men with SPSD in terms of risk factors, symptoms, diagnosis, prognosis, and treatment are not clear.

Hyperkinetic Movement Disorders

Hyperkinetic movement disorders involve excessive involuntary and semi-voluntary movements, including tremors, dystonia, chorea, tics, myoclonus, and others. Tremor is the most prevalent type in clinical practice. Clinical presentation, progression, and treatment vary across these disorders and gender differences have been reported in several of the hyperkinetic movement disorders.

Tremor

Tremor is an involuntary, rhythmic, oscillatory movement in one or more body parts. It can be characterized based on the activation of tremor (Latorre et al., 2022). Rest tremor occurs at rest, while a body part is not activated and supported against gravity. Action tremor occurs while moving a muscle voluntarily. Postural tremor occurs while holding a position against gravity; kinetic tremor occurs during voluntary movement. Classification is based on clinical features including history, tremor characteristics, associated signs, and laboratory tests; and etiology including idiopathic, genetically defined, and acquired (Bhatia et al., 2018). Tremor can present on its own or with other symptoms as a part of a neurological syndrome. Etiology is diverse with essential tremor as the most common disorder (Fig. 6.3). Other tremor

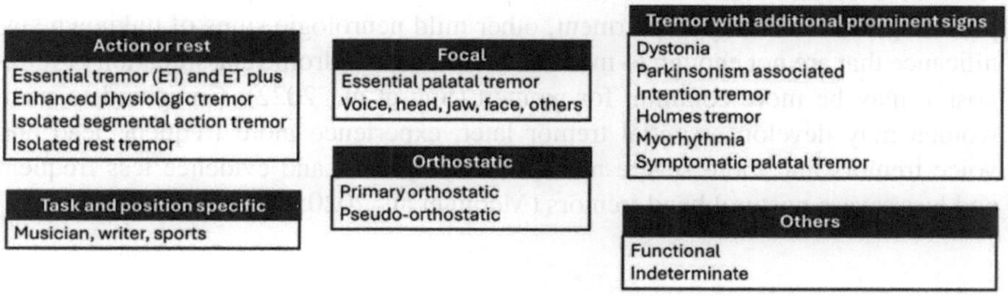

Fig. 6.3 Tremor syndromes based on the predominant presenting symptom

disorders include genetic diseases such as Wilson's disease, degenerative disorders such as Parkinson's disease, neuropathies, and spinal muscular atrophies, drug or toxin-induced, infectious or inflammatory diseases, endocrine and metabolic disorders such as hyperthyroidism and liver failure, neoplasms, injury, vascular, trauma, and functional disorders.

Essential Tremor

Essential tremor is one of the most common neurological disorders (Song et al., 2021). It is defined as an isolated tremor syndrome manifesting as bilateral upper extremity action tremor with at least 3 years of duration, without any other neurological signs such as ataxia, dystonia, or parkinsonism. Tremor can have a variable frequency of 4–10 Hz and also involve the head, vocal cords, or lower limbs (Bhatia et al., 2018).

Epidemiology and Presentation

Tremors can start insidiously early in life with severity increasing over the years. They are typically aggravated by stress, fatigue, exercise, and caffeine and can be improved by certain relaxing methods, small doses of alcohol, and certain medications. Women, however, are less likely than men to have alcohol sensitivity (Sun et al., 2022). Disability can occur if tremors impair voluntary activities. Non-motor symptoms including cognitive decline, depression, anxiety, apathy, and sleep disturbances can also occur and impact the quality of life. A meta-analysis in 2021 noted global prevalence as 0.32% in the general population with lower rates for women than men (0.28% vs. 0.36% overall; Song et al., 2021). Prevalence increased with older age (0.04% for people <20 years vs. 2.87% for people ≥ 80 years). Despite 50% of people with essential tremor having a family history, a single causal gene has not been identified.

Essential tremor plus, defined as essential tremor with additional neurological signs of uncertain significance (i.e., impaired tandem gait, questionable dystonic posturing, mild memory impairment, other mild neurologic signs of unknown significance that are not enough to make an additional syndrome classification or diagnosis), may be more common for women (Sun et al., 2022). Compared to men, women may develop essential tremor later, experience more frequent head and voice tremors and more severe non-motor symptoms, and evidence less frequent and less severe postural hand tremors (Meoni et al., 2020; Sun et al., 2022).

Treatment and Prognosis

The most common medications for essential tremor, primidone and propranolol, have teratogenic potential and are contraindicated in pregnancy (Bordelon & Smith, 2007; Kranick et al., 2010). However, gender differences for treatment response and treatment effects during pregnancy have yet to be clarified. Topiramate and gabapentin are also associated with congenital malformations and toxicity in animal studies and should be avoided during pregnancy. These findings lead to women preferring to avoid medications for their tremor management during pregnancy. Thalamic and subthalamic deep brain stimulation are other potential treatment options for essential tremor and are associated with similar outcomes for women and men, although women may be referred less for surgical treatments (Blomstedt et al., 2011; Reker et al., 2023).

Wilson's Disease

Wilson's disease is a treatable cause of tremors, which, if not appropriately diagnosed, can lead to irreversible damage. It is a rare autosomal recessive disorder with *AT7B* mutations causing excessive copper accumulation in the liver, brain (mainly basal ganglia, thalamus, cerebellum, upper brain stem), and other organs (Członkowska et al., 2018). It typically leads to hepatic, neurologic, and psychiatric symptoms, and Kayser-Fleischer rings in the cornea. Half of the people present with liver disease and hepatic symptoms can precede neuropsychiatric symptoms by up to 10 years. The most common neurologic signs of Wilson's disease include dysarthria, dystonia, parkinsonism, tremor, choreoathetosis, ataxia, and cognitive impairment. Tremor, including rubral (wing-beating), rest, and postural tremor, is one of the most frequent neurological manifestations of Wilson's disease. It is usually asymmetrical with 4–8 Hz frequency and variable amplitude.

Epidemiology and Diagnosis

Diagnosis is based on history, physical examination, laboratory findings, and imaging (Kasztelan-Szczerbinska & Cichoz-Lach, 2021). Determining blood ceruloplasmin level, urinary copper excretion, and molecular analysis is generally sufficient for diagnosis, although liver biopsy can be required for a smaller number of people.

Prevalence is estimated as 1 in 30,000 to 50,000, with overall similar rates for women and men, although lower rates for women compared to men have been suggested for adult-onset Wilson's disease (Cai et al., 2023; Sandahl et al., 2020). The hepatic form of Wilson's disease was suggested to occur more frequently in women, whereas neuropsychiatric form with rigidity, tremor, and psychiatric manifestations may be less common in women than men, with a younger age at onset for women (Cai et al., 2023; Litwin et al., 2012). Delayed diagnosis is frequent for Wilson's disease and may lead to irreversible damage and even death. Thus, early diagnosis with effective treatment is crucial as people on treatment can have a normal lifespan with minimal morbidity.

Treatment and Prognosis

For women with Wilson's disease, it is crucial to provide close monitoring and adequate treatment during pregnancy (Kasztelan-Szczerbinska & Cichoz-Lach, 2021; Pfeiffenberger et al., 2018). Procreative success has been directly associated with treatment efficacy for women with Wilson's disease. Chelators and zinc salts have teratogenic effects; however, the risk of discontinuing therapy outweighs the risk of continuing therapy. Breastfeeding is also not recommended during chelation therapy. D-penicillamine at a daily dose of 0.75–1.5 g and zinc are safe during pregnancy. Providers should also be careful about contraceptive options for women with Wilson's disease, as estrogen may interfere with the copper mechanism, and intrauterine devices contain copper.

Dystonia

Dystonia is a movement disorder characterized by abnormal, involuntary movements and/or postures caused by sustained or intermittent muscle contractions. It is often patterned, repetitive, twisting, triggered, or worsened by voluntary movement, associated with overflow muscle activation, and can be tremulous. It can be isolated or co-occur with different symptoms in multi-systemic disorders. Postural changes can be spasmodic or tonic, fixed or dynamic, or a combination of these (Albanese et al., 2013). Dystonia and dystonic tremor may have a directional nature, with movements worsening in certain positions and improving in others. People with dystonia can have alleviating maneuvers (sensory tricks), which typically involve simple movements that are not forceful opposition to the dystonic movement.

Anxiety, stress, and fatigue can worsen dystonia, while relaxation can improve dystonia with dystonia generally resolving during sleep (Stephen, 2022). Following Parkinson's disease and essential tremor, dystonia is the third most common movement disorder; people with dystonia make up ~20% of people in movement disorders clinics (Balint et al., 2018; Grütz & Klein, 2021). According to the most recent consensus in 2013, dystonia is classified based on two axes (Fig. 6.4; Albanese et al., 2013). The first axis provides categories for the clinical presentation including age at onset, body distribution, temporal pattern, and associated features. The second axis notes categories for etiology including nervous system pathology and whether the disorder is inherited or acquired.

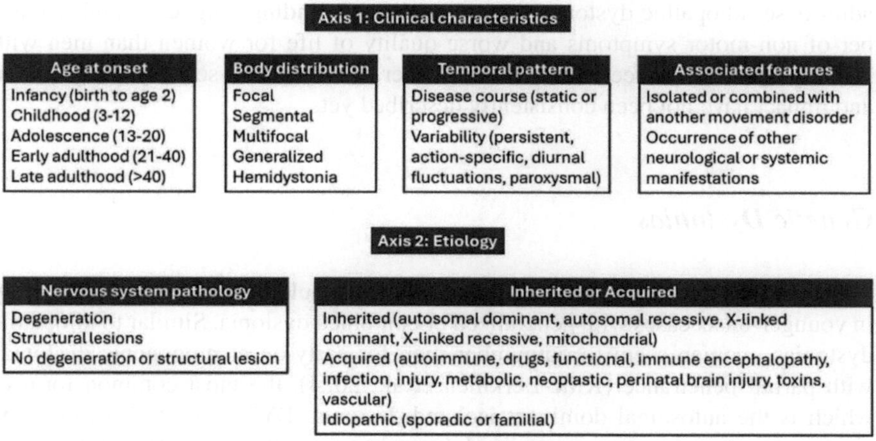

Fig. 6.4 Dystonia classification

Adult-Onset Idiopathic Focal and Segmental Dystonias

Adult-onset idiopathic focal and segmental dystonias are the most common dystonias (focal more common than segmental) and commonly present in the fourth decade of life (Stephen, 2022). These dystonias are not typically generalized, although they can progress to involve other parts or other tasks (if task-specific) over time. They can be differentiated from early-onset dystonias, where symptoms typically begin before age 26 and often generalize, with a frequent underlying genetic cause. Adult-onset idiopathic focal and segmental dystonias can include cervical, cranial, oromandibular, laryngeal, limb, and truncal dystonia. A meta-analysis in 2013 reported a prevalence of 15.36 per 100,000 for focal and segmental dystonias, with a higher prevalence in women than men (22.35 vs. 14.58; Steeves et al., 2012). Prevalence differences in women and men seem to increase with older age (Kilic-Berkmen et al., 2024). Furthermore, age of onset is earlier for women; blepharospasm, laryngeal, oromandibular, and cervical dystonias are more common; and limb dystonia is less common for women than men (Kilic-Berkmen et al., 2024).

Cervical dystonia is the most common type of adult-onset idiopathic focal dystonia, with higher prevalence rates for women than men. Interestingly, women are more likely than men to experience benefits from botulinum toxin treatment and continue treatment compared to men (Supnet et al., 2020). On the contrary, task-specific dystonias, including musician's dystonia with involuntary cramping of the limb at the instrument severely impairing the ability to perform highly trained tasks, as well as writer's cramp, are more common for men (Doll-Lee et al., 2024). Women seem to outnumber men for multifocal and generalized dystonias (Kilic-Berkmen et al., 2024). Positive family history is also more common for women with adult-onset idiopathic dystonia. Although research findings suggest a higher number of non-motor symptoms and worse quality of life for women than men with primary dystonia (Rafee et al., 2021), gender differences in severity, progression, and impact have not been consistently described yet.

Genetic Dystonias

There are many genetic forms of dystonia, which should be investigated thoroughly in younger-onset cases with generalized or combined dystonia. Similar to idiopathic dystonias, women seem to outnumber men for early-onset monogenic dystonias with partial penetrance (Kilic-Berkmen et al., 2024), the most common form of which is the autosomal dominant isolated dystonia. DYT-*TOR1A* (DYT1) is the most common early-onset generalized dystonia, particularly prevalent in people of Ashkenazi Jewish ancestry (Stephen, 2022). Gender differences have not been described for prevalence, presentation, or prognosis. A limited number of studies have suggested that *THAP1*, *GNAL*, *GCH1*, and *ANO3*-related dystonias may be more prevalent in women than men (Arabia et al., 2022; Kilic-Berkmen et al., 2024). In dystonia-plus syndromes, dystonia is associated with another movement disorder such as parkinsonism or myoclonus, without any evidence of neurodegeneration. These include dopa-responsive dystonia, myoclonus dystonia, and rapid-onset dystonia-parkinsonism. Dopa-responsive dystonia seems to be more prevalent in women (2–4:1 compared to men; Phukan et al., 2011).

Neurodegeneration with Brain Iron Accumulation (NBIA)

Another group of disorders that can include dystonia among the symptoms is neurodegeneration with brain iron accumulation (NBIA). NBIA is characterized by abnormal iron accumulation in the basal ganglia, most often in the globus pallidus and/or substantia nigra, with frequent generalized cerebral and cerebellar atrophy. Clinical manifestations are progressive dystonia, dysarthria, parkinsonism, spasticity, psychiatric symptoms, optic atrophy, and retinal degeneration (Kolarova et al., 2022). Onset can range from infancy to adulthood; progression can also have a variable rate, although in most cases the disease leads to severe disability and premature death. The lifetime risk of NBIA disorders is estimated to be 0.88 per 100,000, with an overall similar prevalence for women and men (Kolarova et al., 2022). The majority of the NBIA are autosomal recessive. Beta-propeller protein-associated neurodegeneration is an NBIA caused by a mutation in *WDR45* on the X chromosome, with suspected male lethality, as most cases have been women (Gregory & Hayflick, 1993). Overall, treatment for NBIA is symptomatic without much knowledge of gender differences.

Special Considerations for Prognosis and Treatment of Dystonia in Women

Dystonia severity can fluctuate during pregnancy, potentially due to estrogen fluctuations. Levodopa-responsive dystonia, Wilson's disease, and other young-onset genetic dystonia (i.e., DYT1) are the most common dystonia types reported for women in pregnancy. Providers should be careful about treatment planning. Neuroleptics for hyperemesis gravidarum have been associated with drug-induced dystonia. Low-dose levodopa can be administered without adverse effects. Benzodiazepine does not seem to have a teratogenic effect, although there is only limited data for anticholinergics and caution is recommended. Botulinum neurotoxin injections can be safe, as they do not enter the systemic circulation when injected adequately, and molecules larger than 500 Daltons do not cross the placenta (Arabia et al., 2022). Botulin toxin A and B and deep brain stimulation have not been associated with complications in pregnancy, although data remain limited.

Chorea

Chorea, derived from the Greek word "dance," is an abnormal involuntary movement characterized by sudden, brief, irregular, unpredictable, non-stereotyped movements. The velocity and severity can vary. The flowing component is usually faster than that of dystonia but slower than the jerking component of myoclonus (Termsarasab, 2019). Chorea can also be mistaken as myoclonus when it has a quick velocity with low amplitude, appearing jerky. In people with milder chorea, it can be overlooked as these people can appear clumsy and fidgety with movements seeming purposeful. It can present in various body parts; impact posture, gait, speech, and swallowing; and can resolve during sleep. Ballism is a type of chorea characterized by large-amplitude flinging movements in proximal extremities. Differential diagnosis of chorea is challenging due to the high number of diseases presenting with chorea. Although many diseases can lead to generalized chorea, hemichorea, chorea in orobuccolingual, or forehead regions can hint at a shorter list of potential etiologies.

Hemichorea

Hemichorea can be due to contralateral subthalamic nucleus, basal ganglia, or corona radiata lesions. Asymmetric chorea or hemichorea can be due to systemic disorders such as nonketotic hyperglycemia and polycythemia vera. Hemichorea due to nonketotic hyperglycemia is more common in women and Asian populations. In addition to blood sugar control, symptomatic treatment of chorea for several weeks or months can be needed. Sydenham chorea can also lead to asymmetric chorea or hemichorea; although, the majority experience generalized chorea (Beier et al., 2024). It is a childhood disorder affecting up to 40% of children with rheumatic fever. It is more common in developing countries and can develop up to six months after an infection with group A streptococcus bacteria. It is more prevalent for girls than boys (3:1).

Symptoms can include chorea, diminished muscle tone, muscle weakness, gait disturbances, dysarthria, dysgraphia, tics, and cognitive or emotional disorders. Symptoms usually last for 3 to 6 weeks and usually resolve over time. However, in some cases, symptoms can last longer or recur. It also has strong correlations with the development of carditis and valvular heart disease.

For children, Sydenham chorea is the most common type of acquired chorea, whereas benign hereditary chorea is the most common type of genetic chorea. Benign hereditary chorea, caused by *NKX2.1 (TITF1)* mutations, is a childhood-onset disorder more common in girls than boys (Termsarasab, 2019). Symptoms typically include chorea that does not typically progress to adulthood, ataxia, dystonia, hypotonia, and delayed motor milestones.

Orobuccolingual or Lower Cranial Region Chorea

Orobuccolingual or lower cranial region chorea is typically seen in tardive syndromes or acquired hepatocerebral degeneration. Dystonia in the orobuccolingual region can also occur in some choreic disorders including neuroacanthocytosis syndrome, neurodegeneration with brain iron accumulation disorders, X-linked dystonia-parkinsonism, Wilson's disease, and Lesch-Nyhan syndrome.

Neuroacanthocytosis is a heterogeneous group of disorders with erythrocyte acanthocytosis and progressive neurodegeneration, predominantly in the basal ganglia (Walker et al., 2011). Clinical presentation typically includes chorea, dystonia, and other movement disorders, as well as prominent cognitive and psychiatric symptoms. The two core neuroacanthocytosis syndromes are the autosomal recessive chorea-acanthocytosis and X-linked McLeod syndrome. Chorea-acanthocytosis, caused by *VPS13A* mutations, is estimated to have a prevalence of few cases per 1,000,000, with similar rates for women and men. Feeding dystonia with a person's tongue pushing the food out of the mouth as soon as it comes into contact with the food is pathognomonic for this disease. X-linked McLeod syndrome has a prevalence of less than 1 per 1,000,000 and affects women less than men (Jung et al., 1993). Symptoms include chorea, tics, parkinsonism, dysarthria, dysphagia, cognitive and behavioral symptoms, and seizures. Heterozygous females usually lack central nervous system and neuromuscular symptoms; however, some may develop chorea or late-onset cognitive decline. X-linked dystonia-parkinsonism affects primarily Filipino men (99:1 for men:women) (Evidente, 1993). Women carriers are mostly asymptomatic; compared to men, women often do no present with dystonia, and instead experience chorea, focal tremor, or mild, non-progressive parkinsonism.

Huntington's Disease

Forehead chorea often presents in Huntington's disease, and forehead involvement can help differentiate Huntington's from tardive dyskinesia. Huntington's disease is the most common genetic chorea in adults. It is an autosomal-dominant, progressive neurodegenerative disorder caused by expanded CAG repeat on the *huntingtin (HTT)* gene, with fully penetrant disease when repeats exceed 40 (Caron et al., 1993). Prevalence is estimated to be around 5 per 100,000 globally, although rates differ across the continents with higher rates in Europe and North American than in Africa (Medina et al., 2022). Symptoms include motor, cognitive, and behavioral changes, with cognitive and behavioral changes impacting daily life more at times.

While women were suggested to have a higher prevalence than men in a large American cohort (7.05 vs. 6.10 per 100,000); gender differences have not been consistently reported in prevalence studies (Bruzelius et al., 2019; Risby-Jones et al., 2024). However, studies have noted gender differences in inheritance and clinical profile (Table 6.4). Compared to maternal transmission, paternal transmission results in earlier onset and faster progression due to CAG repeat instability particularly during spermatogenesis; large CAG repeat expansions predominantly occur through paternal transmission (Risby-Jones et al., 2024). Women with Huntington's disease can experience a more severe disease with a faster progression in motor and functional domains (Hentosh et al., 2021). Motor symptoms may affect functional ability and independence more for women than men. Depression can be more prevalent and severe in women than men. Accordingly, women are more likely than men to be prescribed anti-anxiolytic or antidepressants. Reduced plasma testosterone has been associated with depression in women, and more severe disease and cognitive impairment in men (Markianos et al., 2005).

Table 6.4 Gender differences in Huntington's disease

Disease features	Women	Men
Risk	Apolipoprotein E ε2ε3 associated with later onset than men	*PPARGC1A* variant associated with earlier motor onset
Clinical profile	More severe disease More prevalent and severe depression	
Progression	Faster progression on motor and functional domains	Negative association between growth hormone and cognitive impairment
Daily life	Motor symptoms impact functioning and independence more	
Treatment	More likely to be prescribed anti-anxiolytic or antidepressants	

The age of onset for Huntington's disease is typically between 30 and 50 with an average life expectancy of 10 to 25 years after onset. Studies have noted similar age of onset and at death for women and men; although, genotypes and allele frequencies may impact age at onset differently for women and men. A coding variant in *PPARGC1A* is associated with earlier motor onset only in men carriers, and women with apolipoprotein E genotype ε2ε3 have a later onset than men with the same genotype (Meoni et al., 2020; Weydt et al., 2014). Higher levels of insulin-like growth factor are associated with worse cognitive impairment for both genders, although the negative association between growth hormone and cognitive impairment was only present for men in a cohort of 109 people with genetically documented Huntington's disease, aged 21 to 85 years, from five centers of the Francophone Huntington Network in France (Saleh et al., 2010). Currently, only symptomatic treatment options are available with potential gender differences still needing to be explored.

Ataxia

Ataxia is an incoordination of voluntary muscle movement, which is a neurological sign usually caused by cerebellar dysfunction, and impaired vestibular or proprioceptive afferents to the cerebellum. It can be characterized by poor coordination, unsteady gait with a tendency to stumble, wide-based stance, impairment of fine motor skills, dysarthria, dysphagia, and eye movement abnormalities (Rosenthal, 2022; Winchester et al., 2013). It may have an acute onset with rapid progression (e.g., when caused by stroke, hemorrhage, or infection), insidious onset with slower progression (e.g., when caused by spinocerebellar ataxias), subacute onset (e.g., alcohol abuse, paraneoplastic syndrome, infections, certain medications), and can be benign in symptomatic disorders (e.g., vestibular neuritis). As some causes of ataxia have a narrow therapeutic window, prompt and careful assessment to identify the etiology is important.

Ataxia can be classified by the cause: hereditary, acquired, and non-hereditary degenerative (Fig. 6.5; Klockgether & Paulson, 2011). Acquired ataxias may have sudden or subacute onset with quick progression and asymmetrical or focal presentation. Acute onset without progression suggests injury, stroke, hemorrhage, or anoxia, whereas subacute onset with progression suggests infectious, inflammatory, or immune processes, metabolic disease, toxin or drug exposure, or neoplasm. It is important to identify the underlying cause of ataxia as acquired ataxias can resolve once the underlying factor is removed or treated. Hereditary ataxias usually have an insidious onset, progress relatively slowly, and affect both sides of the body. There is currently no cure for hereditary ataxias; however, people's functional abilities can be supported by medications and rehabilitation.

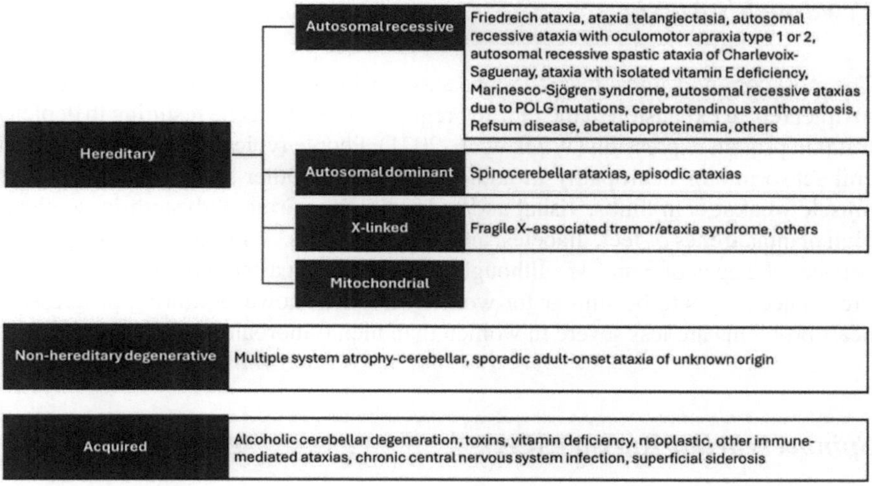

Fig. 6.5 Ataxia classification

Autosomal recessive ataxias or metabolic disorders should be considered for younger people with ataxia onset before the age of 25, or people with siblings who are also affected; autosomal dominant ataxias should be considered for people with parents who are affected; and maternal inheritance can point to mitochondrial or X-linked disorders (Witek et al., 2021). Although genetic testing is becoming more available for the diagnosis of these disorders, new pathogenic variants continue to be identified for ataxia. People with ataxia onset after the age of 40 with no family history are most likely to have sporadic etiology.

Epidemiology

The overall prevalence is estimated as 26 per 100,000 in children for ataxia, 10 per 100,000 for genetic ataxia, 2.7 per 100,000 for dominant cerebellar ataxia, and 3.3 per 100,000 for recessive. Global prevalence of spinocerebellar ataxia (SCA) is estimated as 3 to 5.6 per 100,000 with the most common type being SCA type 3, followed by SCA type 2 and 6 (Ruano et al., 2014). The most common autosomal recessive ataxia is Friedreich ataxia, followed by ataxia with oculomotor apraxia or ataxia-telangiectasia. X-linked ataxias can be less common in women compared to men (Witek et al., 2021). Otherwise, there is no clear gender difference reported for the prevalence of autosomal recessive or dominant cerebellar ataxias. Sporadic adult-onset cerebellar ataxia is less common in women, with women/men prevalence rates of 1/1.3 to 2.3 (Klockgether, 2018). Acquired ataxia can also be less common in women, with women/men prevalence rates of 1/2.1 (Shehata et al., 2011).

Friedreich's Ataxia

The most common autosomal recessive ataxia is Friedreich's ataxia, associated with a triplet repeat expansion in the intronic region of the *FXN* gene resulting in depleted frataxin protein expression (Witek et al., 2021). People typically experience peripheral sensorimotor neuropathy in addition to ataxia. Other symptoms can include muscle weakness in limbs, visual and/or hearing impairment, dysarthria, scoliosis, high plantar arches of feet, diabetes, and heart disorders. Symptom onset is typically between the ages of 5 and 15, although late-onset form after age 25 can also occur. Prevalence seems to be similar for women and men; however, during progression, heart problems are less severe in women than men (Ghorbani et al., 2019).

Spinocerebellar Ataxia (SCA)

The most common cause of autosomal dominant ataxia is SCA. Currently, there are over 40 different SCAs, and the number continues growing with new genetic mutations being discovered (Ashizawa et al., 2018). Symptoms can differ based on the underlying genetic cause for SCAs, with progressive ataxia present in all types. Although prevalence appears to be similar for women and men, symptoms and progression may differ. Women are affected less by ataxia-specific symptoms and more by non-ataxia symptoms; non-ataxia symptoms can progress faster for women; quality of life is better for women with slower decline over time compared to men (Weber et al., 2024; Zielonka & Stawinska-Witoszynska, 2020).

Fragile X-Associated Tremor/Ataxia Syndrome (FXTAS)

The most common X-linked ataxia is fragile X-associated tremor/ataxia syndrome (FXTAS), associated with a 50–200 CGG repeat expansion in the *FMR1* gene and inherited in an X-linked dominant pattern (Witek et al., 2021). It is estimated that around 16% of women and 40% of men carriers develop FXTAS. Premutation occurs in less than 1 in 200 women and 1 in 400 men, resulting in a more balanced prevalence rate for women and men (Cabal-Herrera et al., 2020). FXTAS typically presents after the age of 50 with kinetic tremor, gait ataxia, neuropathy, autonomic dysfunction, cognitive impairment, and parkinsonism (Hall & Hagerman, 2018). Once a person is diagnosed, other family members should also be screened for FXTAS and fragile X-associated primary ovarian insufficiency. FXTAS can be less severe for women than men, and present with clinical features specific for women such as primary ovarian insufficiency (Orsucci et al., 2022; Witek et al., 2021). *FMR1* premutations are the most common monogenic cause of premature ovarian insufficiency and increase the risk for premature menopause. Psychiatric disorders, especially depression, are also more common in women with *FMR1* premutations.

Mitochondrial Disorders

Mitochondrial disorders with ataxia often present with multi-organ dysfunction impacting tissues like the peripheral and central nervous system, muscles, endocrine glands, heart, and gastrointestinal system (Finsterer & Zarrouk-Mahjoub, 2017). Although these disorders are more likely to be maternally inherited, there are some autosomal recessive nuclear genes coding proteins that regulate mitochondrial genes, which can also play a role.

Tics and Tourette Syndrome

Tics are sudden, rapid, repetitive, brief, irregular movements or sounds, which can appear voluntary and are often exaggerated in intensity. Any movement or sound can be a tic, and they can be highly variable within and between individuals. Tics can be classified based on type (motor, vocal, or both) and complexity (simple, complex; Fig. 6.6). They can range from infrequent and not bothersome to frequent, intense, disruptive, and even self-injurious (Singer, 2019). Stress, anxiety, anger, excitement, fatigue, heat, or infections can worsen, while concentrating on a physical or mental task, or sleeping can reduce the tics. Tics are commonly preceded by an urge or sensation, referred to as a "premonitory urge," which includes mounting

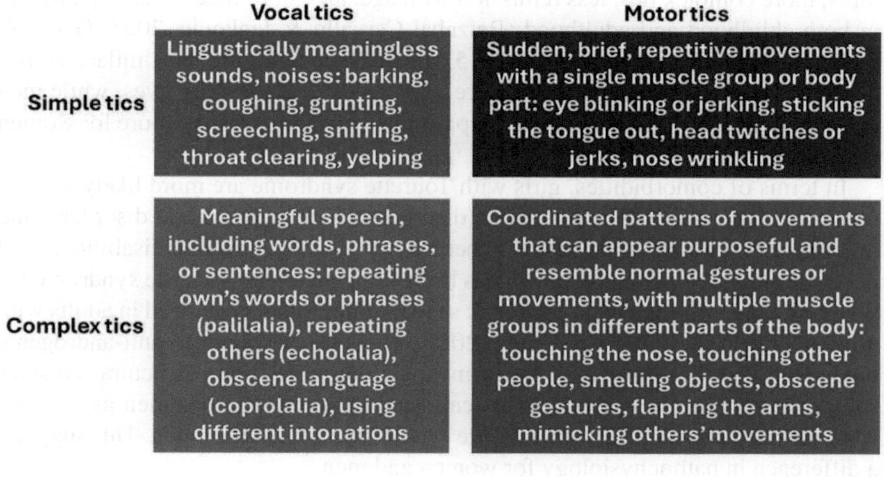

Fig. 6.6 Classification of tics

tension, pressure, itch, or feeling localized to the region of the tic, which resolves when the tic occurs. They can be suppressible at times, although this may worsen the urge or internal tension.

Epidemiology and Presentation

Types of tic disorders include Tourette syndrome, chronic motor or vocal tic disorder, and provisional tic disorder. These can be differentiated based on the type of tics and disease duration. Both motor (two or more) and vocal (at least one) tics occur in Tourette syndrome and symptoms are present for at least 1 year; either motor or vocal tics (one or more) occur in chronic motor or vocal tic disorder with symptoms present for at least 1 year; and symptoms last less than 1 year in provisional tic disorder. Typically, tics are most severe between the ages of 8 and 12 and decline throughout teenagehood and adulthood. However, tics can continue into or start during adulthood and can be severe and disabling.

Simple tics are common in childhood with prevalence suggested to be between 6 and 12%. Global prevalence for Tourette syndrome is estimated to range from 0.3% to 1%. Overall, tic disorders are more common in children than adults, and less common in girls than boys (1:3–4; Knight et al., 2012; Singer, 2019). While prevalence declines with age for boys, it increases for girls (Garris & Quigg, 2021).

Prognosis and Treatment

Compared to boys with Tourette syndrome, girls have later onset, later peak symptoms, more complex tics, less remission with age, and more functional impairment, in both childhood and adulthood (Baizabal-Carvallo & Jankovic, 2023; Garris & Quigg, 2021; Lichter & Finnegan, 2015). In adulthood, despite the similar severity of the tics, women can experience more impairment in their daily lives, while men can experience more pain from tics. Impairment worsens over time more for women than men.

In terms of comorbidities, girls with Tourette syndrome are more likely to have obsessive-compulsive disorder, eating disorders, anxiety, and mood disorders, and less likely to have attention deficit hyperactivity disorder, learning disabilities, and perinatal stress. Hyperandrogenism has been associated with Tourette syndrome for both boys and girls, and neuroanatomic sexual dimorphism is reduced in adults with Tourette syndrome (Garris & Quigg, 2021). However, response to anti-androgenic medication can be less likely for women. Furthermore, brain structural changes such as frontoparietal cortex, corpus callosum thinning, and putamen asymmetry were reported only in men with Tourette syndrome, but not in women. This suggests a difference in pathophysiology for women and men.

Treatment options can include behavioral therapy, pharmacological therapies, non-invasive neuromodulation, and deep brain stimulation. Treatment response can differ by gender, as supported by better response to haloperidol for women. As long-term outcomes are worse for women with more impact on their daily lives, women with tics and Tourette syndrome should be included more in research during adulthood to better understand and address their needs.

Myoclonus

Epidemiology

Myoclonus is an involuntary, sudden, brief (10–50 millisecond duration) jerk caused by muscle contraction (positive myoclonus) or interruption of muscle activity (negative myoclonus including asterixis). It is not a disease, but rather a clinical sign. A study in Olmsted County, Minnesota with a population primarily of Northern and Western European descent estimated the incidence as 0.9 per 100,000 persons/year for women compared to 1.6 for men, and the prevalence as 9.2 per 100,000 person/year for women compared to 7.9 for men (Caviness et al., 1999). Incidence increased after the age of 40, with prevalence increasing with advancing age for both women and men. In general, incidence and prevalence for different age groups were lower for women than for men. These numbers may be higher in the general population, as myoclonus is often secondary to another disease.

Presentation

The classification can be made based on clinical signs, neurophysiology, and etiology (Riva et al., 2024). Clinical classification can be based on the body distribution with focal, multifocal, segmental, or generalized distribution. Myoclonus is usually irregular (arrhythmic) but can also be rhythmic (i.e., palatal or ocular myoclonus). It can occur at rest, while maintaining a posture, or during action, and may be triggered by tactile, acoustic, or visual stimuli (reflex or stimulus-sensitive myoclonus). Etiological classification can include (1) physiologic, with myoclonic jerks occurring as normal phenomena (hiccups, sleep jerks, startle response); (2) essential, with non-progressive, isolated, and minimally disabling myoclonus which can be idiopathic, sporadic, or hereditary (myoclonus-dystonia syndrome); (3) epileptic, with EEG correlate; (4) symptomatic or secondary, with myoclonus due to a post-hypoxic cerebral damage, drug or toxin exposure, metabolic, infectious, inflammatory, neurodegenerative, or structural disorder; and (5) functional myoclonus. Neurophysiological classification is based on identifying the pathophysiologic generators and mechanisms of propagation, which includes cortical, cortical–subcortical, subcortical–nonsegmental, segmental, and peripheral (Caviness, 2019; Merchant et al., 2020).

Diagnosis

Since a wide range of factors can underlie myoclonus, assessment should include a thorough medical history, physical examination as well as laboratory tests, imaging, and neurophysiology as needed. Treatment will differ based on etiology. While gender differences for the etiology, symptom presentation, diagnosis, and prognosis for myoclonus have not been determined, some studies have noted differences in myoclonus-inducing disorders such as juvenile myoclonic epilepsy and myoclonus-dystonia due to *SGCE* mutations. For myoclonus-dystonia due to *SGCE* mutations, the median age at onset was 5 for girls and 8 for boys, and the disease is more commonly paternally inherited (Raymond et al., 2008). For juvenile myoclonic epilepsy, girls are more likely than boys to demonstrate photoparoxysmal response most often manifesting as myoclonus; earlier myoclonus onset age is associated with drug resistance for girls (Cervenka, 2022; Shakeshaft et al., 2022).

Restless Legs Syndrome

Epidemiology

Restless legs syndrome (RLS), also known as Willis-Ekbom disease, is a common disorder where people feel an irresistible urge to move their legs (Allen et al., 2014). It can be idiopathic or secondary to diseases or conditions. Higher RLS risk has been noted in conditions including end-stage renal disease, chronic liver disease, multiple sclerosis, diabetes, peripheral neuropathy, migraine, and pregnancy in the third trimester (Broström et al., 2023). Non-painful sensations typically start at rest, improve by moving the legs, and recur once the movement stops. Sensations may feel like aching, throbbing, itching, pulling, crawling, or creeping. Symptoms commonly occur later in the day and get more intense at night while resting, disturbing sleep. Thus, RLS is also noted as a sleep disorder and is associated with periodic leg movements of sleep. Severity and frequency may vary from day to day and daytime disruption can accompany sleep disturbance. Spontaneous remission can occur, although symptoms often recur. A meta-analysis including 97 studies from 33 different countries published between January 2000 and February 2022 estimated global prevalence as 3% for adults, with 4.7% for women and 2.8% for men (Broström et al., 2023). RLS is considered to be underdiagnosed and undertreated with higher prevalence rates reported in prior studies.

Risk Factors and Presentation

Women are consistently reported to have a higher risk for RLS than men. Pregnancy and increased parity are significant risk factors for women, and menopause increases the frequency of occurrence (Seeman, 2020). RLS is the most common movement disorder during pregnancy for women; prevalence in pregnant women is reported to be two to three times higher than in the general population (Miri et al., 2014). Low iron levels and high estrogen levels, which oscillate, in women impact dopamine and glutamate transmission and can contribute to this increased RLS risk (Seeman, 2020). Common comorbidities in RLS including migraine, depression, and anxiety can also be more prevalent for women. Both the higher prevalence of these conditions and treatments for these conditions can contribute to RLS risk. Symptoms and comorbidities can also differ by gender. RLS can present more with sensory symptoms in women and motor symptoms in men (Holzknecht et al., 2020). Women experience pain, waking up during sleep, sleep disturbance, and depressive mood more than men, whereas men experience motor symptoms, hypertension, and cardiovascular disease more than women with RLS (Kim et al., 2024). However, the severity and impact on quality of life may not differ between women and men (Manconi et al., 2012).

Treatment

In people with mild symptoms, non-pharmacological treatments may be sufficient; however, if needed, several medications are available and helpful for the treatment. Women have lower iron and receive iron supplementation therapy more frequently than men (Kim et al., 2024; Manconi et al., 2012). Given significant differences in risk, symptom presentation, and comorbidities, different treatments may be more beneficial for women and men with RLS.

Paroxysmal Movement Disorders

Paroxysmal movement disorders are a rare heterogeneous group of diseases including paroxysmal dyskinesia and episodic ataxia (Erro et al., 2023). Paroxysmal dyskinesias are intermittent attacks of abnormal involuntary movements (dystonia, chorea, ballism, or a combination of these) without loss of consciousness and include paroxysmal kinesigenic dyskinesia, paroxysmal non-kinesigenic dyskinesia, and paroxysmal exertion-induced dyskinesia (Harvey et al., 2021). Episodic ataxia refers to attacks of cerebellar dysfunction with or without interictal neurological manifestations. Treatment differs based on the subtype.

Epidemiology, Risk Factors, and Presentation

Primary paroxysmal movement disorders typically begin in childhood or adolescence and improve or resolve with age, with a typically normal neurological examination between the attacks. Secondary paroxysmal movement disorders typically after the second decade of life occur sporadically, with a typically abnormal clinical examination between the attacks (Garone et al., 2020). Several genes have been associated with paroxysmal movement disorders (primary), although they can also occur due to secondary or acquired causes such as neurodegenerative, metabolic, structural, or immunological disorders (secondary).

Paroxysmal kinesigenic dyskinesia with dystonia and/or chorea attacks triggered by sudden voluntary movement lasting from a few seconds to a minute is the most common form of paroxysmal dyskinesia. Prevalence is estimated to be 1 per 150,000 with lower rates for women than men (1/4 to 8) in sporadic cases, but not familial cases (Bhatia, 2011).

Paroxysmal non-kinesigenic dyskinesia is characterized by dystonia and/or chorea attacks that last for a few minutes to a few hours and can occur at rest or after coffee, alcohol, or stress (Méneret & Roze, 2016). Prevalence is estimated to be 1 per 1,000,000. The women/men ratio for prevalence varies between 1/2 for sporadic and 1/1 for familial cases (Bhatia, 2011).

Paroxysmal exertion-induced dyskinesia is induced by physical exhaustion after prolonged exercise. Attacks usually last 5 to 30 min and affect the body part involved in the exercise. Prevalence is less than 1 in 1,000,000 people, with the women/men ratio reported to be 3/2 (Bhatia et al., 1997). The incidence of episodic ataxia is estimated to be less than 1 per 100,000 persons/year (Choi & Choi, 2016).

Special Considerations for Prognosis of Paroxysmal Movement Disorders in Women

Interestingly, 50% of women with paroxysmal kinesigenic dyskinesia were noted to experience improvement during pregnancy (Bruno et al., 2004). Women may experience attacks of paroxysmal non-kinesigenic dyskinesia more frequently during ovulation or menstruation. In episodic ataxia type 1, pregnancy or menstruation can trigger attacks in women (Graves et al., 2014). Beyond these limited number of studies, gender differences for the etiology, symptom presentation, diagnosis, prognosis, and treatment are yet to be clarified.

Tardive Syndromes

Tardive syndrome is a group of disorders with persistent hyperkinetic and hypokinetic movements and sensory complaints after chronic neuroleptics and other dopamine receptor-blocking agents. It is distinguishable from similar symptoms presenting as acute side effects of the medications, which resolve shortly after the medication is stopped (Frei et al., 2018). In tardive syndromes, abnormal movements or sensory symptoms persist or worsen for a month or more after the medication is stopped (Frei et al., 2018; Ward & Citrome, 2018). Abnormal movements can include dystonia, chorea, tremor, akathisia, parkinsonism, tics, and myoclonus.

Epidemiology, Risk Factors, and Presentation

Tardive dyskinesia typically manifests as oro-buccal-lingual dyskinesia with stereotyped, involuntary movements of the tongue (protrusion or twisting), lips (smacking or puckering), and jaw (chewing) (Chen et al., 2020). A meta-analysis including 41 studies published between January 1, 2000 and September 30, 2015 identified through PubMed, MEDLINE, and Google Scholar search reported a global mean prevalence of 25.3% in people taking typical and/or atypical antipsychotics, with the highest rate for typical antipsychotics (30%) followed by atypical antipsychotics (20.7%) and the lowest rate for people never exposed to typical antipsychotics (7.7%; Carbon et al., 2017). Female sex is considered a risk factor, with higher prevalence rates and more severe symptoms for women compared to men (Yassa & Jeste, 1992).

Tardive dystonia typically presents focally and progresses into a segmental or generalized form over time. It typically co-occurs with tardive dyskinesia. The face and neck are the most commonly affected parts followed by the arms, trunk, and legs. Prevalence ranges from 0.4% to 5% with a slight male predominance (Macerollo & Deuschl, 2018). The onset age is younger for men than women (Kiriakakis et al., 1998). Tardive akathisia is characterized by a feeling of restlessness and an inability to remain still. Typical manifestations are body rocking and lower body involvement with a prevalence ranging from 20% to 30% (Chen et al., 2020). It is more prevalent in women than men (Burke et al., 1989).

Tardive parkinsonism incidence has decreased after the use of atypical, new-generation neuroleptics that have less affinity for D2 receptors (Badarny et al., 2023). Ceasing the medication improves parkinsonism within a few months or years, although symptoms persist or worsen in a quarter of cases (Martí Massó & Poza, 1996). Similar to the majority of tardive syndromes, tardive parkinsonism is also more prevalent in women than men. Other tardive syndromes can include myoclonus, tremors, tics, and pain. Tardive pain may be more prevalent in women than men (Ford et al., 1994).

Prognosis and Treatment

Overall, tardive syndrome is diverse in both the phenomenology and clinical outcomes, with a higher prevalence for women than men. While prevention is the best course of treatment, there are also treatment options including oral medications, botulinum toxin injections, and deep brain stimulation.

Functional Movement Disorders

Functional movement disorders (FMD) are among the most commonly seen disorders at the neurology clinic and a major source of disability (Galli et al., 2020). FMD were also referred to as psychogenic movement disorder, although there has been a shift to the FMD term to emphasize the biopsychosocial illness model rather than the idea of an unresolved psychological disease expressed through physical symptoms. Changes in temporoparietal junction activity and connectivity between the temporoparietal junction, salience/limbic network, and sensorimotor region have been noted (Aybek & Perez, 2022). The diagnostic approach has shifted from diagnosis of exclusion to positive diagnostic criteria based on clinical features and physical examination (LaFaver, 2020). The current diagnostic approach includes testing for distractibility, enhancement with attention, incongruency, motor inconsistency, suggestibility, and variability of involuntary movements (Gupta & Lang, 2009) (Table 6.5). Neurophysiological assessment is also helpful.

Sudden onset with often a precipitating trigger, spontaneous remission, paroxysmal nature, migration around the body, change of type of movement over time, and association with other FMD or functional neurological disorders serve as clues for diagnosis. Movement symptoms may include tremors, dystonia, myoclonus, and parkinsonism. Psychiatric comorbidity is also common with a history of recent and/or childhood physical or psychological trauma; however, such psychological stressors are not required for the diagnosis (Espay et al., 2018).

Epidemiology, Risk Factors, and Presentation

Studies in North America and Europe suggest the prevalence in neurology clinics for FMD cases ranges from 3.3 to 3.6%, with 40–50% having tremor, 18% dystonia, 4–14% myoclonus, and 7–40% parkinsonism (Galli et al., 2020). It is more prevalent for women than men (2.5/1) with a mean age at onset of 40 to 50. There are also gender differences beyond prevalence. Mean age at onset is older for men than women; sexual abuse is a risk factor for FMD more so for women than men; and functional dystonia is more common for women, whereas gait problems are more common for men (Edwards & Aybek, 2020).

Table 6.5 Positive signs on examination and critical points in the diagnosis and delivering the diagnosis of functional movement disorders

Positive signs on examination	
Distractibility	Abnormal movement resolves if attention is directed elsewhere
Enhancement with attention	Drawing attention to the abnormal movement triggers or worsens the movement
Incongruency	Discordant clinical findings with known movement disorder
Motor inconsistency	Movement inconsistent on exam and when the person is not actively examined, movement impaired at some times, preserved at some times
Suggestibility	Movement emerges or worsens with examiner's instructions, suggestions, or maneuvers
Variability	Movement pattern including frequency, amplitude, distribution, changes over time
Critical points in the diagnosis and delivering the diagnosis	
- Make the diagnosis based on clinical examination, rather than as a diagnosis of exclusion	
- Disclose how the diagnosis was made by outlining the specific features on examination that made the diagnosis definite, if such level of certainty was achieved (e.g., Hoover sign or tremor entrainment)	
- Emphasize the confidence in the diagnosis to prevent the person to feel the need for alternative medical opinions	
- Validate the neurological symptoms and disability	
- Disorder is potentially reversible with treatment, and favorable outcome starts with delivering the diagnosis successfully	
- Ensure the person understands the rationale for tailored multidisciplinary management with a partnership with the provider	

Prognosis and Treatment

Many people living with FMD can have persistent symptoms after years of follow-up (LaFaver, 2020). Although there is still a need for more studies to better determine the course of the disease, timely diagnosis, reduced stigma, and more access to treatment can improve the prognosis. Treatment starts with appropriately informing the person of the diagnosis. Addressing the stressor if identified, medication, rehabilitation therapy, and invasive approaches are available treatment options.

Conclusions

While findings remain limited, literature so far supports unique experiences for women compared to men across several hypokinetic and hyperkinetic movement disorders. Gender differences can include risk factors, prevalence, clinical profile, progression, and treatments (Table 6.6). As pathophysiological mechanisms may

Table 6.6 Ratio of women to men with movement disorders

Movement disorder	Ratio (Women:Men)
Parkinson's disease	0.85:1
Dementia with Lewy bodies	Women < Men[a]
Multiple system atrophy	0.43:1
Progressive supranuclear palsy	~1:1[b]
Corticobasal degeneration	~1:1[b]
Drug-induced parkinsonism	Women > Men[a]
Vascular parkinsonism	0.39:1
Stiff person syndrome	2:1
Essential tremor	0.78:1
Wilson's disease	~1:1[b]
Adult-onset focal and segmental dystonias	1.53:1
DYT-*TOR1A* dystonia	0.9:1
GCH1-deficient dopa-responsive dystonia	2.1:1
GNAL-linked dystonia	2:1
ANO3-related dystonia	1.4:1
DYT-THAP1 dystonia	1:1
TH-deficient dopa-responsive dystonia	0.9:1
Beta-propeller protein-associated neurodegeneration (BPAN)	Women > Men[a]
Sydenham chorea	3:1
Benign hereditary chorea	Girls > Boys
Chorea-acanthocytosis	~1:1[b]
X-linked dystonia-parkinsonism	0.01:1
Huntington's disease	1.15:1
Friedreich's ataxia	~1:1[b]
Spinocerebellar ataxias	~1:1[b]
Fragile X-associated tremor/ataxia syndrome (FXTAS)	0.8:1
Sporadic adult-onset cerebellar ataxia	0.43:1
Acquired ataxia	0.48:1
Tourette syndrome	0.25–0.33:1
Restless legs syndrome	1.68:1
Sporadic paroxysmal kinesigenic dyskinesia	0.13–0.25:1
Sporadic paroxysmal non-kinesigenic dyskinesia	0.5:1
Familial paroxysmal non-kinesigenic dyskinesia	1:1
Paroxysmal exterion-induced dyskinesia	1.5:1
Tardive dyskinesia	1.23:1
Tardive dystonia	Women < Men-
Tardive akathisia	1.9:1
Tardive parkinsonism	Women > Men[a]
Functional movement disorders	2.5:1

Note. [a]While exact ratio is unclear, prevalence is noted to be different between women and men
[b]While exact ratio is unclear, prevalence is noted to be similar for women and men

differ for women and men, considering gender becomes more important to establish effective treatments for movement disorders. Women with movement disorders need to be highlighted and supported more by both clinical and research efforts.

Clinical Takeaways

- Movement disorders characterized by production and control of movements include some of the most common neurological disorders leading to both motor and non-motor symptoms.
- Risk factors, prevalence, and symptoms in a number of hypokinetic and hyperkinetic movement disorders differ by gender, which can inform the diagnosis, prognosis, and treatment plan.
- Reproductive stages and pregnancy should be considered for prognosis and treatment, as they impact symptoms and some common treatments may have teratogenic effects.

Research Takeaways

- Structure and function of the basal ganglia and cerebellum, associated with movement disorders, differ by gender.
- Women remain significantly underrepresented in the research of several movement disorders, underscoring the need for targeted efforts to better understand their experience and to provide better care during different reproductive stages and pregnancy.
- Different pathophysiological processes can contribute to the symptoms for women with movement disorders, requiring different treatment options to be determined by research.

References

Aarsland, D., & Kurz, M. W. (2010). The epidemiology of dementia associated with Parkinson disease. *Journal of the Neurological Sciences, 289*(1–2), 18–22. https://doi.org/10.1016/j.jns.2009.08.034

Abdelzaher Ibrahim, A., Abdelazim, I. A., & Hagras, A. (2022). The risk of Parkinson's disease in women who underwent hysterectomy before the age of menopause. *Menopausal Review, 21*(3), 185–190. https://doi.org/10.5114/pm.2022.119634

Aiba, I., Hayashi, Y., Shimohata, T., Yoshida, M., Saito, Y., Wakabayashi, K., Komori, T., Hasegawa, M., Ikeuchi, T., Tokumaru, A. M., Sakurai, K., Murayama, S., Hasegawa, K., Uchihara, T., Toyoshima, Y., Saito, Y., Yabe, I., Tanikawa, S., Sugaya, K., & Hayashi, K. (2023). Clinical course of pathologically confirmed corticobasal degeneration and corticobasal syndrome. *Brain. Communications, 5*(6), Article fcad296. https://doi.org/10.1093/braincomms/fcad296

Albanese, A., Bhatia, K., Bressman, S. B., DeLong, M. R., Fahn, S., Fung, V. S. C., Hallett, M., Jankovic, J., Jinnah, H. A., Klein, C., Lang, A. E., Mink, J. W., & Teller, J. K. (2013). Phenomenology and classification of dystonia: A consensus update. *Movement Disorders, 28*(7), 863–873. https://doi.org/10.1002/mds.25475

Allen, R. P., Picchietti, D. L., Garcia-Borreguero, D., Ondo, W. G., Walters, A. S., Winkelman, J. W., Zucconi, M., Ferri, R., Trenkwalder, C., & Lee, H. B. (2014). Restless legs syndrome/Willis–Ekbom disease diagnostic criteria: Updated International Restless Legs Syndrome Study Group (IRLSSG) consensus criteria – history, rationale, description, and significance. *Sleep Medicine, 15*(8), 860–873. https://doi.org/10.1016/j.sleep.2014.03.025

Arabia, G., De Martino, A., & Moro, E. (2022). Sex and gender differences in movement disorders: Parkinson's disease, essential tremor, dystonia and chorea. *International Review of Neurobiology, 164*, 101–128. https://doi.org/10.1016/bs.irn.2022.06.010

Armstrong, M. J., Litvan, I., Lang, A. E., Bak, T. H., Bhatia, K. P., Borroni, B., Boxer, A. L., Dickson, D. W., Grossman, M., Hallett, M., Josephs, K. A., Kertesz, A., Lee, S. E., Miller, B. L., Reich, S. G., Riley, D. E., Tolosa, E., Tröster, A. I., Vidailhet, M., & Weiner, W. J. (2013). Criteria for the diagnosis of corticobasal degeneration. *Neurology, 80*(5), 496–503. https://doi.org/10.1212/WNL.0b013e31827f0fd1

Ashizawa, T., Öz, G., & Paulson, H. L. (2018). Spinocerebellar ataxias: Prospects and challenges for therapy development. *Nature Reviews Neurology, 14*(10), 590–605. https://doi.org/10.1038/s41582-018-0051-6

Aybek, S., & Perez, D. L. (2022). Diagnosis and management of functional neurological disorder. *British Medical Journal (BMJ), 376*, Article o64. https://doi.org/10.1136/bmj.o64

Baba, Y., Putzke, J. D., Whaley, N. R., Wszolek, Z. K., & Uitti, R. J. (2006). Progressive supranuclear palsy: Phenotypic sex differences in a clinical cohort. *Movement Disorders, 21*(5), 689–692. https://doi.org/10.1002/mds.20769

Badarny, S., Nassar, R., & Badarny, Y. (2023). Tardive syndrome is a mysterious phenomenon with different clinical manifestations—review. *Journal of Clinical Medicine, 12*(4), Article 1498. https://doi.org/10.3390/jcm12041498

Baizabal-Carvallo, J. F., & Jankovic, J. (2015). Stiff-person syndrome: Insights into a complex autoimmune disorder. *Journal of Neurology, Neurosurgery & Psychiatry, 86*(8), 840–848. https://doi.org/10.1136/jnnp-2014-309201

Baizabal-Carvallo, J. F., & Jankovic, J. (2023). Sex differences in patients with Tourette syndrome. *CNS Spectrums, 28*(2), 205–211. https://doi.org/10.1017/S1092852922000074

Balint, B., Mencacci, N. E., Valente, E. M., Pisani, A., Rothwell, J., Jankovic, J., Vidailhet, M., & Bhatia, K. P. (2018). Dystonia. *Nature Reviews Disease Primers, 4*(1), Article 25. https://doi.org/10.1038/s41572-018-0023-6

Barnes, L. L., Lamar, M., & Schneider, J. A. (2019). Sex differences in mixed neuropathologies in community-dwelling older adults. *Brain Research, 1719*, 11–16. https://doi.org/10.1016/j.brainres.2019.05.028

Bayram, E., Batzu, L., Tilley, B., Gandhi, R., Jagota, P., Biundo, R., Garon, M., Prasertpan, T., Lazcano-Ocampo, C., Chaudhuri, K. R., & Weil, R. S. (2023a). Clinical trials for cognition in Parkinson's disease: Where are we and how can we do better? *Parkinsonism & Related Disorders, 112*, Article 105385. https://doi.org/10.1016/j.parkreldis.2023.105385

Bayram, E., Coughlin, D. G., Banks, S. J., & Litvan, I. (2021). Sex differences for phenotype in pathologically defined dementia with Lewy bodies. *Journal of Neurology, Neurosurgery & Psychiatry, 92*(7), 745–750. https://doi.org/10.1136/jnnp-2020-325668

Bayram, E., Coughlin, D. G., & Litvan, I. (2022). Sex differences for clinical correlates of Alzheimer's pathology in people with Lewy body pathology. *Movement Disorders, 37*(7), 1505–1515. https://doi.org/10.1002/mds.29044

Bayram, E., Coughlin, D. G., Rajmohan, R., & Litvan, I. (2024a). Sex differences for clinical correlates of substantia nigra neuron loss in people with Lewy body pathology. *Biology of Sex Differences, 15*(1), Article 8. https://doi.org/10.1186/s13293-024-00583-6

Bayram, E., Reho, P., Litvan, I., Ding, J., Gibbs, J. R., Dalgard, C. L., Traynor, B. J., Scholz, S. W., & Chia, R. (2024b). Genetic analysis of the X chromosome in people with Lewy body dementia nominates new risk loci. *Nature Partner Journals (npj) Parkinson's Disease, 10*(1), Article 39. https://doi.org/10.1038/s41531-024-00649-7

Bayram, E., Weigand, A. J., & Flatt, J. D. (2023b). Perceived discrimination in health care for LGBTQIA+ people living with Parkinson's disease. *The Journals of Gerontology: Series B, 78*(9), 1459–1465. https://doi.org/10.1093/geronb/gbad046

Beier, K., Lui, F., & Pratt, D. P. (2024). Sydenham chorea. In *StatPearls*. https://www.ncbi.nlm.nih.gov/books/NBK430838/

Bhatia, K. P. (2011). Paroxysmal dyskinesias. *Movement Disorders, 26*(6), 1157–1165. https://doi.org/10.1002/mds.23765

Bhatia, K. P., Bain, P., Bajaj, N., Elble, R. J., Hallett, M., Louis, E. D., Raethjen, J., Stamelou, M., Testa, C. M., & Deuschl, G. (2018). Consensus statement on the classification of tremors. From the task force on tremor of the International Parkinson and movement disorder Society. *Movement Disorders, 33*(1), 75–87. https://doi.org/10.1002/mds.27121

Bhatia, K. P., Soland, V. L., Bhatt, M. H., Quinn, N. P., & Marsden, C. D. (1997). Paroxysmal exercise-induced dystonia: Eight new sporadic cases and a review of the literature. *Movement Disorders, 12*(6), 1007–1012. https://doi.org/10.1002/mds.870120626

Blauwendraat, C., Iwaki, H., Makarious, M. B., Bandres-Ciga, S., Leonard, H. L., Grenn, F. P., Lake, J., Krohn, L., Tan, M., Kim, J. J., Gibbs, J. R., Hernandez, D. G., Ruskey, J. A., Pihlstrøm, L., Toft, M., van Hilten, J. J., Marinus, J., Schulte, C., Brockmann, K., et al. (2021). Investigation of autosomal genetic sex differences in Parkinson's disease. *Annals of Neurology, 90*(1), 35–42. https://doi.org/10.1002/ana.26090

Bloem, B. R., Okun, M. S., & Klein, C. (2021). Parkinson's disease. *Lancet, 397*(10291), 2284–2303. https://doi.org/10.1016/S0140-6736(21)00218-X

Blomstedt, P., Sandvik, U., Hariz, M. I., Fytagoridis, A., Forsgren, L., Hariz, G.-M., & Koskinen, L.-O. D. (2011). Influence of age, gender and severity of tremor on outcome after thalamic and subthalamic DBS for essential tremor. *Parkinsonism & Related Disorders, 17*(8), 617–620. https://doi.org/10.1016/j.parkreldis.2011.05.014

Bordelon, Y., & Smith, M. (2007). Movement disorders in pregnancy. *Seminars in Neurology, 27*(5), 467–475. https://doi.org/10.1055/s-2007-991128

Boxer, A. L., Yu, J. T., Golbe, L. I., Litvan, I., Lang, A. E., & Höglinger, G. U. (2017). Advances in progressive supranuclear palsy: New diagnostic criteria, biomarkers, and therapeutic approaches. *The Lancet Neurology, 16*(7), 552–563. https://doi.org/10.1016/S1474-4422(17)30157-6

Broström, A., Alimoradi, Z., Lind, J., Ulander, M., Lundin, F., & Pakpour, A. (2023). Worldwide estimation of restless legs syndrome: A systematic review and meta-analysis of prevalence in the general adult population. *Journal of Sleep Research, 32*(3), Article e13783. https://doi.org/10.1111/jsr.13783

Bruno, M. K., Hallett, M., Gwinn-Hardy, K., Sorensen, B., Considine, E., Tucker, S., Lynch, D. R., Mathews, K. D., Swoboda, K. J., Harris, J., Soong, B.-W., Ashizawa, T., Jankovic, J., Renner, D., Fu, Y.-H., & Ptacek, L. J. (2004). Clinical evaluation of idiopathic paroxysmal kinesigenic dyskinesia. *Neurology, 63*(12), 2280–2287. https://doi.org/10.1212/01.WNL.0000147298.05983.50

Bruzelius, E., Scarpa, J., Zhao, Y., Basu, S., Faghmous, J. H., & Baum, A. (2019). Huntington's disease in the United States: Variation by demographic and socioeconomic factors. *Movement Disorders, 34*(6), 858–865. https://doi.org/10.1002/mds.27653

Burke, R. E., Kang, U. J., Jankovic, J., Miller, L. G., & Fahn, S. (1989). Tardive akathisia: An analysis of clinical features and response to open therapeutic trials. *Movement Disorders, 4*(2), 157–175. https://doi.org/10.1002/mds.870040208

Cabal-Herrera, A. M., Tassanakijpanich, N., Salcedo-Arellano, M. J., & Hagerman, R. J. (2020). Fragile X-associated tremor/ataxia syndrome (FXTAS): Pathophysiology and clinical implications. *International Journal of Molecular Sciences, 21*(12), Article 4391. https://doi.org/10.3390/ijms21124391

Cai, L., Huang, X., Ye, Y., Yang, D., Xie, L., Fu, D., Peng, L., Zhou, D., & Liao, J. (2023). Role of gender and age in features of Wilson's disease. *Frontiers in Neurology, 14*, Article 1176946. https://doi.org/10.3389/fneur.2023.1176946

Carbon, M., Hsieh, C.-H., Kane, J. M., & Correll, C. U. (2017). Tardive dyskinesia prevalence in the period of second-generation antipsychotic use. *The Journal of Clinical Psychiatry, 78*(3), e264–e278. https://doi.org/10.4088/JCP.16r10832

Caron, N. S., Wright, G. E., & Hayden, M. R. (1993). Huntington disease. In *GeneReviews®*. http://www.ncbi.nlm.nih.gov/pubmed/16383221

Caslake, R., Taylor, K., Scott, N., Harris, C., Gordon, J., Wilde, K., Murray, A., & Counsell, C. (2014). Age-, and gender-specific incidence of vascular parkinsonism, progressive supranuclear palsy, and parkinsonian-type multiple system atrophy in North East Scotland: The PINE study. *Parkinsonism & Related Disorders, 20*(8), 834–839. https://doi.org/10.1016/j.parkreldis.2014.04.013

Caviness, J. N. (2019). Myoclonus. *Continuum: Lifelong Learning in Neurology, 25*(4), 1055–1080. https://doi.org/10.1212/CON.0000000000000750

Caviness, J. N., Alving, L. I., Maraganore, D. M., Black, R. A., Mcdonnell, S. K., & Rocca, W. A. (1999). The incidence and prevalence of myoclonus in Olmsted County. *Minnesota. Mayo Clinic Proceedings, 74*(6), 565–569. https://doi.org/10.4065/74.6.565

Cervenka, M. C. (2022). Let's talk about sex and juvenile myoclonic epilepsy. *Epilepsy Currents, 22*(6), 356–358. https://doi.org/10.1177/15357597221120487

Chen, C.-Y., Chiang, H.-L., & Fuh, J.-L. (2020). Tardive syndrome: An update and mini-review from the perspective of phenomenology. *Journal of the Chinese Medical Association, 83*(12), 1059–1065. https://doi.org/10.1097/JCMA.0000000000000435

Chiu, S. Y., Wyman-Chick, K. A., Ferman, T. J., Bayram, E., Holden, S. K., Choudhury, P., & Armstrong, M. J. (2023). Sex differences in dementia with Lewy bodies: Focused review of available evidence and future directions. *Parkinsonism & Related Disorders, 107*, Article 105285. https://doi.org/10.1016/j.parkreldis.2023.105285

Choi, K.-D., & Choi, J.-H. (2016). Episodic ataxias: Clinical and genetic features. *Journal of. Movement Disorders, 9*(3), 129–135. https://doi.org/10.14802/jmd.16028

Constantinides, V. C., Paraskevas, G. P., Paraskevas, P. G., Stefanis, L., & Kapaki, E. (2019). Corticobasal degeneration and corticobasal syndrome: A review. *Clinical Parkinsonism & Related Disorders, 1*, 66–71. https://doi.org/10.1016/j.prdoa.2019.08.005

Coughlin, D. G., Hurtig, H. I., & Irwin, D. J. (2019). Pathological influences on clinical heterogeneity in Lewy body diseases. *Movement Disorders, 35*(1), 5–19. https://doi.org/10.1002/mds.27867

Currie, L. J., Harrison, M. B., Trugman, J. M., Bennett, J. P., & Wooten, G. F. (2004). Postmenopausal estrogen use affects risk for Parkinson disease. *Archives of Neurology, 61*(6), 886–888. https://doi.org/10.1001/archneur.61.6.886

Członkowska, A., Litwin, T., Dusek, P., Ferenci, P., Lutsenko, S., Medici, V., Rybakowski, J. K., Weiss, K. H., & Schilsky, M. L. (2018). Wilson disease. *Nature Reviews Disease Primers, 4*(1), Article 21. https://doi.org/10.1038/s41572-018-0018-3

de Souza Ferreira, L. P., André da Silva, R., Mesquita, M., da Costa, M., de Paiva, M., Roda, V., Vizcaino, S., Janisset, N. R. L. L., Ramos Vieira, R., Marcos Sanches, J., Maria Soares Junior, J., & de Jesus Simões, M. (2022). Sex differences in Parkinson's Disease: An emerging health question. *Clinics, 77*, Article 100121. https://doi.org/10.1016/j.clinsp.2022.100121

Desai, U., Chandler, J., Kirson, N., Georgieva, M., Cheung, H. C., Westermeyer, B., Lane, H., & Biglan, K. (2022). Epidemiology and economic burden of Lewy body dementia in the United States. *Current Medical Research and Opinion, 38*(7), 1177–1188. https://doi.org/10.1080/03007995.2022.2059978

Digma, L. A., Litvan, I., del Ser, T., & Bayram, E. (2023). Sex differences for cognitive decline in progressive supranuclear palsy. *Parkinsonism & Related Disorders, 112*, Article 105454. https://doi.org/10.1016/j.parkreldis.2023.105454

Doll-Lee, J., Passarotto, E., Altenmüller, E., & Lee, A. (2024). Gender differences in task specific dystonia: What can we learn from musician's dystonia? *Movement Disorders Clinical Practice, 11*(5), 526–533. https://doi.org/10.1002/mdc3.14015

Edwards, M. J., & Aybek, S. (2020). Gender, abuse, and functional movement disorders: From his-story to the future. *Movement Disorders Clinical Practice, 7*(2), 167–168. https://doi.org/10.1002/mdc3.12887

Erro, R., Magrinelli, F., & Bhatia, K. P. (2023). Paroxysmal movement disorders: Paroxysmal dyskinesia and episodic ataxia. *Handbook of Clinical Neurology, 196*, 347–365. https://doi.org/10.1016/B978-0-323-98817-9.00033-8

Espay, A. J., Aybek, S., Carson, A., Edwards, M. J., Goldstein, L. H., Hallett, M., LaFaver, K., LaFrance, W. C., Lang, A. E., Nicholson, T., Nielsen, G., Reuber, M., Voon, V., Stone, J., & Morgante, F. (2018). Current concepts in diagnosis and treatment of functional neurological disorders. *JAMA Neurology, 75*(9), 1132–1141. https://doi.org/10.1001/jamaneurol.2018.1264

Evidente, V. G. H. (1993). X-linked dystonia-parkinsonism. In *GeneReviews®*. 20301662

Finsterer, J., & Zarrouk-Mahjoub, S. (2017). Mitochondrial multiorgan disorder syndrome score generated from definite mitochondrial disorders. *Neuropsychiatric Disease and Treatment, 13*, 2569–2579. https://doi.org/10.2147/NDT.S149067

Ford, B., Greene, P., & Fahn, S. (1994). Oral and genital tardive pain syndromes. *Neurology, 44*(11), 2115–2115. https://doi.org/10.1212/WNL.44.11.2115

Frei, K., Truong, D. D., Fahn, S., Jankovic, J., & Hauser, R. A. (2018). The nosology of tardive syndromes. *Journal of the Neurological Sciences, 389*, 10–16. https://doi.org/10.1016/j.jns.2018.02.008

Galli, S., Béreau, M., Magnin, E., Moulin, T., & Aybek, S. (2020). Functional movement disorders. *Revue Neurologique, 176*(4), 244–251. https://doi.org/10.1016/j.neurol.2019.08.007

Garone, G., Capuano, A., Travaglini, L., Graziola, F., Stregapede, F., Zanni, G., Vigevano, F., Bertini, E., & Nicita, F. (2020). Clinical and genetic overview of paroxysmal movement disorders and episodic ataxias. *International Journal of Molecular Sciences, 21*(10), 3603. https://doi.org/10.3390/ijms21103603

Garris, J., & Quigg, M. (2021). The female Tourette patient: Sex differences in Tourette Disorder. *Neuroscience & Biobehavioral Reviews, 129*, 261–268. https://doi.org/10.1016/j.neubiorev.2021.08.001

GBD 2016 Parkinson's Disease Collaborators. (2018). Global, regional, and national burden of Parkinson's disease, 1990–2016: A systematic analysis for the Global Burden of Disease Study 2016. *The Lancet Neurology, 17*(11), 939–953. https://doi.org/10.1016/S1474-4422(18)30295-3

Ghorbani, M., Pousset, F., Tucker, A., Swift, S., Giunti, P., Parkinson, M., Gilbert, D., Liu, X., & Payne, A. (2019). Analysis of Friedreich's ataxia patient clinical data reveals importance of accurate GAA repeat determination in disease prognosis and gender differences in cardiac measures. *Informatics in Medicine Unlocked, 17*, Article 100266. https://doi.org/10.1016/j.imu.2019.100266

Gibbons, E., Rongve, A., de Rojas, I., Shadrin, A., Westra, K., Baumgartner, A., Rosendall, L., Madaj, Z., Hernandez, D. G., Ross, O. A., Escott-Price, V., Shepherd, C., Parkkinen, L., Scholz, S. W., Troncoso, J. C., Pletnikova, O., Dawson, T., Rosenthal, L., Ansorge, O., … Bras, J. (2022). Identification of a sex-specific genetic signature in dementia with Lewy bodies: A meta-analysis of genome-wide association studies. *MedRxiv*. https://doi.org/10.1101/2022.11.22.22282597

Gonzalez-Latapi, P., Bayram, E., Litvan, I., & Marras, C. (2021). Cognitive impairment in Parkinson's disease: Epidemiology, clinical profile, protective and risk factors. *Behavioral Sciences, 11*(5), Article 74. https://doi.org/10.3390/bs11050074

Gozes, I., Shapira, G., Lobyntseva, A., & Shomron, N. (2023). Unexpected gender differences in progressive supranuclear palsy reveal efficacy for davunetide in women. *Translational Psychiatry, 13*(1), Article 319. https://doi.org/10.1038/s41398-023-02618-9

Graves, T. D., Cha, Y.-H., Hahn, A. F., Barohn, R., Salajegheh, M. K., Griggs, R. C., Bundy, B. N., Jen, J. C., Baloh, R. W., & Hanna, M. G. (2014). Episodic ataxia type 1: Clinical characterization, quality of life and genotype–phenotype correlation. *Brain, 137*(4), 1009–1018. https://doi.org/10.1093/brain/awu012

Gregory, A., & Hayflick, S. (1993). Neurodegeneration with brain iron accumulation disorders overview. In *GeneReviews®*. http://www.ncbi.nlm.nih.gov/pubmed/17167799

Grütz, K., & Klein, C. (2021). Dystonia updates: Definition, nomenclature, clinical classification, and etiology. *Journal of Neural Transmission, 128*(4), 395–404. https://doi.org/10.1007/s00702-021-02314-2

Gupta, A., & Lang, A. E. (2009). Psychogenic movement disorders. *Current Opinion in Neurology, 22*(4), 430–436. https://doi.org/10.1097/WCO.0b013e32832dc169

Hadavi, S., Noyce, A. J., Leslie, R. D., & Giovannoni, G. (2011). Stiff person syndrome. *Practical Neurology, 11*(5), 272–282. https://doi.org/10.1136/practneurol-2011-000071

Hall, D. A., & Hagerman, R. J. (2018). Fragile X-associated tremor/ataxia syndrome: Unmet needs and a path for the future. *Frontiers in Genetics, 9*, Article 100. https://doi.org/10.3389/fgene.2018.00100

Harvey, S., King, M. D., & Gorman, K. M. (2021). Paroxysmal movement disorders. *Frontiers in Neurology, 12*, Article 659064. https://doi.org/10.3389/fneur.2021.659064

Heinzel, S., Berg, D., Gasser, T., Chen, H., Yao, C., & Postuma, R. B. (2019). Update of the MDS research criteria for prodromal Parkinson's disease. *Movement Disorders, 34*(10), 1464–1470. https://doi.org/10.1002/mds.27802

Heinzel, S., Kasten, M., Behnke, S., Vollstedt, E.-J., Klein, C., Hagenah, J., Pausch, C., Heilmann, R., Brockmann, K., Suenkel, U., Yilmaz, R., Liepelt-Scarfone, I., Walter, U., & Berg, D. (2018). Age- and sex-related heterogeneity in prodromal Parkinson's disease. *Movement Disorders, 33*(6), 1025–1027. https://doi.org/10.1002/mds.27349

Hentosh, S., Zhu, L., Patino, J., Furr, J. W., Rocha, N. P., & Furr Stimming, E. (2021). Sex differences in Huntington's disease: Evaluating the Enroll-HD database. *Movement Disorders Clinical Practice, 8*(3), 420–426. https://doi.org/10.1002/mdc3.13178

Höglinger, G. U., Respondek, G., Stamelou, M., Kurz, C., Josephs, K. A., Lang, A. E., Mollenhauer, B., Müller, U., Nilsson, C., Whitwell, J. L., Arzberger, T., Englund, E., Gelpi, E., Giese, A., Irwin, D. J., Meissner, W. G., Pantelyat, A., Rajput, A., van Swieten, J. C., et al. (2017). Clinical diagnosis of progressive supranuclear palsy: The movement disorder society criteria. *Movement Disorders, 32*(6), 853–864. https://doi.org/10.1002/mds.26987

Höllerhage, M. (2019). Secondary parkinsonism due to drugs, vascular lesions, tumors, trauma, and other insults. *International Review of Neurobiology, 149*, 377–418. https://doi.org/10.1016/bs.irn.2019.10.010

Holzknecht, E., Hochleitner, M., Wenning, G. K., Högl, B., & Stefani, A. (2020). Gender differences in clinical, laboratory and polysomnographic features of restless legs syndrome. *Journal of Sleep Research, 29*(3), Article e12875. https://doi.org/10.1111/jsr.12875

Jung, H. H., Danek, A., Walker, R. H., Frey, B. M., & Peikert, K. (1993). McLeod neuroacanthocytosis syndrome. In *GeneReviews®*. http://www.ncbi.nlm.nih.gov/pubmed/13860532

Kaczkurkin, A. N., Raznahan, A., & Satterthwaite, T. D. (2019). Sex differences in the developing brain: Insights from multimodal neuroimaging. *Neuropsychopharmacology, 44*(1), 71–85. https://doi.org/10.1038/s41386-018-0111-z

Kaplan, S. (2024). Prevalence of multiple system atrophy: A literature review. *Revue Neurologique, 180*(5), 438–450. https://doi.org/10.1016/j.neurol.2023.11.013

Kasztelan-Szczerbinska, B., & Cichoz-Lach, H. (2021). Wilson's disease: An update on the diagnostic workup and management. *Journal of Clinical Medicine, 10*(21), Article 5097. https://doi.org/10.3390/jcm10215097

Kilic-Berkmen, G., Scorr, L. M., McKay, L., Thayani, M., Donsante, Y., Perlmutter, J. S., Norris, S. A., Wright, L., Klein, C., Feuerstein, J. S., Mahajan, A., Wagle-Shukla, A., Malaty, I., LeDoux, M. S., Pirio-Richardson, S., Pantelyat, A., Moukheiber, E., Frank, S., Ondo, W., et al. (2024). Sex differences in dystonia. *Movement Disorders Clinical Practice, 11*(8), 973–982. https://doi.org/10.1002/mdc3.14059

Kim, J., Kim, J. R., Park, H. R., & Joo, E. Y. (2024). Sex-specific patterns of discomfort in patients with restless legs syndrome. *Journal of Clinical Sleep Medicine, 20*(2), 253–259. https://doi.org/10.5664/jcsm.10848

Kiriakakis, V., Bhatia, K. P., Quinn, N. P., & Marsden, C. D. (1998). The natural history of tardive dystonia. A long-term follow-up study of 107 cases. *Brain, 121*(11), 2053–2066. https://doi.org/10.1093/brain/121.11.2053

Klockgether, T. (2018). Sporadic adult-onset ataxia. *Handbook of Clinical Neurology, 155*, 217–225. https://doi.org/10.1016/B978-0-444-64189-2.00014-7

Klockgether, T., & Paulson, H. (2011). Milestones in ataxia. *Movement Disorders, 26*(6), 1134–1141. https://doi.org/10.1002/mds.23559

Knight, T., Steeves, T., Day, L., Lowerison, M., Jette, N., & Pringsheim, T. (2012). Prevalence of tic disorders: A systematic review and meta-analysis. *Pediatric Neurology, 47*(2), 77–90. https://doi.org/10.1016/j.pediatrneurol.2012.05.002

Kolarova, H., Tan, J., Strom, T. M., Meitinger, T., Wagner, M., & Klopstock, T. (2022). Lifetime risk of autosomal recessive neurodegeneration with brain iron accumulation (NBIA) disorders calculated from genetic databases. *EBioMedicine, 77*, Article 103869. https://doi.org/10.1016/j.ebiom.2022.103869

Kranick, S. M., Mowry, E. M., Colcher, A., Horn, S., & Golbe, L. I. (2010). Movement disorders and pregnancy: A review of the literature. *Movement Disorders, 25*(6), 665–671. https://doi.org/10.1002/mds.23071

LaFaver, K. (2020). Treatment of functional movement disorders. *Neurologic Clinics, 38*(2), 469–480. https://doi.org/10.1016/j.ncl.2020.01.011

Latorre, A., Hallett, M., Deuschl, G., & Bhatia, K. P. (2022). The MDS consensus tremor classification: The best way to classify patients with tremor at present. *Journal of the Neurological Sciences, 435*, Article 120191. https://doi.org/10.1016/j.jns.2022.120191

Le Guen, Y., Napolioni, V., Belloy, M. E., Yu, E., Krohn, L., Ruskey, J. A., Gan-Or, Z., Kennedy, G., Eger, S. J., & Greicius, M. D. (2021). Common X-chromosome variants are associated with Parkinson disease risk. *Annals of Neurology, 90*(1), 22–34. https://doi.org/10.1002/ana.26051

Leys, F., Eschlböck, S., Campese, N., Mahlknecht, P., Peball, M., Goebel, G., Sidoroff, V., Krismer, F., Granata, R., Kiechl, S., Poewe, W., Seppi, K., Wenning, G. K., & Fanciulli, A. (2024). Sex-related differences in the clinical presentation of multiple system atrophy. *Clinical Autonomic Research, 34*(2), 253–268. https://doi.org/10.1007/s10286-024-01028-1

Lichter, D. G., & Finnegan, S. G. (2015). Influence of gender on Tourette syndrome beyond adolescence. *European Psychiatry, 30*(2), 334–340. https://doi.org/10.1016/j.eurpsy.2014.07.003

Litwin, T., Gromadzka, G., & Członkowska, A. (2012). Gender differences in Wilson's disease. *Journal of the Neurological Sciences, 312*(1–2), 31–35. https://doi.org/10.1016/j.jns.2011.08.028

Lv, M., Zhang, Y., Chen, G., Li, G., Rui, Y., Qin, L., & Wan, Z. (2017). Reproductive factors and risk of Parkinson's disease in women: A meta-analysis of observational studies. *Behavioural Brain Research, 335*, 103–110. https://doi.org/10.1016/j.bbr.2017.07.025

Lyons, S., Trépel, D., Lynch, T., Walsh, R., & O'Dowd, S. (2023). The prevalence and incidence of progressive supranuclear palsy and corticobasal syndrome: A systematic review and meta-analysis. *Journal of Neurology, 270*(9), 4451–4465. https://doi.org/10.1007/s00415-023-11791-2

Macerollo, A., & Deuschl, G. (2018). Deep brain stimulation for tardive syndromes: Systematic review and meta-analysis. *Journal of the Neurological Sciences, 389*, 55–60. https://doi.org/10.1016/j.jns.2018.02.013

Mahale, R. R., Krishnan, S., Divya, K. P., Jisha, V. T., & Kishore, A. (2022). Gender differences in progressive supranuclear palsy. *Acta Neurologica Belgica, 122*(2), 357–362. https://doi.org/10.1007/s13760-021-01599-0

Makawita, C., Ananthavarathan, P., de Silva, R., & Malek, N. (2024). A systematic review of the spectrum and prevalence of non-motor symptoms in multiple system atrophy. *The Cerebellum, 23*(4), 1642–1650. https://doi.org/10.1007/s12311-023-01642-1

Manconi, M., Ulfberg, J., Berger, K., Ghorayeb, I., Wesström, J., Fulda, S., Allen, R. P., & Pollmächer, T. (2012). When gender matters: Restless legs syndrome. Report of the "RLS and woman" workshop endorsed by the European RLS Study Group. *Sleep Medicine Reviews, 16*(4), 297–307. https://doi.org/10.1016/j.smrv.2011.08.006

Markianos, M., Panas, M., Kalfakis, N., & Vassilopoulos, D. (2005). Plasma testosterone in male patients with Huntington's disease: Relations to severity of illness and dementia. *Annals of Neurology, 57*(4), 520–525. https://doi.org/10.1002/ana.20428

Martí Massó, J. F., & Poza, J. J. (1996). Drug-induced or aggravated parkinsonism: Clinical signs and the changing pattern of implicated drugs. *Neurologia, 11*(1), 10–15. http://www.ncbi.nlm.nih.gov/pubmed/8714170

McKeith, I. G., Boeve, B. F., Dickson, D. W., Halliday, G., Taylor, J.-P., Weintraub, D., Aarsland, D., Galvin, J., Attems, J., Ballard, C. G., Bayston, A., Beach, T. G., Blanc, F., Bohnen, N., Bonanni, L., Bras, J., Brundin, P., Burn, D., Chen-Plotkin, A., et al. (2017). Diagnosis and management of dementia with Lewy bodies. *Neurology, 89*(1), 88–100. https://doi.org/10.1212/WNL.0000000000004058

Medina, A., Mahjoub, Y., Shaver, L., & Pringsheim, T. (2022). Prevalence and incidence of Huntington's disease: An updated systematic review and meta-analysis. *Movement Disorders, 37*(12), 2327–2335. https://doi.org/10.1002/mds.29228

Méneret, A., & Roze, E. (2016). Paroxysmal movement disorders: An update. *Revue Neurologique, 172*(8–9), 433–445. https://doi.org/10.1016/j.neurol.2016.07.005

Meoni, S., Macerollo, A., & Moro, E. (2020). Sex differences in movement disorders. *Nature Reviews Neurology, 16*(2), 84–96. https://doi.org/10.1038/s41582-019-0294-x

Merchant, S. H. I., Vial-Undurraga, F., Leodori, G., van Gerpen, J. A., & Hallett, M. (2020). Myoclonus: An electrophysiological diagnosis. *Movement Disorders Clinical Practice, 7*(5), 489–499. https://doi.org/10.1002/mdc3.12986

Miguel-Puga, A., Villafuerte, G., Salas-Pacheco, J., & Arias-Carrión, O. (2017). Therapeutic interventions for vascular parkinsonism: A systematic review and meta-analysis. *Frontiers in Neurology, 8*, Article 481. https://doi.org/10.3389/fneur.2017.00481

Miri, S., Rohani, M., Vahdat, M., Kashanian, M., Sariri, E., Zamani, B., & Shahidi, G. A. (2014). Presenting features of idiopathic versus secondary restless legs syndrome in pregnancy. *Iranian Journal of Neurology, 13*(4), 241–244. http://www.ncbi.nlm.nih.gov/pubmed/25632338

Munhoz, R. P., Bertucci Filho, D., & Teive, H. A. G. (2017). Not all drug-induced parkinsonism are the same: The effect of drug class on motor phenotype. *Neurological Sciences, 38*(2), 319–324. https://doi.org/10.1007/s10072-016-2771-y

Newsome, S. D., & Johnson, T. (2022). Stiff person syndrome spectrum disorders; more than meets the eye. *Journal of Neuroimmunology, 369*, Article 577915. https://doi.org/10.1016/j.jneuroim.2022.577915

Nordengen, K., Cappelletti, C., Bahrami, S., Frei, O., Pihlstrøm, L., Henriksen, S. P., Geut, H., Rozemuller, A. J. M., van de Berg, W. D. J., Andreassen, O. A., & Toft, M. (2024). Pleiotropy with sex-specific traits reveals genetic aspects of sex differences in Parkinson's disease. *Brain, 147*(3), 858–870. https://doi.org/10.1093/brain/awad297

Orsucci, D., Lorenzetti, L., Baldinotti, F., Rossi, A., Vitolo, E., Gheri, F. L., Napolitano, A., Tintori, G., & Vista, M. (2022). Fragile X-associated tremor/ataxia syndrome (FXTAS): A gender perspective. *Journal of Clinical Medicine, 11*(4), Article 1002. https://doi.org/10.3390/jcm11041002

Pantelyat, A. (2022). Progressive supranuclear palsy and corticobasal syndrome. (2022). *Continuum: Lifelong Learning in Neurology, 28*(5), 1364–1378. https://doi.org/10.1212/CON.0000000000001158

Park, H. K., Ilango, S. D., & Litvan, I. (2021). Environmental risk factors for progressive supranuclear palsy. *Journal of Movement Disorders, 14*(2), 103–113. https://doi.org/10.14802/jmd.20173

Pfeiffenberger, J., Beinhardt, S., Gotthardt, D. N., Haag, N., Freissmuth, C., Reuner, U., Gauss, A., Stremmel, W., Schilsky, M. L., Ferenci, P., & Weiss, K. H. (2018). Pregnancy in Wilson's disease: Management and outcome. *Hepatology, 67*(4), 1261–1269. https://doi.org/10.1002/hep.29490

Phukan, J., Albanese, A., Gasser, T., & Warner, T. (2011). Primary dystonia and dystonia-plus syndromes: Clinical characteristics, diagnosis, and pathogenesis. *The Lancet Neurology, 10*(12), 1074–1085. https://doi.org/10.1016/S1474-4422(11)70232-0

Postuma, R. B., Berg, D., Stern, M., Poewe, W., Olanow, C. W., Oertel, W., Obeso, J., Marek, K., Litvan, I., Lang, A. E., Halliday, G., Goetz, C. G., Gasser, T., Dubois, B., Chan, P., Bloem, B. R., Adler, C. H., & Deuschl, G. (2015). MDS clinical diagnostic criteria for Parkinson's disease. *Movement Disorders, 30*(12), 1591–1601. https://doi.org/10.1002/mds.26424

Postuma, R. B., Poewe, W., Litvan, I., Lewis, S., Lang, A. E., Halliday, G., Goetz, C. G., Chan, P., Slow, E., Seppi, K., Schaffer, E., Rios-Romenets, S., Mi, T., Maetzler, C., Li, Y., Heim, B., Bledsoe, I. O., & Berg, D. (2018). Validation of the MDS clinical diagnostic criteria for Parkinson's disease. *Movement Disorders, 33*(10), 1601–1608. https://doi.org/10.1002/mds.27362

Rafee, S., O'Riordan, S., Reilly, R., & Hutchinson, M. (2021). We must talk about sex and focal dystonia. *Movement Disorders, 36*(3), 604–608. https://doi.org/10.1002/mds.28454

Rao, S. C., Li, Y., Lapin, B., Pattipati, S., Ghosh Galvelis, K., Naito, A., Gutierrez, N., Leal, T. P., Salim, A., Salles, P. A., De Leon, M., & Mata, I. F. (2023). Association of women-specific health factors in the severity of Parkinson's disease. *Nature Partner Journals (npj) Parkinson's Disease, 9*(1), Article 86. https://doi.org/10.1038/s41531-023-00524-x

Raymond, D., Saunders-Pullman, R., de Carvalho Aguiar, P., Schule, B., Kock, N., Friedman, J., Harris, J., Ford, B., Frucht, S., Heiman, G. A., Jennings, D., Doheny, D., Brin, M. F., de Leon Brin, D., Multhaupt-Buell, T., Lang, A. E., Kurlan, R., Klein, C., Ozelius, L., & Bressman, S. (2008). Phenotypic spectrum and sex effects in eleven myoclonus-dystonia families with ε-sarcoglycan mutations. *Movement Disorders, 23*(4), 588–592. https://doi.org/10.1002/mds.21785

Reker, P., Jost, S. T., Schiller, P., Gronostay, A., Fink, G. R., Visser-Vandewalle, V., Ashkan, K., Rizos, A., Martinez-Martin, P., Strobel, L., Sattari, A., Timmermann, L., Sauerbier, A., Chaudhuri, K. R., Kalbe, E., & Dafsari, H. S. (2023). Gender differences in referrals for deep brain stimulation for essential tremor. *Parkinsonism & Related Disorders, 112*, Article 105490. https://doi.org/10.1016/j.parkreldis.2023.105490

Rijpkema, M., Everaerd, D., van der Pol, C., Franke, B., Tendolkar, I., & Fernández, G. (2012). Normal sexual dimorphism in the human basal ganglia. *Human Brain Mapping, 33*(5), 1246–1252. https://doi.org/10.1002/hbm.21283

Risby-Jones, G., Lee, J. D., Woodruff, T. M., & Fung, J. N. (2024). Sex differences in Huntington's disease from a neuroinflammation perspective. *Frontiers in Neurology, 15*, Article 1384480. https://doi.org/10.3389/fneur.2024.1384480

Riva, A., D'Onofrio, G., Ferlazzo, E., Pascarella, A., Pasini, E., Franceschetti, S., Panzica, F., Canafoglia, L., Vignoli, A., Coppola, A., Badioni, V., Beccaria, F., Labate, A., Gambardella, A., Romeo, A., Capovilla, G., Michelucci, R., Striano, P., & Belcastro, V. (2024). Myoclonus: Differential diagnosis and current management. *Epilepsia Open, 9*(2), 486–500. https://doi.org/10.1002/epi4.12917

Rosenthal, L. S. (2022). Neurodegenerative Cerebellar Ataxia. *Continuum: Lifelong Learning. Neurology, 28*(5), 1409–1434. https://doi.org/10.1212/CON.0000000000001180

Ruano, L., Melo, C., Silva, M. C., & Coutinho, P. (2014). The global epidemiology of hereditary ataxia and spastic paraplegia: A systematic review of prevalence studies. *Neuroepidemiology, 42*(3), 174–183. https://doi.org/10.1159/000358801

Russillo, M. C., Andreozzi, V., Erro, R., Picillo, M., Amboni, M., Cuoco, S., Barone, P., & Pellecchia, M. T. (2022). Sex differences in Parkinson's disease: From bench to bedside. *Brain Sciences, 12*(7), Article 917. https://doi.org/10.3390/brainsci12070917

Saiz, A., Blanco, Y., Sabater, L., González, F., Bataller, L., Casamitjana, R., Ramió-Torrentà, L., & Graus, F. (2008). Spectrum of neurological syndromes associated with glutamic acid decarboxylase antibodies: Diagnostic clues for this association. *Brain, 131*(10), 2553–2563. https://doi.org/10.1093/brain/awn183

Saleh, N., Moutereau, S., Azulay, J.-P., Verny, C., Simonin, C., Tranchant, C., El Hawajri, N., Bachoud-Lévi, A.-C., & Maison, P. (2010). High insulinlike growth factor I is associated with cognitive decline in Huntington disease. *Neurology, 75*(1), 57–63. https://doi.org/10.1212/WNL.0b013e3181e62076

Sandahl, T. D., Laursen, T. L., Munk, D. E., Vilstrup, H., Weiss, K. H., & Ott, P. (2020). The prevalence of Wilson's disease: An update. *Hepatology, 71*(2), 722–732. https://doi.org/10.1002/hep.30911

Seeman, M. V. (2020). Why are women prone to restless legs syndrome? *International Journal of Environmental Research and Public Health, 17*(1), Article 368. https://doi.org/10.3390/ijerph17010368

Seier, M., & Hiller, A. (2017). Parkinson's disease and pregnancy: An updated review. *Parkinsonism & Related Disorders, 40*, 11–17. https://doi.org/10.1016/j.parkreldis.2017.05.007

Shakeshaft, A., Panjwani, N., Collingwood, A., Crudgington, H., Hall, A., Andrade, D. M., Beier, C. P., Fong, C. Y., Gardella, E., Gesche, J., Greenberg, D. A., Hamandi, K., Koht, J., Lim, K. S., Møller, R. S., Ng, C. C., Orsini, A., Rees, M. I., Rubboli, G., et al. (2022). Sex-specific disease modifiers in juvenile myoclonic epilepsy. *Scientific Reports, 12*(1), Article 2785. https://doi.org/10.1038/s41598-022-06324-2

Shehata, G. A., Farghaly, M. A. W., El-Tallawy, H. N., Rageha, T. A., Hakeem, M., & Abo-Elfetoh, N. M. (2011). Population-based study of acquired cerebellar ataxia in Al-Kharga district, New Valley, Egypt. *Neuropsychiatric Disease and Treatment, 7*, 183–187. https://doi.org/10.2147/NDT.S14497

Shiraiwa, N., Tamaoka, A., & Ohkoshi, N. (2018). Clinical features of drug-induced Parkinsonism. *Neurology International, 10*(4), Article 7877. https://doi.org/10.4081/ni.2018.7877

Singer, H. S. (2019). Tics and Tourette syndrome. *Continuum: Lifelong Learning in Neurology, 25*(4), 936–958. https://doi.org/10.1212/CON.0000000000000752

Song, P., Zhang, Y., Zha, M., Yang, Q., Ye, X., Yi, Q., & Rudan, I. (2021). The global prevalence of essential tremor, with emphasis on age and sex: A meta-analysis. *Journal of. Global Health, 11*, Article 04028. https://doi.org/10.7189/jogh.11.04028

Steeves, T. D., Day, L., Dykeman, J., Jette, N., & Pringsheim, T. (2012). The prevalence of primary dystonia: A systematic review and meta-analysis. *Movement Disorders, 27*(14), 1789–1796. https://doi.org/10.1002/mds.25244

Stephen, C. D. (2022). The dystonias. *Continuum: Lifelong Learning in Neurology, 28*(5), 1435–1475. https://doi.org/10.1212/CON.0000000000001159

Subramanian, I., Mathur, S., Oosterbaan, A., Flanagan, R., Keener, A. M., & Moro, E. (2022). Unmet needs of women living with Parkinson's disease: Gaps and controversies. *Movement Disorders, 37*(3), 444–455. https://doi.org/10.1002/mds.28921

Sun, Q., He, R., Huang, H., Cao, H., Wang, X., Liu, H., Wang, C., Lei, L., Wang, P., Cui, G., Ma, J., Gu, P., An, D., Jia, M., Sun, Z., Wu, H., Lin, J., Tang, J., Zhou, X., et al. (2022). Age and sex affect essential tremor (ET) plus: Clinical heterogeneity in ET based on the national survey in China. *Aging and Disease, 14*(4), 1360–1373. https://doi.org/10.14336/AD.2022.1205

Supnet, M. L., Acuna, P., Carr, S. J., Kristoper de Guzman, J., Al Qahtani, X., Multhaupt-Buell, T., Francoeur, T., Aldykiewicz, G. E., Alluri, P. R., Campion, L., Paul, L., Ozelius, L., Penney, E. B., Stephen, C. D., Dy-Hollins, M., & Sharma, N. (2020). Isolated cervical dystonia: Management and barriers to care. *Frontiers in Neurology, 11*, Article 591418. https://doi.org/10.3389/fneur.2020.591418

Swallow, D. M. A., Zheng, C. S., & Counsell, C. E. (2022). Systematic review of prevalence studies of progressive supranuclear palsy and corticobasal syndrome. *Movement Disorders Clinical Practice, 9*(5), 604–613. https://doi.org/10.1002/mdc3.13489

Termsarasab, P. (2019). Chorea. *Continuum: Lifelong Learning in Neurology, 25*(4), 1001–1035. https://doi.org/10.1212/CON.0000000000000763

Vann Jones, S. A., & O'Brien, J. T. (2014). The prevalence and incidence of dementia with Lewy bodies: A systematic review of population and clinical studies. *Psychological Medicine, 44*(4), 673–683. https://doi.org/10.1017/S0033291713000494

Walker, R. H., Jung, H. H., & Danek, A. (2011). Neuroacanthocytosis. *Handbook of Clinical Neurology, 100*, 141–151. https://doi.org/10.1016/B978-0-444-52014-2.00007-0

Wang, Y., Hu, C., Aljarallah, S., Reyes Mantilla, M., Mukharesh, L., Simpson, A., Roy, S., Harrison, K., Shoemaker, T., Comisac, M., Balshi, A., Obando, D., Maldonado, D. A. P., Koshorek, J., Snoops, S., Fitzgerald, K. C., & Newsome, S. D. (2024). Expanding clinical profiles and prognostic markers in stiff person syndrome spectrum disorders. *Journal of Neurology, 271*(4), 1861–1872. https://doi.org/10.1007/s00415-023-12123-0

Ward, K. M., & Citrome, L. (2018). Antipsychotic-related movement disorders: Drug-induced parkinsonism vs. tardive dyskinesia—Key differences in pathophysiology and clinical management. *Neurology and Therapy, 7*(2), 233–248. https://doi.org/10.1007/s40120-018-0105-0

Weber, N., Buchholz, M., Rädke, A., Faber, J., Schmitz-Hübsch, T., Jacobi, H., Klockgether, T., Hoffmann, W., Michalowsky, B., du Montcel, S. T., Bauer, P., Giunti, P., Cook, A., Labrum, R., Parkinson, M. H., Durr, A., Brice, A., Charles, P., Marelli, C., et al. (2024). Factors influencing health-related quality of life of patients with spinocerebellar ataxia. *The Cerebellum, 23*(4), 1466–1477. https://doi.org/10.1007/s12311-024-01657-2

Wenning, G. K., Stankovic, I., Vignatelli, L., Fanciulli, A., Calandra-Buonaura, G., Seppi, K., Palma, J., Meissner, W. G., Krismer, F., Berg, D., Cortelli, P., Freeman, R., Halliday, G., Höglinger, G., Lang, A., Ling, H., Litvan, I., Low, P., Miki, Y., et al. (2022). The Movement Disorder Society criteria for the diagnosis of multiple system atrophy. *Movement Disorders, 37*(6), 1131–1148. https://doi.org/10.1002/mds.29005

Weydt, P., Soyal, S. M., Landwehrmeyer, G. B., & Patsch, W. (2014). A single nucleotide polymorphism in the coding region of PGC-1α is a male-specific modifier of Huntington disease age-at-onset in a large European cohort. *Boston Medical Center (BMC) Neurology, 14*(1), Article 1. https://doi.org/10.1186/1471-2377-14-1

Wichmann, T. (2018). Pathophysiologic basis of movement disorders. *Progress in Neurological Surgery, 33*, 13–24. https://doi.org/10.1159/000480718

Willis, A. W., Schootman, M., Kung, N., Evanoff, B. A., Perlmutter, J. S., & Racette, B. A. (2012). Predictors of survival in patients with Parkinson disease. *Archives of Neurology, 69*(5), 601–607. https://doi.org/10.1001/archneurol.2011.2370

Winchester, S., Singh, P. K., & Mikati, M. A. (2013). Ataxia. *Handbook of Clinical Neurology, 112*, 1213–1217. https://doi.org/10.1016/B978-0-444-52910-7.00043-X

Witek, N., Hawkins, J., & Hall, D. (2021). Genetic ataxias: Update on classification and diagnostic approaches. *Current Neurology and Neuroscience Reports, 21*(3), Article 13. https://doi.org/10.1007/s11910-021-01092-4

Wyman-Chick, K. A., Chaudhury, P., Bayram, E., Abdelnour, C., Matar, E., Chiu, S. Y., Ferreira, D., Hamilton, C. A., Donaghy, P. C., Rodriguez-Porcel, F., Toledo, J. B., Habich, A., Barrett, M. J., Patel, B., Jaramillo-Jimenez, A., Scott, G. D., & Kane, J. P. M. (2024). Differentiating prodromal dementia with Lewy bodies from prodromal Alzheimer's disease: A pragmatic review for clinicians. *Neurology and Therapy, 13*(3), 885–906. https://doi.org/10.1007/s40120-024-00620-x

Yassa, R., & Jeste, D. V. (1992). Gender differences in tardive dyskinesia: A critical review of the literature. *Schizophrenia Bulletin, 18*(4), 701–715. https://doi.org/10.1093/schbul/18.4.701

Zhu, J., Cui, Y., Zhang, J., Yan, R., Su, D., Zhao, D., Wang, A., & Feng, T. (2024). Temporal trends in the prevalence of Parkinson's disease from 1980 to 2023: A systematic review and meta-analysis. *The Lancet Healthy Longevity, 5*(7), e464–e479. https://doi.org/10.1016/S2666-7568(24)00094-1

Zielonka, D., & Stawinska-Witoszynska, B. (2020). Gender differences in non-sex linked disorders: Insights from Huntington's disease. *Frontiers in Neurology, 11*, Article 571. https://doi.org/10.3389/fneur.2020.00571

Chapter 7
Epilepsy

Yosefa Modiano and Erin Sullivan-Baca

Introduction

Epilepsy refers to the propensity to generate recurrent unprovoked seizures and ranks among the most common neurological diseases (Beghi, 2019). Seizures are paroxysmal events caused by abnormal excessive and hypersynchronous neuronal activity in the brain and are associated with changes in behavior, movement, sensation, and level of consciousness. Seizures can be broadly characterized as generalized or focal, referring to the hemisphere(s) in which aberrant neurophysiological signaling originates, and are further defined based on symptom onset and episode semiology (Fisher et al., 2017). Etiology is varied; epilepsy can emerge following nearly any neurologic insult, congenital malformations, or genetic syndromes. In cases where no clear precipitant is identified, genetic factors are the presumed etiology. In addition to seizure generation, epilepsy impacts physiological, cognitive, psychological, and social functioning.

Epilepsy affects people across the lifespan of all genders, ethnic backgrounds, and socioeconomic classes, though certain demographic factors (e.g., gender and race/ethnicity) confer increased risk for developing epilepsy, as reviewed below. Notably, women with epilepsy (WWE) warrant consideration as a unique subgroup of people with epilepsy based on evidence that they present with distinct seizure etiology (Christensen et al., 2005; Hauser et al., 1993), neuropsychological factors (Lorkiewicz et al., 2023), psychiatric and medical comorbidities (Sullivan-Baca et al., 2022, 2023), and treatment considerations (Knight et al., 2021; Sullivan-Baca et al., 2023; Tomson et al., 2019).

Y. Modiano (✉)
University of Texas Health Neurosciences, Houston, TX, USA
e-mail: Yosefa.A.Modiano@uth.tmc.edu

E. Sullivan-Baca
Neurocognitive Specialty Group, Dallas, TX, USA

E. Sullivan-Baca, R. Ellison (eds.), *Neuropsychology of Women*,
https://doi.org/10.1007/978-3-031-87228-0_7

Given high base rates, neuropsychologists are likely to encounter patients with epilepsy in practice settings or research contexts. Neuropsychological assessment in this population generally focuses on measuring and understanding cognitive and behavioral presentations to aid in diagnosis and treatment planning. Neuropsychologists are well poised to integrate medical, functional, developmental, and social factors in characterizing patients. Accordingly, this chapter will highlight the characteristics of WWE that are important for neuropsychologists to appreciate in administering appropriate patient care and designing informed research.

Base Rates and Prevalence Rates

Epilepsy ranks among the most common neurologic conditions, with a 3.1% cumulative lifetime risk for epilepsy in industrialized countries (McHugh & Delanty, 2008). The lifetime prevalence is 7.60 per 1,000 persons with an annual cumulative incidence of 67.77 per 100,000 (Fiest et al., 2017). Findings regarding sex differences in rates of epilepsy are mixed with most studies showing slightly lower incidence and prevalence among women or non-significant differences (Fiest et al., 2017; Hauser & Beghi, 2008; Kim et al., 2014; Kotsopoulos et al., 2002). In a large meta-analysis, Kotsopoulos et al. (2002) identified a modestly lower incidence of epilepsy among women (46.2 per 100,000 persons) than men (50.7 per 100,000 persons). However, Fiest et al. (2017) failed to identify sex differences in a large systematic review.

Considerations About Base Rates

Inconsistent or null findings regarding sex differences across epidemiological studies may reflect a number of methodological and sociocultural issues (see Beghi & Beghi, 2013). While epidemiological studies ideally include large population-based surveys, many studies are in fact conducted in small urban or rural settings that are not representative of nationally based reports. The definition of epilepsy can vary across studies. Some surveys focus exclusively on generalized seizures and fail to include individuals with mild or infrequent seizures. This could influence outcomes, as sex differences are identified among seizure types and syndromes (Christensen et al., 2005). Community surveys may not account for higher perceived stigma among women reporting epilepsy or sufficiently screen for psychogenic non-epileptic seizures (PNES), which is highly prevalent among community epilepsy clinics and disproportionately affects women.

Risk Factors

Age is a strong risk factor for the development of epilepsy. Incidence is bimodally distributed with highest rates among infants under the age of 1 and older adults above the age of 65 with precipitous increase in risk after age 75 (Hauser et al., 1993; Hauser & Beghi, 2008). There may be a sex by age interaction in epilepsy risk, as one study showed annual incidence of epilepsy was similar among men and women until age 50, at which point incidence decreased for women only (Hesdorffer et al., 2011). Several of the studies on adult epidemiology are drawn from a cohort in Rochester, MN, and data likely do not generalize to populations with different life expectancy rates. Studies in pediatric samples show that girls under the age of 5 have a slightly higher incidence of epilepsy than boys, though this pattern reverses in later childhood (Cowan, 2002). There is a two- to three-fold higher incidence of epilepsy in low to middle income countries (Beghi & Hesdorffer, 2014), though the extent to which this differs across sex is not reported. Low-income individuals living in high income countries are also at greater risk for developing epilepsy and increased mortality due to factors associated with poverty, including perinatal risk factors, higher rates of CNS infection, and risk for traumatic brain injury (TBI).

When examining why men and women are at differential risk of developing epilepsy, it is crucial to consider well-established sex differences in etiologies. For example, women typically have lower rates of risk factors for remote symptomatic epilepsy and acute symptomatic seizures, such as TBI (see Chap. 4), CNS infection, and substance abuse leading to alcohol-related seizures (McHugh & Delanty, 2008). Regarding TBI specifically, the influence of intimate partner violence on TBI among women (both due to blunt force trauma and less identified anoxic events; see Chap. 4 for more details) and downstream risk of post-traumatic epilepsy (PTE) remains an area for future research. Given the link between trauma and PNES (see Chap. 10), such research would require astute discernment of epilepsy versus PNES within the sample.

Diagnosis and Prognosis

There are established sex differences in a number of epilepsy clinical characteristics, including age of onset, propensity toward epilepsy syndromes, and seizure semiology, each of which may confer different prognostic outcomes between men with epilepsy (MWE) and WWE. Hypotheses regarding sex differences in age of epilepsy onset date to the 1960s with purported mechanisms related to different rates of maturation. Taylor (1969) argued that cerebral maturation is more rapid in girls, such that boys are at greater risk for neurologic insult for a longer duration of development. While this remains to be demonstrated mechanistically, research does indicate sex differences in age of development as a function of epilepsy type. Hauser et al. (1993) showed a higher incidence of seizure development among girls in the first five years of life, with highest rates of generalized epilepsy in the first year of life. The incidence appears to converge across childhood and early to mid-adulthood until ages 45 to 50, when women are less likely than men to develop lesional epilepsy.

Epilepsy Syndromes

Despite findings of higher incidence among men, women appear at higher risk for a number of idiopathic generalized epilepsies (IGE; Christensen et al., 2005; Hauser et al., 1993). Christensen et al. (2005) showed that juvenile myoclonic epilepsy (JME) is 1.5 times more common in girls than boys, and Hauser et al. (1993) demonstrated a two- to five-fold increased risk for absence seizures among girls. Age by gender interactions may account for some of these differences, as women between age 15 and 50 were more likely to have IGE, suggesting a possible role of sex hormones (Christensen et al., 2005). Findings are not uniform, as one population study from Rochester, MN showed male predominance for both generalized and focal seizures (Hauser et al., 1993). In terms of etiology, focal cortical dysplasia and periventricular nodular heterotopias are less common among WWE (Ortiz-González et al., 2013; Sisodiya et al., 1999), though others have shown PVNH is more common among WWE in familial cases (Battaglia et al., 2006). In one study of patients with refractory mesial temporal lobe epilepsy (mTLE) in Sweden who underwent anterior temporal lobectomy with hippocampectomy, WWE showed more pronounced subpial and intracortical gliosis compared to MWE, as well as reduced cortical thickness. The degree of hippocampal sclerosis (HS) was similar across sexes (Doherty et al., 2007). The authors posit that sex hormones may influence neuronal and glial cell homeostasis and differentially modulate inflammatory responses contributing to pathological processes.

Seizure Semiology

Aspects of seizure semiology can differ across sexes. Isolated auras appear more common in women with temporal lobe epilepsy (TLE) than men with TLE (Janszky et al., 2004), and the specific aura semiology may differ, with one report showing a higher rate of sexual arousal auras among women than men (Remillard et al., 1983). Ictal fear was more common in women in one sample (Chiesa et al., 2007), though this was only seen in adults, as rates of ictal fear were similar among pediatric girls and boys. Janszky et al. (2004) presented a pathologically homogeneous sample of men and women with mTLE due to identified HS and failed to identify sex differences in a number of clinical characteristics, including age of onset, seizure frequency, seizure duration, or affected hemisphere. Males in their sample were more likely to have focal to bilateral tonic clonic generalizations, and women were more likely to exhibit auras in isolation. Interestingly, concordance between hemisphere of HS and seizure laterality was more common among women, which argues that men may exhibit greater atrophy in the contralateral hippocampus, perhaps as a function of more extensive epileptic networks.

Neuroimaging Results

Structural and functional neuroimaging show sexual dimorphisms among people with epilepsy (PWE). MWE have reduced volume in areas extraneous to the seizure onset zone (e.g., contralateral hippocampus; Briellmann et al., 2000; Janszky et al., 2004). Men with TLE tend to demonstrate more structural abnormalities in frontal regions, whereas women with TLE display more predictable temporal abnormalities (Santana et al., 2014). Similar findings have emerged in functional imaging studies. In contrast to Janszky et al. (2004), Savic & Engel (1998) demonstrated greater hypometabolism among women with TLE contralateral to the hemisphere of seizure onset, whereas men with TLE had greater hypometabolism ipsilateral to seizure onset. Men with mTLE demonstrated greater extra-mesiotemporal hypometabolism compared to women with mTLE, which correlated with reduced performance on cognitive measures of trail making and logical memory (Nickel et al., 2003).

Prognosis

Regarding prognosis, a large prospective longitudinal study measuring seizure remission over a 9-year period showed no sex differences (Cockerell et al., 1997). Another multicenter cohort study demonstrated reduced risk of post-surgical seizure recurrence for men with TLE due to HS with poorer post-surgical prognosis among women with TLE and HS (Burneo et al., 2006).

Morbidity and Mortality

WWE have lower incidence of status epilepticus than MWE, perhaps due to greater risk of other neurologic insult among men or sex hormone-mediated differences in seizure threshold (McHugh & Delanty, 2008). Regarding mortality, WWE had a two-fold higher mortality rate (standardized mortality ratio of 5.4) compared with MWE (standardized mortality ratio of 2.8) in an Italian sample (Beghi et al., 2005). Others have not shown a sex difference in incidence of SUDEP (Nilsson et al., 1999).

Presentation

Neuropsychological Presentation

Research on cognition in epilepsy has primarily focused on TLE. Within that literature base, the majority of studies have emphasized memory functions, as these are the most commonly reported disruptions in individuals with TLE (Bell et al., 2011; Zhao et al., 2014). A similar trend exists in the literature evaluating sex differences in neurocognitive presentation between WWE and MWE, with nearly all studies focused on learning and memory in TLE patients. Table 7.1 describes the primary findings from the current literature.

Table 7.1 Trends in gender-specific differences in cognitive performance

Study	Sample	Cognitive domain	Cognitive measure	Pre-Surgical findings	Post-Surgical findings
Bengston et al. (2000)	22F & 18M (left TLE) 16F & 14M (right TLE)	Verbal LR[C]	WMS Logical Memory (savings score)	No gender differences.	Women demonstrated stronger performances regardless of surgical hemisphere compared to men.
Berenbaum et al. (1997)	30F & 27M (left TLE)	Verbal LR[NC]	CVLT (Total Learning, SDFR, Semantic Clustering)	Women outperformed men due to increased semantic clustering.	Women outperformed men despite similar hippocampal pathology suggesting frontal lobe function may underlie gender differences in learning and memory.
Berger et al. (2017)[‡]	13F & 122M	Verbal LR[NC] Visual LR	RAVLT (German version, Total Learning, DFR) NVLT (Total Learning, Delayed Recognition)	Women performed better than men on verbal but not visual tasks.	Women maintained an advantage over men on verbal tasks despite similar hippocampal pathology.

(continued)

Table 7.1 (continued)

Study	Sample	Cognitive domain	Cognitive measure	Pre-Surgical findings	Post-Surgical findings
Berger et al. (2018)[a]	90F & 93M (TLE) 26F & 24M (FLE)	Verbal LR[NC]	RAVLT (German version; Total Learning, DFR)	Women with TLE performed better than men. FLE was not associated with gender-specific differences in performance.	–
Bjørnæs et al. (2005)[‡]	19F & 22M (left TLE) 27F & 23M (right TLE)	Verbal LR[NC] Visual LR	List Learning Task (Norwegian version adapted from Luria, 1966; DFR, # of trials to reach criterion, % Recall) Modified version of design learning and retention from Jones-Gotman, 1986 (Total Learning, DFR)	Women with right TLE outperformed women with left TLE on verbal tasks. No gender differences were found on verbal or visual tasks.	Women demonstrated less decline on verbal tasks and greater improvement on visual tasks than men following left ATL. Neither group experienced significant declines.
Davies et al. (1998)	60F & 47M (left TLE) 50F & 46M (right TLE)	Verbal LR[NC]	CVLT (Total Learning, SDFR, LDFR, % Loss)	While mean scores for women were relatively higher than men, differences were non-significant.	Left-sided resection and male sex predicted lower performance.
Frings et al. (2006)	8F & 14M (medial TLE)	Verbal LR[NC] Visual LR	RAVLT (German Version) DCS-R fMRI Recognition Paradigm	No gender differences in performance on any task.	Hippocampal activation differed between left and right medial TLE but not gender.

(continued)

Table 7.1 (continued)

Study	Sample	Cognitive domain	Cognitive measure	Pre-Surgical findings	Post-Surgical findings
Helmstaedter et al. (1999)[a]	43F & 42M (left TLE)	Verbal LR^{NC} Visual LR	AVLT (German Version; Total Learning, DFR, Delayed Recognition) Benton Visual Retention Test (Total Correct, Total Errors); DCS-R (Total Correct)	Women performed better than men on verbal tasks whereas men outperformed women on visual tasks. While atypical dominance prevalence was similar between men and women, only women benefited from atypical dominance in task performance.	–
Helmstaedter et al. (2004)	75F & 94M (left TLE)	Verbal LR^{NC} Visual LR	RAVLT (German Version; Total Learning, DFR) DCS-R (Total Correct at Last Trial)	Women performed better on verbal tasks, particularly those with atypical or bilateral dominance. No sex differences were found in visual task performance.	Women with left TLE and atypical language dominance demonstrated greater preservation of verbal abilities but performed worse on visual tasks compared to men.
Smith et al. (2009)[b]	25F & 26M (intractable epilepsy)	Verbal LR^{NC} Verbal LR^{C} Visual LR Facial Recognition	AVLT (Child Version; Total Recall, DFR) Story Recall (IFR, DFR) Rey Complex Figure Test (DFR) Facial Recognition Test (IFR)	Girls demonstrated stronger Verbal LR^{NC} (not significant) and Verbal LR^{C}. No gender differences were found in Visual LR or Facial Recognition.	–

(continued)

Table 7.1 (continued)

Study	Sample	Cognitive domain	Cognitive measure	Pre-Surgical findings	Post-Surgical findings
Strauss et al. (1992)[b]	16F & 8M (left early onset seizures)	General Intelligence Language Verbal LR[C] Visual LR	WISC-R; WAIS-R (Verbal & Performance IQ) Verbal Fluency (FAS); Boston Naming Test; Token Test WMS Logical Memory (IFR, DFR) WMS Visual Retention (IFR, DFR)	Females with atypical language dominance performed significantly lower than women with typical language dominance on language and verbal and visual memory tasks. Males performed below expectation on all tasks, suggesting that early left hemisphere insult has sex-specific cognitive consequences.	–

Note. Table modified from Lorkiewicz et al. (2023)
[a]Only presurgical findings
[b]Pediatric sample with only presurgical findings
[C]Contextual; [NC]Non-contextual. FLE = Frontal lobe epilepsy; TLE = Temporal lobe epilepsy; F = Female/women; M = Male/men; LR = Learning and recall; IFR = Immediate free recall; DFR = Delayed free recall; SDFR = Short delay free recall; LDFR = Long delay free recall; AVLT = Auditory Verbal Learning Test; CVLT = California Verbal Learning Test; DCS-R = Diagnosticum Fur Cerebralschadigung (Revised; Lamberti & Weidlich, 1999)

Across these studies, WWE have been shown to have stronger performances on verbal list learning and retrieval tasks compared to men, with a particular strength in semantic clustering. This finding has remained even when factors such as morphologic pathology, including hippocampal sclerosis (HS), are controlled for (Berenbaum et al., 1997), and differential cognitive findings seem to hold across the lifespan (Smith et al., 2009). While the exact driver of this advantage is unknown, more efficient encoding and preserved frontal lobe functioning are believed to be contributory (Berger et al., 2017). Alternatively, men with TLE appear to have a relative preservation of visuospatial learning and memory compared to women (Helmstaedter, 1999; Helmstaedter & Kockelmann, 2006), although this pattern appears limited to adult samples.

Regarding subjective cognitive concerns, when neurocognitive test performance is controlled for, WWE evidence an increased rate of memory concerns when compared to MWE (Rayner et al., 2020). The relationship between sex and subjective cognitive concerns is likely moderated by depression and other psychological factors, which, as described below, are elevated in WWE. It may also be reflective of a tendency of women to more readily report cognitive complaints, which is not unique to epilepsy. Clinically, elevated subjective cognitive concerns in WWE underline the need for evaluations and feedback sessions that are driven by both empathy and psychoeducation.

Post-Surgical Neurocognitive Outcomes

While there are multiple surgical interventions to address epilepsy, the primary focus of the neurocognitive literature has been on anterior temporal lobectomy (ATL), which typically includes amygdalohippocampectomy (AH). In studies examining the outcomes of men and women post-ATL, findings are mixed. Some studies have shown that women may be more resilient to the potential adverse neurocognitive effects of surgical intervention. Specifically, women may maintain better verbal memory following ATL when compared to men, with small to moderate differences identified across list learning tasks, paired associate learning and memory tasks, and prose recall tasks (Bengtson et al., 2000; Berger et al., 2017; Davies et al., 1998). However, while sex appears to be one factor moderating memory following ATL, it is likely a part of a complex system of influences, including side of resection, seizure freedom, and language lateralization.

However, other studies have found the opposite, with women more significantly impacted by post-surgical declines. In a large study comparing women (n = 202) and men (n = 170) presenting for temporal lobe resection in the UK, there was no effect of sex on laterality of seizure focus or seizure outcome 1 year post surgery (Baxendale, 2023). Likewise, no sex differences were noted in reported anxiety or depression. However, women scored higher than men before surgery on story learning and memory but showed less proficient naming skills in both right and left TLE compared with males in the study. As expected, the overall left TLE group demonstrated more postoperative declines in verbal learning and recall, but sex interactions demonstrated greater decline among women with left TLE resection. The author concluded that preoperative functional reorganization does not protect WWE from postoperative loss. Similarly, in developing nomograms to help predict post-surgical decline following ATL, Busch et al. (2018) found that sex predicted postoperative decline in naming with slightly greater risk of decline among women. The nomograms were derived from a large cohort (n = 719, 54% female) of individuals with TLE from the Midwestern United States and validated with cohorts from other institutions based in the Northeastern, Northwestern, and Southeastern US. The original validation cohort was predominantly Caucasian (93.05%) with a mean of 13 years of education, so generalizations are limited to similar cohorts.

Aging and Cognitive Decline

There is limited literature investigating the differential risk of cognitive decline in MWE and WWE. Animal model research focused on the dual roles of Alzheimer's disease markers and seizures suggests chronic seizures may alter hippocampal neuroinflammation and neuroplasticity in a sex-specific manner, with a differential influence on the cognitive presentation of female and male rodents (Knox et al., 2023). How these neuropathological sex differences may combine with psychosocial, treatment, and other influences in human cognition is less well established. In a recent study of epilepsy, vascular risk factors, and cognitive decline in older adults, researchers found that MWE and vascular risk factors had a lower than expected long-term risk of cognitive decline (measured by a global screener and processing speed performance) compared to women with these same health factors (Choi et al., 2022). Interestingly, sex was the only demographic factor that interacted significantly with epilepsy to influence cognitive decline. Similarly, in two studies of older adults with late-onset epilepsy, women were more likely to have comorbid dementia than men. Increased dementia among women was only statically significant in a large cohort study based on Medicare claims (Martin et al., 2014), whereas a meta-analysis did not find a significant sex effect for late onset epilepsy (Tang et al., 2022). As such, while emerging literature suggests WWE may be at a greater risk of cognitive decline than men, further research is needed to confirm this trend and its underlying contributors.

Psychological Conditions

People with epilepsy are at an increased risk of psychological dysfunction when compared to the general population, with estimates suggesting that anywhere from 25% to 60% of people with epilepsy also have a psychological diagnosis (Bangar et al., 2016; LaFrance et al., 2008; Rai et al., 2012). Psychological conditions likely have a bi-directional relationship with epilepsy, such that epilepsy-related pathological changes place someone at an increased risk for subsequent psychopathology, and pre-existing psychopathology places someone at an elevated risk of epilepsy (Josephson & Jetté, 2017; Martin et al., 2014).

WWE are more greatly impacted by psychological conditions when compared both to women in the general population and men with epilepsy (Chan et al., 2015; Sundar et al., 2017). Specifically, compared to MWE, MWE have higher rates of depression (27%–65% in women versus 17%–33% in men) and anxiety (17%–33% versus 9%–23% in men) (Karouni et al., 2010; Zhong et al., 2021). There is also an elevated risk of traumatic exposure in people with epilepsy and especially WWE, who may be especially prone to exposure to specific types of traumas, including physical and sexual violence (Vederhus et al., 2022). Pregnant women and women with limited access to resources are especially vulnerable to trauma (Birbeck et al.,

2007; Chaudhry et al., 2023). As such, rates of PTSD in WWE are likely also elevated, although further research is needed to explore this risk. Rates of other psychological conditions, such as bipolar disorder and schizophrenia spectrum disorders, have been less thoroughly investigated, but do not appear to meaningfully differ between sexes (Lorkiewicz et al., 2023).

Suicidality is especially crucial to consider in people with epilepsy, as rates of suicidal ideation and completed suicide are vastly greater than those in the general population. Specifically, between 11.5% and 20.8% of people with epilepsy have a history of suicide attempt versus 1.2% of the general population (Jones et al., 2003). While the overall trends of MWE and WWE mimic those of the general population, with women more likely to attempt suicide than men and men more likely to complete suicide, risk factors for suicidality may be unique in this population. Table 7.2 (from Lorkiewicz et al., 2023) describes the influence of seizure characteristics, demographic factors, psychosocial stress, and behavioral characteristics on suicidality in WWE and MWE.

Table 7.2 Gender-specific factors mediating suicide risk and mortality among PWE

Factor	Study	Pattern
Seizure characteristics	Kalinin and Polyanskiy (2005a)	Focal impaired awareness seizures decreased suicide mortality risk in women.
	Kalinin and Polyanskiy (2005a)	Daily dose of phenobarbital, carbamazepine, and valproate increased suicide risk in women with more frequent seizures.
	Kalinin and Polyanskiy (2005a)	Daily dose of classic ASMs increased suicide risk for men.
	Kalinin and Polyanskiy (2005a)	Greater seizure frequency (particularly focal or secondary generalized seizures) increased suicide risk in men.
Demographics	Tian et al. (2016)	Being between ages 30 and 39 increased suicide risk in women.
	Kalinin and Polyanskiy (2005a)	Earlier age of seizure onset increased suicide risk in men.
	Abraham et al. (2019)	Being a man increased suicide risk and mortality among PWE.
	Tian et al. (2016)	Being separated, divorced, or widowed increased suicide risk in women.
Psychosocial	Abraham et al. (2019)	Relationship difficulty in younger PWE increased suicide risk for men and women.
	Abraham et al. (2019)	Financial and/or medical challenges in older PWE increased suicide risk for men and women.
Behavior	Lee et al. (2022)	Impulsivity increased suicide risk in men.

Note. Table from Lorkiewicz et al. (2023)
PWE = people with epilepsy; ASM = anti-seizure medication

Quality of Life

Epilepsy is associated with reduced quality of life (QoL), with QoL levels affected by seizure frequency, epilepsy treatment, psychiatric conditions, neurocognitive symptoms, and other medical conditions (Baranowski, 2018; Strzelczyk et al., 2023). Compared to men, WWE report lower QoL (Grant et al., 2013; Santos et al., 2018). The reason for reduced QoL in WWE is multifactorial and may vary across the lifespan. For example, WWE in their reproductive years are at risk for lower QoL due to hormonal imbalances, obstetric concerns and complications, as well as elevated risk of comorbid depression and anxiety (Beghi et al., 2004). Additional predictors of decreased QoL in WWE include lower education level; being single, divorced, or separated; intractable seizures; ASM side effects; catamenial epilepsy; polycystic ovarian syndrome; depression; fatigue; and/or sexual dysfunction (Lorkiewicz et al., 2023).

Unique Considerations for Women

Catamenial Epilepsy

Catamenial epilepsy highlights the relationship between hormonal fluctuations and seizure presentation in women. Defined as seizure clustering in alignment with the menstrual cycle, catamenial epilepsy has further been divided into three patterns based on the phase of seizure exacerbation: perimenstrual, periovulatory, and luteal phase (Herzog et al., 1997). While there is variability in proposed diagnostic criteria for catamenial epilepsy, a two-fold increase in seizure frequency during the period of exacerbation when compared to baseline is the most generally accepted definition (Herzog et al., 2004). Prevalence of catamenial epilepsy is believed to be at least 40% in WWE (Herzog et al., 2012) and is likely attributable to estrogen to progesterone ratio, with estrogen believed to have excitatory proconvulsant effects and progesterone having anticonvulsant effects (Frank & Tyson, 2020). A single gold-standard treatment for catamenial epilepsy has not yet been identified and thus a treatment regimen may include traditional antiseizure medications (ASMs), natural progesterone, or amenorrhea-inducing drugs, with less support for hormonal contraception.

It is notable that many questions about catamenial epilepsy remain underexplored in the literature. In a recent review of research productivity in catamenial epilepsy, Mirawati and colleagues examined studies spanning 1956 to 2022 on a global scale (Mirawati et al., 2024). While they found that the number of publications has accelerated over the past 20 years, the literature base remains insufficient, particularly in terms of practice guidelines, risk assessment, and medication-related research.

Menstrual Disorders, Infertility, and Obstetric Risk

WWE have consistently been found to be at an increased risk of menstrual disturbances when compared to women without epilepsy, with current estimates suggesting approximately 33% of WWE experience menstrual disorders compared to 12–14% of women without epilepsy (Herzog & Friedman, 2001; Svalheim et al., 2003). This risk is multifactorial and may be the result of epilepsy characteristics, including age of seizure onset and frequency of seizures, as well as the use of specific ASMs and the need for polytherapy (Bosak et al., 2018).

Alongside menstrual disorders, infertility is also a prominent concern among both MWE and WWE. While some of the decreased birth rate among WWE may be attributable to a choice to not become pregnant due to risk of obstetric complications, there is also prominent literature to support the relationship between epilepsy, ASMs, and infertility. Epilepsy likely exhibits a direct effect on the reproductive endocrine system in women, with resulting estrogen and androgen level abnormalities (Markoula et al., 2020). At the same time, the influence of ASMs on women's reproductive health is also well established, with a high risk of secondary endocrine disorders with certain types of ASM treatment, most notably valproate (Sazgar et al., 2024).

Obstetric risk in epilepsy is one of the more thoroughly investigated domains specific to women with this condition (Viale et al., 2015). Risk factors for obstetric complications include seizures and ASMs; conversely, pregnancy may affect seizure control and ASM metabolism. Specific risks during pregnancy include miscarriage, antepartum or postpartum hemorrhage, hypertensive disorders of pregnancy, preterm labor and delivery, and fetal growth restriction (Kaplan et al., 2007). In a report from the International League Against Epilepsy (ILAE) task force on women and pregnancy, it is emphasized that the majority of WWE will have uneventful pregnancies resulting in healthy children; however, a management approach balancing fetal and maternal risks associated with seizures and exposure to teratogenic effects of certain ASMs is crucial (Tomson et al., 2019).

Considerations for Transgender Individuals

While the majority of this chapter has focused on cis-gender PWE, there are unique considerations faced by transgender PWE. Findings from a study of Medicare beneficiaries suggest that transgender people may be at a higher risk of epilepsy (10.5% vs. 3.3%; Dragon et al., 2017). However, few studies have explored reasons for this prevalence discrepancy or differences in the course or prognosis of epilepsy in transgender vs. cis-gender PWE. It has been posited that considering elevated rates of psychological comorbidities in PWE and elevated rates of depression in transgender people, this group may be especially vulnerable to psychological disease burden; however, this area is grossly understudied (Johnson & Kaplan, 2017).

Much of the research that exists on transgender PWE is focused on the potential interactions between ASMs and gender-affirming hormone therapy (GAHT) as well as the influence of GAHT on seizure control. Such research suggests that GAHT may have a direct influence on seizure control due to proconvulsant or anticonvulsant properties and further suggests that estrogen may influence the effectiveness of ASMs, including reducing the serum concentration of lamotrigine (Waldman & Benson, 2022). While such medication considerations generally fall outside the scope of routine neuropsychological practice, neuropsychologists are poised in a position to advance research on the cognitive, neurological, and psychological presentation of transgender PWE.

Research Takeaways

- Most epidemiological studies pool subjects with different epilepsy syndromes, which can mask sex differences and contribute to inter-study inconsistencies/variability. As is stated in Scharfman and MacLusky (2014, p. 16): "Studies are likely to obtain different results unless experimental conditions are carefully controlled, with attention to age, body weight, time of day, housing, diet, and the type of seizure that is studied. Even if conditions are constant, biological variability will require large sample sizes to detect significant differences." Furthermore, in those studies focused on a specific epilepsy syndrome, TLE predominates. Other epilepsy syndromes warrant additional research.
- While there has been significant focus on the construct of memory, and particularly memory in TLE, other cognitive domains warrant additional research. The domains of language, visuospatial function, processing speed, attention, and executive functioning are understudied in the literature and potential gender differences in those domains are uncertain.
- While gender differences in depression, anxiety, and exposure to trauma are becoming more well established, potential gender differences in additional psychological disorders need further study. For example, there is little established research on potential differences between men and women with epilepsy in rates or symptoms of bipolar disorder or schizophrenia-spectrum disorders.

Clinical Takeaways

- Women with TLE have an advantage in verbal memory compared to men with TLE, regardless of the level of hippocampal sclerosis. There is mixed evidence about whether such advantages persist post-surgical intervention. Awareness of such gender differences in cognition may (1) guide the use of cognitive measures and normative data sets to better capture nuances in performance during pre- and post-surgical neuropsychological evaluations and (2) allow for greater accuracy in predicting treatment outcomes and development of more individualized treatment plans.

- Psychological factors may have a substantial influence on the neuropsychological profile of women with epilepsy. WWE are at a higher risk for depressive and anxiety disorders than men with epilepsy as well as than women in the general population. Such factors should be considered in neuropsychological evaluations at any stage of treatment of people with epilepsy, with a goal to reduce the impact of psychological factors and promotion of quality of life.
- Gender-specific intervention for women with epilepsy is in its infancy and warrants further development. While much of the literature focuses on the influence of ASMs on women of reproductive age, there is less of an emphasis on non-pharmacological treatment of neurocognitive and psychological concerns in WWE.

References

Abraham, N. et al. (2019). A Meta-Analysis of the Rates of Suicide Ideation, Attempts and Deaths in People with Epilepsy. International *Journal of Environmental Research and Public Health* 16, 1451.

Bangar, S., Shastri, A., El-Sayeh, H., & Cavanna, A. E. (2016). Women with epilepsy: Clinically relevant issues. *Functional Neurology, 31*(3), 127–134. https://doi.org/10.11138/FNeur/2016.31.3.127

Baranowski, C. J. (2018). The quality of life of older adults with epilepsy: A systematic review. *Seizure, 60*, 190–197. https://doi.org/10.1016/j.seizure.2018.06.002

Battaglia, G., Chiapparini, L., Franceschetti, S., Freri, E., Tassi, L., Bassanini, S., Villani, F., Spreafico, R., D'Incerti, L., & Granata, T. (2006). Periventricular nodular heterotopia: Classification, epileptic history, and genesis of epileptic discharges. *Epilepsia, 47*(1), 86–97. https://doi.org/10.1111/j.1528-1167.2006.00374.x

Baxendale, S. (2023). Sex differences in the pre and postoperative neuropsychological function of epilepsy surgery candidates. *The Clinical Neuropsychologist, 1–13*. https://doi.org/10.1080/13854046.2023.2281706

Beghi, E. (2019). The epidemiology of epilepsy. *Neuroepidemiology, 54*(2), 185–191. https://doi.org/10.1159/000503831

Beghi, E., & Beghi, M. (2013). Gender difference in epidemiology and comorbidities of epilepsy. In C. L. Harden, S. V. Thomas, & T. Tomson (Eds.), *Epilepsy in Women* (1st ed., pp. 1–10). Wiley. https://doi.org/10.1002/9781118531037.ch1

Beghi, E., & Hesdorffer, D. (2014). Prevalence of epilepsy—An unknown quantity. *Epilepsia, 55*(7), 963–967. https://doi.org/10.1111/epi.12579

Beghi, E., Leone, M., & Solari, A. (2005). Mortality in patients with a first unprovoked seizure. *Epilepsia, 46*(s11), 40–42. https://doi.org/10.1111/j.1528-1167.2005.00407.x

Beghi, E., Roncolato, M., & Visonà, G. (2004). Depression and altered quality of life in women with epilepsy of childbearing age. *Epilepsia, 45*(1), Article 1. https://doi.org/10.1111/j.0013-9580.2004.56502.x

Bell, B., Lin, J. J., Seidenberg, M., & Hermann, B. (2011). The neurobiology of cognitive disorders in temporal lobe epilepsy. *Nature Reviews Neurology, 7*(3), 154–164. https://doi.org/10.1038/nrneurol.2011.3

Bengtson, M., Martin, R., Sawrie, S., Gilliam, F., Faught, E., Morawetz, R., & Kuzniecky, R. (2000). Gender, memory, and hippocampal volumes: Relationships in temporal lobe epilepsy. *Epilepsy & Behavior, 1*(2), 112–119. https://doi.org/10.1006/ebeh.2000.0051

Berenbaum, S. A., Baxter, L., Seidenberg, M., & Hermann, B. (1997). Role of the hippocampus in sex differences in verbal memory: Memory outcome following left anterior temporal lobectomy: Neuropsychology. *Neuropsychology, 11*(4), 585–591. https://doi.org/10.1037/0894-4105.11.4.585

Berger, J., Oltmanns, F., Holtkamp, M., & Bengner, T. (2017). Sex differences in verbal and nonverbal learning before and after temporal lobe epilepsy surgery. *Epilepsy & Behavior, 66*, 57–63. https://doi.org/10.1016/j.yebeh.2016.11.037

Berger, J., Demin, K., Holtkamp, M. & Bengner, T. (2018). Female verbal memory advantage in temporal, but not frontal lobe epilepsy. *Epilepsy Research 139*, 129–134.

Birbeck, G., Chomba, E., Atadzhanov, M., Mbewe, E., & Haworth, A. (2007). The social and economic impact of epilepsy in Zambia: A cross-sectional study. *The Lancet Neurology, 6*(1), 39–44. https://doi.org/10.1016/S1474-4422(06)70629-9

Bjørnæs, H., Stabell, K. E., Røste, G. K. & Bakke, S. J. (2005). Changes in verbal and nonverbal memory following anterior temporal lobe surgery for refractory seizures: effects of sex and laterality. *Epilepsy & Behavior 6*, 71–84.

Bosak, M., Cyranka, K., Dudek, D., Kowalik, M., Mołek, P., & Słowik, A. (2018). Psychiatric comedication in patients with epilepsy. *Epilepsy & Behavior, 83*, 207–211. https://doi.org/10.1016/j.yebeh.2018.03.033

Briellmann, R. S., Berkovic, S. F., & Jackson, G. D. (2000). Men may be more vulnerable to seizure-associated brain damage. *Neurology, 55*(10), 1479–1485. https://doi.org/10.1212/WNL.55.10.1479

Burneo, J. G., Black, L., Martin, R., Devinsky, O., Pacia, S., Faught, E., Vasquez, B., Knowlton, R. C., Luciano, D., Doyle, W., Najjar, S., & Kuzniecky, R. I. (2006). Race/ethnicity, sex, and socioeconomic status as predictors of outcome after surgery for temporal lobe epilepsy. *Archives of Neurology, 63*(8), 1106–1110. https://doi.org/10.1001/archneur.63.8.1106

Busch, R. M., Hogue, O., Kattan, M. W., Hamberger, M., Drane, D. L., Hermann, B., Kim, M., Ferguson, L., Bingaman, W., Gonzalez-Martinez, J., Najm, I. M., & Jehi, L. (2018). Nomograms to predict naming decline after temporal lobe surgery in adults with epilepsy. *Neurology, 91*(23), e2144–e2152. https://doi.org/10.1212/WNL.0000000000006629

Chan, J., Chen, J., Makhija, K., Faulkner, M., & Singh, S. (2015). Gender differences in the incidence of psychiatric co-morbidity in patients with epilepsy (P3.196). *Neurology, 84*((14 Supplement), Article 14 Supplement. https://n.neurology.org/content/84/14_Supplement/P3.196

Chaudhry, N., Bergey, G. K., Kaplan, P. W., & Johnson, E. L. (2023). Life stressors during pregnancy in women with epilepsy: Results from the pregnancy risk assessment monitoring system. *Neurology*. https://doi.org/10.1212/WNL.0000000000207274

Chiesa, V., Gardella, E., Tassi, L., Canger, R., Lo Russo, G., Piazzini, A., Turner, K., & Canevini, M. P. (2007). Age-related gender differences in reporting ictal fear: Analysis of case histories and review of the literature. *Epilepsia, 48*(12), 2361–2364. https://doi.org/10.1111/j.1528-1167.2007.01227.x

Choi, H., Elkind, M. S. V., Longstreth, W. T., Boehme, A. K., Hafen, R., Hoyt, E. J., & Thacker, E. L. (2022). Epilepsy, vascular risk factors, and cognitive decline in older adults. *Neurology, 99*(21), e2346–e2358. https://doi.org/10.1212/WNL.0000000000201187

Christensen, J., Kjeldsen, M. J., Andersen, H., Friis, M. L., & Sidenius, P. (2005). Gender differences in epilepsy. *Epilepsia, 46*(6), 956–960. https://doi.org/10.1111/j.1528-1167.2005.51204.x

Cockerell, O. C., Johnson, A. L., Sander, J. W. A. S., & Shorvon, S. D. (1997). Prognosis of epilepsy: A review and further analysis of the first nine years of the British national general practice study of epilepsy, a prospective population-based study. *Epilepsia, 38*(1), 31–46. https://doi.org/10.1111/j.1528-1157.1997.tb01075.x

Cowan, L. D. (2002). The epidemiology of the epilepsies in children. *Mental Retardation and Developmental Disabilities Research Reviews, 8*(3), 171–181.

Davies, K. G., Bell, B. D., Bush, A. J., & Wyler, A. R. (1998). Prediction of verbal memory loss in individuals after anterior temporal lobectomy. *Epilepsia, 39*(8), 820–828. https://doi.org/10.1111/j.1528-1157.1998.tb01175.x

Doherty, M. J., Rostad, S. W., & Haltiner, A. M. (2007). Neocortical gliosis in temporal lobe epilepsy: Gender-based differences. *Epilepsia, 48*(8), 1455–1459. https://doi.org/10.1111/j.1528-1167.2007.01046.x

Dragon, C. N., Guerino, P., Ewald, E., & Laffan, A. M. (2017). Transgender Medicare beneficiaries and chronic conditions: exploring fee-for-service claims data. *LGBT health, 4*(6), 404–411. https://doi.org/10.1089/lgbt.2016.0208

Fiest, K. M., Sauro, K. M., Wiebe, S., Patten, S. B., Kwon, C.-S., Dykeman, J., Pringsheim, T., Lorenzetti, D. L., & Jetté, N. (2017). Prevalence and incidence of epilepsy. *Neurology, 88*(3), 296–303. https://doi.org/10.1212/WNL.0000000000003509

Fisher, R. S., Cross, J. H., French, J. A., Higurashi, N., Hirsch, E., Jansen, F. E., Lagae, L., Moshé, S. L., Peltola, J., Roulet Perez, E., Scheffer, I. E., & Zuberi, S. M. (2017). Operational classification of seizure types by the International League Against Epilepsy: Position paper of the ILAE commission for classification and terminology. *Epilepsia, 58*(4), 522–530. https://doi.org/10.1111/epi.13670

Frank, S., & Tyson, N. A. (2020). A clinical approach to catamenial epilepsy: A review. *The Permanente Journal, 24*(19), 145. https://doi.org/10.7812/TPP/19.145

Frings, L., Wagner, K., Unterrainer, J., Spreer, J., Halsband, U., & Schulze-Bonhage, A. (2006). Gender-related differences in lateralization of hippocampal activation and cognitive strategy. *Neuroreport, 17*(4), 417-421.

Grant, A. C., Prus, N., & Nakhutina, L. (2013). Factors affecting quality of life in epilepsy in a multi-ethnic urban population. *Epilepsy & Behavior, 27*(2), 283–285. https://doi.org/10.1016/j.yebeh.2013.01.031

Hauser, W. A., Annegers, J. F., & Kurland, L. T. (1993). Incidence of epilepsy and unprovoked seizures in Rochester, Minnesota: 1935–1984. *Epilepsia, 34*(3), 453–458. https://doi.org/10.1111/j.1528-1157.1993.tb02586.x

Hauser, W. A., & Beghi, E. (2008). First seizure definitions and worldwide incidence and mortality. *Epilepsia, 49*(s1), 8–12. https://doi.org/10.1111/j.1528-1167.2008.01443.x

Helmstaedter, C. (1999). Sex differences in material-specific cognitive functions related to language dominance: An intracarotid amobarbital study in left temporal lobe epilepsy. *Laterality: Asymmetries of Body, Brain and Cognition, 4*(1), 51–63. https://doi.org/10.1080/713754322

Helmstaedter, C., & Kockelmann, E. (2006). Cognitive outcomes in patients with chronic temporal lobe epilepsy. *Epilepsia, 47*(s2), Article s2. https://doi.org/10.1111/j.1528-1167.2006.00702.x

Helmstaedter, C., Kurthen, M. & Elger, C. E. (1999). Sex differences in material-specific cognitive functions related to language dominance: An intracarotid amobarbital study in left temporal lobe epilepsy. *Laterality: Asymmetries of Body, Brain, and Cognition 4*, 51–63.

Helmstaedter, C., Brosch, T., Kurthen, M. & Elger, C. E. (2004). The impact of sex and language dominance on material-specific memory before and after left temporal lobe surgery. *Brain 127*, 1518–1525.

Herzog, A. G., Fowler, K. M., Smithson, S. D., Kalayjian, L. A., Heck, C. N., Sperling, M. R., Liporace, J. D., Harden, C. L., Dworetzky, B. A., Pennell, P. B., Massaro, J. M., Herzog, A. G., Fowler, K. M., Smithson, S. D., Schomer, D. L., Bromfield, E. B., Dworetzky, B. A., Replansky, S., Gleason, K., et al. (2012). Progesterone vs placebo therapy for women with epilepsy. *Neurology, 78*(24), 1959–1966. https://doi.org/10.1212/WNL.0b013e318259e1f9

Herzog, A. G., & Friedman, M. N. (2001). Menstrual cycle interval and ovulation in women with localization-related epilepsy. *Neurology, 57*(11), 2133–2135. https://doi.org/10.1212/WNL.57.11.2133

Herzog, A. G., Harden, C. L., Liporace, J., Pennell, P., Schomer, D. L., Sperling, M., Fowler, K., Nikolov, B., Shuman, S., & Newman, M. (2004). Frequency of catamenial seizure exacerbation in women with localization-related epilepsy. *Annals of Neurology, 56*(3), 431–434. https://doi.org/10.1002/ana.20214

Herzog, A. G., Klein, P., & Rand, B. J. (1997). Three patterns of catamenial epilepsy. *Epilepsia, 38*(10), 1082–1088. https://doi.org/10.1111/j.1528-1157.1997.tb01197.x

Hesdorffer, D. C., Logroscino, G., Benn, E. K. T., Katri, N., Cascino, G., & Hauser, W. A. (2011). Estimating risk for developing epilepsy. *Neurology, 76*(1), 23–27. https://doi.org/10.1212/WNL.0b013e318204a36a

Janszky, J., Schulz, R., Janszky, I., & Ebner, A. (2004). Medial temporal lobe epilepsy: Gender differences. *Journal of Neurology, Neurosurgery, and Psychiatry, 75*(5), 773–775. https://doi.org/10.1136/jnnp.2003.020941

Jones-Gotman, M. (1986). Right hippocampal excision impairs learning and recall of a list of abstract designs. *Neuropsychologia, 24*(5), 659–670.

Johnson, E. L., & Kaplan, P. W. (2017). Caring for transgender patients with epilepsy. *Epilepsia, 58*(10), 1667–1672. https://doi.org/10.1111/epi.13864

Jones, J. E., Hermann, B. P., Barry, J. J., Gilliam, F. G., Kanner, A. M., & Meador, K. J. (2003). Rates and risk factors for suicide, suicidal ideation, and suicide attempts in chronic epilepsy. *Epilepsy & Behavior, 4*, 31–38. https://doi.org/10.1016/j.yebeh.2003.08.019

Josephson, C. B., & Jetté, N. (2017). Psychiatric comorbidities in epilepsy. *International Review of Psychiatry, 29*(5), Article 5. https://doi.org/10.1080/09540261.2017.1302412

Kalinin, V. V. & Polyanskiy, D. A. (2005a). Gender differences in risk factors of suicidal behavior in epilepsy. *Epilepsy & Behavior* 6, 424–429.

Kaplan, P. W., Norwitz, E. R., Ben-Menachem, E., Pennell, P. B., Druzin, M., Robinson, J. N., & Gordon, J. C. (2007). Obstetric risks for women with epilepsy during pregnancy. *Epilepsy & Behavior, 11*(3), 283–291. https://doi.org/10.1016/j.yebeh.2007.08.012

Karouni, M., Arulthas, S., Larsson, P. G., Rytter, E., Johannessen, S. I., & Johannessen Landmark, C. (2010). Psychiatric comorbidity in patients with epilepsy: A population-based study. *European Journal of Clinical Pharmacology, 66*(11), 1151–1160. https://doi.org/10.1007/s00228-010-0861-y

Kim, D. W., Lee, S.-Y., Chung, S.-E., Cheong, H.-K., Jung, K.-Y., & Society, the K. E. (2014). Clinical characteristics of patients with treated epilepsy in Korea: A nationwide epidemiologic study. *Epilepsia, 55*(1), 67–75. https://doi.org/10.1111/epi.12469

Knight, R., Wittkowski, A., & Bromley, R. L. (2021). Neurodevelopmental outcomes in children exposed to newer antiseizure medications: A systematic review. *Epilepsia, 62*(8), 1765–1779. https://doi.org/10.1111/epi.16953

Knox, K. M., Beckman, M., Smith, C. L., Jayadev, S., & Barker-Haliski, M. (2023). Chronic seizures induce sex-specific cognitive deficits with loss of presenilin 2 function. *Experimental Neurology, 361*, 114321. https://doi.org/10.1016/j.expneurol.2023.114321

Kotsopoulos, I. A. W., Van Merode, T., Kessels, F. G. H., De Krom, M. C. T. F. M., & Knottnerus, J. A. (2002). Systematic review and meta-analysis of incidence studies of epilepsy and unprovoked seizures. *Epilepsia, 43*(11), 1402–1409. https://doi.org/10.1046/j.1528-1157.2002.t01-1-26901.x

LaFrance, W. C., Kanner, A. M., & Hermann, B. (2008). Chapter 20: Psychiatric comorbidities in epilepsy. In *International Review of Neurobiology* (Vol. 83, pp. 347–383). Academic Press. https://doi.org/10.1016/S0074-7742(08)00020-2

Lamberti, G., & Weidlich, S. (1999). DCS a visual learning and memory test for neuropsychological assessment, after F. Hillers: manual.

Lee, S. A., Choi, E. J., Jeon, J. Y., Han, S. H., Kim, H. W., Lee, G. H., ... & Yang, H. R. (2022). Impulsivity in persons with epilepsy: association with seizure severity and suicide risk. *Epilepsy research*, 179, 106825.

Lorkiewicz, S. A., Modiano, Y. A., Miller, B. I., Van Cott, A. C., Haneef, Z., & Sullivan-Baca, E. (2023). The neuropsychological presentation of women with epilepsy: Clinical considerations and future directions. *The Clinical Neuropsychologist, 0*(0), 1–27. https://doi.org/10.1080/13854046.2023.2283937

Markoula, S., Siarava, E., Keramida, A., Chatzistefanidis, D., Zikopoulos, A., Kyritsis, A. P., & Georgiou, I. (2020). Reproductive health in patients with epilepsy. *Epilepsy & Behavior, 113*. https://doi.org/10.1016/j.yebeh.2020.107563

Martin, R. C., Faught, E., Richman, J., Funkhouser, E., Kim, Y., Clements, K., & Pisu, M. (2014). Psychiatric and neurologic risk factors for incident cases of new-onset epilepsy in older adults: Data from U.S. Medicare beneficiaries. *Epilepsia, 55*(7), Article 7. https://doi.org/10.1111/epi.12649

McHugh, J. C., & Delanty, N. (2008). Chapter 2: Epidemiology and classification of epilepsy: Gender comparisons. In *International Review of Neurobiology* (Vol. 83, pp. 11–26). Academic Press. https://doi.org/10.1016/S0074-7742(08)00002-0

Mirawati, D. K., Wiyono, N., Ilyas, M. F., Putra, S. E., & Hafizhan, M. (2024). Research productivity in catamenial epilepsy: A bibliometric analysis of worldwide scientific literature (1956–2022). *Heliyon, 10*(10), e31474. https://doi.org/10.1016/j.heliyon.2024.e31474

Nickel, J., Jokeit, H., Wunderlich, G., Ebner, A., Witte, O. W., & Seitz, R. J. (2003). Gender-specific differences of hypometabolism in mTLE: Implication for cognitive impairments. *Epilepsia, 44*(12), 1551–1561. https://doi.org/10.1111/j.0013-9580.2003.13603.x

Nilsson, L., Farahmand, B., Persson, P., Thiblin, I., & Tomson, T. (1999). Risk factors for sudden unexpected death in epilepsy: A case control study. *The Lancet, 353*(9156), 888–893.

Ortiz-González, X. R., Poduri, A., Roberts, C. M., Sullivan, J. E., Marsh, E. D., & Porter, B. E. (2013). Focal cortical dysplasia is more common in boys than girls. *Epilepsy & Behavior: E&B, 27*(1), 121. https://doi.org/10.1016/j.yebeh.2012.12.035

Rai, D., Kerr, M. P., McManus, S., Jordanova, V., Lewis, G., & Brugha, T. S. (2012). Epilepsy and psychiatric comorbidity: A nationally representative population-based study. *Epilepsia, 53*(6), 1095–1103. https://doi.org/10.1111/j.1528-1167.2012.03500.x

Rayner, G., Siveges, B., Allebone, J., Pieters, J., & Wilson, S. J. (2020). Contribution of autobiographic memory impairment to subjective memory complaints in focal epilepsy. *Epilepsy & Behavior, 102*, 106636. https://doi.org/10.1016/j.yebeh.2019.106636

Remillard, G. M., Andermann, F., Testa, G. F., Gloor, P., Aube, M., Martin, J. B., Feindel, W., Guberman, A., & Simpson, C. (1983). Sexual ictal manifestations predominate in women with temporal lobe epilepsy. *Neurology, 33*(3), 323–323. https://doi.org/10.1212/WNL.33.3.323

Santana, M. T. C. G., Jackowski, A. P., Britto, F. d. S., Sandim, G. B., Caboclo, L. O. S. F., Centeno, R. S., Carrete, H., & Yacubian, E. M. T. (2014). Gender and hemispheric differences in temporal lobe epilepsy: A VBM study. *Seizure, 23*(4), 274–279. https://doi.org/10.1016/j.seizure.2013.12.006

Santos, A. M. C., Castro-Lima, H., Matos, M. A. A., & Brito, M. B. (2018). Quality of life among women with epilepsy during their reproductive years. *Epilepsy & Behavior, 85*, 10–13. https://doi.org/10.1016/j.yebeh.2018.04.028

Savic, I., & Engel, J. (1998). Sex differences in patients with mesial temporal lobe epilepsy. *Journal of Neurology, Neurosurgery, and Psychiatry, 65*(6), 910–912.

Sazgar, M., Mnatsakanyan, L., Pack, A. M., & Harden, C. L. (2024). Epilepsy and anti-seizure medications: Secret agents for endocrine disruption. *Epilepsy Currents, 24*(2), 79–83. https://doi.org/10.1177/15357597231213248

Scharfman, H. E., & MacLusky, N. J. (2014). Sex differences in the neurobiology of epilepsy: a preclinical perspective. *Neurobiology of disease*, 72, 180–192.

Sisodiya, S. M., Free, S. L., Thom, M., Everitt, A. E., Fish, D. R., & Shorvon, S. D. (1999). Evidence for nodular epileptogenicity and gender differences in periventricular nodular heterotopia. *Neurology, 52*(2), 336–336. https://doi.org/10.1212/WNL.52.2.336

Smith, M. L., Elliott, I., & Naguiat, A. (2009). Sex differences in episodic memory among children with intractable epilepsy. *Epilepsy & Behavior, 14*(1), 247–249. https://doi.org/10.1016/j.yebeh.2008.08.010

Strauss, E., Wada, J. & Hunter, M. (1992). Sex-related differences in the cognitive consequences of early lefthemisphere lesions. *Journal of Clinical and Experimental Neuropsychology* 14, 738–748.

Strzelczyk, A., Aledo-Serrano, A., Coppola, A., Didelot, A., Bates, E., Sainz-Fuertes, R., & Lawthom, C. (2023). The impact of epilepsy on quality of life: Findings from a European survey. *Epilepsy & Behavior, 142*. https://doi.org/10.1016/j.yebeh.2023.109179

Sullivan-Baca, E., Modiano, Y. A., Miller, B. I., Fadipe, M., Van Cott, A. C., & Haneef, Z. (2022). Characterizing women veterans receiving seizure care in the veterans affairs healthcare system. *Epilepsy Research, 180*, 106849. https://doi.org/10.1016/j.eplepsyres.2021.106849

Sullivan-Baca, E., Rehman, R., Towne, A. R., & Haneef, Z. (2023). Psychiatric co-morbidity of drug-resistant epilepsy in Veterans. *Epilepsy & Behavior, 139*, 109059. https://doi.org/10.1016/j.yebeh.2022.109059

Sundar, U., Honrao, S. T., & Shah, N. (2017). Psychiatric co-morbidities in women with epilepsy. *The. Journal of the Association of Physicians of India, 65*(12), Article 12.

Svalheim, S., Taubøll, E., Bjørnenak, T., Røste, L. S., Mørland, T., Sætre, E. R., & Gjerstad, L. (2003). Do women with epilepsy have increased frequency of menstrual disturbances? *Seizure - European Journal of Epilepsy, 12*(8), 529–533. https://doi.org/10.1016/S1059-1311(03)00195-X

Tang, T., Zhang, R., & Pan, X. (2022). Meta-analysis of the risk of dementia in elderly patients with late-onset epilepsy. *Clinical Neurology and Neurosurgery, 223*, 107499. https://doi.org/10.1016/j.clineuro.2022.107499

Taylor, D. C. (1969). Differential rates of cerebral maturation between sexes and between hemispheres: Evidence from epilepsy. *The Lancet, 294*(7612), 140–142. https://doi.org/10.1016/S0140-6736(69)92445-3

Tian, N., Cui, W., Zack, M., Kobau, R., Fowler, K. A., & Hesdorffer, D. C. (2016). Suicide among people with epilepsy: a population-based analysis of data from the US National Violent Death Reporting System, 17 states, 2003–2011. *Epilepsy & behavior, 61*, 210–217.

Tomson, T., Battino, D., Bromley, R., Kochen, S., Meador, K., Pennell, P., & Thomas, S. V. (2019). Management of epilepsy in pregnancy: A report from the International League against epilepsy task force on women and pregnancy. *Epileptic Disorders, 21*(6), 497–517. https://doi.org/10.1684/epd.2019.1105

Vederhus, J., Husebye, E. S. N., Eid, K., Gilhus, N. E., & Bjørk, M. H. (2022). Prevalence of self-reported emotional, physical, and sexual abuse and association with fear of childbirth in pregnant women with epilepsy: The Norwegian Mother, Father, and Child Cohort Study. *Epilepsia, 63*(7), 1822–1834. https://doi.org/10.1111/epi.17242

Viale, L., Allotey, J., Cheong-See, F., Arroyo-Manzano, D., Mccorry, D., Bagary, M., Mignini, L., Khan, K. S., Zamora, J., & Thangaratinam, S. (2015). Epilepsy in pregnancy and reproductive outcomes: A systematic review and meta-analysis. *The Lancet, 386*(10006), Article 10006. https://doi.org/10.1016/S0140-6736(15)00045-8

Waldman, G., & Benson, R. (2022). Epilepsy care in transgender patients. *Current Neurology and Neuroscience Reports, 22*(8), 451–458. https://doi.org/10.1007/s11910-022-01208-4

Zhao, F., Kang, H., You, L., Rastogi, P., Venkatesh, D., & Chandra, M. (2014). Neuropsychological deficits in temporal lobe epilepsy: A comprehensive review. *Annals of Indian Academy of Neurology, 17*(4), 374. https://doi.org/10.4103/0972-2327.144003

Zhong, R., Chen, Q., Li, M., Li, N., Zhang, X., & Lin, W. (2021). Sex differences in anxiety in patients with epilepsy: Status and risk factors analysis. *Epilepsy & Behavior: E&B, 116*, 107801. https://doi.org/10.1016/j.yebeh.2021.107801

Chapter 8
Cancer

Rachael L. Ellison, Hannah B. VanLandingham, Joyce W. Tam, Lauren Rynar, and Demy Alfonso

Introduction

Cancer is a leading cause of death and a major public health issue worldwide (National Cancer Institute, 2024). Advances in treatment and early detection also yield exponential growth in the increasing number of long-term cancer survivors (Jemal et al., 2010; Santucci et al., 2020). However, there are known disparities in incidence, prevalence, susceptibility to cancer, early detection and screening, response to treatment, symptom profile, morbidity, mortality, and financial burden across multiple variables including race, ethnicity, age, socioeconomic status, and gender (Dorak & Karpuzoglu, 2012; Islami et al., 2020; NIH Cancer Disparities, 2024). Therefore, incorporating gender differences in cancer-related clinical trials, considering gender differences in oncology-related clinical care as well as in disseminated research, such as this chapter, is vital to optimizing outcomes (Rubin et al., 2020; Unger et al., 2022).

This chapter will focus on differences between women and men across several of these cancer-related measures, with an emphasis on gender differences in cognitive sequelae of cancer and cancer treatment. At the same time, there are multiple etiologies for cognitive sequelae of cancer (Bender & Thelen, 2013), including via direct (e.g., neural inflammation, neurotoxicity, tumor burden) and indirect (e.g., stress, fatigue, mood) pathways (Andreotti et al., 2015; Lange et al., 2019; NCI

R. L. Ellison (✉) · H. B. VanLandingham
Rosalind Franklin University of Medicine and Science, North Chicago, IL, USA
e-mail: rachael.ellison@rosalindfranklin.edu

J. W. Tam · L. Rynar
Rush University Medical Center, Chicago, IL, USA

D. Alfonso
Children's Healthcare of Atlanta, Atlanta, GA, USA

E. Sullivan-Baca, R. Ellison (eds.), *Neuropsychology of Women*,
https://doi.org/10.1007/978-3-031-87228-0_8

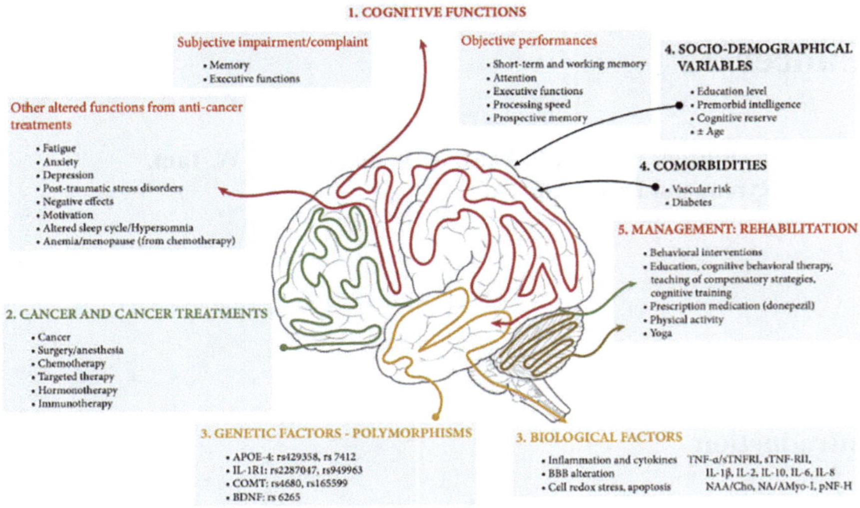

Fig. 8.1 Direct and indirect etiologies of cognitive sequalae of cancer. (*Note:* Reproduced with permission from Lange et al. [2019])

PDQ—Cognitive Impairment in Adults with Cancer), these pathways will not be reviewed in detail. See Fig. 8.1 for an illustrative diagram of direct and indirect etiologies of cognitive sequelae of cancer.

Rather, this chapter will focus on gender differences in cancer-related cognitive impairment across non-central nervous system (CNS) cancers, CNS cancers, and non-CNS cancers with brain metastases. Gender differences in base and prevalence rates, diagnosis and prognosis, symptom presentation, and risk factors, as well as in other clinical factors, will also be reviewed. Of note, the chapter is specific to adult-onset cancer; though not reviewed in the present chapter, women with a history of pediatric cancer may have enduring cognitive impacts.

Lastly, as we will again bring up in this chapter's discussion, although there is some data on differences in incidence rates for sexual and gender minority patients (SGM; Jackson et al., 2023), there is little to no research and published data at this time on cancer-related cognitive impairment in this group. Though we hope future chapters will be able to speak to SGM patients, there unfortunately is currently not enough data to include at this time to make generalizable claims.

Cancer Subtype Overview

Cancers can be categorized broadly into CNS cancer—those originating in the brain or spinal cord—and non-CNS cancer, which develops in almost any other part of the body, including the organs, muscles, and bones. Non-CNS cancer cells can also spread from their original site to the brain, causing brain metastases. Each of the three categories of cancer—non-CNS, CNS, and non-CNS with brain metastases—can lead to cognitive impairment due to the cancer or its treatments. For cancers that can affect both women and men, incidence ratios are typically 1:1.5 to 1:3, indicating that women are less likely to develop cancer as well as have better treatment outcomes (Sun et al., 2015). Gender differences are apparent across multiple domains in cancer (Kim et al., 2018), and this chapter will offer a detailed review of how women are differentially impacted in both CNS and non-CNS cancer in terms of base and prevalence rates, diagnosis and prognosis, symptom presentation, and associated risk factors, as well as in other clinical factors.

Cancer Treatment Overview

Across cancer types, multiple treatment modalities may be applied singularly or in combination, causing a highly variable profile of side effects that impact functioning to varying degrees. Depending on the size and location of the cancer, surgery may be performed before or after treatment or at multiple time points. Treatment(s) may include radiation therapy, chemotherapy, immunotherapy, hormone therapy, targeted therapies, and/or stem cell transplant for some cancers. Chemotherapy delivered before surgery is referred to as neo-adjuvant, administered with the goal of shrinking larger cancers to optimize the chances of successful surgery. Adjuvant chemotherapy is administered after surgery, radiation, or other primary treatments with the goal of eliminating any remaining cancer cells and reducing the risk of recurrence. Long-term maintenance interventions, such as endocrine therapy after primary cancer treatment, are another type of adjuvant treatment. In most cases, treatment involves two or more modalities in combination to yield the most optimal outcome. This is important to consider when trying to understand cognitive sequelae of cancer, as different treatments can have positive and negative impacts on cognitive functioning.

General Gender Differences Related to Cancer Treatment(s)

Women can be uniquely affected by treatment-related side effects across cancer types. Notably, animal studies have begun to suggest taking sex into account when designing radiation-based treatment protocols, given small but significant differences in radiation responses between sexes (De Courcy et al., 2020). In addition, research highlights gender differences related to aspects of multiple treatment modalities (Unger et al., 2022). For example, data indicate differences in radiotherapy sensitivity across genders due to differences in inflammatory response, polymorphism, and estrogen interaction, suggesting radiation protocols should be adjusted by gender to maximize impact (De Courcy et al., 2020).

Across many chemotherapy protocols, there is robust evidence to suggest higher rates of toxicity for women versus men. For example, the commonly used agents

5-fluorouracil and cisplatin (Liaw, 2001) cause more prolonged and burdensome symptoms for women, such as fatigue and leukopenia (Sloan et al., 2002). Women may also metabolize certain chemotherapies differently than men, resulting in longer and less effective elimination (Joerger et al., 2006), as well as higher rates of cardiac risk factors and abnormalities (Lipshultz et al., 1995). In addition, certain chemotherapies can cause higher levels of neurotoxicity and cognitive dysfunction, notably including those that are used to treat cancers predominantly affecting women, such as cisplatin, doxorubicin, paclitaxel, and carboplatin (Park et al., 2008; Taillibert et al., 2016).

Regarding treatment-related effects impacting cognitive outcomes (in a sample of predominately women with breast cancer), chemotherapy-induced cognitive side effects can include impairment in immediate free recall, delayed memory, verbal memory, delayed recognition memory, selective attention, and attention capacity (Dos Santos et al., 2020). For patients receiving immunotherapy, men appear to have greater absolute benefit than women in progression-free survival (Klein & Morgan, 2020); women also have increased hematologic, cardiovascular, and gastrointestinal adverse effects as compared to men.

Hormone therapy is commonly prescribed to reduce the likelihood of growth of hormone-sensitive cancers (e.g., estrogen-positive breast cancer) and is associated with many side effects, including hot flashes, fatigue, and mood lability (Pan et al., 2018). These side effects can be chronic, can negatively affect functioning, and have the potential to interact differently with women versus men across time due to natural hormonal changes (e.g., menopause; Flores et al., 2021). Both forms of hormone therapy—selective estrogen receptor modulators (e.g., tamoxifen) and aromatase inhibitors (e.g., anastrozole, exemestane)—are associated with small negative effects in cognitive functioning, including verbal memory, verbal attention, and working memory; though, significant methodological heterogeneity limits the meaningfulness of results (Bakoyiannis et al., 2015).

Overall, treatment-related factors interact with cancer type to yield specific symptom profiles that significantly interfere with the quality of life of impacted women. In this chapter we review gender differences in prevalence, risk factors, symptom presentation, and cognitive profiles, as well as psychosocial considerations across non-CNS and CNS cancers (Table 8.1).

Non-CNS Cancer

As previously noted, cancers can be categorized into cancers that originate outside of the central nervous system (non-CNS cancers), those that originate within the CNS, and non-CNS cancers that metastasize into the brain. We will first focus specifically on non-CNS system cancers, including gender differences in prevalence and prognosis, unique risk factors for women that impact rates of developing these types of cancers, and lastly, differences in cognitive symptom presentation for

Table 8.1 Gender differences related to cancer treatment

Outcome Type	Differences Between Women vs. Men in Effects
Toxicity	– Higher rates in women vs. men – 5-fluorouracil and cisplatin cause more prolonged and burdensome symptoms for women, such as fatigue and leukopenia – Differences in chemotherapy metabolism; longer and less effective elimination; resulting in higher rates of cardiac risk factors/abnormalities – Cisplatin, doxorubicin, paclitaxel, and carboplatin, chemotherapies used to treat cancer primarily in women, can cause higher levels of toxicity/cognitive dysfunction
Cognitive Outcomes	– Chemotherapy-induced cognitive side effects can include impairment in immediate free recall, delayed memory, verbal memory, delayed recognition memory, selective attention, and attention capacity
Hormone-Related Treatment Outcomes	– Many chronic side effects, including hot flashes, fatigue, and mood lability – Potential to interact differently with women versus men across time due to natural hormonal changes (e.g., menopause)

women. We will follow the same format for CNS cancers and then for CNS metastasizing cancers.

Gender Differences in Prevalence and Prognosis for Non-CNS Cancers

Overall, certain cancer types have higher prevalence rates for women (Jackson et al., 2022). Within non-CNS cancers in particular, breast cancer is more likely to occur in women than men (Cook et al., 2009). In a study using gender-specific incidence rates and women-to-men incidence rate ratios (IRR), five cancer types emerged as having a higher incidence in women compared to men (Cook et al., 2009). These five cancer types are breast, peritoneum, omentum, mesentery, thyroid, gallbladder, and anus, anal canal, and anorectum (Cook et al., 2009). Notably, gynecological cancers (e.g., ovarian, uterine corpus, cervical, and endometrial) appear only in individuals born with primary female sex characteristics and additionally are shown to have high mortality rates (Dorak & Karpuzoglu, 2012; Kim et al., 2018).

Despite the overall prevalence rates not varying by race/ethnicity, women from racial or ethnic minority groups tend to be diagnosed in later disease states (Palmer Kelly et al., 2021). This finding is important as well as concerning because mortality rates are higher for women from multiple minority status groups despite having no difference in overall prevalence rates (Palmer Kelly et al., 2021).

Increased Risk Factors for Cognitive Sequelae in Women with Non-CNS Cancers

The broad picture of cognitive status during and following cancer treatment is complex and nuanced outside of gender differences. Adding to this complexity, there are several documented gender differences that can increase their risk in women for cognitive changes through direct and indirect means. That is, women may experience more frequent and severe symptoms despite undergoing the same treatment protocol as a male counterpart.

The Role of Hormone Therapy

In general, hormone-driven non-CNS cancer types are frequently treated with adjuvant hormone therapy during and after other types of intervention (Bao & Davidson, 2003; De Vos et al., 2012; Emons & Heyl, 2000). Hormone-sensitive cancer types are commonly treated with hormone therapies that influence the growth of hormone-sensitive cancers (e.g., estrogen receptor-positive breast cancer; Pan et al., 2018). The use of hormone therapies can induce significant side effects, including, but not limited to, fatigue, mood changes, and hot flashes (Pan et al., 2018). Such side effects can also further impact sleep quality.

Across the literature, hormone therapies for the treatment of cancer in women have a significant influence on cognitive symptoms and outcomes, and the influence of hormone therapy on women's health is widely documented. Though this significant impact is well documented, the nuances of the influence of hormone therapy on women's unique hormonal presentation are not well understood. For example, there is a need for more research to explicitly focus on the impact of menopause on cancer treatment (specifically hormone therapy) and related outcomes (VanLandingham et al., 2024).

The Role of Chemotherapy

There are documented gender differences in the metabolism of certain chemotherapies that are commonly used to treat non-CNS cancer types that are prevalent in women (Liaw, 2001; Sloan et al., 2002). Certain chemotherapies may cause higher levels of toxicity in women compared to men (e.g., 5-fluorouracil, cisplatin; Liaw, 2001; Sloan et al., 2002). Furthermore, elimination rates of chemotherapies are less effective and longer for women when compared to men for certain chemotherapies, which extend the length of time that women are exposed to toxins (e.g., paclitaxel; Joerger et al., 2006). Many chemotherapies used to treat cancers that disproportionately impact women, such as cisplatin, doxorubicin, paclitaxel, and carboplatin, have shown higher levels of neurotoxicity, meaning they can bypass the blood-brain barrier (Park et al., 2008; Taillibert et al., 2016). Sex differences in the metabolism of certain chemotherapies for women may lead to higher rates of cardiac abnormalities, resulting in ongoing cardiovascular risk factors (use of doxorubicin; Lipshultz et al., 1995).

Gender Differences in Cognitive Symptom Presentation for Non-CNS Cancers

Cancer and its treatments can have direct impacts on cognitive functioning, such as neural inflammation and neurotoxicity, as well as indirect impacts like stress, fatigue, and mood (Andreotti et al., 2015). Symptom presentation, both cognitive and physical, can also vary for women with cancer. Moreover, these differences can be further impacted by the onset of cancer and its treatment. For example, women are more likely to experience worse neurocognitive outcomes compared to men if they are pediatric survivors of non-CNS cancer (Kadan-Lottick et al., 2010). A review of adolescent and young adult cancer survivors documents a consistently high prevalence of cancer-related cognitive impairments, with female gender as a risk factor, in addition to higher doses of chemotherapy as well as several other comorbidities (e.g., fatigue, mental status, medical conditions [diabetes, asthma]; Vizer et al., 2022). However, before addressing specific risk factors for women in detail, a broad overview of the impact of non-CNS cancer and its treatment on cognitive functioning will be provided.

Findings from Neuroimaging

To understand the etiology of cognitive concerns for women undergoing cancer treatment, neural alterations must be included. A non-systematic review of neuroimaging studies of adult patients with non-CNS cancers found consistent evidence of reduced gray matter volume/density and reduced white matter integrity; findings were stronger in patients treated with chemotherapy (McDonald, 2021). Though many of the studies discussed had samples exclusively comprised of women with higher rates of breast cancer, no gender-related data or analyses were reported from studies reviewed. Research also documented alterations in white and gray matter structural network connectivity (McDonald, 2021). Overall, structural abnormalities were predominately located in frontal and temporal regions and associated with objective and subjective cognitive impairment (McDonald, 2021). These findings were consistently reported across a second, similar review, which highlights that structural abnormalities were greatest when patients with cancer who received treatment were compared to healthy controls, versus other patients with cancer (Amidi & Wu, 2019).

Domains of Cognitive Symptoms

A review of non-CNS patients across genders with cancer from 2004 to 2019 found frequent, mild-to-moderate cognitive dysfunction with a significant impact on quality of life (Cerulla Torrente et al., 2020). Though not gender-specific, the most reported cognitive symptoms for non-CNS cancer types include difficulties with working memory, attention, executive functioning, and information processing speed (Cerulla Torrente et al., 2020). Specific cognitive domains and the extent of reported impairment were variable, given mediating factors related to cancer, treatment, lifestyle, and health-related moderating factors (Cerulla Torrente et al., 2020).

Regarding cognitive symptoms in women specifically, women with breast cancer who have undergone chemotherapy, especially when in combination with adjuvant therapies, self-report significant subjective impact in the domains of attention, executive functioning, and memory; however, with mixed corroboration on objective testing results (i.e., in one study only a small subset with objective deficits overall and no differences between breast cancer survivors and healthy controls; Von Ah et al., 2022). Other studies document mixed objective impairment, when found, for verbal and visual memory impairment, attentional deficits, and broad executive functioning difficulties (Deprez et al., 2012; Ganz et al., 2013; Hsu et al., 2021; Jansen et al., 2011; Kjoe et al., 2023; Koppelmans et al., 2012; Kesler et al., 2013; Lange et al., 2023; Lejbak et al., 2010; Palmer et al., 2008; Reid-Arndt et al., 2010; Stewart et al., 2006; Tager et al., 2010; Van Dyk et al., 2018; Wefel et al., 2011; Yao et al., 2016).

Emergent literature documents gender differences in cognitive outcomes from both hormone therapies and chemotherapy reactions. Specifically, Chen and colleagues (2014, 2017) identified specific deficits in objective memory, information processing, and decision-making skills associated with Tamoxifen use, a selective estrogen receptor modulator used in breast cancer treatment, even without chemotherapy. Supporting the significant impact of hormone-targeting therapies, four additional studies (Deprez et al., 2012; Ganz et al., 2013; Hsu et al., 2021; Kjoe et al., 2023) corroborate these findings. Yin and colleagues (2023) also found that longer durations of endocrine therapies predicted greater cognitive impairment in women. However, the treatment status (e.g., current or post-endocrine therapy) was not reported. Conversely, Jenkins et al. (2008) found no cognitive impact in women experiencing natural menopause who were taking anastrozole, a nonsteroidal aromatase inhibitor that decreases estrogen in the body.

Overall, longitudinal outcomes appear to be reassuring, with women treated for breast cancer showing an objective recovery for processing speed and verbal memory 3–4 years post-treatment (Billiet et al., 2018). Moreover, in another study, women who received endocrine therapy within the first year of treatment did not display advanced cognitive changes compared to those who did not receive endocrine therapy (Van Dyk et al., 2019) (Table 8.2).

Table 8.2 Domains of cognitive symptoms in women with non-CNS cancer

Etiology of Cognitive Impairment	Cognitive Domain
Hormone therapies Tamoxifen	– Longer durations of endocrine therapies predict greater cognitive impairment – Deficits in objective memory, information processing, and decision-making skills
Chemotherapies	– Deficits, especially when in combination with adjuvant therapies – Self-report significant subjective impact in the domains of attention, executive functioning, and memory; however, with mixed corroboration on objective testing results – Mixed objective impairment, when found, for verbal and visual memory impairment, attentional deficits, and broad executive functioning difficulties

Cognitive Symptoms in Women with Gynecological Cancer

In general, women with gynecological cancer types are less frequently researched compared to women with primary breast cancer types, which impacts our ability to make generalizations about cognitive sequelae. Most research within gynecological cancer populations focuses on subjective cognitive status with less information on objectively assessed cognitive abilities.

Subjective cognitive complaints are common across gynecological cancer types, treatment protocols, and staging (Areklett et al., 2021; Correa et al., 2010; Correa et al., 2017; DeRosa et al., 2021; Stavraka et al., 2012). Regarding objective findings, there is evidence that women who undergo radiation and chemotherapy, as opposed to surgery alone, demonstrate higher rates of cognitive impairment (Areklett et al., 2021). In addition, about a fourth of women with a primary gynecological cancer self-report a progressive worsening of their cognitive abilities six months after the end of treatment, regardless of their treatment protocol (De Rosa et al., 2021); however, this is not consistent for most patients. Specifically, in a study by Correa and colleagues (2010), 28% of a sample of women with epithelial cancer displayed objective cognitive impairment in at least one domain of functioning 5–10 years post-treatment, with no group differences related to recurrence rates. Conversely, in a later study, they found that only a subgroup of patients (22%) produced test performance scores at or below one standard deviation of normative expectation with no difference when compared to healthy controls (Correa et al., 2017).

Health-Related Moderating Factors

Considering health-related moderating factors, a 2021 systematic review outlines the role of sleep as a part of the complicated etiology of cognitive concerns in women with non-CNS cancer (Duivon et al., 2022). Cancer type and treatment protocol, along with patient characteristics (e.g., medical comorbidities, age, and sex), can produce variations in such side effects, including whether the side effects are brief or become chronic (DeSantis et al., 2014). Chronic pain may also be important to consider when relevant.

CNS Primary Cancers

CNS tumors originate from the brain or spinal cord. For the purpose of this chapter, the review focuses on brain tumors, as spinal cord tumors are less common and published studies related to spinal cord tumors and cognitive sequelae are fewer. A primary brain tumor is a tumor that develops in the brain or in the nerves and tissues of the brain. This type of tumor can be either malignant or non-cancerous. Common brain tumors in adulthood include meningiomas, astrocytomas, oligodendrogliomas, and glioblastomas.

Gender Differences in Prevalence & Prognosis for CNS Primary Cancers

Prevalence rates of primary brain tumors have significantly increased in the past couple of decades, suggested to be due to technological advancements for the identification, diagnosis, and treatment of cancer (Gehrke et al., 2013). Research has consistently shown gender differences in the prevalence and outcomes (including progression and mortality) of brain tumors (Sun et al., 2015).

Although this chapter will not focus on pediatric populations, patients with pediatric onset cancers are important to consider when trying to understand primary brain tumors, given primary brain tumors are the most common tumors in children and, as such, they are widely studied. Pediatric medulloblastomas, ependymomas, and high-grade gliomas (Bosma et al., 2007) also typically occur less often in girls than boys, with a general incidence ratio of 1:2, which suggests there are specific mechanisms of tumor development influenced by gender that are prevalent even when sex hormones are at their lowest (infancy and toddlerhood; Sun et al., 2015). Specifically, Olsson et al. (2014) found that in pediatric brain tumor populations, girls typically presented with smaller brain tumors and decreased intracranial pressure when compared to boys, presumably due to smaller head circumferences.

Glioblastomas are well-documented as the most common malignant primary brain tumor in adulthood; it is also known to have the worst outcomes. In a systematic review on glioblastomas, women exhibited a lower incidence rate and better outcomes when compared with men; it is suggested that estrogen plays a protective role while androgen and testosterone play a pathological role in the development and effects of glioblastomas (Carrano et al., 2021). Another study showed gender differences in the survival rate of primary brain tumors, such that women have a significantly high survival rate at the 5-year mark across age groups and different cancer stages for glioblastomas (Tian et al., 2018).

On the other hand, meningiomas occur at significantly higher rates in women (more than twice as often) when compared to men; however, meningiomas tend to be low grade in women and malignant in men. Meningiomas appear to be related to hormones like estrogen and progesterone, making them uncommon in prepubescent ages. Alternatively, they are more likely to become aggressive if a woman is pregnant (Sun et al., 2015).

Gender Differences in Cognitive Symptom Presentation for CNS Primary Cancers

Cognitive symptom presentation may vary greatly depending on the tumor type, size, location, lateralization, and pathology. However, there are few studies looking at these differences outside of the context of treatment and intervention, so it is difficult to determine whether cognitive deficits are attributed to the tumor versus the potential side effects of treatment.

Cognitive Symptoms by CNS Primary Cancer

Patients with meningiomas typically present with cognitive deficits not specific to the meningioma itself (e.g., memory, attention, executive function) at the time of diagnosis, and although these symptoms significantly improve postoperatively, patients tend to still have cognitive impairments when compared to healthy controls (Meskal et al., 2016). Similarly, a study conducted in Romania showed that patients with glioblastomas had significantly more cognitive deficits (though as measured by cognitive screeners, i.e., the MoCA and CAMCOG, so specific cognitive domains were not adequately assessed) when compared to patients with diffuse astrocytomas; however, there were no significant cognitive differences between patients with meningioma versus diffuse astrocytomas (Bondari et al., 2017).

Cognitive Symptoms Associated with Treatment for CNS Primary Cancer

The most common forms of intervention for primary brain tumors and their most prominent side effects include biopsy, surgical resection, chemotherapy, radiation therapy, and antiseizure medications. It has long been thought that radiation was the leading cause of cognitive deficits in patients with brain tumors; however, studies have shown that the tumor itself contributes to cognitive deficits. For example, patients with diffuse tumors may have more global cognitive impairments as compared to those with a site-specific tumor, leading to localized deficits (Taphoorn & Klein, 2004). Other types of treatments (e.g., surgery, chemotherapy, and antiseizure medications) can also contribute to cognitive impairments.

A systematic review investigating neurocognitive functioning in post-treatment survivors of primary brain tumors (almost all were gliomas) as compared to a non-cancer control group was conducted; of note, though many samples were matched by gender, gender-related differences in cognitive impairment were not reported (Gehrke et al., 2013). Treatments in the four included studies (Bosma et al., 2008; Davidson et al., 2008; Godbout et al., 2005; Klein et al., 2002) included chemotherapy, radiation, antiseizure medications, and surgical intervention (e.g., biopsy, resection). Patients across studies were 6 to 36 post-intervention. Patients in the brain tumor survivor group presented with cognitive impairments in "working memory, cognitive control and flexibility, cognitive processing speed, visual searching, planning and foresight, and general attention" when compared to the non-cancer control group while matched via sex, age, and education (Gehrke et al., 2013). There was mixed evidence concerning performance on tests of executive function, motor speed, and learning and memory between groups. Unfortunately, however, because of the limited number of studies included in the review, small sample sizes, and lack of specificity on intervention types for patients, Gehrke et al. (2013) were unable to delineate differences on neurocognitive deficits between types of treatment. The following sections will provide specific cognitive findings for different intervention methods.

Cognitive Sequelae Related to Surgical Interventions for CNS Primary Cancers

Surgical interventions are often used for biopsy and resection of tumors, as well as for resection of neuroanatomical structures that produce intractable epileptic seizures (i.e., typically the tumor site). Preliminary studies demonstrate cognitive dysfunction across several tumor types (e.g., malignant gliomas, meningiomas, low-grade gliomas), with dominant hemisphere tumors placing patients at higher risk for cognitive dysfunction prior to surgery and those with non-dominant tumors more likely to recover cognitive functioning after surgery (Yoshii et al., 2008). Deep tumors (e.g., pituitary and pineal) have been particularly implicated in simple auditory attention tasks (i.e., Digits Forward; Goldstein et al., 2003), and high-grade gliomas have been associated with a decline in processing speed/efficiency and attention (Klein et al., 2012). Information on gender differences in cognitive functioning prior to or post-surgical intervention in these tumor populations is lacking, given that none of the aforementioned studies examined gender differences. It has been suggested that women may experience lower quality of life than men across timepoints (e.g., prior to surgery and post-operatively at 3 months and 1 year; Mainio et al., 2006).

Cognitive Sequelae Related to Cranial Radiation for CNS Cancers

Cranial radiation is a common treatment used to treat primary and metastatic brain tumors. One of the most researched negative treatment outcomes of cranial radiation is encephalopathy, or significant dysfunction in cognition, behavior, and mood (Crossen et al., 1994). It is imperative that treatment planning is individualized and sensitive to personal factors in order to prevent neurotoxicity; however, even with the appropriate dose for effective radiation, there is still a risk for negative cognitive outcomes (Dropcho, 1991). Related negative outcomes can include asymptomatic focal edema, focal necrosis, periventricular disease, necrotizing leukoencephalopathy, vascular disease, large artery injury, cerebral atrophy, and mineralizing microangiopathy (Abayomi, 2002; Valk & Dillon, 1991). Crossen et al.' (1994) review found that 213 out of 748 patients that received therapeutic cranial irradiation and 100 out of 368 patients that received prophylactic cranial irradiation developed encephalopathy; however, it was difficult to delineate distinct differences in outcomes as most patients had also received chemotherapy. Notably, brain radiation side effects that developed within months were likely to be transient and reversible, while delayed-onset symptoms (i.e., onset after 6 months of radiation) were thought to be irreversible and progressive (Turnquist et al., 2020).

With regard to diffuse infiltrative gliomas, as previously noted, a rare type of low-grade tumor only accounting for 5% of all primary brain tumors and 15% of all gliomas, there is evidence of cognitive deficits in patients who received radiation in all neurocognitive domains when compared to patients who did not receive radiation (Klein et al., 2012).

With regard to gender differences, research is limited and often specific to pediatric samples. For example, Willard et al. (2009) found that female survivors of pediatric brain tumors who did not receive cranial radiation therapy performed better and with fewer errors on facial expression recognition tasks when compared to female survivors who did receive radiation and male survivors who did and did not receive radiation. Although not specifically cranial radiation, in a study examining differences between women and men occupationally and accidentally exposed to ionizing radiation, women were more likely to have higher long-term radiosensitivity when compared to males receiving similar levels of ionizing radiation, and they were more likely to suffer and die from cancer caused by these forms of radiation (Narendran et al., 2019).

Cognitive Sequelae Related to Antiseizure Medications for CNS Cancers

As brain tumors and surgical interventions frequently cause seizures, patients are often treated with antiseizure medications. It is well-known that some antiseizure medications (ASMs) affect cognitive functioning, including attention, working memory, fluency, motor speed, language and comprehension, visuospatial functions, and memory (Eddy et al., 2011). Few studies showed potential beneficial effects of ASMs on certain aspects of cognition, including fluency and processing speed; however, it is difficult to determine whether these positive changes were merely the result of decreased seizure frequency and severity (Eddy et al., 2011). Other studies note that some ASMs have an overall limited impact on cognitive functioning in select populations (e.g., valproate, carbamazepine, and phenytoin with children); however, overall that is likely the most important factor impacting cognition with relation to ASMs is becoming seizure-free (Aldenkamp et al., 1993; Hirsch et al., 2003). For a full overview of gender-related considerations in the use of ASMs, please see Chap. 7 (Epilepsy).

Non-CNS Cancer + CNS Metastases

Information described above for non-CNS cancer and primary brain tumor also apply to individuals with non-CNS cancer that metastasized to the brain. The section below highlights the information specific to individuals with brain metastasis (BM), also known as secondary brain tumor.

Gender Differences in Prevalence and Incidence for Non-CNS Cancer + CNS Metastases

In 2018, over 600,000 individuals in the United States were living with metastatic cancer of the breast, prostate, lung, colorectal, bladder, and skin (melanoma), which are common causes of BM (Gallicchio et al., 2022). Despite metastatic brain tumors being the most common type of CNS tumor, there is no national systematic reporting mechanism (Sacks & Rahman, 2020). It is estimated that metastatic brain tumors affect about 20% of patients with cancer (Achrol et al., 2019). Estimated incidence of brain metastases in the United States ranged from 30,000 to 200,000 (e.g., Amsbaugh & Kim, 2023; Barnholtz-Sloan et al., 2004; Nathoo et al., 2004; Nayak et al., 2012). The number of individuals with metastatic brain tumors is expected to increase given improved treatment outcomes and earlier diagnosis with more sensitive neuroimaging tools.

BMs are often diagnosed following the diagnosis of primary cancer. Synchronous BM is defined as having BM within two months of the primary cancer diagnosis. Metachronous BM indicates when BM develops more than 2 months following the primary cancer diagnosis. Precocious BM is when BM is identified prior to the diagnosis of primary cancer (Shibahara et al., 2018). While data from synchronous BM are most frequently reported in the literature, a recent study showed that individuals with metachronous BM had longer survival than synchronous BM (Jiang et al., 2023). Similar differences in prevalence rates by gender are seen in adults with BM as in other CNS cancers, where women have lower incidence rates than men in almost all cancer types (Sun et al., 2015). However, data is mixed, as a recent study indicated middle-aged women have been found to be at a higher risk of BM but better survival in a study that only included individuals with synchronous BM (Che et al., 2022).

Gender Differences in Prognosis for Non-CNS Cancer + CNS Metastases

Long-term prognosis of BM is poor (Hall et al., 2000); however, there appear to be gender differences in prognosis. The mean survival time in individuals with BM who underwent surgery as the first treatment was significantly longer for women (19.2 months) than men (12.9 months, $p = 0.008$), with gender being the only significant variable affecting survival when also considering age, histological type, location, functional status (i.e., Karnofsky score), chemotherapy, and radiotherapy (Rotta et al., 2018). This was further supported in a study of 127 Turkish breast cancer patients with BM; the median age of BM occurrence was 50.9, with a median time of 29.7 months between breast cancer diagnosis to BM and a median survival time of 7.9 months following BM (Simsek et al., 2022). Prognosis was found to be significantly more favorable in younger women (i.e., less than 40 years old) than for those who were older (i.e., > 40 years old) as well as for those whose breast cancer first metastasized to the brain when compared to those who had brain metastases later (Mustillo et al., 2020).

While lung cancer BM is most common in men, breast cancer BM is most common in women (Achrol et al., 2019; Lin et al., 2004). It is estimated that roughly 20% of BMs occur in women with primary HER2-positive breast cancer (Lin & Winer, 2007). In fact, CNS involvement was identified in the majority of patients with HER-2 positive metastatic breast cancer in the first 3 years following metastatic breast cancer (Bendell et al., 2003). The mean survival from the diagnosis of BM was 13 months. A targeted treatment, adding tucatinib to the standard treatment of trastuzumab and capecitabine, has been approved for treatment of HER-2-based breast cancer BM and was shown to improve median overall survival to 21.9 months (Murthy et al., 2020). Those with triple-negative breast cancer tumors (i.e., estrogen receptor—negative, progesterone receptor—negative, and normal HER-2 levels) have an increased risk of BM (Achrol et al., 2019). Triple-negative breast cancer BM are likely to have a more cystic and necrotic appearance on MRI than other types (Yeh et al., 2015). In comparison to those with moderately abundant necrosis, individuals with highly abundant and sparse necrosis have been shown to be associated with poorer prognosis (Yoo et al., 2022).

While BM is rare in individuals with primary gynecological cancer, the outcome is notably poor. For example, Takeshita et al. (2017) reported the incidence of brain metastasis in a sample of over 2800 patients was 1.7%, and the median survival rate following diagnosis of metastasis was 20 weeks. In a sample of 42 patients with primary gynecological cancer with neuroimaging-confirmed brain metastasis, the interval between the time of primary cancer diagnosis and metastatic CNS diagnosis ranged from 0 to 107.8 months (median age of BM diagnosis = 33; Zhang et al., 2019). The median age of diagnosis of BM due to gestational trophoblastic disease was youngest (Zhang et al., 2019), although it has been reported that BM develops earlier in patients with endometrial cancer than in those with ovarian cancer in a study that included only these two types of primary gynecological cancer (Karpathiou et al., 2022).

When evaluating different CNS involvements, meningeal involvement was significantly higher in individuals with cervical cancer; otherwise, there were no significant differences in brain region involvement across different types of gynecological cancers (Zhang et al., 2019). In the same study, BM was most identified in the frontal lobe, with the majority of patients in the sample having multiple brain lesions. Notably, due to low base rates of BM in primary gynecological cancers, patients are not routinely screened for BM.

Gender Differences in Cognitive Symptoms for Non-CNS Cancer + CNS Metastases

Whole brain radiation therapy (WBRT) and stereotactic radiosurgery (SRS) can be used for treatment of BM. While these techniques decrease the risk for BM recurrence, WBRT alone or combined with SRS has been shown to be associated with increased cognitive decline (see Liu et al., 2019 for a review). Hippocampal-sparing WBRT with the use of memantine for individuals without hippocampal BM has the potential as an alternative option to preserve cognitive abilities than WBRT (Brown et al., 2020). Late effects of whole brain radiation are more chronic and permanent. Less is known regarding potential gender differences in treatment outcome or associated cognitive decline.

It is not uncommon for individuals with BM to experience a significant number of symptoms that can be due to cancer and its related treatments. In a heterogeneous group of patients with BM, the four highest scored symptoms were fatigue, poor sense of well-being, anxiety, and drowsiness and poor appetite (Chow et al., 2008), with fatigue, nausea, appetite loss, coordination, concentration, balance, and depression found to be significantly associated with shorter prognosis (Wong et al., 2016). While there have been no reported gender differences in the reporting of symptoms at baseline, women reported worsening of symptoms following whole brain radiation (Harris et al., 2006).

Cognitive functioning can vary in individuals with BM depending on the brain region(s) involved, the characteristics of the metastatic brain tumors, the effects of cancer-related treatment, and psychosocial factors. There is evidence that BM distribution differs by primary cancer type (Schroeder et al., 2020). In a study of individuals with newly diagnosed BM, many of the participants had cognitive impairments at baseline, with primarily retrieval-based memory difficulties

(Gerstenecker et al., 2014). Individuals with BM were also found to perform poorer than healthy controls on measures of attention, verbal fluency, and executive functioning. Slow processing speed was only found in about 15% of the individuals with BM (Schatz et al., 2000). To our knowledge, potential gender differences in cognitive performance have not been reported.

Psychosocial Factors and Quality of Life for Women Impacted by Cancer Diagnoses

VanLandingham et al. (2024) eloquently summarize the complicated web of intersecting psychosocial factors that affect outcomes for women affected by cancer, in that "women may experience unique challenges related to self-identity, fertility, psychosocial stress, and alterations in hormone levels (e.g., forced menopause, irregular menstruation)" (p. 15). These intersecting psychosocial factors all can intersect and compound to impact women's quality of life (Benedict et al., 2018). Giving higher rates of varying familial-related roles (e.g., primary caregiver and caregiver of elderly parents), women may also experience compounding stress related to the management of continuous social responsibilities.

Notably, these aforementioned factors are not static and can interact differently at different strengths across time. Regarding time out from treatment, research documents a significant cumulative impact from cancer treatment and psychosocial stressors that persists following active treatment phases. Specifically, women report greater emotional distress in the 2–5 years after treatment when compared to the first 1–2 years after treatment (Holzner et al., 2001). This highlights the importance of following women in long-term recovery clinics even after remission to monitor and support mental health and overall quality of life.

Limitations to Understanding Cognitive Sequelae in Women with Cancer

When trying to understand cognitive sequelae of various cancer types for women, there is significant heterogeneity in cancer type, treatment time, inclusion/exclusion criteria of studies, cognitive outcomes assessed, and cognitive assessments utilized. Heterogeneity in treatment protocols and individual differences makes predicting outcomes challenging, but there is also evidence that specific treatments add an additional burden for women's cognitive status. Compounding the issue, there is notable variability in when patients are assessed (e.g., how long post-surgery/treatment vs. when we may expect stabilization of cognitive symptoms) that makes it increasingly difficult to generalize results between studies (e.g., in Bondari et al. (2017), it is unclear when the assessments even took place). In addition, the dearth of large-scale and longitudinal studies limits our understanding of cognitive sequelae for women, especially as outcomes may be variable over time (e.g., more acute post-treatment, later interacting with hormonal factors depending on women's life stage).

Limitations to Understanding Cognitive Sequelae in Women with CNS Cancer

There are increasing difficulties in trying to understand cognitive sequelae specifically of CNS cancer for women. Across this specific area of research, sample sizes are very small, especially in cognitive outcomes post-brain tumor with treatment (Gehrke et al., 2013). For example, the neurocognitive deficits in the brain tumor post-treatment review described that given strict search criteria, as well as variations in chemotherapy dose, radiation dose, and use and dose of anti-seizure medication across studies, it is hard to draw consistent conclusions—and only four studies were included in this review ultimately (Gehrke et al., 2013). In addition, of the few studies that do exist, not all break down analysis by gender; rather, they focus on differences in tumor type among CNS cancers (e.g., Bondari et al., 2017), making it increasingly difficult to understand potential gender differences.

Research Takeaways

- Women can be uniquely affected by treatment-related side effects across cancer types.
- In non-CNS cancers, women may experience more frequent and severe symptoms (including cognitive sequelae) despite undergoing the same treatment protocol as a male counterpart.
- Research has consistently shown gender differences in the prevalence and outcomes (including progression and mortality) of brain tumors (Sun et al., 2015).
- Long-term prognosis of brain metastasis is poor (Hall et al., 2000); however, there appear to be gender differences in prognosis, with more favorable outcomes for women compared to men. Less is known regarding potential gender differences in treatment outcome or associated cognitive decline.
- There are major limitations within the overall cancer research that impact both the reliability and generalizability of these findings (Jansen et al., 2007).
- Though there is a general bias in cancer-related research towards breast cancer, across cancer types, gender differences are under-reported or under-studied (Klein & Morgan, 2020).
- Within cancers that impact women at higher prevalence rates, the focus on breast cancer creates a major limitation in our understanding of gynecological cancer outcomes.

- Small sample sizes in CNS cancer studies in women (i.e., brain tumor studies) also limit our conceptualization of cognitive outcomes in this population. Compounding this issue, recruitment of women (as well as sexual and gender minority patients) in clinical trials is not equitable across cancer types, with some cancer types documenting lower recruitment rates, particularly of women (Duma et al., 2018).
- Even when women are adequately recruited into clinical trials and research, there is a notable dearth of research for women diagnosed with stage IV (i.e., terminal) variants of cancer (VanLandingham et al., 2024).
- Heterogeneity in patient populations and study designs limits the generalizability of results. Future studies should address these problems, including significant heterogeneity in cancer type, treatment time, inclusion/exclusion criteria of studies, cognitive outcomes assessed, cognitive assessments utilized, and timing of cognitive assessments in study designs.
- Neuropsychologists remain uniquely positioned to help in the design of clinical trials to advocate for improvements in study designs assessing cognitive outcomes. Such trials can address underrepresentation issues, including underrepresentation of racial/ethnic minority women, unequal samples of women with stage IV cancer types, and small sample sizes of women with CNS cancer.
- There is insufficient research on the cognitive outcomes of women diagnosed with gynecological cancers, which warrants further exploration.
- Across cancer types, more research is needed that explicitly focuses on the impact of menopause among women (VanLandingham et al., 2024).
- There is a lack of research on gender non-binary individuals in cancer research, including more specifically the exploration of the potential impact of hormonal therapies for gender transition when in close temporal proximity to hormonal treatments for cancer.

Clinical Takeaways

- Clinicians need to be aware of the "unique challenges these patients may face related to self-identity, fertility, psychosocial stress, and alterations in hormone levels (e.g., forced menopause, irregular menstruation)" (p. 15, VanLandingham et al., 2024), all of which have the potential to impact their quality of life (Benedict et al., 2018). At the same time, these variables should be considered on an individual basis, as patient concern about fertility or caregiving will differ between women.
- Given the potential of cumulative impact from cancer treatment and psychosocial stress that may persist following active treatment phases, women are increasingly important to follow in long-term recovery clinics even after remission, to monitor and support both mental health as well as overall quality of life (see Hines et al., 2014).

- In addition to the documented potential benefits of psychosocial interventions for this population, outpatient cognitive rehabilitation shows strong evidence for addressing patients' cognitive concerns post-acute cancer treatments (see Zeng et al., 2016 for a meta-analysis).

References

Abayomi, O. K. (2002). Pathogenesis of cognitive decline following therapeutic irradiation for head and neck tumors. *Acta Oncologica, 41*(4), 346–351.

Achrol, A. S., Rennert, R. C., Anders, C., Soffietti, R., Ahluwalia, M. S., Nayak, L., et al. (2019). Brain metastases. *Nature Reviews, 5*(5), 1–26. https://doi.org/10.1038/s41572-018-0055-y

Aldenkamp, A. P., Alpherts, W. C. J., Blennow, G., Elmqvist, D., Heijbel, J., Nilsson, H. L., et al. (1993). Withdrawal of antiepileptic medication in children–effects on cognitive function: The Multicenter Holmfrid Study. *Neurology, 43*(1_part_1), 41–41.

American Cancer Society (ACS). (n.d.). *Treatment types*. https://www.cancer.org/cancer/managing-cancer/treatment-types.html

Amidi, A., & Wu, L. M. (2019). Structural brain alterations following adult non-CNS cancers: A systematic review of the neuroimaging literature. *Acta Oncologica, 58*(5), 522–536.

Amsbaugh, M. J., & Kim, C. S. (2023, April 3). Brain metastasis. https://www.ncbi.nlm.nih.gov/books/NBK470246/#:~:text=Brain%20metastases%20are%20a%20common,cancer%20will%20develop%20brain%20metastases

Andreotti, C., Root, J. C., Ahles, T. A., McEwen, B. S., & Compas, B. E. (2015). Cancer, coping, and cognition: A model for the role of stress reactivity in cancer-related cognitive decline. *Psycho-Oncology, 24*(6), 617–623. https://doi.org/10.1002/pon.3683

Areklett, E. W., Fagereng, E., Bruheim, K., Andersson, S., & Lindemann, K. (2021). Self-reported cognitive impairment in cervical cancer survivors: A cross-sectional study. *Psycho-Oncology*. https://doi.org/10.1002/pon.5818

Bao, T., & Davidson, N. E. (2003). Adjuvant hormonal therapy for premenopausal women with breast cancer. *Clinical Cancer Research, 9*, 486–494. https://doi.org/10.1186/bcr1830

Barnholtz-Sloan, J. S., Sloan, A. E., Davis, F. G., Vigneau, F. D., Lai, P., & Sawaya, R. E. (2004). Incidence proportions of brain metastases in patients diagnosed (1973 to 2001) in the Metropolitan Detroit Cancer Surveillance System. *Neurooncology, 22*(14), 2865–2872. https://doi.org/10.1200/JCO.2004.12.14

Bendell, J. C., Domchek, S. M., Burstein, H. J., Harris, L., Younger, J., Kuter, I., et al. (2003). Central nervous system metastases in women who receive trastuzumab-based therapy for metastatic breast carcinoma. *Cancer, 97*(12), 2972–2977.

Bender, C. M., & Thelen, B. D. (2013, November). Cancer and cognitive changes: The complexity of the problem. In *Seminars in Oncology Nursing* (Vol. 29, No. 4, pp. 232–237). WB Saunders.

Benedict, C., Thom, B., Friedman, D. N., Pottenger, E., Raghunathan, N., & Kelvin, J. F. (2018). Fertility information needs and concerns post-treatment contribute to lowered quality of life among young adult female cancer survivors. *Supportive Care in Cancer, 26*, 2209–2215. https://doi.org/10.1007/s00520-017-4006-z

Billiet, T., Emsell, L., Vandenbulcke, M., Peeters, R., Christiaens, D., Leemans, A., Van Hecke, W., Smeets, A., Amant, F., Sunaert, S., & Deprez, S. (2018). Recovery from chemotherapy-induced white matter changes in young breast cancer survivors?. *Brain Imaging and Behavior, 12*(1), 64–77. https://doi.org/10.1007/s11682-016-9665-8

Bondari, S., Bondari, D., Pîrşcoveanu, M., Moroşanu, D. V., Muşetescu, A. E., Valerica, T., & Pîrşcoveanu, D. F. V. (2017). Study on cognitive decline in patients diagnosed with brain tumors. *Romanian Journal of Morphology & Embryology, 58*(4), 1185–1192.

Bosma, I., Douw, L., Bartolomei, F., Heimans, J. J., van Dijk, B. W., Postma, T. J., et al. (2008). Synchronized brain activity and neurocognitive function in patients with low-grade glioma: A magnetoencephalography study. *Neuro-oncology, 10*(5), 734–744.

Bosma, I., Vos, M. J., Heimans, J. J., Taphoorn, M. J., Aaronson, N. K., Postma, T. J., et al. (2007). The course of neurocognitive functioning in high-grade glioma patients. *Neuro-oncology, 9*(1), 53–62.

Brown, P. D., Gondi, V., Pugh, S., Tome, W. A., Wefel, J. S., Armstrong, T. S., et al. (2020). Hippocampal avoidance during whole-brain radiotherapy plus memantine for patients with brain metastases: Phase III Trial ORG Oncology CC001. *Journal of Clinical Oncology, 38*(10), 1019–1029.

Carrano, A., Juarez, J. J., Incontri, D., Ibarra, A., & Cazares, H. G. (2021). Sex-specific differences in glioblastoma. *Cells, 10*(7), 1783.

Cerulla Torrente, N., Navarro Pastor, J. B., & de la Osa Chaparro, N. (2020). Systematic review of cognitive sequelae of non-central nervous system cancer and cancer therapy. *Journal of Cancer Survivorship, 14*(4), 464–482.

Che, W., Wang, Y., Wang, X., & Lyu, J. (2022). Midlife brain metastases in the United States: Is male at risk? *Cancer Medicine, 11*(4), 1202–1216. https://doi.org/10.1002/cam4.4499

Chen, X., Li, J., Chen, J., Li, D., Ye, R., Zhang, J., Zhu, C., Tian, Y., & Wang, K. (2014). Decision-making impairments in breast cancer patients treated with tamoxifen. *Hormones and Behavior, 66*(2), 449–456. https://doi.org/10.1016/j.yhbeh.2014.07.005

Chen, X., He, X., Tao, L., Li, J., Wu, J., Zhu, C., ... & Wang, K. (2017). The working memory and dorsolateral prefrontal-hippocampal functional connectivity changes in long-term survival breast cancer patients treated with tamoxifen. *International Journal of Neuropsychopharmacology, 20*(5), 374–382.

Chow, E., Fan, G., Hadi, S., Wong, J., Kirou-Mauro, A., & Filipczak, L. (2008). Symptom clusters in cancer patients with brain metastases. *Clinical Oncology, 20*(1), 76–82.

Cook, M. B., Dawsey, S. M., Freedman, N. D., Inskip, P. D., Wichner, S. M., Quraishi, S. M., et al. (2009). Sex disparities in cancer incidence by period and age. *Cancer Epidemiology Biomarkers & Prevention, 18*(4), 1174–1182.

Correa, D. D., Zhou, Q., Thaler, H. T., Maziarz, M., Hurley, K., & Hensley, M. L. (2010). Cognitive functions in long-term survivors of ovarian cancer. *Gynecologic Oncology, 119*(2), 366–369. https://doi.org/10.1016/j.ygyno.2010.06.02

Correa, D. D., Root, J. C., Kryza-Lacombe, M., Mehta, M., Karimi, S., Hensley, M. L., & Relkin, N. (2017). Brain structure and function in patients with ovarian cancer treated with first-line chemotherapy: A pilot study. *Brain Imaging and Behavior, 11*(6), 1652–1663. https://doi.org/10.1007/s11682-016-9608-4

Crossen, J. R., Garwood, D., Glatstein, E., & Neuwelt, E. A. (1994). Neurobehavioral sequelae of cranial irradiation in adults: A review of radiation-induced encephalopathy. *Journal of Clinical Oncology, 12*(3), 627–642.

Davidson, P. S., Gao, F. Q., Mason, W. P., Winocur, G., & Anderson, N. D. (2008). Verbal fluency, Trail Making, and Wisconsin Card Sorting Test performance following right frontal lobe tumor resection. *Journal of Clinical and Experimental Neuropsychology, 30*(1), 18–32.

De Courcy, L., Bezak, E., & Marcu, L. G. (2020). Gender-dependent radiotherapy: The next step in personalised medicine? *Critical Reviews in Oncology/Hematology, 147*, 102881.

Deprez, S., Amant, F., Smeets, A., Peeters, R., Leemans, A., Van Hecke, W., Verhoeven, J. S., Christiaens, M. R., Vandenberghe, J., Vandenbulcke, M., & Sunaert, S. (2012). Longitudinal assessment of chemotherapy-induced structural changes in cerebral white matter and its correlation with impaired cognitive functioning. *Journal of Clinical Oncology: Official journal of the American Society of Clinical Oncology, 30*(3), 274–281. https://doi.org/10.1200/JCO.2011.36.8571

De Rosa, N., Della Corte, L., Giannattasio, A., Giampaolino, P., Di Carlo, C., & Bifulco, G. (2021). Cancer-related cognitive impairment (CRCI), depression and quality of life in gynecological cancer patients: A prospective study. *Archives of Gynecology and Obstetrics, 303*, 1581–1588.

De Vos, F. Y. F. L., van Laarhoven, H. W. M., Laven, J. S. E., Themmen, A. P. N., Beex, L. V. A. M., Sweep, C. G. J., Seynaeve, C., & Jager, A. (2012). Menopausal status and adjuvant hormonal therapy for breast cancer patients: A practical guideline. *Critical Reviews in Oncology/Hematology, 84*(2), 252–260. https://doi.org/10.1016/j.critrevonc.2012.06.005

DeSantis, C. E., Lin, C. C., Mariotto, A. B., Siegel, R. L., Stein, K. D., Kramer, J. L., et al. (2014). Cancer treatment and survivorship statistics, 2014. *A Cancer Journal for Clinicians, 64*(4), 252–271.

Dorak, M. T., & Karpuzoglu, E. (2012). Gender differences in cancer susceptibility: An inadequately addressed issue. *Frontiers in Genetics, 3*(268), 1–11. https://doi.org/10.3389/fgene.2012.00268

Dos Santos, M., Hardy-Léger, I., Rigal, O., Licaj, I., Dauchy, S., Levy, C., et al. (2020). Cognitive rehabilitation program to improve cognition of cancer patients treated with chemotherapy: A 3-arm randomized trial. *Cancer, 126*(24), 5328–5336. https://doi.org/10.1002/cncr.33186

Dropcho, E. J. (1991). Central nervous system injury by therapeutic irradiation. *Neurologic Clinics, 9*(4), 969–988.

Duivon, M., Giffard, B., Desgranges, B., & Perrier, J. (2022). Are sleep complaints related to cognitive functioning in non-central nervous system cancer? A systematic review. *Neuropsychology Review, 32*(3), 483–505.

Duma, N., Vera Aguilera, J., Paludo, J., Haddox, C. L., Gonzalez Velez, M., Wang, Y., et al. (2018). Representation of minorities and women in oncology clinical trials: Review of the past 14 years. *Journal of Oncology Practice, 14*(1), e1–e10.

Eddy, C., Rickards, H., & Cavanna, A. (2011). The cognitive impact of antiepileptic drugs. *Therapeutic Advances in Neurological Disorders, 4*(6), 385–407. https://doi.org/10.1177/1756285611417920

Emons, G., & Heyl, W. (2000). Hormonal treatment of endometrial cancer. *Journal of Cancer Research and Clinical Oncology, 126*(11), 619–623. https://doi.org/10.1007/pl00008473

Flores, V. A., Pal, L., & Manson, J. E. (2021). Hormone therapy in menopause: Concepts, controversies, and approach to treatment. *Endocrine Reviews, 42*(6), 720–752.

Gallicchio, L., Devasia, T. P., Tonorezos, E., Mollica, M., & Mariotto, A. (2022). Estimation of the number of individuals living with metastatic cancer in the United States. *Journal of National Cancer Institute, 114*(11), djac 158. https://doi.org/10.1093/jnci/djac158

Ganz, P. A., Kwan, L., Castellon, S. A., Oppenheim, A., Bower, J. E., Silverman, D. H. S., Cole, S. W., Irwin, M. R., Ancoli-Israel, S., & Belin, T. R. (2013). Cognitive complaints after breast cancer treatments: Examining the relationship with neuropsychological test performance. *Journal of the National Cancer Institute, 105*(11), 791–801. https://doi.org/10.1093/jnci/djt073

Gehrke, A. K., Baisley, M. C., Sonck, A. L., Wronski, S. L., & Feuerstein, M. (2013). Neurocognitive deficits following primary brain tumor treatment: Systematic review of a decade of comparative studies. *Journal of Neuro-Oncology, 115*, 135–142.

Gerstenecker, A., Nabors, L. B., Meneses, K., Fiveash, J. B., Marson, D. C., Cutter, G., Martin, R. C., Meyers, C. A., & Triebel, K. L. (2014). Cognition in patients with newly diagnosed brain metastasis: profiles and implications. *Journal of Neurooncology, 20*, 179–185.

Godbout, L., Grenier, M. C., Braun, C. M. J., & Gagnon, S. (2005). Cognitive structure of executive deficits in patients with frontal lesions performing activities of daily living. *Brain Injury, 19*(5), 337–348.

Goldstein, B., Armstrong, C. L., John, C., & Tallent, E. M. (2003). Attention in adult intracranial tumors patients. *Journal of Clinical and Experimental Neuropsychology, 25*(1), 66–78.

Hall, W. A., Djalilian, H. R., Nussbaum, E. S., & Cho, K. H. (2000). Long-term survival with metastatic cancer to the brain. *Medical Oncology, 17*, 279–286.

Harris, K., Chow, E., Davis, L., Chiu, H. H., Bradley, N. M. E., Doyle, M., Li, K., Sinclair, E., Barnes, E. A., & Danjoux, C. (2006). Gender differences in patient-rated symptoms following whole brain radiotherapy for brain metastases. *Journal of Cancer Pain & Symptom Palliation, 2*(1), 11–15. https://doi.org/10.3109/J427v02n01_03

Hines, S., Ramis, M. A., Pike, S., & Chang, A. M. (2014). The effectiveness of psychosocial interventions for cognitive dysfunction in cancer patients who have received chemotherapy: A systematic review. *Worldviews on Evidence-Based Nursing, 11*(3), 187–193.

Hirsch, E., Schmitz, B., & Carreno, M. (2003). Epilepsy, antiepileptic drugs (AEDs) and cognition. *Acta Neurologica Scandinavica, 108*, 23–32.

Holzner, B., Kemmler, G., Kopp, M., Moschen, R., Schweigkofler, H. R., Du Nser, M., Margreiter, R., Fleischhacker, W. W., & Sperner-Unterweger, B. (2001). Quality of life in breast cancer patients—Not enough attention for long-term survivors? *Psychosomatics, 42*(2), 117–123. https://doi.org/10.1176/appi.psy.42.2.117

Hsu, Y. H., Chen, V. C. H., Hsieh, C. C., Weng, Y. P., Hsu, Y. T., Hsiao, H. P., Wang, W. K., Chen, H. M., Weng, J. C., Wu, S. I., & Gossop, M. (2021). Subjective and objective cognitive functioning among patients with breast cancer: Effects of chemotherapy and mood symptoms. *Breast Cancer, 28*, 236–245. https://doi.org/10.1007/s12282-020-01168-y

Islami, F., Siegel, R. L., & Jemal, A. (2020). The changing landscape of cancer in the USA—opportunities for advancing prevention and treatment. *Nature Reviews Clinical Oncology, 17*(10), 631–649.

Jackson, S. S., Marks, M. A., Katki, H. A., Cook, M. B., Hyun, N., Freedman, N. D., et al. (2022). Sex disparities in the incidence of 21 cancer types: Quantification of the contribution of risk factors. *Cancer, 128*(19), 3531–3540.

Jackson, S. S., Patel, S., & Parker, K. (2023). Cancer disparities among sexual and gender minority populations. *Journal of the National Medical Association, 115*(2), S32–S37.

Jansen, C. E., Miaskowski, C. A., Dodd, M. J., & Dowling, G. A. (2007). A meta-analysis of the sensitivity of various neuropsychological tests used to detect chemotherapy-induced cognitive impairment in patients with breast cancer. *Oncology Nursing Forum, 34*(5), 997–1005. https://doi.org/10.1188/07.ONF.997-1005

Jansen, C. E., Cooper, B. A., Dodd, M. J., & Miaskowski, C. A. (2011). A prospective longitudinal study of chemotherapy-induced cognitive changes in breast cancer patients. Supportive care in cancer. *Official Journal of the Multinational Association of Supportive Care in Cancer, 19*(10), 1647–1656. https://doi.org/10.1007/s00520-010-0997-4

Jemal, A., Ward, E., & Thun, M. (2010). Declining death rates reflect progress against cancer. *PloS One, 5*(3), e9584.

Jiang, K., Parker, M., Materi, J., Azad, T. D., Kamson, D. O., Kleinberg, L., Ye, X., Rincon-Torroella, J., & Bettegowda, C. (2023). Epidemiology and survival outcomes of synchronous and metachronous brain metastases: A retrospective population-based study. *Neurosurgery Focus, 55*(2), 1–9. https://doi.org/10.3171/2023.5.FOCUS23212

Jenkins, V. A., Ambroisine, L. M., Atkins, L., Cuzick, J., Howell, A., & Fallowfield, L. J. (2008). Effects of anastrozole on cognitive performance in postmenopausal women: a randomised, double-blind chemoprevention trial (IBIS II). *The Lancet. Oncology, 9*(10), 953–961. https://doi.org/10.1016/S1470-2045(08)70207-9

Joerger, M., Huitema, A. D., van den Bongard, D. H., Schellens, J. H., & Beijnen, J. H. (2006). Quantitative effect of gender, age, liver function, and body size on the population pharmacokinetics of paclitaxel in patients with solid tumors. *Clinical Cancer Research, 12*(7), 2150–2157. https://doi.org/10.1158/1078-0432.CCR-05-2069

Kadan-Lottick, N. S., Zeltzer, L. K., Liu, Q., Yasui, Y., Ellenberg, L., Gioia, G., et al. (2010). Neurocognitive functioning in adult survivors of childhood non-central nervous system cancers. *JNCI: Journal of the National Cancer Institute, 102*(12), 881–893.

Karpathiou, G., Camy, F., Chauleur, C., Dridi, M., Dal Col, P., & Peoc'h, M. (2022). Brain metastases from gynecologic malignancies. *Medicina (Kaunas), 58*(4), 548. https://doi.org/10.3390/medicina58040548

Kesler, S., Janelsins, M., Koovakkattu, D., Palesh, O., Mustian, K., Morrow, G., & Dhabhar, F. S. (2013). Reduced hippocampal volume and verbal memory performance associated with interleukin-6 and tumor necrosis factor-alpha levels in chemotherapy-treated breast cancer survivors. *Brain, Behavior, and Immunity, 30*, S109–S116. https://doi.org/10.1016/j.bbi.2012.05.017

Kim, H. I., Lim, H., & Moon, A. (2018). Sex differences in cancer: Epidemiology, genetics and therapy. *Biomolecules & Therapeutics, 26*(4), 335–342. https://doi.org/10.4062/biomolther.2018.103

Kjoe, P. R., Kieffer, J. M., Small, B. J., Boogerd, W., Schilder, C. M., van der Wall, E., ... & Schagen, S. B. (2023). Effects of tamoxifen and exemestane on cognitive function in postmenopausal patients with breast cancer. *JNCI Cancer Spectrum, 7*(2), https://doi.org/10.1093/jncics/pkad022

Klein, M., Duffau, H., & De Witt Hamer, P. C. (2012). Cognition and resective surgery for diffuse infiltrative glioma: An overview. *Journal of Neuro-Oncology, 108*, 309–318.

Klein, M., Heimans, J. J., Aaronson, N. K., Van Der Ploeg, H. M., Grit, J., Muller, M., et al. (2002). Effect of radiotherapy and other treatment-related factors on mid-term to long-term cognitive sequelae in low-grade gliomas: A comparative study. *The Lancet, 360*(9343), 1361–1368.

Klein, S., & Morgan, S. (2020). The impact of sex and gender on immunotherapy outcomes. *Biology of Sex Differences, 11*(24), 1–10. https://doi.org/10.1186/s13293-020-00301-y

Koppelmans, V., Breteler, M., Boogerd, W., Seynaeve, C., Gundy, C., & Schagen, S. (2012). Neuropsychological performance in survivors of breast cancer more than 20 years after adjuvant chemotherapy. *Journal of Clinical Oncology, 30*(10), 1080–1086. https://doi.org/10.1200/JCO.2011.37.0189

Lange, M., Joly, F., Vardy, J., Ahles, T., Dubois, M., Tron, L., et al. (2019). Cancer-related cognitive impairment: An update on state of the art, detection, and management strategies in cancer survivors. *Annals of Oncology, 30*(12), 1925–1940.

Lange, M., Lefevre Arbogast, S., Hardy-Léger, I., Rigal, O., Le Fel, J., Pistilli, B., Petrucci, J., Lévy, C., Capel, A., Coutant, C., Médeau, L., Lerebours, F., Vanlemmens, L., Brion, M., Bourbouloux, E., Blain, M., Binarelli, G., Vaz-Luis, I., Giffard, B., Querel, O., … Joly, F. (2023). Cognitive change in breast cancer patients up to 2 years after diagnosis. *Journal of the National Cancer Institute, 115*(3), 322–331. https://doi.org/10.1093/jnci/djac240

Lejbak, L., Vrbancic, M., & Crossley, M. (2010). Endocrine therapy is associated with low performance on some estrogen-sensitive cognitive tasks in postmenopausal women with breast cancer. *Journal of Clinical and Experimental Neuropsychology, 32*(8), 836–846. https://doi.org/10.1080/13803391003596389

Liaw, C. C. (2001). Gender discrepancy observed between chemotherapy-induced emesis and hiccups. *Supportive Care in Cancer, 9*, 435–441. https://doi.org/10.1007/s005200000231

Lin, N. U., Bellon, J. R., & Winer, E. P. (2004). CNS metastases in breast cancer. *Journal of Clinical Oncology, 22*(17), 3608–3617.

Lin, N. U., & Winer, E. P. (2007). Brain metastases: The HER2 paradigm. *Clinical Cancer Research, 13*(6), 1648–1655.

Lipshultz, S. E., Lipsitz, S. R., Mone, S. M., Goorin, A. M., Sallan, S. E., Sanders, S. P., et al. (1995). Female sex and higher drug dose as risk factors for late cardiotoxic effects of doxorubicin therapy for childhood cancer. *New England Journal of Medicine, 332*(26), 1738–1744. https://doi.org/10.1056/NEJM199506293322602

Liu, Q., Tong, Z., & Wang, J. (2019). Management of brain metastases: History and the present. *Chinese Neurosurgical Journal, 5*, 1–8. https://doi.org/10.1186/s41016-018-0149-0

Mainio, A., Hakko, H., Niemelä, A., Koivukangas, J., & Räsänen, P. (2006). Gender difference in relation to depression and quality of life among patients with a primary brain tumor. *European Psychiatry, 21*(3), 194–199.

McDonald, B. C. (2021). Structural neuroimaging findings related to adult non-CNS cancer and treatment: Review, integration, and implications for treatment of cognitive dysfunction. *Neurotherapeutics, 18*(2), 792–810.

Meskal, I., Gehring, K., Rutten, G. J. M., & Sitskoorn, M. M. (2016). Cognitive functioning in meningioma patients: A systematic review. *Journal of Neuro-oncology, 128*, 195–205.

Murthy, R. K., Loi, S., Okines, A., Paplomata, E., Hamilton, E., Hurvitz, S. A., et al. (2020). Tucatinib, Trastuzumab, and Capecitabine for HER2-positive metastatic breast cancer. *The New England Journal of Medicine, 382*(7), 597–609. https://doi.org/10.1056/NEJMoa1914609

Mustillo, A., Ayoub, J. P., Charpentier, D., Yelle, L., & Florescu, M. (2020). Prognosis in younger women less than 40 years of age with brain metastasis from breast cancer. *Current Oncology: A Canadian Cancer Research Journal, 27*(1), 39–45. https://doi.org/10.3747/co.27.5621

Narendran, N., Luzhna, L., & Kovalchuk, O. (2019). Sex difference of radiation response in occupational and accidental exposure. *Frontiers in Genetics, 10*, 427795.

Nathoo, N., Toms, S. A., & Barnett, G. H. (2004). Metastases to the brain: Current management perspectives. *Expert Review of Neurotherapeutics, 4*(4), 633–640. https://doi.org/10.1586/14737175.4.4.633

National Cancer Institute. (2024). Cancer statistics. Retrieved August 26, 2024, from https://www.cancer.gov/about-cancer/understanding/statistics#:~:text=Cancer%20is%20among%20the%20leading,related%20deaths%20to%2015.3%20million

Nayak, L., Lee, E. Q., & Wen, P. Y. (2012). Epidemiology of brain metastases. *Neuro-oncology, 14*, 48–54.

Olsson, I. T., Perrin, S., Lundgren, J., Hjorth, L., & Johanson, A. (2014). Long-term cognitive sequelae after pediatric brain tumor related to medical risk factors, age, and sex. *Pediatric Neurology, 51*(4), 515–521.

Palmer, J. L., Trotter, T., Joy, A. A., & Carlson, L. E. (2008). Cognitive effects of Tamoxifen in premenopausal women with breast cancer compared to healthy controls. Journal of Cancer Survivorship: *Research and Practice, 2*(4), 275–282. https://doi.org/10.1007/s11764-008-0070-1

Palmer Kelly, E., McGee, J., Obeng-Gyasi, S., Herbert, C., Azap, R., Abbas, A., & Pawlik, T. M. (2021). Marginalized patient identities and the patient-physician relationship in the cancer care context: A systematic scoping review. *Supportive Care in Cancer, 29*(12), 7195–7207. https://doi.org/10.1007/s00520-021-06382-8

Pan, Y., Yang, K., Shi, X., Liang, H., Shen, X., Wang, R., et al. (2018). Clinical benefits of acupuncture for the reduction of hormone therapy–related side effects in breast cancer patients: A systematic review. *Integrative Cancer Therapies, 17*(3), 602–618. https://doi.org/10.1177/1534735418786801

Park, S. B., Krishnan, A. V., Lin, C. S., Goldstein, D., Friedlander, M., & Kiernan, M. C. (2008). Mechanisms underlying chemotherapy-induced neurotoxicity and the potential for neuroprotective strategies. *Current Medicinal Chemistry, 15*, 3081–3094. https://doi.org/10.2174/092986708786848569

Reid-Arndt, S. A., Hsieh, C., & Perry, M. C. (2010). Neuropsychological functioning and quality of life during the first year after completing chemotherapy for breast cancer. *Psycho-Oncology, 19*(5), 535–544. https://doi.org/10.1002/pon.1581

Rotta, J. M., Rodrigues, D. B., Diniz, J. M., Abreu, B. M. D., Kamimura, F., Sousa, U. O., et al. (2018). Analysis of survival in patients with brain metastases treated surgically: Impact of age, gender, oncologic status, chemotherapy, radiotherapy, number and localization of lesions, and primary cancer site. *Revista da Associação Médica Brasileira, 64*, 717–722.

Rubin, J. B., Lagas, J. S., Broestl, L., Sponagel, J., Rockwell, N., Rhee, G., et al. (2020). Sex differences in cancer mechanisms. *Biology of Sex Differences, 11*, 1–29.

Sacks, P., & Rahman, M. (2020). Epidemiology of brain metastases. *Neurosurgery Clinics of North America, 31*(2020), 481–488. https://doi.org/10.1016/j.nec.2020.06.001

Santucci, C., Carioli, G., Bertuccio, P., Malvezzi, M., Pastorino, U., Boffetta, P., et al. (2020). Progress in cancer mortality, incidence, and survival: A global overview. *European Journal of Cancer Prevention, 29*(5), 367–381.

Schatz, J., Kramer, J. H., Ablin, A., & Matthay, K. K. (2000). Processing speed, working memory, and IQ: A developmental model of cognitive deficits following cranial radiation therapy. *Neuropsychology, 14*(2), 189.

Schroeder, T., Bittrich, P., Kuhne, J. F., Noebel, C., Leischner, H., Fiehler, J., Schroeder, J., Schoen, G., & Gillißen. (2020). Mapping distribution of brain metastases: Does the primary tumor matter? *Journal of Neurooncology, 147*(1), 229–235. https://doi.org/10.1007/s11060-020-03419-6

Shibahara, I., Kanamori, M., Watanabe, T., Utsunomiya, A., Suzuki, H., Saito, R., Sonoda, Y., Jokura, H., Uenohara, H., & Tominaga, T. (2018). Clinical Features of Precocious, Synchronous, and Metachronous Brain Metastases and the Role of Tumor Resection. *World Neurosurgery, 113*, e1–e9. https://doi.org/10.1016/j.wneu.2017.10.145

Simsek, M., Aliyev, A., Baydas, T., Besiroglu, M., Demir, T., Shbair, A., et al. (2022). Breast cancer patients with brain metastases: A cross-sectional study. *The Breast Journal, 2022*, 1–5. https://doi.org/10.1155/2022/5763810

Sloan, J. A., Goldberg, R. M., Sargent, D. J., Vargas-Chanes, D., Nair, S., Cha, S. S., et al. (2002). Women experience greater toxicity with fluorouracil-based chemotherapy for colorectal cancer. *Journal of Clinical Oncology, 20*(6), 1491–1498. https://doi.org/10.1200/JCO.2002.20.6.1491

Stewart, A., Bielajew, C., Collins, B., Parkinson, M., & Tomiak, E. (2006). A meta-analysis of the neuropsychological effects of adjuvant chemotherapy treatment in women treated for breast cancer. *The Clinical Neuropsychologist, 20*(1), 76–89.

Sun, T., Plutynski, A., Ward, S., & Rubin, J. B. (2015). An integrative view on sex differences in brain tumors. *Cellular and Molecular Life Sciences, 72*, 3323–3342.

Tager, F. A., McKinley, P. S., Schnabel, F. R., El-Tamer, M., Cheung, Y. K., Fang, Y., Golden, C. R., Frosch, M. E., Habif, U., Mulligan, M. M., Chen, I. S., & Hershman, D. L. (2010). The cognitive effects of chemotherapy in post-menopausal breast cancer patients: A controlled longitudinal study. *Breast Cancer Research and Treatment, 123*(1), 25–34. https://doi.org/10.1007/s10549-009-0606-8

Taillibert, S., Le Rhun, E., & Chamberlain, M. C. (2016). Chemotherapy-related neurotoxicity. *Current Neurology and Neuroscience Reports, 16*, 1–14. https://doi.org/10.1007/s11910-016-0686-x

Takeshita, S., Todo, Y., Furuta, Y., Okamoto, K., Minobe, S., Yamashiro, K., & Kato, H. (2017). Prognostic factors for patients with brain metastasis from gynecological cancer: A significance of treatment-free interval of more than 6 months. *Japanese Journal of Clinical Oncology, 47*(7), 604–610. https://doi.org/10.1093/jjco/hyx047

Taphoorn, M. J., & Klein, M. (2004). Cognitive deficits in adult patients with brain tumours. *The Lancet Neurology, 3*(3), 159–168.

Tian, M., Ma, W., Chen, Y., Yu, Y., Zhu, D., Shi, J., & Zhang, Y. (2018). Impact of gender on the survival of patients with glioblastoma. *Bioscience Reports, 38*(6), BSR20180752.

Turnquist, C., Harris, B., & Harris, C. (2020). Radiation-induced brain injury: Current concepts and therapeutic strategies targeting neuroinflammation. *Neuro-Oncology Advances, 2*(1), 1–10. https://doi.org/10.1093/noajnl/vdaa05

Unger, J., Vaidya, R., Albain, K., LeBlanc, M., Minasian, L., Gotay, C., et al. (2022). Sex differences in risk of severe adverse events in patients receiving immunotherapy, targeted therapy, or chemotherapy in cancer clinical trials. *Journal of Clinical Oncology, 40*(13), 1474–1486. https://doi.org/10.1200/JCO.21.02377

Valk, P. E., & Dillon, W. P. (1991). Radiation injury of the brain. *American Journal of Neuroradiology, 12*(1), 45–62.

Van Dyk, K., Bower, J. E., Crespi, C. M., Petersen, L., & Ganz, P. A. (2018). Cognitive function following breast cancer treatment and associations with concurrent symptoms. *Breast Cancer, 4*(1), 25. https://doi.org/10.1038/s41523-018-0076-4

Van Dyk, K., Crespi, C. M., Bower, J. E., Castellon, S. A., Petersen, L., & Ganz, P. A. (2019). The cognitive effects of endocrine therapy in survivors of breast cancer: A prospective longitudinal study up to 6 years after treatment. *Cancer, 125*(5), 681–689. https://doi.org/10.1002/cncr.31858

VanLandingham, H. B., Ellison, R. L., Turchmanovych-Hienkel, N., Alfonso, D., Oh, A., Tse, K. Y., Kaseda, E. T., & Khan, H. (2024). Neuropsychological assessment, intervention, and best practices for women with cancer: A scoping review of current standards. *The Clinical Neuropsychologist*. https://doi.org/10.1080/13854046.2024.2343147

Vizer, L. M., Mikles, S. P., & Piepmeier, A. T. (2022). Cancer-related cognitive impairment in survivors of adolescent and young adult non-central nervous system cancer: A scoping review. *Psycho-Oncology, 31*(8), 1275–1285.

Von Ah, D., Crouch, A. D., Monahan, P. O., Stump, T. E., Unverzagt, F. W., Storey, S., Cohee, A. A., Cella, D., & Champion, V. L. (2022). Association of cognitive impairment and breast cancer survivorship on quality of life in younger breast cancer survivors. *Journal of Cancer Survivorship: Research and Practice, 16*(4), 812–822. https://doi.org/10.1007/s11764-021-01075-x

Wefel, J. S., Vardy, J., Ahles, T., & Schagen, S. B. (2011). International cognition and cancer task force recommendations to harmonise studies of cognitive function in patients with cancer. *Lancet Oncology, 12*, 703–708. https://doi.org/10.1016/S1470-2045(10)70294-1

Willard, V. W., Hardy, K. K., & Bonner, M. J. (2009). Gender differences in facial expression recognition in survivors of pediatric brain tumors. *Psycho-Oncology: Journal of the Psychological, Social and Behavioral Dimensions of Cancer, 18*(8), 893–897.

Wong, E., Rowbottom, L., Tsao, M., Zhang, L., McDonald, R., Danjoux, C., Barnes, E., Chan, S., & Chow, D. (2016). Correlating symptoms and their changes with survival in patients with brain metastases. *Annals of Palliative Medicine, 5*(4), 253–266.

Yao, C., Rich, J. B., Tirona, K., & Bernstein, L. J. (2016). Intraindividual variability in reaction time before and after neoadjuvant chemotherapy in women diagnosed with breast cancer. *Psycho-Oncology, 26*(12), 2261–2268. https://doi.org/10.1002/pon.4351

Yeh, R., Yu, J., Chu, C., Ho, C., Kao, H., Liao, G., et al. (2015). Distinct MR imaging features of triple-negative breast cancer with brain metastasis. *Journal of Neuroimaging, 25*(3), 337–516.

Yin, Y., Jin, L., Chu, M., Zhou, Y., Tu, S., Cheng, Y., Ye, M., Wu, J., & Chen, H. (2023). Association between endocrine therapy and cognitive decline in breast cancer based on propensity score matching. *Frontiers in Medicine, 10*. https://doi.org/10.3389/fmed.2023.1132287

Yoo, J., Cha, Y. J., Park, H. H., Park, M., Joo, B., Suh, S. H., & Ahn, S. J. (2022). The extent of necrosis in brain metastases may predict subtypes of primary cancer and overall survival in patients receiving craniotomy. *Cancers (Basel), 14*(7), 1694–1702. https://doi.org/10.3390/cancers14071694

Yoshii, Y., Tominaga, D., Sugimoto, K., Tsuchida, Y., Hyodo, A., Yonaha, H., & Kushi, S. (2008). Cognitive function of patients with brain tumor in pre-and postoperative stage. *Surgical Neurology, 69*(1), 51–61.

Zeng, Y., Cheng, A. S., & Chan, C. C. (2016). Meta-analysis of the effects of neuropsychological interventions on cognitive function in non–central nervous system cancer survivors. *Integrative Cancer Therapies, 15*(4), 424–434.

Zhang, Y., Grant, M. S., Stepp, W. H., & Clark, L. H. (2019). Clinical characteristics of CNS metastases from primary gynecologic cancers. *Gynecologic Oncology Reports, 30*, 100518.

Chapter 9
Autoimmune Disorders

Erin Logue and Robin C. Hilsabeck

Introduction

Autoimmune disorders, affecting approximately 10% of the population, are the third most common type of disorder in the United States. These disorders cause the body's immune system to mistakenly attack its own healthy tissues, which can affect a single organ or multiple organ systems (Cornelius, 2019). Women are significantly more likely to develop autoimmune disease, representing 64% of individuals diagnosed between 2000 and 2019. This translates to a 13% prevalence among women compared to 7% in men (Angum et al., 2020). Table 9.1 provides a summary of gender differences in prevalence for each of the autoimmune conditions discussed in this chapter.

There are multiple physiological reasons for these observed differences, including the influences of sex hormones, sex chromosomes, genetic and epigenetic factors, and the gut microbiome (Cincinelli et al., 2018; Cornelius, 2019; Dupuis et al., 2019; Kedia & Ravindran, 2020). Sex hormones in women cause a more vigorous immune response, which puts them at a higher risk (Cincinelli et al., 2018; Cornelius, 2019; Dupuis et al., 2019). For example, prolactin stimulates the release of proinflammatory cytokines (Cornelius, 2019). Furthermore, the X chromosome contains a large number of immune-related genes, and given that females have two X chromosomes, some X-linked genes that influence immune response may be overexpressed (Dupuis et al., 2019). However, environmental factors also play an important role in gender differences (Angum et al., 2020; Siegel & Sammaritano, 2024).

E. Logue (✉)
The University of Texas at Austin Dell Medical School, Austin, TX, USA
e-mail: erin.logue@austin.utexas.edu

R. C. Hilsabeck
UT Health San Antonio, San Antonio, TX, USA

E. Sullivan-Baca, R. Ellison (eds.), *Neuropsychology of Women*,
https://doi.org/10.1007/978-3-031-87228-0_9

Table 9.1 Ratio of women to men with autoimmune conditions

Autoimmune condition	Ratio (women:men)
Multiple sclerosis (MS)	3:1
Systemic lupus erythematosus (SLE)	9:1
Rheumatoid arthritis (RA)	3:1
Autoimmune thyroid disease (AITD)	5–10:1
Autoimmune encephalitis (AE)	4:1
Type 1 diabetes	1:1.4

Autoimmune disorders have been historically stigmatized and poorly understood, often questioned as to their veracity (Gunning, 2023). This can lead to feelings of frustration, helplessness, and invalidation. Women may also be more likely to have pain associated with many of these conditions dismissed or underrated, or to be misdiagnosed due to gender bias (Samulowiz et al., 2018).

In the following sections, we delve deeper into the gender-related aspects of specific autoimmune conditions, including multiple sclerosis (MS); Systemic lupus erythematosus (SLE); rheumatoid arthritis (RA); autoimmune thyroid disease (AITD); autoimmune encephalitis (AE), particularly anti-N-methyl-D-aspartate receptor (NMDAR) encephalitis; and type I diabetes. Additionally, we discuss how the consequences of autoimmune diseases can go beyond physical health and direct impacts on cognition, as women with these conditions are at greater risk for developing mental health problems (Table 9.2).

Multiple Sclerosis

Epidemiology

Multiple Sclerosis (MS) is a disease of the central nervous system characterized by chronic, inflammatory demyelination of brain axons (Baecher-Allan et al., 2018). Wallin et al. (2019) estimated a 2010 prevalence of MS in the U.S. adult population over 10 years at 309.2 per 100,000, with a disparity between genders. Women were afflicted at a rate nearly triple that of men (450.1 per 100,000 compared to 159.7 per 100,000). This female predominance was further supported by Hittle et al. (2023), who identified 76% of adults with MS as women in a large cohort study. The prevalence of MS also demonstrated a geographical trend, with a stronger association with latitude observed in women, Black/African American individuals, and older patients.

A confluence of factors likely accounts for the gender disparity, including hormonal fluctuations, immunological response differences, genetic predisposition, and environmental influences. As discussed, hormonal and X-chromosome factors

Table 9.2 Gender differences in clinical presentation of autoimmune conditions

Autoimmune condition	Clinical presentation in women	Clinical presentation in men
Multiple sclerosis	– Broader range of symptoms across multiple systems (e.g., digestive, musculoskeletal, and mental) – Higher fatigue and pain – Greater sadness and helplessness – Earlier disease onset – More inflammatory relapses – Slower disease progression – More white matter atrophy	– The reproductive system affected more often – More weakness, sexual dysfunction, and bowel and bladder difficulties – Non-acceptance, relationships negatively impacted – Worse long-term outcomes – Primary progressive phenotype more common – Greater visuospatial/ constructional and memory deficits – More gray matter atrophy
Systemic lupus erythematosus	– Musculoskeletal, dermatological, and alopecia more common – Greater negative effect on quality of life	– More severe and aggressive disease course – Cardiovascular disease, nephritis, and seizures more common
Rheumatoid arthritis	– Pain and joint swelling more frequent – Higher levels of depression – More aggressive disease course – Greater levels of disability – Less likely to achieve remission – Increased mortality in older women	– Organs outside of the joints more often affected
Autoimmune thyroid disease	– Unknown	– Unknown
Autoimmune encephalitis	– Tumors, especially ovarian teratomas, more prevalent – More clinical symptoms – Worse peak stage background EEG activity – Higher likelihood of ICU stay – Poorer prognosis with increasing age	– Prevalence of tumors increases with age
Type 1 diabetes	– Poorer metabolic control leading to more long-term complications	– Unknown

Note. EEG = electroencephalogram, ICU = intensive care unit

contribute to a more robust immunological response in women. Notably, as with many other autoimmune diseases, women experience changes in disease activity during pregnancy and postpartum, likely related to changes in adaptive immune response and hormones during those time periods. Disease activity tends to be lower during pregnancy, and relapses are common during the postpartum period (Angeloni et al., 2021). Regarding environmental factors, Epstein-Barr Virus, a significant risk factor for MS and other autoimmune disorders, is more prevalent in women. Other environmental factors (e.g., lack of sun exposure, cigarette smoking) also appear to interact with sex-related mechanisms (Angeloni et al., 2021; Krysko et al., 2020).

Risk Factors and Presentation

There are distinct presentations of MS symptomatology between genders. Perwieniec et al. (2021) found that women are more likely to experience a broader range of symptoms, including headaches as well as digestive, musculoskeletal, ophthalmic, laryngological, mental, and cardiovascular issues. Men, however, tend to present more frequently with reproductive system problems. Similarly, in a multicenter study conducted in China, Zhao et al. (2020) reported higher levels of fatigue and pain in women, whereas men experienced more weakness, sexual dysfunction, and difficulties with urination and defecation. Psychologically, the women with MS in this study reported greater sadness and helplessness, whereas men expressed more non-acceptance and a negative impact on relationships (Zhao et al., 2020). Cornelius (2019) also pointed out a worsening of symptoms in women after menopause, possibly due to lower estradiol, which stimulates pro-inflammatory cytokines (Cincinelli et al., 2018).

Diagnostic and prognostic considerations for MS also differ between genders. For example, there is an earlier onset of the disease in women (Gilli et al., 2020). The prodromal phase, often characterized by increased healthcare utilization, reveals another pattern consistent with differences in initial symptomology. In a large population-based cohort study, Yusuf et al. (2022) found that Canadian women visited general practitioners and ophthalmologists more frequently during this period, whereas women had a lower rate of genitourinary-related visits. Additionally, although women experience more frequent inflammatory relapses, evidence points point to a slower disease progression compared to men (Gilli et al., 2020). This suggests that men may face worse long-term outcomes. However, being female and of childbearing age appears to offer some protection against both a more aggressive disease course and cognitive decline (D'hooghe et al., 2013). This protective effect seems to wane with ovarian aging, as there is an acceleration of disability progression in women after menopause (Krysko et al., 2020).

Cognitive Outcomes

Neurocognitive impairment, including in social cognition, is a common early symptom in MS (Benedict et al., 2020; Doskas et al., 2021). Regarding risk factors for cognitive decline in MS, there is a correlation between clinical phenotype and gender. Women are more likely to experience all phenotypes of MS except for primary progressive MS (PPMS), which is associated with the most severe and widespread cognitive deficits (Brochet & Ruet, 2019). These deficits include information processing speed, attention, working memory, executive functions, and verbal episodic memory, with more tests and domains impaired than relapsing remitting MS (Brochet & Ruet, 2019). This suggests that men, who are more prone to PPMS, may have a greater vulnerability to cognitive decline in MS (Beatty & Aupperle, 2002). Brain scans also reveal gender differences in atrophy patterns. Women tend to have more white matter atrophy, whereas men exhibit greater gray matter atrophy (Gilli et al., 2020). Taken together, these findings suggest distinct pathological processes at play in the brains of women and men with MS. As such, the cognitive impact of MS also shows gender disparity. Specifically, Schoonheim et al. (2012) matched females and males on lesion load and length of MS and found that females in their study evidenced less impairment than males in visuospatial memory. In a larger sample, in which women had a lower rate of PPMS than men, Donaldson et al. (2019) reported better verbal memory performance in women. These findings echo those of Beatty and Aupperle (2002), who found that women performed worse than men on memory and visuoconstruction measures, and there were no significant demographic differences between women and men in this sample. On average, the individuals in the Schoonheim et al. (2012), Donaldson et al. (2019), and Beatty and Aupperle (2002) studies had at least a high school level of education. No race or ethnicity demographics were provided.

Systemic Lupus Erythematosus

Epidemiology

Systemic Lupus Erythematosus (SLE) is a complex autoimmune disease with a multifactorial origin, involving genetic, epigenetic, and environmental factors manifesting in a variable clinical presentation and course (Lichtnekert et al., 2022; Siegel & Sammaritano, 2024). It can impact almost every tissue and organ system in the body but preferentially affects the kidneys, joints, and skin (Hoi et al., 2024). The epidemiology of SLE is variable too, differing by region, age, sex, and race. With regard to region, the United States has one of the highest estimated incidences in the world at 12.13 per 100,000 person-years, second only to Poland (Tian et al., 2023). Although high-income countries/regions have higher rates of SLE, disease burden, morbidity, and mortality are greater in countries/regions with lower socioeconomic status (Carter et al., 2016; Scherlinger et al., 2020; Tian et al., 2023). Regardless of region, adults are more likely to be affected than children, and women are more likely to be affected than men at a ratio of about 9 to 1 (Tian et al., 2023). In the United States, Black/African American women are most likely to be affected, at rates two to three times higher than Asian/Pacific Islander, Hispanic/Latinx, and white women (Izmirly et al., 2021). White women typically have less severe disease than Black/African American, Asian, and Hispanic/Latinx women (Izmirly et al., 2021).

Risk Factors and Presentation

Given this large sex bias, SLE is often referred to as the prototypical sexually dimorphic disease. Sex hormones, X-linked genes, sex differences in the immune system, and epigenetic regulation of gene expression are all thought to play a role in the differing risk factors, clinical presentation, and prognosis for women and men (Bose & Jefferies, 2022). Men typically have a more severe and aggressive disease course with regard to organ involvement and prognosis (Jolly et al., 2019; Nusbaum et al., 2020; Ramírez Sepúlveda et al., 2019). Smoking, alcohol use, and renal involvement are more common in men with SLE, and they tend to experience cardiovascular disease, serositis, cytopenias, nephritis, thrombotic events, and seizures more frequently than women (Gui et al., 2022; Murphy & Isenberg, 2013; Nusbaum et al., 2020). Risk factors for women include early age at menarche, early age at menopause, surgical menopause, oral contraceptive use, and postmenopausal use of hormones, although it is important to note that results are based on data from predominantly White samples (Costenbader et al., 2007). Women are more likely to experience musculoskeletal involvement, malar rash, alopecia, photosensitivity, retinitis pigmentosa, oral ulcers, and arthritis (Murphy & Isenberg, 2013; Ramírez Sepúlveda et al., 2019). Women also report greater negative effects of SLE on quality of life in the domains of lupus symptoms, cognition, and procreation than age-matched men (Jolly et al., 2019).

Cognitive Outcomes

Neuropsychiatric manifestations of SLE, including cognitive impairment, seizures, mood disorders, psychosis, and headaches, are common (Emerson et al., 2023; Santos et al., 2021; Sarwar et al., 2021). Although the prevalence of cognitive impairment varies widely depending on sample characteristics, measures used, and how impairment is defined, approximately 38–40% of people with SLE exhibit cognitive impairment when examined with a comprehensive neuropsychological battery using cut-offs at or below 1.5 standard deviations below a normative mean on more than one measure (Rayes et al., 2018; Emerson et al., 2023; Raghunath et al., 2023; Yuen et al., 2021). Attention, working memory, processing speed, executive functioning, and verbal fluency are usually most affected, but performance is worse than healthy controls across all cognitive domains (Raghunath et al., 2023; Seet et al., 2021). Individuals with cognitive impairment report significantly reduced quality of life and negative effects on employment and academic performance for adults and children, respectively (Mendelsohn et al., 2021). To our knowledge, gender differences in cognitive performance have not been examined in SLE.

Rheumatoid Arthritis

Epidemiology

Rheumatoid Arthritis (RA) is a chronic autoimmune disease characterized by inflammation of the joints (Maranini et al., 2022). In the United States, it is estimated that roughly 1.3 million adults, or 0.6–1% of the adult population, are afflicted with RA (Helmick et al., 2008). Women are disproportionately affected, at a ratio of 3 to 1 compared to men, and socioeconomic deprivation further increases risk (Angum et al., 2020; Maranini et al., 2022). This disparity is even more pronounced in Latin American and Caribbean populations, where women not only have a higher prevalence of RA but also tend to experience an earlier onset of the disease (Barragan-Martinez et al., 2012). However, there is a reversal of this trend after age 75 years, with a lower women-to-men ratio observed (Cornelius, 2019). Socioeconomic factors also appear to play a role. Xu and Wu (2021) reported a significantly higher risk and prevalence of RA among Black/African Americans and individuals with lower socioeconomic status between 2005 and 2018.

Risk Factors and Presentation

There are unique risk factors for women with RA, with studies suggesting that earlier menarche and menopause may increase a woman's susceptibility (Hernandez-Avila et al., 1990; Pikwer et al., 2012). Furthermore, the presentation and comorbidities of RA differ between genders. Women with RA generally experience more pain and swelling in their joints than men (Intriago et al., 2019). Additionally, Barragan-Martinez et al. (2012) found that in Latin American and Caribbean populations, women with RA were more likely to experience polyautoimmunity (i.e., the presence of multiple autoimmune diseases) and abdominal obesity, whereas men had more extra-articular manifestations (symptoms affecting organs outside the joints).

Psychological considerations are also important. Women with RA report higher levels of depression and negative mood than men with RA (Dowdy et al., 1996). Although longitudinal findings indicate this may be influenced by factors such as the quality of emotional support they receive, their use of passive pain coping mechanisms, and the physical limitations imposed by the disease, the correlation between depression and RA in women is stronger with increased disease activity (Dowdy et al., 1996; Sautner et al., 2020).

The prognosis of RA is also less favorable for women. Women tend to have a more aggressive disease course, experience greater disability, and are less likely to achieve remission compared to men (Intriago et al., 2019; Shin et al., 2021; Sokka et al., 2009). The additional physical and psychological burdens faced by women with RA may further impact their overall well-being (Meade et al., 2018). Furthermore, Anderson (1996) reported an increased mortality rate among elderly women with RA.

Cognitive Outcomes

Greater than 2/3 of patients show signs of cognitive dysfunction in RA, associated with disease activity, linked to greater functional limitations, and often associated with anxiety and depression (Chaurasia et al., 2020; Petersen et al., 2018; Vitturi et al., 2019). Although a meta-analysis found that individuals with RA performed significantly worse on cognitive function tests (especially on tests of verbal function, memory, and attention) compared to healthy controls, no significant gender differences were observed (Meade et al., 2018). Underlying mechanisms for cognitive dysfunction in RA are not fully understood, and possibilities include altered brain-derived neurotrophic factor signaling, increased inflammatory cytokines, and some of the treatments for RA (Olah et al., 2020; Pedard et al., 2021).

Autoimmune Thyroid Disease

Epidemiology

Autoimmune thyroid disease (AITD), or thyroiditis, affects approximately 2–8% of the U.S. population and is the most prevalent organ-specific autoimmune disease (Franco et al., 2013; Hu et al., 2022; Pyzik et al., 2015). Like other autoimmune diseases, the etiology of AITD is thought to be a complex interaction of environmental factors in genetically susceptible individuals. Women are 5–10 times more likely to develop AITD than men (Franco et al., 2013; Pyzik et al., 2015), and pregnancy-related immune system and hormonal changes are hypothesized to play a pathophysiological role (Bogović Crnčić et al., 2023). However, the effect of puberty did not differ between genders in a study of the onset of AITD in children and adolescents, supporting the importance of factors in addition to hormones (Calcaterra et al., 2020). Risk for AITD increases with age, is more common in individuals who suffer from other autoimmune diseases, such as MS, SLE, and RA, and can worsen disease activity associated with these conditions (Lichtiger et al., 2024; Pyzik et al., 2015). Little information is known about racial and ethnic differences, and there is conflicting information about the impact of economic status (Hu et al., 2022).

Risk Factors and Presentation

One of the most common AITDs is Graves' disease (GD), which is the primary cause of hyperthyroidism (Franco et al., 2013; Pyzik et al., 2015). Hyperthyroidism is defined as increased synthesis and secretion of thyroid hormones, thyroxine (T4) and triiodothyronine (T3), in the context of suppressed serum concentrations of thyroid-stimulating hormone (TSH) (Chaker et al., 2024). The clinical presentation of hyperthyroidism is variable and not strongly linked to circulating thyroid hormone concentrations (Vox et al., 2009). Symptoms can be present in multiple systems, including skin, eyes, cardiovascular, gastrointestinal, skeletal, neurological, and psychiatric (Chaker et al., 2024). Common neuropsychiatric symptoms include anxiety, restlessness, tremor, emotional lability, psychosis, poor concentration, and irritability (Chaker et al., 2024).

A rare but serious complication of hyperthyroidism is referred to as thyroid storm. Thyroid storm occurs when one or more organ systems decompensate, which can result in congestive heart failure, stupor, and/or coma. Clinical signs that raise suspicion for GD specifically include thyroid eye disease, alopecia, acropachy (i.e., clubbing of nails), and thymic enlargement (Chaker et al., 2024). Sex differences in hyperthyroidism have not been widely investigated, with only one study in children reporting no differences (Wang et al., 2020b).

The second most common AITD is hypothyroidism or an underactive thyroid gland (Bernal & Meager, 2019; Zamwar & Muneshwar, 2023). Primary hypothyroidism, which constitutes 99% of cases, is caused by a deficiency of T4, which regulates metabolism and can cause complications in several organs of the body if left untreated (Zamwar & Muneshwar, 2023). It presents with increased levels of TSH and decreased levels of T4 concentrations in the blood.

Subclinical hypothyroidism, a milder form of hypothyroidism, presents with elevated TSH levels in the context of normal T4 levels. Common signs of hypothyroidism are lethargy, weight gain, cold intolerance, and dry skin and hair, but the symptomatology can range from non-existent to life-threatening (i.e., myxedema coma) (Bernal & Meager, 2019; Zamwar & Muneshwar, 2023). Symptoms of depression and anxiety are also common (Karakiewicz-Krawczyk et al., 2022). Hypothyroidism commonly occurs as a consequence of treating GD, iodine deficiency, and Hashimoto's thyroiditis (HT), which is chronic inflammation secondary to an autoimmune response that damages the thyroid gland.

HT, also known as autoimmune thyroiditis or chronic lymphocytic thyroiditis, is the most common cause of primary hypothyroidism in regions with sufficient iodine (Franco et al., 2013; Pyzik et al., 2015; Zamwar & Muneshwar, 2023). Although greater body mass index and waist circumference are associated with increased risk of HT for both women and men, only metabolically unhealthy women with obesity are at higher risk, whereas men who are metabolically unhealthy or obese are at higher risk (Yang et al., 2022).

Cognitive Outcomes

Cognitive impairment is associated with both hyper- and hypothyroidism, with the latter sometimes referred to as a "reversible" cause of dementia, although it is unclear how many patients this type of reversible dementia actually affects (Bernal & Meager, 2019; Lekurwale et al., 2023; Zamwar & Muneshwar, 2023). Meta-analytic studies of the association of thyroid disease with risk of cognitive impairment and dementia did not confirm a relationship with hypothyroidism (Ma et al., 2023; Ye et al., 2022) but did find that hyperthyroidism was predictive of dementia (Ma et al., 2023). Congenital hypothyroidism, on the other hand, is a leading cause of preventable cognitive and intellectual disability (Bernal & Meager, 2019), and Hashimoto's Encephalopathy (HE), also known as steroid-responsive autoimmune encephalopathy associated with autoimmune thyroiditis (SREAT), presents with cognitive impairment, altered mental status, seizures, psychosis, movement disorders, and stroke-like symptoms (Chaudhuri et al., 2023; Chiarello et al., 2020; Figgie et al., 2024; Zhou et al., 2017). Following resolution of the acute confusional state, cognitive impairment is typically diffuse with gradual improvement, although residual deficits may be present in executive dysfunction (Mazzu et al., 2012). Gender differences in cognitive impairment or neuropsychiatric profiles in AITDs, if any, are unknown.

Autoimmune Encephalitis

Epidemiology

Autoimmune encephalitis (AE) refers to a heterogeneous group of diseases mediated by autoimmune mechanisms and sometimes strong genetic predispositions that commonly cause neuropsychiatric symptoms (Altintas et al., 2020; Kvam et al., 2024). NMDAR encephalitis was the first of these diseases to be reported in 2007 and is the most common, accounting for approximately 54–80% of AE cases (Zhao et al., 2023). Incidence is estimated at 1.5 per million population per year (Dalmau et al., 2019). Women are overrepresented at a rate about four times higher than men, although sex differences are less apparent in ages 12 and younger and 45 and older (Altintas et al., 2020). AE secondary to high-titer antibodies against glutamic acid decarboxylase (GAD) also has a strong female predominance and usually manifests between the ages of 10–39 years (Altintas et al., 2020). Antibodies targeting Leucine-rich glioma-inactivated 1 (LGI1) are thought to be the second most common cause of AE, followed by contactin-associated protein-like 2 (Caspr2), which confers a strong male predominance (Altintas et al., 2020; Kvam et al., 2024).

Risk Factors, Presentation, and Cognitive Outcomes

In NMDAR AE, psychiatric and behavioral symptoms, seizures, and cognitive impairment are common clinical features (Dalmau et al., 2019; Zhao et al., 2023). Tumors, particularly ovarian teratomas, are significantly more prevalent in women, particularly between ages 12 and 45 years, whereas the prevalence of tumors in men increases with age (Altintas et al., 2020; Zhao et al., 2023). The presence of teratomas is associated with milder neurological symptoms and better long-term outcomes post-tumor resection (Zhang et al., 2020). Women experience more clinical symptoms and worse peak stage background activity on EEG than men and have a higher probability of needing ICU support, all of which are associated with poorer outcomes (Wang et al., 2020a, 2020b; Zhao et al., 2023). In addition, increasing age is associated with a poorer prognosis in women but not men (Sun et al., 2020). Information about long-term cognitive outcomes is limited but suggests pervasive impairment with 40–88% of patients exhibiting cognitive impairment greater than 1.5 standard deviations below the normative mean in at least one domain (Kvam et al., 2024). Domains most likely to be impaired are memory, attention, processing speed, and executive functioning (Galioto et al., 2023; Kvam et al., 2024).

Type 1 Diabetes

Epidemiology

Type 1 diabetes, previously referred to as juvenile diabetes, is an autoimmune disease in which the body destroys cells in the pancreas that produce insulin. This results in a lifelong need for insulin injected to control blood sugar levels (Bullard et al., 2019). A meta-analysis found a global incidence of 15 per 100,000 people and a prevalence of 9.5% (Mobasseri et al., 2020). Research suggests gender and ethnic disparities in type 1 diabetes; men and non-Hispanic/Latinx White individuals appear to have a higher incidence compared to Hispanic/Latinx individuals (Bullard et al., 2018).

Risk Factors and Presentation

Although the core symptoms of and risk factors for type 1 diabetes are similar between genders, there are some gender differences in terms of prognosis. Women with this condition tend to have poorer metabolic control, leading to more long-term complications (Manicardi et al., 2016). Furthermore, Evers et al. (2004) noted an increased risk of complications during pregnancy among women with type 1 diabetes. These findings underscore the importance of an approach to managing type 1 diabetes that considers gender.

Cognitive Outcomes

Regarding cognitive dysfunction in type 1 diabetes, meta-analysis indicates lower performances than healthy controls, of mild to moderate magnitude, in multiple cognitive domains. These include intelligence, information processing speed, sustained attention, cognitive flexibility, and visual perception; however, there were no differences on measures of learning and memory (Brands et al., 2005). Multiple investigations have shown a relationship between these deficits and microvascular complications associated with type 1 diabetes (Brands et al., 2005; Sharma & Brown, 2022), and disease duration and younger age of onset are among the strongest predictors of lower scores across neuropsychological measures (Brismar et al., 2007). Clinically significant impairments, defined as at least 1.5 standard deviations below the normative mean on at least two cognitive tests, in older adults with type 1 diabetes have also been found, with one study citing 48% of their sample as having these impairments (Chaytor et al., 2019). Findings were consistent with those in younger populations in that the number of lifetime hypoglycemic events was not related to cognitive performances; however, neither were disease duration and age of onset. Furthermore, the number of recent hypoglycemic events was negatively associated with performances on cognitive tasks. Together, these findings suggest other factors may be contributing to cognitive dysfunction in older adults with type 1 diabetes. However, whether there are significant differences in cognitive performance between genders has not been specifically examined to our knowledge.

Research Takeaways

There is growing recognition of the influence gender plays on the prevalence, presentation, and prognosis of autoimmune diseases. As discussed in this chapter, women are disproportionately affected by many autoimmune conditions, and their experiences often differ from those of men. However, the impact of intersecting identities, such as race, ethnicity, sexual orientation, and gender identity on autoimmune diseases remains largely unexplored. This lack of data on individuals with marginalized identities creates significant gaps in our understanding and a barrier to providing truly equitable healthcare.

Much of the existing research focuses on biological factors like hormonal fluctuations and variations in the immune response between women and men. This biological focus is undoubtedly important. However, for a more complete picture, we need to broaden our scope and delve deeper into how environmental and sociocultural factors differentially contribute to stress and the immune response in women and men. Disparities in stress levels, access to healthcare, and environmental exposures may differentially impact women and men. For example, women often face unique stressors related to childcare, work-life balance, and societal expectations. Chronic stress is a well-established activator of the immune system, and understanding how these external factors influence disease development and progression is crucial. Furthermore, we must explore the intricate interplay between biological predispositions and environmental factors across different developmental stages—childhood, adolescence, and adulthood—for a more holistic understanding. Below are key takeaways to guide future research:

- *Gender Differences in Cognitive Concerns:* Although research has begun to illuminate the gendered aspects of autoimmune diseases, a critical question remains largely unanswered: Are there gender-specific risk factors for cognitive decline and dysfunction? Research in this area has been scarce. Future studies should prioritize investigating this question, with a particular focus on environmental factors. Specifically, we need to understand how stressors unique to understudied populations with intersecting identities might influence cognitive function. For example, we could ask questions such as: How do childhood experiences of discrimination or social isolation in individuals with understudied intersecting identities interact with their genetic makeup to influence their risk of developing an autoimmune disease later in life? By investigating how stressors at different life stages interact with the immune system and influence cognitive function, we can gain valuable insights into the complex interplay between gender, environment, and autoimmune disease.
- *Understanding Cognitive Impairment Across Autoimmune Diseases:* Even though research on cognitive decline in MS is commendable, we need to understand the underlying mechanisms of cognitive impairment in other autoimmune diseases. This knowledge is crucial for developing targeted interventions and improving overall patient well-being. For instance, do the inflammatory processes characteristic of RA or SLE impact cognitive function differently in women and men? By investigating these questions, we can move beyond a one-size-fits-all approach to cognitive dysfunction in autoimmune diseases and develop interventions tailored to the specific needs of different patient populations.
- *Diversity in Clinical Trials:* Strait (2019) and Finalyson et al. (2023) rightly emphasize the need for more diverse representation in clinical trials for RA and MS, respectively. We extend this call to action to all autoimmune diseases. Currently, many clinical trials lack sufficient representation from racial and ethnic minorities, LGBTQ+ individuals, and those from lower socioeconomic backgrounds. This homogeneity in research populations leads to findings that may not be generalizable to the broader patient community. By including individuals from various backgrounds and identities, we can ensure that research findings are generalizable and inform equitable treatment strategies.

Clinical Takeaways

Cognitive impairment affects a subset of patients in each of the autoimmune diseases reviewed in this chapter. In most cases, deficits are mild and nonprogressive, and the pattern is suggestive of frontal subcortical dysfunction. Exceptions are PPMS, which involves more severe and widespread deficits with decline over time, and HE and AE, which present with altered mental status and a diffuse pattern of deficits that recover with treatment but often do not return to baseline and may interfere with return to work or school activities. Psychiatric symptoms, such as depression, anxiety, mania, and psychosis, are also common across diseases, along with pain and fatigue. In many cases, it may be difficult to discern whether cognitive deficits are secondary to the disease process, its treatments, and/or comorbid conditions or disease complications. Identification of cognitive impairment is important for treatment planning and safety purposes. Patients, families, and caretakers will benefit from knowledge of cognitive strengths and weaknesses and the need for compensatory strategies or assistance. Below are key takeaways for clinical practice:

- *Gender Differences in Diagnosis and Treatment:* Across autoimmune diseases, there are gender differences in epidemiology, risk factors, clinical presentation, prognosis, and treatment response that need to be considered for diagnosis and treatment planning. Integrating what is known (and not known) about environmental, sociocultural, and genetic factors and communicating those to patients during feedback will be important to facilitate understanding of cause and effects on neuropsychological functioning.
- *Disease-Specific Neuropsychological Assessment:* Use of shorter neuropsychological test batteries that are sensitive to cognitive deficits typically found in a particular autoimmune disease would help ensure that routine assessment of cognitive functioning occurs and subtle deficits are not missed. Disease-specific batteries of an hour or less have been proposed for MS, SLE, and AE and could be utilized for other autoimmune diseases.
- *Interventions for Cognitive Impairment:* Patients with cognitive impairment secondary to autoimmune diseases may benefit from cognitive rehabilitation techniques, as well as from holistic approaches that align with patients' beliefs and preferences to address emotional and behavioral symptoms. Understanding whether there are gender differences in response to interventions for cognitive impairment is an area in need of future study.

References

Altintas, A., Dargvainiene, J., Schneider-Gold, C., Asgari, N., Ayzenberg, I., Ciplea, A. I., Junker, R., Leypoldt, F., Wandinger, K. P., & Hellwig, K. (2020). Gender issues of antibody-mediated diseases in neurology: (NMOSD/autoimmune encephalitis/MG). *Therapeutic Advances in Neurological Disorders, 13*. https://doi.org/10.1177/1756286420949808

Anderson, S. T. (1996). Mortality in rheumatoid arthritis: Do age and gender make a difference? *Seminars in Arthritis and Rheumatism, 25*(5), 291–296. https://doi.org/10.1016/s0049-0172(96)80015-1

Angeloni, B., Bigi, R., Bellucci, G., Mechelli, R., Ballerini, C., Romano, C., Morena, E., Pellicciari, G., Reniè, R., Rinaldi, V., Buscarinu, M. C., Romano, S., Ristori, G., & Salvetti, M. (2021). A case of double standard: Sex differences in multiple sclerosis risk factors. *International Journal of Molecular Sciences, 22*(7). https://doi.org/10.3390/ijms22073696

Angum, F., Khan, T., Kaler, J., Siddiqui, L., & Hussain, A. (2020). The prevalence of autoimmune disorders in women: A narrative review. *Cureus, 12*(5). https://doi.org/10.7759/cureus.8094

Barragán-Martínez, C., Amaya-Amaya, J., Pineda-Tamayo, R., Mantilla, R. D., Castellanos-de la Hoz, J., Bernal-Macías, S., Rojas-Villarraga, A., & Anaya, J. M. (2012). Gender differences in Latin-American patients with rheumatoid arthritis. *Gender Medicine, 9*(6), 490–510. https://doi.org/10.1016/j.genm.2012.10.005

Baecher-Allan, C., Kaskow, B. J., & Weiner, H. L. (2018). Multiple sclerosis: Mechanisms and immunotherapy. *Neuron, 97*(4), 742–768. https://doi.org/10.1016/j.neuron.2018.01.021

Beatty, W. W., & Aupperle, R. L. (2002). Sex differences in cognitive impairment in multiple sclerosis. *The Clinical Neuropsychologist, 16*(4), 472–480. https://doi.org/10.1076/clin.16.4.472.13904

Benedict, R. H. B., Amato, M. P., DeLuca, J., & Geurts, J. J. G. (2020). Cognitive impairment in multiple sclerosis: Clinical management, MRI, and therapeutic avenues. *The Lancet. Neurology, 19*(10), 860–871. https://doi.org/10.1016/S1474-4422(20)30277-5

Bernal, S. Y., & Meager, M. R. (2019). Hypothyroidism and Hashioto's thyroiditis: Mechanisms, diagnosis, neuropsycholgca phenotypes, and treatments. In C. Armstrong & L. Morrow (Eds.), *Handbook of medical neuropsychology*. Springer. https://doi.org/10.1007/978-3-030-14895-9_25

Bogović Crnčić, T., Girotto, N., Ilić Tomaš, M., Krištofić, I., Klobučar, S., Batičić, L., Ćurko-Cofek, B., & Sotošek, V. (2023). Innate immunity in autoimmune thyroid disease during pregnancy. *International Journal of Molecular Sciences, 24*(20). https://doi.org/10.3390/ijms242015442

Bose, M., & Jefferies, C. (2022). Sex bias in systemic lupus erythematosus: A molecular insight. *Immunometabolism, 4*(3). https://doi.org/10.1097/IN9.0000000000000004

Brands, A. M., Biessels, G. J., de Haan, E. H., Kappelle, L. J., & Kessels, R. P. (2005). The effects of type 1 diabetes on cognitive performance: A meta-analysis. *Diabetes Care, 28*(3), 726–735. https://doi.org/10.2337/diacare.28.3.726

Brismar, T., Maurex, L., Cooray, G., Juntti-Berggren, L., Lindström, P., Ekberg, K., Adner, N., & Andersson, S. (2007). Predictors of cognitive impairment in type 1 diabetes. *Psychoneuroendocrinology, 32*(8–10), 1041–1051. https://doi.org/10.1016/j.psyneuen.2007.08.002

Brochet, B., & Ruet, A. (2019). Cognitive impairment in multiple sclerosis with regards to disease duration and clinical phenotypes. *Frontiers in Neurology, 10*, 261. https://doi.org/10.3389/fneur.2019.00261

Bullard, K. M., Cowie, C. C., Lessem, S. E., Saydah, S. H., Menke, A., Geiss, L. S., Orchard, T. J., Rolka, D. B., & Imperatore, G. (2018). Prevalence of diagnosed diabetes in adults by diabetes type – United States, 2016. *Morbidity and Mortality Weekly Report, 67*(12), 359–361. https://doi.org/10.15585/mmwr.mm6712a2

Calcaterra, V., Nappi, R. E., Regalbuto, C., De Silvestri, A., Incardona, A., Amariti, R., Bassanese, F., Clemente, A. M., Vinci, F., Albertini, R., & Larizza, D. (2020). Gender differences at the onset of autoimmune thyroid diseases in children and adolescents. *Frontiers in Endocrinology, 11*, 229. https://doi.org/10.3389/fendo.2020.00229

Carter, E. E., Barr, S. G., & Clarke, A. E. (2016). The global burden of SLE: Prevalence, health disparities and socioeconomic impact. *Nature Reviews. Rheumatology, 12*(10), 605–620. https://doi.org/10.1038/nrrheum.2016.137

Chaker, L., Cooper, D. S., Walsh, J. P., & Peeters, R. P. (2024). *Hyperthyroidism. Lancet, 403*(10428), 768–780. https://doi.org/10.1016/S0140-6736(23)02016-0

Chaurasia, N., Singh, A., Singh, I. L., Singh, T., & Tiwari, T. (2020). Cognitive dysfunction in patients of rheumatoid arthritis. *Journal of Family Medicine and Primary Care, 9*(5), 2219–2225. https://doi.org/10.4103/jfmpc.jfmpc_307_20

Chaudhuri, J., Mukherjee, A., & Chakravarty, A. (2023). Hashimoto's encephalopathy: Case series and literature review. *Current Neurology and Neuroscience Reports, 23*(4), 167–175. https://doi.org/10.1007/s11910-023-01255-5

Chaytor, N. S., Barbosa-Leiker, C., Ryan, C. M., Germine, L. T., Hirsch, I. B., & Weinstock, R. S. (2019). Clinically significant cognitive impairment in older adults with type 1 diabetes. *Journal of Diabetes and Its Complications, 33*(1), 91–97. https://doi.org/10.1016/j.jdiacomp.2018.04.003

Chiarello, P., Talarico, V., Nicoletti, A., Rodio, B., Arcuri, P. P., Bosco, D., Gigliotti, F., Galati, M. C., & Raiola, G. (2020). Hashimoto encephalopathy: A case report and a short revision of current literature. *Acta Bio-Medica, 91*(3), 10.23750/abm.v91i3.10157.

Cincinelli, G., Generali, E., Dudam, R., Ravindran, V., & Selmi, C. (2018). Why women or why not men? Sex and autoimmune diseases. *Indian Journal of Rheumatology, 13*(1), 44–50. https://doi.org/10.4103/injr.injr_1_18

Cornelius, D. C. (2019). The role of sex differences in inflammation and autoimmune diseases. In B. LaMarca & B. T. Alexander (Eds.), *Sex differences in cardiovascular physiology and pathophysiology* (pp. 205–217). Academic Press. https://doi.org/10.1016/B978-0-12-813197-8.00013-0

Costenbader, K. H., Feskanich, D., Stampfer, M. J., & Karlson, E. W. (2007). Reproductive and menopausal factors and risk of systemic lupus erythematosus in women. *Arthritis and Rheumatism, 56*(4), 1251–1262. https://doi.org/10.1002/art.22510

Dalmau, J., Armangué, T., Planagumà, J., Radosevic, M., Mannara, F., Leypoldt, F., Geis, C., Lancaster, E., Titulaer, M. J., Rosenfeld, M. R., & Graus, F. (2019). An update on anti-NMDA receptor encephalitis for neurologists and psychiatrists: Mechanisms and models. *The Lancet. Neurology, 18*(11), 1045–1057. https://doi.org/10.1016/S1474-4422(19)30244-3

D'hooghe, M. B., D'Hooghe, T., & De Keyser, J. (2013). Female gender and reproductive factors affecting risk, relapses and progression in multiple sclerosis. *Gynecologic and Obstetric Investigation, 75*(2), 73–84. https://doi.org/10.1159/000346319

Donaldson, E., Patel, V. P., Shammi, P., & Feinstein, A. (2019). Why sex matters: A cognitive study of people with multiple sclerosis. *Cognitive and Behavioral Neurology, 32*(1), 39–45. https://doi.org/10.1097/WNN.0000000000000188

Doskas, T., Vavougios, G. D., Karampetsou, P., Kormas, C., Synadinakis, E., Stavrogianni, K., Sionidou, P., Serdari, A., Vorvolakos, T., Iliopoulos, I., & Vadikolias, K. (2021). Neurocognitive impairment and social cognition in multiple sclerosis. *The International Journal of Neuroscience, 132*(12), 1229–1244.

Dowdy, S. W., Dwyer, K. A., Smith, C. A., & Wallston, K. A. (1996). Gender and psychological well-being of persons with rheumatoid arthritis. *Arthritis Care and Research, 9*(6), 449–456. https://doi.org/10.1002/art.1790090606

Dupuis, M. L., Maselli, A., Pagano, M. T., Pierdominici, M., & Ortona, E. (2019). Immune response and autoimmune disease: A matter of sex. *International Journal of Gender-Specific Medicine, 5*(1), 11–20. https://doi.org/10.1723/3148.31294

Emerson, J. S., Gruenewald, S. M., Gomes, L., Lin, M. W., & Swaminathan, S. (2023). The conundrum of neuropsychiatric systemic lupus erythematosus: Current and novel approaches to diagnosis. *Frontiers in Neurology, 14*, 1111769. https://doi.org/10.3389/fneur.2023.1111769

Evers, I. M., de Valk, H. W., & Visser, G. H. (2004). Risk of complications of pregnancy in women with type 1 diabetes: Nationwide prospective study in the Netherlands. *British Medical Journal, 328*(7445), 915. https://doi.org/10.1136/bmj.38043.583160.EE

Figgie, M. P., Jr., Kelly, H., Pyatka, N., Chu, C., & Abboud, H. (2024). Neurological morbidity associated with thyroid antibodies: Hashimoto's encephalopathy and beyond. *Journal of Neurology Science, 458*(122908). https://doi.org/10.1016/j.jns.2024.122908

Finlayson, M., Al-Mashita, L., & Sandhu, R. (2023). Participant diversity in clinical trials of rehabilitation interventions for people with multiple sclerosis: A scoping review. *Multiple Sclerosis, 29*(9), 1149–1157. https://doi.org/10.1177/13524585231189670

Franco, J. S., Amaya-Amaya, J., & Anaya, J. M. (2013). Thyroid disease and autoimmune diseases. In J. M. Anaya, Y. Shoenfeld, A. Rojas-Villarraga, R. A. Levy, & R. Cervera (Eds.), *Autoimmunity: From bench to bedside*. El Rosario University Press. Accessed July 8, 2023, from https://www.ncbi.nlm.nih.gov/books/NBK459466/

Galioto, R., Grezmak, T., Swetlik, C., Abbatemarco, J. R., Titulaer, M. J., Finke, C., & Kunchok, A. (2023). Neuropsychological testing in autoimmune encephalitis: A scoping Review. *Neurology Neuroimmunology & Neuroinflammation, 11*(1). https://doi.org/10.1212/NXI.0000000000200179

Gilli, F., DiSano, K. D., & Pachner, A. R. (2020). SeXX matters in multiple sclerosis. *Frontiers in Neurology, 11*, 616. https://doi.org/10.3389/fneur.2020.00616

Gui, Y., Bai, W., Xu, J., Duan, X., Zhan, F., Zhao, C., Jiang, Z., Li, Z., Wu, L., Liu, S., Yang, M., Wei, W., Wang, Z., Zhao, J., Wang, Q., Leng, X., Tian, X., Li, M., Zhao, Y., Zeng, X., et al. (2022). Sex differences in systemic lupus erythematosus (SLE): An inception cohort of the Chinese SLE Treatment and Research Group (CSTAR) registry XVII. *Chinese Medical Journal, 135*(18), 2191–2199. https://doi.org/10.1097/CM9.0000000000002360

Gunning, J. N. (2023). "But you don't look sick:" Memorable messages of emerging adulthood autoimmune disease. *Journal of Social and Personal Relationships, 40*(6), 2008–2030. https://doi.org/10.1177/02654075221137548

Helmick, C. G., Felson, D. T., Lawrence, R. C., Gabriel, S., Hirsch, R., Kwoh, C. K., Liang, M. H., Kremers, H. M., Mayes, M. D., Merkel, P. A., Pillemer, S. R., Reveille, J. D., Stone, J. H., & National Arthritis Data Workgroup. (2008). Estimates of the prevalence of arthritis and other rheumatic conditions in the United States. Part I. *Arthritis and Rheumatism, 58*(1), 15–25. https://doi.org/10.1002/art.23177

Hernández-Avila, M., Liang, M. H., Willett, W. C., Stampfer, M. J., Colditz, G. A., Rosner, B., Roberts, W. N., Hennekens, C. H., & Speizer, F. E. (1990). Reproductive factors, smoking, and the risk for rheumatoid arthritis. *Epidemiology, 1*(4), 285–291. https://doi.org/10.1097/00001648-199007000-00005

Hittle, M., Culpepper, W. J., Langer-Gould, A., Marrie, R. A., Cutter, G. R., Kaye, W. E., Wagner, L., Topol, B., LaRocca, N. G., Nelson, L. M., & Wallin, M. T. (2023). Population-based estimates for the prevalence of multiple sclerosis in the United States by race, ethnicity, age, sex, and geographic region. *Journal of the American Medical Association Neurology, 80*(7), 693–701. https://doi.org/10.1001/jamaneurol.2023.1135

Hoi, A., Igel, T., Mok, C. C., & Arnaud, L. (2024). Systemic lupus erythematosus. *Lancet, 403*(10441), 2326–2338. https://doi.org/10.1016/S0140-6736(24)00398-2

Hu, X., Chen, Y., Shen, Y., Tian, R., Sheng, Y., & Que, H. (2022). Global prevalence and epidemiological trends of Hashimoto's thyroiditis in adults: A systematic review and meta-analysis. *Frontiers in Public Health, 10*. https://doi.org/10.3389/fpubh.2022.1020709

Intriago, M., Maldonado, G., Cárdenas, J., & Ríos, C. (2019). Clinical characteristics in patients with rheumatoid arthritis: Differences between genders. *The Scientific World Journal, 8103812*. https://doi.org/10.1155/2019/8103812

Izmirly, P. M., Parton, H., Wang, L., McCune, W. J., Lim, S. S., Drenkard, C., ... & Somers, E. C. (2021). Prevalence of systemic lupus erythematosus in the United States: estimates from a meta-analysis of the Centers for Disease Control and Prevention National Lupus Registries. *Arthritis & Rheumatology, 73*(6), 991–996.

Jolly, M., Sequeira, W., Block, J. A., Toloza, S., Bertoli, A., Blazevic, I., Vila, L. M., Moldovan, I., Torralba, K. D., Mazzoni, D., Cicognani, E., Hasni, S., Goker, B., Haznedaroglu, S., Bourre-Tessier, J., Navarra, S. V., Mok, C. C., Weisman, M., Clarke, A. E., Wallace, D., et al. (2019). Sex differences in quality of life in patients with systemic lupus erythematosus. *Arthritis Care & Research, 71*(12), 1647–1652. https://doi.org/10.1002/acr.23588

Karakiewicz-Krawczyk, K., Knyszyńska, A., Wieder-Huszla, S., Zabielska, P., Włodarska, J., & Jurczak, A. (2022). A preliminary assessment of the impact of women's susceptibility to Hashimoto's thyroiditis on the occurrence of anxiety and depressive disorders. *Archives of Psychiatry and Psychotherapy, 24*(1), 65–72. https://doi.org/10.12740/APP/139475

Kedia, A. K., & Ravindran, V. (2020). Influence of gender on autoimmune rheumatic diseases. In S. Sharma (Ed.), *Women's health in autoimmune diseases*. Springer. https://doi.org/10.1007/978-981-15-0114-2_2

Krysko, K. M., Graves, J. S., Dobson, R., Altintas, A., Amato, M. P., Bernard, J., Bonavita, S., Bove, R., Cavalla, P., Clerico, M., Corona, T., Doshi, A., Fragoso, Y., Jacobs, D., Jokubaitis, V., Landi, D., Llamosa, G., Longbrake, E. E., Maillart, E., Marta, M., et al. (2020). Sex effects across the lifespan in women with multiple sclerosis. *Therapeutic Advances in Neurological Disorders, 13*. https://doi.org/10.1177/1756286420936166

Kvam, K. A., Stahl, J. P., Chow, F. C., Soldatos, A., Tattevin, P., Sejvar, J., & Mailles, A. (2024). Outcome and sequelae of autoimmune encephalitis. *Journal of Clinical Neurology, 20*(1), 3–22. https://doi.org/10.3988/jcn.2023.0242

Lekurwale, V., Acharya, S., Shukla, S., Kumar, S., & Lekurwale, V. Y. (2023). *Neuropsychiatric Manifestations of Thyroid Diseases. Cureus, 15*(1).

Lichtiger, A., Fadaei, G., & Tagoe, C. E. (2024). Autoimmune thyroid disease and rheumatoid arthritis: Where the twain meet. *Clinical Rheumatology, 43*(3), 895–905. https://doi.org/10.1007/s10067-024-06888-6

Lichtnekert, J., Anders, H. J., & Lech, M. (2022). Lupus nephritis: current perspectives and moving forward. *Journal of Inflammation Research*, 6533–6552.

Ma, L. Y., Zhao, B., Ou, Y. N., Zhang, D. D., Li, Q. Y., & Tan, L. (2023). Association of thyroid disease with risks of dementia and cognitive impairment: A meta-analysis and systematic review. *Frontiers in Aging Neuroscience, 15*. https://doi.org/10.3389/fnagi.2023.1137584

Manicardi, V., Russo, G., Napoli, A., Torlone, E., Li Volsi, P., Giorda, C. B., Musacchio, N., Nicolucci, A., Suraci, C., Lucisano, G., Rossi, M. C., & AMD Annals Study Group. (2016). Gender-disparities in adults with Type 1 Diabetes: More than a quality of care issue. A cross-sectional observational study from the AMD Annals Initiative. *PLoS One, 11*(10). https://doi.org/10.1371/journal.pone.0162960

Maranini, B., Bortoluzzi, A., Silvagni, E., & Govoni, M. (2022). Focus on sex and gender: What we need to know in the management of rheumatoid arthritis. *Journal of Personalized Medicine, 12*(3), 499. https://doi.org/10.3390/jpm12030499

Mazzù, I., Mosti, S., Caltagirone, C., & Carlesimo, G. A. (2012). Hashimoto's encephalopathy: Neuropsychological findings. *Neurological Sciences, 33*(3), 653–656. https://doi.org/10.1007/s10072-011-0813-z

Meade, T., Manolios, N., Cumming, S. R., Conaghan, P. G., & Katz, P. (2018). Cognitive impairment in rheumatoid arthritis: A systematic review. *Arthritis Care & Research, 70*(1), 39–52. https://doi.org/10.1002/acr.23243

Mendelsohn, S., Khoja, L., Alfred, S., He, J., Anderson, M., DuBois, D., Touma, Z., & Engel, L. (2021). Cognitive impairment in systemic lupus erythematosus is negatively related to social role participation and quality of life: A systematic review. *Lupus, 30*(10), 1617–1630. https://doi.org/10.1177/09612033211031008

Mobasseri, M., Shirmohammadi, M., Amiri, T., Vahed, N., Hosseini Fard, H., & Ghojazadeh, M. (2020). Prevalence and incidence of type 1 diabetes in the world: A systematic review and meta-analysis. *Health Promotion Perspectives, 10*(2), 98–115. https://doi.org/10.34172/hpp.2020.18

Murphy, G., & Isenberg, D. (2013). Effect of gender on clinical presentation in systemic lupus erythematosus. *Rheumatology, 52*(12), 2108–2115. https://doi.org/10.1093/rheumatology/ket160

Nusbaum, J. S., Mirza, I., Shum, J., Freilich, R. W., Cohen, R. E., Pillinger, M. H., Izmirly, P. M., & Buyon, J. P. (2020). Sex differences in systemic lupus erythematosus: Epidemiology, clinical considerations, and disease pathogenesis. *Mayo Clinic Proceedings, 95*(2), 384–394. https://doi.org/10.1016/j.mayocp.2019.09.012

Oláh, C., Schwartz, N., Denton, C., Kardos, Z., Putterman, C., & Szekanecz, Z. (2020). Cognitive dysfunction in autoimmune rheumatic diseases. *Arthritis Research & Therapy, 22*(1), 78. https://doi.org/10.1186/s13075-020-02180-5

Pedard, M., Quirié, A., Tessier, A., Garnier, P., Totoson, P., Demougeot, C., & Marie, C. (2021). A reconciling hypothesis centered on brain-derived neurotrophic factor to explain neuropsychiatric manifestations in rheumatoid arthritis. *Rheumatology, 60*(4), 1608–1619. https://doi.org/10.1093/rheumatology/keaa849

Perwieniec, J., Podwójcic, K., Maluchnik, M., Szeląg, M., Walkiewicz, D., Zakrzewski, M., Droździkowska, A., Kamiński, B., Zasybska, A., Wnuk, M., Słowik, A., & Rejdak, K. (2021). Gender-related differences in prodromal multiple sclerosis characteristics: A 7-year observation study. *Journal of Clinical Medicine, 10*(17). https://doi.org/10.3390/jcm10173821

Petersen, L. E., Baptista, T. S. A., Molina, J. K., Motta, J. G., do Prado, A., Piovesan, D. M., de Nardi, T., Viola, T. W., Vieira, É. L. M., Teixeira, A. L., Grassi-Oliveira, R., & Bauer, M. E. (2018). Cognitive impairment in rheumatoid arthritis: Role of lymphocyte subsets, cytokines and neurotrophic factors. *Clinical Rheumatology, 37*(5), 1171–1181. https://doi.org/10.1007/s10067-018-3990-9

Pikwer, M., Bergström, U., Nilsson, J. Å., Jacobsson, L., & Turesson, C. (2012). Early menopause is an independent predictor of rheumatoid arthritis. *Annals of the Rheumatic Diseases, 71*(3), 378–381. https://doi.org/10.1136/ard.2011.200059

Pyzik, A., Grywalska, E., Matyjaszek-Matuszek, B., & Roliński, J. (2015). Immune disorders in Hashimoto's thyroiditis: What do we know so far? *Journal of Immunology Research*. https://doi.org/10.1155/2015/979167

Raghunath, S., Glikmann-Johnston, Y., Vincent, F. B., Morand, E. F., Stout, J. C., & Hoi, A. (2023). Patterns and prevalence of cognitive dysfunction in systemic lupus erythematosus. *Journal of the International Neuropsychological Society, 29*(5), 421–430. https://doi.org/10.1017/S1355617722000418

Ramírez Sepúlveda, J. I., Bolin, K., Mofors, J., Leonard, D., Svenungsson, E., Jönsen, A., Bengtsson, C., DISSECT consortium, Nordmark, G., Rantapää Dahlqvist, S., Bengtsson, A. A., Rönnblom, L., Sjöwall, C., Gunnarsson, I., & Wahren-Herlenius, M. (2019). Sex differences in clinical presentation of systemic lupus erythematosus. *Biology of Sex Differences, 10*(1), 60. https://doi.org/10.1186/s13293-019-0274-2

Rayes, H. A., Tani, C., Kwan, A., Marzouk, S., Colosimo, K., Medina-Rosas, J., Mustafa, A., Su, J., Lambiris, P., Mosca, M., & Touma, Z. (2018). What is the prevalence of cognitive impairment in lupus and which instruments are used to measure it? A systematic review and meta-analysis. *Seminars in Arthritis and Rheumatism, 48*(2), 240–255. https://doi.org/10.1016/j.semarthrit.2018.02.007

Samulowitz, A., Gremyr, I., Eriksson, E., & Hensing, G. (2018). "Brave Men" and "Emotional Women": A theory-guided literature review on gender bias in health care and gendered norms towards patients with chronic pain. *Pain Research & Management*. https://doi.org/10.1155/2018/6358624

Santos, F. P. S. T., Nascimento, B. R., Calderaro, D. C., Ferreira, G. A., & Correa, H. (2021). Neuropsychiatric syndromes in childhood-onset systemic lupus erythematosus: A systematic review and meta-analysis. *Journal of Clinical Rheumatology, 27*(5), 206–214.

Sarwar, S., Mohamed, A. S., Rogers, S., Sarmast, S. T., Kataria, S., Mohamed, K. H., Khalid, M. Z., Saeeduddin, M. O., Shiza, S. T., Ahmad, S., Awais, A., & Singh, R. (2021). Neuropsychiatric systemic lupus erythematosus: A 2021 update on diagnosis, management, and current challenges. *Cureus, 13*(9). https://doi.org/10.7759/cureus.17969

Sautner, J., Puchner, R., Alkin, A., & Pieringer, H. (2020). Depression: A common comorbidity in women with rheumatoid arthritis-results from an Austrian cross-sectional study. *British Medical Journal Open, 10*(1). https://doi.org/10.1136/bmjopen-2019-033958

Scherlinger, M., Mertz, P., Sagez, F., Meyer, A., Felten, R., Chatelus, E., Javier, R. M., Sordet, C., Martin, T., Korganow, A. S., Guffroy, A., Poindron, V., Richez, C., Truchetet, M. E., Blanco, P., Schaeverbeke, T., Sibilia, J., Devillers, H., & Arnaud, L. (2020). Worldwide trends in all-cause mortality of auto-immune systemic diseases between 2001 and 2014. *Autoimmunity Reviews, 19*(6). https://doi.org/10.1016/j.autrev.2020.102531

Schoonheim, M. M., Hulst, H. E., Landi, D., Ciccarelli, O., Roosendaal, S. D., Sanz-Arigita, E. J., Vrenken, H., Polman, C. H., Stam, C. J., Barkhof, F., & Geurts, J. J. (2012). Gender-related differences in functional connectivity in multiple sclerosis. *Multiple Sclerosis, 18*(2), 164–173. https://doi.org/10.1177/1352458511422245

Seet, D., Allameen, N. A., Tay, S. H., Cho, J., & Mak, A. (2021). Cognitive dysfunction in systemic lupus erythematosus: Immunopathology, clinical manifestations, neuroimaging and management. *Rheumatology and Therapy, 8*(2), 651–679. https://doi.org/10.1007/s40744-021-00312-0

Sharma, S., & Brown, C. E. (2022). Microvascular basis of cognitive impairment in type 1 diabetes. *Pharmacology & Therapeutics, 229*. https://doi.org/10.1016/j.pharmthera.2021.107929

Shin, S., Park, E. H., Kang, E. H., Lee, Y. J., Song, Y. W., & Ha, Y. J. (2021). Sex differences in clinical characteristics and their influence on clinical outcomes in an observational cohort of patients with rheumatoid arthritis. *Joint Bone Spine, 88*(3). https://doi.org/10.1016/j.jbspin.2020.105124

Siegel, C. H., & Sammaritano, L. R. (2024). Systemic lupus erythematosus: A review. *Journal of the American Medical Association, 331*(17), 1480–1491. https://doi.org/10.1001/jama.2024.2315

Sokka, T., Toloza, S., Cutolo, M., Kautiainen, H., Makinen, H., Gogus, F., Skakic, V., Badsha, H., Peets, T., Baranauskaite, A., Géher, P., Ujfalussy, I., Skopouli, F. N., Mavrommati, M., Alten, R., Pohl, C., Sibilia, J., Stancati, A., Salaffi, F., Romanowski, W., et al. (2009). Women, men, and rheumatoid arthritis: Analyses of disease activity, disease characteristics, and treatments in the QUEST-RA study. *Arthritis Research & Therapy, 11*(1). https://doi.org/10.1186/ar2591

Strait, A., Castillo, F., Choden, S., Li, J., Whitaker, E., Falasinnu, T., Schmajuk, G., & Yazdany, J. (2019). Demographic characteristics of participants in rheumatoid arthritis randomized clinical trials: A systematic review. *Journal of the American Medical Association Network Open, 2*(11).

Sun, Y., Ren, G., Ren, J., Shan, W., Han, X., Lian, Y., Wang, T., & Wang, Q. (2020). The association between age and prognosis in patients under 45 years of age with anti-NMDA receptor encephalitis. *Frontiers in Neurology, 11*. https://doi.org/10.3389/fneur.2020.612632

Tian, J., Zhang, D., Yao, X., Huang, Y., & Lu, Q. (2023). Global epidemiology of systemic lupus erythematosus: A comprehensive systematic analysis and modelling study. *Annals of the Rheumatic Diseases, 82*(3), 351–356. https://doi.org/10.1136/ard-2022-223035

Vitturi, B. K., Nascimento, B. A. C., Alves, B. R., de Campos, F. S. C., & Torigoe, D. Y. (2019). Cognitive impairment in patients with rheumatoid arthritis. *Journal of Clinical Neuroscience, 69*, 81–87. https://doi.org/10.1016/j.jocn.2019.08.027

Vos, X. G., Smit, N., Endert, E., Brosschot, J. F., Tijssen, J. G., & Wiersinga, W. M. (2009). Age and stress as determinants of the severity of hyperthyroidism caused by Graves' disease in newly diagnosed patients. *European Journal of Endocrinology, 160*, 193–199.

Wallin, M. T., Culpepper, W. J., Campbell, J. D., Nelson, L. M., Langer-Gould, A., Marrie, R. A., Cutter, G. R., Kaye, W. E., Wagner, L., Tremlett, H., Buka, S. L., Dilokthornsakul, P., Topol, B., Chen, L. H., LaRocca, N. G., & U.S. Multiple Sclerosis Prevalence Workgroup. (2019). The prevalence of MS in the United States: A population-based estimate using health claims data. *Neurology, 92*(10). https://doi.org/10.1212/WNL.0000000000007035

Wang, Y., Miao, A., Shi, Y., Ge, J., Wang, L., Yu, C., Xu, H., Yu, Y., Huang, S., Li, Y., & Wang, X. (2020a). Influencing electroclinical features and prognostic factors in patients with anti-NMDAR encephalitis: A cohort follow-up study in Chinese patients. *Scientific Reports, 10*(1). https://doi.org/10.1038/s41598-020-67485-6

Wang, S. Y., Wang, C. T., Tien, K. J., Chang, C. C., & Liu, T. H. (2020b). Thyroid-stimulating hormone receptor antibodies during follow-up as remission markers in childhood-onset Graves' disease treated with antithyroid drugs. *Kaohsiung Journal of Medical Sciences, 36*(4), 281–286. https://doi.org/10.1002/kjm2.12167

Xu, Y., & Wu, Q. (2021). Prevalence trend and disparities in rheumatoid arthritis among U.S. adults, 2005-2018. *Journal of Clinical Medicine, 10*(15). https://doi.org/10.3390/jcm10153289

Yang, H., Xia, Q., Shen, Y., Chen, T. L., Wang, J., & Lu, Y. Y. (2022). Gender-specific impact of metabolic obesity phenotypes on the risk of Hashimoto's thyroiditis: A retrospective data analysis using a health check-up database. *Journal of Inflammation Research, 15*, 827–837. https://doi.org/10.2147/JIR.S353384

Ye, Y., Wang, Y., Li, S., Guo, J., Ding, L., & Liu, M. (2022). Association of hypothyroidism and the risk of cognitive dysfunction: A meta-analysis. *Journal of Clinical Medicine, 11*(22), 6726. https://doi.org/10.3390/jcm11226726

Yuen, K., Green, R., Bingham, K., Ruttan, L., Lee-Kim, V., Tartaglia, M. C., Anderson, M., Zandy, M., Choi, M. Y., Fritzler, M. J., Wither, J. E., Beaton, D. E., Katz, P., & Touma, Z. (2021). Metrics and definitions used in the assessment of cognitive impairment in systemic lupus erythematosus: A systematic review. *Seminars in Arthritis and Rheumatism, 51*(4), 819–830. https://doi.org/10.1016/j.semarthrit.2021.05.018

Yusuf, F. L. A., Wijnands, J. M. A., Karim, M. E., Kingwell, E., Zhu, F., Evans, C., Fisk, J. D., Zhao, Y., Marrie, R. A., & Tremlett, H. (2022). Sex and age differences in the multiple sclerosis prodrome. *Frontiers in Neurology, 13*. https://doi.org/10.3389/fneur.2022.1017492

Zamwar, U. M., & Muneshwar, K. N. (2023). Epidemiology, types, causes, clinical presentation, diagnosis, and treatment of hypothyroidism. *Cureus, 15*(9), e46241. https://doi.org/10.7759/cureus.46241

Zhang, L., Lu, Y., Xu, L., Liu, L., Wu, X., Zhang, Y., Zhu, G., & Hong, Z. (2020). Anti-N-methyl-D-aspartate receptor encephalitis with accompanying ovarian teratoma in female patients from East China: Clinical features, treatment, and prognostic outcomes. *Seizure, 75*, 55–62. https://doi.org/10.1016/j.seizure.2019.12.016

Zhao, X., Teng, Y., Ni, J., Li, T., Shi, J., & Wei, M. (2023). Systematic review: Clinical characteristics of anti-N-methyl-D-aspartate receptor encephalitis. *Frontiers in Human Neuroscience, 17*. https://doi.org/10.3389/fnhum.2023.1261638

Zhao, Z., Zhang, Y., Du, Q., Chen, H., Shi, Z., Wang, J., Qiu, Y., Yan, C., & Zhou, H. (2020). Differences in physical, mental, and social functions between males and females in multiple sclerosis: A multicenter cross-sectional study in China. *Multiple Sclerosis and Related Disorders, 48*. https://doi.org/10.1016/j.msard.2020.102693

Zhou, J. Y., Xu, B., Lopes, J., Blamoun, J., & Li, L. (2017). Hashimoto encephalopathy: A literature review. *Acta Neurologica Scandinavica, 135*(3), 285–290.

Chapter 10
Chronic Health Conditions

Maddy Myers and Mary Jo Pugh

Introduction

Understanding the intricate interplay between gender and health reveals striking differences in how women and men experience, report, and manage complex medical conditions. Experiences by gender for chronic pain, fibromyalgia, chronic fatigue syndrome, sleep disorders, psychogenic nonepileptic seizures (PNES), and long COVID exhibit particularly pronounced variation. Despite these clear differences, there remains a notable gap in gender-specific research, often leading to generalized treatment approaches that may not be equally effective for all. Focusing on these complex conditions, we shed light on how biological, psychological, and social factors uniquely shape the experiences of women. By exploring the latest epidemiological data, we aim to provide a comprehensive understanding of unique presentations in women, illuminate research gaps, and ultimately guide more personalized and effective healthcare interventions (Table 10.1).

Chronic Pain

Chronic pain is characterized as pain that persists or recurs for at least 3–6 months, often extending beyond the usual healing period of an injury or illness (Dydyk & Conemann, 2024). It encompasses a diverse group of conditions characterized by complex interactions among physical, psychological, and social factors, which can

M. Myers (✉)
University of Utah School of Medicine, Salt Lake City, UT, USA
e-mail: Maddy.Myers@hsc.utah.edu

M. J. Pugh
VA Salt Lake City, University of Utah School of Medicine, Salt Lake City, UT, USA

E. Sullivan-Baca, R. Ellison (eds.), *Neuropsychology of Women*,
https://doi.org/10.1007/978-3-031-87228-0_10

Table 10.1 Ration of Women to Men with Chronic Health Conditions

Chronic health condition	Ratio (women:men)
Chronic pain	1.2 : 1
Fibromyalgia	7–9 : 1
Myalgic encephalitis / chronic fatigue syndrome	1.9 : 1
Sleep disorders	1.4 : 1
Psychogenic nonepileptic seizures	2–3 : 1
Long COVID	1.6 : 1

significantly impair daily functioning, quality of life, as well as social support. Moreover, biological mechanisms, such as neuroinflammation and central sensitization, alongside psychosocial stressors, contribute to the persistence and complexity of chronic pain syndromes (Tracey & Mantyh, 2007; Vardeh et al., 2016).

Epidemiology

Chronic pain—in this case defined as pain that persists on most days or every day for at least 3 months—affected 20.5%–21.8% of U.S. adults across genders between 2019 and 2021. High-impact chronic pain, a more severe form that limits daily activities or work on most days, affected 6.9%–7.8% of U.S. adults during the same period (Rikard et al., 2023). Women exhibited a higher prevalence of chronic pain, both in nonadjusted and age-adjusted analyses (22% vs. 19.7% and 20.5% vs. 18.8%, respectively; Rikard et al., 2023). This trend persisted with high-impact chronic pain, with women reporting rates of 7.6% compared to 6.2% in men (nonadjusted) and 7.0% vs. 5.8% (age-adjusted) (Rikard et al., 2023).

Data from the National Health and Nutrition Examination Survey (NHANES) spanning from 1999 to 2004 reveal that women had a higher prevalence of both localized and widespread chronic pain (e.g., knee, hip, or shoulder pain) at 56.4% compared to 43.6% in men. Similarly, widespread chronic pain—characterized by bilateral pain above and below the waist with axial involvement (e.g., spine or chest)—was reported by 59.7% of women compared to 40.3% of men (Umeda et al., 2019). Together, these findings demonstrate that women consistently report higher rates of both localized and widespread chronic pain across different time periods and datasets. This trend, observed across decades, underscores the persistent gender disparity in chronic pain prevalence.

Chronic pain disparities extend beyond gender, with significant differences across demographic factors such as race, ethnicity, and sexual orientation. Intersectional analysis from the CDC MMWR highlighted that certain populations, such as American Indian/Alaska Native (AI/AN) adults and individuals identifying as bisexual, also exhibited significantly higher rates of high-impact chronic pain. Age-adjusted prevalence of high-impact chronic pain among AI/AN adults was more than six times higher than non-Hispanic/Latinx Asian adults (12.8% vs. 2.1%, respectively; Rikard et al., 2023) and almost two times as high as among non-Hispanic/Latinx White adults (12.8% vs. 6.5%, respectively; Rikard et al., 2023). The age-adjusted prevalence of chronic pain among adults identifying as bisexual was 32.9% compared with 20.7% among those identifying as gay or lesbian and 19.3% among adults identifying as straight (Rikard et al., 2023). These disparities underscore the need for intersectional approaches in chronic pain research and healthcare, ensuring that prevention, diagnosis, and treatment strategies are equitable and responsive to the diverse pain experiences of affected populations.

Risk Factors and Presentation

The experience and management of chronic pain can vary greatly between women and men. Research indicates that the genotypic and phenotypic differences in pain between the sexes are influenced by a combination of anatomical, physiological, neural, hormonal, psychological, social, and cultural factors (Casale et al., 2021; see Fig. 10.1). Women are more likely to experience pain related to the genitourinary system (Casale et al., 2021), postpartum chronic pain (Lavand'homme, 2019), and chronic pelvic pain syndrome (Grinberg et al., 2020; Vincent & Evans, 2021). Additionally, women often utilize different coping mechanisms for pain compared to men. For example, women might seek social support more frequently, while men may be more inclined to use problem-focused strategies (El-Shormilisy et al., 2015).

Animal models, particularly rodent models, suggest gender differences in pain sensitivity are influenced by hormonal fluctuations, particularly in females during the estrous and menstrual cycles. These cycles, which include phases like proestrus and diestrus in rodents and the follicular and luteal phases in humans, are characterized by varying estrogen levels (Mota-Carrillo et al., 2024). A study by

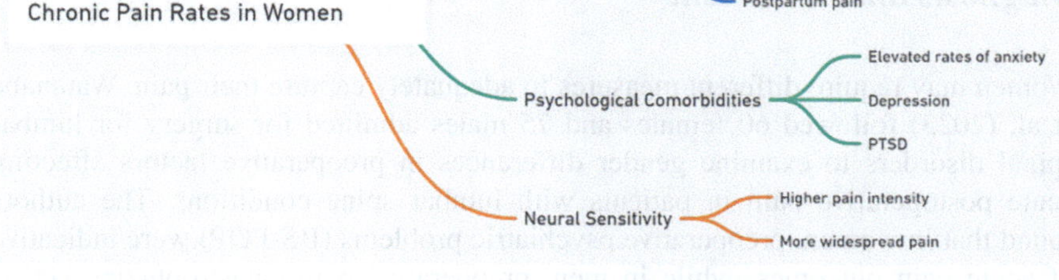

Fig. 10.1 Key factors contributing to higher chronic pain rates in women

Mota-Carrillo et al. (2024) examined pain responses in female mice at different estrous cycle phases and male mice. They found that female mice had a lower pain threshold during the proestrus phase compared to other phases. During the proestrous phase, female mice had a lower pain threshold than male mice. Additionally, they observed that transient receptor potential vanilloid 1 (TRPV1) protein levels were higher in females during proestrus than in other phases and in male mice (Mota-Carrillo et al., 2024). TRPV1 is an ion channel crucial for pain perception, as it detects and responds to noxious stimuli such as high temperatures and chemical irritants like capsaicin, which cause a burning sensation (Caterina et al., 2000; Mota-Carrillo et al., 2024). Thus, these findings suggest that hormonal changes, particularly related to sex steroid hormones, play a significant role in regulating pain sensitivity.

Chronic pain presents differently in women and men, with women often reporting higher pain sensitivity, greater intensity, and more widespread discomfort (Casale et al., 2021). Pain in women is more frequently accompanied by comorbid conditions like anxiety, depression, and PTSD, with these conditions intensifying each other's severity when present together (Casale et al., 2021; Gasperi et al., 2021). Women Veterans face heightened vulnerability to chronic pain due to increased exposure to various forms of trauma, including interpersonal violence and childhood abuse, as well as more life stressors and limited social support (Lehavot et al., 2018). In a 2021 cohort of 1,936,859 Veterans with chronic pain—12.5% of whom were women—Hadlandsmyth et al. (2024) found that women Veterans had higher rates of depression, anxiety, PTSD, and sleep disturbances. These mental health conditions contributed to pain catastrophizing (where individuals feel overwhelmed by their pain), which further worsened outcomes (Hadlandsmyth et al., 2024). Women also reported more intense pain and greater interference in daily activities compared to men, reflecting the severe impact chronic pain has on their functioning (Hadlandsmyth et al., 2024). Furthermore, women Veterans exhibited higher rates of multiple overlapping pain conditions (MOPCs), with an average of 2.3 conditions compared to 1.9 among men. PTSD emerged as an independent risk factor for MOPCs, highlighting the importance of integrated, trauma-informed care that addresses both mental health and chronic pain challenges (Hadlandsmyth et al., 2024).

Diagnosis and Treatment

Women may require different measures to adequately capture their pain. Watanabe et al. (2023) followed 60 females and 75 males admitted for surgery for lumbar spinal disorders to examine gender differences in preoperative factors affecting acute postoperative pain in patients with lumbar spine conditions. The authors found that in women, preoperative psychiatric problems (BS-POP) were indicative of acute pain outcomes, while in men, preoperative pain catastrophizing (PCS) scores were a significant predictor of acute pain. These findings suggest that while

PCS should be specifically assessed in men to predict pain severity, women may require a broader evaluation including BS-POP in addition to PCS to better understand and manage acute postoperative pain (Watanabe et al., 2023).

Differences in symptom presentation and pain diagnoses are further complicated by gendered norms about pain expression. Societal expectations can influence how women and men report and cope with pain (Samulowitz et al., 2018). Women are more likely to be diagnosed with chronic pain conditions, partly due to their higher reported prevalence and severity of symptoms. However, gender biases in the treatment of chronic pain are documented—with women receiving less aggressive pain management compared to men (Samulowitz et al., 2018). Additionally, racial and ethnic disparities influence the treatment and management of chronic pain. As the research area grows, so does the body of evidence showing that racial and ethnic differences affect both opioid treatment and long-term monitoring of opioid use (Morales & Yong, 2021). For example, in a survey of a 310-system sample encompassing 2,197,153 person-years, Morden et al. (2021) found that while the crude annual prevalence of opioid use differed slightly between Black/African American and White patients (50.2% vs. 52.2%), the mean annual dose was 36% lower among Black/African American patients (5190 morphine milligram equivalents [MME]) compared to White patients (8082 MME). These complex associations among patient sociodemographic characteristics and chronic pain can significantly impact quality of life and the effectiveness of pain management strategies. Moreover, pharmacological treatment approaches may exacerbate the cognitive impact of chronic pain (e.g., opioids, anticonvulsants; Salinsky et al., 2023). Thus, it is critical to examine both the pain and treatment contributions to cognitive function.

Notable differences exist in the utilization and efficacy of opioids for chronic pain management between women and men. According to the 2019 CDC National Health Statistics Reports, women with chronic pain were more likely to have used a prescription opioid in the past 3 months (24.3%) compared to men (19.4%; Dahlhamer et al., 2021). Interestingly, the efficacy of pain management drugs, such as opioids, may differ between women and men. Research by Wang et al., (2006) shows that female experience significantly less and shorter-lasting relief from morphine than frats. Additionally, Huhn et al. (2018) reviewed evidence suggesting that mu opioid receptors are influenced by sex hormones, with receptor availability fluctuating according to the estrous phase. These findings underscore the complexity of gender differences in opioid efficacy and suggest that similar gender-related factors may influence responses to various pain management strategies. Given these gender-based differences, research suggests that women often benefit more from interdisciplinary pain management programs than men (Keogh et al., 2005; Racine et al., 2020).

Cognitive Outcomes

Chronic pain (including fibromyalgia) and its subsequent treatment are also associated with several distinct cognitive effects linked to well-being, productivity, and mental health. Chronic pain is associated with difficulties or deficits of memory, attention and concentration, executive function, information processing speed, and cognitive flexibility, as well as declines in mental fatigue and overall mood (Berryman et al., 2013). Chronic pain is consistently associated with memory problems in humans—particularly working memory, recall, attention, and recognition (Hagger et al., 2021; Muñoz & Esteve, 2005; van der Leeuw et al., 2018). Memory problems associated with chronic pain are thought to derive from decreased hippocampal volume and plasticity and activation of the basolateral amygdala in context of chronic pain (Mutso et al., 2012; Roozendaal et al., 2006; Tajerian et al., 2018). Similar findings have also been obtained in animal studies (Ji et al., 2010).

Studies in both animals and humans demonstrate pathway overlap between the attention matrix and pain pathways (Filley, 2002). As a result, painful stimuli can interfere with attention, and interestingly, cognitively complex tasks are associated with decreased pain sensitivity, reinforcing the idea that there is a bidirectional relationship between cognition and chronic pain (Villemure & Bushnell, 2002). However, this ability to use cognitive distraction to reduce pain perception is not generally effective in older adults and those with mood-related comorbidities (e.g., depression/anxiety) (van der Leeuw et al., 2018).

Because pathways in the brain associated with executive function and pain also overlap, chronic pain is also associated with impaired executive function (including information processing speed and decision making). Gray matter reduction found in aging also occurs more quickly in the setting of chronic pain, leading to these executive function problems (Ceko et al., 2013; Minkova et al., 2017; Planchuelo-Gómez et al., 2020). However, the type of chronic pain is important as not all types of pain have been associated with impairment of executive function. For instance, fibromyalgia is commonly associated with emotional decision making in women while neuropathic pain is not (Verdejo-García et al., 2009). Studies have also implicated chronic pain in emotional decision making (Apkarian et al., 2004; Barnhart et al., 2019). Taken together, these findings suggest the possibility of personality interactions with pain and cognition.

Fibromyalgia

Fibromyalgia is an often overlooked and misunderstood complex chronic pain disorder. It is defined by widespread musculoskeletal pain, fatigue, and cognitive disturbances (colloquially referred to as "fibro fog") and often coexists with other conditions such as depression, anxiety, and irritable bowel syndrome (IBS; Bhargava & Hurley 2023; Wolfe et al., 2016). Although its exact cause remains unclear, it is understood to involve abnormal pain processing in the central nervous system (Bhargava & Hurley 2023). Given the unique symptom complex and the more gendered presentation, we now describe unique features of fibromyalgia that are not addressed in our discussion of chronic pain above.

Epidemiology

The prevalence of fibromyalgia varies across studies, reflecting differences in methodology and population demographics. The Rochester Epidemiology Project, a population-based study conducted in Olmsted County, Minnesota, identified potential 3410 patients, with 1115 having a documented fibromyalgia diagnosis confirmed through chart review (Vincent et al., 2013). Of these, 492 completed a survey, and 370 met the criteria for fibromyalgia (Vincent et al., 2013). The use of both clinical diagnoses and survey data ensured a more comprehensive capture, including cases that might have otherwise gone undiagnosed. Investigators reported a prevalence of fibromyalgia in women of 7.7% vs. 4.9% in men—suggesting a significant gender gap (Vincent et al., 2013).

A scoping review by Ruschak et al. (2023), which included 10 articles published in the years 2016–2022, reported that fibromyalgia affects up to 5% of the world's population with the incidence in the United States estimated at 2.41% (lower than Europe at 2.64%; Ruschak et al., 2023). It found the female predominance to be from 80% and 96% (Ruschak et al., 2023). A study by Arout et al. (2018) focused specifically on U.S. Veterans receiving a pain diagnosis in FY2012 (October 1, 2011, to September 30, 2012). The cohort included 2,216,621 Veterans who had a pain diagnosis and within this group; 77,087 (3.48%) were diagnosed with fibromyalgia, while 2,139,534 (96.52%) received other pain diagnoses. Of those diagnosed with fibromyalgia, 19,620 (25.5%) were female and 57,467 (74.5%) were male. However, it is critical to note the sample was predominantly male. The authors found that among Veterans with a pain diagnosis in 2012, the strongest independent predictor of fibromyalgia was being female (SRC = 0.177; OR = 3.2, 95% CI: 3.1–3.2) (Arout et al., 2018).

Risk Factors and Presentation

While the estimates vary, research consistently identifies gender as a significant risk factor. Women diagnosed with fibromyalgia tended to be younger and have higher rates of comorbid conditions such as headaches, connective tissue diseases, and psychiatric disorders (e.g., depression, anxiety) compared to men (Arout et al., 2018; Thieme et al., 2004). Women are also less likely to delay in seeking care (Conversano et al., 2021). In contrast, men with fibromyalgia often presented with more medical comorbidities but experienced fewer psychiatric symptoms (Arout

Table 10.2 Gender differences in Fibromyalgia presentation

	Women with Fibromyalgia	Men with Fibromyalgia
Pain	Widespread, more severe	Localized to tender points
Fatigue and fibro fog	Greater fatigue and cognitive disturbances	Milder cognitive impact
Comorbidities	Headaches, connective tissue diseases, psychiatric disorders (anxiety, depression)	More medical comorbidities, fewer psychiatric symptoms
Hormonal influence	Symptoms influenced by menstrual cycle (pain, mood changes)	N/A
Sexual dysfunction	Higher incidence (86.9%)	Lower incidence (76.5%)
Care-seeking behavior	Early diagnosis, proactive care-seeking	Delay in seeking care until symptoms become severe

et al., 2018; Wolfe et al., 2018). In men, the pain is often less widespread pain and more localized ("tender points"; Clauw, 2014; Conversano et al., 2021) (Table 10.2).

Recent research indicates that fibromyalgia in women may be linked to specific biochemical markers. For example, fibromyalgia patients showed higher serum levels of amino acids like glutamic acid and histidine while alanine levels were lower compared to controls (Rus et al., 2018). Additionally, plasma norepinephrine, serotonin or 5-hydroxytryptamine (5-HT), 5-hydroxyindolacetic acid (5-HIAA), and 5-hydroxytryptophan (5-HTP) levels are elevated in patients with fibromyalgia compared to healthy controls (Jurado-Priego et al., 2024; Rus et al., 2018). Norepinephrine levels above 694.69 pg/mL are a strong predictor of fibromyalgia (Jurado-Priego et al., 2024; Rus et al., 2018). In contrast, dopamine and serotonin levels are reduced in fibromyalgia patients. Increased oxytocinase activity and low EDA activity are also observed, which may influence pain sensitivity and the overall severity of symptoms (Aguilar-Ferrándiz et al., 2021; Jurado-Priego et al., 2024; Martínez-Martos et al., 2019). These biomarkers could be valuable in diagnosing and understanding fibromyalgia's pathophysiology.

Symptom presentation in fibromyalgia varies widely, but studies consistently show that women report more symptoms and higher levels of symptom severity compared to men (Wolfe et al., 2018). Women living with fibromyalgia commonly experience greater subjective pain perception, increased fatigue, and altered responses to pain stimuli. The latter may be influenced by hormonal fluctuations and central nervous system (CNS) effects related to the menstrual cycle (Ruschak et al., 2023; Siracusa et al., 2021). In a sample comprised 293 patients with fibromyalgia (276 females and 17 males) and 86 healthy controls (72 females and 14 males), Rico-Villademoros et al. (2012) found that the frequency of sexual dysfunction (e.g., desire, arousal, orgasm) was significantly higher in patients with fibromyalgia than in controls for both females (86.9% vs. 23.6%) and males (76.5% vs. 6.7). Further complicating the picture is that antidepressants (e.g., SSRIs) can exacerbate sexual dysfunction, which is a challenge as they are commonly prescribed for fibromyalgia and fibromyalgia-related depression and/or anxiety (Rico-Villademoros et al., 2012). Taken together, these findings highlight how the pervasive nature of fibromyalgia symptoms significantly impairs overall quality of life, leading to considerable challenges in daily functioning and well-being for those affected.

Diagnosis and Treatment

Diagnosing fibromyalgia remains challenging due to its subjective nature and overlapping symptoms with other conditions—especially those rheumatologic in nature. Thorough clinical evaluation and consideration of symptom patterns, tender points, and patient-reported outcomes are paramount in making an accurate diagnosis (Wolfe et al., 2018). Prognosis varies widely, with some individuals experiencing periods of remission or symptom improvement, while others may face chronic symptoms that significantly impact daily functioning and quality of life (Wolfe et al., 2018).

Manual therapy, which includes techniques such as gentle stretching, joint manipulation, and myofascial release, is gaining attention as a treatment for fibromyalgia. Studies investigating both women and men (Algar-Ramírez et al., 2020; Jurado-Priego et al., 2024; Schulze et al., 2020) and only women (Audoux et al., 2023; Nadal-Nicolas et al., 2020) show that manual therapy can reduce pain perception, improve muscle fatigue, and alleviate tension anxiety in individuals living with fibromyalgia. While a promising path forward, the evidence for manual therapy is mixed and further research is needed. A systematic review of randomized controlled trials (RCTs) examined the impact of manual therapy on pain, quality of life, and disease burden across seven studies involving 368 patients (Schulze et al., 2020). The authors concluded that the available evidence, ranging from very low to moderate quality, is inconclusive and insufficient to endorse the use of manual therapy for patients with FM (Schulze et al., 2020). The authors did note that general osteopathic treatment has achieved clinically relevant improvements in pain relief compared to controls (Schulze et al., 2020). Additionally, manual lymphatic drainage and myofascial therapy demonstrate potential benefits. Again, the quality of evidence is variable, highlighting the need for individualized and comprehensive management strategies for fibromyalgia. Other proposed nonpharmacological treatment options include exercise therapy, electrotherapy, and hydrotherapy (Jurado-Priego et al., 2024; Velioglu et al., 2023).

Cognitive Function

The heterogeneity of the studies describing the impact of fibromyalgia on cognition makes it difficult to perform a comprehensive systematic review. However, a 2021 meta-analysis by Bell et al. identified 37 eligible studies for analysis where persons with fibromyalgia (total $n = 964$) were compared to participants from age-matched control groups without fibromyalgia (total $n = 1025$) on a range of neuropsychological measures. The results demonstrated that, compared to healthy controls, fibromyalgia was associated with lower cognitive function broadly, with the largest impact on inhibitory control and both long- and short-term memory (Bell et al., 2018). Tobacco smoking and high body mass index (BMI) showed an inverse impact on cognitive dysfunction and quality of life in fibromyalgia.

Although most studies on fibromyalgia and cognitive function focus primarily on women due to the higher prevalence of the disease among females, there is limited research directly comparing cognitive function between women and men with fibromyalgia. A review by Ibraheem et al. (2021) suggests that hormonal fluctuations (e.g., estrogen) may contribute to greater cognitive impairment in women with FM. Moreover, women with FM frequently report higher levels of sleep disturbances, fatigue, and anxiety, all of which are known to exacerbate cognitive symptoms (Ibraheem et al., 2021). In contrast, while men with FM also report cognitive dysfunction, most studies on male patients tend to focus on physical comorbidities rather than cognitive issues (Ibraheem et al., 2021). This disparity makes it challenging to clearly distinguish gender-specific symptom profiles from potential underreporting of cognitive complaints in men.

Myalgic Encephalomyelitis/Chronic Fatigue Syndrome

Myalgic encephalomyelitis (ME), also known as chronic fatigue syndrome (CFS), is a debilitating disorder characterized by profound and persistent fatigue that is not alleviated by rest and cannot be explained by another medical or psychiatric condition (CDC, 2023). Beyond chronic fatigue, individuals with ME/CFS often experience a range of other symptoms, including unrefreshing sleep, muscle and joint pain, headaches, cognitive difficulties, and flu-like symptoms (CDC, 2023). These symptoms significantly impair daily functioning, and the unclear etiology of the condition presents challenges for both diagnosis and treatment.

A closely related concept is severe fatigue, which shares some characteristics with ME/CFS but differs in important ways. Severe fatigue is defined as persistent exhaustion lasting for at least 6 months, with a marked reduction in normal activities at work or home (Palacios et al., 2023). However, unlike ME/CFS, severe fatigue lacks at least four of the additional symptoms, such as cognitive impairment, unrefreshing sleep, or postexertional malaise, which are necessary for a ME/CFS diagnosis (Palacios et al., 2023). This distinction underscores the complexity of fatigue-related disorders and the need for nuanced diagnostic approaches.

Epidemiology

Per the CDC's National Center for Health Statistics (NCHS) Data Brief from 2021/2022, approximately 1.3% of adults in the United States reported ME/CFS. The prevalence of ME/CFS is notably higher among women, with 1.7% of women affected compared to 0.9% of men (CDC). Additionally, the prevalence varies by race and ethnicity with 1.5% of white non-Hispanic/Latinx adults report having ME/CFS, compared to 0.8% of Hispanic/Latinx adults and 0.7% of Asian non-Hispanic/Latinx adults. Additionally, Collin and Crawley's (2017) cohort study, which analyzed trends across 660 general practices in the UK between 2001 and 2013, found that women were 2.4 times more likely to be diagnosed with ME/CFS than men. This aligns with broader findings indicating the gendered burden of chronic fatigue syndromes (Collin & Crawley, 2017). The study also reported a peak incidence in women aged 40–49, reinforcing evidence that middle-aged women are particularly vulnerable.

In a 2022 CDC report, 13.5% of adults aged 18 and older reported feeling very tired or exhausted most days or every day in the past 3 months, though these cases did not meet the threshold for severe fatigue (CDC, 2023). Across all age groups, women consistently reported higher levels of fatigue than men. Specifically, 20.3% of women aged 18–44 years, 15.3% aged 45–64 years, and 11.5% aged 65 and older reported fatigue, compared to 11.0% of men aged 18–44 years, 9.7% aged 45–64 years, and 8.9% aged 65 and older (CDC, 2023). Notably, fatigue levels among women declined steeply with age, while the decline among men was more gradual. These data emphasize that fatigue, regardless of meeting severe fatigue or ME/CFS criteria, is more prevalent among women than men.

Risk Factors and Presentation

The risk factors and clinical presentation of ME/CFS differ notably by gender, with women showing unique vulnerabilities linked to biological, social, and psychological factors. Insights from cross-sectional research, such as the UK ME/CFS Biobank, highlight the connection between reproductive health and ME/CFS. These studies reveal that conditions like endometriosis, pelvic pain, and amenorrhea frequently co-occur with ME/CFS, potentially exacerbating fatigue and other symptoms (Lacerda et al., 2019). Cohort data from the Nurses' Health Study II underscores that postpartum periods pose a heightened risk for ME/CFS, with hormonal shifts and postpartum depression often linked to disease onset or symptom worsening. Among the 41,802 female nurses who completed the online questionnaire, 102 met the criteria for ME/CFS. These findings emphasize the significant influence of reproductive health on the expression of ME/CFS in women (Palacios et al., 2023) (Table 10.3).

Table 10.3 Key factors contributing to ME/CFS in women

Risk factor	Details
Gender prevalence	ME/CFS significantly more prevalent in women (~3:1 female-to-male ratio)
Gynecological conditions	Higher prevalence of pelvic pain, endometriosis, and amenorrhea among women with ME/CFS
Postpartum fatigue/depression	Strong correlation between postpartum depressive symptoms and ME/CFS onset
Infections (mononucleosis/viral onset)	Frequently reported postinfectious onset, particularly in adolescent girls and young women
Family history of mental health issues	Family history of anxiety linked to higher ME/CFS
Social and marital	Higher risk among single, divorced, or separated women
Socioeconomic factors	Women with lower income more likely to develop ME/CFS

Note: ME = myalgic encephalomyelitis; CFS = chronic fatigue syndrome

Severe fatigue—distinct from ME/CFS in diagnostic criteria but still a significant clinical concern—was experienced by 522 female participants in the Nurses' Health Study II cohort. The study found that severe fatigue was associated with older age, higher BMI, and hormone therapy use, which contrasts with ME/CFS cases that did not show these associations (Palacios et al., 2023). Additionally, participants with severe fatigue had lower caffeine intake and higher alcohol consumption, suggesting that lifestyle and behavioral factors may contribute to the severity of fatigue in ways distinct from ME/CFS (Palacios et al., 2023). These findings underscore the importance of differentiating between fatigue syndromes, as the risk factors and clinical patterns of severe fatigue may diverge from those of ME/CFS, requiring distinct management approaches.

Infections, particularly viral illnesses like infectious mononucleosis (typically caused by the Epstein–Barr virus (EBV)), are major risk factors for ME/CFS, disproportionately affecting women—especially adolescent girls and young women. Data from the UK ME/CFS Biobank, a cross-sectional resource of biosamples and clinical data, found that frequent colds and viral infections often preceded symptom onset in women, underscoring the role of immune activation in disease progression (Lacerda et al., 2019). This biobank collects various biological samples, including blood, plasma, and RNA, alongside detailed clinical histories, facilitating research into immunological and genetic markers relevant to ME/CFS (Lacerda et al., 2019). Complementing these findings, Hempel et al.'s systematic review (2008)—based on an initial screening of 643 studies, 11 of which met inclusion criteria—reaffirms that infections frequently trigger ME/CFS. However, inconsistencies in diagnostic methods across studies have complicated efforts to compare findings, particularly regarding gender-specific patterns (Hempel et al., 2008). The gendered nature of immune responses, influenced by hormonal and genetic factors, likely heightens women's vulnerability to postinfectious fatigue syndromes, further highlighting the need for targeted research on gender differences (Klein & Flanagan, 2016).

Psychosocial risk factors also play a significant role in ME/CFS development. A family history of anxiety elevates risk—suggesting that psychological stress may interact with biological susceptibilities to shape disease onset (Lacerda et al., 2019). Social instability compounds these risks, with studies finding that being single, divorced, or separated is associated with more severe disease in women (Palacios et al., 2023). Socioeconomic factors also contribute, as highlighted by findings from the UK ME/CFS Biobank, which identified that women with lower income are more likely to develop ME/CFS, likely due to compounded stress and limited access to care (Lacerda et al., 2019). These studies emphasize the need for multidisciplinary, biopsychosocial, gender-sensitive research, as women disproportionately experience the social and economic burdens that can exacerbate chronic illness.

The clinical presentation of ME/CFS in women is marked by more pronounced postexertional malaise, cognitive dysfunction, and chronic pain compared to men (Hempel et al., 2008; Lacerda et al., 2019). These findings draw on both cross-sectional clinical data and systematic reviews, which provide a broad overview of patient-reported symptoms. Symptom fluctuations tied to menstrual cycles and severe sleep disturbances—including unrefreshing sleep—pose additional challenges for disease management (Lacerda et al., 2019). Women with severe ME/CFS report greater physical and mental impairment, as well as reduced participation in social and economic activities, reinforcing the need for individualized care strategies (Hempel et al., 2008). The integration of biobank-based studies with large-scale longitudinal data enhances the ability to uncover nuanced gender differences in symptom severity and disease trajectory. Understanding these distinct risk factors and clinical patterns is essential for developing effective, evidence-based interventions and ensuring equitable treatment for women with ME/CFS.

Diagnosis and Treatment

Diagnosing ME/CFS remains challenging due to the absence of definitive biomarkers and the overlap of symptoms with conditions like fibromyalgia, depression, and postviral fatigue syndromes (Collin & Crawley, 2017; Hempel et al., 2008; Jason et al., 2015). Physicians primarily use exclusion criteria to rule out infections, autoimmune diseases, and psychiatric disorders (Hempel et al., 2008). While earlier frameworks like the Canadian Consensus Criteria and CDC-1994 guidelines emphasized core symptoms, these lacked consistency in clinical use (Jason et al., 2015; Lacerda et al., 2019).

The latest diagnostic frameworks—the NAM/IOM 2015 criteria and NICE 2021 guidelines—offer more refined criteria (Barry et al., 2024; National Academies of Sciences, Engineering, and Medicine, 2015). Both frameworks emphasize worsening symptoms after exertion, unrefreshing sleep, and cognitive impairment or orthostatic intolerance (Barry et al., 2024; National Academies of Sciences, Engineering, and Medicine, 2015). These guidelines require symptoms to persist for at least 6 months, causing significant reductions in activity, with no alternative medical explanation. The NICE guidelines highlight fluctuating symptom severity, necessitating long-term patient monitoring and referrals to specialists when appropriate (Barry et al., 2024). Additionally, the NICE framework advises against graded exercise therapy (GET), given reports of symptom exacerbation, advocating instead for individualized care strategies (Barry et al., 2024).

Unfortunately, despite treatment advances, recovery rates of ME/CFS remain low. A systematic review of 28 studies by Cairns and Hotopf (2005) found a median full recovery rate of 5%, with rates varying from 0% to 31%. Partial improvements are more common, with 39.5% showing some symptom relief, although relapses remain frequent (Cairns & Hotopf, 2005). Collin and Crawley (2017) similarly found that 0–8% of patients fully recover, while around 40% report gradual improvement with unpredictable relapses. Employment outcomes remain poor, with only 8–30% of patients returning to work, though primary care patients often fare better than those treated in specialized clinics (Cairns & Hotopf, 2005). This discrepancy may result from the severity or chronicity of symptoms in specialized settings, where patients tend to present with more complex cases, whereas primary care patients may have milder symptoms or receive earlier interventions, which can improve prognosis (Cairns & Hotopf, 2005).

Overall, better outcomes are linked to individualized, multidisciplinary approaches tailored to the patient's needs (Barry et al., 2024; Lacerda et al., 2019). Psychological support, including cognitive behavioral therapy (CBT), may help some patients manage symptoms, though the effectiveness of treatments varies (Hempel et al., 2008; Lacerda et al., 2019).

Cognitive Function

Cognitive dysfunction, including "brain fog," is a hallmark symptom of ME/CFS and carries significant gender-specific implications. It manifests through memory lapses, difficulties in concentration, impaired information processing, and executive dysfunction (Hempel et al., 2008; Lacerda et al., 2019). These impairments are notably more severe and frequent in women, especially when exacerbated by physical exertion or hormonal fluctuations, such as during menstrual cycles or postpartum periods (Lacerda et al., 2019; Palacios et al., 2023). Research suggests that hormonal changes related to reproductive health, including pregnancy and menopause, further amplify cognitive difficulties, increasing the burden on affected women (Palacios et al., 2023).

The cognitive burden women with ME/CFS experience compounds other challenges, including more severe postexertional symptom exacerbation and chronic pain compared to men (Hempel et al., 2008; Palacios et al., 2023). These fluctuations complicate both disease management and daily functioning, reducing participation in social, professional, and economic activities. Many women report that cognitive dysfunction impairs their ability to maintain employment, manage household responsibilities, and engage in personal relationships, highlighting the broader impact of ME/CFS on quality of life (Palacios et al., 2023).

Neuroimaging studies suggest structural and functional brain changes in ME/CFS patients, such as reduced gray matter in the frontal regions responsible for memory, decision making, and cognitive flexibility, which correlate with higher fatigue levels (de Lange et al., 2005; Shan et al., 2016). Disrupted connectivity between brain areas like the anterior cingulate cortex, hippocampus, and dorsolateral prefrontal cortex may also underlie cognitive dysfunction, contributing to challenges in multitasking, word retrieval, and decision making (Shan et al., 2016). Moreover, chronic neuroinflammation and immune system dysregulation, including elevated proinflammatory cytokines such as IL-6 and TNF-α, exacerbate cognitive symptoms (Shan et al., 2016). These immune-related mechanisms align with gendered patterns in immune responses, further supporting the notion that women with ME/CFS are particularly vulnerable to cognitive decline (Klein & Flanagan, 2016).

Given the complexity and variability of cognitive dysfunction in ME/CFS, particularly among women, effective management requires gender-sensitive, multidisciplinary interventions. Cognitive pacing strategies—where patients regulate cognitive and physical activities to prevent exacerbations—are essential to maintaining stability (Lacerda et al., 2019). These interventions should address both biological and psychosocial factors, ensuring that fluctuations in symptom severity and cognitive decline do not become barriers to care or recovery.

Sleep Disorders

Sleep disorders encompass a diverse range of conditions that affect the quality, timing, and duration of sleep, leading to disturbances in sleep patterns (Karna et al., 2024). These conditions include insomnia, sleep-disordered breathing, central disorders of hypersomnolence, circadian rhythm sleep-wake disorders, parasomnia (e.g., sleepwalking, sleep talking, bed-wetting), and sleep-related movement disorders. Sleep disturbances can significantly impact daily functioning and overall health (Karna et al., 2024).

Epidemiology

According to the CDC's National Health Interview Survey (NHIS) 2020, across genders, 14.5% of adults reported trouble falling asleep and 17.8% had trouble staying asleep. However, gender-specific patterns are evident. Women (20.7%) were significantly more likely than men (14.7%) to have trouble staying asleep (Adjaye-Gbewonyo et al., 2022). The disparities align with a meta-analysis by Zeng et al. (2020) that pooled 13 articles meeting strict inclusion criteria. The articles covered 326,908 participants in total (139,349 females and 187,559 males) and were published between 1994 and 2017. From the analysis, Zeng et al. found that women had a significantly higher prevalence of insomnia compared to men (OR = 1.58, 95% CI: [1.35, 1.85], $p < 0.0001$) (Zeng et al., 2020). Additionally, non-Hispanic/Latinx White adults (21.0%) were more likely to have trouble staying asleep than non-Hispanic/Latinx Black/African American (15.4%), Hispanic/Latinx (10.6%), and non-Hispanic/Latinx Asian (8.7%) adults, indicating significant racial and ethnic disparities in sleep disturbances (Adjaye-Gbewonyo et al., 2022).

Sleep disturbances are notably prevalent among women with noncancerous gynecologic conditions, with 33.7% reporting poor sleep quality and 6.8% reporting short sleep duration of less than 6 hours (Singh et al., 2014). This disparity in sleep disturbances once again underscores the complex interplay between gynecological conditions and other health issues, revealing how conditions specific to women can intersect with broader medical concerns. In a similar vein, hormonal etiologies largely unique to women contribute to sleep disorders, including the hormonal changes associated with menarche, pregnancy, perimenopause, and menopause, which significantly affect sleep patterns (Pengo et al., 2018). Please see Chap. 11 for more details on the relationship between hormonal changes and sleep. In brief, pregnancy induces physiological changes that can lead to sleep disturbances, such as increased urinary frequency, discomfort, and hormonal fluctuations (Driver & Shapiro, 1992; Pengo et al., 2018). Menopause, or the end of menstruation, is associated with an increase in insomnia symptoms, especially difficulty staying asleep (Baker et al., 2018). Sleep disturbances are considered a core symptom of menopause by the NIH State-of-the-Science Conference (National Institutes of Health, 2005).

Risk Factors and Presentation

Gender differences in sleep disorders, particularly insomnia and obstructive sleep apnea (OSA), reveal significant health disparities. While women are more likely to experience insomnia, men are diagnosed with OSA more frequently. However, OSA is underdiagnosed in women, who often present with nonclassic symptoms like fatigue, anxiety, or depression, instead of snoring or daytime sleepiness typical in men (Fabozzi et al., 2024). McDermott et al. (2018) found that OSA affects 9% of women and 17% of men aged 50–70. Women with OSA tend to experience more hypopneas—partial obstructions—compared to men, who exhibit more full apneas (Fabozzi et al., 2024). Additionally, women have fewer desaturation events (drops in blood oxygen), which further complicates diagnosis and delays treatment (Fabozzi et al., 2024). Women's OSA cases are often complicated by coexisting conditions such as PTSD, anxiety, and depression, making clinical management more challenging (Foster et al., 2017) (Table 10.4).

Women's vulnerability to stroke due to sleep apnea is particularly concerning. In an analysis of 29,961 patients with sleep apnea syndrome (SAS) and 119,844 matched controls using Taiwan's national health database, women under 35 years of

Table 10.4 Key factors contributing to sleep disorders in women

Risk factor	Details
Gender-specific OSA patterns	– More hypopneas (partial airway obstructions) – Fewer desaturation events – Nonclassic symptoms (e.g., fatigue, anxiety, and depression rather than snoring or sleepiness)
Stroke risk and OSA	– Overall increased stroke risk
Comorbid conditions and OSA	– PTSD, depression, and anxiety
Hormonal transitions	– **Pregnancy:** Hormonal changes, weight gain, and increased airway resistance – **Postpartum:** Hormonal shifts, caregiving, RLS, and hot flashes – **Menopause:** Increases insomnia risk linked to anxiety, depression, and physical symptoms (e.g., night sweats)
Chronic conditions	– Migraines, osteoporosis, chronic pain
Protective aspects	– More stable circadian rhythms and less fragmented sleep

Note. OSA = obstructive sleep apnea; PTSD = posttraumatic stress disorder; RLS = restless leg syndrome

age exhibited the highest stroke risk (Chang et al., 2014). This cohort showed a 19% higher stroke risk overall, with younger women surpassing both older women and men of the same age group in stroke incidence (Chang et al., 2014). This suggests that OSA and sleep disorders may have a more detrimental effect on younger women, especially when comorbid with psychological stressors or cardiovascular risks.

The impact of sleep disorders on women is amplified during transitional life stages, such as pregnancy, postpartum, and menopause. During pregnancy, hormonal fluctuations, physical discomfort, and sleep disorders such as insomnia, restless legs syndrome (RLS), and OSA significantly disrupt sleep (Baker et al., 2018; Xu et al., 2018). These disruptions worsen as pregnancy progresses, with OSA becoming particularly severe in the third trimester due to weight gain and increased airway resistance, which narrow the upper airway and lead to more frequent apneic or hypopneic events (Facco et al., 2010). Additionally, insomnia and RLS exacerbate sleep difficulties, contributing to fatigue and impaired daytime functioning (Facco et al., 2012). Postpartum sleep disturbances can worsen due to hormonal changes, caregiving demands, and the onset of RLS or hot flashes (Xu et al., 2018). During menopause, these disruptions increase the risk of chronic insomnia, which is linked to anxiety and depression (Baker et al., 2018).

Beyond life transitions, chronic conditions that are more prevalent in women—such as migraines, osteoporosis, and chronic pain—also disrupt sleep quality. Research indicates that women experience migraines at three times the rate of men, further disrupting their circadian rhythms (Rossi et al., 2022). In addition, women are more likely to experience conditions like osteoporosis, fractures, and back problems that impair sleep quality, leading to fragmented sleep patterns and reduced daytime functioning (Lai et al., 2024; Zeng et al., 2020).

While women are more likely to experience insomnia, they tend to have more stable circadian rhythms than men, which may result in less fragmented sleep at baseline. However, the long-term effects of insomnia are more detrimental to men's life expectancy, as shown by Pajėdienė et al. (2024). This reinforces the need to consider both the protective and harmful aspects of gender-specific sleep patterns when designing effective intervention.

Diagnosis and Treatment

The prognosis and treatment of sleep disorders are influenced by the underlying causes and the individual's overall health. Effective management often requires a multifaceted approach that addresses both the physiological and psychological aspects of sleep disturbances. For example, women metabolize prescription insomnia medications, notably zolpidem, differently. Low levels of free plasma testosterone may contribute to lower CYP3A (a cytochrome enzyme present in the liver and important in drug metabolism) which results in up to 50% higher plasma levels than men. Clinically, this means women may require a lower dose than men to achieve the same clinical effects of zolpidem (Cubala et al., 2010).

While cognitive behavioral therapy for insomnia has been identified as an evidence-based treatment for insomnia broadly, and more effective in the long-run than sleep medications, gender-specific situations require more complex multifaceted approaches (Mitchell et al., 2012). For example, treatment for sleep disorders in menopausal women may include hormone replacement therapy, cognitive-behavioral therapy for insomnia, lifestyle modifications to improve sleep hygiene, and regular physical activity and social engagement to promote long-term brain health in aging women (Caretto et al., 2019; Choshen-Hillel et al., 2021; Gelfo, 2024). Recognizing and addressing the gender-specific factors that contribute to sleep disorders can enhance the effectiveness of interventions and improve long-term outcomes for affected individuals.

Cognitive Function

Sleep disorders in women, particularly during menopause, are strongly associated with cognitive decline and increased risk of neurodegenerative conditions (Guarnieri, 2019; Ma et al., 2020; Mosconi et al., 2021). Fluctuations in estrogen and progesterone impact both sleep quality and cognitive performance, as these hormones regulate serotonin and other neurotransmitters essential for maintaining restful sleep (Guarnieri, 2019; Harvard Health, 2022). Declines in estrogen during menopause lead to disrupted sleep cycles, which impair memory consolidation and exacerbate cognitive issues such as brain fog and forgetfulness (Ma et al., 2020).

Additionally, poor sleep impairs the brain's ability to clear amyloid plaques, increasing the risk of Alzheimer's disease (Ma et al., 2020; Mosconi et al., 2021).

Postmenopausal women are particularly vulnerable to sleep disruptions, such as insomnia and obstructive sleep apnea (OSA), which further compromise cognitive functioning if left untreated (Guarnieri, 2019). Hormone replacement therapy (HRT) has been effective in alleviating sleep disturbances and improving cognitive outcomes, but it is most beneficial when initiated early in menopause (Mosconi et al., 2021). Previously, there have been concerns about the safety of hormone replacement therapy. However, Manson et al. (2017) found that among postmenopausal women, hormone therapy was not associated with risk of all-cause, cardiovascular, or cancer mortality during a cumulative follow-up of 18 years. These findings came from observational follow-up of U.S. multiethnic postmenopausal women aged 50–79 years ($N = 27{,}347$) enrolled in two randomized clinical trials between 1993 and 1998 and followed up through December 31, 2014 (Manson et al., 2017).

Psychogenic Nonepileptic Seizures (PNES)

Psychogenic Non-Epileptic Seizures (PNES) are episodes that mimic epileptic seizures but occur without abnormal neuronal activity, meaning they do not show the characteristic electrical discharges on electroencephalograms (EEGs) (Benbadis & Hauser, 2000; Popkirov et al., 2020). These events are thought to arise from psychological stressors or unresolved emotional conflicts, often linked to trauma, anxiety, or dissociative processes. PNES is classified as a functional neurological disorder (FND) or conversion disorder in the Diagnostic and Statistical Manual of Mental Disorders (DSM-5), reflecting the complex interaction between psychological and somatic symptoms (American Psychiatric Association, 2013; Popkirov et al., 2020). Unlike epilepsy, PNES involves behavioral and emotional manifestations such as shaking, unresponsiveness, or crying, without the physical after-effects (such as postictal confusion) typically associated with epileptic seizures (American Psychiatric Association, 2013; Popkirov et al., 2020). Diagnosis relies heavily on clinical history and video-EEG monitoring to capture typical events and exclude epilepsy, as misdiagnosis is common due to overlapping symptoms (Beimer & LaFrance, 2022).

Epidemiology

The CDC has not reported on PNES and estimates of PNES prevalence vary. Villagrán et al. (2021), who focused on a Norwegian sample, found a prevalence of 23.8 per 100,000 across all levels of diagnostic certainty. For the highest level of diagnostic certainty, which included confirmed video-electroencephalographically, the prevalence was 10.6 per 100,000 (Villagrán et al., 2021). The authors reported a mean annual incidence rate (2010–2019) as 3.1 per 100,000 per year (Villagrán et al., 2021). In a systematic review investigating the prevalence and incidence of PNES, Asadi-Pooya further examined five peer-reviewed publications. From an analysis of the primary studies conducted in Iceland, Scotland, and the United States, the calculated incidence rate was 3.1 per 100,000 population year (Asadi-Pooya et al., 2023). This finding supports the study results of Villagrán et al. (2021). Additionally, Asadi-Pooya (2023) estimated prevalence rate in 2019 for the United States was 108.5 per 100,000 population.

PNES appears to predominantly affect women, with female-to-male ratios typically reported between 2:1 and 4:1 (Asadi-Pooya et al., 2019; Türe et al., 2019; Villagrán et al., 2021). The condition is more common in younger adult women, with a bimodal distribution particularly noticeable after puberty and before the age of 55 (Dworetzky & Baslet, 2017). Türe et al. (2019) identified specific age peaks at 20–23 years and 40–43 years in women, highlighting critical periods of increased risk. This data came from a sample of 150 patients (female:male = 92:63) aged 13–67 who were diagnosed with PNES via video monitoring electroencephalogram (EEG) between 2010 and 2017 (Türe et al., 2019).

These recent epidemiological studies underscore that PNES is not uncommon, especially in epilepsy monitoring units, where it accounts for 10–40% of cases evaluated for refractory seizures (Asadi-Pooya et al., 2023; Villagrán et al., 2021). This suggests that PNES is often underdiagnosed in community settings, as many cases are initially mistaken for epilepsy due to overlapping motor and cognitive symptoms (Beimer & LaFrance, 2022). The variability in prevalence and incidence estimates may reflect methodological differences and limited access to specialized care across regions. For example, delays in diagnosis range from 5 to 10 years, which may contribute to underestimating the true prevalence (Asadi-Pooya et al., 2023). Additionally, socioeconomic and cultural factors influence recognition and reporting, particularly in men, whose emotional distress may be culturally discouraged, contributing to diagnostic delays (Beimer & LaFrance, 2022).

Risk Factors and Presentation

Although PNES shares several overlapping features between women and men—such as the absence of abnormal brain activity on EEG and the presence of physical symptoms—specific manifestations differ between genders (Oto et al., 2005). For instance, weeping episodes are far more common among women. Oto et al. (2005) found that women were three times more likely than men to cry during or after seizures ($p = .012$), and Türe et al. (2019) reported that 20.6% of women with PNES exhibited crying episodes during events, whereas none of the men did. In contrast, intense physical movements, including jerking or shaking actions that mimic generalized or tonic–clonic seizures, tend to appear more frequently in men (Türe et al., 2019). Additionally, arched-body postures and repetitive hip movements are more often seen in men (Türe et al., 2019). Although aggressive behavior is more commonly observed during episodes in men, the difference was not statistically significant (Oto et al., 2005). These patterns may reflect cultural norms and societal expectations about emotional expression—where women are more socially accepted in expressing distress through crying, while men tend to externalize stress through physical actions or aggressive movements. Interestingly, both women and men experience fainting-like episodes at similar rates, challenging the notion that responses to psychological stressors are entirely gender-specific (Türe et al., 2019). When discussing the origins of their seizures, men were more likely to attribute their PNES to factors related to epilepsy ($p = .001$), while women were over eight times more likely to report sexual abuse as a predisposing factor ($p = .001$; Oto et al., 2005). This further supports the notion that trauma-related experiences are disproportionately reported by female PNES patients (Table 10.5).

Psychiatric comorbidities are significantly associated with PNES, with depression, anxiety disorders, and trauma histories—including physical and sexual abuse—more prevalent among women than men (Asadi-Pooya et al., 2019; Dworetzky & Baslet, 2017). Borderline personality disorder (BPD) is also more frequently diagnosed in women with PNES, consistent with findings that trauma and emotional dysregulation are key features of this population (Jones & Rickards, 2021).

In a recent study of United States military Veterans, similar patterns were observed: women with PNES were nearly three times more likely than men to be diagnosed with depression (76.7% vs. 26.3%), BPD (18.9% vs. 4.7%), or a history of childhood sexual abuse (37.8% vs. 11.6%) (Sullivan-Baca et al., 2022). Women were also nearly twice as likely to report suicidality (65.6% vs. 33.7%). In contrast, men were more than four times as likely to be diagnosed with a substance use disorder (37.2% vs. 8.9%). This study drew on matching (age and seizure diagnosis) a sample of male Veterans (PNES $n = 87$, ES $n = 28$) with a previously

Table 10.5 Gender differences in PNES risk factors and symptoms

	Women with PNES	Men with PNES
Key PNES factors		
Psychiatric comorbidities	Higher rates depression, borderline personality disorder, suicidality	Higher rates substance use disorders
Attribution of seizures	Sexual abuse	Epilepsy-related causes
Trauma histories	Higher report childhood sexual abuse	Less likely to report trauma history
Symptoms		
Emotional	Crying, weeping episodes	Rarely report crying
Motor	Less frequent motor activity	Jerking, hip thrusting, arched back positions (opisthotonos)
Aggression	Less commonly aggressive	More aggressive behavior observed
Fainting	Fainting episodes common in men and women	

Note. PNES = Psychogenic nonepileptic seizures

gathered female Veteran sample (PNES $n = 90$, ES $n = 28$). Conversely, men were over four times more likely to be diagnosed with substance use disorders (SUDs), reflecting distinct gendered coping mechanisms (Sullivan-Baca et al., 2022).

Diagnosis and Treatment

The prognosis for individuals with PNES remains uncertain, with mixed outcomes reported across different populations. Durrant et al. (2011), who examined 18 studies (published from 1990 to 2010) in their systematic review, found that prognosis tends to be poor for adults with PNES, especially when seizure recurrence is used as the primary outcome measure. However, children with PNES showed better outcomes, likely due to earlier intervention and family involvement in treatment plans (Durrant et al., 2011). These findings underscore the importance of early diagnosis and timely therapeutic intervention to improve prognosis.

Research demonstrates that cognitive behavioral therapy (CBT) is effective in reducing seizure frequency and improving quality of life in PNES patients, though studies have used varying sample sizes and methodologies. For example, LaFrance et al. (2014) conducted a randomized controlled trial (RCT) with 38 participants across three sites. The authors compared cognitive behavioral therapy informed psychotherapy (CBT-ip) alone, CBT-ip plus sertraline, sertraline alone, and care as usual. Their findings revealed that CBT-ip led to significant reductions in seizure frequency (51.4%) and significant improvement in secondary measures such as depression, anxiety, global functioning, and daily life over the course of the 16-week study period (LaFrance et al., 2014). The CBT-ip with sertraline arm also showed seizure reduction (59.3%) and significant improvements in global functioning (LaFrance et al., 2014). Interestingly, the sertraline-only arm did not show a reduction in seizures (LaFrance et al., 2014). This distinction is important because PNES patients often experience comorbid psychiatric conditions such as anxiety and depression, which are typically managed with selective serotonin reuptake inhibitor (LaFrance et al., 2014). Thus, clinicians should know that the SSRI, while important for other conditions, is not sufficient treatment for PNES. Critically, the authors of the study noted that further research is needed to evaluate the durability of these effects beyond the trial period (LaFrance et al., 2014). In a later report, LaFrance et al. (2020) noted that the flexibility of CBT delivery through both in-person sessions and telehealth platforms has improved access to care, particularly for patients in rural areas or regions lacking specialized clinicians (LaFrance et al., 2020).

Gender-related differences have also been observed in PNES treatment outcomes. In a retrospective cohort study of 260 participants seen in a PNES clinic from 1999 to 2004, McKenzie et al. (2010) reported that women exhibited less sustained improvements in seizure outcomes than men. The study suggested that structured interventions targeting externalized symptoms—such as physical agitation—were more beneficial for men (McKenzie et al., 2010). By contrast, Carton et al. (2003), in a study of 84 patients diagnosed with PNES who answered questionaries and participated in interviews, found that females were more likely to have a better prognosis (e.g., reduced seizure frequency, improved coping) when treatment included psychological interventions. These findings point to the need for gender-sensitive treatment approaches that account for the distinct ways men and women express and cope with stress (Carton et al., 2003; McKenzie et al., 2010; Oto et al., 2005). Women, for instance, may benefit from trauma-focused interventions due to their higher likelihood of reporting abuse histories, while men may require treatments that address substance use disorders and externalized stress responses (Sullivan-Baca et al., 2022).

Cognitive Function

Cognitive dysfunction, including frontal lobe domain deficits and attention deficits (Simani et al., 2019), is frequently reported in individuals with PNES, but the nature and impact of cognitive impairment often differ between women and men. Women with PNES are more likely to report subjective memory complaints and emotional interference with cognitive functioning, often linked to co-occurring depression, anxiety, and trauma histories (Carton et al., 2003; Oto et al., 2005; Sullivan-Baca et al., 2022). These emotional comorbidities appear to amplify cognitive issues, as emotional regulation and cognitive processing are closely intertwined (Storbeck & Clore, 2007). In contrast, men with PNES are more prone to display externalizing behaviors, such as impulsivity or aggression, which can interfere with cognitive performance, particularly in tasks requiring sustained attention and problem-solving (Sullivan-Baca et al., 2022). Additionally, substance use disorders, which are more common in men with PNES, further impair cognitive function by disrupting memory and executive control processes. While women's cognitive difficulties are often tied to emotional dysregulation and trauma-related dissociation, men's cognitive challenges may reflect behavioral dysregulation and external stressors, such as difficulties managing interpersonal conflicts. These differences highlight the need for gender-sensitive neuropsychological assessments that account for both emotional and behavioral factors contributing to cognitive dysfunction. Tailoring cognitive interventions—such as trauma-focused therapy for women and executive functioning support for men—may improve outcomes and enhance quality of life for individuals with PNES (LaFrance et al., 2014; Popkirov et al., 2020).

Long COVID

Postacute sequelae of SARS-CoV-2 infection (PASC), commonly called long COVID, describes symptoms that persist for at least 3 months beyond the acute phase of COVID-19 (Ely et al., 2024a, 2024b). Common symptoms include persistent fatigue, respiratory difficulties (e.g., dyspnea), chest pain, cognitive dysfunction ("brain fog"), and sleep disturbances (Ely et al., 2024a, 2024b). These symptoms can significantly impair daily functioning and quality of life, making long COVID a relatively new public health issue. The research into long COVID is ongoing and continues to evolve

Epidemiology

According to a 2022 report from the CDC, 6.9% of U.S. adults reported experiencing long COVID in their lifetime, with prevalence rates exceeding 8.8% in seven states. Additionally, 3.4% of adults were currently experiencing long COVID symptoms. A 2022 National Center for Health Statistics CDC report indicated that 8.5% of women and 5.2% of men reported having ever had long COVID, with 4.4% of women and 2.3% of men currently experiencing it. Symptom clusters are more common in women aged 20 years or older (10.6%) compared to men (5.4%) 3 months after symptomatic SARS-CoV-2 infection (Global Burden of long COVID Collaborators, 2022).

Risk Factors and Presentation

A prospective cohort study at San Paolo Hospital in Milan, Italy, enrolled 377 patients hospitalized for COVID-19 through the outpatient service and monitored them during follow-up. Long COVID was observed in 69% of patients, with 81.7% of these being women. In terms of symptoms, women were more than twice as likely to present with myalgia–arthralgia (11.7% vs. 5.0%) and almost three times as likely to present with chest pain (7.3% vs. 2.5%; Bai et al., 2022). In contrast, women were less likely smokers and presented with lower rates of respiratory symptoms such as cough (44.5% vs. 57.1%) and dyspnea (39.4% vs. 44.6%; Bai et al., 2022). Interestingly, while women are more likely to develop long COVID, they are slightly less likely than men to report activity limitations due to the condition (women 78.8% vs. men 81.0%) (Cohen & van der Meulen Rodgers, 2023).

Cognitive Function

Cognitive dysfunction is a key feature of long COVID, with growing evidence suggesting that its impact differs between women and men. In a cohort from the Real-Time Assessment of Community Transmission (REACT) study in England, Hampshire et al. (2024) estimated a global cognitive score across eight tasks. Out of the 112,964 participants who completed the cognitive assessment and questionaries, women were found to report cognitive impairments more frequently than men, particularly in the form of concentration difficulties and memory problems. These impairments also translated into functional challenges—women reported difficulty managing household responsibilities and work-related tasks due to issues with memory recall and focus. In contrast, men primarily experienced slower decision making, particularly in tasks that required rapid responses.

This finding aligns with research by Zhao et al. (2024), who employed objective cognitive assessments such as the simple reaction time (SRT) and number vigilance test (NVT). Their results confirmed gender-based differences in cognitive dysfunction, with women experiencing greater difficulties in attention and memory, while men showed more pronounced impairments in psychomotor speed and response time.

One possible explanation for the higher prevalence of cognitive dysfunction in women is the greater burden of comorbidities such as anxiety, depression, and sleep disturbances—conditions known to impair cognitive function (Zhao et al., 2024). A multicenter study involving 270 participants with post-COVID condition from Germany and the UK found that fatigue and anxiety were more prevalent among women with long COVID, exacerbating the severity of their cognitive symptoms (Zhao et al., 2024). This combination of physical and psychological factors may contribute to a greater cognitive burden in women, impacting their ability to function in daily life more significantly than in men.

In addition, the inflammatory response to COVID-19 may influence cognitive outcomes differently across genders. Research suggests that women tend to have stronger immune responses, which could intensify neuroinflammatory processes associated with long COVID-related cognitive dysfunction (Hampshire et al., 2024). This heightened immune activation may help explain the higher prevalence of brain fog and memory problems reported by women.

Research Takeaways

The gender-based differences in the experience, diagnosis, and treatment of chronic medical conditions such as chronic pain, fibromyalgia, CFS, sleep disorders, PNES, and long COVID highlight the critical need for more nuanced and targeted research. These disparities reflect not only biological differences but also the significant influence of psychological, social, and cultural factors on health outcomes. Future research should prioritize the following:

- Identification and validation of gender-specific biomarkers and gender-specific differences in immune response, which could lead to more accurate diagnoses and personalized treatments.

- Adopting an intersectional approach in studies is essential to understanding how factors like race, ethnicity, socioeconomic status, and sexual orientation interact with gender to affect the prevalence, severity, and management of these conditions. Addressing these complexities can help mitigate the disparities observed in certain populations, such as the higher prevalence of chronic pain among American Indian/Alaska Native adults.
- There is a pressing need for long-term studies to assess the effectiveness of gender-specific treatments. For instance, while cognitive-behavioral therapy (CBT) has shown promise in treating PNES, its long-term efficacy across different genders remains underexplored. Similarly, understanding the long-term outcomes of various treatment approaches for chronic pain, sleep disorders, and other conditions will be crucial in developing more effective and equitable healthcare strategies.

Clinical Takeaways

Clinicians should be acutely aware of the gender-based differences in the presentation, diagnosis, and treatment of chronic conditions. A personalized approach to care is essential, recognizing that women and men may experience symptoms differently, respond to treatments variably, and face unique challenges due to societal and psychological factors. The following points are of particular salience:

- Women may require a more comprehensive evaluation that includes consideration of hormonal influences and psychosocial stressors, particularly in conditions like fibromyalgia and chronic fatigue syndrome.
- In managing chronic pain, it is important to consider that women are more likely to report higher pain intensity and may benefit more from interdisciplinary pain management programs.
- Gender-specific risks, such as the higher likelihood of sleep disorders and PNES in women, should guide the selection of appropriate diagnostic tools and therapeutic interventions.
- Trauma informed care—women with PNES are more likely to have trauma histories, clinicians should integrate trauma-informed approaches into their care plans.
- Clinicians must also be vigilant about the potential for gender biases in treatment, ensuring that all patients receive equitable care tailored to their individual needs.

References

Adjaye-Gbewonyo, D., Ng, A. E., & Black, L. I. (2022). Sleep difficulties in adults: United States, 2020. *NCHS Data Brief,* (436), 1–8.

Adjaye-Gbewonyo, D., Vahratian, A., Perrine, C. G., & Bertolli, J. (2023). Long COVID in adults: United States, 2022. *NCHS Data Brief, 480*, 1–8.

Aguilar-Ferrándiz, M. E., Casas-Barragán, A., Rus, A., Tapia-Haro, R. M., Martínez-Martos, J. M., Molina, F., & Correa-Rodríguez, M. (2021). Associations among nitric oxide and enkephalinases with fibromyalgia symptoms. *Nursing Research, 70*(2), E11–E20. https://doi.org/10.1097/NNR.0000000000000496

Algar-Ramírez, M., Ubeda-D'Ocasar, E., & Hervás-Pérez, J. P. (2020). Efficacy of manual lymph drainage and myofascial therapy in patients with fibromyalgia: A systematic review. *Schmerz (Berlin, Germany), 35*(5), 349–359.

American Psychiatric Association. (2013). *Diagnostic and statistical manual of mental disorders* (5th ed.). American Psychiatric Publishing. https://doi.org/10.1176/appi.books.9780890425596

Apkarian, V. A., Sosa, Y., Krauss, B. R., Thomas, S. P., Fredrickson, B. E., Levy, R. E., et al. (2004). Chronic pain patients are impaired on an emotional decision-making task. *Pain, 108*(1–2), 129–136. https://doi.org/10.1016/j.pain.2003.12.015

Arout, C. A., Sofuoglu, M., Bastian, L. A., & Rosenheck, R. A. (2018). Gender differences in the prevalence of fibromyalgia and in concomitant medical and psychiatric disorders: A National Veterans Health Administration study. *Journal of Women's Health (2002), 27*(8), 1035–1044. https://doi.org/10.1089/jwh.2017.6622

Asadi-Pooya, A. A. (2023). Incidence and prevalence of psychogenic nonepileptic seizures (functional seizures): A systematic review and an analytical study. *International Journal of Neuroscience, 133*(6), 598–603. https://doi.org/10.1080/00207454.2021.1942870

Asadi-Pooya, A. A., Myers, L., Valente, K., Restrepo, A. D., D'Alessio, L., Sawchuk, T., et al. (2019). Sex differences in demographic and clinical characteristics of psychogenic nonepileptic seizures: A retrospective multicenter international study. *Epilepsy & Behavior, 97*, 154–157. https://doi.org/10.1016/j.yebeh.2019.05.045

Asadi-Pooya, A. A., Brigo, F., Lattanzi, S., & Blumcke, I. (2023). Adult epilepsy. *Lancet (London, England), 402*(10399), 412–424. https://doi.org/10.1016/S0140-6736(23)01048-6

Audoux, C. R., Estrada-Barranco, C., Martínez-Pozas, O., Gozalo-Pascual, R., Montaño-Ocaña, J., García-Jiménez, D., et al. (2023). What concept of manual therapy is more effective to improve health status in women with fibromyalgia syndrome? A study protocol with preliminary results. *International Journal of Environmental Research and Public Health, 20*(2), 1061.

Bai, F., Tomasoni, D., Falcinella, C., Barbanotti, D., Castoldi, R., Mulè, G., Augello, M., Mondatore, D., Allegrini, M., Cona, A., Tesoro, D., Tagliaferri, G., Viganò, O., Suardi, E., Tincati, C., Beringheli, T., Varisco, B., Battistini, C. L., Piscopo, K., Vegni, E., … Monforte, A. D. (2022). Female gender is associated with long COVID syndrome: A prospective cohort study. *Clinical Microbiology and Infection, 28*(4), 611.e9–611.e16. https://doi.org/10.1016/j.cmi.2021.11.002

Baker, F. C., Lampio, L., Saaresranta, T., & Polo-Kantola, P. (2018). Sleep and sleep disorders in the menopausal transition. *Sleep Medicine Clinics, 13*(3), 443–456. https://doi.org/10.1016/j.jsmc.2018.04.011

Barnhart, W. R., Buelow, M. T., & Trost, Z. (2019). Effects of acute pain and pain-related fear on risky decision-making and effort during cognitive tests. *Journal of Clinical and Experimental Neuropsychology, 41*(10), 1033–1047. https://doi.org/10.1080/13803395.2019.1646711

Barry, P. W., Kelley, K., Tan, T., & Finlay, I. (2024). NICE guideline on ME/CFS: Robust advice based on a thorough review of the evidence. *Journal of Neurology, Neurosurgery, and Psychiatry, 95*(7), 671–674. https://doi.org/10.1136/jnnp-2023-332731

Beimer, N. J., & LaFrance, W. C., Jr (2022). Evaluation and treatment of psychogenic Nonepileptic Seizures. *Neurologic Clinics, 40*(4), 799–820. https://doi.org/10.1016/j.ncl.2022.03.017

Bell, T., Trost, Z., Buelow, M. T., Clay, O., Younger, J., Moore, D., & Crowe, M. (2018). Meta-analysis of cognitive performance in fibromyalgia. *Journal of Clinical and Experimental Neuropsychology, 40*(7), 698–714. https://doi.org/10.1080/13803395.2017.1422699

Benbadis, S. R., & Allen Hauser, W. (2000). An estimate of the prevalence of psychogenic non-epileptic seizures. *Seizure, 9*(4), 280–281. https://doi.org/10.1053/seiz.2000.0409

Berryman, C., Stanton, T. R., Jane Bowering, K., Tabor, A., McFarlane, A., & Moseley, G. L. (2013). Evidence for working memory deficits in chronic pain: A systematic review and meta-analysis. *Pain, 154*(8), 1181–1196. https://doi.org/10.1016/j.pain.2013.03.002

Bhargava, J., & Hurley, J. A. (2023). Fibromyalgia. In *StatPearls*. StatPearls Publishing. https://www.ncbi.nlm.nih.gov/books/NBK540974/

Cairns, R., & Hotopf, M. (2005). A systematic review describing the prognosis of chronic fatigue syndrome. *Occupational Medicine (Oxford, England), 55*(1), 20–31. https://doi.org/10.1093/occmed/kqi013

Caretto, M., Giannini, A., & Simoncini, T. (2019). An integrated approach to diagnosing and managing sleep disorders in menopausal women. *Maturitas, 128*, 1–3. https://doi.org/10.1016/j.maturitas.2019.06.008

Carton, S., Thompson, P. J., & Duncan, J. S. (2003). Non-epileptic seizures: Patients' understanding and reaction to the diagnosis and impact on outcome. *Seizure, 12*(5), 287–294. https://doi.org/10.1016/S1059-1311(02)00354-4

Casale, R., Atzeni, F., Bazzichi, L., Beretta, G., Costantini, E., Sacerdote, P., & Tassorelli, C. (2021). Pain in women: A perspective review on a relevant clinical issue that deserves prioritization. *Pain and Therapy, 10*(1), 287–314. https://doi.org/10.1007/s40122-021-00244-1

Caterina, M. J., Leffler, A., Malmberg, A. B., Martin, W. J., Tominaga, M., Petersen, J., et al. (2000). Impaired nociception and pain sensation in mice lacking the capsaicin receptor. *Science, 288*(5464), 306–313. https://doi.org/10.1126/science.288.5464.306

Ceko, M., Bushnell, M. C., Fitzcharles, M.-A., & Schweinhardt, P. (2013). Fibromyalgia interacts with age to change the brain. *NeuroImage: Clinical, 3*, 249–260. https://doi.org/10.1016/j.nicl.2013.08.015

Centers for Disease Control and Prevention. (2023). *Chronic fatigue syndrome (CFS)*. https://www.cdc.gov/me-cfs/about/index.html

Centers for Disease Control and Prevention. (2023). QuickStats: Percentage of adults aged ≥18 years who felt very tired or exhausted most days or every day in the past 3 months, by sex and age group—National Health Interview Survey, United States, 2022. *MMWR Morbidity and Mortality Weekly Report, 72*(45), 1248. https://doi.org/10.15585/mmwr.mm7245a7

Chang, C. C., Chuang, H. C., Lin, C. L., Sung, F. C., Chang, Y. J., Hsu, C. Y., & Chiang, L. L. (2014). High incidence of stroke in young women with sleep apnea syndrome. *Sleep Medicine, 15*(4), 410–414. https://doi.org/10.1016/j.sleep.2013.12.011

Choshen-Hillel, S., Ishqer, A., Mahameed, F., Reiter, J., Gozal, D., Gileles-Hillel, A., & Berger, I. (2021). Acute and chronic sleep deprivation in residents: Cognition and stress biomarkers. *Medical Education, 55*(2), 174–184. https://doi.org/10.1111/medu.14296

Clauw, D. J. (2014). Fibromyalgia: A clinical review. *JAMA, 311*(15), 1547–1555. https://doi.org/10.1001/jama.2014.3266

Cohen, J., & van der Meulen Rodgers, Y. (2023). An intersectional analysis of long COVID prevalence. *International Journal for Equity in Health, 22*(1), 261. https://doi.org/10.1186/s12939-023-02072-5

Collin, S. M., & Crawley, E. (2017). Specialist treatment of chronic fatigue syndrome/ME: A cohort study among adult patients in England. *BMC Health Services Research, 17*, 488. https://doi.org/10.1186/s12913-017-2437-3

Conversano, C., Ciacchini, R., Orrù, G., Bazzichi, M. L., Gemignani, A., & Miniati, M. (2021). Gender differences on psychological factors in fibromyalgia: A systematic review on the male experience. *Clinical and Experimental Rheumatology, 39 Suppl 130*(3), 174–185. https://doi.org/10.55563/clinexprheumatol/73g6np

Cubała, W. J., Wiglusz, M., Burkiewicz, A., & Gałuszko-Wegielnik, M. (2010). Zolpidem pharmacokinetics and pharmacodynamics in metabolic interactions involving CYP3A: Sex as a differentiating factor. *European Journal of Clinical Pharmacology, 66*(9), 955–958. https://doi.org/10.1007/s00228-010-0854-x

Dahlhamer, J. M., Connor, E. M., Bose, J., Lucas, J. W., & Zelaya, C. E. (2021). *Prescription opioid use among adults with chronic pain: United States, 2019.* (National Health Statistics Reports No. 162). National Center for Health Statistics. https://doi.org/10.15620/cdc:107641

De Lange, F. P., Kalkman, J. S., Bleijenberg, G., Hagoort, P., Van der Meer, J. W., & Toni, I. (2005). Gray matter volume reduction in the chronic fatigue syndrome. *Neuroimage, 26*(3), 777–781.

Driver, H. S., & Shapiro, C. M. (1992). A longitudinal study of sleep stages in young women during pregnancy and postpartum. *Sleep, 15*(5), 449–453. https://doi.org/10.1093/sleep/15.5.449

Durrant, J., Rickards, H., & Cavanna, A. E. (2011). Prognosis and outcome predictors in psychogenic nonepileptic seizures. *Epilepsy Research and Treatment, 2011*, Article 274736. https://doi.org/10.1155/2011/274736

Dworetzky, B. A., & Baslet, G. (2017). Psychogenic nonepileptic seizures in women. *Seminars in Neurology, 37*(6), 624–631. https://doi.org/10.1055/s-0037-1607971

Dydyk, A. M., & Conermann, T. (2024, May 6). Chronic pain. In StatPearls. *StatPearls Publishing*. https://www.ncbi.nlm.nih.gov/books/NBK553030/

El-Shormilisy, N., Strong, J., & Meredith, P. J. (2015). Associations between gender, coping patterns and functioning for individuals with chronic pain: A systematic review. *Pain Research & Management, 20*(1), 48–55. https://doi.org/10.1155/2015/490610

Ely, E. W., Brown, L. M., Fineberg, H. V., & National Academies of Sciences, Engineering, and Medicine Committee on examining the working definition for long covid. (2024a). Long covid defined. *The New England Journal of Medicine*, https://doi.org/10.1056/NEJMsb2408466. Advance online publication.

Ely, E. W., Mehta, S., Devlin, J. W., & Iwashyna, T. J. (2024b). Long COVID: A new frontier in critical care. *Journal of Intensive Care Medicine, 39*(1), 15–22. https://doi.org/10.1177/08850666231145432

Fabozzi, A., Pasqualotto, F., Laguardia, M., Natuzzi, P. F., Capone, R., Steffanina, A., Pellegrino, D., Olmati, F., Antonaglia, C., & Palange, P. (2024). Gender differences in obstructive sleep apnea syndrome: A pilot study. *Sleep & Breathing = Schlaf & Atmung, 28*(4), 1645–1650. https://doi.org/10.1007/s11325-024-03052-x

Facco, F. L., Ouyang, D. W., Zee, P. C., & Grobman, W. A. (2010). Sleep-disordered breathing in a high-risk cohort: Prevalence and severity across pregnancy. *American Journal of Obstetrics and Gynecology, 203*(5), 495.e1–495.e5. https://doi.org/10.1016/j.ajog.2010.05.017

Facco, F. L., Parker, C. B., Reddy, U. M., et al. (2012). Development of a pregnancy-specific screening tool for obstructive sleep apnea. *Journal of Clinical Sleep Medicine, 8*(4), 389–394. https://doi.org/10.5664/jcsm.2032

Filley, C. M. (2002). The neuroanatomy of attention. *Seminars in Speech and Language, 23*(2), 89–98. https://doi.org/10.1055/s-2002-24985

Foster, S. N., Mednick, S. C., Nakazawa, M., & Vgontzas, A. N. (2017). Gender differences in PTSD, sleep, and trauma-related insomnia. *Journal of Traumatic Stress, 30*(5), 518–525. https://doi.org/10.1002/jts.22209

Gasperi, M., Afari, N., Goldberg, J., Suri, P., & Panizzon, M. S. (2021). Pain and trauma: The role of criterion a trauma and stressful life events in the pain and PTSD relationship. *The Journal of Pain, 22*(11), 1506–1517. https://doi.org/10.1016/j.jpain.2021.04.015

Gelfo, F. (2024). The complex relationship between sleep and cognitive reserve: A narrative review. *Brain Sciences, 14*(7), 654. https://doi.org/10.3390/brainsci14070654

Global Burden of Long COVID Collaborators. (2022). Burden of long COVID: Systematic review and meta-analysis. *Lancet Global Health, 10*(12), e1600–e1613. https://doi.org/10.1016/S2214-109X(22)00443-1

Grinberg, K., Sela, Y., & Nissanholtz-Gannot, R. (2020). New insights about chronic pelvic pain syndrome (CPPS). *International Journal of Environmental Research and Public Health, 17*(9), 3005. https://doi.org/10.3390/ijerph17093005

Guarnieri, B. (2019). Sleep disorders and cognitive alterations in women. *Maturitas, 126*, 25–27. https://doi.org/10.1016/j.maturitas.2019.04.214

Hadlandsmyth, K., Driscoll, M. A., Johnson, N. L., Mares, J. G., Mengeling, M. A., Thomas, E. B. K., Norman, S. B., & Lund, B. C. (2024). Veterans with chronic pain: Examining gender differences in pain type, overlap, and the impact of post-traumatic stress disorder. *European Journal of Pain, 28*(2), 402–414. https://doi.org/10.1002/ejp.2258

Hagger, M. S., Keech, J. J., & Hamilton, K. (2021). Managing stress during the coronavirus disease 2019 pandemic and beyond: Reappraisal and mindset approaches. *Frontiers in Psychology, 12*, 673962. https://doi.org/10.3389/fpsyg.2021.673962

Hampshire, A., Azor, A., Atchison, C., Trender, W., Hellyer, P. J., Giunchiglia, V., Husain, M., Cooke, G. S., Cooper, E., Lound, A., Donnelly, C. A., Chadeau-Hyam, M., Ward, H., & Elliott, P. (2024). Cognition and memory after COVID-19 in a large community sample. *New England Journal of Medicine, 390*(9), 806–818. https://doi.org/10.1056/NEJMoa2311330

Harvard Health. (2022). *Menopause and memory: Know the facts*. Harvard Health Publishing. https://www.health.harvard.edu

Hempel, S., Chambers, D., Bagnall, A. M., Forbes, C., & Geddes, J. (2008). Risk factors for chronic fatigue syndrome/myalgic encephalomyelitis: A systematic scoping review of multiple predictor studies. *Psychological Medicine, 38*(7), 915–926. https://doi.org/10.1017/S0033291707002321

Huhn, A. S., Berry, M. S., & Dunn, K. E. (2018). Systematic review of sex-based differences in opioid-based effects. *International Review of Psychiatry, 30*(5), 107–116. https://doi.org/10.1080/09540261.2018.1514295

Ibraheem, W., Mckenzie, S., Wilcox-Omubo, V., Abdelaty, M., Saji, S. E., Siby, R., Alalyani, W., & Mostafa, J. A. (2021). Pathophysiology and clinical implications of cognitive dysfunction in fibromyalgia. *Cureus, 13*(10), e19123. https://doi.org/10.7759/cureus.19123

Jason, L. A., McManimen, S., Sunnquist, M., Brown, A., Newton, J. L., & Strand, E. B. (2015). Examining the Institute of Medicine's recommendations regarding chronic fatigue syndrome: Clinical versus research criteria. *Journal of Neurology and Psychology, 2015*(Suppl. 2) http://www.avensonline.org/wp-content/uploads/JNP-2332-3469-S2-0002.pdf

Ji, G., Sun, H., Fu, Y., Li, Z., Pais-Vieira, M., Galhardo, V., & Neugebauer, V. (2010). Cognitive impairment in pain through amygdala-driven prefrontal cortical deactivation. *The Journal of Neuroscience, 30*(15), 5451–5464. https://doi.org/10.1523/JNEUROSCI.0225-10.2010

Jones, L. L., & Rickards, H. (2021). History of abuse and psychogenic nonepileptic seizures: A systematic review. *Seizure, 92*, 200–204. https://doi.org/10.1016/j.seizure.2021.09.009

Jurado-Priego, L. N., Cueto-Ureña, C., Ramírez-Expósito, M. J., & Martínez-Martos, J. M. (2024). Fibromyalgia: A review of the pathophysiological mechanisms and multidisciplinary treatment strategies. *Biomedicines, 12*(7), 1543. https://doi.org/10.3390/biomedicines12071543

Karna, B., Sankari, A., & Tatikonda, G. (2024). Sleep disorder. In *StatPearls*. StatPearls Publishing. https://www.ncbi.nlm.nih.gov/books/NBK560720/

Keogh, E., McCracken, L. M., & Eccleston, C. (2005). Do men and women differ in their response to interdisciplinary chronic pain management? *Pain, 114*(1), 37–46. https://doi.org/10.1016/j.pain.2004.12.009

Klein, S. L., & Flanagan, K. L. (2016). Sex differences in immune responses. *Nature Reviews Immunology, 16*(10), 626–638. https://doi.org/10.1038/nri.2016.90

Lacerda, E. M., Geraghty, K., Kingdon, C. C., Palla, L., & Nacul, L. (2019). A logistic regression analysis of risk factors in ME/CFS pathogenesis. *BMC Neurology, 19*(1), 275. https://doi.org/10.1186/s12883-019-1468-2

LaFrance, W. C., Jr., Baird, G. L., Blum, A. S., & Price, B. H. (2020). Telehealth delivery of treatment for psychogenic nonepileptic seizures. *Epilepsy & Behavior, 103*(Part B), Article 106512. https://doi.org/10.1016/j.yebeh.2019.106512

LaFrance, W. C., Baird, G. L., Barry, J. J., Blum, A. S., Webb, A. F., Keitner, G. I., et al. (2014). Multicenter pilot treatment trial for psychogenic nonepileptic seizures: A randomized clinical trial. *JAMA Psychiatry, 71*(9), 997–1005. https://doi.org/10.1001/jamapsychiatry.2014.817

Lai, H. L., Chen, C. I., Lin, Y. C., Lu, L. C., & Huang, C. Y. (2024). A path analysis investigation into menopausal osteoporosis, sarcopenia risk, and their impact on sleep quality, depressive symptoms and quality of life. *International Journal of Orthopaedic and Trauma Nursing, 52*, 101080. https://doi.org/10.1016/j.ijotn.2023.101080

Lavand'homme, P. (2019). Postpartum chronic pain. *Minerva Anestesiol, 85*(3), 320–324.

Lehavot, K., Goldberg, S. B., Chen, J. A., Katon, J. G., Glass, J. E., Fortney, J. C., Simpson, T. L., & Schnurr, P. P. (2018). Do trauma type, stressful life events, and social support explain women Veterans' high prevalence of PTSD? *Social Psychiatry and Psychiatric Epidemiology, 53*(9), 943–953. https://doi.org/10.1007/s00127-018-1550-x

Ma, Y., Liang, L., Zheng, F., Shi, L., Zhong, B., & Xie, W. (2020). Association between sleep duration and cognitive decline. *JAMA Network Open, 3*(9), e2013573. https://doi.org/10.1001/jamanetworkopen.2020.13573

Manson, J. E., Aragaki, A. K., Rossouw, J. E., Anderson, G. L., Prentice, R. L., LaCroix, A. Z., Chlebowski, R. T., Howard, B. V., Thomson, C. A., Margolis, K. L., Lewis, C. E., Stefanick, M. L., Jackson, R. D., Johnson, K. C., Martin, L. W., Shumaker, S. A., Espeland, M. A., Wactawski-Wende, J., & Investigators, W. H. I. (2017). Menopausal hormone therapy and long-term all-cause and cause-specific mortality: The Women's Health Initiative Randomized Trials. *JAMA, 318*(10), 927–938. https://doi.org/10.1001/jama.2017.11217

Martínez-Martos, J. M., Correa-Rodríguez, M., Rus, A., Molina, F., Ramírez-Expósito, M. J., & Aguilar-Ferrandiz, M. E. (2019). Altered serum oxytocinase and enkephalin-degrading aminopeptidase activities in patients with fibromyalgia. *Biological Research for Nursing, 21*(4), 431–439. https://doi.org/10.1177/1099800419854207

McDermott, M., Brown, D. L., Li, C., Garcia, N. M., Case, E., Chervin, R. D., ... & Lisabeth, L. D. (2018). Sex differences in sleep-disordered breathing after stroke: Results from the BASIC project. *Sleep Medicine, 43*, 54–59.

McKenzie, P., Oto, M., Graham, C. D., & Duncan, R. (2010). Predicting outcome in psychogenic nonepileptic seizures: A prospective cohort study. *Epilepsy & Behavior, 18*(3), 247–251. https://doi.org/10.1016/j.yebeh.2010.04.007

Mitchell, M. D., Gehrman, P., Perlis, M., & Umscheid, C. A. (2012). Comparative effectiveness of cognitive behavioral therapy for insomnia: A systematic review. *BMC Family Practice, 13*, 40. https://doi.org/10.1186/1471-2296-13-40

Minkova, L., Habich, A., Kaller, C. P., Eickhoff, S. B., & Klöppel, S. (2017). Gray matter asymmetries in aging and neurodegeneration: A review and meta-analysis. *Human Brain Mapping, 38*(12), 5890–5904. https://doi.org/10.1002/hbm.23772

Morales, M. E., & Yong, R. J. (2021). Racial and ethnic disparities in the treatment of chronic pain. *Pain Medicine (Malden, Mass.), 22*(1), 75–90. https://doi.org/10.1093/pm/pnaa427

Morden, N. E., Chyn, D., Wood, A., & Meara, E. (2021). Racial inequality in prescription opioid receipt – Role of individual health systems. *The New England Journal of Medicine, 385*(4), 342–351. https://doi.org/10.1056/NEJMsa2034159

Mosconi, L., Berti, V., Dyke, J., et al. (2021). Menopause impacts human brain structure, connectivity, energy metabolism, and amyloid-beta deposition. *Scientific Reports, 11*(1), 10867. https://doi.org/10.1038/s41598-021-90084-y

Mota-Carrillo, E., Juárez-Contreras, R., González-Ramírez, R., Luis, E., & Morales-Lázaro, S. L. (2024). The influence of sex steroid hormone fluctuations on capsaicin-induced pain and TRPV1 expression. *International Journal of Molecular Sciences, 25*(15), 8040. https://doi.org/10.3390/ijms25158040

Muñoz, M., & Esteve, R. (2005). Reports of memory functioning by patients with chronic pain. *The Clinical Journal of Pain, 21*(4), 287–291. https://doi.org/10.1097/01.ajp.0000173993.53733.2e

Mutso, A. A., Radzicki, D., Baliki, M. N., Huang, L., Banisadr, G., Centeno, M. V., Radulovic, J., Martina, M., Miller, R. J., & Apkarian, A. V. (2012). Abnormalities in hippocampal functioning with persistent pain. *The Journal of Neuroscience, 32*(17), 5747–5756. https://doi.org/10.1523/JNEUROSCI.0587-12.2012

Nadal-Nicolas, Y., Rubio-Arias, J. A., Martinez-Olcina, M., Reche-Garcia, C., Hernandez-Garcia, M., & Martinez-Rodriguez, A. (2020). Effects of manual therapy on fatigue, pain, and psychological aspects in women with fibromyalgia. *International Journal of Environmental Research and Public Health, 17*(12), 4611.

National Academies of Sciences, Engineering, and Medicine. (2015). *Beyond myalgic encephalomyelitis/chronic fatigue syndrome: Redefining an illness*. The National Academies Press. https://doi.org/10.17226/19012

National Institutes of Health. (2005). National Institutes of Health State-of-the-Science Conference statement: Management of menopause-related symptoms. *Annals of Internal Medicine, 142*(12 Pt 1), 1003–1013.

Oto, M., Conway, P., McGonigal, A., Russell, A. J., & Duncan, R. (2005). Gender differences in psychogenic non-epileptic seizures. *Seizure, 14*(1), 33–39. https://doi.org/10.1016/j.seizure.2004.09.005

Pajėdienė, E., Urbonavičiūtė, V., Ramanauskaitė, V., Strazdauskas, L., & Stefani, A. (2024). Sex differences in insomnia and circadian rhythm disorders: A systematic review. *Medicina (Kaunas, Lithuania), 60*(3), 474. https://doi.org/10.3390/medicina60030474

Palacios, N., Molsberry, S., Fitzgerald, K. C., & Komaroff, A. L. (2023). Different risk factors distinguish myalgic encephalomyelitis/chronic fatigue syndrome from severe fatigue. *Scientific Reports, 13*(1), 2469. https://doi.org/10.1038/s41598-023-29329-x

Pengo, M. F., Won, C. H., & Bourjeily, G. (2018). Sleep in women across the life span. *Chest, 154*(1), 196–206. https://doi.org/10.1016/j.chest.2018.04.005

Planchuelo-Gómez, Á., García-Azorín, D., Guerrero, Á. L., Rodríguez, M., Aja-Fernández, S., & de Luis-García, R. (2020). Gray matter structural alterations in chronic and episodic migraine: A morphometric magnetic resonance imaging study. *Pain Medicine (Malden, Mass.), 21*(11), 2997–3011. https://doi.org/10.1093/pm/pnaa271

Polasek, T. M., & Miners, J. O. (2010). Response to "Zolpidem pharmacokinetics and pharmacodynamics in metabolic interactions involving CYP3A: Sex as differentiating factor." *European Journal of Clinical Pharmacology, 66*(9), 957–958. https://doi.org/10.1007/s00228-010-0855-9

Popkirov, S., Asadi-Pooya, A. A., & Duncan, R. (2020). The aetiology of psychogenic non-epileptic seizures: Risk factors and comorbidities. *Epileptic Disorders, 22*(6), 563–578. https://doi.org/10.1684/epd.2020.1215

Racine, M., Solé, E., Sánchez-Rodríguez, E., Tomé-Pires, C., Roy, R., Jensen, M. P., Miró, J., Moulin, D. E., & Cane, D. (2020). An evaluation of sex differences in patients with chronic pain undergoing an interdisciplinary pain treatment program. *Pain practice: The Official Journal of World Institute of Pain, 20*(1), 62–74. https://doi-org.ezproxy.lib.utah.edu/10.1111/papr.12827

Rico-Villademoros, F., Calandre, E. P., Rodríguez-López, C. M., García-Carrillo, J., Ballesteros, J., Hidalgo-Tallón, J., & García-Leiva, J. M. (2012). Sexual functioning in women and men with fibromyalgia. *The Journal of Sexual Medicine, 9*(2), 542–549. https://doi.org/10.1111/j.1743-6109.2011.02513.x

Rikard, S. M., Strahan, E. E., Schmit, K. M., & Guy, G. P., Jr. (2023). Chronic pain among adults—United States, 2019–2021. *MMWR Morbidity and Mortality Weekly Report, 72*, 379–385. https://doi.org/10.15585/mmwr.mm7215a1

Roozendaal, B., Okuda, S., de Quervain, D. J., & McGaugh, J. L. (2006). Glucocorticoids interact with emotioninduced noradrenergic activation in influencing different memory functions. *Neuroscience, 138*(3), 901–910. https://doi.org/10.1016/j.neuroscience.2005.07.049

Rossi, M. F., Tumminello, A., Marconi, M., Gualano, M. R., Santoro, P. E., Malorni, W., & Moscato, U. (2022). Sex and gender differences in migraines: A narrative review. *Neurological Sciences, 43*(9), 5729–5734. https://doi.org/10.1007/s10072-022-06178-6

Ruschak, I., Montesó-Curto, P., Rosselló, L., Aguilar Martín, C., Sánchez-Montesó, L., & Toussaint, L. (2023). Fibromyalgia syndrome pain in men and women: A scoping review. *Healthcare (Basel, Switzerland), 11*(2), 223. https://doi.org/10.3390/healthcare11020223

Rus, A., Molina, F., Del Moral, M. L., Ramírez-Expósito, M. J., & Martínez-Martos, J. M. (2018). Catecholamine and indolamine pathway: A case-control study in fibromyalgia. *Biological Research for Nursing, 20*(5), 577–586. https://doi.org/10.1177/1099800418787672

Salinsky, L. M., Merritt, C. R., Zamora, J. C., Giacomini, J. L., Anastasio, N. C., & Cunningham, K. A. (2023). μ-opioid receptor agonists and psychedelics: Pharmacological opportunities and challenges. *Frontiers in Pharmacology, 14*, 1239159. https://doi.org/10.3389/fphar.2023.1239159

Samulowitz, A., Gremyr, I., Eriksson, E., & Hensing, G. (2018). "Brave Men" and "Emotional Women": A theoryguided literature review on gender bias in health care and gendered norms towards patients with chronic pain. *Pain Research & Management*, 2018, 6358624. https://doi.org/10.1155/2018/6358624

Schulze, N. B., Salemi, M. M., de Alencar, G. G., Moreira, M. C., & de Siqueira, G. R. (2020). Efficacy of manual therapy on pain, impact of disease, and quality of life in the treatment of fibromyalgia: A systematic review. *Pain Physician, 23*(5), 461–476.

Shan, Z. Y., Kwiatek, R., Burnet, R., & Staines, D. R. (2016). Brain function characteristics of chronic fatigue syndrome: A task fMRI study. *NeuroImage: Clinical, 12*, 439–444. https://doi.org/10.1016/j.nicl.2016.08.006

Simani, L., Roozbeh, M., Rostami, M., Pakdaman, H., Ramezani, M., & Asadollahi, M. (2019). Attention and inhibitory control deficits in patients with genetic generalized epilepsy and psychogenic nonepileptic seizures. *Epilepsy & Behavior, 101*, Article 106672. https://doi.org/10.1016/j.yebeh.2019.106672

Singh, J. K., Learman, L. A., Nakagawa, S., Gregorich, S. E., & Kuppermann, M. (2014). Sleep problems among women with noncancerous gynecologic conditions. *Journal of Psychosomatic Obstetrics and Gynaecology, 35*(1), 29–35. https://doi.org/10.3109/0167482X.2013.868880

Siracusa, R., Paola, R. D., Cuzzocrea, S., & Impellizzeri, D. (2021). Fibromyalgia: Pathogenesis, mechanisms, diagnosis and treatment options update. *International Journal of Molecular Sciences, 22*(8), 3891. https://doi.org/10.3390/ijms22083891

Storbeck, J., & Clore, G. L. (2007). On the interdependence of cognition and emotion. *Cognition and Emotion, 21*(6), 1212–1237. https://doi.org/10.1080/02699930701438020

Sullivan-Baca, M. K., Chen, Z., McKenzie, P., & LaFrance, W. C. (2022). Gender differences in comorbidities and treatment outcomes among Veterans with PNES. *Epilepsy & Behavior, 131*, Article 108680. https://doi.org/10.1016/j.yebeh.2022.108680

Tajerian, M., Hung, V., Nguyen, H., Lee, G., Joubert, L. M., Malkovskiy, A. V., Zou, B., Xie, S., Huang, T. T., & Clark, J. D. (2018). The hippocampal extracellular matrix regulates pain and memory after injury. *Molecular Psychiatry, 23*(12), 2302–2313. https://doi.org/10.1038/s41380-018-0209-z

Thieme, K., Turk, D. C., & Flor, H. (2004). Comorbid depression and anxiety in fibromyalgia syndrome: relationship to somatic and psychosocial variables. *Psychosomatic Medicine*, (6), 837–844. https://doi.org/10.1097/01.psy.0000146329.63158.40

Tracey, I., & Mantyh, P. W. (2007). The cerebral signature for pain perception and its modulation. *Neuron, 55*(3), 377–391. https://doi.org/10.1016/j.neuron.2007.07.012

Türe, H. S., Tatlidil, I., Kiliçarslan, E., & Akhan, G. (2019). Gender-related differences in semiology of psychogenic non-epileptic seizures. *Noro Psikiyatri Arsivi, 56*(3), 178–181. https://doi.org/10.29399/npa.23420

Umeda, M., & Kim, Y. (2019). Gender differences in the prevalence of chronic pain and leisure time physical activity among US adults: A NHANES study. *International Journal of Environmental Research and Public Health, 16*(6), 988. https://doi.org/10.3390/ijerph16060988

van der Leeuw, G., Leveille, S. G., Dong, Z., Shi, L., Habtemariam, D., Milberg, W., Hausdorff, J. M., Grande, L., Gagnon, P., McLean, R. R., & Bean, J. F. (2018). Chronic pain and attention in older community-dwelling adults. *Journal of the American Geriatrics Society, 66*(7), 1318–1324. https://doi.org/10.1111/jgs.15413

Vardeh, D., Mannion, R. J., & Woolf, C. J. (2016). Toward a mechanism-based approach to pain diagnosis. *Journal of Pain, 17*(9 Suppl), T50–T69. https://doi.org/10.1016/j.jpain.2016.03.001

Velioglu, O., Yildizgoren, M. T., Ogut, H., Guler, H., & Turhanoglu, A. D. (2023). Short-term effects of pregabalin plus exercise therapy on pain, emotional status, physical function and nociceptive responses in patients with fibromyalgia. *Medicine International, 3*(4), 1–7.

Verdejo-García, A., López-Torrecillas, F., Calandre, E. P., Delgado-Rodríguez, A., & Bechara, A. (2009). Executive function and decision-making in women with fibromyalgia. *Archives of Clinical Neuropsychology, 24*(1), 113–122. https://doi.org/10.1093/arclin/acp014

Villemure, C., & Bushnell, C. M. (2002). Cognitive modulation of pain: how do attention and emotion influence pain processing?. *Pain, 95*(3), 195–199. https://doi.org/10.1016/S0304-3959(02)00007-6

Villagrán, A., Ursin, M. H., Enevoldsen, C., & Hecimovic, H. (2021). Incidence and prevalence of psychogenic nonepileptic seizures in a Norwegian county: A population-based study. *Epilepsia, 62*(2), 388–396. https://doi.org/10.1111/epi.16787

Vincent, K., & Evans, E. (2021). An update on the management of chronic pelvic pain in women. *Anaesthesia, 76 Suppl 4*, 96–107. https://doi.org/10.1111/anae.15421

Vincent, A., Lahr, B. D., Wolfe, F., Clauw, D. J., Whipple, M. O., Oh, T. H., Barton, D. L., & St Sauver, J. (2013). Prevalence of fibromyalgia: A population-based study in Olmsted County, Minnesota, utilizing the Rochester Epidemiology Project. *Arthritis Care & Research, 65*(5), 786–792. https://doi.org/10.1002/acr.21896

Wang, X., Traub, R. J., & Murphy, A. Z. (2006). Persistent pain model reveals sex difference in morphine potency. *American Journal of Physiology. Regulatory, Integrative and Comparative Physiology, 291*(2), R300–R306. https://doi.org/10.1152/ajpregu.00022.2006

Watanabe, Y., Nikaido, T., Yabuki, S., Abe, J., Suzuki, H., Shishido, K., Kobayashi, H., Yoshida, R., Iinuma, K., Nagamine, S., Ono, Y., Sato, M., & Oi, N. (2023). Gender differences on preoperative psychologic factors affecting acute postoperative pain in patients with lumbar spinal disorders. *Journal of Orthopaedic Science: Official Journal of the Japanese Orthopaedic Association*, S0949-2658(23)00258-0. Advance online publication. https://doi-org.ezproxy.lib.utah.edu/10.1016/j.jos.2023.08.019

Wolfe, F., Brähler, E., Hinz, A., & Häuser, W. (2013). Fibromyalgia prevalence, somatic symptom reporting, and the dimensionality of polysymptomatic distress: Results from a survey of the general population. *Arthritis Care & Research, 65*(5), 777–785. https://doi.org/10.1002/acr.21931

Wolfe, F., Clauw, D. J., Fitzcharles, M. A., Goldenberg, D. L., Häuser, W., Katz, R. S., Mease, P., Russell, A. S., Russell, I. J., & Winfield, J. B. (2011). Fibromyalgia criteria and severity scales for clinical and epidemiological studies: A modification of the ACR Preliminary Diagnostic Criteria for Fibromyalgia. *The Journal of Rheumatology, 38*(6), 1113–1122. https://doi.org/10.3899/jrheum.100594

Wolfe, F., Clauw, D. J., Fitzcharles, M. A., Goldenberg, D. L., Häuser, W., Katz, R. L., Mease, P. J., Russell, A. S., Russell, I. J., & Walitt, B. (2016). 2016 Revisions to the 2010/2011 fibromyalgia diagnostic criteria. *Seminars in Arthritis and Rheumatism, 46*(3), 319–329. https://doi.org/10.1016/j.semarthrit.2016.08.012

Wolfe, F., Walitt, B., Perrot, S., Rasker, J. J., & Häuser, W. (2018). Fibromyalgia diagnosis and biased assessment: Sex, prevalence and bias. *PloS One, 13*(9), e0203755. https://doi.org/10.1371/journal.pone.0203755

Xu, Q., Lang, C. P., & Elavsky, S. (2018). Sleep quality and menopausal status in midlife women: The moderating role of physical activity. *Menopause, 25*(9), 1011–1018. https://doi.org/10.1097/GME.0000000000001128

Zeng, L. N., Zong, Q. Q., Yang, Y., Zhang, L., Xiang, Y. F., Ng, C. H., Chen, L. G., & Xiang, Y. T. (2020). Gender difference in the prevalence of insomnia: A meta-analysis of observational studies. *Frontiers in Psychiatry, 11*, 577429. https://doi.org/10.3389/fpsyt.2020.577429

Zhao, S., Martin, E. M., Reuken, P. A., Scholcz, A., Ganse-Dumrath, A., Srowig, A., Utech, I., Kozik, V., Radscheidt, M., Brodoehl, S., Stallmach, A., Schwab, M., Fraser, E., Finke, K., & Husain, M. (2024). Long COVID is associated with severe cognitive slowing: A multicentre cross-sectional study. *eClinicalMedicine, 68*, 102434. https://doi.org/10.1016/j.eclinm.2024.102434

Chapter 11
Pregnancy, Menopause, and Other Hormonal Factors

Jessica Rohr, Elisabeth Netherton, and Hannah Combs

Introduction

Historically, the medical community has often viewed puberty, pregnancy, and menopause through the narrow scope of their effects on female reproductive organs, emphasizing their roles in physiological readiness for conception and childbearing. This perspective has traditionally overlooked the critical neuroendocrine signals and pathways essential for these processes, which have systemic effects throughout the body. Recent decades of research have shed light on how fluctuations in reproductive hormones can have significant, system-wide physiological impacts. These effects are far-reaching, both spatially within the body and temporally over time, with some persisting long after the initial hormonal changes. While research in this domain has traditionally focused on reproductive hormones and cognitive function during pregnancy, it is now recognized that these hormones fluctuate continuously over the lifespan. This has opened new avenues of research into how these hormonal variations correlate with cognitive shifts at various stages of a woman's life.

This chapter will explore the latest research on subjective cognitive experiences and objective cognitive functioning as they relate to changes in reproductive hormones throughout a woman's life. It will cover key developmental milestones such as puberty, pregnancy, postpartum, and menopause, as well as examine other factors influencing reproductive hormones, including hormonal contraception, hormone replacement therapy, as well as gender-affirming hormonal therapy. Additionally,

J. Rohr (✉)
Houston Methodist, Houston, TX, USA

E. Netherton
Rock Springs Behavioral Health, Georgetown, TX, USA

H. Combs
Baylor College of Medicine, Houston, TX, USA

E. Sullivan-Baca, R. Ellison (eds.), *Neuropsychology of Women*,
https://doi.org/10.1007/978-3-031-87228-0_11

the chapter will offer insights for researchers and healthcare professionals looking to incorporate this knowledge into their practice.

Overview of Women's Reproductive Hormones

Reproductively active hormones we will outline here include estrogen, progesterone, testosterone, anti-Müllerian hormone, follicular stimulating hormone, and luteinizing hormone. These hormones are well conserved across mammalian species and while they are known for effects within the reproductive system, we increasingly appreciate their role in mediating other biological processes, particularly those processes with cascading changes seen during puberty, the menstrual cycle, pregnancy, or menopause. These effects occur far from their location of production as the hormones are carried through the bloodstream and act on hormone-specific receptors, and rather than being uniform effects of hormones on cognitive processes are often variable depending on timing, concentration, duration, and presence of other regulatory factors.

Estrogen

See Table 11.1 for an abbreviated overview of reproductive hormones. Estrogen is a neuroactive steroid that has historically been considered "the" female hormone but, in fact, has important effects in both women and men and is found across vertebrate species. Estrogen acts on estrogen receptors both on the cell membrane and inside the cell, where it impacts gene expression. The effects of estrogen are myriad, and many are beyond the scope of this chapter, including in the development of muscle, bone density, health of connective tissue, regulation of weight and metabolism, regulation of fluid balance, anti-inflammatory properties, and health of blood vessels. Here, we will focus our attention on estrogen's regulatory effects for the menstrual cycle and the nervous system.

Estrogen is produced from testosterone and androstenedione through the action of aromatase and is found in four forms in the human body: estrone (E1), estradiol (E2), estriol (E3), and estetrol (E4). During reproductive years in women, serum levels of estradiol are highest, whereas, during pregnancy, estriol predominates and after menopause estrone predominates. During puberty, estrogen is responsible for development of mammary gland tissue, and in the menstrual cycles that follow, it regulates growth of the endometrial lining. While estrogen is predominantly produced by the ovaries in reproductive age women, it is also synthesized in other body tissues including adipose tissue, brain, bone, liver, pancreas, and skin (Gardner & Shoback, 2007).

Animal studies, predominantly conducted in rodents, inform our understanding of the role of estrogen in specific domains of cognitive functioning, both through

Table 11.1 Overview of reproductive hormones and influence on the brain

Hormone	Purpose	Influence on the brain
Estrogen	Numerous, including regulation of menstrual cycle, development of mammary gland tissue, regulation of bone density, and more	Improves verbal working memory and attention, potentially reducing cognitive decline risk postmenopause
Progesterone	Thickens endometrium, maintains pregnancy, prevents uterine contractions	Anxiolytic and mood-supporting properties through its metabolite allopregnanolone
Testosterone	Sexual functions, cardiovascular health, muscle development, bone functions	Neuroprotective in men, potential improvement in cognitive functioning in older men
Follicle-stimulating hormone (FSH)	Triggers development of ovarian follicles prior to ovulation	No direct influence on the brain
Luteinizing hormone (LH)	Regulates estrogen production, triggers ovulation	Affects hypothalamus and hippocampus, potentially involved in Alzheimer's disease pathology
Anti-Mullerian hormone (AMH)	Regulates folliculogenesis, indicates ovarian reserve	Receptors found in hypothalamus, pituitary, and neurons; regulated by inflammatory markers

rapid effects mediated by estrogen receptors embedded in cell membranes and through slower effects mediated via changes in gene expression. Decreased estrogen following menopause is associated with increased risk of cognitive decline, and that risk increases for women who experience that decrease in estrogen earlier due to ovariectomy. Some studies find this risk may improve through use of hormone replacement therapy; though, other findings have not supported this effect. Variability in estrogen formulations and timing may contribute to inconsistency in these findings (Burnham et al., 2017). However, trends seen with estradiol administration generally indicate improvement in verbal working memory and attention, likely via effects in prefrontal circuits (Duff & Hampson, 2000; Joffe et al., 2006; Krug et al., 2006).

Progesterone

Progesterone is a neuroactive steroid produced in the adrenal cortex and ovaries. Its reproductive impacts include thickening of the endometrium to facilitate implantation during pregnancy, thickening of the cervical mucus, and helping to maintain the pregnancy. During the menstrual cycle, progesterone is produced by the ovary, which prevents further development of the endometrium and contributes to cellular changes that allow for the lining of the uterus to be sloughed. During pregnancy, the corpus luteum secretes progesterone, which helps to maintain the pregnancy, as the pregnancy progresses progesterone is produced by the placenta and plays a critical role in preventing uterine contractions until labor begins. Progesterone may also have some effects in preventing immunologic rejection of the pregnancy (Gardner & Shoback, 2007).

Like estrogen, receptors for progesterone are found throughout the body, including in the GI tract, lungs, pituitary, liver, kidney, bladder, adrenals, skin, and the brain (Asavasupreechar, 2020). Much of recent work on cognitive effects of progesterone involves research into allopregnanolone, a progesterone metabolite with findings supporting anxiolytic and mood-supporting properties (Edinoff et al., 2021; Schiller et al., 2016). Research examining the benefit of direct administration of progesterone and progesterone derivatives for mood and anxiety is highly mixed, likely indicating importance of timing and formulation on disease states and outcomes. For example, while allopregnanolone has now come to market as Brexanolone for postpartum depression (Hutcherson et al., 2020), altered response to allopregnanolone in women with premenstrual dysphoric disorder (PMDD) may be implicated in the negative mood changes associated with PMDD. Symptoms of PMDD have not shown benefit from administration of progesterone (Freeman et al., 1995). Rather, Freeman et al. found in their study examining allopregnanolone levels in women with PMDD treated with antidepressants that in patients whose depression improved allopregnanolone levels in fact decreased (Freeman et al., 2002). Administration of progesterone-only hormonal contraception, along with combined hormonal contraception, has further been associated with depression in some women (Skovlund et al., 2016).

Testosterone

Testosterone, often overlooked in female physiology, is present at higher concentrations than estrogen in reproductive age women and is synthesized in the ovaries as well as in other organs, including the skin and adipose tissue, from steroid precursors made in the adrenal glands and the ovaries. While the ovaries begin to produce testosterone as women begin to ovulate, production peaks in the 20s and 30s and then declines thereafter. It is associated with sexual functions, including libido and arousal, cardiovascular health, muscle development, and bone functions (Gardner & Shoback, 2007).

Testosterone is found in some studies to be neuroprotective in men, with lower testosterone levels found in men diagnosed with Alzheimer's disease, and some studies finding improvement in cognitive functioning through administration of testosterone in older men (Holland et al., 2011). While the role of testosterone replacement postmenopause is understudied in women, evidence supports improvement in sexual functioning and sense of general well-being when given as part of hormone replacement therapy regimens (Davis & Wahlin-Jacobsen, 2015). At this time, there is insufficient evidence of how changes in testosterone level with aging may impact cognition in women or whether testosterone replacement postmenopause is indicated for neuroprotective properties; however, multiple small studies have indicated potential benefit for cognitive domains such as verbal learning, and this remains a promising area for future research (please see Davis and Wahlin-Jacobsen (2015) and Islam et al. (2019) for excellent reviews of this topic).

Other Reproductive Hormones

Follicle-stimulating hormone (FSH) and luteinizing hormone (LH) are glycoprotein hormones produced by gonadotropic cells in the adenohypophysis of the pituitary gland. FSH is released as it is made, whereas LH is produced, stored, and then released when triggered. Gonadotropin releasing hormone (GnRH) triggers the release of both FSH and LH. FSH triggers the development of ovarian follicles prior to ovulation, and FSH receptors are found on developing follicles (Gardner & Shoback, 2007).

LH is involved in regulation of estrogen production in the ovaries, and high estrogen levels suppress LH production. While FSH triggers development of ovarian follicles prior to ovulation, during the menstrual cycle a surge in LH concentration for around 48 h mid-cycle leads to the development of the oocyte with progression of Meiosis 1 and triggers ovulation. LH also triggers production of vascular endothelial growth factors by the granulosa cells.

LH crosses the blood brain barrier and is noted to have effects on the hypothalamus and the hippocampus. Human chorionic gonadotropin (HCG), produced by the placenta during pregnancy, also crosses the blood brain barrier and, given its structural similarity to LH, binds to LH receptors. There is observational evidence that high LH, resulting from low estrogen levels, may be involved in the pathology of Alzheimer's disease, and rodent studies support a link between difficulties with special memory and high LH levels concomitant with low estradiol/testosterone levels (Holland et al., 2011).

Anti-Mullerian hormone (AMH) is produced by the granulosa cells of developing follicles and serves to regulate folliculogenesis; levels of AMH change as the follicles develop. Levels of AMH in the serum also indicate degree of ovarian reserve. AMH is produced throughout the female lifespan, beginning by the time gestation is complete until menopause. Similar to other hormones discussed above, AMH receptors are found throughout the body, including in the hypothalamus, pituitary, and neurons (including motor neurons) (see Di Clemente et al., 2021 for review). AMH is also made in the hypothalamus and the pituitary and is regulated by levels of estrogen, LH, and FSH. Studies suggest that in both animals and humans AMH is likely regulated by inflammatory markers, including vascular endothelial growth factor and TNF-alpha. Fu et al. (2018) further showed a decrease in AMH in response to chronic unpredictable mild stress in rodents, and Hardy et al. (2016) showed dysregulation of AMH in human women with chronic abdominal pain, a disease state associated with stress. This is notable because data supports an association between both interfertility and early ovarian failure and increased risk for onset of dementia (Liang et al., 2024; Karamitrou et al., 2023).

Puberty and the Menstrual Cycle

Postinfancy (during which the GnRH secretory system is temporarily active; Morris et al., 2004) reproductive hormones are in a quiescent state until the initiation of puberty. Puberty begins when the GnRH system secretes GnRH in a pulsatile manner, thus leading to the release of LH and FSH and subsequent steroidogenesis and gametogenesis in the gonads (DiVall & Radovick, 2008). Though there is detectable LH and FSH activity prior to menarche, primarily during sleep, reproductive hormones levels increase as girls progress through stages of puberty (Apter et al., 1993; Hansen et al., 1975). Toward the end of the pubertal transition, after a year-long increase in estradiol, menarche occurs (Legro et al., 2000). Regulation of the cycle varies among girls, though it generally takes up to a year for the cycle to become fully established, including ovulation (DiVall & Radovick, 2008).

The menstrual cycle is divided into the follicular phase and the luteal phase (Chappell et al., 2014). The first days of the follicular phase are marked by menses, during which time estrogen and progesterone are relatively low (i.e., low for the menstruating person). After menstruation, in the mid-follicular phase, levels of circulating estradiol increase. Over the late follicular phase, there is a steep increase in estrogen immediately prior to ovulation and a rapid decline at and after ovulation (Farage et al., 2009). Also, during the late follicular phase, there is a surge in LH which then initiates an increase in progesterone, leading to an increase in FSH (Reed & Carr, 2015). At this time, testosterone concentration peaks and remains high through the luteal phase (Rothman et al., 2011). If there is no implantation of a fertilized egg, progesterone then decreases in the luteal phase, leading to the sloughing of the endometrial lining (menses) and the cycle beginning again (Reed & Carr, 2015). See Fig. 11.1 for a visualization of hormonal variation across the menstrual cycle (reproduced with permission from Iacovides et al., 2015).

Subjective Cognitive Concerns

For healthy women, there is little data regarding the prevalence of cognitive complaints during different phases of the menstrual cycle, although limited data on women's perception of their memory abilities suggests that perceived memory worsens in the luteal phase (Zare et al., 2013). Cognitive complaints are a common feature of disorders associated with the menstrual cycle, including premenstrual syndrome and premenstrual dysphoric disorder (PMDD). Research on PMDD suggests increased subjective cognitive concerns (such as worse executive functioning, concentration difficulties, and forgetfulness) in the mid- to late-luteal phase, often referred to as the premenstrual phase (Meza-Moreno et al., 2021; Souza et al., 2012).

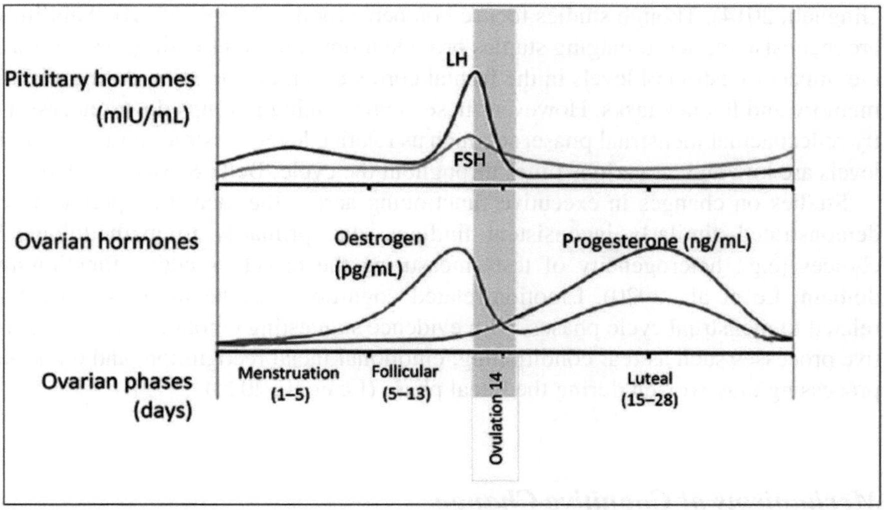

Fig. 11.1 Hormonal variations across the menstrual cycle. *Note:* Adapted from Iacovides et al. (2015)

Objective Cognitive Change

Overall, objective findings of cognitive changes and deficits across the menstrual cycle are equivocal. Sex dimorphism of cognitive skills has predominated as the prevailing theory linking menstrual cycle phases to cognition. This theory suggests that the early follicular phase is associated with better performance on visuospatial tasks, or "male-favoring" tasks, due to lower levels of female reproductive hormones, and the late follicular through mid-luteal phases (marked by increased estrogen and/or progesterone) are associated with improved verbal fluency and verbal memory, or "female-favoring" tasks (Sundström & Gingnell, 2014). However, in a comprehensive review of primarily longitudinal (within-subject) designs by Sundström and Gingnell in 2014 (replicated in 2018), visuospatial ability (assessed as mental rotation performance, spatial perception, spatial visualization, navigation tests, and object location tests) did not show a consistent relationship with menstrual cycle phase. Several reports do suggest improved functioning during phases of low estrogen and progesterone (Courvoisier et al., 2013; Hampson et al., 2014; Haussman et al., 2000; Maki et al., 2002), though several others reported no effect of phase (Dietrich et al., 2001; Epting & Overman, 1998; Gordon & Lee, 1993; Griksiene & Ruksenas, 2011; Halari et al., 2005; Kozaki & Yasukochi, 2009; Mordecai et al., 2008; Schoning et al., 2007). The same review also suggests no consistent pattern across the menstrual cycle for verbal tasks (assessed as verbal fluency, verbal recall, semantic retrieval, and implicit verbal memory; Sundström &

Gingnell, 2014). Though studies focused on behavioral measures of verbal abilities are inconsistent, neuroimaging studies provide more consistent findings supporting the impact of estradiol levels in the frontal cortex on brain activation during verbal memory and fluency tasks. However, these neuroimaging findings do not necessarily reflect actual menstrual phase, so much as relative level of estradiol (as estradiol levels are low/high at various times throughout the cycle; Beltz & Moser, 2020).

Studies on changes in executive functioning across the menstrual period have demonstrated similarly inconsistent findings, due primarily to methodological choices (e.g., heterogeneity of tests measuring the broad executive functioning domain; Le et al., 2020). Emotion-related cognition may be more consistently related to menstrual cycle phases, with evidence suggesting emotion-related cognitive processes such as fear conditioning, emotional facial recognition, and emotion processing may worsen during the luteal phase (Le et al., 2020).

Mechanisms of Cognitive Change

Though findings are inconclusive regarding the traditional sex dimorphism hypothesis, there is evidence of hormonal influence on brain activation patterns that fluctuates through the cycle. A 2019 fMRI study in 36 naturally cycling women demonstrated enhanced hippocampal activity during the late follicular (higher estradiol) phase and enhanced fronto-striatal activation during the luteal (high progesterone) phase in the absence of impact on task performance (Pletzer et al., 2019). This and other neuroimaging studies support the likely influence of sex hormones on cognitively important brain structures, potentially in subtle ways that are not accurately captured by tasks attempting to demonstrate male- and female-favoring skills (Le et al., 2020).

Because studies on cognitive change across the menstrual cycle are observational, determination of causality by sex hormones is hindered by several concomitant factors that also impact cognition. Sleep issues are common in the premenstrual period, with one-third of women reporting disruption premenstrually and up to 66% of women with PMDD reporting sleep disturbance (Bakhshani et al., 2009; Meers & Nowakowski, 2020). Given the well-documented relationship between sleep issues and impaired cognition (Leong & Chee, 2023), any hormonal influence on cognitive performance must be understood in the context of sleep disturbances. Mood changes and their impact on cognitive performance may also contribute to the pattern across the menstrual cycle (Walters & Hines-Martin, 2018).

Risk and Resilience Factors

Severity of premenstrual symptomatology may act as a risk factor for cognitive changes across the menstrual cycle. Importantly, women with PMS/PMDD do not have absolute differences in hormone levels from healthy controls; rather, they are theorized to have a unique vulnerability to hormone changes (Hantsoo & Epperson, 2015). Studies are limited in nature and marked by methodological concerns, but current evidence is consistent with cognitive deficits specifically in some aspects of executive functioning when premenstrual symptoms are more severe (Le et al., 2020).

Pregnancy and Postpartum

A woman becomes pregnant when a fertilized egg successfully implants in the endometrium after ovulation. Progesterone levels remain elevated and increase throughout pregnancy so that the endometrial lining does not slough, lactation does not prematurely occur, and contractions do not prematurely occur (Putnam et al., 1991). At and after birth, progesterone levels drop sharply, promoting lactation and continued expulsion of uterine matter through contractions (Goletiani et al., 2007). Estrogen also rises steadily throughout the pregnancy with a sharp drop at delivery, reaching prepregnancy levels by day 5 postpartum (Speroff & Fritz, 2005).

Subjective Cognitive Concerns

"Mom brain" or "pregnancy brain" has been the subject of popular news articles, blog posts, and books for decades. Reviews and meta-analyses strongly support the subjective memory concerns of pregnant and postpartum women. In a meta-analysis of 11 studies evaluating subjective memory concerns, significant and moderate negative effects for pregnancy and the postpartum period were found (Anderson & Rutherford, 2012). Consistently, over 80% of women report some level of cognitive change from baseline during pregnancy and postpartum (Parsons & Redman, 1991; Poser et al., 1986). Most reported that these concerns did not become impairing until the second or third trimester of pregnancy. In many studies, risk factors for experiencing more cognitive difficulties include being older, married, having a higher level of education, and having a career (Parsons & Redman, 1991; Welch, 1991). Cognitive complaints by pregnant and postpartum women include forgetfulness, distractibility, weak concentration, word-finding difficulties, poor coordination, and general cognitive slowing (Brett & Baxendale, 2001).

In addition to subjective complaints relative to baseline, pregnant, and postpartum, women also report more memory complaints than nonpregnant and postpartum women, even in the absence of differences in physical health complaints, emotional health, and anxiety level (Janes et al., 1999).

Objective Cognitive Changes

To date, meta-analyses and reviews suggest a small decrement in cognitive functioning during pregnancy, primarily driven by changes during the third trimester in performance on tasks of memory (Orchard et al., 2023). These decrements are small, unlikely to impact functioning, and scores are still at normative levels. This suggests that subjective concerns are reflective of a relative change from baseline rather than a cognitive decline (Orchard et al., 2023). Here, we summarize the most recent available meta-analytic data (Anderson & Rutherford, 2012; Davies et al., 2018) for different neuropsychological domains. Importantly, all studies provide results based on comparisons between nonpregnant/postpartum and pregnant/postpartum women or between pregnant women and themselves across pregnancy. To our knowledge, there are no methodologically sound studies comparing women during pregnancy and postpartum to themselves at baseline or prepregnancy.

General cognitive functioning In their meta-analysis, Davies et al. (2018) conceptualized general cognitive functioning as encompassing memory, attention, executive functioning, processing speed, and verbal and visuospatial abilities. Meta-analytic results demonstrate that overall functioning was worse in pregnant women than in nonpregnant women but only during the third trimester (Davies et al., 2018). Anderson and Rutherford's (2012) meta-analysis suggested a trend toward decrements in cognitive functioning in pregnant women, though it was nonsignificant. There are no consistent significant findings of worse cognitive functioning in the postpartum period. Table 11.2 demonstrates findings of meta-analyses examining differences in performance by cognitive domain.

Mechanisms of Cognitive Change

To understand the possible mechanisms of cognitive change, we must highlight the discrepancy between subjective experience of significant cognitive changes and objective evidence of cognitive decrement. In pregnancy and postpartum, the vast majority of women report significant and impairing cognitive changes from baseline. Empirical objective data supports a small to moderate cognitive difference between pregnant/postpartum women and nonpregnant/postpartum women. Data also suggests changes in some neuropsychological variables across pregnancy, but cognition remains at normative levels. This discrepancy may result from methodological issues in the study of cognition during pregnancy. See Fig. 11.2 for details.

Table 11.2 Differences in performance by cognitive domain

Cognitive domain	Study authors	Findings (control vs. pregnancy)	Findings (control vs. postpartum)
General cognitive functioning	Davies et al. (2018)	Worse in pregnant women	–
	Anderson and Rutherford (2012)	NS	NS
Overall memory[a]	Davies et al. (2018)	Worse in pregnant women only during third trimester	–
Working memory	Anderson and Rutherford (2012)	Worse in pregnant women	NS
Free recall	Anderson and Rutherford (2012)	Worse in pregnant women	NS
Delayed free recall	Anderson and Rutherford (2012)	Worse in pregnant women	NS
Recognition	Anderson and Rutherford (2012)	Improved in pregnant women	NS
Laboratory prospective memory	Anderson and Rutherford (2012)	NS	NS
Natural prospective memory	Anderson and Rutherford (2012)	Worse in pregnant women ($p < .01$)	NS
Overall executive functioning[b]	Davies et al. (2018)	NS	–
Processing speed	Anderson and Rutherford (2012)	Worse in pregnant women ($p < .05$)	NS

Note. [a]Overall memory defined by authors as working memory and retrieval from long-term memory via recognition and recall

[b]Overall executive functioning defined by authors as attention, planning, shifting between ideas, generating new responses, problem-solving, abstraction, and inhibition. Findings considered significant at $p < .01$ or lower. *NS* = nonsignificant, – = not reported

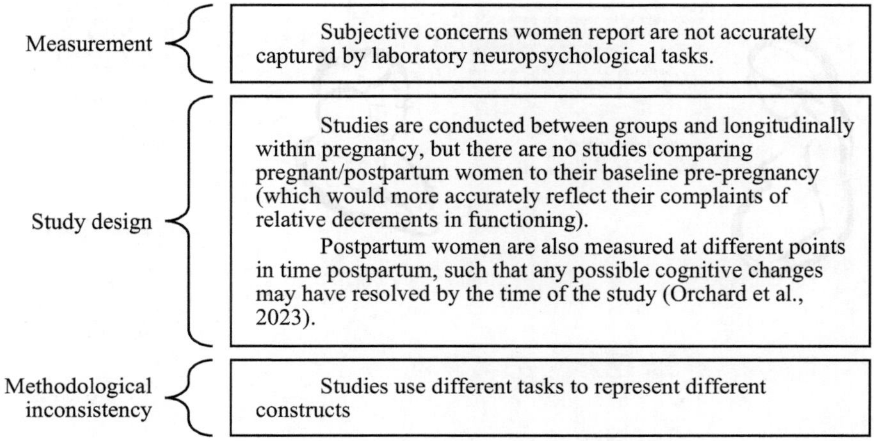

Fig. 11.2 Methodological issues inhibiting the study of cognition in pregnancy

Currently, the available evidence supports (1) differences in cognitive functioning between women in the third trimester and nonpregnant women, and (2) widespread subjective experience of poor cognitive functioning. When considering mechanisms of cognitive change, we then consider how hormones and other factors impact both the subjective experience of cognitive dysfunction and the measurable difference during the pregnancy period in memory and executive functioning.

The profusion of reproductive hormones in the body during pregnancy is implicated in a number of neurological changes, both functionally and structurally. Theoretically, levels of estrogen and progesterone, which drop dramatically following birth, are responsible for changes in memory function; however, studies linking absolute values of pregnancy hormones and cognition do not demonstrate significant relationships (Orchard et al., 2023). The relationship between pregnancy hormones and cognition is likely more complex and mediated by brain changes consistent with improved maternal caregiving behaviors.

Throughout pregnancy, reproductive hormones exert influence on the brain to prepare the mother to be able to care for her infant as successfully as possible. Rodent studies have demonstrated this structural and functional plasticity unequivocally, suggesting the existence of a maternal circuit or maternal motivation system that encourages prioritization of the infant and the mother's safety in order to support survival (Numan, 2007). Human studies have begun to point to the occurrence of an inherent and human-specific structural brain plasticity as well (Barba-Müller et al., 2019). Structurally, there appear to be gray matter reductions in the theory of mind (ToM) network during pregnancy (Hoekzema et al. 2017). See Fig. 11.3 for

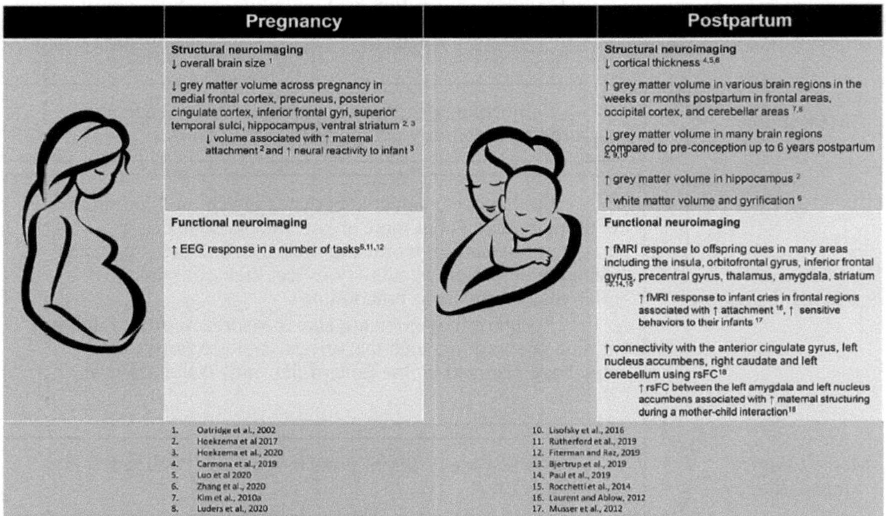

Fig. 11.3 Summary of key changes in pregnancy and postpartum. *Note:* From Pawluski et al. (2022)

Pawluski et al.'s (2022) overview of structural and functional brain changes in human pregnancy and postpartum.

In the postpartum period, increases in gray matter volume in the parietal lobe, prefrontal cortex, and midbrain can be seen (Kim et al., 2010). With some overlap with areas of reduction, this may reflect a recovery of volume in these areas across the postpartum period. The structural changes in these studies were significantly related to caregiving behaviors, such as a positive perception of the baby and the quality of mother-to-infant attachment (Hoekzema et al., 2017; Kim et al., 2010). Functionally, an increase in brain activation in certain regions reflects a recruitment of neural resources above and beyond that of nonpregnant and nonpostpartum women (Barba-Müller et al., 2019). Regions of increased activation include the reward system (also called the maternal motivation system; includes the medial preoptic area and the bed nucleus of the stria terminalis), the salience network (activated to detect and respond to threats; includes paralimbic structures such as the dorsal anterior cingulate and orbital frontoinsular cortices), the emotion regulation network (activated to manage own and children's emotions; includes prefrontal and cingulate control systems), and the empathy and ToM networks (activated to process social cognitive tasks such as perspective-taking and reflecting on the needs of another person; includes medial prefrontal cortex, precuneus, and posterior cingulate cortex), anterior temporal lobes, temporoparietal junction, and the inferior frontal gyri (Barba-Müller et al., 2019). Studies that have assessed changes in cognition without evaluating neuroimaging have observed enhanced social cognitive abilities and vigilance toward threatening emotional signals (Anderson & Rutherford, 2011; Pearson et al., 2009). This is a significant redistribution of neural resources and may account for the relative decrement in cognitive abilities that evolution has deemed less important during the transition to motherhood.

Additionally, the impact of sleep on cognition cannot be ignored in the pregnant and postpartum population. Over 90% of women report sleep disturbances in the pregnancy and postpartum period. In the abovementioned study examining subjective cognitive complaints between pregnant and nonpregnant groups, while there was no difference in the groups on physical health or anxiety, sleep disturbance did significantly predict cognitive issues in the pregnant group (Janes et al., 1999). The link between mood and memory also continues to be important, as higher levels of depression predict poorer memory (Burt et al., 1995). With close to one-third of women reporting perinatal mood and anxiety concerns, cognitive complaints may be related to mood issues (Orchard et al., 2023). In fact, in one study comparing 26 nonpregnant women to 21 pregnant women, perinatal cognitive changes were no longer significant when corrected for mood and sleep (Onyper et al., 2010). Finally, the increase in cognitive load secondary to caregiving in the context of modern social pressures and limited social supports likely reduces resource availability for cognitive abilities (Callaghan et al., 2024).

Risk and Resilience Factors

As mentioned above, women at higher risk for experiencing subjective cognitive decrements tend to be older, married, and have reached a higher level of education (Parsons & Redman, 1991). Given that research on objective cognitive changes is relatively new and ongoing, strong support for risk and resilience factors does not yet exist. As social determinants of health such as SES, race/ethnicity, and food insecurity significantly impact cognition and risk for dementia in the general population (Majoka & Schimming, 2021), it can be hypothesized that these factors are also risk factors for cognitive changes during pregnancy and postpartum. Further research is needed.

Menopause

The menopausal transition is marked by unpredictable variations in estradiol and progesterone levels due to the slowing down and eventual cessation of ovarian function. Perimenopause, or the beginning of the transition, typically begins around age 40, and natural menopause, or the lack of a menstrual period for 12 consecutive months, typically occurs around age 51. The menopausal transition is accompanied by vasomotor symptoms (e.g., hot flushes/flashes, night sweats), urogenital symptoms (e.g., vaginal dryness), and mood/neurological symptoms (e.g., changes in sex drive, changes in depression/anxiety, and changes in cognition; Baber et al., 2016; Stuenkel et al., 2015).

Subjective Cognitive Concerns

Reuben et al. (2021) conducted a systematic review of the extant literature between 1996 and 2020 and identified 19 studies for review. They found that the majority of women across the menopausal transition reported cognitive complaints. Subjective complaints include difficulty retrieving words or numbers, forgetting the purpose of a behavior, losing train of thought, and forgetting appointments (Sullivan-Mitchell & Fugate Woods, 2001). The literature is equivocal regarding whether perimenopausal or postmenopausal women report more subjective complaints (Reuben et al., 2021; Weber et al., 2014). Subjective reports of forgetfulness are significantly associated with worse vasomotor symptoms (Drogos et al., 2013; LeBlanc et al., 2007; Mitchell & Woods, 2011).

Objective Cognitive Changes

Studies differentiate between changes due to "natural menopause," or the menopause transition occurring in the absence of external medical changes, and "surgical menopause," or the removal of ovaries (oophorectomy) due to medical reasons. Natural menopause is associated with decreases in verbal memory and verbal fluency that appear to be independent of those expected to occur with normal aging (Weber et al., 2014). In addition, women experiencing natural menopause demonstrate lower scores on measures of verbal memory, attention, and working memory, though scores were still in the normative ranges (Schaafsma et al., 2010; Unkenstein et al., 2016; Weber et al. 2012). Effects tend to be small and may be time dependent, persisting for approximately 4 years surrounding menopause or peaking after menopause (Baber et al., 2016; Epperson et al., 2013; Maki, 2015; Weber et al., 2014). In fact, a large longitudinal study ($N = 2000$) reported a temporary decrement in cognitive skills in perimenopause which resolved after menopause (Greendale et al., 2009, 2010). Vasomotor symptoms as measured objectively (with an ambulatory hot flash monitor) are associated with poorer verbal memory (Maki et al., 2008).

Surgical menopause and the abrupt decline of reproductive hormones are predictive of an increased risk for cognitive impairment and dementia based on the woman's age at the time of surgery (Rocca et al., 2007; see Chap. 5 on Alzheimer's disease for more detail).

In terms of brain activation during tasks, there is evidence of changes across the menopausal period. Postmenopausal women show the least hippocampal activation during verbal processing tasks and increased bilateral hippocampi connectivity as compared to both premenopausal and perimenopausal women (Jacobs et al., 2016).

Mechanisms of Cognitive Change

The robust medical literature connecting higher levels of estrogen with protected cognitive abilities implies that fluctuating levels of estrogen in the menopausal transition may impact cognition; however, this has yet to be studied in a methodologically sound manner that supports causality (Conde et al., 2021). There is general support for the relationship between absolute levels of estrogen and cognitive performance. Studies have suggested a functional increase in frontal and temporal activation when performing verbal tasks during perimenopause with an accompanying decrement in verbal cognition and estradiol (Berent-Spillson et al., 2012). Higher concentrations of estrogen/estradiol are associated with better verbal memory and less susceptibility to interference (Wolf & Kirschbaum, 2002). Importantly, there are considerable intraindividual differences in the way in which hormones fluctuate across the transition (Burger et al., 2002). Given these considerations, identifying the absolute impact of reproductive hormones on cognition through the menopausal transition is difficult.

Risk and Resilience Factors

Objective experience of vasomotor symptoms has a direct impact on cognitive performance, as do mood disorder symptoms and sleep disturbances (Greendale et al., 2020). The impact of number of births on future cognition and risk for dementia is inconsistently reported and cannot be utilized as a risk or resilience factor at this time (Barha et al., 2023).

Hormonal Contraceptives

The effect of birth control on cognition is a complex topic that has garnered increasing attention in recent years. As hormonal contraceptives (HC) are widely used by millions of women worldwide, understanding their potential impact on cognitive functions such as memory, attention, and executive function is crucial. This section delves into the latest research findings, exploring both the positive and negative cognitive effects associated with various forms of birth control. By examining these studies, we aim to provide a comprehensive overview of how hormonal contraceptives may influence cognitive processes, ultimately contributing to a more informed discussion on women's health and well-being.

Subjective Cognitive Concerns

Estrogen contraceptives work by preventing ovulation, altering the uterine lining to prevent implantation, and thickening cervical mucus to block sperm. Progesterone contraceptives, often called the "minipill," primarily thicken cervical mucus and sometimes prevent ovulation. Combination birth control pills contain both estrogen and progestin, working together to stop ovulation, thicken cervical mucus, and change the uterine lining, making it less likely for sperm to reach an egg or for a fertilized egg to implant. There are limited studies examining subjective cognitive concerns of HC. One study, which recruited women in Indonesia from young adulthood, found no significant associations between HCs and subjective memory complaints (Pradono et al., 2020). This suggests that, at least in this demographic, the use of HCs did not appear to impact self-reported memory issues. However, more research is needed to fully understand the broader implications and to explore these associations in different populations and age groups.

Objective Cognitive Change

Neuroactive steroid hormones play a crucial role in regulating learning and memory, and several studies have explored the impact HC on women's cognition, yielding mixed results. HC use is associated with improvements (Gurvich et al., 2020; Plamberger et al., 2021), no changes (Gravelsins et al., 2021; Mihalik et al., 2009), or declines (Bradshaw et al., 2020; Griksiene et al., 2018) in cognitive abilities compared to naturally cycling women. These discrepancies may arise from variations in the cognitive domains studied, such as verbal fluency, visuospatial abilities, and mental rotation tasks, as well as differences in treatment duration, dosage, and the type of progestin used. Specifically, HC can lead to improvements (Gogos et al., 2014) or no changes (Roodenrys et al., 2008) in verbal memory, a domain typically favoring females, while visuospatial abilities, generally favoring males, remain unaffected except in cases where the type of progestin (androgenic or antiandrogenic) influences outcomes (Wharton et al., 2008). Overall, HC may enhance cognitive performance in verbal memory and visuospatial abilities but could potentially decrease accuracy in mental arithmetic and emotion recognition tasks (Gurvich et al., 2023).

Mechanisms of Cognitive Change

The mechanisms of how HC may affect cognition have been explored through neuroimaging and animal studies. Neuroimaging studies show increased mean diffusivity in the fornix of HC users compared to nonusers, indicating microstructural changes in white matter (De Bondt et al., 2013). Additionally, there are modified volumes in specific brain regions and altered functional connectivity in the frontal nodes of the executive network, which can significantly impact emotional regulation (Engman et al., 2018; Gingnell et al., 2016; Petersen et al., 2021; Pletzer, 2019). These effects can vary between adolescent and adult HC users (Sharma et al., 2020), may depend on the duration of HC use and the type of progestin, and might not be entirely reversible. The underlying mechanisms are not fully understood, but animal models could help investigate the neurobiological mechanisms behind HC's impact on brain function (see review by Concas et al., 2022). For instance, a study by Simone and colleagues found that impaired memory in rats on the novel object recognition test was linked to reduced hippocampal BDNF mRNA expression, a neurotrophin involved in learning and memory (Simone et al., 2015). This reduction was also positively correlated with tyrosine hydroxylase mRNA expression in the locus coeruleus, suggesting that noradrenergic transmission might play a role in HC-induced cognitive performance changes.

Risk and Resilience Factors

Research by Beltz et al. (2015) highlights that college-aged women using monophasic oral contraceptives with second generation progestins performed better on cognitive tasks compared to those who were naturally cycling. The dose of ethinyl estradiol in the pill was a significant predictor of cognitive performance. Several factors can modulate the influence of oral contraceptives (OCs) on cognition, including task-related factors like reporting results at a task level and considering task difficulty. Control group factors, such as accurately reporting the menstrual cycle phase of naturally cycling participants, are also important. Additionally, OC-related factors like the duration of use, timing of ingestion, and the specific hormonal profile of the OC formulation can differentially impact cognitive outcomes (Gurvich et al., 2023).

Gender-Affirming Hormone Therapy

Gender affirming hormonal therapy (GAHT) is a crucial aspect of the transition process for many transgender individuals, offering significant benefits in aligning one's physical appearance with their gender identity. The National Transgender Discrimination Survey Report on Health and Health Care reveals that at least 80% of transgender individuals have either undergone GAHT or wish to do so at some point (Grant et al., 2011). Beyond the physical changes, GAHT can also lead to cognitive changes. This section explores the various cognitive effects associated with GAHT.

Subjective Cognitive Concerns

Research by Van Heesewijk et al. (2021) found that transgender women reported memory problems similar to those of cisgender groups, indicating they did not experience more cognitive hindrance. However, other studies have highlighted that older transgender individuals (aged 45 and above) reported increased confusion or memory loss over the past year compared to their cisgender counterparts. This suggests that while younger transgender individuals may not face significant cognitive issues, older transgender individuals might experience more pronounced subjective cognitive concerns (Cicero et al., 2023; Flatt et al., 2021).

Objective Cognitive Change

Research on cognitive performance effects of gender-affirming hormone therapy (GAHT) overwhelmingly supports its impact on cognitive tasks that exhibit well-established sex differences (Nguyen et al., 2019). Androgens, which are administered to female-to-male (FTM) individuals, enhance "male-like" characteristics and are associated with decreases in performance on typically male-dominated cognitive tasks among male-to-female (MTF) individuals. Longitudinal studies suggest that hormone manipulations used by MTF result in a reduction in performance on 3D visuospatial tasks and increased verbal fluency. Estrogen therapy in MTFs has been shown to impact performance on some cognitive tasks, such as paired associate learning (both immediate and delayed recall). These effects align with the typical sex differences observed in these cognitive domains.

A systematic review and meta-analysis of ten studies (seven cohort and three cross-sectional studies published between 1995 and 2016) by Karalexi et al. (2020) highlighted significant enhancements in visuospatial ability in FTM individuals following GAHT. Cross-sectional studies pooled together showed improved performance in verbal working memory among treated compared to nontreated birth-assigned female individuals. FTM transgender individuals who had been on androgen treatment for at least 6 months performed better on two visual memory tasks compared to those not on treatment (Gomez-Gil et al., 2009). However, performance assessed by reaction time among FTMs using high-dose testosterone was slower than that of cisgender females, suggesting that testosterone treatment did not consistently make FTMs more "masculine" in their performance (Carrillo et al., 2010).

Mechanisms of Cognitive Change

Research on the mechanisms of cognitive change with GAHT reveals notable differences in brain activation between trans and cisgender individuals. Carrillo et al. (2010) found that during mental rotation tasks, brain activation patterns, as measured by the blood oxygen level dependent (BOLD) signal, differ significantly between these groups. Sommer et al. (2008) observed changes in brain activation during language and mental rotation tasks after 3 months of GAHT, though lateralization of these functions remained stable. Additionally, smaller studies highlight that parietal activation decreases with longer GAHT duration in MTF individuals, who also tend to use verbal strategies more than cisgender males during task performance (Schnoing et al., 2009). Both transgender groups showed increased temporo-occipital activation compared to male controls. However, Nota et al. (2017) reported no significant changes in functional connectivity after 4 months of GAHT.

Hormone Replacement Therapy

Hormone Replacement Therapy (HRT) is a medical treatment designed to supplement the body with hormones that are at deficient levels, particularly in the context of menopause. It primarily involves the administration of estrogen and, often, progesterone to alleviate symptoms associated with decreased hormone levels in postmenopausal women, such as hot flashes, night sweats, and vaginal dryness. HRT is associated with various cognitive changes, although the literature surrounding HRT and cognition largely focuses on its relationship to Alzheimer's disease, which will be discussed in Chap. 5. This section will discuss the remaining literature on HRT, which is unfortunately limited.

Subjective Complaints and Objective Cognitive Changes

Subjectively, some HRT users report increased forgetfulness (Hogervorst et al., 1999). Objectively, there is evidence suggesting that estrogen alone may benefit verbal memory in younger postmenopausal women, with more consistent findings in those who are surgically postmenopausal (Maki & Sundermann, 2009). However, a combination of conjugated equine estrogen and medroxyprogesterone acetate appears to detrimentally affect verbal memory across different age groups. Additionally, some studies indicate that hormone therapy may enhance executive function (Maki & Sundermann, 2009).

Mechanisms of Cognitive Change

Research indicates that HRT in postmenopausal women may preserve brain matter. Studies by Erickson et al. (2005) and Boccardi et al. (2006) found that current and former HT users had more gray and white matter in key brain regions compared to nonusers, suggesting HRT leads to greater sparing of gray and white matter tissue in the aging brain. Conversely, Zhang et al. (2016) utilized a novel method to detect brain differences in older women undergoing HRT and found reduced gray matter volumes in HRT recipients, particularly in the prefrontal and hippocampal regions. In a study by Albert et al. (2017), 75 postmenopausal women aged 51–75 living in the United States were given varying doses of 17β-estradiol or a placebo over 3 months. No racial/ethnic information about the sample was provided. MRI scans revealed that only the group receiving the higher 2 mg dose experienced an increase in hippocampal gray matter volume, suggesting HRT's effect on grey and white matter may be dose dependent (Table 11.3).

Table 11.3 Hormone therapy research highlights

Hormonal contraceptives (HC)	• Limited studies have found no significant association between HC use and self-reported memory issues • HC use may lead to mild improvements in verbal memory and visuospatial abilities but may decrease accuracy in mental arithmetic and emotion recognition tasks • Neuroimaging and animal studies suggest HC use can cause microstructural changes in white matter and alter brain region volumes and functional connectivity, affecting cognitive performance • Factors such as the type of progestin, duration of use, and specific hormonal profiles can influence cognitive outcomes
Gender-affirming hormone therapy (GAHT)	• Younger transgender women report similar memory issues as cisgender women, while older transgender individuals report more cognitive concerns • GAHT impacts cognitive tasks with sex differences, enhancing visuospatial ability in female-to-male (FTM) individuals and affecting verbal fluency and memory in male-to-female (MTF) individuals • Brain activation patterns differ between trans individuals on GAHT and cisgender individuals, with changes observed in brain regions and functional connectivity
Hormone replacement therapy (HRT)	• Although many HRT users report increased forgetfulness, estrogen may benefit verbal memory in younger postmenopausal women • Some studies indicate hormone therapy may enhance executive function • HRT may preserve brain matter, with varying effects on gray and white matter volumes depending on dosage and duration

Research Takeaways

Research on cognitive changes across a woman's lifespan concomitant with hormonal changes is, in many ways, in its infancy. Though there are decades worth of studies examining objective cognitive differences between women at certain stages (e.g., pregnancy, menopausal) and control groups, the question of whether women themselves experience objectively verified cognitive shifts congruent with their subjective experience remains unanswered. Patterns of objective findings are equivocal and trends depend on whether or not major covariates have been acknowledged. Many questions remain regarding the nature of cognitive difficulties in the context of social determinants of health, differential dosing of hormones, and racial and ethnic differences. Major takeaways include:

- People experiencing major hormonal shifts are also likely to experience significant subjective decrements in cognitive functioning.
- Patterns of objective cognitive dysfunction are inconsistent and vary more based on population studied, methodology, study design, and covariates acknowledged than on hormonal changes.
- The relationship between reproductive hormones and cognitive change is complex and necessitates further exploration of integrated neural frameworks.

Evaluating absolute levels of hormones in relation to cognitive change may artificially oversimplify relationships.

Clinical Takeaways

Presumably, the purpose of clinical research on the nature of cognitive changes is to be able to respond appropriately to patients wanting to understand their lived experience of new-onset difficulties with cognitive functioning. As demonstrated in this chapter, objective findings may not fully validate patients' experiences, and it is clinically useful to help them understand the meaning of these findings and find ways to improve their own functioning. The subjective experience of cognitive dysfunction may lead to increased stress which may then lead to further interference in cognitive functioning, creating a cycle which can be difficult to interrupt. Mood, stress, cognitive load, physiological symptoms associated with hormonal changes, and social determinants of health can be understood as potentially modifiable factors that impact cognition. Major takeaways include:

- It is both valid and important to normalize the experience of cognitive changes. Subjective cognitive deficits are common, and the patient experiencing them is not alone.
- Because objective cognitive testing leads to equivocal and inconsistent results, pursuing neuropsychological testing and/or considering neurocognitive disorder diagnoses should only occur in the context of serious and sustained impairment in functioning in the patient's daily life after other factors have resolved.
- Education and treatment related to the cognitive impact of sleep disturbance, mood issues, vasomotor symptoms (if relevant), premenstrual symptoms (if relevant), cognitive load of caregiving (if relevant), and other applicable factors known to impact perceived or actual cognitive functioning can be therapeutic and lessen hormonally related cognitive difficulties.

References

Albert, K., Hiscox, J., Boyd, B., Dumas, J., Taylor, W., & Newhouse, P. (2017). Estrogen enhances hippocampal gray-matter volume in young and older postmenopausal women: A prospective dose-response study. *Neurobiology of Aging, 56*, 1–6.

Anderson, M. V., & Rutherford, M. D. (2011). Recognition of novel faces after single exposure is enhanced during pregnancy. *Evolutionary Psychology, 9*(1), 47–60.

Anderson, M. V., & Rutherford, M. D. (2012). Cognitive reorganization during pregnancy and the postpartum period: An evolutionary perspective. *Evolutionary Psychology, 10*(4), 147470491201000402.

Apter, D., Bützow, T. L., Laughlin, G. A., & Yen, S. S. (1993). Gonadotropin-releasing hormone pulse generator activity during pubertal transition in girls: Pulsatile and diurnal patterns of circulating gonadotropins. *The Journal of Clinical Endocrinology & Metabolism, 76*(4), 940–949.

Asavasupreechar, T., Saito, R., Miki, Y., Edwards, D. P., Boonyaratanakornkit, V., & Sasano, H. (2020). Systemic distribution of progesterone receptor subtypes in human tissues. *The Journal of Steroid Biochemistry and Molecular Biology, 199*, 105599.

Baber, R. J., Panay, N., & Fenton, A. (2016). IMS Recommendations on women's midlife health and menopause hormone therapy (MHT). *Climacteric, 201*, 109–150.

Bakhshani, N. M., Mousavi, M. N., & Khodabandeh, G. (2009). Prevalence and severity of premenstrual symptoms among Iranian female university students. *Journal of the Pakistan Medical Association, 59*(4), 205.

Barba-Müller, E., Craddock, S., Carmona, S., & Hoekzema, E. (2019). Brain plasticity in pregnancy and the postpartum period: Links to maternal caregiving and mental health. *Archives of Women's Mental Health, 22*(2), 289–299.

Barha, C. K., Best, J. R., Rosano, C., Yaffe, K., Catov, J. M., & Liu-Ambrose, T. (2023). Walking for cognitive health: Previous parity moderates the relationship between self-reported walking and cognition. *The Journals of Gerontology: Series A, 78*(3), 486–493.

Beltz, A. M., Hampson, E., & Berenbaum, S. A. (2015). Oral contraceptives and cognition: A role for ethinyl estradiol. *Hormones and Behavior, 74*, 209–217.

Beltz, A. M., & Moser, J. S. (2020). Ovarian hormones: A long overlooked but critical contributor to cognitive brain structures and function. *Annals of the New York Academy of Sciences, 1464*(1), 156–180.

Berent-Spillson, A., Persad, C. C., Love, T., Sowers, M., Randolph, J. F., Zubieta, J.-K., & Smith, Y. R. (2012). Hormonal environment affects cognition independent of age during the menopause transition. *The Journal of Clinical Endocrinology & Metabolism, 97*(9), E1686–E1694.

Boccardi, M., Ghidoni, R., Govoni, S., Testa, C., Benussi, L., Bonetti, M., et al. (2006). Effects of hormone therapy on brain morphology of healthy postmenopausal women: A Voxel-based morphometry study. *Menopause, 13*(4), 584–591.

Bradshaw, H. K., Mengelkoch, S., & Hill, S. E. (2020). Hormonal contraceptive use predicts decreased perseverance and therefore performance on some simple and challenging cognitive tasks. *Hormones and Behavior, 119*, 104652.

Brett, M., & Baxendale, S. (2001). Motherhood and memory: A review. *Psychoneuroendocrinology, 26*(4), 339–362.

Burger, H. G., Dudley, E. C., Robertson, D. M., & Dennerstein, L. (2002). Hormonal changes in the menopause transition. *Recent Progress in Hormone Research, 57*, 257–276.

Burnham, V., Sundby, C., Laman-Maharg, A., & Thornton, J. (2017). Luteinizing hormone acts at the hippocampus to dampen spatial memory. *Hormones and Behavior, 89*, 55–63.

Burt, D. B., Zembar, M. J., & Niederehe, G. (1995). Depression and memory impairment: A meta-analysis of the association, its pattern, and specificity. *Psychological Bulletin, 117*(2), 285.

Callaghan, B. L., McCormack, C., Kim, P., & Pawluski, J. L. (2024). Understanding the maternal brain in the context of the mental load of motherhood. *Nature Mental Health*, 1–9.

Carrillo, B., Gómez-Gil, E., Rametti, G., Junque, C., Gomez, Á., Karadi, K., et al. (2010). Cortical activation during mental rotation in male-to-female and female-to-male transsexuals under hormonal treatment. *Psychoneuroendocrinology, 35*(8), 1213–1222.

Chappell, C. A., Rohan, L. C., Moncla, B. J., Wang, L., Meyn, L. A., Bunge, K., & Hillier, S. L. (2014). The effects of reproductive hormones on the physical properties of cervicovaginal fluid. *American Journal of Obstetrics and Gynecology, 211*(3), 226.e1–226.e2267.

Cicero, E. C., Lett, E., Flatt, J. D., Benson, G. P., & Epps, F. (2023). Transgender adults from minoritized ethnoracial groups in the US report greater subjective cognitive decline. *The Journals of Gerontology: Series B, 78*(6), 1051–1059.

Concas, A., Serra, M., & Porcu, P. (2022). How hormonal contraceptives shape brain and behavior: A review of preclinical studies. *Frontiers in Neuroendocrinology, 66*, 101017.

Conde, D. M., Verdade, R. C., Valadares, A. L., Mella, L. F., Pedro, A. O., & Costa-Paiva, L. (2021). Menopause and cognitive impairment: A narrative review of current knowledge. *World Journal of Psychiatry, 11*(8), 412.

Courvoisier, D. S., Renaud, O., Geiser, C., Paschke, K., Gaudy, K., & Jodan, K. (2013). Sex hormones and mental rotation: An intensive longitudinal investigation. *Hormones and Behavior, 63*, 345–351.

Davies, S. J., Lum, J. A., Skouteris, H., Byrne, L. K., & Hayden, M. J. (2018). Cognitive impairment during pregnancy: A meta-analysis. *Medical Journal of Australia, 208*(1), 35–40.

Davis, S. R., & Wahlin-Jacobsen, S. (2015). Testosterone in women—the clinical significance. *The Lancet Diabetes & Endocrinology, 3*(12), 980–992.

De Bondt, T., Jacquemyn, Y., Van Hecke, W., Sijbers, J., Sunaert, S., & Parizel, P. M. (2013). Regional gray matter volume differences and sex-hormone correlations as a function of menstrual cycle phase and hormonal contraceptives use. *Brain Research, 1530*, 22–31.

Di Clemente, N., Racine, C., Pierre, A., & Taieb, J. (2021). Anti-Müllerian hormone in female reproduction. *Endocrine Reviews, 42*(6), 753–782.

Dietrich, T., Krings, T., Neulen, J., Willmes, K., Erberich, S., Thron, A., et al. (2001). Effects of blood estrogen level on cortical activation patterns during cognitive activation as measured by functional MRI. *Neuroimage, 13*, 425–432.

DiVall, S. A., & Radovick, S. (2008). Pubertal development and menarche. *Annals of the New York Academy of Sciences, 1135*(1), 19–28.

Drogos, L. L., Rubin, L. H., Geller, S. E., Banuvar, S., Shulman, L. P., & Maki, P. M. (2013). Objective cognitive performance is related to subjective memory complaints in midlife women with moderate to severe vasomotor symptoms. *Menopause, 20*(12), 1236–1242.

Duff, S. J., & Hampson, E. (2000). A beneficial effect of estrogen on working memory in postmenopausal women taking hormone replacement therapy. *Hormones and Behavior, 38*(4), 262–276.

Edinoff, A. N., Odisho, A. S., Lewis, K., Kaskas, A., Hunt, G., Cornett, E. M., et al. (2021). Brexanolone, a GABAA modulator, in the treatment of postpartum depression in adults: A comprehensive review. *Frontiers in Psychiatry, 12*, 699740.

Engman, J., Sundström Poromaa, I., Moby, L., Wikström, J., Fredrikson, M., & Gingnell, M. (2018). Hormonal cycle and contraceptive effects on amygdala and salience resting-state networks in women with previous affective side effects on the pill. *Neuropsychopharmacology, 43*(3), 555–563.

Epperson, C. N., Sammel, M. D., & Freeman, E. W. (2013). Menopause effects on verbal memory: Findings from a longitudinal community cohort. *The Journal of Clinical Endocrinology & Metabolism, 98*(9), 3829–3838.

Epting, L. K., & Overman, W. H. (1998). Sex-sensitive tasks in men and women: A search for performance fluctuations across the menstrual cycle. *Behavioral Neuroscience, 112*, 1304–1317.

Erickson, K. I., Colcombe, S. J., Raz, N., Korol, D. L., Scalf, P., Webb, A., et al. (2005). Selective sparing of brain tissue in postmenopausal women receiving hormone replacement therapy. *Neurobiology of Aging, 26*(8), 1205–1213.

Farage, M. A., Neill, S., & MacLean, A. B. (2009). Physiological changes associated with the menstrual cycle: A review. *Obstetrical & Gynecological Survey, 64*(1), 58–72.

Flatt, J. D., Cicero, E. C., Lambrou, N. H., Wharton, W., Anderson, J. G., Bouldin, E. D., et al. (2021). Subjective cognitive decline higher among sexual and gender minorities in the United States, 2015–2018. *Alzheimer's & Dementia: Translational Research & Clinical Interventions, 7*(1), e12197.

Freeman, E. W., Frye, C. A., et al. (2002). Allopregnanolone levels and symptom improvement in severe premenstrual syndrome. *Journal Clinical Psychopharmacolgoy, 22*(5), 516–520.

Freeman, E. W., Rickels, K., Sondheimer, S. J., & Polansky, M. (1995). A double-blind trial of oral progesterone, alprazolam, and placebo in treatment of severe premenstrual syndrome. *JAMA, 274*(1), 51–57.

Fu, X. Y., Chen, H. H., Zhang, N., Ding, M. X., Qiu, Y. E., Pan, X. M., et al. (2018). Effects of chronic unpredictable mild stress on ovarian reserve in female rats: Feasibility analysis of a rat model of premature ovarian failure. *Molecular Medicine Reports, 18*(1), 532–540.

Gardner, D. G., & Shoback, D. (2007). *Greenspan's basic and clinical endocrinology* (8th ed.). McGraw Hill Medical.

Gingnell, M., Bannbers, E., Engman, J., Frick, A., Moby, L., Wikström, J., & Sundström-Poromaa, I. (2016). The effect of combined hormonal contraceptives use on brain reactivity during response inhibition. *The European Journal of Contraception & Reproductive Health Care, 21*(2), 150–157.

Gogos, A., Wu, Y. C., Williams, A. S., & Byrne, L. K. (2014). The effects of ethinylestradiol and progestins ("the pill") on cognitive function in pre-menopausal women. *Neurochemical Research, 39*, 2288–2300.

Goletiani, N. V., Keith, D. R., & Gorsky, S. J. (2007). Progesterone: Review of safety for clinical studies. *Experimental and Clinical Psychopharmacology, 15*(5), 427.

Gómez-Gil, E., Canizares, S., Torres, A., De La Torre, F., Halperin, I., & Salamero, M. (2009). Androgen treatment effects on memory in female-to-male transsexuals. *Psychoneuroendocrinology, 34*(1), 110–117.

Gordon, H. W., & Lee, P. A. (1993). No difference in cognitive performance between phases of the menstrual cycle. *Psychoneuroendocrinology, 18*, 521–531.

Grant, J. M., Mottet, L. A., Tanis, J. J., & Min, D. (2011). Transgender discrimination survey. *National Center for Transgender Equality and National Gay and Lesbian Task Force: Washington, DC, USA, 1*(1), 2–7.

Gravelsins, L., Duncan, K., & Einstein, G. (2021). Do oral contraceptives affect young women's memory? Dopamine-dependent working memory is influenced by COMT genotype, but not time of pill ingestion. *PLoS One, 16*(6), e0252807.

Greendale, G. A., Huang, M. H., Wight, R. G., Seeman, T., Luetters, C., Avis, N. E., et al. (2009). Effects of the menopause transition and hormone use on cognitive performance in midlife women. *Neurology, 72*(21), 1850–1857.

Greendale, G. A., Wight, R. G., Huang, M. H., Avis, N., Gold, E. B., Joffe, H., et al. (2010). Menopause-associated symptoms and cognitive performance: Results from the study of women's health across the nation. *American Journal of Epidemiology, 171*(11), 1214–1224.

Greendale, G. A., Karlamangla, A. S., & Maki, P. M. (2020). The menopause transition and cognition. *JAMA, 323*(15), 1495–1496.

Griksiene, R., Monciunskaite, R., Arnatkeviciute, A., & Ruksenas, O. (2018). Does the use of hormonal contraceptives affect the mental rotation performance? *Hormones and Behavior, 100*, 29–38.

Griksiene, R., & Ruksenas, O. (2011). Effects of hormonal contraceptives on mental rotation and verbal fluency. *Psychoneuroendocrinology, 36*, 1239–1248.

Gurvich, C., Nicholls, I., Lavale, A., & Kulkarni, J. (2023). Oral contraceptives and cognition: A systematic review. *Frontiers in Neuroendocrinology, 69*, 101052.

Gurvich, C., Warren, A. M., Worsley, R., Hudaib, A. R., Thomas, N., & Kulkarni, J. (2020). Effects of oral contraceptive androgenicity on visuospatial and social-emotional cognition: A prospective observational trial. *Brain Sciences, 10*(4), 194.

Halari, R., Hines, M., Kumari, V., Mehrotra, R., Wheeler, M., Ng, V., et al. (2005). Sex differences and individual differences in cognitive performance and their relationship to endogenous gonadal hormones and gonadotropins. *Behavioral Neuroscience, 119*, 104–117.

Hampson, E., Levy-Cooperman, N., & Korman, J. M. (2014). Estradiol and mental rotation: Relation to dimensionality, difficulty, or angular disparity? *Hormones and Behavior, 65*, 238–248.

Hansen, J. W., Hoffman, H. J., & Ross, G. T. (1975). Monthly gonadotropin cycles in premenarcheal girls. *Science, 190*(4210), 161–163.

Hantsoo, L., & Epperson, C. N. (2015). Premenstrual dysphoric disorder: Epidemiology and treatment. *Current Psychiatry Reports, 17*(11), 87.

Hardy, T. M., McCarthy, D. O., Fourie, N. H., & Henderson, W. A. (2016). Anti-Müllerian hormone levels and urinary cortisol in women with chronic abdominal pain. *Journal of Obstetric, Gynecologic & Neonatal Nursing, 45*(6), 772–780.

Hausmann, M., Slabbekoorn, D., Van Goozen, S. H., Cohen-Kettenis, P. T., & Gunturkun, O. (2000). Sex hormones affect spatial abilities during the menstrual cycle. *Behavioral Neuroscience, 114*, 1245–1250.
Hoekzema, E., Barba-Müller, E., Pozzobon, C., Picado, M., Lucco, F., García-García, D., et al. (2017). Pregnancy leads to long-lasting changes in human brain structure. *Nature Neuroscience, 20*(2), 287–296.
Hogervorst, E., Boshuisen, M., Riedel, W., Willeken, C., & Jolles, J. (1999). The effect of hormone replacement therapy on cognitive function in elderly women. *Psychoneuroendocrinology, 24*(1), 43–68.
Holland, J., Bandelow, S., & Hogervorst, E. (2011). Testosterone levels and cognition in elderly men: A review. *Maturitas, 69*(4), 322–337.
Hutcherson, T. C., Cieri-Hutcherson, N. E., & Gosciak, M. F. (2020). Brexanolone for postpartum depression. *American Journal of Health-System Pharmacy, 77*(5), 336–345.
Iacovides, S., Avidon, I., & Baker, F. C. (2015). Does pain vary across the menstrual cycle? A review. *European Journal of Pain, 19*(10), 1389–1405.
Islam, R. M., Bell, R. J., Green, S., Page, M. J., & Davis, S. R. (2019). Safety and efficacy of testosterone for women: A systematic review and meta-analysis of randomised controlled trial data. *The Lancet Diabetes & Endocrinology, 7*(10), 754–766.
Jacobs, E. G., Weiss, B. K., Makris, N., Whitfield-Gabrieli, S., Buka, S. L., Klibanski, A., & Goldstein, J. M. (2016). Impact of sex and menopausal status on episodic memory circuitry in early midlife. *Journal of Neuroscience, 36*(39), 10163–10173.
Janes, C., Casey, P., Huntsdale, C., & Angus, G. (1999). Memory in pregnancy. I: Subjective experiences and objective assessment of implicit, explicit and working memory in primigravid and primiparous women. *Journal of Psychosomatic Obstetrics & Gynecology, 20*(2), 80–87.
Joffe, H., Hall, J. E., Gruber, S., Sarmiento, I. A., Cohen, L. S., Yurgelun-Todd, D., & Martin, K. A. (2006). Estrogen therapy selectively enhances prefrontal cognitive processes: A randomized, double-blind, placebo-controlled study with functional magnetic resonance imaging in perimenopausal and recently postmenopausal women. *Menopause, 13*(3), 411–422.
Karalexi, M. A., Georgakis, M. K., Dimitriou, N. G., Vichos, T., Katsimpris, A., Petridou, E. T., & Papadopoulos, F. C. (2020). Gender-affirming hormone treatment and cognitive function in transgender young adults: A systematic review and meta-analysis. *Psychoneuroendocrinology, 119*, 104721.
Karamitrou, E. K., Anagnostis, P., Vaitsi, K., Athanasiadis, L., & Goulis, D. G. (2023). Early menopause and premature ovarian insufficiency are associated with increased risk of dementia: A systematic review and meta-analysis of observational studies. *Maturitas*, 107792.
Kim, P., Leckman, J. F., Mayes, L. C., Feldman, R., Wang, X., & Swain, J. E. (2010). The plasticity of human maternal brain: Longitudinal changes in brain anatomy during the early postpartum period. *Behavioral Neuroscience, 124*(5), 695.
Kozaki, T., & Yasukouchi, A. (2009). Sex differences on components of mental rotation at different menstrual phases. *International Journal of Neuroscience, 119*, 59–67. https://doi.org/10.1080/00207450802480101
Krug, R., Born, J., & Rasch, B. (2006). A 3-day estrogen treatment improves prefrontal cortex-dependent cognitive function in postmenopausal women. *Psychoneuroendocrinology, 31*(8), 965–975.
Le, J., Thomas, N., & Gurvich, C. (2020). Cognition, the menstrual cycle, and premenstrual disorders: A review. *Brain Sciences, 10*(4), 198.
LeBlanc, E. S., Neiss, M. B., Carello, P. E., Samuels, M. H., & Janowsky, J. S. (2007). Hot flashes and estrogen therapy do not influence cognition in early menopausal women. *Menopause, 14*(2), 191–202.
Legro, R. S., Lin, H. M., Demers, L. M., & Lloyd, T. (2000). Rapid maturation of the reproductive axis during perimenarche independent of body composition. *The Journal of Clinical Endocrinology & Metabolism, 85*(3), 1021–1025.
Leong, R. L., & Chee, M. W. (2023). Understanding the need for sleep to improve cognition. *Annual Review of Psychology, 74*(1), 27–57.

Liang, C., Dobson, A. J., Chung, H. F., van der Schouw, Y. T., Sandin, S., Weiderpass, E., & Mishra, G. D. (2024). Association of infertility and recurrent pregnancy loss with the risk of dementia. *European Journal of Epidemiology*, 1–9.

Majoka, M. A., & Schimming, C. (2021). Effect of social determinants of health on cognition and risk of Alzheimer disease and related dementias. *Clinical Therapeutics, 43*(6), 922–929.

Maki, P. M., Drogos, L. L., Rubin, L. H., Banuvar, S., Shulman, L. P., & Geller, S. E. (2008). Objective hot flashes are negatively related to verbal memory performance in midlife women. *Menopause, 15*(5), 848–856.

Maki, P. M., & Sundermann, E. (2009). Hormone therapy and cognitive function. *Human Reproduction Update, 15*(6), 667–681.

Maki, P. M. (2015). Verbal memory and menopause. *Maturitas, 82*(3), 288–290.

Maki, P. M., Rich, J. B., & Rosenbaum, R. S. (2002). Implicit memory varies across the menstrual cycle: Estrogen effects in young women. *Neuropsychologia, 40*, 518–529.

Meers, J. M., & Nowakowski, S. (2020). Sleep, premenstrual mood disorder, and women's health. *Current Opinion in Psychology, 34*, 43–49.

Meza-Moreno, F. I., Pimienta-Alcaraz, M. J., Vázquez-Valdez, M. F., Balderas-Sánchez, C. P., & Toledo-Fernández, A. (2021). Self-reported executive function, and not performance-based measures, strongly associates with symptoms of premenstrual syndrome/premenstrual dysphoric disorder. *Salud Mental, 44*(2), 83–90.

Mihalik, J. P., Ondrak, K. S., Guskiewicz, K. M., & McMurray, R. G. (2009). The effects of menstrual cycle phase on clinical measures of concussion in healthy college-aged females. *Journal of Science and Medicine in Sport, 12*(3), 383–387.

Mitchell, E. S., & Woods, N. F. (2011). Cognitive symptoms during the menopausal transition and early postmenopause. *Climacteric, 14*(2), 252–261.

Mordecai, K. L., Rubin, L. H., & Maki, P. M. (2008). Effects of menstrual cycle phase and oral contraceptive use on verbal memory. *Hormones and Behavior, 54*, 286–293.

Morris, J. A., Jordan, C. L., & Breedlove, S. M. (2004). Sexual differentiation of the vertebrate nervous system. *Nature Neuroscience, 7*(10), 1034–1039.

Nguyen, H. B., Loughead, J., Lipner, E., Hantsoo, L., Kornfield, S. L., & Epperson, C. N. (2019). What has sex got to do with it? The role of hormones in the transgender brain. *Neuropsychopharmacology, 44*(1), 22–37.

Nota, N. M., Burke, S. M., den Heijer, M., Soleman, R. S., Lambalk, C. B., Cohen-Kettenis, P. T., et al. (2017). Brain sexual differentiation and effects of cross-sex hormone therapy in transpeople: A resting-state functional magnetic resonance study. *Neurophysiologie Clinique, 47*(5–6), 361–370.

Numan, M. (2007). Motivational systems and the neural circuitry of maternal behavior in the rat. *Developmental Psychobiology: The Journal of the International Society for Developmental Psychobiology, 49*(1), 12–21.

Onyper, S. V., Searleman, A., Thacher, P. V., Maine, E. E., & Johnson, A. G. (2010). Executive functioning and general cognitive ability in pregnant women and matched controls. *Journal of Clinical and Experimental Neuropsychology, 32*(9), 986–995.

Orchard, E. R., Rutherford, H. J., Holmes, A. J., & Jamadar, S. D. (2023). Matrescence: Lifetime impact of motherhood on cognition and the brain. *Trends in Cognitive Sciences, 27*(3), 302–316.

Parsons, C., & Redman, S. (1991). Self-reported cognitive change during pregnancy. *The Australian Journal of Advanced Nursing, 9*(1), 20–29.

Pawluski, J. L., Hoekzema, E., Leuner, B., & Lonstein, J. S. (2022). Less can be more: Fine tuning the maternal brain. *Neuroscience & Biobehavioral Reviews, 133*, 104475.

Pearson, R. M., Lightman, S. L., & Evans, J. (2009). Emotional sensitivity for motherhood: Late pregnancy is associated with enhanced accuracy to encode emotional faces. *Hormones and Behavior, 56*(5), 557–563.

Petersen, N., Kearley, N. W., Ghahremani, D. G., Pochon, J. B., Fry, M. E., Rapkin, A. J., & London, E. D. (2021). Effects of oral contraceptive pills on mood and magnetic resonance imaging measures of prefrontal cortical thickness. *Molecular Psychiatry, 26*(3), 917–926.

Plamberger, C. P., Van Wijk, H. E., Kerschbaum, H., Pletzer, B. A., Gruber, G., Oberascher, K., et al. (2021). Impact of menstrual cycle phase and oral contraceptives on sleep and overnight memory consolidation. *Journal of Sleep Research, 30*(4), e13239.

Pletzer, B. (2019). Sex hormones and gender role relate to gray matter volumes in sexually dimorphic brain areas. *Frontiers in Neuroscience, 13*, 592.

Pletzer, B., Steinbeisser, J., Van Laak, L., & Harris, T. (2019). Beyond biological sex: Interactive effects of gender role and sex hormones on spatial abilities. *Frontiers in Neuroscience, 13*, 675.

Poser, C. M., Kassirer, M. R., & Peyser, J. M. (1986). Benign encephalopathy of pregnancy preliminary clinical observations. *Acta Neurologica Scandinavica, 73*(1), 39–43.

Pradono, J., Sudikno, S., Suswanti, I., & Turana, Y. (2020). Incidence and risk factors of subjective memory complaints in women in central Bogor city, Indonesia. *Aging Medicine and Healthcare, 11*(3), 95–101.

Putnam, C. D., Brann, D. W., Kolbeck, R. C., & Mahesh, V. B. (1991). Inhibition of uterine contractility by progesterone and progesterone metabolites: Mediation by progesterone and gamma amino butyric acidA receptor systems. *Biology of Reproduction, 45*(2), 266–272.

Reed, B. G., & Carr, B. R. (2015). *The normal menstrual cycle and the control of ovulation*.

Reuben, R., Karkaby, L., McNamee, C., Phillips, N. A., & Einstein, G. (2021). Menopause and cognitive complaints: Are ovarian hormones linked with subjective cognitive decline? *Climacteric, 24*(4), 321–332.

Rocca, W. A., Bower, J. H., Maraganore, D. M., Ahlskog, J. E., Grossardt, B. R., De Andrade, M., & Melton Iii, L. J. (2007). Increased risk of cognitive impairment or dementia in women who underwent oophorectomy before menopause. *Neurology, 69*(11), 1074–1083.

Roodenrys, S. J., Astheimer, L., Islam, F., & Sparkes, C. (2008). Short-term changes in endogenous estrogen levels and consumption of soy isoflavones affect working and verbal memory in young adult females. *Nutritional Neuroscience, 11*(6), 251–262.

Rothman, M. S., Carlson, N. E., Xu, M., Wang, C., Swerdloff, R., Lee, P., et al. (2011). Reexamination of testosterone, dihydrotestosterone, estradiol and estrone levels across the menstrual cycle and in postmenopausal women measured by liquid chromatography–tandem mass spectrometry. *Steroids, 76*(1–2), 177–182.

Schaafsma, M., Homewood, J., & Taylor, A. (2010). Subjective cognitive complaints at menopause associated with declines in performance of verbal memory and attentional processes. *Climacteric, 13*(1), 84–98.

Schiller, C. E., Johnson, S. L., Abate, A. C., Schmidt, P. J., & Rubinow, D. R. (2016). Reproductive steroid regulation of mood and behavior. *Comprehensive Physiology, 6*(3), 1135.

Schöning, S., Engelien, A., Bauer, C., Kugel, H., Kersting, A., Roestel, C., et al. (2009). Neuroimaging differences in spatial cognition between men and male-to-female transsexuals before and during hormone therapy. *The Journal of Sexual Medicine, 7*(5), 1858–1867.

Schoning, S., Engelien, A., Kugel, H., Schafer, S., Schiffbauer, H., Zwitserlood, P., et al. (2007). Functional anatomy of visuo-spatial working memory during mental rotation is influenced by sex, menstrual cycle, and sex steroid hormones. *Neuropsychologia, 45*, 3203–3214.

Sharma, R., Fang, Z., Smith, A., & Ismail, N. (2020). Oral contraceptive use, especially during puberty, alters resting state functional connectivity. *Hormones and Behavior, 126*, 104849.

Simone, J., Bogue, E. A., Bhatti, D. L., Day, L. E., Farr, N. A., Grossman, A. M., & Holmes, P. V. (2015). Ethinyl estradiol and levonorgestrel alter cognition and anxiety in rats concurrent with a decrease in tyrosine hydroxylase expression in the locus coeruleus and brain-derived neurotrophic factor expression in the hippocampus. *Psychoneuroendocrinology, 62*, 265–278.

Skovlund, C. W., Mørch, L. S., Kessing, L. V., & Lidegaard, Ø. (2016). Association of hormonal contraception with depression. *JAMA Psychiatry, 73*(11), 1154–1162.

Sommer, I. E. C., Cohen-Kettenis, P. T., Van Raalten, T., Vd Veer, A. J., Ramsey, L. E., Gooren, L. J. G., et al. (2008). Effects of cross-sex hormones on cerebral activation during language and mental rotation: An fMRI study in transsexuals. *European Neuropsychopharmacology, 18*(3), 215–221.

Souza, E. G. V., Ramos, M. G., Hara, C., Stumpf, B. P., & Rocha, F. L. (2012). Neuropsychological performance and menstrual cycle: A literature review. *Trends in Psychiatry and Psychotherapy, 34*, 5–12.

Speroff, L., & Fritz, M. A. (Eds.). (2005). *Clinical gynecologic endocrinology and infertility*. Lippincott, Williams & Wilkins.
Stuenkel, C. A., Davis, S. R., Gompel, A., Lumsden, M. A., Murad, M. H., Pinkerton, J. V., & Santen, R. J. (2015). Treatment of symptoms of the menopause: An endocrine society clinical practice guideline. *The Journal of Clinical Endocrinology & Metabolism, 100*(11), 3975–4011.
Sullivan Mitchell, E., & Fugate Woods, N. (2001). Midlife women's attributions about perceived memory changes: Observations from the Seattle Midlife Women's Health Study. *Journal of Women's Health & Gender-Based Medicine, 10*(4), 351–362.
Sundström Poromaa, I., & Gingnell, M. (2014). Menstrual cycle influence on cognitive function and emotion processing—from a reproductive perspective. *Frontiers in Neuroscience, 8*, 380.
Unkenstein, A. E., Bryant, C. A., Judd, F. K., Ong, B., & Kinsella, G. J. (2016). Understanding women's experience of memory over the menopausal transition: Subjective and objective memory in pre-, peri-, and postmenopausal women. *Menopause, 23*(12), 1319–1329.
van Heesewijk, J. O., Dreijerink, K. M., Wiepjes, C. M., Kok, A. A., van Schoor, N. M., Huisman, M., et al. (2021). Long-term gender-affirming hormone therapy and cognitive functioning in older transgender women compared with cisgender women and men. *The Journal of Sexual Medicine, 18*(8), 1434–1443.
Walters, M., & Hines-Martin, V. (2018). Overview of executive functions in mood and depressive disorders: A review of the literature. *Archives of Psychiatric Nursing, 32*(4), 617–637.
Weber, M. T., Maki, P. M., & McDermott, M. P. (2014). Cognition and mood in perimenopause: A systematic review and meta-analysis. *The Journal of Steroid Biochemistry and Molecular Biology, 142*, 90–98.
Weber, M. T., Mapstone, M., Staskiewicz, J., & Maki, P. M. (2012). Reconciling subjective memory complaints with objective memory performance in the menopausal transition. *Menopause, 19*(7), 735–741.
Welch, J. (1991). Labouring brains. *BMJ: British Medical Journal: International Edition, 303*(6796), 253–253.
Wharton, W., Hirshman, E., Merritt, P., Doyle, L., Paris, S., & Gleason, C. (2008). Oral contraceptives and androgenicity: Influences on visuospatial task performance in younger individuals. *Experimental and Clinical Psychopharmacology, 16*(2), 156.
Wolf, O. T., & Kirschbaum, C. (2002). Endogenous estradiol and testosterone levels are associated with cognitive performance in older women and men. *Hormones and Behavior, 41*(3), 259–266.
Zare, H., Abazarian Tehrani, M., & Alipour, A. (2013). The effect of menstrual cycle on metamemory, everyday memory and prospective memory in women aged 18-45 years. *The Iranian Journal of Obstetrics, Gynecology and Infertility, 15*(41), 1–8.
Zhang, T., Casanova, R., Resnick, S. M., Manson, J. E., Baker, L. D., Padual, C. B., et al. (2016). Effects of hormone therapy on brain volumes changes of postmenopausal women revealed by optimally-discriminative voxel-based morphometry. *PLoS One, 11*(3), e0150834.

Index

E. Sullivan-Baca, R. Ellison (eds.), *Neuropsychology of Women*,
https://doi.org/10.1007/978-3-031-87228-0

MIX
Papier aus verantwortungsvollen Quellen
Paper from responsible sources
FSC® C105338

If you have any concerns about our products,
you can contact us on
ProductSafety@springernature.com

In case Publisher is established outside the EU,
the EU authorized representative is:
Springer Nature Customer Service Center GmbH
Europaplatz 3, 69115 Heidelberg, Germany

Printed by Libri Plureos GmbH
in Hamburg, Germany